ECKWEEK, PEASEDOWN ST JOHN, SOMERSET

Survey and Excavations
at a Shrunken Medieval Hamlet 1988–90

by

Andrew Young MCIfA

with contributions by

Alexander Kidd

and

Nigel Blades, Wendy Carruthers, Dr Nick Corcos, Dr Michael Costen, Dr Simon Davis, Prof Gilbert Kelling, Dr Matthew Law, Dr Peter Marshall, Dr Elaine Morris, Sarah Newns, Andrew Payne, Vince Russett, Ann Thompson, Dr Frank Thorn, Dr Jane Timby and Dr D F Williams

THE SOCIETY FOR MEDIEVAL ARCHAEOLOGY MONOGRAPH 40

First published 2020
by Routledge
2 Park Square, Milton Park, Abingdon, Oxon OX14 4RN

and by Routledge
52 Vanderbilt Avenue, New York, NY 10017

Routledge is an imprint of the Taylor & Francis Group, an informa business

© 2020 The Society for Medieval Archaeology and authors

The right of Andrew Young to be identified as author of the editorial material, and of the authors for their individual chapters, has been asserted in accordance with sections 77 and 78 of the Copyright, Designs and Patents Act 1988..

All rights reserved. No part of this book may be reprinted or reproduced or utilised in any form or by any electronic, mechanical, or other means, now known or hereafter invented, including photocopying and recording, or in any information storage or retrieval system, without permission in writing from the publishers.

Trademark notice: Product or corporate names may be trademarks or registered trademarks, and are used only for identification and explanation without intent to infringe.

British Library Cataloguing-in-Publication Data
A catalogue record for this book is available from the British Library

Library of Congress Cataloging-in-Publication Data
A catalog record for this book has been requested

ISBN: 978-0-367-86029-5 (hbk)
ISBN: 978-0-367-86031-8 (pbk)
ISBN: 978-1-003-01652-6 (ebk)

Typeset in Bembo MT Pro
by Oxford Book Projects

Publisher's Note
This book has been prepared from camera-ready copy provided by the author.

This publication has been made possible by a grant from Historic England.

The Society for Medieval Archaeology www.medievalarchaeology.co.uk

Cover: *Detail of reconstruction drawing showing the 11th-century Period III settlement at Eckweek. Looking north*

CONTENTS

List of Figures iv
Acknowledgements ix
Summaries (English/French/German/Spanish) x
Abbreviations xii

1 Introduction
1.1 Background to the project 1
1.2 Geology, topography and land use 5

2 Documentary and Archaeological Background
2.1 Documentary, archaeological and landscape evidence (by Dr Nick Corcos, 2013) 9
2.2 The placename Eckweek (by Dr Michael Costen) 28
2.3 Eckweek in Domesday Book (by Dr Frank Thorn) 29

3 Surveys
3.1 Preliminary surveys 44
3.2 Geophysical survey (by Andrew Payne of Historic England, 1989, updated 2015) 45

4 Excavations
4.1 Excavation areas and methodologies 51
4.2 Summary of structural phasing 52
4.3 The excavated evidence 53
4.4 Watching brief 109

5 Artefacts and Environmental Evidence
5.1 Prehistoric ceramics – pottery, briquetage and a bronze-working crucible (by Dr Elaine Morris, 1992, updated 2015) 113
5.2 Romano-British pottery (by Dr Jane Timby, 2015) 118
5.3 The late Saxon, Saxo-Norman, medieval and post-medieval pottery (by Andrew Young and Alexander Kidd, 1990–1991, updated 2015) .. 119
5.3.1 *The petrology of medieval pottery (by D F Williams PhD FSA – Department of Archaeology, University of Southampton, 1991)* .. 155
5.4 Coins (by Sarah Newns, 2015) 165
5.5 Iron and lead objects (by Ann Thompson, 1991) 167

5.6 Copper alloy objects (by Sarah Newns, 2015) 182
5.7 Flint (by Vince Russett, 1991) 190
5.8 Worked stone objects (by Alexander Kidd and Andrew Young, 1991) 196
5.8.1 *The petrology of medieval whetstones of sandstone from Eckweek (by Professor Gilbert Kelling – Department of Geology, University of Keele, 1991)* 208
5.9 Clay tobacco pipe (by Sarah Newns, 2014) 208
5.10 The composition of a group of later medieval copper alloy 'ingots' and other objects (by Nigel Blades, 1991) 210
5.11 Worked bone objects (by Sarah Newns, 2015) 212
5.12 The jet bead SF627 (by Sarah Newns, 2015) 214
5.13 Faunal remains (by Dr Simon Davis, 1992, updated 2015) 214
5.14 Charred plant remains (by Wendy Carruthers, 1995, updated 2015) 222
5.15 Molluscs (by Dr Matthew Law, 2014) 233

6 Independent Dating
6.1 Radiocarbon dating (Queens University Belfast, 1991, reviewed and updated by Dr Peter Marshall, 2015) 237
6.2 Comment on the 1991 radiocarbon dates (by Andrew Young, 1991, revised 2015) 238

7 Reconstructing Late Saxon and Medieval Eckweek (2015)
7.1 The medieval buildings and structures 239
7.2 Artefacts: the character and distribution of Late Saxon and medieval finds 255
7.3 Artefactual evidence for settlement development – continuity and change 278
7.4 Artefacts and ecofacts – general conclusions .. 284
7.5 The agricultural and domestic economy 285

8 Synthesis
8.1 Prehistoric activity 289
8.2 Late Saxon and medieval settlement 290

Bibliography 300

Index 309

LIST OF FIGURES

1.1 England and Wales showing Somerset and modern unitary authorities 1
1.2 Historic Somerset showing the location of Eckweek with principal towns and modern regional authorities 2
1.3 Peasedown St John and surrounding area showing Eckweek and other settlements in Wellow parish 2
1.4 Peasedown St John showing the Eckweek site, local settlements and recorded monuments 3
1.5 Eckweek excavation and survey areas superimposed onto the modern Ordnance Survey showing the site of the former Eckweek House Farm 4
1.6 The study area in 1988 showing the location of excavation and survey areas and the recording and excavation base line 6
1.7 The study area showing earthworks, geophysical survey and excavation areas plus principal geophysical features 7
2.1 HER events 10
2.2 HER monuments 11
2.3 Extract from the 1843 Wellow tithe award 12
2.4 Medieval and early modern documentary sources for Eckweek 18
2.5 The Wellow tithe map of 1843 with principal settlements added by the author (reproduced courtesy of Somerset Record Office) 20
2.6 Extract from the Wellow tithe map of 1843 showing the settlements at Eckweek and White Ox Mead. Annotated by the author (reproduced courtesy of Somerset Record Office) 21
2.7 Extract from the Wellow tithe map of 1843 showing the settlement at Eckweek and surrounding fields (reproduced courtesy of Somerset Record Office) 21
2.8 Extract from the Wellow tithe map of 1843 showing the settlements at Eckweek and Shoscombe with the area of the 2004–2005 excavations by Cotswold Archaeology indicated. Annotated by the author (reproduced courtesy of Somerset Record Office) 22

2.9 Extract from the First Edition Ordnance Survey map of 1887 showing Eckweek settlement. Somerset Sheet XX NE. Not to scale 28
2.10 Domesday estates in Wellow Hundred 40
3.1 The Eckweek earthwork survey 44
3.2 Detail of earthworks in OS Field 2000 at Eckweek, immediately north of the excavation areas 45
3.3 Earthworks in OS Field 0033 at Home Farm, White Ox Mead 45
3.4 The areas of magnetometer and earth resistance geophysical survey 46
3.5 Geophysical data from magnetometer and earth resistance surveys 47
3.6 Detail of magnetometer and earth resistance survey data from OS Field 2470 48
3.7 Detail of magnetometer survey data from OS Field 2756 (Area H) 49
3.8 Interpretation of geophysical survey data from OS Fields 2470 and 2756 50
4.1 Detail of magnetometer survey greyscale data from OS Field 2756 (Area H) with location of excavation areas superimposed 53
4.2 Excavation Area A – summary of structural phasing 54
4.3 Area H as excavated 55
4.4 Area A showing Period IV features 56
4.5 Area A showing Period V features 57
4.6 Area H showing Iron Age Ditch 3161 in the SW-facing section of Cutting 1 58
4.7 Area H showing Iron Age features as excavated in Cutting 2 59
4.8 SW-facing section of Iron Age ditch 3161 in Cutting 1. Scales 2m 60
4.9 Area H – W-facing section in Cutting 2 showing Iron Age ditch 3076 and late Saxon ditch 3023 60
4.10 Trench I – detail of SW-facing section showing Iron Age ditch 3213 and late Saxon features 60
4.11 Iron Age ditch 3213 in Trench I. Facing NE. Scale 1m 61
4.12 Area A showing Period III.1 features of Structure 468 as excavated 62

LIST OF FIGURES

4.13	Area A showing Period III features of Structure 467 as excavated	63
4.14	Area H showing detail of Structures 475, 476 and 477 as excavated	65
4.15	Area A – West to East section showing Period III to V structures and deposits	66
4.16	Area A – North to South section (west) showing Period III to V structures and deposits	66
4.17	Area A – North to South section (east) showing Period III to V structures and deposits	67
4.18	Photographs A–F: A) Area A showing Period III features as excavated. Facing E. Scales 2m	68
	B) Area A showing Period III Building 467 sunken-floor features fully excavated. Facing W. Scales 2m	68
	C) Area A showing Period III features 223, 284 and 228 as excavated. Facing SW. Scale 2m	68
	D) Area A showing detail of offset between Period III features 251 and 457. Facing E. Scale 2m	69
	E) Area A showing detail of relationship between Period III gully 171 and sunken-floor features. Facing N. Scales 2m	69
	F) Area A showing Period III pit 416 during excavation and the top (base) of buried pot 490. Facing NW. Scale 1m.	69
4.19	Area A – the Yard area as excavated showing Period III to V features	70
4.20	Area A – detail of Period III Pit Group 469 as excavated	71
4.21	Period III Pit Group 469 in Area A as excavated. Looking NE. Scale 2m	71
4.22	Area A – section through Period III Gully 171/387 and Pit 179	72
4.23	Area A – section through Period III Pit 416 showing Pot 490	72
4.24	Area H – profiles of principal earthfast features of Period III Building 477	74
4.25	Area H – section through Period III Post-pits 3013 and 3015	74
4.26	Photographs A and B: A) Area H – section through Period III Post-pit 3137 showing burnt daub layer 3144/3145. Facing W. Scales 2m	75
	B) Area H – detail of Period III Post-pit 3009 showing secondary stone foundation layer 3041. Facing SW. Scale 2m.	75
4.27	Period III features 3005, 3007 and 3009 before excavation. Features 3007 and 3009 circled. Facing SW. Scales 2m	76
4.28	Area H – detail of Iron Age and Period III features as excavated	76
4.29	Area H – Period III features as excavated	77
4.30	Area H – Period III features exposed in section at the SE end of Cutting 1	77
4.31	Area H – section through Period III Pits 3029 and 3061. Facing E	78
4.32	Area H – Period III Pits 3029 and 3061 during excavation, showing daub layer 3063. Facing NE. Scales 2m	78
4.33	Area H – profiles across Structure 476	79
4.34	Area H – Structure 476 as excavated. Facing NE. Scales 2m	79
4.35	Area H – Structure 475 in foreground prior to excavation. Facing SW. Scales 2m	79
4.36	Area H – north-facing section in Cutting 3 showing Period III enclosure ditches and bank deposits	80
4.37	Area H – south-facing section in Cutting 3 showing Period III enclosure ditches and bank deposits	80
4.38	Area H – east-facing section in Cutting 4 showing Period III enclosure ditches	80
4.39	Photographs A and B: A) Area H during excavation. Facing NE	81
	B) As 4.39A above with principal Period III features indicated. Facing NE.	81
4.40	Area A – Period III Structure 467 with Period III.3 features highlighted	82
4.41	Area A showing Period IV and V walls overlying the fill of Period III pits 221 and 234. Facing E. Scales 2m	83
4.42	Trench D – SE-facing section showing Period III ditches overlain by Period IV–V earth bank and rubble revetment 438	85
4.43	Trench C – south-facing section	85
4.44	Trench E – NW-facing section showing Period III trackway ditches, Period III–V trackway metalling and Period IV–V earth bank and rubble revetment 119	86
4.45	Area H – arrangement and interpretation of Period III features	88
4.46	Photographs A and B: A) Area A – Period IV Wall 13 overlying fill of Period III Pit 234. Facing N. Scales 2m	89
	B) Area A – masonry forming the SE corner of Period IV Building 462. Facing W. Scale 2m	89
4.47	Area A – Period IV Building 462 and associated features and deposits	90
4.48	Area A – the SE corner of Period IV Building 465 as indicated by wall fragments 55 and 391, the former reused as the entrance threshold of Period V Building 463. Facing N. Scale 2m	91
4.49	Area A – north-facing section through Wall 20 of Period V Building 463 showing remnant Period IV floor layer 315 and inferred line of Period IV wall 391	91
4.50	Area A – Period V Building 460 showing remnant Period V.1 floor layers and deposits preserved in the western bay	92
4.51	Area A showing Period V Building 460 during excavation with the south wall [10] overlying Period III cut features. Facing N. Scales 2m	93
4.52	Area A showing Period V Building 460 during excavation and fully excavated	

	Period III features 251 and 385 of Building 467 in the foreground. Facing N. Scales 2m 94		demolition rubble (3 and 12) yet to be excavated. Also showing post-medieval robber pits (37 and 45) 108
4.53	Area A showing the eastern end of Period V Building 460 as excavated and the southeast corner of Period IV Building 462, revealed by the excavation of Period V floor layer 18. Facing S. Scales 2m 95	4.70	Area B – section drawing showing rock-cut platform prepared for Period V Building 461. Facing N 108
4.54	Area A – Period V Building 460 during excavation showing Period III trackway metalling and ditches partly exposed in the left foreground. Facing E. Scales 500mm and 2m 96	4.71	Plan showing location of features recorded during the watching brief stage 110
		4.72	Detail showing features recorded during the watching brief adjacent to Excavation Areas A, B and G 111
4.55	Area A – the western part of Period V Building 460 during excavation with Feature numbers added. Showing Period III trackway metalling [174] and Period IV wall fragment [187] in the foreground. Facing S. Scales 500mm and 2m 96	4.73	Detail showing features recorded during the watching brief adjacent to Excavation Area H 111
		4.74	Walls 3258 and 3259 revealed during the watching brief immediately west of Area B. Facing W. Scales 2m 112
		4.75	Wall 3255 recorded during the watching brief defining the east side of the medieval trackway. Facing E. Scale 2m 112
4.56	Area A – plan showing Period V Building 463 and part of Structure 466 as excavated with remnants of Period IV Building 465 98	5.1	Quantification of the prehistoric ceramics by fabric type 113
4.57	Area A showing Period V Building 463 during excavation. Facing SE. Scale 2m 98	5.2	Relative frequency of Iron Age pottery and briquetage by fabric type 113
4.58	Area A showing the south wall [242] of Period V Building 463 with demolition rubble and small cobbled path immediately outside. Structure 466 and the southern part of the Yard beyond. Facing E. Scales 2m 99	5.3	The prehistoric pottery 114
		5.4	Correlation of Iron Age fabric types to visible evidence of use 115
		5.5	Prehistoric pottery fabric descriptions 115
		5.6	Illustrated prehistoric pottery and briquetage . 116
4.59	Area A – plan showing Period V Kiln 466 and associated features as excavated 100	5.7	Summary of Romano-British pottery and ceramic material 119
4.60	Area A showing Period V Kiln 466 during excavation. Facing S. Scales 1m and 2m 100	5.8	Description of late Saxon and medieval pottery fabrics 121
4.61	Area A – plan showing Period V Building 460 as excavated with latest CP5 features and floor layers 102	5.9	Medieval pottery illustrations Nos 1–16 135
		5.10	Medieval pottery illustrations Nos 17–37 136
		5.11	Medieval pottery illustrations Nos 38–54 138
4.62A	Area A – plan showing the eastern end of Period V Building 460 with demolition rubble [3 and 12] yet to be excavated and post-medieval Robber Pit 37 103	5.12	Medieval pottery illustrations Nos 55–69 139
		5.13	Medieval pottery illustrations Nos 70–86 141
		5.14	Medieval pottery illustrations Nos 87–108 ... 143
		5.15	Medieval pottery illustrations Nos 109–124 . 146
4.62B	Area A showing the eastern end of Period V Building 460 with demolition rubble [3 and 12] in situ and cut of post-medieval Robber Pit 37 in the foreground. Facing S. Scale 2m . 103	5.16	Medieval pottery illustrations Nos 125–138 . 148
		5.17	Medieval pottery illustrations Nos 139–145 . 149
		5.18	Medieval pottery illustrations Nos 146–166 . 150
		5.19	Medieval pottery illustrations Nos 167–172 . 152
4.63	Area A – detail of Period V haystack base (Structure 473) as excavated. Facing NE. Scale 2m 104	5.20	Medieval pottery illustration No. 149. FPN62 153
		5.21	No. 149. The Stag's Head Cistern. FPN62 .. 153
4.64	Plan showing Area B and Period V Building 461 as excavated 105	5.22	No. 167. Leaf Jug. FPN74 154
		5.23	No. 13. Reconstructed cooking pot. FPN251 154
4.65	Area B showing detail of the entrance steps to Period V Building 461. Facing W. Scale 2m .. 106	5.24	No. 140. Reconstructed Period V fish dish. FPN48 155
4.66	Area G – plan as excavated showing Structure 472 106	5.25	No. 111. Reconstructed Period V jug. FPN50 155
4.67A and B	Area G – section drawings showing possible Period III sunken-floor feature (Cut 448) overlain by later medieval wall foundation (446) 107	5.26	No. 46. Reconstructed Period III cookpot. FPN246 156
		5.27	No. 79. Reconstructed Period IV Westcountry dish. FPN35 156
4.68	Testpit Area K showing Period V wall 3155. Facing E. Scale 200mm graduations 107	5.28	Plot showing incidence of external to internal sooting by medieval fabric type 161
4.69	Area A – plan showing Period V Building 460 after the removal of topsoil only with	5.29	Plot showing incidence of vessel sooting and calcareous concretions by medieval fabric type 161
		5.30	Plot showing incidence of vessel sooting and wiping by medieval fabric type 162

LIST OF FIGURES

5.31	Plot showing incidence of vessel glaze and calcareous concretions by medieval fabric type	162
5.32	Plot showing incidence of vessel glaze and wiping by medieval fabric type	163
5.33	Plot showing incidence of vessel sooting and glaze by medieval fabric type	163
5.34	Plot showing relative proportions of medieval ceramic wares by ceramic phase and date	164
5.35	Coins in chronological order	166
5.36	Coins in context number order	166
5.37	Catalogue of coins	166
5.38	Illustrated coins	166
5.39	1) Edward I penny SF938, 2) Edward III groat SF586, 3) Edward I penny SF548	166
5.40	Metalwork illustrations Nos 1–8. Knives	170
5.41	Metalwork illustrations Nos 9–21	172
5.42	Metalwork illustrations Nos 22–35	174
5.43	Metalwork illustrations Nos 36–48	176
5.44	Metalwork illustrations Nos 49–58	178
5.45	Metalwork illustrations Nos 59–74	180
5.46	Metalwork illustrations Nos 68 and 75–82	181
5.47	Catalogue of copper alloy objects	184
5.48	Copper alloy Illustrations Nos 1–18	186
5.49	Copper alloy Illustrations Nos 19–27, 33 and 35–40	188
5.50	Copper alloy Illustrations Nos 28–32 and 34. Vessel feet	189
5.51	Copper alloy vessel feet from Period V Building 460	190
5.52	Catalogue of flint cores and other flint tools	192
5.53	Description of flint objects	193
5.54	Illustrated flint arrowheads	195
5.55A	Worked stone by ceramic phase and function	197
5.55B	Worked stone by ceramic phase and source geology	197
5.56	Worked stone illustrations Nos 1–5	198
5.57	Worked stone illustrations Nos 6–20	200
5.58	Worked stone illustrations Nos 21–27	201
5.59	Worked stone illustrations Nos 28–32	203
5.60	Worked stone illustrations Nos 33–42	205
5.61	Worked stone illustrations Nos 43–48	206
5.62	Worked stone illustrations Nos 49–54	207
5.63	Examples of whetstone types I, III and II	208
5.64	Catalogue of clay tobacco pipes	209
5.65	Illustrated clay tobacco pipes	210
5.66	Results of ICPS analysis of copper alloy objects	211
5.67	Catalogue of worked bone objects	212
5.68	Illustrated medieval worked bone objects	213
5.69	Medieval worked bone objects including pin-beaters, a decorated fragment and a knife guard	213
5.70	Medieval animal fauna by period	215
5.71	Medieval animal fauna and body parts in ceramic phases 1–4 (Periods III–IV)	216
5.72	Medieval animal fauna and body parts in ceramic phases 5–6 (Period V)	217
5.73	Medieval sheep/goat and cattle body parts	218
5.74	Medieval small mammal, bird and amphibian fauna from sieved samples	218
5.75	Payne large mammal tooth wear stages by ceramic phase	219
5.76	Eckweek medieval cattle mandibular wear stages (after Grant 1982)	219
5.77	Eckweek medieval pig mandibular wear stages (after Grant 1982)	219
5.78	Distinction between mandibles of *Apodemus sylvaticus* and *A. flavicollis* and the identity of the Eckweek Apodemus from contexts 273 and 213	220
5.79	Display of the data in Figure 5.73. Each cross represents a MN of 3	220
5.80	Measurements in millimetres of sheep bones compared to modern unimproved Shetland sheep in the Ancient Monuments Laboratory (Davis 2000; now in Portsmouth; above) and sheep from medieval and post-medieval levels at Launceston Castle, Cornwall (Albarella and Davis 1996)	221
5.81	The percentage compositions of the 24 richest medieval charred plant assemblages	223
5.82	Charred plant species list by period and medieval ceramic phase	225
5.83	Charred plant remains count by medieval ceramic phase	226
5.84	The proportions of charred medieval plant remains by type and ceramic phase	227
5.85	Cereals by percentage across the medieval ceramic phases	230
5.86	Minimum number of snail (MNI) values for the vertical sequence of samples.	234
6.1	Radiocarbon dating results	237
6.2	Probability distributions of radiocarbon dates. The distributions are the result of simple radiocarbon calibration (Stuiver and Reimer 1993)	238
7.1	Structural interpretation of Period III Building 467 in Area A	242
7.2	General structural interpretation of Period III features in Area H	245
7.3A	Structural interpretation of Period III Building 477 in Area H – Option 1	246
7.3B	Structural interpretation of Period III Building 477 in Area H – Option 2	247
7.4	Comparison of Building 477/476 at Eckweek and Structure A at Bonhunt Farm, Essex	248
7.5	Structural interpretation of Period V Building 460 in Area A	252
7.6	Period V Building 460 – distribution of structural metalwork	256
7.7	Period V Building 460 – distribution of structural objects including nails and staples	256
7.8	Period V Building 460 – distribution of Phase V.1 objects	257
7.9	Period V Building 463 – distribution of structural objects	259
7.10	Period IV Building 462 – distribution of structural and other objects	260
7.11	Period V.3 Building 460 – distribution of pottery vessels and sherds	262

7.12	Period V.3 Building 460 – distribution of animal bone	262
7.13	Period V Building 460 – distribution of tools	263
7.14	Period V Building 460 – distribution of furnishings	263
7.15	Period V Building 460 – distribution of domestic objects	264
7.16	Period V Building 460 – distribution of domestic metalwork	264
7.17	Period V Building 460 – distribution of personal and domestic stone objects	265
7.18	Period V Building 460 – distribution of metal vessel parts	265
7.19	Period V Building 460 – distribution of personal items	266
7.20	Period V Building 460 – distribution of equestrian objects including fiddle-key nails	266
7.21	Period V Building 460 – distribution of miscellaneous objects	267
7.22	Period V Building 463 – distribution of tools and personal objects	268
7.23	Period V Building 463 – distribution of horse gear and worked stone	269
7.24	Area A Period V – distribution of ceramic ware 14 during CP5–6	270
7.25	Area A Period V – distribution of ceramic ware 15 during CP5	270
7.26	Area A Period V – distribution of ceramic ware 16 during CP5	271
7.27	Area A Period IV – distribution of ceramic ware 4 during CP4–5	271
7.28	Area A Building 460 Period V.3 – breakage and movement of domestic pottery after abandonment	272
7.29	Area B Period V Building 461 – distribution of iron and lead objects	273
7.30	Area A Period III – distribution of structural metalwork	274
7.31	Area A Period III – distribution of domestic and other objects	274
7.32	Area A Period III – distribution of ceramic ware 1 pottery sherds (CP2–4)	274
7.33	Area A Period III.1 – distribution of later 10th-century pottery sherds (CP1)	274
7.34	Area H Period III – distribution of structural nails	276
7.35	Area H Period III – distribution of domestic and furnishing items	276
7.36	Area H Period III – distribution of horse gear and personal items	277
7.37	Inventory of domestic objects from Period V Building 460	278
7.38	Frequency of Area A Period V artefacts expressed as a percentage of the total number of pottery sherds	278
7.39	Total quantities of finds by excavation area and category	279
7.40	Total numbers of finds by excavation area, ceramic phase and material type	279
7.41	Total numbers of pottery sherds by excavation area and ceramic phase	280
7.42	Total numbers of iron objects by excavation area and ceramic phase	280
7.43	Total numbers of stone objects by excavation area and ceramic phase	280
7.44	Total numbers of copper alloy objects by excavation area and ceramic phase	280
7.45	Comparative ratios of iron objects to pottery sherds in Areas A and H by ceramic phase	280
7.46	Comparative ratios of copper alloy objects to pottery sherds in Areas A and H by ceramic phase	280
7.47	Comparative ratios of stone objects to pottery sherds in Areas A and H by ceramic phase	280
7.48	Inventory of finds recovered from late Saxon and medieval contexts in Area A by category and ceramic phase	281
7.49	Inventory of finds recovered from late Saxon and medieval contexts in Area H by category and ceramic phase	282
7.50	Total numbers of finds by count, area, category and ceramic phase	283
8.1	Reconstruction drawing showing the interior of Period III Building 467 in Area A. Looking north	293
8.2	Detail of the magnetometer greyscale data from Area H with principal 11th-century Period III features superimposed	294
8.3	Reconstruction drawing showing the 11th-century Period III 'thegnly hall' and its compound in Area H. Looking north east	295
8.4	Reconstruction drawing showing the 11th-century Period III settlement at Eckweek. Looking north	296
8.5	Reconstruction drawing showing the interior of 14th-century Period V Farmhouse 460 in Area A. Looking north	297
8.6	Reconstruction drawing showing the 14th-century Period V farmstead in Area A. Looking north	299

ACKNOWLEDGEMENTS

The preparation of this very long-overdue report is thanks firstly to funding by Historic England, formerly English Heritage, with significant additional time and resources also provided over some twenty-five years in between by the writer and Avon Archaeological Unit Limited. In addition, thanks are due to the Maltwood Fund for Archaeological Research in Somerset and the late Professor Mick Aston for supporting the examination of documentary sources for the site undertaken in 2012 by Dr Nick Corcos. Particular thanks are also due to all the named specialist contributors, both those of the 1990s and more recently, whilst special thanks are due to Dr Michael Costen and Dr Frank Thorn for their respective analyses of the placename and Domesday entries for Eckweek, who both gave up their time and knowledge freely.

I also need to thank the very many members of the Manpower Services Commission (MSC) workforce that undertook the excavation work in the late 1980s and in particular to my former colleague at Avon County Council, Alexander Kidd, whose knowledge (particularly of all things to do with 1989 computers), meticulous fieldwork and many post-excavation contributions played a large part in the successful completion of the fieldwork and initial post-excavation analyses. With regard to the fieldwork, particular thanks are due to John Turner and Mike Chapman, both very able excavators, and to student volunteers who included Vince Devine and David Radford, along with others whose names were sadly lost in our office fire of 2001. Special thanks are due to Lynn Hume for her many hours of work given to the project over many years, both during the fieldwork and thereafter in salvaging many of the primary drawings from the residues of the 2001 fire. More recently, I am deeply indebted to Dr Mark Gardiner for his time and enthusiasm in discussing the project in detail in Belfast in 2015; to my wife Donna, for managing to correct my numerous errors during many long hours of copy editing and proof reading, and to Jennie Anderson for producing such excellent reconstruction drawings. To all those above and the many others who have been involved in the project that have not been named, my very sincere thanks.

Finally, this report is dedicated to the late Professor Mick Aston who with his now well-known enthusiasm and knowledge introduced the writer to the rural medieval world whilst an undergraduate at Bristol University. Subsequently, in the years between 1992 and until shortly before his death in 2013, he never failed to gently remind me that '*you really should get on and publish the Eckweek site*' – it is a great personal regret that he did not get to see it finally completed.

All errors contained in this report are of course solely the responsibility of the writer.

SUMMARIES

Eckweek Summary

This report is based on excavations undertaken by the writer for Avon County Council at the medieval rural settlement of Eckweek, Peasedown St John, near Bath, Somerset, between 1988 and 1990.

The excavations yielded a stratified sequence of rural medieval buildings dating between the late 10th and later 14th centuries, augmented by a rich assemblage of finds, including structural, domestic, agricultural and personal objects. The occupation was initiated by a large 11th-century earthfast timber building which displayed a number of key indicators of late Saxon *thegnly* status, supporting its identification as the focal centre of one of two separate manors documented at Domesday. The settlement culminated in a 14th-century farmhouse that produced a very complete assemblage of structural and domestic objects whose distribution provides a clear picture of its internal organisation. The abandonment of the settlement coincides with documented episodes of epidemic in Somerset.

The excavated building remains are particularly significant for documenting the transition from earthfast timber to stone building traditions in 11th- to 12th-century England, and for illustrating a previously unrecorded rural building practice in Somerset, which incorporates elements of the Anglo-Saxon *Grubenhäuser* tradition.

Environmental evidence and faunal remains document broad continuities in farming regime throughout the occupation sequence, including the insight that an open field system of agriculture was already established at Eckweek by the turn of the 11th century. Other finds, including a large assemblage of domestic pottery, iron and stone objects and personal items, detail the day-to-day lives of the inhabitants.

Altogether, the evidence provides a vivid portrait of Eckweek's evolution as a manorial centre over a 400-year period, one which contributes new knowledge of continuity and change in patterns of medieval rural life both regionally and nationally.

Résumé Eckweek

Les fouilles de l'habitat rural médiéval d'Eckweek, Peasedown St John (Somerset), ont été menées entre 1988 et 1990, sous la direction du présent auteur, par le *County Council* d'Avon. Cette opération a permis la mise au jour d'une séquence stratifiée de bâtiments ruraux, accompagnée d'un large assemblage de mobiliers à usage domestique et agricole, l'ensemble datant de la fin du Xe au XIVe siècles.

La première phase d'occupation est matérialisée par un grand bâtiment en bois du XIe siècle, indiquant un occupation privilégiée caractéristique de la fin de la période anglo-saxonne. Le site a été identifié comme un centre élitaire et mis en parallèle avec l'un des deux domaines manoriaux, identifiés dans le livre du *Domesday*. Le site a atteint son apogée au XIVe siècle, et a pris la forme d'une ferme fortifiée. À l'intérieur de celle-ci, la distribution spatiale des artefacts a permis l'identification précise de son organisation interne. L'abandon du site a coïncidée avec une série documentée d'épidémies, qui se sont déclarées dans le Somerset à la fin de ce siècle.

La fouille des bâtiments du site s'est révélée essentielle à la documentation et à la compréhension du passage de l'usage du bois à l'usage de la pierre dans les constructions aux XIe et XIIe siècles. Ces derniers ont également permis d'illustrer les composants traditionnels des constructions rurales du Somerset, et leur incorporation d'éléments plus anglo-saxons tels que les *Grubenhauser*.

Les études environnementales et archéozoologiques ont révélées une continuité des régimes agraires tout au long de l'occupation du site, et ont permis de soutenir l'hypothèse d'un système agraire à champ ouvert déjà établi à Eckweek au tournant du XIe siècle. Enfin, le petit mobilier du site, riche en objet ferreux, céramiques, ustensiles et objets en pierre, a offert une image détaillée du quotidien des habitants d'Eckweek.

La prise en compte de l'ensemble des vestiges offre finalement un portrait vivant du développement du site d'Eckweek et de son évolution, sur près de 400 ans, en une résidence privilégiée. Le site constitue un nouvel apport à la connaissance des modes de vie en espace rural – leur continuité et leur transformation – autant à l'échelle régionale que nationale.

Eckweek Zusammenfassung

Diser Bericht beschreibt die Ausgrabungen der mittelalterlichen Dorfsiedlung Eckweek, Peasedown St John in der Nähe von Bath, Somerset, die der Autor im Auftrag von Avon County Council in den Jahren 1988–1990 unternommen hat.

Die Ausgrabungen bekunden eine stratigraphische Abfolge der mittelalterlichen Dorfgebäude, die zwischen dem späten 10. bis zum späteren 14. Jahrhundert datieren und die durch eine reichhaltige Fundmenge, bestehend aus strukturellen, häuslichen, landwirtschaftlichen und persönlichen Gegenständen, noch ergänzt werden. Die Erstbesiedlung erfolgte in Form eines grossen Gebäudes in Pfostenbauweise, das eine Reihe von wichtigen Hinweissen bezüglich seines spätsächsischen Adel-Status aufzeigte, die eine Interpretation als Zentrum eines von zwei getrennten Herrenhäusern, die im *Domesday Book* dokumentiert sind, zulässt. Die Siedlung kulminierte in einem Farmhaus des 14. Jahrhunderts, das eine vollständige Fundgruppe von strukturellen und häuslichen Objekten hervorbrachte, deren Verbreitung eine deutliches Bild seiner inneren Organisation lieferte. Die Auflassung der Siedlung erfolgte zeitgleich mit dokumentierten Epidemien in Somerset.

Die ausgegrabenen Gebäudereste sind von besonderer Bedeutung um den Übergang von einer Pfostenbauweise zu Steinbautraditionen des englischen 11.–12. Jahrhunderts zu belegen und um eine bisher in Somerset unbekannte ländliche Bauweise zu dokumentieren, die Elemente der angelsächsischen Grubenhaustradition einbezieht.

Umweltdaten und Faunen-Überreste dokumentieren eine weitgehende Kontinuität der Bewirtschaftungsmethode während der Besiedlungzeit, insbesondere die Erkenntnis, dass auf einem offenen Feldsystem basierende Landwirtschaft bereits um die Wende zum 11. Jahrhundert in Eckweek betrieben wurde. Weitere Funde, insbesondere eine grosse Anzahl von Haushaltskeramik, Gegenständen aus Eisen und Stein, sowie persönliche Objekte, dokumentieren das tägliche Leben der Bewohner.

Zusammengefasst liefert dies ein lebendiges Bild der 400-jährigen Entwicklung Eckweeks von seinem Ursprung als herrschaftliches Zentrum, dass uns erlaubt, neue Erkenntnisse zum Fortbestand und Wandel des ländlichen Lebens im Mittelalter auf regionaler und überregionaler Ebene zu gewinnen.

Excavaciones en Eckweek

Este libro presenta los resultados de las excavaciones realizadas por el autor para el *Avon County Council* en el asentamiento rural medieval de Eckweek, Peasedown St John, cerca de Bath, Somerset, entre 1988 y 1990.

Las excavaciones han proporcionado una secuencia estratificada de edificios medievales rurales fechados entre finales del siglo X hasta finales del XIV, junto con un rico conjunto de materiales estructurales, domésticos, agrícolas y personales. La primera estructura en el yacimiento fue construida en arcilla y madera, con características que apuntan a un status de *thegnly* tardo-sajón, lo que confirma su identificación como el centro focal de uno de los dos feudos independientes documentados en *Domesday*. El asentamiento culminó en una casa dedicada a la explotación agrícola en el siglo XIV, en una fase de ocupación que proporcionó un conjunto muy completo de objetos estructurales y domésticos cuya distribución refleja fielmente la organización espacial interna. El abandono del asentamiento coincide con epidemias documentadas en Somerset en esa fecha.

Los restos estructurales excavados son importantes para documentar la transición entre la construcción en arcilla y madera a la construcción con piedra en los siglos XI–XII en Inglaterra, y para ilustrar un tipo de construcción rural previamente no documentada en Somerset, una que incorpora elementos de la tradición *Grubenhäuser* anglosajona.

La evidencia medioambiental y los restos de fauna documentan la continuidad en la explotación agrícola durante toda la ocupación, a la vez que apuntan a la existencia de un sistema de campos abiertos para la agricultura en Eckweek ya a fines del siglo XI. Además se cuenta con un gran conjunto de cerámica doméstica, objetos de hierro y piedra y artículos personales que nos evocan la vida cotidiana de los habitantes.

En conjunto, la evidencia consta la evolución de Eckweek como centro señorial durante un período de 400 años, aportando nuevos matices sobre la continuidad y el cambio en los patrones de la vida rural medieval tanto a nivel regional como nacional.

ABBREVIATIONS

AAU	Avon Archaeological Unit Ltd	OS	Ordnance Survey
DMS	Deserted Medieval Settlement	SAM	Scheduled Ancient Monument
HER	Historic Environment Record	SRO	Somerset Record Office
NGR	National Grid Reference	SRS	Somerset Record Society
NHL	National Heritage List	TNA	The National Archives
OD	Ordnance Datum	VCH	Victoria County History

Aerial photograph showing the earthworks at Eckweek. Facing NE. Taken by the late Mick Aston in 1985

1
INTRODUCTION

1.1 BACKGROUND TO THE PROJECT

In 1988 agricultural land attached to Eckweek House Farm at Eckweek Lane, Peasedown St John, near Bath, centred at NGR ST 7121 5762 (Figures 1.1 to 1.5), was earmarked for a new road bypass and associated housing development. The modern town of Peasedown St John is located some 6 miles to the southwest of Bath and developed during the 19th century in response to the expanding coal-mining industry of the Radstock area, alongside the Bath Road, the A367, a major route that closely follows the course of the Roman *Fosse Way*, Ivan Margary's Road 5B (Margary 1973). By 1988 the modern settlement had expanded eastwards as far as Eckweek Lane and plans for the new development, including an extensive belt of new housing in the fields attached to Eckweek House Farm, were well advanced.

In response to the proposed development, an archaeological project was set up by the then County Archaeologist, Rob Iles, of Avon County Planning Department, in order to survey and assess a series of well-preserved earthworks in pasture attached to the farm and first identified by the late Mick Aston during one of his regular aerial photographic surveys of land in Somerset (one of Mick's first images taken around 1985 is reproduced opposite). The preliminary survey work involved measured contour surveys and subsequent geophysical surveys (Section 3.2), the latter undertaken by Andrew Payne of English Heritage. The earthwork

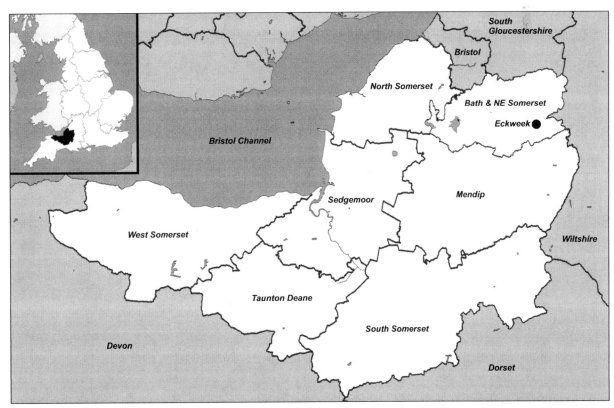

Figure 1.1

England and Wales showing Somerset and modern unitary authorities

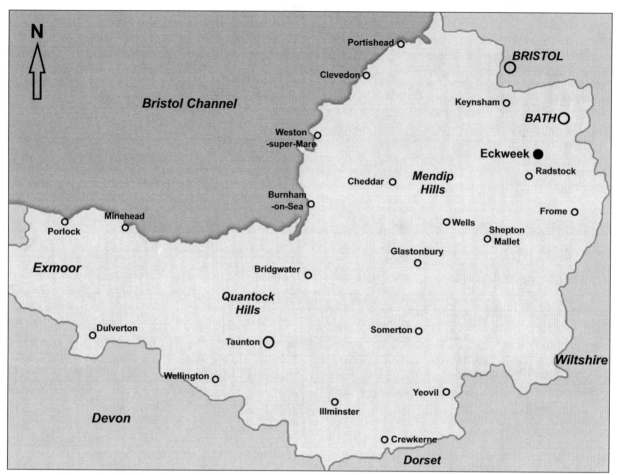

FIGURE 1.2

Historic Somerset showing the location of Eckweek with principal towns and modern regional authorities

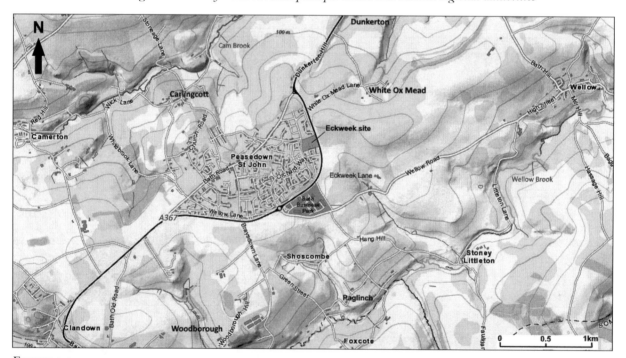

FIGURE 1.3

Peasedown St John and surrounding area showing Eckweek and other settlements in Wellow parish

surveys indicated two, and possibly three, individual farmstead sites located in grassland immediately to the north of Eckweek House Farm. The subsequent geophysical surveys identified a further group of linear negative geophysical anomalies of unknown origin in open grassland immediately to the south of the farm. On the basis of the survey data it was agreed that a selective programme of

INTRODUCTION

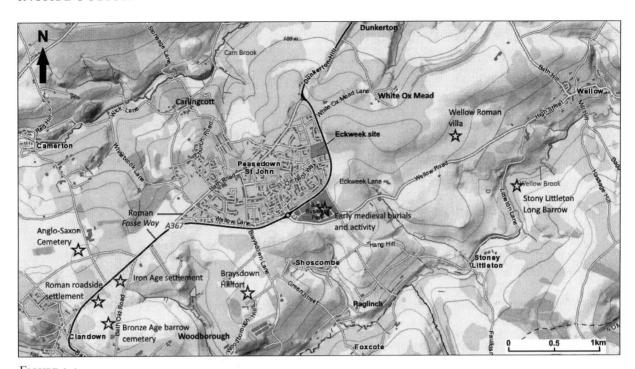

FIGURE 1.4
Peasedown St John showing the Eckweek site, local settlements and recorded monuments

excavation work was needed to investigate the site, in particular the possible farmstead sites indicated by extant earthworks, prior to the impending road and housing development. In the event three of the four zones of archaeological interest indicated by either earthworks or geophysical survey (Figure 1.7, Areas A-G and Area H) were investigated in detail by means of area excavation and trial trenching. The fourth area of interest, located immediately to the north of Eckweek House Farm, between Areas A and H, was investigated by means of geophysical survey. Excavation of the latter, however, was restricted to two small trial trenches (Areas J and K), which revealed shallowly buried medieval structures and deposits. Regrettably the greater part of this area has since been developed for new housing without any detailed investigation or recording, although some archaeology may yet survive in that part adopted as an extension to the parish cemetery (Figure 1.5).

The survey and excavation fieldwork and the initial post-excavation programme was directed by the writer with the great assistance of Alexander Kidd, both initially employed as staff of the former Avon County Council and thereafter on a freelance basis. The fieldwork was supported by a grant from the developers, Beazer Homes Limited and Westbury Homes Limited, with further funding of excavation in Area H and the initial post-excavation programme supported entirely by English Heritage. In addition, the review of documentary evidence for the site undertaken by Dr Nick Corcos (Section 2.1) was supported by a grant from the Maltwood Fund for Archaeological Research in Somerset. The later stages of the project were managed by the late Jan Roberts, who was appointed Avon County Archaeological Officer in January 1989, whilst the bulk of the twelve-man excavation team was initially provided by the former Avon County Community Environment Scheme (ACCES), part of the then Manpower Services Commission (MSC), and later on a freelance basis. MSC involvement in the project ceased in March 1989 when that programme was replaced by the Government's 'Employment Training'.

Excavation and Post-excavation Work

Site investigations began in September 1988 and continued until April of the following year. The intrusive fieldwork initially involved a series of selective evaluation trenches subsequently followed by two larger open area excavations in Areas A and B (Figures 1.6 and 1.7). Further records were made during the initial development groundwork stages of the road carriageway construction by means of an unfunded watching brief. Due to a delay in the development programme a further programme of area excavation was undertaken in May and June 1989 to investigate the geophysical anomalies located to the south of Eckweek House Farm, the part of the study area designated Area H (Figures 1.6 and 1.7). The additional excavation work was undertaken over a period of two months led by the writer with a team of six archaeologists funded by English Heritage, as was the succeeding programme of preliminary post-excavation work. This involved the seriation of the large assemblage of medieval pottery, initial site phasing and the commissioning of a number of key in-house and specialist reports, including those for prehistoric ceramics by Elaine Morris (Section 5.1), iron and lead

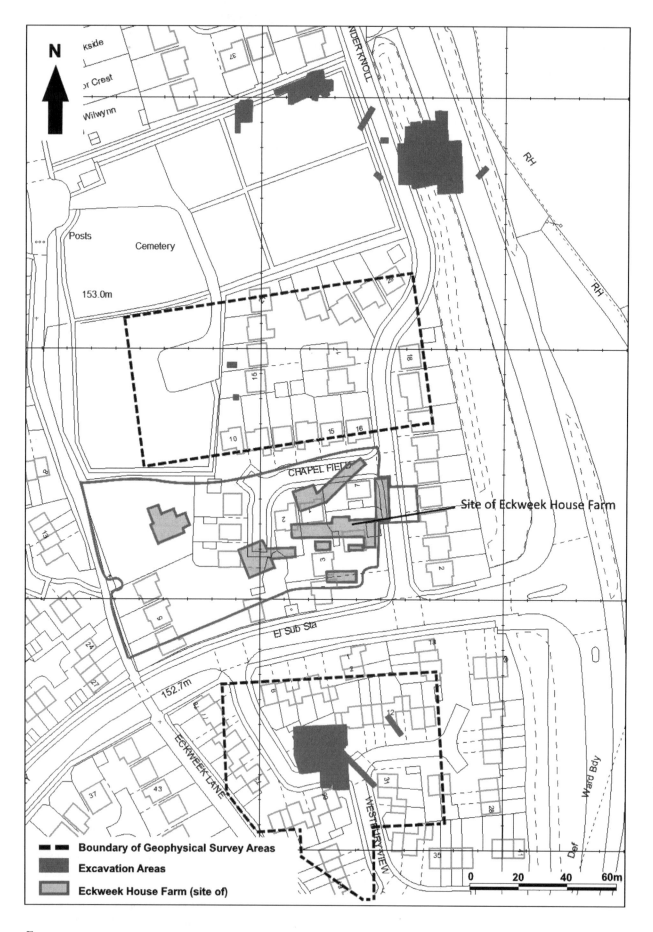

FIGURE 1.5

Eckweek excavation and survey areas superimposed onto the modern Ordnance Survey showing the site of the former Eckweek House Farm

objects by Ann Thompson (Section 5.5), lithics by Vince Russett (Section 5.7), animal bone by Simon Davis (Section 5.13) and charred plant remains by Wendy Carruthers (Section 5.14). In addition, a series of five radiocarbon determinations for medieval deposits was produced by Queens University Belfast (Section 6.1). Other artefact reports, including those for the medieval pottery and worked stone objects, were produced in-house by the writer and Alexander Kidd.

Avon County Council disbanded its archaeology service in 1992 and disappeared both as an organisation and County in 1996. By that time the Eckweek project effectively had been shelved and the slow progress made between then and 2014 was entirely the responsibility of the writer, as indeed was the curation of the project archive (BATRM 1997.1), a part of which (most notably a number of original field drawings and many of the best photographs) was destroyed in an office fire in 2001.

Project Strategy

The initial aim of the project was to characterise the complex of earthworks located in the fields around Eckweek House Farm before they were destroyed by impending development. To do so, it was agreed that initial excavation should be concentrated in OS Field 2477 (Figure 1.7, Area A), where a complex of well-preserved earthworks almost certainly reflected the site of a small farmstead that appeared to incorporate the remains of at least one building located alongside a well-defined hollow-way. These earthworks were located directly within the corridor of the proposed new bypass carriageway and the aim therefore was to complete at least one detailed area excavation plus a series of trial trenches, in order to fully characterise the range of settlement-related activity from earliest to latest in this part of the site – this goal was achieved, along with considerably more.

Structure of the Report

This report is the product of over 25 years of intermittent work by the writer and many other specialists and contributors and staff at Avon Archaeological Unit Limited. In agreeing to fund its preparation, Historic England was at pains to point out that in most respects the report would need to be 'of its time', as a wholesale review of the data that already existed was neither affordable nor indeed justified. As a result some of the contributions that follow, for example the reports on the medieval pottery, worked stone and iron objects, are largely unchanged from those produced in the early 1990s. Other specialist contributions, notably those for the charred plant remains, animal bone, radiocarbon dates, geophysical surveys, prehistoric pottery, coins, copper alloy objects, clay tobacco pipe and molluscs, have either been reviewed or recently updated by their respective authors or, in the case of the documentary evidence (including the contributions by Dr Costen and Dr Thorn), the clay tobacco pipe and the evidence from molluscs, have been produced entirely afresh from primary data or samples. In addition, the structural and stratigraphic evidence from the site has been comprehensively reviewed as part of the work for publication.

No synthesis of the excavated data was produced in the 1990s and as a consequence Chapters 7 and 8 of the report represent a new body of work produced by the writer in 2015. The review and reinterpretation of the excavated data has benefited from a wide range of archaeological research undertaken in the intervening years and moreover from the advice and guidance of Dr Mark Gardiner of Queens University Belfast, whose insight in respect of the late Saxon and medieval structures has been invaluable.

Finally, the project archive including the finds and primary field documentation is held by The Roman Baths Museum, Bath, under accession number BATRM 1997.1. The archive can be consulted for detailed elements of the project, for example stratigraphic matrices, primary context records and background documentation, not reproduced in this report, as well as other reference material such as the portable Fabric Type Series for the late Saxon and medieval pottery.

1.2 GEOLOGY, TOPOGRAPHY AND LAND USE

Eckweek lies towards the southern end of the Cotswold Hills in a region of complex geology consisting of basement rocks ranging in date from the Silurian to the Holocene. This complexity has given rise to variously undulating land and steeper slopes to the northwest and southeast where the Cam and Wellow brooks cross the area (Figure 1.3). The underlying solid geology of the Peasedown St John area can be divided into two principal terrains; to the east, beds of Greater Oolitic Limestone form a capping layer that gives way to beds of limestone interbedded with Fullers Earth clay, the latter representing an important raw material used since the Middle Ages to process and clean wool, exposures of which are found in the valley at nearby Dunkerton. The Inferior Oolite lies below the Fullers Earth and comes to the surface along the edge of the Peasedown ridge. To the west of the town the surface geology consists of Inferior Oolitic Limestone, overlying Liassic clays. The study area itself is situated upon Fullers Earth Rock Member and Lower Fullers Earth Member of the Jurassic Great Oolite Series (British Geological Survey 2000), part of an extensive oolitic ridge that extends to the east of the Mendip hills. In addition to the extensive outcrops of Great and Inferior Oolite Limestone

FIGURE 1.6

The study area in 1988 showing the location of excavation and survey areas and the recording and excavation base line

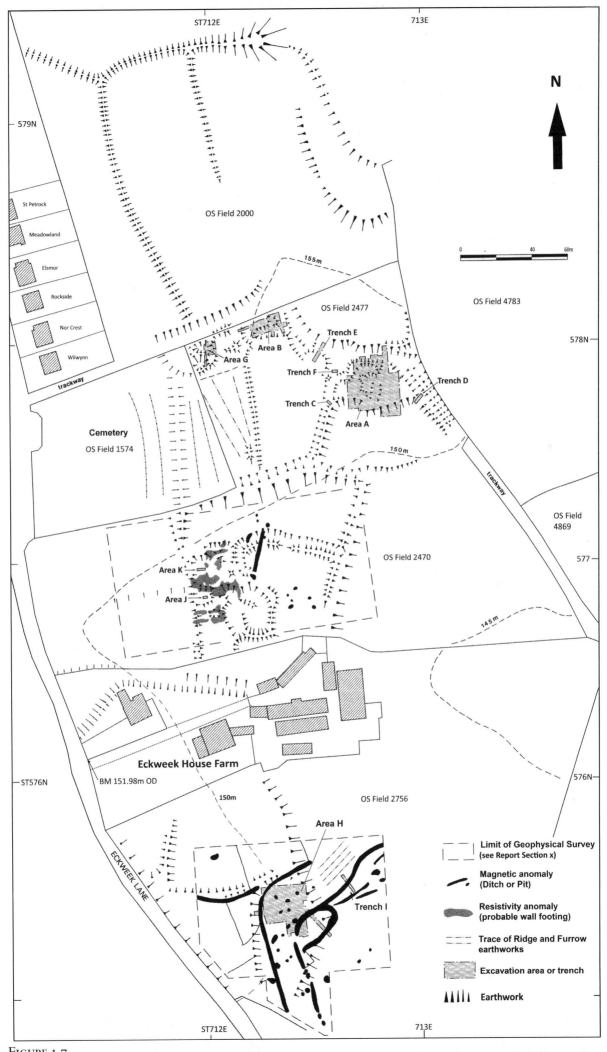

FIGURE 1.7

that locally was most commonly used for building, there are also exposures of Pennant Grit to the west; the most extensive outcrops are of Carboniferous Coal Measure date and occur some 5km southwest of Eckweek around Radstock. The underlying solid geology mainly gives rise to shallow, moderate to well-drained brashy calcareous clays. These soil types are suitable for arable crops and permanent pasture, both of which form part of modern farm regimes in the area, although pasture remains the predominant agricultural land use.

The modern settlement of Peasedown St John is situated on a limestone ridge at around 160m above ordnance datum along a relatively flat, if undulating, plateau. Both the modern town and the settlement at Eckweek lie above the spring line of the ridge and so open water is generally absent. The northern part of the Eckweek site (Figures 1.3 and 1.7) is situated on a gentle south-facing slope, which continues to rise to the north to a height of *c*168m OD at White Ox Mead Knoll and thereafter descends to Dunkerton, situated in the valley of the Cam Brook. The land becomes flatter to the south around Eckweek House Farm (*c*150m OD) and rolls gently towards Camerton before descending to the town of Radstock, situated in the valley of the Wellow Brook, a tributary of the River Avon.

The modern landscape is characteristically open and in places can be somewhat windswept. Hedges are the most common modern land boundary and enclose a pattern of mainly regular, small enclosures, whose pattern alone indicates episodes of land enclosure during the post-medieval period. Mature trees of ash and oak are common in the hedgerows but not abundant, whilst woodland is infrequent and generally small, less than one hectare. Some of the surrounding fields were under cultivation at the time of the project and OS Field 4783 (Figure 1.7), immediately to the east of Area A, was under arable at the time of the fieldwork (this area was fieldwalked but contained remarkably few finds). In contrast, OS Fields 2477 and 2470 (Figure 1.7) contained such well-defined earthworks it was considered unlikely that they had been ploughed since the Middle Ages. Several ponds are noted on the 1st edition and later OS maps of the area and two were still indicated as being open in the 1970s immediately to the east of the settlement, in OS Fields 4783 and 6670.

At the time of the project, prior to the construction of the Peasedown St John A367 bypass, roads in the area were relatively few and narrow. The exception to this was, and remains, the A367, part of the Roman *Fosse Way*, a major route to and from Bath, whose straight alignment cuts diagonally across the limestone plateau.

2
DOCUMENTARY AND ARCHAEOLOGICAL BACKGROUND

2.1 DOCUMENTARY, ARCHAEOLOGICAL AND LANDSCAPE EVIDENCE
by Dr Nick Corcos (2013)

Introduction

The following account examines the archaeological, historical and landscape evidence as background to the programme of survey and excavation that took place at the shrunken medieval settlement of Eckweek. This element of the post-site reporting has been funded by a grant from the Maltwood Fund for Archaeological Research in Somerset, which is gratefully acknowledged.

The campaign of fieldwork at Eckweek was centred around the then extant Eckweek House (formerly Eckweek Farm, now removed) at NGR ST 71244 57709, with the largest of the excavation trenches lying about 175m NNE of the farmhouse; the site of the latter may well have represented the last surviving vestige of the original Eckweek settlement. The work was intended to elucidate, to modern standards of excavation and recording, a type of occupation site, which although well known in Somerset, had up to that date been subjected to only very limited archaeological investigation. The fieldwork indicated that Eckweek had been established by the late Anglo-Saxon period, the archaeology for which is represented by a series of timber structures and associated activity. At the time of their discovery, these were the first rural timber buildings of this date to be identified in Somerset, *apart* from the royal complex at Cheddar, which of course is exceptional and cannot therefore be regarded as comparable. The site continued to be occupied into the high Middle Ages and late medieval period, with substantial stone buildings replacing at least some of the earlier timber structures, and with a rich finds assemblage being recovered from the best preserved of the later buildings.

The site of the Eckweek settlement now lies within the modern civil parish of Peasedown St John, which was carved out only in 1955 from the neighbouring, ancient ecclesiastical parishes of Camerton, Dunkerton and Wellow; historically, however, the settlement of Eckweek itself would always have lain in Wellow parish.

Archaeological Background: The Historic Environment Record and Associated Sources

A trawl of the Bath and North East Somerset Historic Environment Record (HER), covering an area of about 10 sq km and centred on the study site itself at NGR ST 712 576, was carried out. The results of the trawl are tabulated in summary form in Figures 2.1 and 2.2, the split representing the organisation of the HER itself between those records relating to 'Events' and those to 'Monuments'. From a consideration of these sources together, it seems fairly clear that there are in fact few items which could be said to have direct archaeological implications for the purposes of this review, but a few of the more relevant records do need to be reviewed in the context of the fieldwork results which is the subject of the larger report presented here. There are no designated Scheduled Ancient Monuments in the vicinity of the Eckweek settlement, but these do occur in the wider area and those of particular relevance to Eckweek are considered below.

The HER entries clearly attest to human activity in the vicinity of the study site from at least the Bronze Age (HER MBN1594; Rowe and Alexander 2011), and landscape manipulation on a considerable scale from the Iron Age is suggested by the sheer size of the ditch recorded in HER MBN11201, as part of the Eckweek excavations. That this feature is probably associated with settlement seems perfectly reasonable and indeed, is reinforced by the occurrence, just over 1km to the southwest, of another, much more extensive Iron Age site complete with human burials, metalworking debris, a possible defensive ditch, and pottery (HER MBN1595). These finds should come as no surprise – the area around Wellow and Peasedown St John today constitutes good-quality farmland, and there is no reason to think that this was not also the case in the Iron Age. This is therefore very

HER Number	Site Name	NGR (ST)	Record Type and Date of Work	Edited Description
EBN2519	Home Farm, White Ox Mead, Wellow	72019 58244	Buildings survey 1998	A measured survey of two agricultural buildings, formerly belonging to Home Farm was based on architect's measured survey. This in turn was checked for inaccuracies and generalisations and used as the basis for a detailed survey based on rectified photography, hand measurement and written notes.
EBN2520	White Ox Mead	72011 58250	Watching brief 1998	An archaeological watching brief was conducted during the demolition of existing buildings and the excavation of footings for the construction of a new dwelling on the site of two adjoining barns. Initial excavation demonstrated the existence of medieval features probably associated with occupation of the site from the 13th or 14th century. Documentary evidence would however suggest continuous occupation...between the 17th and 19th centuries and observations made during the removal of one building produced clear evidence for the existence of earlier, post-medieval structures within the area of works.
EBN2544	Peasedown St John	71181 57080	Geophysical survey 2000	Geophysical survey following on from a desktop study in relation to a development proposal on allocated land in the local plan. Three areas of potential archaeological anomalies were identified.
EBN2594	Eckweek medieval settlement	71212 57724	Geophysical survey and excavation 1988–1989	Investigations in advance of development for housing, geophysical survey carried out by the Ancient Monuments Laboratory. Excavation at Eckweek yielded evidence of a well preserved and stratified rural occupation that is unique in Avon and Somerset. Continuity of occupation is likely from the 10th to the 15th centuries and incorporates a transition from timber to stone building traditions.
EBN2595	Peasedown St John	71171 57123	Evaluation 2000	Archaeological remains were found widely distributed across the study area within 26 evaluation trenches. Part of the site was covered by a blanket of colluvium which originated from the higher ground to the northwest of the study area. This colluvium both sealed and was also cut by archaeological features. However, over most of the site the natural substrate was covered only by a thin topsoil suggesting soil erosion caused by soil instability following early land clearance and later episodes of agriculture. A cemetery of unknown date was found in the northern corner of the study area (Area 1). However, it may be bounded by a wide shallow ditch and associated with the late Anglo-Saxon and medieval settlement previously excavated at Eckweek Farm approximately 400m to the north of the study area. In Areas 3–5 numerous undated features in the form of pits, postholes, gullies and ditches were apparent. It is possible that these features represent part of a wider rural prehistoric landscape suggested by other prehistoric sites in the vicinity of the study area. However, the presence of a large linear ditch with easterly curving terminals in Area 2 does not fit well into the general picture of a prehistoric rural farming economy and the reasons for its construction and abandonment remain unclear.
EBN2643	Peasedown St John	71186 57073	Desk-based assessment 2000	No sites or artefacts of archaeological significance were recorded from within the study area, which does, though, lie in close proximity to two Iron Age sites. One has been responsible for the designation of an adjacent field to the southwest as a Site of Particular Importance for Archaeology in the Wansdyke Local Plan of 1995 and the other lies to the north at Eckweek Farm. It is possible that remains associated with these sites extend into the study area. It is likely that during the medieval and post-medieval periods the study area was farmland although it is possible that features associated with an Anglo-Saxon and medieval settlement, also identified at Eckweek Farm, may extend into the study area. Also of note are earthworks approximately 100m to the south of the study area which may represent traces of a former medieval settlement.
EBN3110	Peasedown St John	71118 57135	Watching brief 2006–2007	The site was at Plot B, Bath Business Park during groundworks. No features or deposits of archaeological interest and no material pre-dating the modern period was recovered.
EBN3113	Peasedown St John	70371 56950	Desk-based assessment Not dated in HER	Site at Wellow Lane, Peasedown St John. No findings specified in HER.
EBN2960	Peasedown St John	70784 57833	Watching brief 2004	Observation of the excavation of foundation trenches for a small house in Ashgrove. The deposits observed all relate to modern disturbance, and there was no sign of Roman or early activity. Works secured through a planning condition in view of the proximity of Roman road and other finds.
EBN3049	Peasedown St John	71200 57100	Watching brief 2006	Work undertaken during groundworks at Bath Business Park. No features or deposits of archaeological interest were identified and no material pre-dating the modern period was recovered.

FIGURE 2.1

HER events

DOCUMENTARY AND ARCHAEOLOGICAL BACKGROUND

HER Number	Site Name	NGR (ST)	Edited Description
MBN1593	North of Eckweek Lane	7098 5805	Probable site of a ploughed down barrow. The area is under pasture and no trace of a barrow can be seen. Air photographs show a circular crop mark at ST70985811, approximately 80m in diameter. The field has been used as a horse paddock and the crop mark has been caused by a training ring. Grinsell gives the grid reference at ST70985806 as the site of a possible barrow reported by N Quinnell, 1964. Nothing seen by Grinsell in 1970. Possibly 'Aescbeore' in an Anglo-Saxon Charter.
MBN1594	Bath Road	703 574	A looped bronze palstave was found in 1920 whilst digging a trench through one of the workshops of Messrs Coles Bros (Builders) of Peasedown St John. 17cm long, 6.5m wide on cutting edge, weight 17 ounces. Now in Taunton Museum.
MBN1595	Peasedown St John, Braysdown Road	7047 5691	A V-shaped defensive ditch, similar to those at Camerton (Iron Age 'A' and Wheeler's Maiden Castle Phase II – about 200 BC) and containing pottery of the same type, was revealed during sewer laying alongside the Peasedown St John–Braysdown Road, in field 900 on the OS 25 inch map. A human skeleton was also found in this ditch. In addition a pit was found which produced a quantity of early Iron Age late 'A' type pottery, together with several fragments of a crucible with bronze dross still adhering. Mr Wedlake indicated on the map the approximate position of the ditch which ran from ST70475691 to ST70545671. The site is under barley and nothing is visible. Majority of artifacts went to Bristol Museum. Provenance of records unknown.
MBN1605	South of White Ox Mead	720 580	White Ox Mead has been suggested as a deserted medieval village. It is mentioned in the Domesday Book. Possibly only a shrunken settlement. Series of lynchets and platforms. One long bank running northeast–southwest.
MBN1615	Eckweek House (now demolished)	710 580	Roman foundations, coins and potsherds were recorded by Skinner at Eckweek Farm, a mile southwest of the Wellow villa. There is no local knowledge of Roman foundations at Eckweek House (formerly Eckweek Farm) and nothing is visible on the ground or on RAF air photographs. Wedlake (of Meadgate, Camerton) also investigated the area but without success.
MBN1616	Dunkerton Hill	710 580	A Roman stone coffin 'was dug up not long since, near the Fosse, to the right of the Turnpike as you descend Dunkerton Hill going to Bath'. No further information on the coffin. Dunkerton Hill, east of the turnpike, is largely centred on ST7158.
MBN2296	Eckweek Deserted Medieval Settlement	712 578	Earthworks in fields to the north of Eckweek House, and beside the road in the field to the south. Recorded in Domesday Book as the settlement of Ecewiche. Excavations and survey work in 1988/89 identified three individual farmstead sites in the fields to the north of Eckweek House and a further farmstead to the south. A total of eight house structures were identified.
MBN5191	SE of White Ox Mead Knoll	715 578	'In the field adjoining the Ridgeway Rd to the SE of the clump of trees on top of the ick, or where farmer Pontings ploughman informed me he found so many coins formerly while ploughing, I clearly noticed different places on the height where habitations had been erected'. Skinner seems to think that Roman settlement spreads from here eastwards to the site of the Hayes.
MBN5372	White Ox Mead	720 583	Earthworks between the present farms suggest a larger or shifted settlement. Earthwork survey shows several banks and platforms possibly relating to medieval occupation in the fields between Home Farm and White Ox Mead. The banks appear to form rectilinear enclosures that bear little relation to the modern boundaries, particularly the lane between Home Farm and Hays Farm that apparently truncates the southern enclosure/former field.
MBN6178	Not stated	710 570	Location not stated other than centred on 710 570. No date, and no description other than 'earthworks'.
MBN6437	Not stated	711 576	After topsoil stripping (by machine) of the whole field in preparation for road construction and adjacent housing development, a possible pit filled with dark brown clayey loam was observed (28 June 1990). The feature was cut into a brashy brown clay [?natural]. A single pit contrasts with the myriad of features on the opposite side of the road. Site due for redevelopment.
MBN 11079	Eckweek Lane Burial Ground	71241 57248	Inhumation cemetery located by a 50m long evaluation trench. Undated. Graves were shallow, just beneath subsoil. 16 graves...on an approximate west–east or southwest–northeast alignment, with a single grave...on more of a SSW–NNE alignment in trench 1 the graves cut colluvium and the upper fills are at a depth of 0.28m below ground level. Evidence of cemetery organisation was apparent. None was excavated. The full extent of the cemetery is uncertain. It is possibly associated with the late Saxon and medieval settlement at Eckweek Farm. Organised burial argues for a Roman or later date.
MBN11201	Eckweek Iron Age Occupation	71230 57521	Deep curvilinear ditch, first identified by geophysics and then excavated. Sections were excavated in three locations. The ditch was 5.5m wide and 2.1m deep. Ditch profile was irregular and incorporated a number of possible re-cuts or erosion gullies. The base was cut slightly more deeply and contained a primary fill which contained significant quantities of pottery and bone. Postholes were found associated with an entrance. Interpretation not clear but the ditch is most likely to be associated with occupation.
MBN30100	Home Farm, White Ox Mead	720 583	Group of two traditional stone built barns associated with a farm now demolished but presumably part of the group. Now in the ownership of Home Farm. All are in a ruinous state but retain many original features. A third barn is modern but replaces a stone version. Field has some features within it which may represent buried walls associated with the original farm. Documents from the SRO demonstrate that the site was occupied in the seventeenth century. The Tithe Map of 1840 shows the existence of (both) buildings with an additional building between the surviving structures.

FIGURE 2.2

HER monuments

Landowner	Occupier	No.	Name & Description	Cultivation	A	R	P
Wm Skuse	In hand	1007	Eckwick Tyning	Arable	29	0	29
Do.	Do.	1008	(Eckwick) Farmhouse & outbuildings				
Do.	Do.	1009	(Eckwick) Garden		0	1	8
Do.	Do.	1087	Thirteen Acres	Arable	12	0	16
Do.	Do.	1089	Upper Tyning	Arable	9	0	26
		1113	Fosse Tyning	Arable	26	0	35
			Total of Eckweek Farm		76	3	34
William Collins	William Skuse	1113a	Two Acres in Fosse Tyning	Arable & Quarry	1	3	32
John Hill, Joseph Hellicar, Lessees under St John's Hospital, Bath	Elihu Gibbs	1114	Hullicks (Huddox) Hill	Arable	10	1	0
		1115					
J Purnell Esq.	Geo. Matthews	1116	Clay Batch Paddock	Arable	0	3	22
John, Eliz. and Julia Hill, and J L Simmons	John Parker	1117	The Folly	Arable	6	3	25
W C James Esq.	John Parker	1118	The Folly	Arable	2	3	8
James Brimble, Lessee under Wm. Gore-Langton Esq.	In Hand	1119	The Folly	Arable	0	2	33
J D Brodribb Esq.	John Parker	1120	Stolbrow	Arable	6	2	39
Henry Keel, Lessee under St John's Hospital, Bath	In Hand	1121	Foxcote Path	Arable	5	0	3
John Hill, Joseph Hellicar, Lessees under St John's Hospital, Bath	Elihu Gibbs	1122	Hullicks (Huddox) Hill	Arable	5	0	13
John Hill, Joseph Hellicar, Lessees under St John's Hospital, Bath	Elihu Gibbs	1123	Part of Hullicks (Huddox) Hill	Arable	7	2	36
John, Eliz. and Julia Hill, and J L Simmons	John Parker	1124	Fourteen Acres	Arable	13	0	12
J. Purnell Esq.	James Gibbons	1125	Little Hullicks (Huddox) Hill	Arable	1	1	25
Phoebe Flower	Elihu Gibbs	1126	Shoscombe Field	Arable	7	0	29
John Hill	James Brimble	1127	Foxcote Path	Arable	1	2	2
Miss E J Bury	Micah Gibbs	1128	Hullicks (Huddox) Hill	Arable	2	3	12
James Brimble, Lessee under Wm. Gore-Langton Esq.	In Hand	1129	Cottage and Garden		0	0	17
Numerous – Trustees of Mary Smith, deceased	Elihu Gibbs	1130	Folly	Arable	1	3	39
J Purnell Esq.	Geo. Matthews	1131	Clay Batch	Pasture	5	3	29
J Purnell Esq.	Geo. Matthews	1132	Red Post Inn etc				
J Purnell Esq.	Geo. Matthews	1133	Garden and yard		0	1	34
J Purnell Esq.	Wm. Loder	1134	Cottage, smith's shop & garden				19
J Purnell Esq.	Geo. Matthews	1135	Red Post Tyning	Pasture	10	1	38
J Purnell Esq.	Geo. Matthews & James Gibbons	1136	Julius Caesar	Pasture	3	0	2
John Balne, Lessee under Wm. Long Esq.	John Skeates	1137	Wall Mead	Arable	3	2	22
Numerous – trustees of Mary Smith, deceased	Elihu Gibbs	1138	Wall Mead	Arable	7	1	13
John, Eliz. and Julia Hill, and J L Simmons	John Parker	1140	The Lands	Arable	6	0	13
Eliz. Bury	Micah Gibbs	1141	Hullicks (Huddox) Hill	Arable	4	0	27
W C James Esq.	John Parker	1142	Galloping Tyning	Arable	9	0	36
W C James Esq.	John Parker	1143	Galloping Tyning	Arable	8	2	27
Henry Keel, Lessee under St John's Hospital, Bath	In Hand	1144	Shoscombe Field Tyning	Arable	8	0	10
W Long Esq.	J Oxenham	1145	Two Acres	Arable	1	3	14
J H Hill, Eliz. Hill, J L Simmons	John Parker	1146	Five Yards	Arable	1	1	5
Geo. Matthews	In Hand	1147	Harry	Arable	1	2	35
John Craddock	Elihu Gibbs	1148	White Hill Tyning	Arable	7	2	35
Walter Long Esq.	Joseph Ponting	1149	Yonder Tyning	Arable	20	0	34
John Balne, Lessee under Wm Long Esq.	John Skeates	1150	Pye	Arable	2	0	1
W Long Esq.	J Oxenham	1151	Seven Acres	Arable	7	2	13
W Long Esq.	J Oxenham	1010	Eckwick Mead	Pasture	2	2	22
Mary Dovell, copyholder under Walter Long Esq.	James Armstrong	1011	Eckweek	Pasture	1	2	36
Hon. H H Tracey	Daniel Mattock	1012	Knowles	Arable	13	3	21
Hon. H H Tracey	Daniel Mattock	1013	Twelve Acres	Arable	10	3	7
Hon. H H Tracey	Daniel Mattock	1014	Eighteen Acres	Pasture	16	0	21
Hon. H H Tracey	Daniel Mattock	1060	Eight Acres	Pasture	7	1	25
Hon. H H Tracey	Daniel Mattock	1061	Little Knowle	Pasture	7	0	17
Hon. H H Tracey	Daniel Mattock	1062	Plantation		0	3	2
Hon. H H Tracey	Daniel Mattock	1063	Knowle	Pasture	22	1	14
W Long Esq.	J Oxenham	1064	Eckwick Paddock	Pasture	1	2	25
Bury, Miss E J	Micah Gibbs	1065	Eckwick Paddock	Pasture	7	3	36
Do.	Do.	1066	Barn Close	Arable	5	0	21
Do.	Do.	1067	Chit Grove	Pasture	3	3	15
Do.	Do.	1068	Seven Acres	Arable	7	0	35
Wm Collins	Wm Collins	1069	Over Rusham	Arable	3	0	7
Hon. H H Tracey	Daniel Mattock	1070	Grass Rusham	Pasture	5	1	31
Wm Collins	Himself	1071	Middle Rusham	Pasture	1	3	35
Bury, Miss E J	Micah Gibbs	1111	Tyning	Arable	12	3	25
Wm. Collins	Himself	1085	Lower Rusham	Arable	3	3	23
W Long Esq.	J Oxenham	1086	Rusham	Arable	4	0	13
W Long Esq.	J Oxenham	1088	Watershore	Arable	10	3	8
W Long Esq.	J Oxenham	1090	Watershore	Arable	4	0	34
Wm Collins	Himself	1091	Watershore	Pasture	3	1	29
Bury, Miss E	Micah Gibbs	1092	Watershore Mead	Pasture	3	1	22
W Long Esq.	J Oxenham	1093	Watershore	Arable	10	2	7
James Hancock	In Hand	1094	Cottage and garden		0	2	32
Hon. H H Tracey	James Hancock	1095	Garden		0	1	38

FIGURE 2.3

Extract from the 1843 Wellow tithe award

likely to have been an area of dense settlement and land use at that time, of which the known sites give merely the faintest glimpse. For example, at Tunley, about 3.2km northwest of the Eckweek settlement, there exists a Scheduled Ancient Monument (SAM No BA170), described as a 'hillfort', although it is probably more accurately characterised as a 'hilltop enclosure' and it is almost certainly Iron Age in date. In addition, a deep ditch of probable middle Iron Age date was revealed during the course of excavations on a large, multi-period site about 400m or so south of Eckweek and may have been part of a much more extensive field system (Rowe and Alexander 2011). In the wider Iron Age landscape it seems likely that the usual kind of settlement pattern, occupied by the overwhelming majority of the rural population at that date, consisted of open, undefended single farmsteads, or small hamlet-type, kinship farmstead groups.

The site of the Eckweek shrunken medieval settlement was itself devoid of evidence for occupation or activity during the Romano-British period. There are indications of such activity in the immediate vicinity, although some of the 'evidence' is best described as equivocal. For example, HER MBN5191 is an antiquarian account by the redoubtable Reverend John Skinner, Rector of Camerton, of Roman finds and an occupation site, not precisely located but placed by the HER at a point about 300m NNE of the Eckweek settlement. The site is unproven to modern archaeology however, and at present its existence cannot be assumed. Skinner was also responsible for the identification of a further site that he characterised as 'Roman', at a location which appears to have lain immediately north of Eckweek and indeed the HER (MBN1615) places this site at Eckweek Farm (latterly Eckweek House), on whose land the shrunken medieval settlement was situated. Skinner apparently discovered 'foundations, coins and potsherds' at this location, but like his earlier 'site', this one also has remained elusive to modern archaeology and thereby its existence is unproven. Another of Skinner's 'discoveries', related to a near-contemporary report on the unearthing of a stone coffin on Dunkerton Hill about 300m or so northwest of Eckweek (HER MBN1616), conforms to the established pattern of his reports as unproven. None of this is necessarily to say that Skinner was in error in his reporting and characterisation of any or all of these sites, but at present it is simply the case that they cannot be admitted as firm evidence for Romano-British occupation or activity in the context of the present discussion. In contrast, just over 1.5km east of Eckweek, and just outside the area of the HER trawl (although its location is shown on Figure 1.4), lies the Wellow Roman villa (HER MBN1604), a Scheduled Ancient Monument (BA91), the site of which is well attested archaeologically.

At present, it does not look as though Eckweek itself was one of those places for which its well-attested *–wic* placename can be taken as an indication of an origin in the Romano-British period, although the name probably does suggest that it is at least very likely to have been an element in the local post-Roman landscape and, in Michael Costen's words, of 'continuing agricultural relevance' (Costen 2011, 57).

That there was indeed activity, and in fact probably occupation, in the area of the Eckweek settlement in the post-Roman period appears likely, as excavation work carried out just under 0.5km to the south (Rowe and Alexander 2011) recorded a D-shaped enclosure that is tentatively dated by radiocarbon assay to between cal AD 650 and 860. In addition, this work identified a series of badly-preserved inhumation burials, which, although returning a series of conflicting radiocarbon dates, seem nonetheless to represent part of what was a long-lived cemetery. These burials clearly seem to be related to a further series of inhumations discovered during an earlier evaluation on the northern side of the same site, only about 300m south of the Eckweek settlement and completely undated (HER MBN11079), but contextually almost certainly post-Roman in origin. This is *contra* the HER, which gives the possible date range simply as 'Saxon to Medieval – AD 410 to AD 1539'. Zadora-Rio (2003) has shown that the mere fact of the existence of a local church by no means precluded the possibility that Christian burial could, for a time at least, continue in open, unbounded cemeteries. This perspective is very much the one adopted by the excavators at Peasedown St John, who point out that the discovery of early medieval burials *outside* the formal Christian ritual compass of a churchyard, almost by definition argues for a date no later than the 10th to 11th century, but at the same time by no means precludes the likelihood that the burials themselves were Christian.

Although the burials are undated in any absolute sense, it nonetheless remains a distinct possibility that the small, late Anglo-Saxon community attested at Eckweek both archaeologically and in the Domesday record, buried its dead in the Peasedown cemetery, at least in the period before the formal foundation of the main estate church. This church, later the parish church at Wellow, was founded at some unknown date before 1066 and almost certainly, given the estate's clear size and importance in the pre-Conquest period, by the year 1000 and probably well before that date (Morris 1989, 140–167). Even if it were known, the date of foundation of Wellow church could not necessarily be taken as a reliable guide to the date at which any 'unbounded' cemetery in the vicinity ceased in use. In the specific case of Eckweek, one wonders whether the simple fact of its distant relationship to the parish church at Wellow, from which it lay no less than 3km to the east, may have contributed to a degree of inertia in terms of preferred burial location and tended to favour continued use of the Peasedown cemetery even after a more formalised burial ground around the later parish church had become established.

Eckweek: Antecedents of Settlement, Territory and Landscape

Historically, Eckweek always lay firmly within Wellow parish, however, it is worth noting that there are quite strong indications that, at different times and to varying extents, the bounds of Eckweek manor, or manors, seem to have 'bled over' into adjacent parishes. Manorial jurisdiction and landholding were no respecters of parish boundaries: individual manors under a single, unifying jurisdiction, could be and often were scattered across numerous parishes, which did not even have to be contiguous. While most of the time Eckweek is placed in Wellow parish by the documents, occasionally, it is described as 'Eckweek in Camerton', or 'Eckweek in Wellow and Camerton'. The likely explanation in most cases is simply that this is probably the result of a combination of misidentification by scribes unfamiliar with the local manorial geography and local patterns of landholding and tenure, and that those tenants who held the manor or manors of Eckweek also held lands in Camerton, which were then counted under Eckweek.

The two tiny estates that emerge in the documentary record as *Eckwick*, or any one of numerous variable medieval spellings thereof, make their first appearance in the pages of Domesday Book, the entry for which is considered by Dr Frank Thorn below.

Wellow, the wider estate of which, historically at least, Eckweek always appears to have been part, can be first discerned before the Norman Conquest, in the form of an Anglo-Saxon royal land grant made originally to the church of Sherborne. The grant was later modified to favour Wells, which had inherited part of the Sherborne estate upon the creation of its see in or after AD 909 (Costen 2011, 194). These records have recently been subjected to a meticulous review by Dr Susan Kelly (Kelly 2007), as part of her wider reassessment of the corpus of surviving pre-Conquest charters, and the reader is referred to that source for the detailed arguments underpinning the brief summary of those records that follow here.

It should be noted as a prelude to the Anglo-Saxon material that, somewhat oddly for what clearly must have been a large estate in the late 11th century, Wellow itself does not appear in Domesday Book, or more accurately, there are no manorial resources recorded under an estate which explicitly bears that name. This is all the more strange considering that from the late Anglo-Saxon period, and into the 19th century, Wellow lay at the head of its own Hundred. Kelly (2007, 198) has suggested that a small (two-hide) estate at Wellow, which appears to be the subject of a pre-Conquest charter (S262) and eventually came to the church of Wells, may be identical to that found 'tacked on' to the main 50-hide Wells estate enumerated in detail in Domesday (Thorn and Thorn 1980). As already noted, this little holding seems to have originated as a grant to the church at Sherborne. Dr Thorn is of the view that Domesday Book's failure to identify Wellow by name becomes explicable if one considers that by far the greater part of the Wellow estate itself was in fact unhidated, and that its resources were likely to have been subsumed within the account of the massive, and ancient, royal manor of Frome; his argument in this respect is laid out in detail below.

There is as yet no edition of the Somerset *Victoria County History* covering Wellow and the surrounding area, which means that, by default, the most accessible treatment of any real detail remains that contained in the Reverend John Collinson's late 18th-century survey of the entire county (Collinson 1791, III, 325–329), a perfectly sound and worthy enough work in its own day, but not in any way comparable with modern historiographical and landscape archaeological approaches.

Wellow takes its name from the Wellow Brook, which flows southwest to northeast through the central part of the parish, forming Wellow's parish boundary with Hinton Charterhouse northeast of the village itself, and with Foxcote (or 'Forscote') to its southwest. The brook flows immediately to the south of Wellow village in a valley the southern side of which is steep-sided, with the settlement itself sitting somewhat strung out along a northeast/southwest road occupying a narrow break of slope above the brook. The slope continues upwards, although at a rather gentler gradient, north of the village. While it is certainly fortunate that pre-Conquest spellings are available (for which see further below), the meaning of the river name, and hence of the placename, is unknown; but it is certainly pre-English in origin. Ekwall, comparing the Somerset example with an identical name in Hampshire, considers that it is from Welsh *gwelw*, 'pale blue' (Ekwall 1960, 505). Mills (2011, 488) agrees that the provenance is British, but prefers a meaning of 'winding', and indeed in this respect he is following an earlier suggestion by Michael Costen (1979, 14).

Historically, Wellow's large size is clearly attested. At the time of the formal confirmation of the tithe apportionment in 1841, the parish contained something just over 5,140 acres (2,080ha) of land (SRO D/D/Rt 303). The cumulative effect of this large size, the estate's location on a river with a simplex pre-English name, the fact that Wellow was a hundredal centre, and the known existence about 1km west of the present-day village of what was clearly a large and opulent Roman villa complex, to which reference has already been made, is to give the very strong impression that Wellow was an important estate with ancient, and perhaps even

DOCUMENTARY AND ARCHAEOLOGICAL BACKGROUND

pre-English origins. Studies elsewhere in Somerset and beyond have demonstrated that these attributes taken together may be considered diagnostic features of so-called 'seminal' estates (see for example Corcos 2011, 275–285 for a case in north Somerset), and indeed to this list can be added the evidence of the Anglo-Saxon documentary record, which attests very strongly to Wellow's origins as a royal holding.

There is, however, one respect in which Wellow does not appear to conform to the general model of major, ancient royal estates that emerge in the documentary record before 1066 and that is in its lack of a minster church. There do not seem to have been any fully parochial daughter churches in the medieval period that originated as dependencies of Wellow – chapelries there were (at Peasedown and Shoscombe), but these were later 19th-century in origin and can be discounted for present purposes (Youngs 1979, 441).

As a general rule, one would usually expect a church at the centre of a hundred, with a simplex placename derived from a river name and likely pre-Conquest royal antecedents, to show at least some remnant evidence of a structure of ecclesiastical dependencies. It is possible that Wellow's very close ties to, and indeed administrative dependency on, the large and ancient royal manor of Frome, as suggested by Frank Thorn, meant that its church never had the opportunity to break away and acquire dependencies in its own right. It is also possible, however, that such ties did exist in the pre-Conquest period, but that they were severed at an early date, before a meaningful level of documentation for local administration usually becomes available, which for most places is the late 12th to 13th century. At present then, it might be unwise to assert categorically that Wellow was never a minster church, at least in the sense of possessing a group of dependent 'daughter' churches, apart from anything else because it is now well established that once important churches could, for a wide variety of reasons, decline in status over time (Blair 2005, 508–512).

The existence of a coherent, bounded estate at Wellow can be first inferred from an Anglo-Saxon royal charter purported to date to the mid 8th century (the given date is AD 766), which granted two hides of land at a location simply described as being 'on' the River Wellow. Kelly's basic assessment of this source is that

> There can be little doubt that a genuine eighth-century diploma underlies the received text: positive features include the Latin bounds and the entirely consistent witness list. But there are grounds for believing that in its present form [it] should be treated as a forgery …… It seems most likely that [it] is …… based on a diploma that was originally in favour of a different beneficiary [i.e. the church of Sherborne] ……

> These Latin surveys [ie bounds] seem to represent a genuine West Saxon innovation [of the 8th–9th centuries], later superseded by the sequential bounds in Old English which had become the norm in West Saxon charters by the mid-ninth century …… the identification of an estate by reference to a natural feature (here a river), rather than by a fixed placename, is another detail that is generally an early symptom (Kelly 2007, 195–197).

The bounds of this estate as given in the charter are best regarded as awaiting a plausible solution, although of course, various suggestions have been made about how the boundary points may translate into an entity on the ground that might admit of reconstruction on modern maps (Kelly 2007, 198). The difficulty with these bounds is that 'there is not a single landmark in it which can be identified with any name in the modern [parish of] Wellow' (Grundy 1935, 197–198). The place that later emerged as being identified with the placename Eckweek may well have fallen within these bounds, but this is problematic and there is now no way to be sure if this was the case. The extent of the grant, purportedly only two hides, also seems rather too small to have encompassed an estate of the size of the later parish, although that is exactly what Peter Kitson has apparently suggested, albeit with the exclusion of Peasedown St John and Shoscombe (Kelly 2007, 198). There is still much debate as to what, if anything, the hide actually equated to on the ground before its adaptation purely as a unit of tax from the late Anglo-Saxon period (Faith 1997, 91–92; Costen 2011, 82–84 and 128–132; Higham 1990; Ryan 2011), however it seems counter-intuitive to suggest that an ancient ecclesiastical parish later amounting to over 5,000 acres (2,080ha) in size, a very large proportion of it consisting of good quality agricultural land, could be represented by an estate rated at only two hides at the time of its *original* transfer from the royal fisc. It must therefore remain highly probable that the AD 766 charter was not transferring all the land that later emerged within the bounds of the ecclesiastical parish of Wellow.

Following directly on from this, there is another point about the 8th-century bounds of S262 that seems not to have been noted by previous commentators. On the western side of Wellow parish, the entire length of its ancient boundary with both Dunkerton (north) and Camerton (south) marches with the Fosse Way, a total of some 3.5km of boundary altogether, and yet there is no mention whatsoever of this major routeway in the boundary clause of S262. This seems inconceivable if the road had indeed formed any part of the boundary of the estate which was being transferred; a point reinforced by those cases where Somerset Anglo-Saxon charters do make explicit reference to the Fosse Way, where the bounds of their estates march with it

(Costen 2011, 13). Even where the Fosse Way is not explicitly named, as in the boundary clause attached to S692, it seems clear that use of the term *Bæþ herpoð*, 'Bath main road', is intended to refer specifically to it (Kelly 2007, 120). Michael Costen has highlighted further examples of this kind of usage in the Bath charters for the area around Stantonbury (Costen 1983). In her own translation of the AD 766 estate circuit, Kelly notes the occurrence of a boundary point identified as a 'public road', but it follows immediately after a bound called 'Wellow ford', which clearly must be a point actually on the River Wellow itself and so cannot by definition be anywhere near the Fosse Way (Kelly 2007, 198). On this measure alone, and *contra* Kitson, it seems highly improbable that S262 is dealing with an entity that can in any way be equated with the area of the later ecclesiastical parish. The bounds do, however, give the distinct impression that whatever the extent of the estate, the River Wellow itself formed its backbone; as Susan Kelly notes, 'the estate clearly included land on both sides of the river' (Kelly 2007, 198).

In fact, consideration of the topography, and of the local road pattern that was in existence at least by the time of the tithe map, lend support to the idea that the 'Wellow ford' of the charter can be equated with the present river crossing immediately south of the village, and that by extension, the charter is very likely to be dealing with a block of land in the centre of, but probably smaller than, the mid 19th-century 'tithe' parish straddling the Wellow Brook and including the area later occupied by the settlement of Wellow itself. The pattern of lanes north and south of Wellow village is extremely striking. To the north, two main lanes, one coming from the direction of Combe Hay and the other from Twinhoe, converge on the southwest/northeast main road through Wellow village and then effectively 'funnel' sharply southwards, as a single, deeply cut lane down the short but steep slope to the main crossing of the River Wellow, where there is now a bridge, but which originally is likely to have been the site of a ford. Immediately the river has been crossed however, the single lane branches out and diverges fan-like into no fewer than four separate routes heading for different locations on the southern side of the river, all except one (a lane which leads ultimately to Norton St Philip) serving places inside Wellow parish (namely Stony Littleton, Hassage and Baggeridge).

As with so many local road networks which converge on or 'funnel' towards river crossing points, it is highly likely that this is an extremely ancient pattern and may indeed pre-date the establishment of the 'modern' settlement of Wellow, at least in its present form and on its present site. The lane to Hassage, for example, clearly has been partially truncated towards its southern end by the establishment of field boundaries that were in existence at least by the time of the mid 19th-century tithe map (SRO DD/SAS/c2401/7). The probable antiquity of the road pattern north and south of Wellow village, therefore lends support to the suggestion that the 'Wellow ford' of the AD 766 charter is most likely to be represented by the point at which the later 'packhorse' bridge spans the river immediately south of the present village.

As well as S262, other charters survive which may also record pre-Conquest land transfers involving estates in or near Wellow, although like the earlier document, these also bring their own problems of interpretation and authenticity. S692 is a royal charter, carrying a date of AD 961, and transferring a relatively small holding of one hide to a faithful retainer at a place identified only as *Geofanstige*, translated in modern accounts as 'Evesty'. It carries a fairly full boundary clause in Old English, but this remains to all intents and purposes unsolved. In its favour however, Kelly regards the basis of the document as perfectly authentic. This same holding appears in Domesday, unchanged in size, as *Evestie*, by which time ownership had passed to the church at Bath and indeed its transfer to that house after AD 961, probably between AD 1061 and AD 1077/78, can be traced through the survival of a writ by an abbot of Bath, who claimed to have inherited the estate from his father. Following Grundy, and considering the views of other authorities, Kelly suggests that the bounds of 'Evesty' place it not in the later parish of Wellow, but probably as a block of land on the eastern side of Dunkerton parish, south of the Cam Brook and abutting the Fosse Way, which here marks Dunkerton's common boundary with Wellow (Kelly 2007, 120).

S854, of purported date AD 984, records a grant of three and one half hides at a location generally identified from the Old English boundary clause as Radstock (Kelly 2007, 133–136). Its interest for present purposes is that the estate, which is the charter's subject, is named as *Welewestoce*. Kelly comments that

> *The placename ... could mean 'stoc [place, secondary settlement] on the river Wellow' or 'stoc belonging to Wellow village'; in the Domesday entry the manor is called simply Stoche, and this was later prefixed with the element rod, rad, 'road', no doubt because of the manor's association with the place where the Fosse Way crossed the river* (Kelly 2007, 135).

The suggestion that Radstock may have originated as a dependency of the 'main' estate, downstream along the Wellow, hints at an entirely expected local hierarchy of territorial organisation in the pre-Conquest period. A large, nucleated settlement such as exists today may well be a later development, and indeed it is rather more likely that hamlet-type occupation somewhere in the vicinity of the church site was merely one of several dispersed and isolated

DOCUMENTARY AND ARCHAEOLOGICAL BACKGROUND

hamlets and farmsteads scattered around the area of the later parish.

Finally, for the pre-Conquest documentation of a Wellow estate, and leaving aside questions of its exact extent, origin or development, it is worth noting that King Alfred's will, probably drawn up originally at some point between AD 872 and AD 888, includes a bequest to his eldest daughter of an estate *æt Welewe*, the size of which is not specified (S1507). Unfortunately, it is not possible to be certain about the location of this estate, and while Keynes and Lapidge favour East Wellow in Hampshire, they also admit West Wellow (also Hants) or the Somerset Wellow as possibilities (Keynes and Lapidge 1983, 173–178). This question must for the time being be regarded as unresolved, but it may be relevant to consider that in the post-Conquest period, as Dr Thorn demonstrates later on in his analysis of the Domesday evidence, Wellow was certainly officially regarded as a royal manor at least as late as the late 13th century, although by then wrested from the crown by the Earl of Gloucester. This in turn may help to explain the occasional appearance of Wellow lands among the records of the Berkeley family at Berkeley Castle (Figure 2.4).

Fields and Settlement in Wellow

Fields

There is little direct evidence concerning the nature or disposition of the field systems operated at Wellow and its outlying hamlets and farmsteads, one of which was Eckweek, in the medieval period and the level of meaningful inference that we can make is therefore limited. Figure 2.4 makes the point that only a single document, of the late 14th century, could be found relating directly to lands worked from Eckweek, which contained any detail whatsoever about the possible nature of farming arrangements at this date. That said, the lease of 1386, although rather brief, is in fact very revealing. As with some of the other documents in Figure 2.4, the *messauge* described actually contains lands in both Eckweek and White Ox Mead and it seems possible that together these two isolated hamlets may have a long common history and have shared a field system. Of exactly what that may have consisted is however unclear. The small sizes of the parcels (usually one or two acres) and the mention of furlongs demonstrate beyond doubt that at least some of the arable land worked from these two isolated hamlets was in the form of strips in open fields. Also, the document mentions an East and a West Field, and when the acreages for the various individual pieces of land are totalled up, they amount to 7½ acres in the East Field, and 9 acres in the West Field. While not exact, this relatively even distribution of the tenement's holding between the two fields is completely typical of a fairly regular arrangement of open-field strips. Indeed, the outlines of what are palpably remnant or fossilised open-field strips survived late enough to be recorded on the Wellow tithe map of the mid 19th century, and appear to represent a very final expression of land that was still, in the mid 19th century, actually being operated as open-field.

This does not, however, mean that all the arable farmed from Eckweek and its neighbours, and indeed in Wellow itself, was in the form of open field strips. Indeed, in Somerset, a county of early enclosure where open fields had existed (Whitfield 1981) and possessing large swathes of territory which had either never operated open-fields, or where they were of highly irregular types (Aston 1988), this is actually inherently unlikely. At Shapwick for example, even by the early 16th century, a proportion of the formerly open field arable had been taken within consolidated and enclosed plots (Corcos 2007). It is an important question whether the East and West Fields mentioned in the 1386 lease related to the entire parish of Wellow, or whether they represent, in fact, far more localised fields in the NW part of the parish serving, shared by the hamlets of Eckweek and White Ox Mead alone, both of which were characterised as manors, albeit rather small ones, by Domesday Book three centuries earlier. Collation of the mid 19th-century tithe map and the 1386 lease may allow us at least to suggest that on balance, the former is probably the case.

The tithe map, (Figure 2.5) contains few references to fields named from the cardinal points, and even for those which are noted, caution is necessary as it is possible that such names could be of post-medieval origin. If, however, we take the Wellow examples at face value, and presume that they are indeed medieval survivals, then a distinct pattern emerges. The tithe map shows two separate, but closely related enclosures, tithe plots 1030 and 1034 (Figure 2.6), lying about 870m NNE of White Ox Mead Farm and further again from the former settlement of Eckweek. Both enclosures still survive with their mid 19th-century boundaries still pretty much intact, and both were called 'Eastfield' at that time. Tithe plot 1030 was actually called Little East Field in the Wellow tithe award and consisted of just over an acre of arable, while plot 1034 was straightforwardly Eastfield and contained 9½ acres, also of arable. Whatever else that name relates to, it certainly cannot have been Wellow village, the centre of which lies about 1.6km away to the SE. It is suggested here that these fields took their name from their relationship to Eckweek and White Ox Mead and that they may be a remnant of a once larger subdivided open field called East Field, which can be equated with that mentioned as part of the lease of 1386.

There are, unfortunately, no 'West Field' names recorded in the tithe survey, but elsewhere in the

Date	Reference	Type, and Parties Involved	Lands
Late 12th cent.	Jeayes 1892, *Berkeley Charters*, No. 64, 27–28	Grant, from Philip, son of Elias Wace, to Robert de Berkeley, [of land] which John, son of Walter Wace, held. Witn: Henry de Munford; Roger de Munford; Reginald de Herlega; Richd. Parc[arius] de *Heutona*; William de *Hagelega*; John de *Cranlega*; Herebert de *Echewicha*; Baldwin de *Hechewicha*; Robert, son of Ivor.	A virgate of land in Tellisford.
1200	Jeayes 1892, *Berkeley Charters*, No. 71, 30	Grant from Baldwin de *Ekewike*, to Maurice de Berkeley (terms of grant specified). Witn. incl. William Malreward, William, Chaplain of Horton; and Thomas, Chaplain of Foxcote.	All the meadow which he [Baldwin] held on the bank [of the River Wellow] near Foxcote, lying between Foxcote and *Pekelinge* [Peglinch].
Early 13th cent.	Jeayes 1892, *Berkeley Charters*, No. 120, 46	Grant by Baldwin de *Ekewike* to Maurice de Berkeley. Witn. incl. Thomas de Foxcote.	All his [Baldwin's] meadow under Foxcote lying between Foxcote and Pekelinge [Peglinch].
Early 13th cent.	DD/WHb/465	Quitclaim, by Reginald de Knold and Eva his wife to Reginald Pincerna and his heirs in any land of theirs in *Hekewike* Manor especially the land which William Paer son of Walter de Frome held. For this quitclaim Reginald Pincerna has given the said Reginald and Eva seven shillings. Witn. Alexander de Munford, Henry de *Hekewike*, Geoffrey de Hersig, etc.	Eckwick Manor
1243	*Somerset Pleas*, SRS 11, 1897, 200, No. 626.	Withdrawal of case of disseisin originally brought by Henry of *Ekewyk*.	Pasture in Downhead, pertaining to Henry's free tenement of 'Worlite' [location unknown].
1243	As above, 218, No. 709	The same Henry of *Ekewyk* also withdrew a case he had originally brought against one his own tenants (at the same court as above).	A tenement in *Ekewyk*.
1256	*Feet of Fines*, SRS 6, 1892, 168	Lease	A messuage, 16 acres of land and half an acre of meadow in Ecwike.
1258	*Two Cartularies of Bath Priory*, SRS 7, 1893, 71	Quitclaim in favour of Bath Priory, witnessed by, *inter alia*, Richard of *Ekewike*.	Land in Priston.
1312	SRO DD/Whb/513	Grant, by Wm Cherm, to Sir Andrew de Corston, and Sir Wm Hardyng.	Unspecified lands in Eckweek and elsewhere.
1312	SRO DD/Whb/514	Grant and sale, same lands and main parties as above	As above
1315/16	*Nomina Villarum*, in SRS 3, 1889, 61	*Wellewe cum hamelettis* – lists *inter alia* Henricus de *Ekwyk*	
1315/16	*Feet of Fines*, SRS 12, 1898, 58, No. 70	Land specified which Reginald de *Ekewyke*, Gunhilde his wife, and John their son, held for the lives of Gunhilde and John.	16 acres of land in Cridlingcote.
1321	SRO DD/Whb/562	Lease, by John de Forde to Edelina his sister for her life. Witnesses include Roger de *Wytokkesmede* and Henry de *Ekewyk*.	Twerton
1327	*Exchequer Lay Subsidy*, in SRS 3, 1889, 85	Reginald de *Ekewyke*, listed as a taxpayer rendering 12d, under White Ox Mead.	
1349	SRO DD/Whb/308	Lease, for lives, by James Husee, of Hampton, and William FitzWilliam of ?Baa to John Lovel and Alice his wife, and John and Robert their sons. Witn. by, *inter alia*, Thomas *Ekewyke*.	Messuage etc in 'Batheneston'. Rent specified.
1349	SRO DD/Whb/309	Lease for life, by James Husee……to Henry de Ford. Witn. by, *inter alia*, Thomas *Ekewyke*.	A meadow, a dovecote and four acres of land in 'Batheneston'. Rent specified.
1350	SRO DD/Whb/310	Lease by James Husee of Hampton to Thomas Tannere and Edith his wife. Witn. by, *inter alia*, Thomas *Ekewyke*.	The lands which Wm. Smith formerly held of him in 'Batheneston'.
1351	SRO DD/Whb/311	Lease, by James Husee of Hampton, to Stephen Breware. Witn. by, *inter alia*, Thomas *Ekewyke*.	Three cottages, two acres, and a rod of land in 'Batheneston'.
1351	SRO DD/Whb/312	Lease, for lives, by James Husee, of Hampton, to Walter Threshare and the wife whom he shall first marry, and to Adam son of the said Walter. Witn. by, *inter alia*, Thomas *Ekewyke*.	Messuage with close and two acres of land and a piece of meadow called *Paradys* in 'Batheneston'.
1352	DD/Whb/426	Lease for lives by John de Forde, son of John de Forde, to Henry de Forde his brother. Witn. by, *inter alia*, John *Whitokkesmede* and Thomas *Ekewyke*.	All his land in Forde by Bath [now Bathford] and in Le Boxe (excepting those sometime held by Henry Piert in the same place).
1361/62	DD/Whb/515	Grant, by Joan, widow of Richard Criste jnr, to Henry de Forde.	Unspecified lands in Eckweek and elsewhere.
1361/62	DD/Whb/516	Quitclaim by Joan, widow of Richard Criste jnr, and daughter and heir of Wm Cherm, to Henry de Forde her cousin	Unspecified lands in Eckweek and elsewhere, presumably same as in DD/Whb/515.
1362	SRO DD/Whb/632	Grant, by Thomas fil. Will. Boteler of Farlegheswyke to Henry fil. John de Forde. Witn. John Whittokesmede, Richard Cryst, John Lambrigge.	The rents and services issuing from a messuage, close and 17 acres of land which Ralph fil. John Toukere of *Ekewyke* holds for term of his life in Welewe.
1362 (36 Edw. III)	TNA C/143/344/13 printed in *Calendar of Patent Rolls, Edw. III, 1361–64*, 223 (Vol. 12 for reign of Edw. III, 1912).	Grant by Walter de Rodeneye, knight, to Hinton Priory.	The manor of Peglinch, and three carucates of land and 12 acres of meadow in East Wick in Camerton (*Ekewyk*) and Woodborough and Whiteoxmead [in Wellow].
1369	SRO DD/Whb/517	Quitclaim, by Walter son of Walter Osbern, to Henry, son of Jn De Forde, of all right in all lands etc formerly held by Wm Cherm	Unspecified lands in *Eckweek*, White Ox Mede and elsewhere.
1374	*Calendar of Patent Rolls, Edw. III, 1374*, 31 (Vol. 16 for reign of Edw. III)	Royal licence to Hinton Priory to alienate the lands already specified in the earlier grant of 1362 by Walter de Rodeneye, who died before he could do this himself.	

FIGURE 2.4

Medieval and early modern documentary sources for Eckweek

Date	Reference	Type, and Parties Involved	Lands
1375 (48 Edw. III)	TNA E/326/1488	Release by Laurence le Botyler, of Monkton Farley (Farlegh' Monachorum) to John de Puteo, of the same place, of his right in a yearly rent and the reversion of a tenement and lands in *Ekewyk*, and in a curtilage and croft called 'Chacecroft' and other lands in the vill and fields of Monkton Farley, of which the said Laurence had enfeoffed the said John upon the marriage of his daughter Joan with him.	
1384	SRO DD/Whb/467	Grant by Agnes atte Putte, dau. and heir of John atte Putte, of Monks Farleigh, widow of Walter Hoseberne of Frome, to John Balon, Robert Feylond, John de la Lynde and Hugh de la Lynde. Witn. Thomas Gore, John Asshlegh, John Mareys, etc.	All her lands, etc in *Ekewyke*.
1386	SRO DD/Whb/469	Lease by Hugh de la Lynde to Jn Wodebergh snr. And Alice his wife.	*Detailed schedule of lands. See separate note following this table.*
1395	SRO DD/Whb/446	Grant by Robert Poynce, John Rolves and Richard Godefelagh, to Thos. Berlegh, Alice his wife, and John their son.	Unspecified lands in *Ekewyke* and elsewhere.
1395	SRO DD/Whb/447	Letter of attorney, main parties as above.	Same lands as above.
1402/3	SRO DD/Whb/624	Record of suit brought by Edmund Forde against Richard Godefelawe, clerk.	Lands in various locations, but Incl. a messuage in Eckweek held by Ralph *Ekewyke*.
1403/4	SRO DD/Whb/470	Grant, by Hugh de la Lynde to Richard Plente.	All Hugh's lands etc in Eckweek.
1406	SRO DD/Whb/471	Grant by Richard Plente to Jn. Plente his son, and Jn. Frankeleyn.	Same lands as above.
1465	SRO DD/Whb/488	Quitclaim, by Edw. Forde, son and heir of Jn Forde, to Edmund Blounte esq.	Unspecified lands in Eckweek, *Whyttokesmede* and elsewhere.
1440	SRO DD/Whb/472	Lease for lives, by Jn. Blount esq and Willelma his wife, to Jn. Kelveston, Joan his wife, and Jn their son.	A toft formerly a messuage, with courtyard and adjoining close, formerly belonging to Ralph de *Ekewyke*, and Jn. his son, and all appurtenant lands in Eckweek, Peglinch in Wellow, and in Woodborough in Camerton.
1535	*Valor Ecclesiaticus* (Brett 2007, xiv and 2)	Whittockysmede & *Ettewyke* is worth in rents of assize there yearly. Clear. £4 11s 4d.	
1539	Reeves' Accounts (Brett 2007, xiv and 12–13)	Puglege [Peglinch] with Shewiscombe [Shoscombe] and Whittoksmede. '….and of 18d for the rent of 1 burgage there [location unspecified] with appurtenances in the tenure of George Welle of Ebwike [Eckweek]…'	
1544	SRO DD\NCB/C1499/57 This is a copy of TNA C66/762 m. 14 (Brett 2007, 21–22, n175)	Letters patent: grant to John Bysse of Publow, Somerset, of lordship and manor of Peglynche and Hundreds of Showescombe, Whittokkesmede and E[kwik], late the property of the Priory of Henton, otherwise Charterhouse Henton, and all lands in Shewescombe, Whittokkesmede, Woodborough, *Eckewyke* in the parishes of Camerton and Wellow, late of the priory aforesaid; and all lands, courts, etc., in Peglynche, Shewescombe, Whittokkesmede, Woodborough, *Eckewike*, Wellow, and Camerton.	
1566	Calendar of Patent Rolls, 8 Eliz., Part VII, 446, No. 2557, 1960	Report of *Inquisition Post Mortem* on the lands and possessions of John Bysse jnr. The commission found that he died seised of …	(*Inter alia*), the Manor of Peglinch with lands in Shoscombe, Whittocksmead, Woodborough and *Eckwyck* in Wellow and Camerton. Annual value of all these lands, 77s 9½d.
1608	Wellow glebe terrier, SRO D/D/Rg 184/1		In *Ecqwick* al[ia]s oldburie at the gate called old burie gate on[e] acre shuting south and north hauing oldburie hedge on the west and willliam Baber on the east.
1847-76	DD/BR/snt/6	Deed of land, belonging to St. Mary Magdalen Hospital, Lyncombe and Widcombe, 1847, 1867; by Isaac Golledge of Bath, tea-dealer, to Thomas Cousins of Bath, gent., 1861.	Two cottages built on plot number 315 on Dunkerton tithe map. Discharge of mortgage of land (number 1087 on Wellow tithe map), formerly part of Eckwick Farm.

NOTE: Schedule of lands detailed in lease SRO DD/Whb/469, of 1386 (*with abutments omitted except where necessary*):

One messuage with courtyard, garden, close and land adjoining … in Eckweek and White Ox Mead; of this land, 2 acres lie in the East Field opposite la Knoll hull next to the land of John de Ekewyke on both sides, 1 acre lies in the same furlong …1 acre lies upon Knollehull … 1 acre lies below Webegrove … 2 acres lie between the lands of John de Ekewyke on both sides and abut upon a little field belonging to the said John, and ½ an acre lies upon la Quere … and abut [sic] upon la Greneweie …… and in the West Field, 2 acres lie in the furlong called Syx acrys …… 1 perch lies in the same furlong …… 2 acres lie under Ryssham …… 2 acres lie in Langebrech …… 1 acre lies between the three ways near the lands of the hospital and the Fosse …… 1 acre lies in Berforlong …… 1 perch lies opposite …… 1 acre lies on the west part of Hylocschulf.

Totals amount to: **EAST FIELD**: 7½ acres (or 7 acres, 2 roods, or 7 acres, 80 perches)
                     WEST FIELD: 9 acres, 2 perches

Source: Kemp and Shorrocks 1974, 190.

NOTE: It is likely that all the references to a place called *Batheneston* around the mid 14th century are mistranscriptions for either Bathweston (ie Weston by Bath), or Batheaston.

NOTE: 1 perch = 3.25 sq yds
1 rood = 1,210 sq yds or 40 perches
1 acre = 4,840 sq yds or 160 perches or 4 roods

FIGURE 2.4 CONT.

FIGURE 2.5

The Wellow tithe map of 1843 with principal settlements added by the author (reproduced courtesy of Somerset Record Office)

DOCUMENTARY AND ARCHAEOLOGICAL BACKGROUND

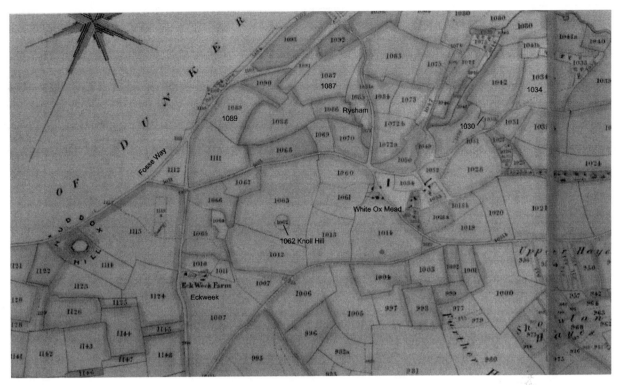

FIGURE 2.6

Extract from the Wellow tithe map of 1843 showing the settlements at Eckweek and White Ox Mead. Annotated by the author (reproduced courtesy of Somerset Record Office)

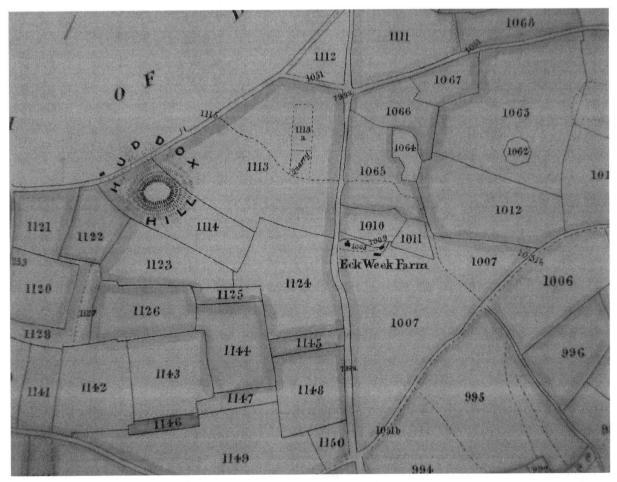

FIGURE 2.7

Extract from the Wellow tithe map of 1843 showing the settlement at Eckweek and surrounding fields (reproduced courtesy of Somerset Record Office)

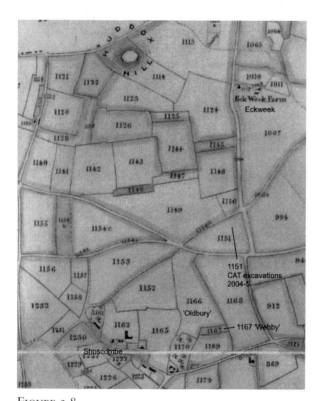

FIGURE 2.8

Extract from the Wellow tithe map of 1843 showing the settlements at Eckweek and Shoscombe with the area of the 2004–2005 excavations by Cotswold Archaeology indicated. Annotated by the author (reproduced courtesy of Somerset Record Office)

parish there are further indications of an original system of cardinally-named fields that seem clearly to be related to isolated hamlets well away from the main village. Away from the immediate Eckweek/ White Ox Mead area, tithe plot 739 is, for example, recorded as an arable enclosure of just over 17 acres (just under 7ha) called Eastfield. What is significant in this context is the location, for it lay, and indeed still lies, just over 1km SSW of the centre of Wellow village. This does not, therefore, seem an appropriate name for this field in terms of its spatial relationship to Wellow itself and a far better candidate in this instance would be Stoney Littleton, represented today by Stoney Littleton Farm only, which lies some 600m or so SW of the old Eastfield enclosure.

Apart from the East and West fieldnames, there are, fortunately, other names recorded in the lease of 1386 that have survived onto the Wellow tithe map, and so the locations can be identified with some confidence. Knoll Hill lies exactly equidistant between Eckweek and White Ox Mead; its summit (170m AOD) still capped by a small, circular plantation just as it was at the time of the tithe survey (Figure 2.6, tithe plot 1062). The description that includes Knoll Hill is actually using it as a reference point for strips in East Field ('in the East Field opposite *la Knoll hull*') and the two East Field names on the tithe map (tithe plots 1087 and 1089) could indeed be said to be 'opposite' Knoll Hill, a short

distance away to its north. Huddox Hill is marked on the tithe map (Figure 2.7, tithe plot 1114), although it now lies underneath the extensive grounds of a large house and is surrounded by modern development in Peasedown St John, about 500m WSW of Eckweek. The tithe award however, reveals that an alternative name for this feature was 'Hullick's Hill' and it seems highly probable that this location is the *Hylocschulf* of 1386. The second element is likely to be the Middle English form of OE *scylfe*, 'shelf', which, as part of a toponym, Margaret Gelling has argued strongly is a specific reference to relatively flat, level ground that can be at either high or low level (Gelling and Cole 2000, 216–219). Contours on the modern 1:25,000 map do indeed show that south of the summit of the hill, represented by a closed contour of 175m OD, the ground levels out markedly into the form of a wide and flat 'plateau' area.

It is not possible to identify the majority of the other furlong names of 1386 from the tithe map, namely *Webegrove, La Quere, Greenweie, Langebreche* and *Berfurlong*; although it is at least possible that *Webegrove* is represented by the 19th-century fieldname 'Webby' (Figure 2.8, tithe plot 1167). Lying as it does over 1km SSE of the site of Eckweek, it does however, seem rather distant to have been part of a messuage in a small, and highly localised open-field system centred on Eckweek and White Ox Mead.

The 1386 lease seems to be very clear that *Ryssham* at that date was part of the West Field, although the reference is actually to two acres (of arable) lying 'under *Ryssham*'. On the 19th-century tithe map, *Ryssham* is represented by an extensive series of enclosures collectively called Rusham, which lie together in a group almost immediately north of White Ox Mead Farm, and about 800m NE of Eckweek. This group of enclosures butts against the SE side of tithe plot 1087 (Figure 2.6), which, as already noted, carries one of the two surviving East Field names in this area. This raises the question of why the Rusham fields lie adjacent to enclosures called East Field, if an arable strip or strips described as 'under *Ryssham*' in 1386 was said to lie in the *West* Field? There is always the possibility of renaming over the course of nearly five centuries, but otherwise this is not easily explained.

Fieldnames

It is not possible to reach a clear judgement about the proportion of medieval fieldnames that had been lost before 1843. For example, only one of the early sources noted in Figure 2.4, a lease of the late 14th century, actually identifies by name some of the individual plots or fields making up the tenement that is the subject of the conveyance (SRO DD/Whb/469). Virtually all the other leases or deeds listed here only make very general reference to 'lands in Eckweek', or some similar vague expression, so that within this corpus toponymic detail relating to minor names is almost entirely lacking.

This said, one of the fieldnames that occurs in the mid 19th-century tithe records is of very great interest in terms of its archaeological implications. *Oldbury* is tithe number 1166 (Figure 2.8) and is the name applied to a field lying about 750m SSW of the former site of Eckweek House, on the western side of the modern development of Peasedown St John. The site has been included on the HER because it contains 'earthworks', and indeed some of these can be seen even on Google Earth (HER MBN6178). The HER contains however, no detail whatsoever about the nature or possible date of these remains and it does not note their crucial coincidence with the fieldname *Oldbury*. Neither is this name a purely modern coining, for it can be traced back at least to the early 17th century, when, as noted in Figure 2.4, it occurs as *oldburie* in a glebe terrier for Wellow dated 1608. This being so, it is very likely to be derived from a medieval precursor. This name is now widely regarded as being archaeologically highly indicative and its meaning in many occurrences appears to relate to '*the old fortified place*'.

Wellow parish has a number of fieldnames that may be indicative of extensive areas of woodland in the late Anglo-Saxon and post-Conquest periods, and especially in the high Middle Ages when woodland was particularly susceptible to opening up for agriculture (Dyer 1994, 62–76). It is possible that there are hints of this process in operation in the Wellow landscape and it may well have implications for the way that we understand the nature of settlement and land use within the parish, including at Eckweek, which cannot be fully understood in isolation. A fieldname 'High Barrow' on the Wellow tithe map (tithe plots 328, 345 and 346) lies immediately north of Upper Twinhoe, close to Wellow's northern boundary with South Stoke parish. The shape of these fields combined is that of a highly regular oval and the SW/NE lane that passes through Upper Twinhoe and heads for the Cam Brook beyond (which forms this part of the Wellow parish boundary) takes a sharp, dog-leg diversion to the west and north around the western boundary of tithe plot 328, instead of simply carrying on in a straight line through to the Cam Brook. In other words, it looks very much as though the lane is aligned so as to skirt around an obstacle in its path. This suggests the possibility that the 'Barrow' fieldname originates in OE *bearu*, 'a small wood', a name that is rare outside of Somerset and Devon and a relationship that has been proven from documentary research elsewhere in Somerset (Corcos 2002a; Gelling and Cole 2000, 221–223). By the mid 19th century, of the 21 or so acres carrying the name 'Barrow', no fewer than 19¾ acres were arable with the remainder woodland. The regular shape of the 'Barrow' fields in the mid 19th century suggests a small piece of bounded, managed woodland on the outer fringes of the parish just where it would be expected to survive, but originating as part of a much larger extent of woodland that was brought progressively under cultivation in the post-Conquest period.

Other fieldnames are also redolent of areas of former woodland being brought under the plough, particularly forms that emerged in the mid 19th century: 'Breach' or 'Brake' derived from OE *brēc* or *bræc*, meaning 'land broken up for cultivation' (Gelling and Cole 2000, 266–7), or similar (Corcos 2002b). The Wellow tithe records show a scattering of such names from locations all over the parish, and indeed, immediately west of Upper Twinhoe, the tithe map marks an enclosure of 13½ acres (5.5ha) called 'Brakes Wood'. Like the 'Barrow' fields, its outline is markedly curvilinear, possibly reflecting an area of remnant woodland that had been cleared in the post-Conquest period and then allowed to regenerate. A whole series of 'Breach' names also occurs just to the east and south of Baggeridge (Figure 2.5) in the SE quarter of the parish (tithe numbers 578, 579, 580, 581, 582, 583, 584 and 585), along with a field called Great Lye (tithe plot 586), which may ultimately be from *leah*, a term to which modern toponymists attribute the explicit meaning of 'a wood pasture', now usually found in the modern form -ley (Gelling and Cole 2000, 237–242; Hooke 2011). Adjoining Great Lye was a field called Middle Wood, but by the mid 19th century, neither of these large fields was woodland, both were arable. Elsewhere in Wellow, it is likely that *leah* may well have given rise to other –ley field names such as Hankley, Blockley and Stenley.

All this being so it is doubly interesting that the 1386 lease records that two acres of the arable land in Eckweek and White Ox Mead belonging to the messuage being described, is recorded as *la Langebrech*, which is presumably 'the long breach'. There is regrettably, no indication of this name in the mid 19th century tithe records. It may well be significant that at least some of these names are directly associated with the individual hamlets in the parish, which acted as foci of progressive woodland clearance in both the late Anglo-Saxon and post-Conquest periods.

Settlement in Wellow Parish

The only occupation site within the bounds of Wellow parish, including the 'modern' village of Wellow itself, which to date has archaeologically proven pre-Conquest antecedents, is Eckweek (Figure 2.5). Despite this, it is inconceivable that Eckweek was alone in its contemporary landscape and it has already been suggested that the late Anglo-Saxon/early post-Conquest settlement pattern is very likely to have consisted of dispersed hamlets and ring-fence farmsteads, although it is probable that by the early 11th century incipient nucleation may have been in progress on the present village site.

Pre-Conquest charters rarely provide clear indications of the existence of actual occupation sites, but this is almost certainly because they deal, by definition, with the *peripheries* of estates and so tell us little or nothing, in landscape terms, about what is going on in the estate centre. While it was not their intended purpose, however, occasionally it is possible to pick up charter references that seem strongly to hint at settlement 'activity', if not necessarily the exact positions of sites, within the bounds of the recorded estates. In the bounds of the Evesty charter, S692, there is a reference to a *ceorla gemære*, 'ceorls' boundary' (Kelly 2007, 120). The status of the *ceorl* in Anglo-Saxon society has been discussed at length by Faith (1997, 126–129), and the word has found its way into placenames of the 'Carlton' type (Finberg 1964b). Whether these people were indeed landless, semi-servile demesne labourers or not, the clear implication of the occurrence of this word in a boundary clause is that somewhere in the vicinity there was a settlement or farmstead occupied, *inter alia*, by people of, at best, low social status. This might be a type of site that archaeologically would be expected to show a fairly low level of material culture, in terms of both finds and buildings. The Wellow charter dated AD 766, S262, twice describes boundary points using the formula 'which the inhabitants call x' (Kelly 2007, 198). By definition, these 'inhabitants' must have been local enough to be familiar with sometimes small and topographically insignificant landmarks and are likely to have lived within the area of the later parish. Indeed, it may well be that the charter explicitly intends us to understand that these people were inhabitants of the estate that is being transferred.

There are, though, more direct indications of a dispersed settlement pattern within the parish. Michael Costen has noted the fieldname 'Baneworth', now lost, within Wellow (Costen 1988, 43). Presuming that the name has not undergone undue garbling from its original form during the course of its transmission, it is almost certainly from Old English *wyrðig*, 'an enclosure, a ring-fence farmstead, a settlement'. Dr Costen has made a detailed study of the occurrence of this name in Somerset (1992), especially as regards fieldnames, and is of the view that it represents an entire stratum of late-Anglo-Saxon, dispersed, ring-fence farmstead and hamlet-type settlement, much of which was swept away and subsumed beneath newly-established, sub-divided open fields in the relatively restricted part of the county where that process occurred. The sites of former settlement were, however, often commemorated in later post-Conquest fieldnames, which can be recovered from both medieval and post-medieval documentation, particularly surveys of various kinds. None, however, could be identified either in the vicinity of Eckweek itself, or in the wider landscape of Wellow parish. It is surprising that for a parish of Wellow's large size, there are so few settlement-type fieldnames preserved into the mid 19th century to be recorded on the tithe map of 1843, although as in so many cases this may well be explicable to nothing more than an accident of survival. This leaves open the question of the location of the habitation sites that were occupied by the people buried in the post-Roman cemetery reported by Rowe and Alexander (2011).

White Ox Mead

Eckweek is not exceptional in Wellow parish in being the only small, subsidiary settlement that is recorded in Domesday Book. White Ox Mead is described as a holding of 1 hide held by two thanes before 1066 (Thorn and Thorn 1980) and there is no reason why the archaeological affinities of that site should not be very similar to those of Eckweek. White Ox Mead remains a largely undeveloped agricultural hamlet dominated by two farms surrounded by fields, White Ox Mead Farm and Home Farm, the latter lies only 750m NE of the Eckweek site. A little south of the present farmsteads at White Ox Mead, the HER identifies the site of what it characterises as a 'deserted medieval village' (MBN1605). It hardly needs be said that this is misleading on both counts, as the date of this supposed settlement is entirely unknown and whatever it was, it was almost certainly not, in morphological terms, a village. That said, earthworks preserved adjacent to White Ox Mead Farm, recorded as part of the Eckweek project (see Figure 3.3), indicate a period of undated settlement shrinkage, whilst a watching brief carried out in 1998 at a site roughly halfway between the two farms recorded evidence that the site was occupied at least from the 13th century (EBN2520). It is by no means beyond the bounds of possibility that the two surviving farms, around which the present hamlet of White Ox Mead has coalesced, may directly reflect the two late Anglo-Saxon thane holdings which were recorded at Domesday. Certainly the very loose, agglomerative morphology of the surviving hamlet is strongly reinforced by its depiction on the tithe map, although after Domesday, the settlement does not appear again in the written record until 1321, as the surname de Wyttokesmede (Figure 2.4).

Stoney Littleton

Elsewhere in Wellow, on the southern side of the Wellow Brook, Stoney Littleton (Figure 2.5) is now represented by a single farm of that name and is recorded on the HER as possessing a probable abandoned medieval settlement site (MBN1609). In the late 11th century, Domesday Book recorded it as a manor. The HER specifically remarks that it is 'mentioned in the Domesday Book as a hamlet with a mill'. Domesday says no such thing and, in fact, gives no indication whatsoever (and never does) of the physical nature, size or layout of settlement(s) for that is not its concern. To call Stoney Littleton a 'hamlet' and to claim Domesday Book as the authority for that suggestion is to misrepresent its evidence. The Domesday entry for Stoney Littleton describes a tiny estate of only two hides with a single smallholder (or 'bordar', ie not even a man of villein status) and six slaves. In 1086 therefore, it was probably not even a hamlet, but a single, low-status farmstead with the slaves accommodated on the farm. There is no reason, therefore, why the visible earthworks need be any earlier than the 12th or 13th century and might indeed be much later. It is however, interesting to note that despite its proximity to Eckweek, Stoney Littleton does not make a single appearance within the various medieval document sources (Figure 2.4), either as a straightforward placename in its own right, or a locative surname. The situation at Stoney Littleton is worth considering because it strikingly highlights the contrast with Eckweek and makes the point that, in part, Eckweek probably can be directly related to the evidence of Domesday precisely because its nature and chronology have been closely characterised by high-quality archaeological fieldwork carried out to modern standards.

Peglynch

Paglinch or Peglynch is another site that is now represented by only a single isolated farmstead (as indeed may always have been the case) located in the extreme SW corner of the historic parish of Wellow, about 3.5km southwest of the parochial settlement and downstream of it. It lies on the northern bank of the Wellow Brook very close to the stream. Unlike White Ox Mead, Eckweek and Stoney Littleton, it is not recorded in Domesday, but its intermittent appearance in documents from 1200 onwards (Figure 2.4) suggests very strongly that it may well, nonetheless, have been a pre-Conquest foundation and certainly the second element of its placename (*hrycg*) is purely Old English in origin (Gelling and Cole 2000, 190–192) with, perhaps, a personal name as prefix (giving a meaning of 'the hillslope/terrace/ridge associated with a man called X'). If, as seems likely, Paglinch was indeed in existence by the late 11th century, the assessment of its resources for the purposes of the Domesday inquest would have been subsumed silently within those for another manor, although it is not at present possible to suggest which. Paglinch Farmhouse as it stands today is a Grade II Listed Building with, according to the formal EH listing description, 'medieval origins', although a date, or even a date range, is not specified. In 1362, Paglinch was described as a 'manor' with appurtenant arable lands amounting to three 'carucates' and a small amount of meadow apparently scattered across Eckweek, Woodborough, and White Ox Mead. Indeed as late as 1566, Paglinch was still being described in this way and at that date its appurtenances were listed as 'lands in Shoscombe, Whittoksmede, Woodborough and *Eckwyck*' (Figure 2.4 and further below). Although by no means certain, it nonetheless seems reasonable to suggest that Paglinch could be added to the list of farmsteads and hamlets known or strongly suspected to have been in existence by the late 11th century, and probably before.

Shoscombe

Like Paglinch, Shoscombe, which lies just over 1km pretty much due south of Eckweek, is not recorded in Domesday, but again like Paglinch there are good reasons for at least suggesting that it may well have been in existence in the late 11th century. Shoscombe is now probably best described as a village of overwhelmingly modern development, but the Wellow tithe map shows that in the mid 19th century it consisted of a somewhat long, straggling hamlet that seems to contain several 'empty' plots giving the distinct impression of shrinkage from a rather denser pattern of occupation. Shoscombe, however, appears different from those places in Wellow parish already examined in that its first appearance in the documents occurs in 1539 (Figure 2.4), which is relatively very late. Within Shoscombe itself, the National Heritage List records only two Listed Buildings, the earlier being of only mid 18th-century date. Of course, there is the usual proviso that listings can only, by definition, include structures that have been examined, or of which there is some prior knowledge. In any event, although Shoscombe is now a civil parish in its own right, the historical indications are that as an occupation site it is of relatively late foundation and may not pre-date the late medieval period.

Foxcote

Foxcote, although it came ultimately to fall outside Wellow parish (albeit only just), clearly had connections with it. Historically, for example, it seems always to have lain in the Hundred of Wellow (Thorn and Thorn 1980, 408–409), within which it had survived as an ancient parish, a status that it retained until well into the 20th century. It lies just over 2km due south of the site of Eckweek, on the southern bank of the Wellow Brook, and 3.6km SW of Wellow itself, from which it is now also in a different local authority area, namely Mendip District. It today consists of a small, loose agglomeration of farms and houses with a redundant church listed at Grade II*, which the National Heritage List assigns to the early 18th century, although significantly, incorporating 15th- and 16th-century structural elements. A Grade II listed field barn at the southern end of the hamlet is said to be a 19th-century rebuild of an original 16th-century structure and there is a listed farmhouse of supposed 17th-century date also located towards the southern end of the settlement. Unlike both Shoscombe and Paglinch, however, Foxcote is recorded as a manor in the pages of Domesday Book, and at five hides and possessing of a mill, it would be regarded as a respectable holding. Interestingly however, it appears on only two occasions in medieval documents (Figure 2.4), in two of the earliest records in the list, one dated to 1200 and another to the early 13th century. The contents show that the two are closely related; having at least one witness in common and dealing with what are clearly the same lands. In both records, Foxcote appears as a surname (see further below) and as a landmark involving a grant of meadow lying 'on the bank [of the Wellow Brook] near Foxcote...between Foxcote and Paglinch'. Thereafter however, Foxcote disappears from the records and even the later items do not include it. It seems likely that we should infer from this that, although within Wellow Hundred, Foxcote was actually not tied in very closely in landholding terms to some of the other places that we have already examined, which occur with far more frequency in medieval documents (Figure 2.4), and most notably to Eckweek itself, but also particularly Paglinch, White Ox Mead, and Woodborough. Finally, it is worth noting that in both the grants relating to Foxcote one of the witnesses is named as Thomas, but in the earlier record we have the additional information that he was at that time 'Chaplain of Foxcote'. The very strong implication of this is that the present church has antecedents, almost certainly on the same site judging from the surviving late medieval elements, which extend back at least to the late 12th century.

Baggeridge and Hassage

South of the Wellow Brook and historically firmly within the SE quarter of Wellow parish are two further settlement sites, which remain to this day probably what they always were, isolated farmsteads, and for both there is at least a likelihood that they reflect sites that were occupied in the medieval period. Both places also appear today pretty much as they did on the Wellow tithe map of the mid 19th century. Baggeridge lies about 1.6km SSE of the centre of Wellow and consists of two separate settlement foci, identified as Upper and Lower Baggeridge Farms. Upper Farm was recorded in some detail by the Somerset Vernacular Architecture Group in 1980 (SRO DD\V\BAR/25/1) and both are protected by statutory listing at Grade II level. The listings describe both as 17th-century in origin in their present form. In the case of Upper Baggeridge Farm, however, the listing description adds the information that it may be a 'possible remodelling of an earlier building', although how much earlier is not specified. Baggeridge's claim to antiquity may, however, be best expressed not in the fabric of the surviving farmhouses, but in its location for it lies at the southern end of, and is clearly served by, one of the several north/south lanes that fan out southwards from the southern bank of the Wellow Brook, having crossed it at a single point now marked by the stone bridge across the stream. Today this road is known as Baggeridge Lane. The possible nature and early origins of these routes are noted above and it has been suggested that they may represent very early features in the local landscape. Furthermore, the second element of the name 'Baggeridge' exactly describes the site's topographical affinities, for it lies at the NE end of a ridge running NE/SW for a distance of about 1.5km, and close to its highest point, which is marked by a trig post with a value of 157m OD slightly to the SW of Upper Baggeridge Farm. The ground slopes away steeply in all directions except to the SW. Given the landscape context it seems unthinkable that 'Baggeridge' is not a genuine topographical placename and as such, an origin in Old English *hrycg* is likely (Gelling and Cole 2000, 190–192). Both the commanding location and the placename could, therefore, be seen as further supporting an early origin for Baggeridge.

Somewhat south of Baggeridge again, lies the hamlet of Hassage, which is situated just under 3km SSE of the centre of Wellow and consists of two foci centred on houses called Hassage Farm and Lower Hassage Farm on the First Edition of the 6" OS map (surveyed 1884, published 1886), but now known as Hassage Manor (recorded by the Somerset Group on Vernacular Architecture; SRO DD\V\BAR/25/5) and Hassage House respectively. In this case, the two parts of the hamlet are much more closely related physically than are the two Baggeridge Farms. Like Baggeridge, Hassage also is connected to the southwards route from the crossing point of the Wellow Brook, by a separate lane called Hassage Hill. This route is *not* continuous, since at least the time of the tithe map, it becomes truncated south of Baggeridge, and is only picked up by a 400m stretch of lane that runs NW from Hassage hamlet. Again as already noted, it seems clear that the route originally ran straight to Hassage, and indeed its 'missing' section may be marked even today by the line of a modern footpath. If the establishment of a medieval field system had indeed interrupted the line of a pre-existing, traditional routeway, of which Hassage or a farmstead on that site was the destination, it suggests that Hassage itself may represent an extremely early (ie pre-Conquest) foundation. Hassage Manor (the building formerly known as Hassage Farm), is a Grade II* Listed Building now recorded as part of Norton St Philip parish, which it never was historically, in Mendip District local authority area.

DOCUMENTARY AND ARCHAEOLOGICAL BACKGROUND

According to the listing description, the earliest extant fabric in the present building dates to the mid 17th century, however even considered purely as a tenement or tenements (ie working farms consisting of farmsteads and associated land), Hassage can lay claim to rather earlier origins for it is mentioned in a quitclaim of 1525, which refers to

messuages, etc. in Hassage in the parish of Wellow and Philippys Norton (SRO DD\WHb/635).

At the other end of the 16th century, in 1595, there is rather more detail, for a notice of fines to be levied on various properties notes that one of them was 'Hassage Farm', which there is no reason to think is not a reference to the present Hassage Manor (SRO DD\WHb/1460). Neither Hassage nor Baggeridge appear among the local placenames noted in Figure 2.4, but this is of course no certain test of medieval antecedents.

Twinhoe

In the NE quarter of Wellow parish lies the extremely dispersed hamlet of Twinhoe, consisting of Upper, Middle and Lower Twinhoe at the time of the tithe map (and indeed still some 40 years later at the time of the OS large-scale First Edition maps), with Upper Twinhoe representing the largest single cluster and at a distance of about 1.5km from the centre, NE of Wellow village. The most distant cluster is Lower Twinhoe, about 2.25km NE of Wellow. Twinhoe is in fact the most dispersed hamlet covered by a single toponym within Wellow parish, as the following breakdown of straight-line distances indicates.

Upper to Middle Twinhoe:	400m
Middle to Lower Twinhoe:	540m
Upper to Lower Twinhoe:	800m

Each of these three parts is composed of a very loose agglomeration of only one or two farms and a few cottages, and while the placename does not appear among any of the documentation cited in Figure 2.4, Twinhoe is recorded in documents of the medieval period. Upper Twinhoe and Lower Twinhoe both contain Listed Buildings, but the National Heritage List appears to confuse the settlement names: two are listed in the cluster that historically was always called Upper Twinhoe, but which are described by the National Heritage List as Upper and Middle Twinhoe; both are Grade II listed and both described as of late 17th-century date in their present form. The hamlet cluster always known historically as Middle Twinhoe contains no listed buildings, however Lower Twinhoe contains two, with what is clearly the more important of the two, the former Lower Twinhoe Farm, recorded as Lower Twinhoe Cottage and listed at Grade II, where it is described as 17th-century in its present form.

Twinhoe does not appear as a separate, named estate in Domesday Book and it is perfectly possible that it represents a post-Conquest 'colonising' hamlet in an outlying and formerly unoccupied part of the Wellow estate; the result of being established in or close to woodland and then with subsequent woodland clearance expanding progressively outwards from the core farmsteads. Like all the other places reviewed here that are not explicitly named at Domesday, this fact alone by no means counts against Twinhoe's well-established existence by the late 11th century, and indeed its documented credentials in that respect are in fact rather better than some. We are extremely fortunate to be able to say with confidence that a farmstead or farmsteads with associated agricultural land were in existence at Twinhoe by the late 13th or early 14th century, because tenements identified by that name appear in a series of early deeds and leases held at the Somerset Record Office beginning at that date and running through to the late 16th century (SRO DD/GL/71). It is not unreasonable to suggest that, like Eckweek and probably most of the other outlying hamlets in Wellow parish that have already been noted, Twinhoe originated in the pre-Conquest period.

Surnames and Other Evidence

The documentation outlined in Figure 2.4, although sparse in terms of detail, does provide occasional glimpses of people who, from their surnames, seem clearly either to have actually lived at Eckweek, or at the least had some close connection with it, since in the period up to about the mid 14th century locative surnames had not yet become fully hereditary and a person bearing such a name can in most cases be presumed to have dwelt at the settlement concerned (Aston 1983, McKinley 1990). The surname *Eckweek*, or *de Eckweek*, or numerous variations thereon, occurs many times in Figure 2.4, and there can be little doubt that small-scale familial relationships and networks lie at the heart of some of this evidence. Other locative surnames occur occasionally in the 14th century, which reinforce what little other evidence there is from the documentary sources to suggest that, as we have already seen, Eckweek was merely one of several dispersed hamlets and isolated farmsteads in Wellow parish at that date. In 1352, for example, John *Whittokesmede* was among the witnesses to a lease involving land at Ford and at Box, and it may well be the same man who is also recorded exactly ten years later witnessing a grant of lands at some unspecified location on the Wellow estate.

The detail of the documents cited in Figure 2.4 also fails to give any indication of changing circumstances at a time at which it might be most expected, at Eckweek and elsewhere in the mid 14th century, and specifically in the years after 1348/9. There is a small group of six leases, closely dated from 1349 to 1352, but in fact these have been captured in the table only because they contain the name of the same man, Thomas *Ekewyke*, as a witness in all six cases. Thomas' appearance as a witness is confined to these documents; he does not appear again after 1352 in the records listed here. It is likely that this Thomas lived at, or was somehow closely associated with Eckweek in the years around the time of the Black Death and its aftermath, and although, as already stated, he disappears from this small corpus of documentary material after 1352, nonetheless, it is highly unlikely that total abandonment of the Eckweek settlement itself occurred as a direct, causal consequence of the various sporadic visitations of disease that occurred during the second half of the 14th century. Indeed, it is clear even from the small sample of documentary evidence outlined in Figure 2.4, as demonstrated by a grant of 1362 mentioning John Toukere (ie Tucker) of Ekewyke, and the release of 1375 that explicitly involved a tenement and lands in Ekewyk, that Eckweek continued in existence as an occupied settlement of some sort well into the 14th century, but probably not much beyond, even though the documents tell us nothing about population levels or the nature or state of its economy in that period.

Eckweek Farm in the Mid 19th Century

The main sources of information for the size and disposition of Eckweek Farm as it emerged in the mid 19th century are the tithe map of 1843 (Figures 2.5 to 2.7) and the subsequent First Edition Ordnance Survey plan (Figure 2.9). Figure 2.3 shows an extract from the tithe award for Wellow (SRO DD/SAS c/2401/7) showing, as the first few entries, the lands that almost certainly belong directly to Eckweek Farm at that date, and also a selection of other properties in the immediate area. It is perhaps surprising that in Wellow parish the farm's holding only ran to some 76 acres (31ha). This was in the form of two large enclosures adjacent to both each other and to the farm itself and two smaller ones, lying close together but physically separate in isolated locations over 500m to the north of the farm buildings.

The farm was owned by one William Skuse, who at the time of the tithe survey held it in hand. Although because this is merely a snapshot taken at one instant, there is of course no way of knowing just from this evidence alone, whether he was actually operating it himself as a going concern, or whether it was being held temporarily on a 'care and maintenance' basis until a new tenant could be found to occupy it. It is also notable that all the Wellow lands belonging to the farm consisted of arable, although the lack of even a small amount of

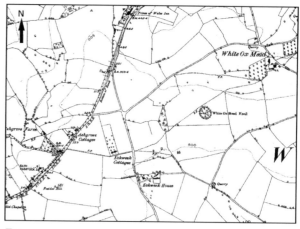

FIGURE 2.9

Extract from the First Edition Ordnance Survey map of 1887 showing Eckweek settlement. Somerset Sheet XX NE. Not to scale

pasture actually belonging to the farm need not necessarily be surprising; we may assume that Eckweek Farm would have operated several draught animals, almost certainly horses by this date, for ploughing and hauling, and while they could of course be fed entirely on grain output from the arable fields, even a small amount of grazing land would have provided a rather more balanced regime. This may well have been the case, however immediately adjacent to Eckweek Farm, to its north, two small enclosures (Figure 2.5, tithe plots 1010 and 1011) were both used for pasture and, although they were not part of the farm by this time, being in the hands of different owners and occupiers, it would be surprising given their very close proximity to the farmstead if they had not once been. It is possible that Eckweek Farm's operational requirements in terms of pasture for draught animals were so small that it may have made more economic sense simply to rent grazing land from other farmers.

2.2 THE PLACENAME ECKWEEK
by Dr Michael Costen

Eckweek is only one of a large number of similar placenames to be found across Somerset. The second element is derived from the Old English *wic* and appears typically with the variants 'wick', 'week' and 'wyke' in modern placenames. The classic definition of this element comes from the work of A H Smith, where it is described as 'a dwelling, a building or collection of buildings for special purpose, a farm, a dairy farm' and where the element appears in its plural form 'a hamlet or village' (Smith 1970, part 2, 257). Ekwall also emphasises the width of meaning available in the word, but suggests that the most common meaning is a dairy farm (Ekwall 1960, 515–516). Dr Margaret Gelling first studied a special case of *'wics'* when she wrote about *wichams*, showing that they were closely related to the Roman settlement pattern (Gelling 1967) and revisited the subject ten years later (Gelling 1977). More recently another scholar, Richard Coates, has produced an elegant and insightful examination of the element (Coates 1999). His conclusions are complex, but he shows that there is running through the many uses of the word a sense of 'dependency'. Other scholars have seen it as describing dependencies such as outlying dairy farms (Hooke 1998, 134). There has been a tendency to regard the element as a fairly late introduction into the landscape, based upon the view that settlements expanded through their estate, creating minor settlements, such as the 'wicks'. However, 10th-century charter bound material strongly suggests that the element was already well established in the landscape by that time, although there can be little doubt that the name was normally attached to settlements of minor importance. Simon Draper, writing about Wiltshire, has tried to establish that *wic*, either as a simplex or in compound forms, can have a relationship to the Roman landscape (Draper 2002, 37–44). Writing in 1992 I suggested that there was a statistical relationship between *wic* sites, and villa sites (Costen 1992, 66). Such a relationship need not be causal, but might suggest that many *wics* are part of the landscape as it was before the expansion of agriculture and the replanning of settlements in the 9th and 10th centuries. Whether this is the case or not can only be settled by archaeological survey and investigation of a number of different *wics*.

Eckweek is an outlier of a group of *wic* settlements in the northeast of Somerset, many of which are close to Bath and include, among extant sites, Shockerwick in Bathford parish, Hunterwick, Swainswick and Tadwick in Batheaston parish, Bathwick, Barrack House in Lincombe (originally Berwick) and Week Farm in Combe Hay. Lost sites include Woodix in Freshford and Old Wick in Weston. Closer to Eckweek, in Wellow parish, was *prestweeke*, which was extant in the later 16th century (SRO DD\SE28, Box 4) and survives as the field names 'lower and middle pressick', tithe numbers 526 and 527 (SRO D\D/Rt/M/303 & D\D/Rt/A/303).

The forms for the placename 'Eckweek' are given below in ascending date order:

ecchewica, 1086, (DB Exon.)
ecewiche, 1086 (DB)
de ekewike, c1200, (Berkeley)
ecwik, 1255–6, (Feet of Fines)
ekwyke, 1315–16 (Nom. Vill.).

The first element is probably a male personal name '*Ecca*'. Hence this is '*Ecca's*' or possibly '*Hecca's*' wick. It is notable that this dithematic placename contains a personal name form. One might hazard the guess that it was initially simply a 'wic', but that its transfer to a named individual, perhaps in the 9th or 10th century caused it to attract the personal name. Placenames of the form personal name+*tun* are relatively common in Somerset, with 15 examples appearing in the Domesday Book (DB). The writer has argued that they are a placename type not developed before the earlier 10th century, but they continued to be formed in the post-Norman Conquest period (Costen 2011, 72). They mark the point at which the estate passed into the hands of a permanent land owner, who could pass the estate on to a descendant or sell it, an owner by 'bookright', or if the name arose after the Conquest, a feudal tenant. This would point to the placename not assuming its final form until quite late, though by the Conquest in the case of Eckwick. Other wics in the area were still going through this process in the post-Conquest period. Swainswick is not noted until c1291 (*Taxatio*) when it appears as *Sweyneswyk*, Swein's wic.

2.3 ECKWEEK IN DOMESDAY BOOK
by Dr Frank Thorn

Note – Words marked with an asterisk on their first appearance in the text are explained in the Glossary of Technical Terms at the end of this chapter.

This section aims to set Eckweek in its Domesday context. Especially since the 900th anniversary of the Domesday Enquiry in 1986 and the publication of a full facsimile, Domesday studies have a new vibrancy and non-specialists have no good general study to which they can turn to update themselves (but see Finn 1963, Williams and Erskine 1987, Hallam and Bates 2001). There is now a fuller understanding of the 'Domesday process' although a number of points are still obscure or controversial. Thus the scene-setting for a study of the entries for Eckweek needs to be considerable, as well as balanced.

Most references to 'Domesday Book' refer either to Great Domesday Book or to Little Domesday Book individually or to both together. The two are often referred to as Exchequer Domesday Book, but as documents they are significantly different. Great Domesday (GDB) is an abbreviated survey of 31 of the English counties occupying 382 folios in double column. It omits three counties (Essex, Norfolk and Suffolk) that are the subject of the more detailed writing-up (itself occupying 450 folios), which is called Little Domesday Book (LDB). Together these volumes contain some of the results of a survey of the whole of England as then constituted, except for Durham and Northumberland, where the Bishop of Durham exercised civil and religious authority and his 'palatinate' contained what became the counties of Durham and Northumberland, stretching from the Tees to the Tweed. With these exceptions, the northern boundary of the surveyed counties ran from the River Esk to the River Tees. Lancashire was a creation of the 12th century and in

Domesday its southern third ('Between the Ribble and the Mersey') was included in a separate section of the folios for Cheshire, while the rest, north of the River Ribble, together with parts of the future Cumberland and Westmorland, was included in the Yorkshire pages. There is a further Domesday, the Exeter or Exon Domesday (EDB), so called from the present location of the manuscript (Thorn and Thorn 1985 and 2001). This contains a fuller, but now fragmentary, survey of the five southwestern counties (Wiltshire, Dorset, Somerset, Devon and Cornwall) and is roughly comparable in scope to LDB. It was the document from which GDB was abbreviated for these counties and it is probable that LDB would also have been similarly reduced had work on GDB not broken off in uncertain circumstances in about 1088.

GDB, which is the most frequently cited, is arranged internally by county and within each by landholder. Each county schedule begins with a city or borough (or boroughs) if there were such there, then continues with a list of those people or institutions who held directly from the king (the tenants-in-chief*), generally in the order of king, ecclesiastical holders, laymen. There are several different ways in which their fiefs* are organised internally, but the general principle is that lands in one hundred* follow those in another. Hundred heads appear in the text, although many can be shown to be missing and they are entirely so for the five southwestern counties, both in EDB and in GDB. Their purpose is unclear: they seem above all to reflect the way in which the Domesday material was collected and processed.

It is as true of Domesday as of any other historical document that no part of it can be adequately interpreted without understanding the whole. The particular difficulty with Domesday is that the 'when?' and the 'how?' can be investigated from contemporary evidence but the 'why?' is elusive.

The Decision

The decision to conduct the Domesday survey (Latin *descriptio* in the double sense of 'describing' and 'writing-down') was made at Gloucester at what is now reckoned as the beginning of 1086, although under the calendar then in use 1085 lasted until Lady Day (March 25th). This decision and its immediate aftermath are recorded in the Anglo-Saxon Chronicle:

> Then at Christmas, the king was at Gloucester with his council, and held his court there for five days, and then the archbishop and clerics had a synod for three days. There Maurice was elected bishop of London, and William for Norfolk and Robert for Cheshire: they were all clerics of the king.
>
> After this, the king had much thought and very deep discussion with his council about this country – how it was occupied and with what sort of people. Then he sent his men all over England into every shire and had them find out how many hundred hides* there were in each shire, or what land and cattle the king himself had in the country, or what dues he ought to have in twelve months from the shire. Also he had a record made of how much land his archbishops had, and his bishops and his abbots and his earls – and (though I relate it at too great length) – what or how much everybody had who was occupying land in England, in land or in cattle, and how much money it was worth. So very narrowly did he have it investigated, that there was no single hide nor virgate* of land, nor indeed (it is a shame to relate it, but it seemed no shame to him to do) one ox nor one cow nor one pig which was there left out, and not put down in his record; and all these records were brought to him afterwards (translation is from Whitelock et al 1965, 161–162).

The tone is indignant, but there is no reason to doubt the essential facts given in this account. If the chronicler for this year is the same man who wrote the annal for the next year (1087), then he knew William personally and had once lived at his court. As the author is aspiring to a literary account there is a certain vagueness about detail and there are emphases that are his own. It is unlikely that the rhetoric of his account should be pinned down, as some have wished, to implying that there were separate surveys of the royal land and of the others' possessions. Allowing for the precedence of style over detail, this account can easily be reconciled with a typical Domesday entry. Even the oxen, cows and pigs (as well as goats and sheep) are included in LDB and in EDB, although they were abbreviated out of GDB. This is one reason why one should not assume that the 'records' that were brought to King William were what became known as GDB. The final format could have been decided at that stage.

The chronicler underlines the unprecedented thoroughness of the survey and there must have been a list of more than a dozen precise matters for investigation. This list resurfaced and is on record as such when the gathered material was processed by the shire-court (Whitelock *et al* 1965, 163). William and his counsellors must have established a timetable for the surveying and reporting and must also have decided how and by whom it was to be carried out. The chronicler says: 'Then he sent his men all over England into every shire and had them find out...' The Latin version of the chronicle uses the term *servi* ('servants', 'ministers') which suggests that these were not King William's magnates or barons, but a lower administrative layer. These servants most probably addressed themselves to the sheriff (the 'shire-reeve') of each county, most of whom will not have been present at Gloucester.

DOCUMENTARY AND ARCHAEOLOGICAL BACKGROUND

The Reasons for the Survey

No contemporary account explains why Domesday Book was made. For the chronicler it appears to have been a result of one of William's traits of character: his greed. In summing up his life and character in the annal for 1087 he says:

The king and his chief men loved gain much and over much – gold and silver – and did not care how sinfully it was obtained, provided that it came to them. The king sold his land on very hard terms – as hard as he could get (Whitelock et al, 1965, 163).

And referring once more to Domesday, he says:

He ruled over England and by his cunning it was so investigated that there was not one hide of land in England that he did not know who owned it and what it was worth, and then set it down in the record (Whitelock et al, 1965, 164).

Nonetheless, William had been on the throne of England for 20 years and it is more likely that Domesday was the product of a particular crisis, rather than the final eruption of his avarice, and certainly not, as some have suggested, of mere curiosity. Reasons are not far to seek. Firstly, in 1085, William faced the prospect of a joint invasion of England by King Cnut of Denmark and Robert the Frisian, Count of Flanders. The Chronicle describes how William returned from Normandy

with a larger force of mounted men and infantry from France and Brittany than had ever come to this country, so that people wondered how this country could maintain all that army. And the king had all the army dispersed all over the country among his vassals, and they provisioned the army each in proportion to his land (Whitelock et al, 1965, 161).

One might deduce that William would have been short of funds to pay any mercenaries and that his vassals will have suffered under the burden and complained much about poverty and iniquity, especially if the king's knowledge of what land each vassal held was inaccurate. The initial awarding of fiefs after the Conquest must have been a messy process and during the 20 years that King William had held the throne of England some of the initial holders of fiefs had died, renounced their holdings in England or been exiled. In these last two circumstances some sub-tenants had been promoted to tenants-in-chief. Other tenants-in-chief had had their fiefs amplified; yet others were also sub-tenants of other lords, and held a bigger fief than might have been thought. It would have been impossible to keep track of this process from the centre.

Secondly, if invasion were to happen, the loyalty of William's magnates would be crucial and it may be that he envisaged some trade-off: confirmation of their lands and exemptions in return for an oath of fidelity. Thirdly, William had levied in 1084 an exceptionally heavy geld★ (at 72d. to the hide) and if the so-called 'geld accounts' that are bound up with EDB are related to that imposition then they record massive exemptions, as well as under-payments and failures to pay. If William knew the overall hidage of each shire, he would have been angered by sums of money that did not reflect it.

Fourthly, some of his followers had systematically seized land that was not theirs, and especially ecclesiastical land. While in some ways this was expected of the Normans, it had provoked some very public litigation. There had been great lawsuits concerning Hampton and Bengeworth in Worcestershire, as well as a great gathering at Penenden Heath (in Kent) to consider lands taken by Odo Bishop of Bayeux, King William's own uterine half-brother, from Saint Augustine's church at Canterbury, and a series concerning the lands of Ely Abbey (see Bigelow 1879 and Van Caenegem 1990–1991). Domesday Book itself lists many less major encroachments. What was needed was an investigation of the rightful transfer of individual estates from those who held them in 1066 on King Edward's death, to those holding them 20 years later at the time of the Domesday Enquiry.

There is a tedious debate among scholars as to whether Domesday Book is primarily fiscal or feudal; does it seek to collect expected revenue efficiently and to raise it by scrutinising exemptions and trying new forms of taxation, or does it check that a man's tenure is legitimate and, if it is, confirm him in his lands and, if it is not, restore those lands to the rightful holder. But if Domesday was a response to a crisis of tenure and revenue, there is no reason why it could not address both issues. The Chronicler ('*there was not one hide of land in England that he [William] did not know who owned it and what it was worth*') implies this, and the physionomy of Domesday entries suggests it. As an example we can take Foxcote, a 5-hide manor★ lying just to the south of Eckweek. It is here translated from EDB, with the GDB abbreviation following:

EDB (folio 145b1)
§ The bishop of Coutances has 1 manor which is called FOXCOTE which Aldgyth held on the day that King E[dward] was alive and dead1 and it paid geld for 5 hides. 4 ploughs can plough these. William of Monceaux holds these from the Bishop. There W[illiam] has 3 hides and 3 virgates and 2 ploughs in demesne★ and the villans★ [have] 1 hide and 1 virgate and 2 ploughs. On it W[illiam] has 3 villans and 6 bordars★ and 2 cottars★ and 3 slaves★ and 20 beasts and 29 pigs and 160 and 17 sheep and a mill, which pays 10 shillings a year, and 20 acres★ of underwood and 19 acres of meadow [....] and 6 acres of pasture. This manor is worth 4 pounds a year and, when the Bishop received [it], it was worth as much.

GDB (SOM 5,42)

> *[The Land of the Bishop of Coutances]*
> *William holds FOXCOTE. Aldgyth held it in King Edward's time and it gelded for 5 hides. There is land for 4 ploughs★. In demesne there are 2 ploughs and 3 slaves and 2 cottars and 3 villans and 6 bordars with 2 ploughs. A mill there, which pays 10 shillings, and 19 acres of meadow, and 6 acres of pasture and 20 acres of underwood. It was and is worth 4 pounds.*

It will be seen that such an entry (whose content is typical) contains:

- The name of the 1066 holder, its 1086 holder and his or her sub-tenant.
- The name of the estate and, in the case of EDB, a statement as to whether it was a manor or not.
- Its assessment for geld in terms of hides and their division between the lord (the demesne land) and the villans.
- An estimate of the number of ploughs that would be needed for full exploitation of its arable potential, sometimes called 'ploughlands★'.
- Its actual resources in terms of ploughs, people (here divided into various categories: villans, bordars, cottars, slaves), pasture, meadow, woodland, mills. The demesne population is given separately.

Other entries list other population categories and other resources such as churches and fisheries. They may also contain additional information such as listing outliers or lands in the jurisdiction of the manor, or recording any parts of the estate that are sub-infeudated, let out by the tenant-in-chief to a sub-tenant, and have separate resources and valuation. There can be a note concerning disputed tenure or the fusion or fission of the manor.

The designation of an estate as a manor (rather than some form of dependency) seems to have been important since it was the manor that was liable to geld and other imposts and it was through its hall that these were channelled. Merging one manor with another would allow one of them, and its potential revenues, to disappear. The sense given to the word *mansio* in EDB and the word *manerium* itself used in GDB, together with the tighter definition of this form of estate which these words imply, seem to have been a Norman import (Maitland 1897, 107–128 and Lewis 2011). Likewise, the terms for the commonest categories of population (*uillani*, *bordarii*, *cotarii*) seem to have been new. Any attempt to compare them with those layers of population described in Anglo-Saxon documents from earlier in the century (the *geneat*, the *gebur*, the *ceorl* and the *cotsetla*) (see the Rectitudines Singularum Personarum in Liebermann 1903, 1. 444–453, translated in part in Douglas and Greenaway 1981, 875–880 (no. 172), and the survey of Tidenham (Gloucestershire), Robertson 1956, 204, 451–454 (no. CIX); Faith 1994) shows that these are not simply Latin names for Anglo-Saxon classes, but a new classification: the old groups find themselves split between the new categories. Unfortunately there is no description of these new categories, but an examination of the Domesday evidence suggests that the basis is primarily economic.

It is clear that such an entry could serve both tenurial and fiscal purposes. Tenurially, it identifies the tenant-in-chief of each holding and the first layer of sub-tenancy. It also gives the 1066 holder, and in some cases, his or her tenant or tenants. Since it was generally clear who or what, in 1086, should hold the 1066 estates of individuals and institutions, here was the information to allow a rapid check of the legitimacy of descent. Thus a church would be expected to have retained its 1066 lands in 1086; while the lands of King Edward, Queen Edith, Earl Harold and of various other earls or countesses should have been in King William's hands in 1086. In many cases, all the lands of one man with a Saxon name passed to one Norman and the concept of legitimate descent from a named *antecessor* or *antecessores* ('predecessor(s)') seems embedded in the process. Nonetheless, this is a weak part of the Domesday record, partly because the manner in which land was held in 1066 (leased from a church for life or for the lives of three men; held in freehold) is often not stated, nor the status of the holder (holding in his own right or from or under someone else) and partly because individuals are rarely identified for 1066, nor are the sub-tenants for 1086. Nonetheless, the Domesday process clearly produced a large number of disputes about tenure, sometimes resolved during the court proceedings, and sometimes listed for future decision.

From the point of view of revenue, it would be possible to:

- identify the holder or holders (the tenant-in-chief and if he defaulted, the first sub-tenant), responsible for the geld and other renders;
- deduce the status of the land (whether a manor or dependency) to determine whether it was directly chargeable, or part of something else;
- consider whether additions or subtractions and the reduction in the number of 1066 manors has affected the integrity (and therefore the geld and value) of the estate;
- know the taxable hidage, as well as any exemptions from geld and the size of the demesne land (which did not pay tax in 1084 according to the geld-accounts as perhaps also in 1086);
- use the number of ploughs at work and the estimate of plough-potential (the 'ploughland') to check if the hidation was beneficial, or now too generous as the basis for a new assessment;

- use the number of people as the basis for a capitation tax or poll tax;
- use the resources (including the numbers and classes of people) to determine if the estate is properly exploited and valued and to consider if revenue could be raised on the basis of these valuations.

Any idea, however, that Domesday could be used as the basis for a new fiscality never came to fruition as William died within a year of having the 'writings' brought to him and his successor, his son William Rufus, did not take the project forward.

The Domesday Process

There is good testimony for a number of the stages and arrangements of the Enquiry:

1. The decision to hold the Enquiry was made by the king and his counsellors at Gloucester at Christmas 1085. Probably at that time the 'terms of reference' were drawn up.
2. The Enquiry had a double format, with 'other investigators following the first'.
3. The country was divided into groups or shires (or 'circuits') each with their set of *barones* or *legati* ('magnates' or 'envoys', often called 'commissioners').
4. The material was processed in the shire-court 'by the oath of the sheriff of the shire and of all the barons and their Frenchmen and of the whole hundred, the priests, the reeves and 6 villans of each and every vill'. One county volume survives (the *Inquisitio Comitatus Cantabrigiensis* for Cambridgeshire) (Hamilton 1876), which probably reflects the proceedings of this court. It is arranged territorially, by shire, hundred, vill and estate.
5. The material was then (re-)arranged feudally, by county, fief, hundred and estate: the volumes for two circuits (East Anglia, the southwest) survive as LDB and EDB.
6. The results of the Domesday Enquiry were probably available in some format (possibly the circuit returns) to the king by 1 August 1086.
7. These circuit returns were condensed and abbreviated to form GDB, although work ceased abruptly, possibly in 1088, with the three East Anglian counties (forming LDB) remaining untreated.
8. Great Domesday itself was subsequently further and more stringently abbreviated and a number of other partial shortenings and extracts made.

Valuable though this good evidence is, it cannot account for all the stages of the inquest, nor give full detail about each one. This lack can be made good by inference, by examining later references to Domesday Book and by trying to assign to a particular stage in the process the fifty-or-so schedules which are generally and unhelpfully called satellites (Clarke 1985). Using these methods, the Domesday process becomes a little more extended and detailed.

The double nature of the Enquiry is mentioned in Robert of Lozinga's description of the Domesday process. In fact his description is really a digression attached to the year 1086 in a technical tract that he was writing about chronology. However, as Bishop of Hereford (1079–95), he may well have been present at the Gloucester court and at the subsequent discussions in council (Bates 1998, 482–484 (146)).

This is the 20th year of William, king of the English on whose orders a written survey was made of the whole of England in this year, concerning the fields in individual counties, concerning the possessions of individual barons in terms of their fields, manors, men, not only slaves but also free men* not only in terms of those only living in huts, but in terms of those possessing houses and fields in terms of ploughs and horses and the other animals in terms of the service and dues from the entire land of everyone. Some enquirers were sent after others and unknown men were sent to unknown counties so that different men should find fault with the written survey of others and place them as guilty men before the king. And the land was troubled by many disasters arising from the amassing of the royal money (See Stevenson 1907. His own translation, frequently reproduced, is more rhetorical than accurate.)

Incidentally, this text contains the only contemporary description of the population categories of Domesday, albeit expressed with a rhetorical vagueness: through it the four principal layers of Domesday society are apparent: free men (not found in Somerset), villans, bordars (or cottars) and slaves.

If the first set of investigators were men sent at once after the Gloucester meeting to visit each sheriff and to charge them with the task, the second set was probably those who presided over the hearings in the shire-court. They are implicitly distinguished from the first by being strangers to the counties where they were sent. They are also likely to have been of higher status. There must have been a collection of material, in response to the visit to the shires by the first group of investigators. There are indications in Domesday that the tenants-in-chief and perhaps some of their major sub-tenants submitted information and that some came from examination of the records held by the sheriff, if not by individual hundreds. This would have been an essential preparation for a hearing in the county court if that was not to be a protracted affair.

The division of the country into circuits is attested by the monk Heming, who names those who presided over the West-Midlands shires (Hearne 1723 i. 288. This is part of the text known as 'Worcester F', translated and discussed in Thorn and Thorn 1982, Appendix V). The conclusion that there were seven or so circuits depends on a study of the minute differences in layout, phrasing and the treatment of the material (Eyton 1880, 9–10; Ballard 1906, 12; Stephenson 1947; Moore 1986).

The procedure in the shire court is described in a preface to the *Liber Eliensis* (Hamilton 1876, 97).

'Written here below is the Land Enquiry as the King's barons made the enquiry, that is, by the oath of the sheriff of the shire and of all the barons and their Frenchmen and of the whole hundred, the priest, the reeve and 6 villans of each and every vill'. Then:

1. *What is the manor called?*
2. *Who held it in King Edward's time?*
3. *Who holds it now?*
4. *How many hides?*
5. *How many ploughs in demesne; how many belong to the men?*
6. *How many villans, how many cottars, how many slaves?*
7. *How many free men, how many sokemen*?*
8. *How much woodland, how much meadow, how many pastures, how many mills, how many fisheries?*
9. *How much has been added or taken away?*
10. *How much was it worth altogether and how much now?*
11. *How much each free man or sokeman had or has there?*
12. *All this in triplicate; that is, in the time of King Edward, when William gave it and as it may be now.*
13. *And if more can be assessed there than may [currently] be assessed* (This last question is often mistranslated as 'If more can be had than is had', through ignorance of the range of meanings of the Latin verb habeo and of the use of the subjunctive).

In view of the number and detail of the questions, it is difficult to imagine that the material was only written down at this stage from oral question and answer; it is more probable that what material had been pre-assembled was nodded through or amended and amplified.

The *Inquisitio Comitatus Cantabrigiensis* probably represents the written outcome of this stage. Its primary arrangement by hundred accurately reflects the most efficient way of swearing to the information, by dealing with one hundred after another. Within each hundred the arrangement is by vill* and all the holdings in each vill are treated together, whereas in Domesday Book they are assigned to their respective holders' fiefs or chapters. Thus the entry for Swaffham in 'Staine' Hundred contains the holdings of Hugh [of Bolbec] from Walter Giffard (CAM 17,2), of Geoffrey from Count Alan [of Brittany] (CAM 14,63), of Aubrey of Vair (CAM 29,4) of the Abbot of Ely (CAM 5,9) also land alienated from Ely Abbey and held by Hugh [of Bolbec] from Walter Giffard (CAM 17,3) and by Hardwin of Les Échelles (CAM 26,1) and further land held by Hardwin (CAM 26,53) and by Count Alan (CAM 14,64) in their own right. Such entries contain all the detail asked for by the Enquiry, including livestock.

If similar documents were produced for each county and circuit, the information would have been full enough to satisfy William's requirements; we have seen that we do not know what form if any was envisaged for the information when collected and testified to. However, if he needed to know at a glance who the major holders of land were and henceforth wished to make the tenant-in-chief (rather than the hundred or vill) responsible for tax and service, he needed a document whose arrangement reflected these changes. Hence a document for each shire was required, in which the fief took precedence over the hundred and where parts of the same vill would appear in different chapters if different landholders held manors there. The result of this conversion would have been volumes like EDB and LDB, but to aid the transfer from format to format, some form of conversion table would probably be needed; indeed some documents which might have been exactly these have been found among the so-called 'satellite' surveys (Clarke 1985, 67).

The substance of the Enquiry will not simply have been accepted by those present at the shire-moot, then passed without further alteration into the *Inquisitio Comitatus Cantabrigiensis* -type volume then into the circuit volume. Certainly at the shire-moot, and possibly later, there will have been disputes between landholders, and a number of other miscellaneous claims which were either too important to be settled on the spot, or where the evidence pointed either way. These seem to have been drawn up as separate schedules: as *Clamores* ('shouts', 'claims'). They form separate lists attached to the GDB folios for Yorkshire and Lincolnshire, similar to the untitled list in Huntingdonshire, usually known as 'Declarations' or 'Declarations of the Jurors'. As *Invasiones* ('land-seizures', 'purprestures'), they appear in LDB for all three counties and as *Terrae Occupatae* they appear in EDB. They mostly record disputed tenure, often because one party claimed land by right of his *antecessor* ('predecessor'). They also record encroachments and land added to or taken from manors, as well as the failure to pay customary dues, and many of the *Terrae Occupatae* are not about annexation or encroachment at all, but about the combining of 1066 manors.

Even after such a process of gathering, swearing and re-formatting, a written survey such as EDB might have been available by the summer of 1086, so feared was William's vicious impatience. The situation was militarily and fiscally urgent and William was a cruel and powerful king:

Also, he was a very stern and violent man, so that no one dared do anything contrary to his will. He had earls in his fetters, who acted against his will. He expelled bishops from their sees, and abbots from their abbacies, and put thegns in prison, and finally, he did not spare his own brother who was called Odo (Whitelock et al, 1965, 164).

The Anglo-Saxon Chronicle records a great meeting at Salisbury (that is at Old Sarum) on 1 August 1086:

In this year [1086] the king wore his crown and held his court at Winchester for Easter, and travelled so as to be at Westminster for Whitsuntide, and there he dubbed his son, Henry, a knight. Then he travelled about so as to come to Salisbury at Lammas [August 1st]; and there his councillors came to him, and all the people occupying land who were of any account all over England, no matter whose vassals they might be; and they all submitted to him and became his vassals and swore oaths of allegiance to him, and that they would be loyal to him against all other men. From there he went to the Isle of Wight, because he meant to go to Normandy and so he did later. But all the same, he first acted according to his custom, that is to say, he obtained a very great amount of money from his men where he had any pretext for it either just or otherwise (Whitelock et al, 1965, 162).

Certainly, the existence of a 'circuit return' such as EDB would have allowed William to discover 'all the people occupying land who were of any account all over England' and to have made hasty summations of the values of fiefs; a few such 'summaries' are among the extant folios of EDB. Certainly it was at Salisbury and probably at this meeting that the king awarded Lydeard St Lawrence and Leigh in Somerset to the Bishop of Winchester and ordered the Bishop of Durham to write this down in the 'documents' (*in brevibus*) which may well have been the extant EDB itself.

and King William granted these lands to St Peter and Bishop Walkelin to have, as he himself acknowledged at Salisbury with the Bishop of Durham listening and he instructed to write down this actual grant of his in the documents (EDB 174b4 = GDB SOM 2,9).

Certainly the Anglo-Saxon Chronicle records that *'all these records were brought to him afterwards'*, and if that was not before he left England for Normandy in the autumn of 1086, never to return, it will certainly have been within a year for he died on the continent in the autumn of 1087.

The Writing of Great Domesday Book

It may be that with the production of these circuit volumes, the aim of the Enquiry as articulated at the Gloucester assembly was fulfilled, but that, if EDB is taken as typical, the bulk, the extravagance of certain formulae, the lack of rubrication and indices, the number of composite chapters, the variety of hands (some of them very poor) made the circuit volumes difficult (though not impossible) to handle. William and his advisers may well have taken fright at the sheer mass of the material (perhaps 3000 folios) at its density and unhighlighted impenetrability. This may also have taken them back to the original questions and led them to ask what answers, with hindsight, were less important and could be jettisoned.

It seems likely that it was now that GDB was envisaged as a highly structured, clarified, easier-to-read and simpler-to-search abbreviation. This was to be achieved by:

— a clearer layout, by the use of ruling and rubrication, the latter being employed both at the heads of pages and within entries;
— the use of shorter formulae;
— separating out individual fiefs from composite chapters;
— reorganising fiefs internally, by, for example, separating the demesne from the sub-infeudations, or by bringing all the lands of one sub-tenant together;
— trying to achieve a standard order of fiefs from county to county (king, archbishop, bishops, abbot, earls or counts, Frenchmen, surviving English thanes);
— the elimination of information, judged at that time to be non-essential, such as bynames, livestock, the repetitive designation of an estate as a manor, the quantity of non-demesne land (which last could usually be deduced from other figures that were retained);
— a more rigorous use of standard terms, in some cases one being substituted for another;
— a revised treatment of placenames and personal names.

Attempts have been made from references in the text and elsewhere to determine how long work would have continued. This is not the place to explore these questions except to say firstly that GDB contains nothing that can be certainly dated to the reign of William Rufus (1087–1100) or later, apart that is from the fief of Robert of *Bruis* which was added to the finished manuscript *c*1120 (GDB YKS 42 (folios 332c–333a)). Thus, the manuscript essentially represents the situation as it was in 1086 and has not been significantly updated. Secondly, work on the manuscript ceased abruptly with gaps still unfilled, marginal queries unanswered, rubrication incomplete and leaving Essex, Norfolk and Suffolk (LDB) uncondensed. The most obvious moments for this cessation of work would be the death of the Conqueror (autumn 1087), or the exile of William of Saint-Calais, Bishop of Durham in the spring of 1088, if he was the man behind the survey or charged with overseeing the writing of GDB (Chaplais 1986). GDB is essentially the work of one scribe and if this man was the Bishop's own scribe he will no doubt have gone into exile with him. Henceforth, the Domesday Project will have lacked a controlling mind and a writer.

Interpreting an entry

The implications for interpretation of this account of the making of Domesday are considerable. Firstly, the focus of the whole enterprise is only on revenue and tenure; it does not present information on that wider range of matters which interest modern users of it. Secondly, the survey contained in GDB, which is all that survives for much of the country, is an abbreviation of fuller originals in similar format: while there is no loss of substance in compressing formulae, considerable quantities of material important in other ways have been jettisoned as not serving its increasingly narrow purposes. Thirdly, material is only sporadically included concerning questions that were not asked but probably should have been. Thus there is no systematic treatment of churches and priests; boroughs are handled in several markedly different ways and the surveys of some (such as London, Winchester and Bristol) are missing completely. Fourthly, the complex reality on the ground in the late 11th century has been forced by central *diktat* into a series of standard names and categories, which have evolved during the survey without systematic revision. Conversely, local individuals will have interpreted the categories differently and introduced their own ways of classifying and measuring, which have found their way into the finished text without standardisation. Fifthly, resources and categories of population have been introduced by local people, when they have either not been included in the questions that framed the Survey, or have not been placed in the correct category. Thus oak trees are mentioned only in Warwickshire and Worcestershire (GDB WAR 12,11; WOR 2,13), and there are noted a mere 7 quarries and 45 vineyards in the whole country (Darby 1977, 287, 362–363). Here the oaks should probably have been categorized as 'a small wood' and the quarries and vineyards have probably survived from a much larger number mentioned but mostly eliminated because they were not the subject of a question in the 'terms of reference'. Ten shepherds are mentioned for the whole country yet there are 48,868 sheep in the five southwestern counties alone. There are 759 *bovarii* ('oxmen') and 556 *porcarii* ('pigmen'), 17 *hospites* ('settlers'), 2 *vaccarii* ('cowmen'), 2 *caementarii* ('masons') and only 1 *carpentarius* ('carpenter') and one *joculatrix* ('female jester') (Darby 1977, 338–345 with additions). Most of these are named by occupation, whereas Domesday is primarily concerned with status (and the possessions, income and obligations) of its various classes.

The successive writings-up and restructurings will inevitably have degraded the Inquest material: words, phrases, sentences, even whole entries will have fallen out; estates will have sometimes been entered twice in the circuit volumes; words and especially figures will have been misread or miscopied; abbreviations will have been wrongly expanded; the names of places, persons and administrative units will have been mangled beyond recall. And this damage will have overlain any errors that were already present in the source material that were not corrected at the shire-court, where there would have been a linguistic cacophony, with Celt, Anglo-Saxon, Norman-French, Fleming, Picardian and Dane trying to communicate with each other and the Latinists. Yet, to understand the complex process that produced Domesday Book is a reason only for caution, not for despair.

The Domesday Entries for Eckweek

(1) The Count of Mortain

EDB (folio 276b3)
§ *The Count [of Mortain] has 1 manor which is called ECKWEEK which Alstan of Boscombe held on the day that King E[dward] was alive and dead and it paid geld for 1 virgate. 1 plough can plough this. Now Alfred [? the butler] holds it from the Count and he has 1 villan there and 1 slave; and it is worth 10 shillings a year and, when the Count received [it], it was worth as much.* (Square brackets enclose editorial additions and explanations).

GDB SOM 19,61
[Land of the Count of Mortain]
Alfred [?the butler] holds ECKWEEK from the Count. Alstan [of Boscombe] held it before 1066 and it gelded for 1 virgate of land. 1 villan there and 1 slave.
It was and is worth 10 shillings.

(2) Walter [*alias* Walscin of Douai]

EDB (folio 354b3)
§ *Walter has 1 manor which is called ECKWEEK which Alwaker held on the day when King Edward was alive and dead and it paid geld for 1 virgate and a half and 8 acres. 1 plough can plough this. Ralph [?of Conteville] holds this from Walter and he has the whole in demesne and he has 1 bordar; and it is worth 10 shillings a year, and it was worth as much when Walter received [it].*

GDB SOM 24,32
[Land of Walter of Douai]
Ralph holds ECKWEEK from W[alter]. Alwaker held it before in King E[dward']s time and
it gelded for one virgate and a half of land and 8 acres.
There is land for 1 plough.
There is 1 bordar there.
It is worth 10 shillings.

Commentary

It will be seen that in both cases the EDB account has been considerably shortened, partly by the adoption of more compact formulae, but also by omissions of substance. Thus, neither holding is described as a manor in GDB; EDB shows that the Alstan of GDB 19,61 is the great Anglo-Saxon thane Alstan of Boscombe. In the case of Walter of Douai's manor (24,32), GDB does not mention that the whole is held in demesne, while in both cases, the earlier of the two values in EDB is the more precise ('when he received it'). Not all of the 1066 holders received their lands at the Conquest.

SOM 19,61

The 1066 holder of this manor was Alstan of Boscombe. He was an important thane of King Edward and Domesday records men holding under him before the Conquest. His full name appears only here and in GLS 58,4. HRT 28,1–3;5;7–8. BDF 18,1;4;6. SOM 26,7 (in this last he is as Alstan Boscombe accounting for all of SOM 26,1–7) and WIL 32,2;14. Since these lands in Bedfordshire and Hertfordshire passed to William of Eu, it is a reasonable assumption that any Alstan named as William's predecessor was Alstan of Boscombe: thus further holdings (HAM 32,4. BDF 18,2–3;7. BRK 23,1. DOR 34,1;9–11;13. HRT 28,4;6. GLS 31,4;7;11. WIL 32,1;3–13) can be added. An Alstan held 1 hide under Malmesbury Abbey (WIL 8,12), which likewise passed to William of Eu. William's post-Conquest predecessor was probably Ralph of Limésy and this makes it probable that the Alstan who held land by freehold in Hampshire (HAM 1,32) and which passed to this Ralph, was Alstan of Boscombe. There are remoter possibilities: one estate held by an Alstan (HAM 32,4) was said to be held in freehold from King Edward and that an Alstan held land from King Edward (rather than in his own right) is mentioned at BDF 18,1. BRK 23,1. HRT 28,4;6;8 and implied in GLS 58,4. It has been suggested that the Alstan, who held land in Somerset that passed to Roger of Courseulles (SOM 21,92) was this Alstan, as was the Alstan whose holding in Dorset went to the Count of Mortain (DOR 26,70). However, the urge to identify individuals in a list of undifferentiated frequently occurring names can sometimes override common sense, and it is only really safe to identify an Alstan as Alstan of Boscome if Domesday names him thus, or if a connection can be established with William of Eu or Ralph of Limésy. From the above, it will be apparent that Eckweek's being surveyed as part of the Count of Mortain's land is surprising. It would have been expected to pass to William of Eu. However, William of Eu held nothing else in the vicinity and it is possible that he was the rightful holder, but that the Count of Mortain had occupied it, in an unrecorded alienation, from his adjacent manor of Carlingcott, the previous entry in GDB (19,60).

Robert, Count of Mortain, was son of Herluin of Conteville and Herlève, mother of William the Conqueror. He was thus the half-brother of the Conqueror, also the full brother of Bishop Odo of Bayeux who granted him the comté of Mortain c1048. Count Robert fought at Hastings and, when William became king of England, he was put in charge of Pevensey Rape (Sussex) where he built a castle. His holdings in Cornwall (which he received later) dominated the county of which he was *de facto* earl. Altogether he held estates in 20 counties. He was twice married, first to Matilda daughter of Roger of Montgomery (the Earl of Shrewsbury) and Mabel of Bellême, and secondly to Almodis. Robert's son William inherited his estates, but rebelled in 1104 and the enormous fief was broken up. Some lands, however, retained the title of Mortain fees and the tenants of others became tenants-in-chief and their lands became separate honours or baronies (see Keats-Rohan 1999, 371-373). It is possible that Alfred who held Eckweek under the count was his butler, thus titled in SOM 19,39;80;86, but it should be noted that an Alfred was a tenant of the Count of Eu in Sussex (SUS 9,1)

SOM 24,32

The 1066 tenant is called Alwaker and he is presumably the same man who held under Walter of Douai in Wiltshire (WIL 36,2) and elsewhere in Somerset (SOM 24,2;9;18;28;30–31).

Walter himself (also known as Walscin) of Douai (and of Flanders and of Bampton, Bampton was his principal holding in Devonshire (GDB DEV 23,5)) was a man of and perhaps related to Walter I the castellan of Douai in Flanders (now in Belgium). He held a small fief in the southwest (in Devon, Dorset, Somerset and Wiltshire) and (as Walter of Flanders) had lands in Bedfordshire, Buckinghamshire and Northamptonshire. His two marriages were firstly to Eadgyth, the widow of Hemming the 1066 holder of Uffculme in Devon (GDB DEV 23,9), and secondly to Emma, by whom he had two sons, Geoffrey and Robert. On his death c1107 his fief was divided between the Honour of Bampton held by his son Robert and the Honour of Castle Cary held by Ralph Lovel. His tenant Ralph here is possibly Ralph of Conteville, so named in SOM 8,33. 24,11;36–37. He will probably have come from one of the two places (now communes) called Conteville in the French département of Pas de Calais, either Conteville-en-Ternoise, or Conteville-lès-Boulogne; the former being closer to Douai (see Keats-Rohan 1999, 450).

The term manor (*mansio* in EDB, *manerium* in GDB) seems to have been so important to the compilers of Domesday that it must have had a technical significance. Identifying the manors in the landscape was tantamount to identifying the sources of revenue and their focal point. A manor would be expected to have a hall (*halla, aula*) or court (*curia*) that organized its affairs. It was the manor that paid geld for the whole estate including any dependencies. However, the fact that there were two manors in Eckweek says nothing about their relative disposition on the ground. It does not imply separate settlements; there might have been a single settlement with adjacent halls (the term implies nothing grand) each looking out on their dependent lands, or these same lands might be intermingled so as to share resources, especially if the separation of Eckweek from some parent estate and its division into two parts was quite late.

What is striking here is the smallness of the two units: 1 virgate and 1½ virgates with 8 acres respectively. Estates of this small taxable size are more usually found in Domesday for Somerset on the edge of the Brendon Hills or of the Quantocks or of Exmoor. It is true that the potential for exploitation is as 1 ploughland each, thus more approximating to 1 hide in the old measure, but these are tiny estates to be in the hands of such great men.

In fact they are so small that it is surprising to find them qualified as manors at all, except in the narrowest sense as units of taxation. It is probable that they both originated as grants of land from the nearest estate, which is Wellow. In the case of Alstan of Boscombe's portion, it is likely that he had not acquired it by inheritance, but was given this land by King Edward or was allowed to lease it from him in recognition of his status or in gratitude for a particular service. It would thus be similar to the estates listed above that he held from King Edward, sometimes in freehold. In normal circumstances, it might have been expected to return to King Edward, but the post-Conquest arrangements meant that the land of one man went to one Norman, even though in this particular case, William of Eu (if he ever held it) seems to have lost it to the Count of Mortain. This passage from predecessor to successor took place irrespective of how the former had held the land, or from whom. The most striking instances of this are when the land of an Englishman, who held land from a church for his lifetime or for the lives of three men, passed to that man's Norman successor and was thus effectively alienated from the church. It is possible that Alwaker's land had similar history, although there is no hint of this in the text of Domesday. What is notable is that neither holding has been found among the lands of these Norman magnates' respective successors. It is thus possible that they were reabsorbed by Wellow, having never been intended to be more than temporary grants. They may fall into the category of lands which have been 'taken away' from another manor, as illustrated, for example by the GDB entries for South Petherton, Curry Rivel and Bruton (SOM 1,4–5;9).

There is a difficulty with this thesis in that Wellow is not named in Domesday Book. It is however, the subject of three pre-Conquest charters: an early grant (766 x 774) by Cynewulf, King of the West Saxons giving 2 *manentes* [hides] beside the River Wellow to the minster at Wells (Sawyer 1968, no. 262 = Kelly 2007, 193–8 (no 27) = Finberg 1964a, 117); a gift of Wellow by King Alfred in his will to his eldest daughter (Sawyer 1968, no. 1507 = Finberg 1964a, 126 (no 25)); the 3½ *mansae* [hides] at *Welewestoce* granted (1006 x 1009) by King Æthelred to the church of Bath (Sawyer 1968, no. 854 = Kelly 2007, 133–136 (no. 20) = Finberg 1964a, 148 (no. 525)).

Thus, Wellow was in existence at the time of the Domesday survey. It was also named from the river on which it lay, a characteristic of ancient estates. It seems, in fact, to be included silently in the entry for the royal manor of Frome;

EDB (90b2)
The King has 1 manor which is called FROME, which King Edward held on the day that he himself was alive and dead and it is not known how many hides are in it because it has never paid geld. 50 ploughs can plough the land of this manor. In it the king has 3 ploughs in his demesne and the villans have 40 ploughs. The King has 31 villans there and 36 bordars {and 6 coliberts★} and 24 pigs and 100 sheep less 7 and three mills, which pay 25 shillings a year, and 1 market, which pays 46 shillings and 8 pence, and woodland 1 league in length and as much in width, and 30 acres of meadow and 50 acres of pasture; and it pays 53 pounds and 5 pence a year at 20 [pence] in an ora★.

Of this manor the church of Saint John of Frome has 8 carucates★ of land which the church itself held from King E[dward] in alms on the day that he himself was alive and dead. Rainbald [the priest] now holds this and he held it in the time of [King] E[dward]. (Curly brackets enclose material that appears in the margin of the manuscript.)

GDB (SOM 1,8)
The King holds FROME. King E[dward] held it. It has never gelded, and it is not known how many hides are there. There is land for 50 ploughs. In demesne are 3 ploughs and 6 coliberts and 31 villans and 36 bordars with 40 ploughs. There are 3 mills there, which pay 25 shillings, and a market, which pays 46 shillings and 8 pence, There are 30 acres of meadow there and 50 acres of pasture. Woodland 1 league long and as much wide. It pays 53 pounds and 5 pence at 20 [pence] to the ora. Of this manor St John's Church of Frome holds 8 carucates of land; it held them similarly King Edward's time. Reinbald is a priest there.

The argument for including Wellow in Frome is as follows: contrary to its normal practice, Domesday does not include hundred headings in the text for any of the five southwestern counties. However, the hundreds that existed at that time can be known from two plain lists of hundred names bound up with EDB (EDB folios 63–64) and from the so-called Tax Returns or Geld Accounts, which are in the same volume (EDB folios 75–82, 526–527: that for Frome Hundred is on folio 527). The order of names in the second of these lists of hundreds is very similar to the order in which places in those hundreds are entered in blocks in EDB and it is likely that the two documents are closely related: this second list might be a checklist of the hundreds that needed to be or had been entered in EDB, or a copy of a document sent out to fief-holders to prescribe a standard order of hundreds for their returns. The hundreds in which Domesday places must have lain, can also be determined independently from later evidence, as the changes over time in the Somerset hundreds are more of name than of content.

The lists of hundreds in EDB refer to the Hundreds of Frome, Kilmersdon and Wellow, while the Geld Accounts simply record a triple Hundred of Frome, amounting to 298 hides. Wellow Hundred must therefore have been one of the hundreds dependent on Frome, and it follows that Wellow (also, like Frome, a British river name) itself already existed as a place and that its lands, as they do not appear in Domesday as an independent estate, must be counted under Frome.

Frome had a simplex river-name; was unhidated; paid at 20d to the *ora;* had an exceptionally well-endowed minster church that was not assessed in hides (therefore not taxed); the manor shared with Bruton a food-rent of one-night's revenue (see EDB 90b3). These are all judged to be characteristics of the most ancient royal estates (Thorn 2014). Bruton too, was head of three hundreds separately named in the EDB lists, but treated as a unit by the Tax Returns. There were three hundreds based on Yeovil, or around the River Yeo and there is a strong argument at least for Somerset that all the hundreds arose from the division (or in some cases recombination) of royal territories that were centred on less than a dozen ancient royal manors (GDB SOM 1,1–10), so it is probable that some of Frome's estimated 50 ploughlands lay at Wellow and Kilmersdon, which continued to be royal manors and heads of hundreds.

Like Wellow, the manor of Kilmersdon itself is not mentioned in Domesday Book, though its church is (GDB SOM 16,14). Half a hide of land was attached to it and it was then in the king's hands, having previously been held by Bishop Peter [of Lichfield]. With such an amount of land and a holder of high status, it is likely that this was a minster church, like Frome's. There must have been an estate here, probably part of the 50 ploughlands of Frome itself. In 1275–1276 it was stated that Kilmersdon had been *antiquum dominicum coronae* ('ancient crown demesne/lordship land'), implying that it had belonged to the crown before 1086 (Illingworth and Caley 1818, 136). Unlike Kilmersdon, Wellow is not later described as *antiquum dominicum coronae*, but it is called a *villa regalis* ('royal vill') in 1284–85 (Feudal Aids, iv. 279) and entries in the *Rotuli Hundredorum* of a few years earlier seem to imply that the manor and hundred had been alienated from the king by the Earl of Gloucester (Illingworth and Caley 1818, ii. 134, 136). Nonetheless, despite these later differences, it is likely that Kilmersdon and Wellow shared a similar origin in being satellites of the royal demesne of Frome.

The aims of the Domesday survey were satisfied by identifying the name of the manor and leaving unmentioned all its constituent parts. Wellow itself was an unnamed part of Frome and its own members and appendages are passed over in silence. In the *Nomina Villarum* of 1316 these are listed as: Banworth [unidentified], Stoney Littleton [ST 7356], Paglinch [ST 7155], Eckweek [ST 7137], White Ox Mead [ST 7258], Twinhoe [ST 7459], and Hassage [ST 7555] (Feudal Aids, iv. 323). Shoscombe [ST 7156] appears in the 1327 *Lay Subsidy* (Dickinson 1889, 84) and the Ancient Parish of Wellow also contained part of Peasedown St John [ST 7057] (Youngs 1979, 433). Of these, Stoney Littleton, Eckweek and White Ox Mead are separately listed in Domesday (GDB SOM 5,56 Stoney Littleton; 19,61 and 24,32 Eckweek; 21,89 White Ox Mead), though only Stoney Littleton continues to feature regularly as a separate estate in feudal lists. Eckweek and White Ox Mead do not do so and seem to have been reabsorbed by Wellow, being held from the lords (long the Earls of Gloucester) of that manor. Additionally, Woodborough is listed in Domesday, but seems to have been of little administrative importance later (GDB SOM 39,3). It was probably later counted silently as part of Wellow, from which it may initially have been granted out.

Wellow was also head of a hundred and a tabulation of its extent and presumed contents (see Figure 2.10) throws more light on the ancient estate of Wellow itself.

In the northern part of the hundred, a series of four vills are assessed individually at 10 hides making a total of 40 hides. These are Corston (10 hides), Newton St Loe (3 + 7 hides), Twerton (7½ + 2½ hides) and Englishcombe (10 hides). These form a geographically discrete unit within the hundred, on a slope running down to the River Avon, whereas the rest of the hundred is south of a watershed and clustered around Wellow. The northern group might already have been separate estates before hidation took place, or represent an early areal hidation (with or without existing estates) at 40 hides. They belong more naturally in the areas which became Bath Hundred (south of the Avon) and Keynsham Hundred. However, geography is not the sole determinant of boundaries and one could speculate that this part of the original territory of Frome contributed to its balanced resources by allowing access to the Avon.

South of here, there are a number of estates whose hidage is regular: Camerton, Hinton

Modern name	Domesday placename	Domesday holder(s)	Size (+)
Camerton	*Camelertone*	8,31 Glastonbury Church	10-0-0
Carlingcott	*Credlincote*	19,60 Richard from the Count of Mortain	3-2-0
Combe (Hay)	*Cume*	47,20 Aethelric	2-0-0
Corston	*Corstune*	7,13 The Church of Bath	10-0-0
Dunkerton	*Duncretone*	36,13 Bernard paunch-face from Thurstan the son of Rolf	3-1-0
Eckweek	*Ecewiche*	9,61 Alfred from the Count of Mortain	0-1-0
	Ecewiche	24,32 Ralph from Walter of Douai	0-1-2 plus 8 acres
Englishcombe	*Engliscome*	5,44 Nigel of Gournai from the Bishop of Coutances	10-0-0
'Eversy' [in Dunkerton]	*Evestie*	7,14 The Church of Bath	1-0-0
Farleigh (Hungerford)	*Ferlege*	21,88 Aelmer from Roger of Courseulles	0-2-0
Foxcote	*Fuscote*	5,42 William of Monceaux from the Bishop of Coutances	5-0-0
Hinton (Charterhouse)	*Hantone*	40,1 Edward of Salisbury	10-0-0
(Stony) Littleton	*Liteltone*	5,56 Osmund from the Bishop of Coutances	2-0-0
Newton (St Loe)	*Niwetone*	5,57 The Bishop of Coutances	10-0-0
Norton St Philip	*Nortune*	40,2 Edward of Salisbury	10-0-0
Tellisford	*Tablesford*	5,53 Moses and Roger from the Bishop of Coutances	5-0-0
Twerton	*Tivvertone*	5,45 Nigel of Gournai from the Bishop of Coutances	7-2-0
	Tivvertone	5,46 Geoffrey *malregard* from the Bishop of Coutances	2-2-0
White Ox Mead	*Witochesmede*	21,89 Roger *grenon* from Roger of Courseulles	1-0-0
Woodborough	*Vdeberge*	39,3 Osbern *giffard*	1-0-0
		TOTAL	94-3-2 plus 8 acres

+ Figures are given in the format hide-virgate-ferding. A virgate is a quarter of a hide and a ferding a quarter of a virgate. The number of acres in a hide is uncertain.

FIGURE 2.10

Domesday estates in Wellow Hundred

[Charterhouse], Norton [St Philip] at 10 hides each, Foxcote (5 hides) and Tellisford (2 + 3 hides) but some whose hidage includes odd fractions, which cannot be made into whole numbers (let alone multiples of 5, which is something of a norm in hidation) by adding together adjacent estates. Although the Domesday total for the hundred is an unsatisfactory 94 hides 3½ virgates and 8 acres, it is unlikely that multiple errors can explain all the odd fractions and totals for adjacent estates. It is more likely that these odd numbers represent the granting out of a number of separate estates over time from a central core originally assessed at a round number of hides, perhaps 55 or 60, if Wellow was at the centre of the area which became the southern half of its hundred. As the northern part of the hundred is clearly evidenced as 40 hides, Wellow was probably also assessed at a round number and the discrepancy between the 54 hides 3½ virgates and 8 acres and a likely total of 55 or 60 (depending if Wellow Hundred was ever a true hundred hides) is due to a single figure error (perhaps involving Eckweek) and/or a missing estate.

It might be thought that Wellow was not the only major estate in the south of the hundred. Hinton Charterhouse, Norton St Philip and Tellisford form a unit of 25 hides, but the half hide at Farleigh Hungerford upsets this neat arrangement. This too, had a connection with Wellow and its Domesday extent compared to its parochial acreage, as well as its name, suggests that it might have been the 'faraway leigh' for Wellow, much of it occupied not by arable but by woodland (Feudal Aids, iv. 279). Thus, when Norton St Philip, Hinton Charterhouse and Tellisford were granted from the fringes of the Wellow estate, the intimate and necessary connection with Farleigh Hungerford remained. Even without these four estates, it is likely that the others depended on Wellow. The second element of Eckweek (Old English *wic*) implies some sort of dependency. The two names with a termination from Old English *cot* (Carlingcott and Foxcote (Sawyer 1968, no. 1711)) are unlikely to have been independent estates at the outset, nor will Woodborough or White Ox Mead have been. The former may have provided timber for Wellow and the latter may have been a monoculture estate for it. Thus, the greater Wellow would have been a classic ancient royal estate, albeit a dependent one, consisting of an unhidated core, with a series of hidated dependencies perhaps amounting to 55 or 60 hides and encompassing all the 14 places named by Domesday in the south of the hundred. By 1086, the unhidated core of Wellow remained as part of the royal lordship land of Frome, but all the hidated parts, including Eckweek, had been lost or granted away.

Those estates according to the Domesday figures actually amount to 54 hides, 3½ virgates and 8 acres, but it is possible that those 2 hides beside the River Wellow mentioned above, granted (766 × 774) by Cynewulf, King of the West Saxons, to the minster at Wells, are the unnamed 2 hides that Domesday lists as added to the 50 hides of Wells itself (GDB SOM 6 1). This would increase the total to nearly 57 hides. The Geld Account for Frome Hundred speaks of a total of 298 hides, which, with the

2 hides attached to Wells and no doubt assessed in Wells Hundred, although they lay on that of Wellow, would make a perfect 300 hides. The most recent study of the individual hundreds allots 96-3-2 plus 8 acres to Wellow, 92-3-0 to Kilmersdon and 111-1-0 to Frome amounting to a total of 300-3-2. Since much of the evidence for the composition of these hundreds is drawn from the 13th and 14th centuries, it is possible that a few hides allotted to Kilmersdon Hundred lay in Wellow Hundred in 1086 and, if so, a larger figure would need to be shifted northwards from Frome Hundred to attain true equality. However, since the hundreds are late to arrive on the scene (in the mid 10th century), they would have to have taken account of a landscape occupied by estates of different sizes, which were essentially subdivisions of the land of Frome, and which the new hundredal boundaries would need to avoid splitting for fear of administrative, legal and fiscal complications. Thus, while the land of Frome was a round 300 hides, its subdivisions could only aspire to be true hundreds. There must have been some fluidity before and after the creation of the hundreds. That the delineation of the land and subsequently the Hundred of Wellow out of an ancient 300-hide unit of Frome was later than the creation of the royal estate there, might be indicated by the fact that the important estate of Norton [St Philip], though it was placed in Wellow Hundred, cannot have been the 'northern *tūn*' of Wellow (it lies to its southeast), but of Frome. Moreover *Welewestoce*, subject of the charter grant mentioned above, was an earlier name for Radstock, so the latter will have been part of the ancient estate of Wellow, although it was ultimately in Kilmersdon Hundred (GDB SOM 5,47).

Thus in terms of the hierarchy of estates in the landscape, it seems that Eckweek looked to Wellow, and Wellow to Frome, which was one of the ten major and ancient royal estates that dominated and, until the advent of the hundreds, administered the whole of Somerset.

Glossary of Technical Terms

Acre (Latin *acra*, cognate with Classical Latin *ager* ('field')). This was a unit of land measurement, sometimes linear (containing four perches), usually square. It is mostly used in Domesday of meadow, woodland and pasture, in which cases it is intended to be a true areal measurement, although there will have been practical difficulties and local variations. It is also used as a subdivision of the hide★, which was an estimate of the land needed to support a family or to keep a plough occupied for a year; thus it was of uncertain and variable size, but a fixed unit of tax and service.

Bordar (Latin *bordarius*, from Continental Latin *borda*, a 'plank' or '(planked) hut'). Sometimes called a 'smallholder'. A cultivator of inferior status, the second layer (below villan★ in its restricted sense) of the unfree population, usually with a little land and sometimes with a share of a plough. See also Cottar below.

Carucate (Latin *car(r)ucata* from Continental Latin *car(r)uca*, 'plough'). A ploughland★. In the ex-Danelaw shires it was the equivalent of a hide and so a measure of tax and service; in Wessex it is used of land, usually ancient and often the core of a major royal estate, which has never been measured in hides. It is thus land that does not pay tax. The phrase *una carucata* ('one carucate) is sometimes used as a substitute for *terra unius carucae* ('land for one plough') in the so-called 'plough estimate' which appears to be a contemporary reassessment of the hide; see ploughland★.

Colibert (Continental Latin *colibertus*, strictly a 'slave freed with others'). They were sometimes called 'freedmen' and often treated as the fourth layer of the unfree population, just above the slaves★, but were sometimes evidenced holding land and a share in a plough. They are occasionally glossed as *buri* ('boors') a Latinization of Old English *(ge)bur*, who had been of higher status in the earlier 11th century.

Cottar (Latin *cot(t)arius*, from Medieval Latin *cota*, a Latinization of Old English *cot* or *cote* 'a hut', 'a cottage'). Sometimes called a 'cottager' or 'cottage-holder'. In cases where cottars and bordars★ appear in the same entry, the cottars were probably inferior to the bordars, being the third layer of the unfree population, living in a mean dwelling often without land. The 'Terms of Reference' in the *Liber Eliensis* do not mention *bordarii*, only *cotarii* and it may be that some Norman Frenchmen behind the survey preferred *bordarii* (a word with which they would be familiar since it produced French *bordier*) to *cotarii* based on an Old English word. It also seems that in some cases *bordarii* were introduced as a further category but that in some hundreds and counties, *cotarii* were simply converted to *bordarii* and vice versa. The categories evidently overlapped so much that there was a problem of definition and allocation.

Demesne (Latin *dominium*, from *dominus*, 'lord'). Demesne (or 'lordship') land was the portion of an estate worked directly for the lord, who received all the revenue and whose men were often slaves. The cultivators of the rest of the estate (often loosely called villans★ in Domesday) rendered various dues, tithes and services to the lord, but kept some profits for themselves.

Fief (Continental Latin *feum*, *feudum*). The total of the holdings of an individual tenant-in-chief, sometimes called a 'fee' or an 'honour' and corresponding to a 'feudal chapter' in EDB and GDB.

Free man (Latin *liber homo*). With sokemen and 'riding men', these formed the free population of the vill. They could 'commend themselves' to another lord or 'go where they wished with their land'. Free men and sokemen★ are sometimes found in the same entry, so at least in these cases, there was some distinction intended, but the categories must have greatly overlapped. The Latin *homo* means a 'member of the human race', 'a person', so the term can also denote free women.

Geld (Latin *geldum* from Old English). This was a tax instituted by Ethelred the Unready and levied on the hide. It was at first intended to pay Scandinavian mercenaries used against the Vikings, but it subsequently became a regular, possibly annual, levy to finance the army and navy of the Anglo–Danish kings. The term included more than one type of geld but only one (the 'army-tax') was abolished by Edward the Confessor in 1051. The repeated statement in GDB that an estate 'gelded for x hides in King Edward's time' shows that the geld continued and was regularly imposed. It is evidenced in King William's reign and there was a particularly heavy imposition in 1084. It is sometimes confused with the Danegeld which consisted of large sums of money raised to pay off the Danes in the reign of the same Ethelred the Unready.

Hide (Latin *hida*, a Latinized form of Old English *hid*). The word 'hide' is connected with the Old English word for 'family' and 'marriage' and was probably in origin enough land to support a household, or to keep a plough occupied for one year. It appears as a well-established form of assessment in Bede and in the 'Tribal Hidae', but there is a distinction to be made between the overall assessment of a 'tribe' or 'people' and that of a smaller area of land, say that based on a royal vill. Neither is it a measure in a strict sense. It seems likely that large areas (say a river basin viewed from a hill ridge) were roughly hidated in round figures and estates were granted out from these in subdivisions, often, though not exclusively of five hides. Some overall hidation of the lands that were later in Somerset was probably made in the 7th century, before the earliest surviving grants by charter. By its nature, the hide will have varied according to the terrain and the judgement of the estimator. It was not generally revised and even in Domesday there is no reason to think that it was a standard measure of land, although it was grounded in agriculture and its size will not have been infinitely variable. Originally, it seems that when, for example, five hides were granted, they were a rough measure of the whole estate including woodland, meadow and rough grazing and not just of the arable land. It was a unit from which service and food, or money in lieu, were demanded, these various obligations being known in Latin as *consuetudo* ('custom' or 'customary dues'); for example in the early 10th century men from each hide were responsible for the construction and upkeep of each fortified *burh* as part of the effort to expel the Danes and, later in that century, Danegeld and geld were levied on each hide to buy off these same Danes and to finance operations against them. Thus, the hide shifted from an agrarian estimate of uncertain and variable size to a regular measure of tax and other liabilities. It is possible that the original purpose of hidation was to establish just such a network of obligations related to the holding of land. Thus, charters appear to be acts of generosity, but dues and services would be implied. In extreme cases, if the tax burden was reduced, the number of hides could be similarly reduced, even though the actual size of the estate remained the same. The hide was divided into four virgates★ and a varying number of acres★, both divisions, being, by implication smaller measures of tax and service.

Hundred (Latin *hundretum, hundredum*, a Latinization of Old English *hundret* meaning originally the figure 100). These were units of administration intermediate between the vill★ and the shire. They originated in the mid 10th century and finally lost their importance in the 19th. Their main responsibilities were taxation, policing, justice and raising the army. Many will have arisen as subdivisions of royal estates and they replace much of the administration that was formerly done by such estates, which were increasingly being granted away or partially or wholly dismembered.

Land for ... ploughs (Latin *terra est ... carucis* etc.) This 'ploughland formula' appears to be an attempt at reassessment, in order to bring the hidation up to date. The hide was originally land for one plough, but for various reasons (including the expansion of the available arable and the increasing use of the hide★ as a measure of tax and service) had drifted away from reality on the ground. The new assessment is not recorded for all counties in Domesday Book, but its intention was probably to increase revenue by surveying the amount of ploughland available and the number of ploughs that could be employed. The number of ploughs in actual use would (as an interim measure) give some indication of the exploitation of the hides available and their possible additional profitability.

Manor (Lain *mansio* (EDB) or *manerium* (GDB)). An estate held by an individual which was treated as a unit of tax, service and justice. It will have had a 'hall' or 'court' at its centre. A typical manor would consist of a portion in demesne★ and a part worked by 'men' or 'villans'★ (in the wider sense), as a series of small estates or tenancies tied to the central core and owing it various obligations. Some manors had major subdivisions held by named individuals (usually French) often with their own valuation.

Ora (Latinized from Scandinavian). Literally 'an ounce', this was a Scandinavian unit of currency (though not an actual coin in England), reckoned at either 16d or 20d. The 16d was the normal rate; the 20d rate was found on estates in the king's hands and was payment 'at face value'. Thus, for every 16d due in revenue, 20d was collected to allow for alloying or clipping, the result being equivalent to a payment in assayed or 'blanched' money.

Ploughland: see **Land for … ploughs**

Slave (Latin *servus*, feminine *ancilla*). The lowest class of the manorial population, the unfreest of the unfree, slaves were totally tied to the estate and to the lord and without a share in any of its resources. For these reasons they were usually found among the demesne★ population.

Sokeman (Latin *sochemannus*, *socmannus*, Latinized from Old English *soc* and *man*) A man who exercised soke (jurisdiction) over others and had the duty of soke to his lord, including attendance at the manorial court. With free men★ and 'riding men' these formed the free population of the vill. They could 'commend themselves' to another lord or 'go where they wished with their land'. Free men and sokemen are sometimes found in the same entry, so at least in these cases, there was some distinction intended, but the categories must have greatly overlapped and they are treated as alternatives in the 'Terms of Reference' prefaced to the *Inquisitio Eliensis* (Hamilton 1876).

Tenant-in-chief A term used by historians to describe those individuals or institutions who held land directly from the king. Their tenants are often described as sub-tenants or sub-holders and their holdings as sub-holdings, sub-tenancies or sub-infeudations.

Vill (Latin *villa*, originally meaning a 'house' or 'rural estate'). It is sometimes, misleadingly rendered as 'village', but the name implies nothing about the form of any settlement. The Old English equivalent is *tunscipe*. A vill was a small administrative unit and a subdivision of the hundred★, whose representatives attended the hundred-court. It is 'the priest, the reeve and 6 villans of each and every vill' hundred by hundred who answer on oath the questions contained in the so-called Terms of Reference, which preface the *Inquisitio Eliensis*. A vill was an area of land akin to the much later civil parishes and will normally have the name of a single place, however many separate settlements with their own names it contained. Manors★ were subdivisions of the vill. Sometimes a vill contained only one manor, in which case the two were equivalent, sometimes more than one. The vill might contain the estates of several landholders, whereas a manor was an estate held by an individual lord.

Villan (Latin *villanus*, from *villa*). Sometimes rendered as 'villager'. The word has a general use in describing the whole non-demesne population of the estate, and a particular one referring to one social or economic class. In this sense, a villan was the topmost layer of the unfree population of the manor or estate, with more land and a greater share of ploughs than a bordar★.

Virgate (Latin *virga*, *virgata*). The latter is derived from the former and *virga* has the sense of a rod or 'measuring-rod'. Nonetheless, a virgate is a quarter of a hide★ and as such is a quarter of the land needed to support a family or to keep a plough occupied for a year; thus it is of uncertain and variable size, but a fixed unit of tax and service.

3
SURVEYS

3.1 PRELIMINARY SURVEYS

At the time of the fieldwork, the land use around Eckweek appeared to have been predominantly for pasture, although the landowner indicated that most of the fields attached to the farm had been ploughed at one time or another in living memory, a fact seemingly confirmed by the low and spread nature of earthworks preserved in OS Fields 2000 and 2756 (Figure 1.7). Only OS Field 4783 was cultivated at the time of the fieldwork, however, the earthworks in OS Fields 2477 and 2470 were so well preserved that it seemed very unlikely that they had ever undergone anything more than the shallowest cultivation. At the time of the fieldwork, OS Field 1574 was used as a modern cemetery, although the area retained faint traces of earthworks at its eastern end. Eckweek House Farm is shown on the 1843 tithe map (Figure 2.5) pretty much as per the layout in 1988 and the farmhouse itself carried a date stone of 1837. The First Edition Ordnance Survey 25 inch map (Figure 2.9) suggests little change in the intervening period, although a pond is shown in the centre of OS Field 2477, probably indicated in 1988 by a hollow located between Area A and Trench F. A second pond is also shown at the southwest corner of OS Field 4783, which was only filled in the winter of 1988–1989.

The preliminary non-intrusive survey work aimed to locate and record the overall extent, preservation and organisation of the earthworks on the site along with others in the vicinity, primarily features such as trackways, former field boundaries and possible building plots (Figure 1.7). The following areas of the Eckweek site and other areas in the locale not directly associated with settlement at Eckweek were surveyed during the course of the project:

1. 1984 – Aerial photographs taken from the south-west by Mick Aston show complex of well-preserved earthworks (see front cover of this report).
2. June 1988 – Earthwork survey of OS Fields 2477, 2470 and 2756 undertaken by R Iles, C Bond and A Kidd (Figures 1.7 and 3.1).

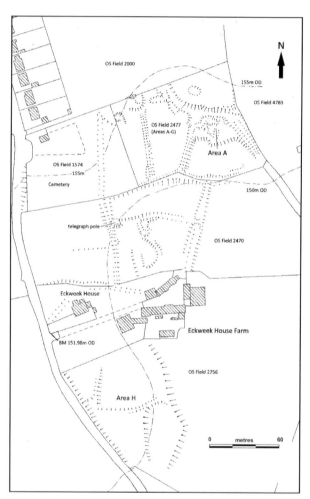

FIGURE 3.1
The Eckweek earthwork survey

3. September 1988 – Contour survey undertaken of Excavation Areas A and B in OS Field 2477 (project archive).
4. October 1988 – Earthwork survey of OS Field 0033 at White Ox Mead; Avon SMR 5372; NGR ST 719 582). The results of the survey show the remains of one of a series of contemporary rural medieval settlements in the area (Section 2.1) and are reproduced here because they form part of the Eckweek project

SURVEYS

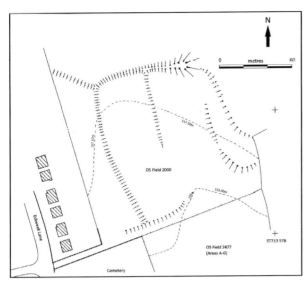

FIGURE 3.2

Detail of earthworks in OS Field 2000 at Eckweek, immediately north of the excavation areas

archive and have not been published previously (Figure 3.3).

5   November 1988 – Fieldwalking of OS Field 4783.
6   December 1988 – Earthwork survey of OS Field 2000 (Figures 1.7 and 3.2).
7   February 1989 – Contour survey in OS Field 2477 (centred on Area G) (project archive).
8   February 1989 – Earthwork survey in the western quarter of OS Field 2477 (Figure 1.7).
9   February 1989 – Minor earthworks in the cemetery (OS Field 1574) noted and photographed (project archive).
10 February 1989 – Line of the ring road in OS Fields 2456 and 2470 walked after topsoil stripping.
11 April 1989 – Resurvey of earthworks in OS Field 2470 including minor earthworks in the garden of Eckweek House Farm (Figure 1.7).
12 August 1989 – Geophysical survey by English Heritage (Section 3.2): magnetometer survey in OS Field 2470 (Test Pit Areas G and K) and OS Field 2756 (Excavation Area H and Trench I) and resistivity survey in OS Field 2470 (Figure 1.6).

The earthwork surveys were carried out by line and tape using an optical square. The results were drawn up in the field at 1:500m scale and reproduced at the same scale as hachure plans. Minor earthworks around Eckweek House were plotted from aerial photographs complemented by a site inspection. In addition, a detailed contour survey (in the project archive) was undertaken in OS Field 2477 prior to topsoil stripping (by hand) and the excavation work in Areas A and B. The survey involved taking spot heights at 1m or 2m intervals related to the overall excavation grid, which extended from a base line orientated north to south (Figure 1.6) from OS Field 2756 to the northern edge of OS Field 2477.

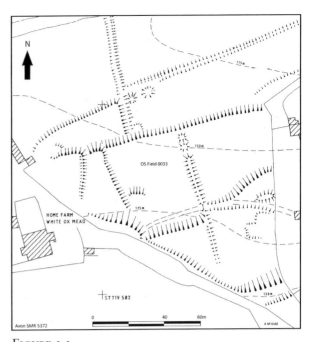

FIGURE 3.3

Earthworks in OS Field 0033 at Home Farm, White Ox Mead

The geophysical surveys were undertaken by Andrew Payne and Stephen Noon of the former English Heritage Ancient Monuments Laboratory (AML Report 119/90) after the completion of the excavation work in Area A. In OS Field 2470 (Figures 1.6 and 1.7), an area of 7200 square metres was covered by resistivity survey; a smaller area (3150 square metres) of magnetometer survey was also centred on the most prominent earthworks in this field. A further area of some 5850 square metres of magnetometer survey was undertaken in OS Field 2756 (Figures 1.6 and 1.7). The geophysical data was set out in a preliminary report containing 1:500m plots provided by the Ancient Monuments Laboratory (Archaeometry Division). The results were updated by Andrew Payne of Historic England in 2015 and are set out below in Section 3.2.

3.2 GEOPHYSICAL SURVEY
by Andrew Payne of Historic England (1989, updated 2015)

Introduction

The purpose of the geophysical survey was to supplement the rescue excavations situated in the fields around Eckweek House Farm (Figures 1.5 to 1.7). At the time of the survey, the excavation work was mainly restricted to the northeastern area of the site (Area A), where the earthworks were more readily interpreted from topographic survey. The aim of the geophysical survey was to provide more precise detail of the form of the settlement in the remaining fields immediately to the north and south of Eckweek House Farm (these areas subsequently incorporating Excavation Areas H, J and K). In these areas

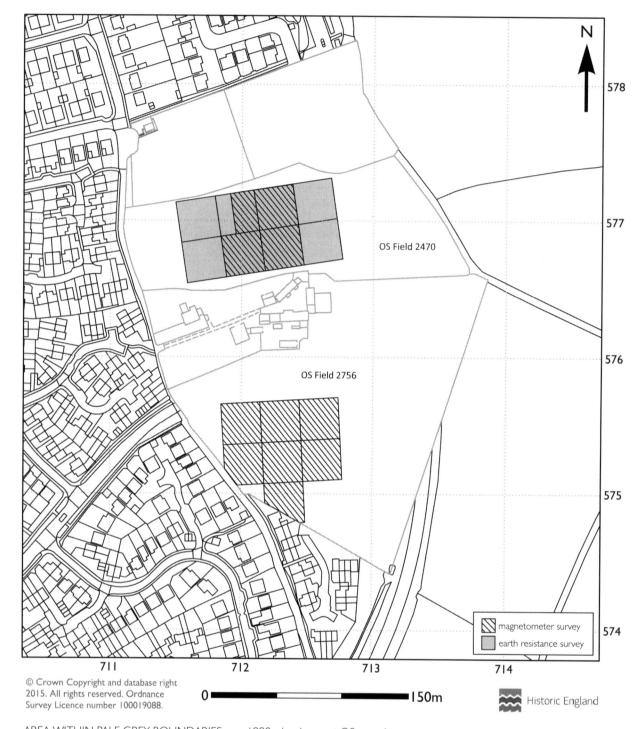

AREA WITHIN PALE GREY BOUNDARIES: pre-1990s development OS mapping

FIGURE 3.4

The areas of magnetometer and earth resistance geophysical survey

(Figures 1.6 and 1.7) the earthworks were less easily interpreted due to loss of definition, probably from past ploughing. Sample excavations in Area A had demonstrated that the site consisted of trackways and stone buildings with associated yards and enclosures, then provisionally dated to the 14th century.

The site lies on a clayey subsoil overlying Jurassic Inferior Oolite limestone and Great Oolite Series Fuller's Earth clays (Geological Survey of Great Britain 1965; Soil Survey of England and Wales 1983).

Method

Geophysical survey was carried out in two separate areas (Figures 1.6 and 3.4): in the field directly to the north of Eckweek House (OS Field 2470) and in the field to the south of the house (OS Field 2756). The majority (120m × 60m) of the field to the north of the farm was covered by earth resistance survey, within which a smaller 60m × 60m area – overlying anomalous resistance readings – was also covered by magnetometer survey. The survey

SURVEYS

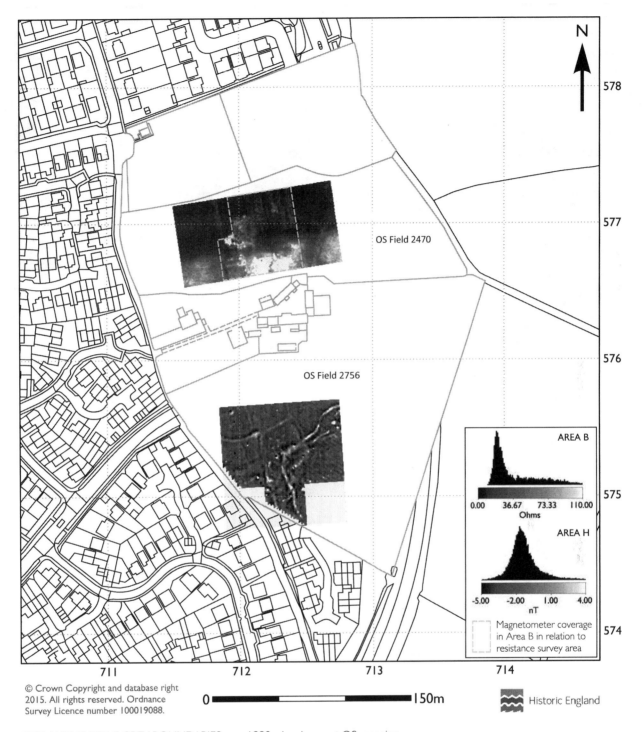

AREA WITHIN PALE GREY BOUNDARIES: pre-1990s development OS mapping

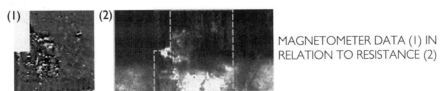

MAGNETOMETER DATA (1) IN RELATION TO RESISTANCE (2)

FIGURE 3.5
Geophysical data from magnetometer and earth resistance surveys

area in OS Field 2756 was covered by magnetometer survey only. These areas are now both covered by modern housing development constructed in the 1990s.

Earth Resistance Survey

A local grid of 30m squares was set out over each survey area (Figure 1.6) using an optical square, tapes and ranging poles. Earth resistance data was recorded

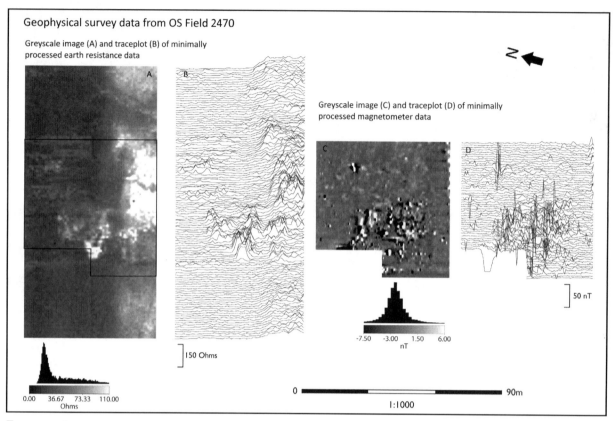

FIGURE 3.6
Detail of magnetometer and earth resistance survey data from OS Field 2470

over eight 30m grid squares in OS Field 2470 using a Geoscan RM4 resistance meter and DL10 data logger in the 0.5m twin electrode configuration with readings collected at 1m intervals along traverses spaced 1m apart. Post-acquisition processing of the data included the application of a thresholding median filter with radius 2m to remove occasional extreme values caused by high contact resistance (Scollar *et al* 1990). The results are presented as a linear greyscale image superimposed over the OS mapping in Figure 3.5. Additional larger scale (1:1000) trace plot and greyscale images of the resistance data are presented in Figure 3.6 (A and B).

Magnetometer Survey

Magnetometer survey was conducted over the 30m grid squares indicated on Figures 1.6 and 3.4 using a Geoscan FM36 fluxgate gradiometer with readings recorded on the 0.1 nanotesla (nT) resolution setting of the instrument at 0.25m intervals along successive parallel traverses spaced 1m apart. The magnetometer data is presented in Figure 3.5 in relation to the Ordnance Survey base mapping after minimal post-acquisition processing, including the truncation of extreme values outside the range of ±50 nT and the setting of each traverse to a zero mean, to remove any effects of directional sensitivity and instrument drift. Additional larger scale (1:1000) trace plot and greyscale images of the magnetic data are presented in Figures 3.6 (C and D) and 3.7.

Results

Graphical summaries of the significant earth resistance [**r1-5**] and magnetic [**m1-17**] anomalies discussed in the following text, superimposed on the OS base mapping, are presented in Figure 3.8.

OS Field 2470

Earth Resistance Survey

Resistance values were relatively subdued over much of this area owing to water retention by the clay subsoil, but showed a significant increase along the southern side of the field adjacent to the mid 19th-century farm. The higher readings here [**r1**] suggested the accumulation of building material or rubble from former structures related to the farm buildings around Eckweek House, or associated with house platforms of the medieval settlement. Due to the absence of structural definition within the broad area of high resistance [**r1**], no clear wall alignments or building foundations could be identified and these areas were therefore interpreted as built up platforms of stonier material perhaps including spreads of rubble deposits from former buildings. A further more conspicuous rectilinear grouping of high resistance anomalies at [**r2-4**] enclosed by a series of linear boundaries defined by the earthwork survey, were interpreted as possible indications of wall footings of medieval or later building structures.

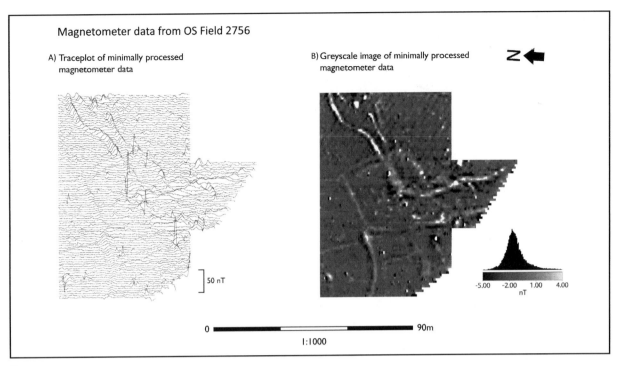

FIGURE 3.7
Detail of magnetometer survey data from OS Field 2756 (Area H)

Unusually, the resistance survey did not detect visible earthwork remains very clearly in OS Field 2470, although an exception was a high resistance alignment at [**r5**], which corresponded with a linear bank. A series of weak linear 'anomalies' rectilinear with the survey grid, in the central northern part of OS Field 2470, were a spurious effect resulting from an intermittent cable wiring fault.

Magnetometer Survey

Magnetometer survey in OS Field 2470 was restricted to the central four grid squares (Figure 1.6, survey squares 9 to 12 and Figure 3.4), in which the possible presence of building structures was suspected from observation of the resistance survey results (anomalies [**r2-4**], above). Distinctive magnetic activity characteristic of demolition deposits such as buried ferrous material, bricks, tile or burnt stone was located [**m1**] and coincided with the area of interest [**r2-4**] defined by the resistance survey, confirming its potential archaeological significance.

In addition, the magnetometer survey detected a faint alignment at [**m2**], possibly representing a ditch coinciding with a linear earthwork feature, and some clusters of small localised anomalies [**m3-4**] potentially indicative of pits or further activity associated with the suggested former occupation in this area.

OS Field 2756

The magnetometer survey carried out in this field detected elements of a field system or a system of enclosures and trackways suggestive of past settlement activity and associated agricultural land use. Several curving ditches (interrupted in places) were clearly detected as linear positive magnetic anomalies [**m5-14**] and these appeared to subdivide the area into various plots or enclosures with a possible double ditched lane, possibly a droveway [**m5-6**], running into a central enclosure (defined by **m8-11**) from the south. Smaller, more localised anomalies were detected interspersed amongst the enclosure ditches, in particular at [**m15**], possibly indicative of pits associated with occupation activity in the central part of the complex. Remnants of former ridge and furrow cultivation on two distinctive alignments were faintly detected in the eastern part of the survey area [**m16** and **m17**].

Conclusions

The survey was successful in defining buried archaeological features in OS Field 2470 likely to be related to the remains of the medieval settlement, although it was not possible to interpret their nature with confidence. In OS Field 2756, magnetometer survey substantially supplemented the evidence of the earthwork survey by identifying previously unsuspected ditch alignments. While some of the linear anomalies detected appeared to share alignments in common with the earthwork evidence, there were further linear anomalies present that suggested a more elaborate and extensive complex of archaeological features, or a complex of several phases that may indicate the presence of an underlying earlier phase of pre-medieval activity on the site.

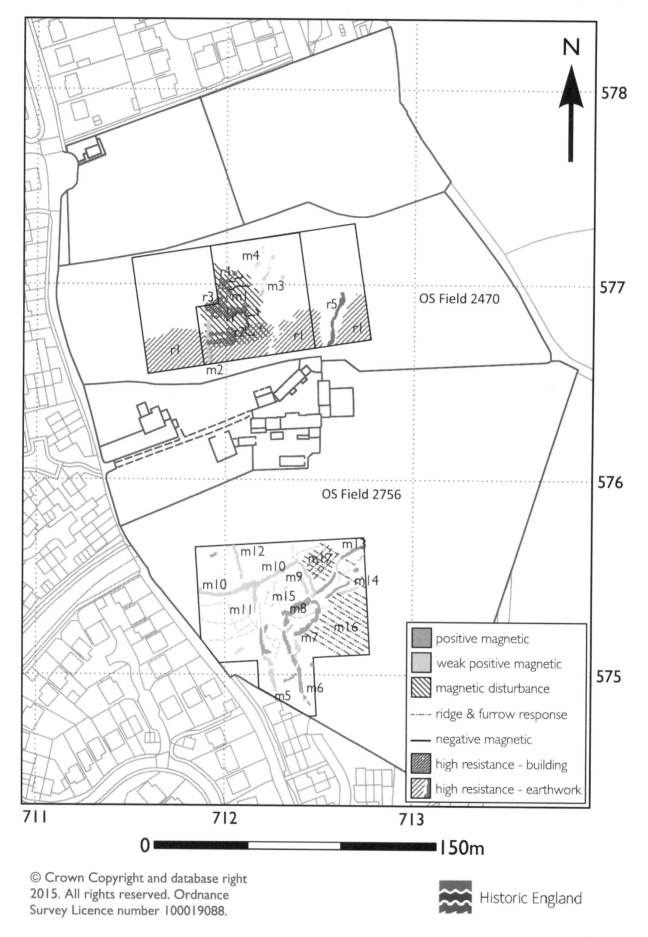

FIGURE 3.8
Interpretation of geophysical survey data from OS Fields 2470 and 2756

4
EXCAVATIONS

4.1 EXCAVATION AREAS AND METHODOLOGIES

Areas of Investigation

From the outset, total excavation was proposed in Area A (Figures 1.6 and 1.7), an area which contained a complex of very well preserved earthworks that appeared to represent the northernmost of the farmstead plots. Other features were to be dated and characterised by means of less extensive evaluation trenching.

For the purposes of recording, a series of three base lines were set out, aligned north to south and east to west across the site (Figure 1.6). A false origin (x=100/y=100) was created at their intersection in OS Field 2477, just to the south of Excavation Area A. An excavation grid was extended from these base lines across the excavation areas and pegged at 5m intervals. The north–south baseline was also extended to the south, into OS Fields 2470 and 2756, to tie in the geophysical surveys and other excavation work.

Each discrete area of investigation was designated by a letter (Figures 1.6 and 1.7, Areas A–K) in the order in which they were investigated. Areas A, B, G and H each consisted of open area excavations; Areas C, D, E, F, I, J and K represented evaluation trenches that were opened by machine and further investigated and recorded by hand. The principal objectives of the work in each survey area were as follows:

1. Area A – total excavation and recording of an area of some 450 square metres. All excavation was done by hand, as rubble, presumed to be remains of demolished structures, was exposed either at the surface in places, or immediately below a thin topsoil. Structures and deposits representing a stratified sequence of archaeology of later 10th- to late 14th-century date were revealed.
2. Area B – an area of 200 square metres was opened by hand to examine a possible building platform located adjacent to the trackway and c50m to the northwest of Area A. The remains of a 14th-century stone dwelling were revealed.
3. Area C – a small trench 1.85m long was opened across a narrow hollow-way running southwest from Area A. Deposits of late 10th- to 14th-century date were revealed.
4. Area D – a 4.5m long trench was opened across a bank that separated the earthworks in Area A from the main trackway through the site.
5. Area E – a 12m long trench was opened across the trackway where the hollow-way earthwork feature was deepest. Deposits of late 10th- to 14th-century date were revealed.
6. Area F – opened to examine a small ridge to the east of Area A. Natural clay was revealed throughout directly below the topsoil and at shallow depth. No archaeological features or finds were revealed and no drawings were made.
7. Area G – a small area totalling 30 square metres was opened by hand to examine a small platform and circular depression in the northwest corner of Field 2477. The cutting revealed an area of disturbance and the remains of a stone building and associated deposits that produced artefacts of 17th-century date.
8. Area H – full area excavation of some 400 square metres, which was initially opened by machine to remove topsoil, in order to characterise a complex arrangement of anomalies identified by the geophysical survey. Archaeological deposits and features of early-middle Iron Age and 11th-century date were revealed.
9. Area I – evaluation trench opened to the east of Area H to investigate a linear geophysical anomaly. Archaeological deposits and features of early-middle Iron Age and 11th-century date were revealed.
10. Area J – a small hand-dug test pit measuring 2m by 1m opened to evaluate earthworks and geophysical anomalies immediately north of Eckweek House Farm in OS Field 2470.
11. Area K – a second hand-dug test pit measuring c4m by 1m opened to evaluate the same features

as Area J above. Later medieval structures and deposits were revealed.

The winter of 1988-1989 was generally exceptionally mild and dry, which enabled rapid progress to be made in the hand-excavation of Area A, such that by the beginning of February 1989 when the late Jan Roberts was appointed County Archaeologist, the later (Period V) medieval activity in this area had been fully defined, excavated and recorded and earlier (Period IV and III) features were in the process of being revealed and excavated. Heavy rain throughout February 1989 caused much delay to the excavation fieldwork, although by March conditions had improved. During April and May the weather changed once again, to a period of consistent and blistering heat and it was in these conditions that the majority of the Period III cut soil features in Area A were excavated – as such, despite continual use of water carried from the cemetery, it is quite likely that some minor stratigraphic details of the Period III (Late Saxon) activity were missed.

Recording Methods

A standard context-based recording system was used throughout the excavation work, pretty much as set out in the Central Excavation Unit recording manual (1985). Further information was recorded in two site notebooks. All primary archaeological plans and sections were drawn at a scale of 1:20m and 1:10m respectively and around 500 photographic prints and slides were taken. Sadly a substantial number of the photographs were lost in an office fire in 2001. The primary site records detailing archaeological contexts, small finds, common artefacts, samples and other material can be found in the project archive (BATRM 1997.1).

Finds were either designated as 'Small Finds' (SFs) and recorded three dimensionally in relation to the site grid, or 'Common Artefacts' (CARs), in which case they were recorded by context. In certain areas, principally inside the buildings, Common Artefacts were further subdivided on a 1m grid. In the case of the yard area in Area A, they were subdivided by larger 5m grid squares. The criteria for recording an object as a Small Find (numbered from SF501 to SF1000) were as follows:

1. Pottery was only recorded as a SF if a substantial proportion of the vessel survived, or if the sherd had distinctive properties or decoration.
2. All worked stone was recorded except for a few fragments that were missed during the clearance of demolition rubble.
3. Only clearly recognisable flint tools were recorded as SFs.
4. All coins, copper alloy and exotic items were recorded as SFs.
5. All iron objects located inside the stone or timber buildings were recorded as SFs. Elsewhere, particularly inside the adjacent 'yard', some nails were treated as Common Artefacts.

The recording of Common Artefacts (Common Artefact Record) covered all cultural material other than unworked building stone, which was not collected. All non-metal finds were subsequently washed and marked with the site code (EK89) and catalogued by context and material type. Charred plant remains were recovered from bulk soil samples by wet sieving through a 500 micron mesh. Finds were sorted by hand into four categories: pottery, bone, metalwork and miscellaneous, and, where finds were not recorded as Small Finds, each category was assigned a unique CAR number for each excavated context running from CAR1001 onwards. In each case, the location, quantification and description of the finds recorded for each individual CAR were included on each record sheet.

In addition, it is worth noting that a group of unstratified metalwork was recovered from the spoil heaps in Area A. The collection was recorded as CAR1744 and included eight lead objects that were visually almost indistinguishable from the local weathered Oolitic Limestone. In view of this, it is quite likely that other lead objects were missed during hand excavation and that lead objects as a whole are therefore underrepresented.

4.2 SUMMARY OF STRUCTURAL PHASING

The description and discussion of the structural evidence (Section 4.3) recorded during the fieldwork is period based (Periods I–VI) and, where appropriate, subdivided into structural phases (SP). The chronology for the development of the late Saxon and medieval settlement (Periods III–V) is based upon a detailed seriation of the large assemblage of 10th- to 14th-century pottery (ceramic phases (CPs) 1–6; Section 5.3) supported by a series of radiocarbon determinations (Section 6) and a small collection of stratified coins (Section 5.4). The excavated evidence is described chronologically, in reverse order, from earliest to latest.

Summary of Site Phasing

PERIOD I *Prehistoric*

Represented by residual Bronze Age flint and pottery and by early to middle Iron Age ditches and postholes in Area H dated by stratified pottery.

PERIOD II *Romano-British*

Activity represented by residual pottery only.

EXCAVATIONS

PERIOD III Late Saxon and Early Medieval structures and deposits – cAD 950–1200

(Medieval ceramic phases 1–4)
Phase III.1: ceramic phase 1; cAD 950–1000
Phase III.2: ceramic phases 2–3; c1000–1100
Phase III.3: ceramic phase 4; c1100–1200

PERIOD IV Medieval structures and deposits – c1200–1275

Phase IV: ceramic phases 4–5

PERIOD V Later Medieval structures and deposits – c1275–1400

(Medieval ceramic phases 5–6)
Phase V.1: ceramic phases 5–6; c1275–c1325
Phase V.2: ceramic phase 6; c1325–c1375
Phase V.3: ceramic phase 6; c1375–1400

PERIOD VI Late Medieval, Post-medieval and Modern structures and deposits

Late medieval activity in the period after AD 1400 and subsequent, post-medieval activity (ceramic phase 7)

4.3 THE EXCAVATED EVIDENCE

Summary by Period

Period I: Late Prehistoric

Later prehistoric activity on the site was represented by Iron Age features revealed in Area H that produced a collection of stratified early-middle Iron Age pottery (Section 5.1). Evidence of Bronze Age activity, on or near the site, was also indicated by a collection of residual flint tools (Section 5.7), including leaf-shaped and barbed and tanged arrowheads recovered from medieval layers in Area A and sherds of residual pottery (Section 5.1) from the primary silts filling the Iron Age ditch in Area H.

The principal evidence for Iron Age activity consisted of a set of well-defined curvilinear features that crossed Area H and extended beyond it to the northeast and south. These features were initially identified by the geophysical survey as a group of strongly positive magnetic anomalies (Figure 3.8, Features m6, m8, m13 and possibly m7 and m14) and were subsequently investigated at three locations by means of two cuttings in Area H, Cuttings 1 and 2 (Figure 4.1), and a further evaluation trench, Trench I (Figures 4.1 and 4.10) located slightly to the north (see Figures 1.6 and 1.7 for trench locations). The excavations in Area H Cutting 1 revealed a full section across a large ditch and a deep sequence of stratified ditch fills. A further part of the same ditch, plus a group of associated postholes, were revealed in Cutting 2, which appeared to be located adjacent to a ditch terminal. The ditch complex is dated to the early middle Iron Age on the basis of an assemblage of stratified pottery recovered from the primary ditch silts identified by Elaine Morris (Section 5.1).

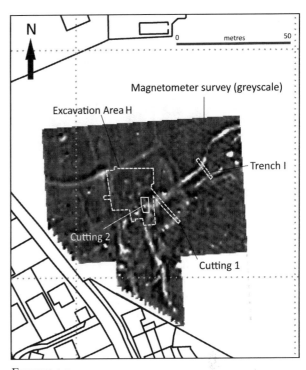

FIGURE 4.1

Detail of magnetometer survey greyscale data from OS Field 2756 (Area H) with location of excavation areas superimposed

Period II: Romano-British

No Roman structures or deposits were identified during the excavation, although a small collection of residual Roman pottery (Section 5.2) and coins (Section 5.4) were recovered from medieval layers in Area A.

Period III: Late Saxon, Saxo-Norman and Medieval – cAD 950–1200

Three phases of late Saxon and earlier medieval activity (Periods III.1–III.3), including evidence for a number of separate timber structures, were recorded on the site. The evidence was most completely examined in Areas A and H (Figures 1.5 and 1.6), where a series of earthfast timber structures were well-preserved and represented by groups of substantial postholes and post-pits, alongside a range of associated ditches, pits and soil features. The three subphases of structural development (Phases III.1–III.3) that subdivide Period III were defined and dated by stratified pottery assigned to ceramic phases 1 to 4, supported by a series of five radiocarbon dates (Section 6.1), to between the late 10th and late 12th centuries AD.

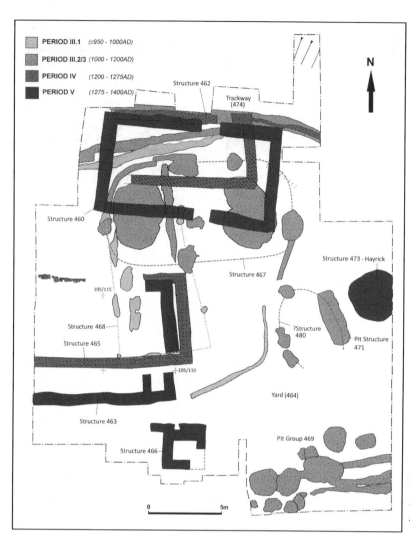

FIGURE 4.2
Excavation Area A – summary of structural phasing

Two distinct Period III timber structures, Structures 467 and 468, were recorded in Area A (Figure 4.2), in addition to the remains of one, or possibly two, further timber structures (Structures 471 and 480). Features associated with the earlier of the two principal structures, Structure 468, were interpreted to reflect a late 10th-century timber building, possibly a small dwelling, whilst the later structure defined a very much more substantial 11th-century timber dwelling, a farmhouse (Figure 4.2, Structure 467), which appears to have continued in use, albeit with some modification, well into the 12th century. The 10th-century structure (Structure 468) is dated by a well-defined group of stratified pottery assigned to ceramic phase 1 (CP1), the second half of the 10th century and, although the physical remains were relatively poorly preserved, appeared to represent a small rectangular timber structure aligned north to south and measuring approximately 9m long and 5m wide that was situated just to the south of a metalled and ditched track and hollow-way. Evidence for later 10th-century activity in Area A aside from this building was very limited.

By the early 11th century, the 10th-century timber structure (468) had been replaced by a more substantial earthfast principal-post timber building (Figure 4.2; Structure 467) that was aligned west to east and measured some 13m long and 7.5m wide. The building was structurally complex and almost certainly represented a principal dwelling that incorporated at least two interior bays, both of which contained sunken-floor or pit-storage areas. Although no contemporary floor layers were identified, the principal foundations and internal features of the building were well preserved (described in detail below) and from these it was possible to identify an initial phase of construction (Figure 4.40, Period III.2) and a later phase of substantial rebuilding (Figure 4.40, Period III.3). Evidence of associated activity in Area A included a variety of pits, ditches and postholes set within a small ditched enclosure or yard (Figure 4.19), a number of which are tentatively considered to reflect further earthfast and timber structures. The northern boundary of the farmstead, already established by a ditch alongside the trackway in the 10th century, was maintained by further recut ditches and continued to separate the farm tenement from the roughly metalled trackway. To the south and east of the farmhouse, the boundary of the farmstead was defined and maintained by a series of ditches and pits, as demonstrated by features recorded by area excavation and in Trench D (Figures 4.19 and 4.42).

EXCAVATIONS

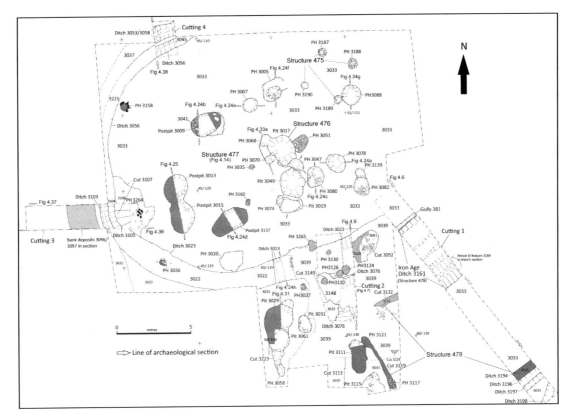

FIGURE 4.3
Area H as excavated

A third, slightly larger, earthfast timber building (Figure 4.3; Structure 477) was erected in Area H during the first half of the 11th century (Period III.2, ceramic phase 2). The building was founded upon a small number of large earthfast posts, as indicated by a group of large postholes and larger post-pits, and set inside an oval or D-shaped enclosure that was defined by an earth bank with an internal ditch. In addition, this substantial building was further separated inside the enclosure from an adjacent rectangular earthfast timber building (Structure 479 – which was only partially investigated), by a shallow curving ditch that was subsequently replaced by a fence. The differences in the size and layout of the principal building's earthfast foundations, in conjunction with a complex of associated internal features, indicate that it may well have incorporated some form of raised superstructure, possibly a small tower, as indicated by the contemporary internal features (Figure 4.3, Structure 476). These features alone suggest that the building had significant status. Contemporary activity around the building was indicated by a range of associated pits, ditches and postholes, a group of which are likely to represent elements of the associated, but slightly later timber structure (Figure 4.3; Structure 479) that is dated to ceramic phase 3, the later 11th century, by pottery and stratigraphy. Pottery recovered from stratified contexts indicates that the occupation and use of Building 477 and Structure 479 were wholly confined to the 11th century (Period III.2; ceramic phases 2–3) and that the farmstead plot in Area H was essentially abandoned by the end of the 11th century and seemingly never reoccupied thereafter.

Period IV: Medieval – 13th Century

The evidence for Period IV activity was relatively poorly preserved and confined to Area A, where occupation of the Saxo-Norman farmstead continued with the construction of two new stone buildings, which replaced the earlier timber farmhouse, Structure 467 during ceramic phase 4. The new buildings (Figures 4.2 and 4.4; Structures 462 and 465) were constructed partially over the remains of the earlier timber farmhouse (see Figure 4.2), at a time when pit and ditch digging appears to have largely ceased generally throughout the settlement. This fundamental change of building technique is echoed elsewhere in the farmstead in Area A, where long established boundary ditches and pits were filled and replaced by earth banks and simple stone revetment walls.

The precise dimensions of these first stone buildings were not established, although each was more than 9m long and around 5m wide. They were laid out parallel to one another with their long axis aligned west to east and constructed later in ceramic phase 4, around or shortly before AD 1200. The excavated evidence relating to their occupation and use was limited due to later disturbance, but

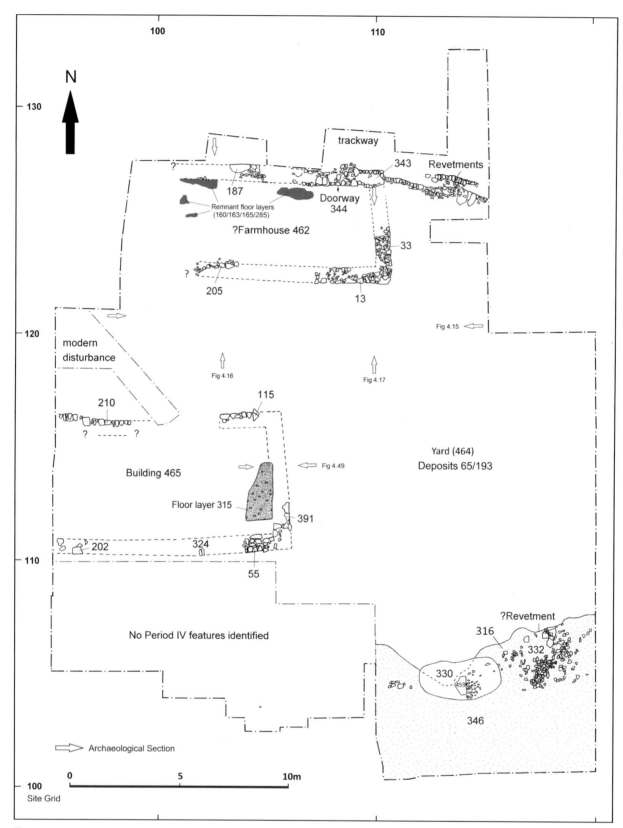

FIGURE 4.4
Area A showing Period IV features

was associated with pottery fabrics of early ceramic phase 5 (*c*1250–1275). Both structures were built in local limestone rubble using drystone technique although neither was well preserved with surviving sections of masonry preserved to no more than three courses of drystone work. Only a few scraps of internal floor layers, probably relating to the latest phase of occupation, were preserved, mostly where the deposits had been sealed beneath subsequent (Period V) medieval walls.

EXCAVATIONS

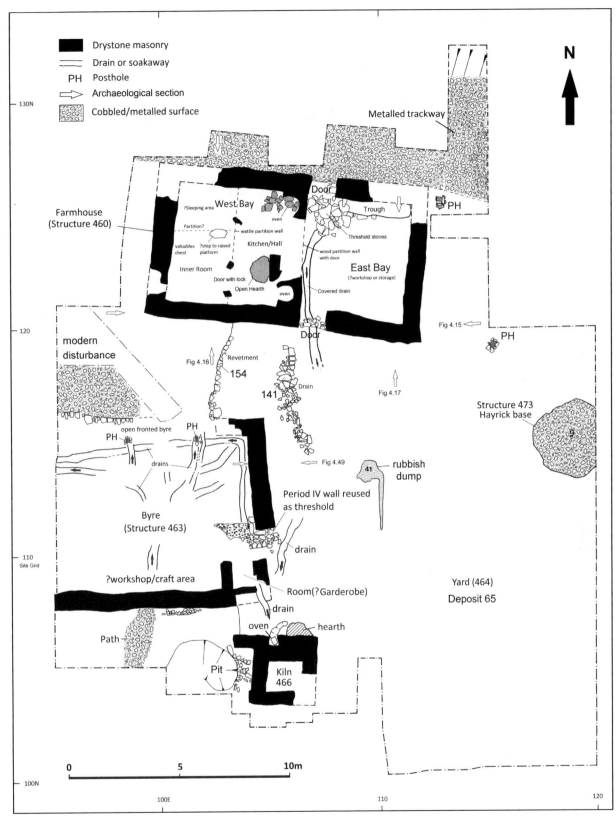

FIGURE 4.5
Area A showing Period V features

Period V: Later Medieval – Later 13th to Late 14th century

During the late 13th century (ceramic phase 5), a second period of major rebuilding took place in Area A and elsewhere across the settlement. The first Period IV stone buildings in Area A (Structures 462 and 465) were replaced by two larger stone buildings (Figures 4.2 and 4.5), one a farmhouse (Structure 460), the other (Structure 463) an open-fronted byre or barn. A new kiln or corn drying structure (Structure 466) was also built. Around

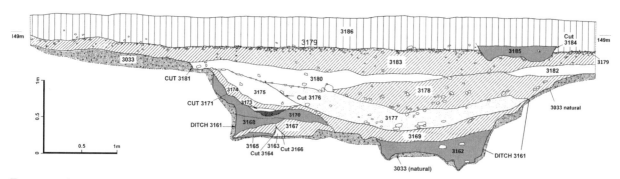

FIGURE 4.6
Area H showing Iron Age Ditch 3161 in the SW facing section of Cutting 1

the same time a large new stone building was constructed in excavation Area B (Figures 1.5, 4.64 and 4.65; Structure 461) in an area that had not been occupied previously. Evidence from the geophysical survey (Section 3.2), Trenches J and K, plus the final watching brief stage, indicates that a further range of substantial stone buildings were also constructed to the south of Area A, in OS Field 2470 (Figures 1.5 to 1.7), at this time. Whether these stone buildings were also preceded by earlier phases of timber structures remains unknown, although the writer considers this quite likely.

Period V represented the zenith of medieval occupation in Area A and it was the remains of these 14th-century buildings that were the most substantially preserved features on the site and in the main defined the site earthworks (Figure 1.7). The dating for this phase of activity is again based upon stratigraphy and the finely seriated pottery sequence, although it is supported by a number of stratified coins, in particular a silver penny of Edward III (1351–1352) recovered from one of the latest floor layers (context 46) inside Structure 460. The coin provides a solid *terminus post quem* for the abandonment of the dwelling and for the range of other typologically distinct domestic, personal and farming artefacts that were preserved along with it.

The combined archaeological and documentary evidence indicates that habitation and associated agricultural activity had diminished very substantially (although had not disappeared completely) across the entire settlement by the early 15th century (Period VI, ceramic phase 7).

Period VI: Post-medieval

Evidence of post-medieval settlement was confined to Area G, located in the northwestern corner of the site, where a poorly preserved stone structure (Figure 4.66, Structure 472), probably the remains of a building, produced a small assemblage of post-medieval pottery. Further evidence of activity during the 17th and early 18th century was provided by a collection of clay tobacco pipes (Section 5.9) that was also recovered from the same excavation area. The only other post-medieval building recorded within the settlement at the time of the fieldwork, Eckweek House Farm (Figures 1.5 to 1.7), was built in 1836 and remained a working farm until 1990. The building was demolished in advance of the modern housing development, but sadly without any archaeological recording.

Detailed Descriptions of the Excavated Evidence

Period I: Prehistoric

Introduction

The geophysical survey in Area H (Figure 3.8) identified a series of localised and linear magnetic anomalies, the most extensive of which (Features m6–m8 and m13–14) clearly extended beyond the survey area. The strong positive linear anomaly, collectively Features m6 to m8 and m13, was investigated by area excavation and trenching at three locations; two cuttings in excavation Area H (Figures 4.1 and 4.3, Cuttings 1 and 2) and by Trench I (Figures 4.10 and 4.11) located just to the northeast. At each point a ditch cut and a sequence of stratified fills were located. A deep sequence of ditch fills was recorded in the SW facing section of Cutting 1 (Figure 4.6); the same feature was investigated in plan in Cutting 2 (Figure 4.7). Both investigations produced stratified early-middle Iron Age pottery (Section 5.1). A group of related postholes (Figure 4.7; Features 3027, 3110, 3124 and 3126) were sited along the northern shoulder of the ditch in Cutting 2, close to where it appeared to reach a terminal (Figure 4.7, Cut 3076). The precise function of both the ditch and postholes was unclear from the excavated evidence, although the location of the postholes suggests they may have represented part of a timber fence or palisade set along the northern side of the ditch, either adjacent to or across a break or entrance point through the ditch.

EXCAVATIONS

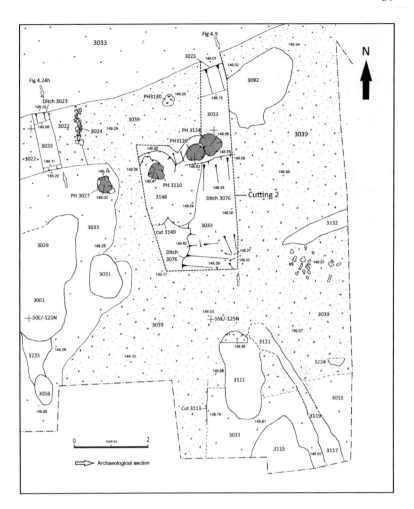

FIGURE 4.7
Area H showing Iron Age features as excavated in Cutting 2

Ditch Structure 478 in Area H, Cutting 1

Here the ditch was cut into brashy natural clay of the Fullers Earth Rock and was up to 5.5m wide and 2.1m deep. Where most completely exposed, the ditch profile (Figures 4.6 and 4.8, Cut 3161) was irregular and incorporated a number of possible early recuts or erosion gullies [Cuts 3164 and 3166]. The northern face was stepped but steep, vertical in places, whilst the southern face was more gently sloping. The base was slightly deeper and more irregular next to the southern scarp; it reached solid rock in this area and contained a primary fill [3162], from which quantities of pottery, bone and environmental samples were recovered. A shallower gully or slot (Figure 4.3, Feature 3181) ran parallel to the main ditch, immediately outside the northern shoulder.

The main ditch fills were well stratified (Figure 4.6) and appeared to indicate at least two likely episodes of recutting or cleaning [Cuts 3171 and 3176] before the entire sequence was sealed by a later stony occupation surface [Layer 3179] associated with subsequent Saxo-Norman activity in Period III. The ditch was sealed by a thick layer of sterile gravely loam [Deposit 3183], into which further 11th-century features (such as Feature 3184) had been cut. The lower ditch fills (earlier than 3176) consisted of relatively pure clays or redeposited natural Fullers Earth clay. They all contained sparse fragments of charcoal and sporadic carbonised cereal grains, although Fill 3172 was rich in woody charcoal. The fabric of the later ditch fills (later than 3176) was generally coarser and contained considerably more small stone, whilst Deposit 3075 also produced a small collection of mollusc shells (Section 5.15).

The Ditch Terminal in Area H, Cutting 2

Excavation of a second cutting in Area H (Figure 4.3, Cutting 2), approximately 5m to the southwest of Cutting 1 where the geophysical survey had indicated a break in the feature, revealed a shallower ditch profile close to a possible terminal and a group of related postholes (Features 3027, 3110, 3124 and 3126). Here, the ditch was shallower, but also cut into the natural clay (Figure 4.9) and ended in a steep irregular scarp [3076]. Originally, it appeared to have extended slightly further west (PH 3149), although this was filled with thick reddish clay (Deposit 3148) prior to the cutting of Posthole 3110. The later terminal [3076] was filled with homogeneous brown silty clay [3075], which produced significant quantities of Iron Age pottery including sherds of Droitwich Salt Container (Section 5.1) and snails (Section 5.15), the latter possibly indicative of slow deposition in relatively dry conditions. Pieces of metallic

FIGURE 4.8
SW facing section of Iron Age ditch 3161 in Cutting 1. Scales 2m

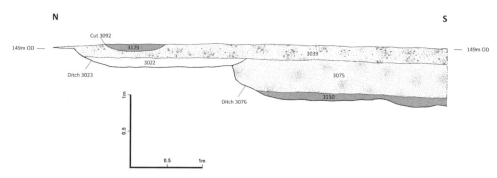

FIGURE 4.9
Area H – W facing section in Cutting 2 showing Iron Age ditch 3076 and late Saxon ditch 3023

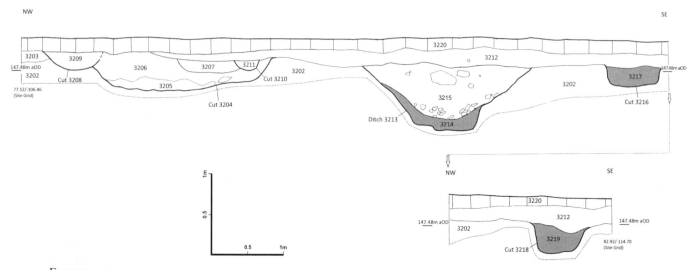

FIGURE 4.10
Trench I – detail of SW facing section showing Iron Age ditch 3213 and late Saxon features

EXCAVATIONS

FIGURE 4.11
Iron Age ditch 3213 in Trench I. Facing NE. Scale 1m

slag were also recovered, as well as a small strip or wire object of copper alloy (Figure 5.49, 33), possibly a personal item. Unfortunately the object has since been lost.

The group of associated postholes (Figure 4.7; features 3124, 3126, 3110 and 3027) was orientated from northeast to southwest along the northern shoulder of the ditch. Three of the four features produced Iron Age pottery (Section 5.1), although Feature 3027 was aceramic. A small amount of charred plant material (Section 5.14) was recovered from the two Iron Age ditch samples indicating cultivated land in the vicinity of the ditch. These included remains of indeterminate cereals including wheat (*Triticum* sp.) and hulled barley (*Hordeum* sp.), plus a few typical arable and disturbed ground weed seeds, including fat hen (*Chenopodium album*), clover-type (*Trifolium/Medicago/Lotus* sp.), knotgrass (*Polygonum aviculare*), dock (*Rumex* sp.) and black bindweed (*Fallopia convolvulus*).

Ditch Structure 478 in Trench I

The trench confirmed the line of the ditch as indicated by geophysical survey (Figure 3.8, Features m8 and m13), although at this point the ditch cut [3213] was narrower and significantly shallower (Figure 4.10), at approximately 2m wide and 1m deep, than the ditch revealed in Cutting 1. This possibly was due to later ploughing, as very faint traces of medieval ridge and furrow cultivation were visible as earthworks in this area and the same was indicated by the geophysical survey (Features m16 and m17). The ditch contained a primary silting [Fill 3214] and a more mixed secondary fill [3215], which incorporated moderate quantities of angular limestone rubble. The deposits filling the ditch failed to produce any finds.

Period III: Late Saxon, Saxo-Norman and Medieval (cAD 950–1200)

Introduction

Structures, features and deposits associated with Period III activity were recorded in Areas A and H. Related features were also revealed in Trenches D, E and I (Figure 1.6). Overall the evidence was interpreted to reflect three distinct phases (Period III, Phases III.1 to III.3) of settlement activity represented by earthfast timber buildings and associated agricultural features and deposits. The evidence for the earliest, 10th-century, activity (Period III.1) was confined to Area A and, with the exception of a few remnant soil layers, all the Period III evidence consisted of negative soil features, chiefly postholes, post-pits and ditches. Overall, the evidence recorded for the Period III activity reflected some 250 years of continuous settlement on the site.

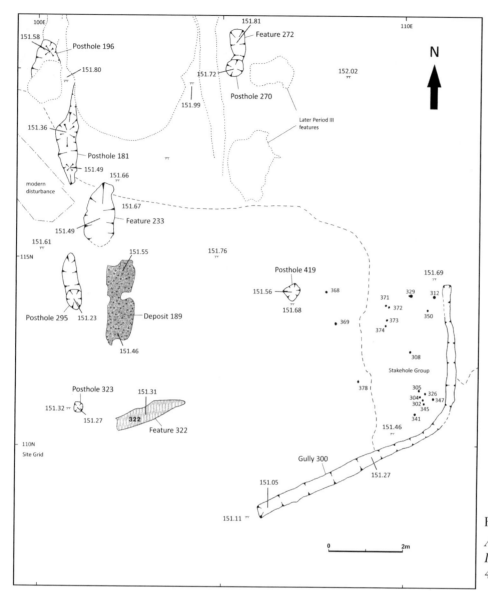

FIGURE 4.12
Area A showing Period III.1 features of Structure 468 as excavated

Period III.1: Area A (ceramic phases CP1–2, cAD 950–1000)

STRUCTURE 468 (FIGURES 4.2 AND 4.12)
The earliest Period III structure was identified in Area A (Figure 4.2, Structure 468) and appeared to reflect the remains of a small rectangular earthfast timber building, although the physical remains of the structure were generally poorly preserved and its precise character was not ascertained with certainty. The structure was defined by a group of shallow 'tadpole' or irregularly-shaped postholes (Figure 4.12, Features 181, 196, 295, 270, 272, 323 and 419) a shallow linear gully [322] and remnants of a compacted clay floor layer (189). The earthfast features were characterised by a similar morphology and a closely related pottery group assigned to ceramic phase 1, which included fabrics strongly analogous to late Saxon Cheddar 'E' from the high status late Saxon site at Cheddar Palace (Rahtz 1979). The fabric type has been recognised at a number of other sites in the region and is dated to the second half of the 10th century at Cheddar Palace and is considered to provide an equivalent chronology for the construction of Structure 468 at Eckweek, a building whose use may have continued into the early 11th century.

The remains of the structure were heavily disturbed by subsequent medieval activity and its overall dimensions can only be estimated (see Figure 4.2). It was located just to the south of the track and hollow-way that ran through Area A and was separated from it by a shallow ditch (Figures 4.2 and 4.16, Ditch 248). The boundary formed by the ditch, and the principal structural features, indicate that Structure 468 would have been rectangular and around 10m long and 5.5m wide, with a long axis orientated north-south. A small remnant of compacted clay floor (Figure 4.12, 189) preserved inside the structure produced sherds of CP1 pottery; further sherds were embedded in the upper surface of the adjacent natural, Layers 201 and 289. A shallow gully [300] defined an area containing a concentration of small stakeholes immediately to the southeast. This appeared to reflect evidence for a small enclosed area, possibly a yard or pen, which adjoined the corner of the structure.

EXCAVATIONS

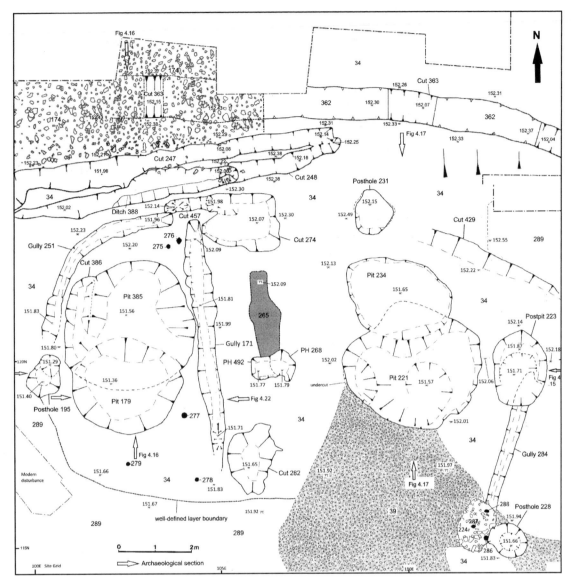

FIGURE 4.13
Area A showing Period III features of Structure 467 as excavated

Postholes 181, 196, 295 and 270/272 (Figure 4.12) were of similar shape and size. Their long axes were all orientated north–south and each had a U-shaped socket that varied in depth between approximately 200mm and 300mm with a shallower, scoured tail. The southernmost postholes [323 and 419] had suffered greater erosion and were shallower (less than 120mm deep respectively) and rounded. Posthole 196 was cut by later Period III Posthole 195, a feature associated with the subsequent building (Building 467). Feature 322 represented the southernmost element of the group. The deposit filled a shallow cut, possibly the remains of a foundation trench, and produced a sealed group of CP1 pottery. The overall extent of the feature [322] was not preserved, as it was truncated at the western end by the foundation stones of a Period IV wall [Wall 324].

Features that appeared to have been located inside Structure 468 included a shallow irregular cut [Feature 233], which could potentially have signified the position of an entrance threshold located between Postholes 181 and 295, and the remnant of rammed clay flooring [Deposit 189]. Both features produced pottery of CP1. Layer 189 was 100mm thick and roughly rectangular, and consisted of a well consolidated layer of reworked natural clay and small stones that filled a shallow depression. The deposit was cut by a series of later soakaways [Features 47, 79, and 190] relating to Period V Building 463.

STRUCTURE 468: ASSOCIATED FEATURES (FIGURES 4.2, 4.12 AND 4.19)

A shallow gully [300] appeared to join or curve around the southeastern corner of the structure. The feature was truncated and sealed by a layer of brashy limestone [39]. It was slightly deeper and wider towards the southwest, where it ended in a squared terminal. The gully also appeared to define the extent of a concentration of small stakeholes (Figure 4.12, Features 301–368 etc), although these formed no discernible spatial pattern.

A boundary ditch located immediately to the north of Structure 468 (Figures 4.2, 4.13 and 4.16, Ditch 248) was aligned west to east and followed the southern side of the hollow-way. Its eastern end was formed by a squared terminal, which had been disturbed by a later Period III ditch [247]. The feature continued beyond the excavation area towards the west, at which point it appeared to deepen (up to 400mm) and had a U-shaped profile with vertical or slightly undercut sides. The base of the ditch contained a number of shallow irregular depressions that could have represented heavily eroded stakeholes. The western end of the ditch was filled by a thick homogeneous loam soil [deposit 249 =192], which produced pottery of CP1 (although note that the eastern end of the feature had been disturbed and produced a few sherds of intrusive CP3 fabrics).

PERIOD III.1, STRUCTURE 468 – INTERPRETATION (FIGURE 4.2)

Pottery of CP1 recovered from the features relating to Structure 468 dates to the later 10th to early 11th centuries, although the principal physical evidence was limited and does not allow the building to be reconstructed in any precise detail. It seems to have been a rectangular structure, founded upon a symmetrical arrangement of at least eight light earthfast posts, each roughly 250mm in diameter, with a long axis orientated very nearly north–south. Feature 322 may have represented the remains of a slot for a foundation beam, in which case it could reflect the southern end of the structure overall, although this remains speculative. The alignment of the building, broadly north to south, is certainly significant and distinguishes it from all subsequent earthfast timber and masonry buildings erected in Area A.

Layer 189 indicates the building contained a compacted clay floor whilst Feature 233 could reflect erosion immediately inside the threshold of a west-facing entrance defined by Postholes 181 and 295. The relationship of Gully 300 suggests the building also may have had a small enclosed yard, although it is at least possible that this feature represented the remains of a once more extensive eavesdrip gully. The presence of Ditch 248 indicates that the route of the trackway was already established when the structure was built in the later 10th century.

Period III.2 in Areas A and H (ceramic phases CP2–4)

INTRODUCTION

During the earlier 11th century (ceramic phases 2–3), the settlement appears to have expanded as substantial new earthfast timber buildings were constructed in Areas A and H (Figures 1.6, 4.2 and 4.3), the former set within a small plot with a yard, the latter including a major principal-post building set inside a well-defined oval or D-shaped enclosure that was initially defined by a shallow ditch with external bank and subsequently by a timber fence. Despite this, the period of expansion appears to have been relatively short lived as the buildings in Area H, and indeed activity as a whole in this area, was abandoned by the end of the century (Period III.2, CP3), and possibly well before AD 1100. Subsequent (CP4) activity was confined to the continued occupation and development of the farmstead in Area A.

In Area A, Structure 468 was replaced by a larger subrectangular timber building (Figures 4.2 and 4.13; Structure 467) interpreted as a dwelling, which measured approximately 13m long and 7m wide. A range of other contemporary features, including ditches, pits and postholes, were also recorded (Figures 4.19 and 4.20) reflecting associated activity. These features either related to the maintenance of the farmstead boundary, or associated activity represented by negative features in a small enclosure or farmyard immediately to the south of the farmhouse.

To the south of Area A, a complex of pits, ditches, large postholes and post-pits (Figure 4.3) included the principal foundations of a major new timber building erected in Area H (Figure 4.14). The building was slightly larger in plan than that erected in Area A, measuring approximately 14.7m long and 7.5m wide, and may also have incorporated a partial upper storey or possibly a small tower. The assemblage of stratified domestic artefacts recovered from Area H is almost exclusively of 11th-century date and indicates that activity in this part of the settlement after the turn of the 12th century was minimal and restricted to the recutting of ditches or the construction of stone revetments, which, combined with the absence of any significant 12th-century or later settlement-related material culture, relate solely to the maintenance of agricultural boundaries rather than a continuation of habitation.

PERIOD III.2 – AREA A

Timber Building 467 (Figures 4.2 and 4.13) was subrectangular in plan, with at least three rounded corners, measuring approximately 13m long by 7m wide externally. Its long axis was orientated west–east and the structure was founded upon two earthfast principal-posts at each gable end, which were represented by a posthole [195] and a larger post-pit [223] (Figure 4.13). Preparation of the site prior to construction was indicated by a curved terrace [Cut 429], which was cut into the natural clay to level the northern corner of the building plot. This mirrored a curved wall foundation trench [Gully 251] at the northwest corner of the building. Pottery recovered from the principal earthfast features indicates that the building was constructed during CP2, when the structure appears to have been founded mainly upon the large gable posts plus a single central support (Figure 4.13, Postholes 492 and 268). The earthfast

EXCAVATIONS

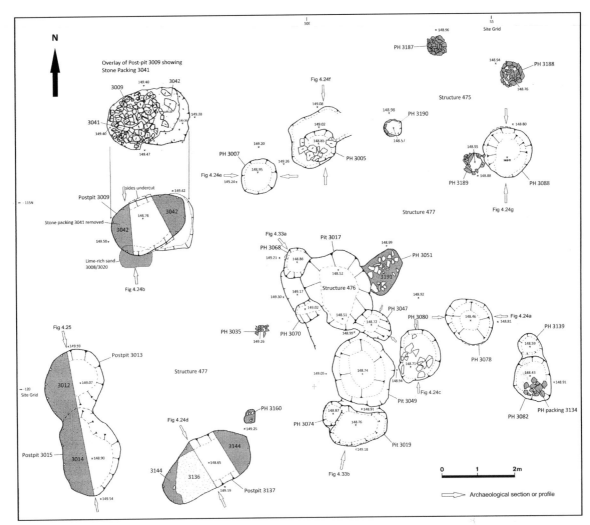

FIGURE 4.14
Area H showing detail of Structures 475, 476 and 477 as excavated

features located along either side of the structure (Figure 4.13, Features 231, 274, 457 and 282) all produced pottery of CP3 and consequently appeared to represent a subsequent development of the building (Period III.3), where at least one of the principal gable-posts, indicated by the larger and recut post-pit [231] was replaced. Features 274 and 282 also produced pottery of CP3, although its presence may have reflected material incorporated into the fills at opposing doorway thresholds during the occupation of the building. Internal structural support seems to have been confined to a single, less substantial, central post throughout the occupation of the building, which was recut at least once (Figure 4.13, Postholes 492 and 268), and therefore presumably replaced, on at least one occasion. The building appears to have had at least one internal division from the outset that separated the interior of the building into at least two bays, as indicated by an irregular trench or beam slot [Gully 171]. Each bay contained a sunken floor area defined by a pair of intercut pits (Figures 4.13 and 4.15–4.17; Pits 385/179 and 221/234). These sunken-floor features (Figures 4.18 A and B) appear to have formed elements of the building from its inception, although in the east bay Pit 221 appears to have replaced Pit 234 (Figure 4.17).

Outside and immediately to the north of Building 467, adjacent to the trackway, the line of the earlier (Period III.1) boundary ditch was maintained and recut on at least two, and probably three, occasions (Figures 4.2, 4.13 and 4.16; Ditches 247 and 363, and 388). To the south of the building, a series of pits and postholes were also dug, a number of which are tentatively interpreted to reflect further earthfast timber structures (Figures 4.2 and 4.19, Structures 471 and 480), albeit of uncertain function. In addition, during the later 11th and early 12th centuries, a series of pits and ditches were dug in the extreme south of Area A (Figures 4.19, 4.20 and 4.21). The group of intercut linear and pit features reflected activity at the southern boundary of the farmstead plot, although their stratigraphic relationships were unclear due to the similarity of fill material. It remains uncertain whether they represented a series of boundary ditches cut by a series of shallow pits (the latter possibly for the extraction of the natural Fullers Earth clay), or a contemporary group of shallow pits that were linked by short ditches.

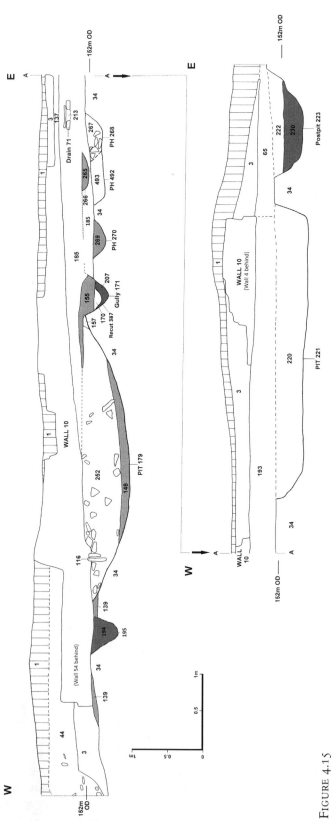

FIGURE 4.15

Area A – West to East section showing Period III to V structures and deposits

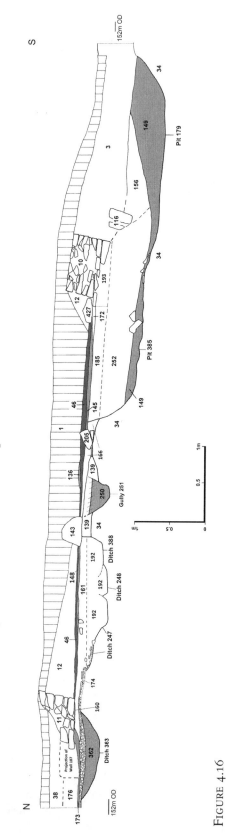

FIGURE 4.16

Area A – North to South section (west) showing Period III to V structures and deposits

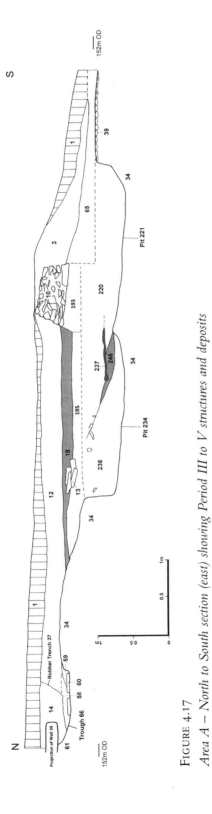

FIGURE 4.17
Area A – North to South section (east) showing Period III to V structures and deposits

STRUCTURE 467 (FIGURES 4.2, 4.13 AND 4.15–4.19)

Structure 467 replaced Structure 468 in CP2 (Period III.2) during the first half of the 11th century and was modified during CP4 (Period III.3), the later 11th century. Some of the principal structural and internal features associated with the original layout, for example the western gable posthole (Figure 4.13, Posthole 195) and Foundation Trench 251, appear to have been maintained throughout its entire use. The structural features associated with the initial building that were preserved unaltered consisted of Postholes 195 and 492 (Figure 4.13), a carefully curved foundation trench [251] located at the northwestern corner and a short steep terrace [Cut 429] cut into the natural at the northeastern end of the building. Internal features associated with its earlier form included three sunken floor areas or pits [Pits 179, 234 and 385] and a ditch or slot (Gully 171) for an internal partition wall. Although the form of the gully provided no clear indication as to the precise nature of the partition wall it originally contained, faint traces of sinuous carbonised material interpreted to reflect wattle burnt in-situ were noted during its excavation. Evidence of associated activity or occupation was generally lacking and confined to a rectangular soil layer [265], which is interpreted to indicate the position of a further internal partition or division.

The western gable posthole (Figures 4.13 and 4.15, Posthole 195) was roughly oval in plan and comprised a shallow shelf and a deeper post-socket up to 500mm deep. It cut an earlier (Period III.1) posthole [Feature 196]. The precise relationship between the posthole and Foundation Trench 251 was not preserved, although their arrangement clearly demonstrated that Feature 251 represented a wall foundation as opposed to an eaves-drip gully, since drip gullies do not ever discharge into postholes. The fill [194] contained tabular limestone rubble, possibly remnant post-packing, and produced pottery of CP2.

Gully 251 appeared to be cut through a thin layer of sterile red clay (Layer 139) into natural Fullers Earth clay [34], although the character of Layer 139 and the gully fill [250] was very similar indeed. The gully profile varied, but in general it was steep-sided with a flat base (Figure 4.16), which became shallower towards the gable posthole [195]. The clay fill [250] was texturally indistinguishable from Layer 139 and produced pottery of CP2. Cut 429 terraced the side of a ridge of natural clay [34] at the northeastern corner of the building, the plan-form of this terrace mirroring the curvature of Foundation Gully 251 at the other end of the structure. Posthole 492 was located approximately centrally inside the building. The feature was roughly squared in plan and up to 250mm deep with a flat base. It was cut by a slightly later posthole [268] of similar depth and size. Both postholes produced pottery of

FIGURE 4.18A
Area A showing Period III features as excavated. Facing E. Scales 2m

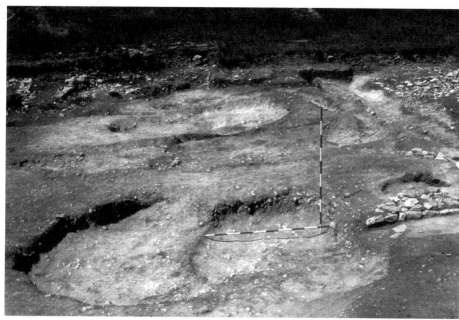

FIGURE 4.18B
Area A showing Period III Building 467 sunken-floor features fully excavated. Facing W. Scales 2m

FIGURE 4.18C
Area A showing Period III features 223, 284 and 228 as excavated. Facing SW. Scale 2m

EXCAVATIONS

FIGURE 4.18D

Area A showing detail of offset between Period III features 251 and 457. Facing E. Scale 2m

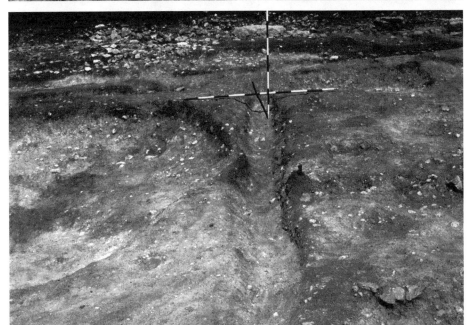

FIGURE 4.18E

Area A showing detail of relationship between Period III gully 171 and sunken floor features. Facing N. Scales 2m

FIGURE 4.18F

Area A showing Period III pit 416 during excavation and the top (base) of buried pot 490. Facing NW. Scale 1m

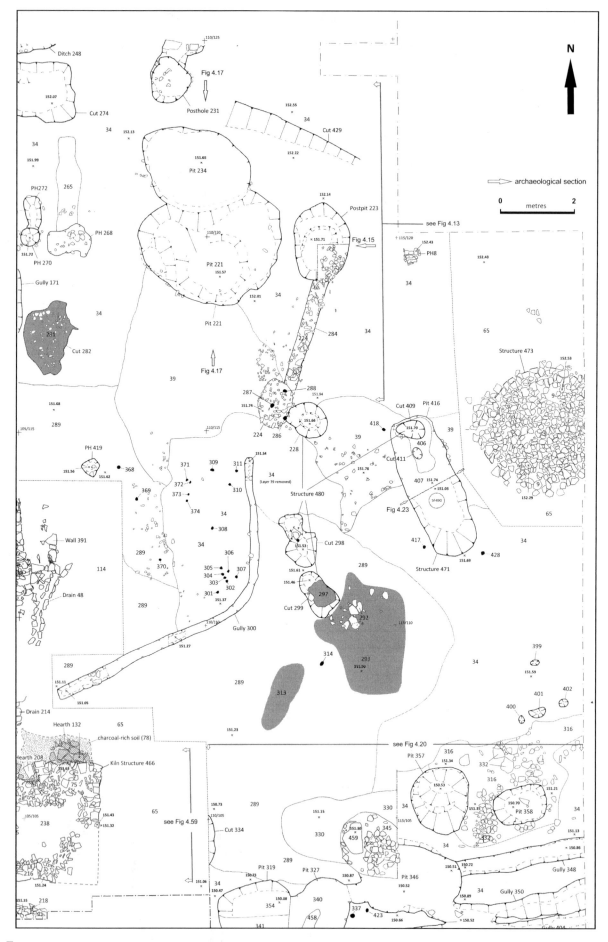

FIGURE 4.19

Area A – the Yard area as excavated showing Period III to V features

EXCAVATIONS

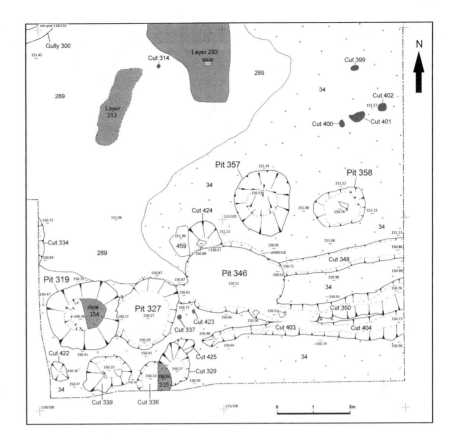

FIGURE 4.20
Area A – detail of Period III Pit Group 469 as excavated

CP3, although Fill 267 was clearly distinguishable during excavation, as it contained loose limestone rubble that appeared to represent the remnants of a post-packing.

Gully 171 represented an internal trench or wall slot that had an irregular, but generally U-shaped, profile (Figures 4.13 and 4.15) and a series of pronounced curved scoops along its edges that possibly reflected individual spade-spits. The feature became shallower from north to south and, at its mid-point, respected the edge of Pit 385, leaving a very narrow ridge of natural clay. The gully was recut during CP4 (Figure 4.22; Cut 387) although the remains of its primary fill [207] produced pottery of CP2.

The two sets of sunken floor features (Figure 4.13) were subrounded in plan and intercut in pairs at the western and eastern ends of the building. Three of them [Features 385, 179 and 234] were associated with the earlier use of the building during Phase III.2, as their primary fills [Deposits 149 and 236] produced pottery of CP3. Pits 179 and 385 clearly intercut in plan, although they shared a single primary fill (Figures 4.15 and 4.16, Fill 149) which indicated that they formed a large single sunken feature during that phase. Pit 234 was filled by Deposit 236 during CP3, a homogeneous loam soil, which, unlike Fill 149, appeared to represent rapid and perhaps deliberate backfilling. In general, the morphology of the sunken floor features was similar; all were round or subrounded in plan with fairly flat bottoms and moderately or steeply sloping sides, although Pits 234 and 221 were occasionally

FIGURE 4.21
Period III Pit Group 469 in Area A as excavated. Looking NE. Scale 2m

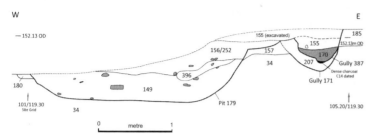
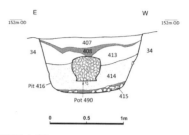

FIGURE 4.22

Area A – section through Period III Gully 171/387 and Pit 179

FIGURE 4.23

Area A – section through Period III Pit 416 showing Pot 490

slightly undercut, possibly as a result of erosion whilst open.

Layer 265 (Figures 4.13 and 4.15) consisted of a subrectangular patch of charcoal-rich silty soil and produced pottery of CP2. The layer extended north from the edge of Postholes 268 and 492 and filled a shallow cut [Cut 266] in Layer 185. The relationship between Layers 265 and 185 (Figure 4.15) indicated that the latter also began to accumulate inside Building 467 during CP2, although, despite this, no discrete horizon relating to Period III occupation alone could be identified.

STRUCTURE 467: ASSOCIATED PERIOD III.2 FEATURES

The northern boundary of the farmstead plot in Area A, established in Period III.1 by a ditch [248], was redefined and extended slightly by a larger ditch, Ditch 363 (Figures 4.2 and 4.16). Where exposed the ditch was approximately 12m long although it clearly continued further to both the west and east. It extended the original farmstead boundary by approximately 2m to the north and, unlike the Period III ditches that succeeded it, appears to have formed a continuous rather than intermittent boundary on the south side of the hollow-way. During CP2, the ditch was filled by an olive clay [362] and the western end was subsequently sealed by a cobbled trackway surface (Figure 4.16, Metalling Layer 174), stones from which slumped down the north face of a subsequent Period III boundary ditch (Figure 4.16, Ditch 247).

Ditch 247 replaced Ditch 363 during Period III.3 as the northern boundary of the farmstead after a thin layer of stone metalling [174] was laid that extended the surface of the adjacent trackway to the south. The eastern end of the ditch shallowed and ended in a squared terminal whilst the western end clearly continued beyond the excavation area. The feature had a thin primary fill of limestone stones and cobbles [174] derived from the adjacent trackway metalling, which were impressed into the north face of the cut. The bulk of the ditch was filled with a homogeneous clay [192] that produced pottery of CP3.

A thin layer of small limestone cobbles [39] extended into the footprint of Building 467 in the south eastern corner (Figures 4.13, 4.17 and 4.19).

The cobbling was very well consolidated and set into the surface of the natural clay and partially sealed the northern end of the earlier Phase III.1 gully [300]. The deposit was cut and thereby dated by a large rectangular pit (Figure 4.19, Pit 416) whose primary fill (Figure 4.23, Fill 415) produced pottery of CP3.

Layer 39 extended as far as the southern edge of Pit 221 (Figure 4.13) and therefore appeared to have originally extended inside Building 467. The layer may have been laid or formed at and across a south-facing entrance to the building. The well-defined boundary separating Layers 289 and 34 (Figure 4.13), to the west of Cobbling 39 clearly indicated the line of the south wall of the building, where a thin veneer of natural red clay [289] had been completely eroded inside the west bay of the building but preserved immediately outside it.

Posthole 228 (Figure 4.19) produced pottery of CP2, suggesting it was broadly contemporary with Layer 39. Pit 416 cut Layer 39 and was rectangular in plan and steep sided (Figure 4.23) although the southern end had a more gently sloping face. The primary fill [415] consisted of an irregular layer of limestone cobbles, some of which were scorched. Later fills varied and included lenses of pure clay [414] and reworked natural clay [408]. A large complete earthenware cookpot (Figure 4.23, Featured Pot Number 490), filled with small cobbles and stones, was set upside-down within Fill 414. The reason for this was unclear, although one possible explanation is that the pot provided an ad-hoc foundation for a later timber post (but see Section 7 below). Three small stakeholes (Figure 4.19, Features 417, 418 and 428), all aceramic, were located close to the corners of the pit, suggesting that it may have been fenced or possibly covered.

PIT GROUP 469 (FIGURES 4.19, 4.20 AND 4.21)

A group of intercutting pits, ditches and postholes were cut into a slight terrace in the natural Fullers Earth clay in the southeastern corner of Area A (Figures 4.20 and 4.21). Three of the pits [Cuts 319, 357 and 358], a ditch [348] and a single posthole [339] produced pottery of CPs 2 and 3 and were interpreted to be the earliest elements of the group. The remaining features produced pottery of CP4. Two of the pits [357 and 358] were set slightly to the north of the complex at the shoulder of the slope.

Pit 357 had an asymmetric profile with a steep northern face and a southern face that was more gently stepped in a series of ledges. The feature contained a thick (400mm) primary fill (359), which was extremely rich in carbonised cereal grains (Section 5.14) and pottery of CP3. Two radiocarbon determinations (Section 6.1, UB 3204 and UB3205) from samples of carbonised grain from the fill were obtained: these provide a weighted mean calibrated date range between AD 1020 and 1210, whilst the overlap of the one sigma probability distributions suggests a late 11th-century date. The charred cereal-rich primary fill was sealed by a subsequent deposit [355] that produced pottery of CP4. Pit 358 was similar in morphology to Pit 416, although it was smaller; the cut being roughly rectangular in plan, steep-sided and flat-bottomed. The homogeneous clay fill [356] produced only a few sherds of pottery of CP3 and sparse limestone cobbles.

Posthole 339 contained pottery of CP2 and as such may have represented the earliest feature of the group. It contained the remnants of stone packing and a probable padstone. Pit 319 was roughly circular and up to 1m deep. Its asymmetric U-shaped profile (not illustrated) was formed by a series of stepped cuts. Both the thick clay primary fill [354] and the secondary fill produced small amounts of pottery of CP3. The upper fill [318] consisted of charcoal-rich soil, which also contained significant quantities of carbonised cereal grain, again in association with pottery of CP3. Ditch 348 was steep-sided and had a flat base. It clearly continued beyond the excavation area to the east, towards the trackway [474], although its western end was cut by a later shallow pit [346], which produced pottery of CP4.

PERIOD III.2 – AREA H
During the first half of the 11th century (CP2), a large earthfast timber building (Figures 4.3 and 4.14, Structure 477) was built in Area H inside a small compound defined, at least in part, by a curved enclosure ditch [Ditch 3023]. Evidence from the geophysical survey (Figure 3.7) indicates that this in turn may have lain within a larger, oval or D-shaped enclosure. The building was founded upon nine principal earthfast timber posts, which were either set into large post-pits or slightly smaller, but still substantial, postholes (Figures 4.39A and 4.39B).

The building defined by these earthfast foundations would have been approximately 14m long, 7m wide and either rectangular or subrectangular in plan. No corner posts were present and for that reason it is suggested that either all four corners were curved, as appears to have been the case in Building 467 in Area A (above), or that the structure incorporated a pair of end-crucks. A number of the principal foundations appeared to have been replaced or added during the lifetime of the building, as some of the post-pits were recut. Unfortunately, no substantial contemporary occupation layers were preserved inside the building. This, and the similarity of most of the ceramic groups recovered from the features (ie the entire associated assemblage was restricted to CP2–3), makes the identification of fine detail in the structural sequence problematic.

A group of three shallow pits (Figure 4.14, Structure 476, Pits 3017, 3049 and 3019), one of which was surrounded by four postholes [Features 3047, 3051, 3068 and 3070] or sockets, was located inside or immediately outside the footprint of the building as defined by the principal timber foundations. None of these features had any direct stratigraphic relationship with the principal foundations of Structure 477, as all were sealed below topsoil alone, although the pottery they contained was securely stratified and entirely of CP3. Other Period III features in Area H included a range of postholes, pits and shallow ditches. Some of these features, for example Structures 479 (Figure 4.3) and 475 (Figure 4.14) were interpreted to represent elements of a second rectangular timber structure [Structure 479] and a four-posted structure [Structure 475], both of uncertain function.

TIMBER BUILDING 477 (CERAMIC PHASE 2; FIGURES 4.3 AND 4.14)
This large earthfast timber building was represented by a group of nine postholes and post-pits (Figure 4.3, Features 3005, 3007, 3009, 3013, 3015, 3078, 3080, 3088 and 3137), all of which were cut into the natural clay (3033). These principal earthfast foundations appeared to define what was, overall, a subrectangular building [Structure 477] that was approximately 14.7m long and 7.4m wide. The morphology of the earthfast features was variable. Some were circular in plan with broad U-shaped profiles (Figure 4.24, Features 3005, 3007, 3078, 3080 and 3088), two of which (3005 and 3080) contained the remnants of stone post-packing. The features forming the southwestern end of the structure (Figure 4.14, Features 3009, 3013, 3015 and 3137) consisted of significantly larger and deeper (up to 750mm deep and 2m diameter) oval-shaped pits, with variable conical or U-shaped profiles (Figure 4.25, Post-pits 3013 and 3015). None of these pits contained evidence of either post-pipes or stone post-packing and the fills varied from stone-free homogeneous loam to redeposited natural clay (Figure 4.25, Fill 3071), some containing patchy concentrations of fragmentary heat-affected daub (Fill 3144, Figures 4.24d and 4.26A).

The diameter of the smaller postholes (Figure 4.24, Features 3005, 3007, 3078, 3080 and 3088) ranged between 900mm and 1.4m and their depth between 250mm and 650mm. The post-pits [3009, 3013, 3015 and 3137] varied in size between 1.75m × 1.6m and 2.7m × 1.4m, and were between 450 and 750mm deep. The majority of the post-pit

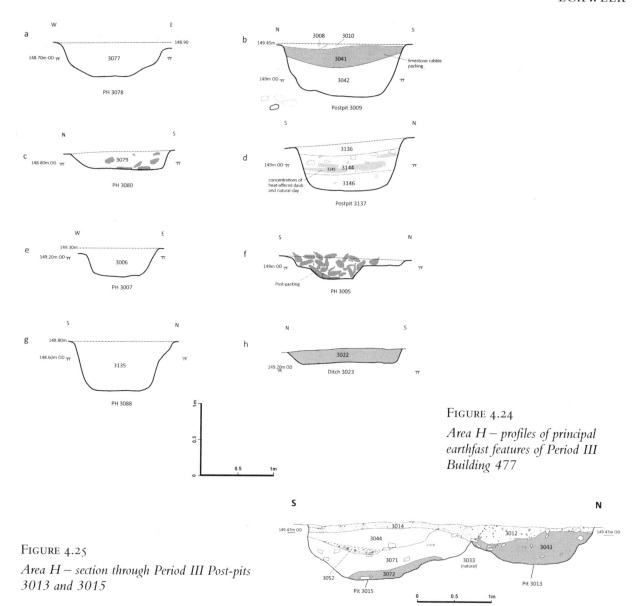

FIGURE 4.24

Area H – profiles of principal earthfast features of Period III Building 477

FIGURE 4.25

Area H – section through Period III Post-pits 3013 and 3015

and posthole fills consisted of rather homogeneous, sometimes stony, loam, although Posthole 3088 contained distinctive greenish, cess-like, silt [Fill 3135]. Pottery from the posthole fills, with the exception of Posthole 3078, was dated to CP2. Posthole 3078 also produced a few sherds of pottery of CP3, although these were considered to be intrusive in that context.

Overall, the building (Figure 4.14; Structure 477) appears to have been initially founded upon two large gable posts (Features 3088 and 3013) and six side-wall posts [Features 3005, 3007, 3009, 3078, 3080 and 3137]. The original western gable-post (Figure 4.14, Pit 3013) appears to have been replaced or, more likely, doubled in size by the addition of Post-pit 3015 during the use of the building, although the ceramic phasing of pottery recovered from Pits 3013 and 3015 was indistinguishable. The addition of a second large gable post at the western end of the building is considered significant and could reflect the need for additional structural support or, alternatively, evidence for the insertion of a door jamb as part of a later remodelling.

The groups of three principal-post settings along the northern (Figures 4.14 and 4.27, Features 3005, 3007 and 3009) and southern (Figure 4.14, Features 3078, 3080 and 3137) sides of the building appeared large enough to have provided ample support for internal partition walls, although no direct evidence for such was identified other than a concentration of burnt daub forming the secondary fill of post-pit 3137 (Fill 3144, Figure 4.24) and two small postholes (Figure 4.14, Features 3035 and 3160) that were located inside the footprint of the building. Both were small with a dense stone packing and located in the western half of the building. Posthole 3035 was also positioned close to its axial line and could have represented a roof or rafter support. Some variation was evident in the material filling the smaller postholes at the eastern end of the building where Posthole 3005 was filled by a dense packing of limestone rubble (Figure 4.27), and Posthole 3080 retained some possible post-packing rubble, whereas the fills of Postholes 3007, 3078 and 3088 were essentially stone-free.

EXCAVATIONS

FIGURE 4.26A
Area H – section through Period III Post-pit 3137 showing burnt daub layer 3144/3145. Facing W. Scale 2m

FIGURE 4.26B
Area H – detail of Period III Post-pit 3009 showing secondary stone foundation layer 3041. Facing SW. Scale 2m

The sequence of deposits filling Post-pit 3009 (Figure 4.24b) provided evidence that some elements of the building were replaced or repaired during CP2, as the majority of the upper fill [3041, Figure 4.26B] consisted of a well-consolidated packing of limestone cobbles and rubble, which had been set into the residue of a thick primary fill [3042]. The stone layer was bowl-shaped and appeared to have provided a firm, if shallower, foundation, for a replacement timber. The difference in the size and morphology of the structural features at the western end of Building 477 [Post-pits 3009, 3013, 3015 and 3137], from those at its eastern end [Postholes 3005, 3007, 3078, 3080 and 3088] was considered significant and important. The distinct morphology of each group suggests that there may have been significant differences in the form and character of the western and eastern ends of the building.

No occupation layers were preserved inside Building 477. Indeed, in Area H as a whole the distinction between the artefact-rich pit and posthole fills and the absence of associated occupation soils suggested a significant degree of post-abandonment erosion, most likely due to some 700 years of subsequent agriculture.

A small, but distinctive patch of lime-rich sand (Figure 4.14, 3008/3020) containing pottery of CP2 overlay the latest fill of Post-pit 3009. The deposit filled a shallow scour less than 100mm deep in the upper fill [3010] of Post-pit 3009 and the natural clay respectively. The significance of this feature in relation to the principal structural elements of Building 477 was not clear at the time of excavation, but the deposit could have represented the vestiges of an internal floor layer or a remnant of internal wall plaster.

BUILDING 477: ASSOCIATED FEATURES (FIGURES 4.3, 4.14 AND 4.28)

A complex of postholes (Figures 4.3 and 4.28, Features 3082, 3139, 3092, 3031, 3058, 3117, 3224 and 3121), pits [3029, 3061, 3111 and 3115], shallow

FIGURE 4.27
Period III Features 3005, 3007 and 3009 before excavation. Features 3007 and 3009 circled. Facing SW. Scales 2m

ditches [3132, 3119, and 3223] and localised charcoal layers (3130) were also revealed to the south of Building 477 in Area H. All the features contained pottery of CP2 and related to activity broadly associated with the occupation of the building. However, evidence from the section in Cutting 1 (Figure 4.6) indicated that at least some of these features, specifically Feature 3132, as indicated by Feature 3184 in Cutting 1, were stratigraphically later than Ditch 3023 and, as a consequence, also the earliest phase of Building 477. As a result, it appears likely that whilst the features only produced pottery of CP2 the majority, excluding PHs 3082 and 3020 (below), probably related to the slightly later phase of 11th-century activity in this area during CP3.

Postholes 3082 and 3139 were intercut and appeared to represent a raked post-setting, which was later replaced. Posthole 3082 was cut more deeply than 3139 and contained the remnants of a limestone cobble packing [3134]. Its location, adjacent to Posthole 3078, and its position, off-centre and to one side of the posthole, indicated that it held an angled timber buttress or support for the south wall (ie post-setting 3078) of the building. A second feature (Figure 4.3, Feature 3020) was located immediately to the south of Post-pit 3137, adjacent to the shallow enclosure ditch – this feature was not excavated (with hindsight, remarkably) although, on the basis of its position alone, it is considered very likely to have represented the foundation for a second raking support post.

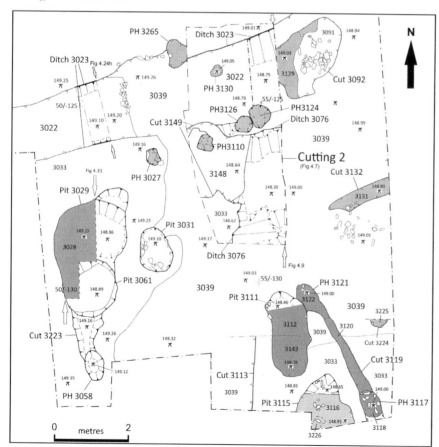

FIGURE 4.28
Area H – detail of Iron Age and Period III features as excavated

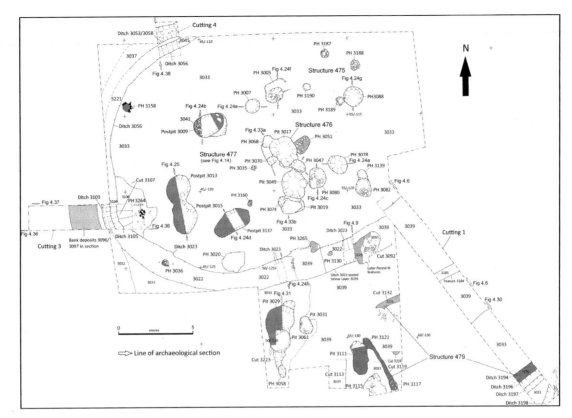

FIGURE 4.29

Area H – Period III features as excavated

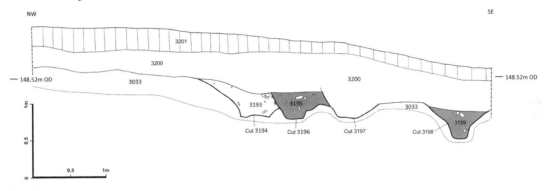

FIGURE 4.30

Area H – Period III features exposed in section at the SE end of Cutting 1

STRUCTURE 479 (FIGURES 4.3, 4.28 AND 4.29)
Ditches 3132 and 3119, Postholes 3121 and 3117, and Pit 3115, appeared to represent a related group of features. With the exception of Pit 3115, they were all cut into the same layer of gravelly soil [Layer 3039]. Ditches 3132 and 3119 were shallow and U-shaped; Postholes 3121 and 3117 were intercut at the ends of Ditch 3119; the northern end of Pit 3115 was cut to a depth of 250mm. The ditch and posthole fills [3131, 3122, 3120 and 3118] were, in general, homogeneous and contained sparse limestone rubble. In the vicinity of these features the surface of Layer 3039 contained small amounts of fragmentary pottery and bone and other (unexcavated) features, such as Feature 3224, which appeared to represent a posthole sealed by Layer 3039. Whilst the evidence was not conclusive, this group of associated features appeared to represent the northwestern corner of a second timber structure [Structure 479], which was founded upon a rectangular arrangement of medium sized earthfast posts and timber sleepers. Further evidence to support this interpretation was provided by Cutting 1 (Figure 4.3), the southeastern end of which revealed a sequence of linear cut features (Figures 4.29 and 4.30, Features 3194, 3196 and 3197), the earliest of which appeared to reflect a recut linear wall-trench that defined the southeastern side of the structure [479].

A further group of intercutting pits (Figure 4.28; Features 3029 and 3061), shallow postholes [3031 and 3058], and a shallow ditch [3223] also appeared to reflect a group of related features. Pits 3029 and 3061 were intercut, Pit 3029 representing the earlier of the two (Figures 4.31 and 4.32) although they both produced pottery of CP2. Pit 3029 was sub-rectangular and had a deep U-shaped profile. Its

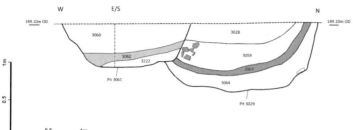

FIGURE 4.31
Area H – section through Period III pits 3029 and 3061. Facing E

FIGURE 4.32
Area H – Period III pits 3029 and 3061 during excavation showing daub layer 3063. Facing NE. Scales 2m

sequence of fills [3028, 3059, 3063 and 3064] provided no direct indication of its function, although it had at one time been deliberately relined with puddled natural clay [3063]. Pit 3061 was subcircular, flat bottomed, and up to 500mm deep (Figure 4.31). It cut Pit 3029 and contained a secondary fill [3062] rich in fragmentary charcoal and carbonised cereal grains (Section 5.14). A shallow ditch [3223] appeared to link a posthole [3058] with Pit 3061, whilst a larger cut feature, 3031, possibly the remains of a further posthole, was subrounded and shallower. Its fill [3030] contained remnants of a stone packing and produced significant amounts of woody charcoal and daub.

Feature 3092, possibly representing a further Period III.3 posthole or small pit, was also cut into gravelly clay layer 3039, which in section (Figure 4.9) sealed the fill of Period III.2 Ditch 3023 and deposits filling the Period I Iron Age ditch. The posthole had an irregular outline and U-shaped profile. Its fill [3091/3129] contained intermixed limestone rubble and reworked natural clay, but no clear post-packing.

Area H (ceramic phase 3 – Later 11th Century)

STRUCTURE 476 (FIGURES 4.3, 4.14, 4.33 AND 4.34)
This group of associated cut soil features defining Structure 476 were located inside Building 477 and appeared to represent elements of the same overall building. The group consisted of three subrounded pits (Figure 4.14; Features 3017, 3049 and 3019), one of which [3017] was surrounded at the pit-shoulder by a roughly rectangular arrangement of postholes/sockets [Features 3068, 3051, 3070 and 3047]. Some of the pits and postholes were intercut, although the material filling them [Fills 3018, 3016 and 3048], and the pottery they produced (CP3) were indistinguishable. All three of the pits had rather irregular profiles (Figure 4.33), although in general they were broadly U-shaped with a roughly flat base. Pit 3017 was the deepest (at 650mm) and contained a thick silty primary fill [3040]. The four shallow postholes cut into the shoulder of the feature were similar, although of slightly different size and depth, at between 200mm and 350mm deep; one [3051] contained a large number of limestone cobbles [3191], possibly the remains of a post-packing. The remainder [Postholes 3068, 3070 and 3047] were filled with soil which was indistinguishable from that which filled the pit. Pit 3019 did contain a different thin primary fill (c100mm thick) that was rich in fragmentary charcoal and charred cereal grains (Section 5.14). Further evidence that the pit group represented contemporary features was provided by the relationship between Pits 3049 and 3047 (Figure 4.33b), which were separated by an extremely narrow ridge of natural clay.

STRUCTURE 475 (FIGURES 4.3, 4.14, 4.29 AND 4.35)
Structure 475 was represented by a group of four stone-lined post settings [Features 3187, 3188, 3189 and 3190]. All four features were of similar size, between 400mm and 500mm in diameter, although their depths varied between 200mm and 330mm.

EXCAVATIONS

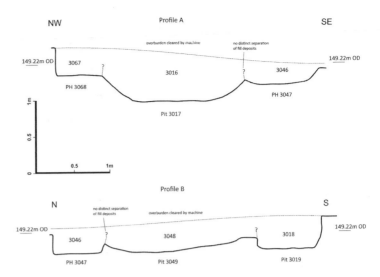

FIGURE 4.33
Area H – profiles across Structure 476

FIGURE 4.34
Area H – Structure 476 as excavated. Facing NE. Scales 2m

FIGURE 4.35
Area H – Structure 475 in foreground prior to excavation. Facing SW. Scales 2m

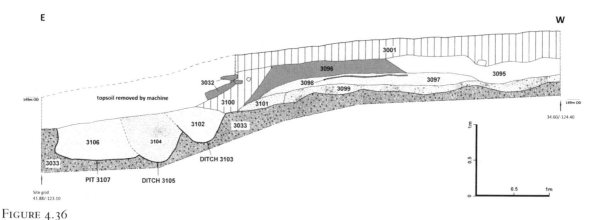

FIGURE 4.36

Area H – north-facing section in Cutting 3 showing Period III enclosure ditches and bank deposits

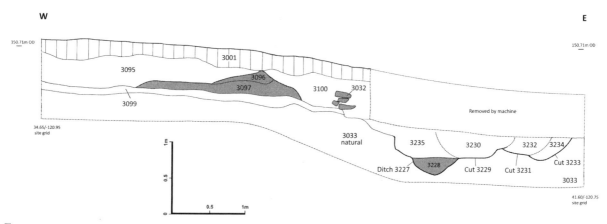

FIGURE 4.37

Area H – south-facing section in Cutting 3 showing Period III enclosure ditches and bank deposits

Each would have accommodated a timber of approximately 250mm diameter. The stone linings had been carefully set into the posthole and in places the sides of the packing even seemed to have been crudely coursed. Overall, the structure would have been roughly 2m square, although no other direct evidence was preserved to determine its original form above ground or function. Dating of the structure must be considered tentative, as the postholes were all aceramic, although there was no evidence to indicate that the structure was not associated with Period III activity in Area H. It is possible that the structure represented an extension or addition to Building 477, perhaps a grain store or a latrine, built against its northeastern corner although, if so, the position of Posthole 3189 is difficult to explain structurally, as it would therefore have been located immediately inside the northeast gable post (ie inside either of the inferred wall-lines of Building 477). Similarly, the post-packings (Figure 4.35) were relatively sophisticated constructions, unlike most other Period III features associated with Building 477, as such they could conceivably reflect a structure that was free-standing and associated with later Period III.2 Structure 479 just to the south. If so, this could indicate that Building 477 had been abandoned and destroyed when Structure 475 was constructed. Of course, a further interpretation is that Structure 475 reflects a distinct and separate phase of medieval (or indeed later) activity in Area H, one for which there was no artefactual or dating evidence of any kind.

OTHER FEATURES (CERAMIC PHASE 3)

In ceramic phase 2 Building 477 was bounded to the west and south by an oval enclosure ditch (Figures 4.3 and 4.29, Cuts 3023, 3056, 3103 and 3105) that was revealed and sectioned at several locations. The presence of an earth bank outside this small ditched boundary, as identified to the southwest in section (Figures 4.29, 4.36 and 4.37),

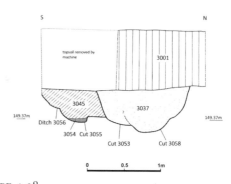

FIGURE 4.38

Area H – east-facing section in Cutting 4 showing Period III enclosure ditches

EXCAVATIONS

FIGURE 4.39A
Area H during excavation. Facing NE

FIGURE 4.39B
As 4.39A above with principal Period III features indicated. Facing NE

combined with the geophysical survey data, suggests that the oval enclosure around Building 477 was in turn set within a larger oval or D-shaped enclosure or compound (Figure 8.2).

The boundary formed by Ditch 3023/3056 etc was clearly recut on at least one occasion (Figures 4.36, 4.37 and 4.38, Cuts 3053/3058) although this sequence was not evident at all the locations where it was investigated (Figure 4.9) and in its final form in CP3, the ditch appears to have been replaced entirely by a timber structure, most likely a fence, as indicated by a group of similar postholes (Figure 4.3; Postholes 3130, 3158, 3264, 3036 and 3265), three of which were sited around the internal shoulder of the earliest ditch cut and one set within its fill. The relationship of the sequence of recut enclosure ditches [Features 3055, 3056 and 3058] was recorded in section at the northwestern corner of the excavation area (Figure 4.38) and to the west of Building 477, where the evidence indicated that the ditch was accompanied by an external bank (Figures 4.36 and 4.37, Deposits 3096, 3097/3098), itself possibly formed in two phases, as indicated by later Deposit 3096 in the north facing section (Figure 4.36).

In addition to Ditch 3023, the earliest enclosure surrounding Building 477 was also revealed in the northwestern corner of the excavation area by a shallow, narrow and flat-bottomed cut (Figure 4.38, Cut 3055) that appeared to be truncated by slightly later recut Ditch 3056. The ditch possibly could have provided a foundation trench for a fence, although in its later form it appeared too wide for such. The silt fill [3054] produced a collection of pottery of CP3. A further recutting of the same boundary was evident in section (Figure 4.38, Cut 3058) and in section at other locations (Figures 4.36 and 4.37; Ditches 3103 and 3105 and Cuts 3227, 3229, 3231

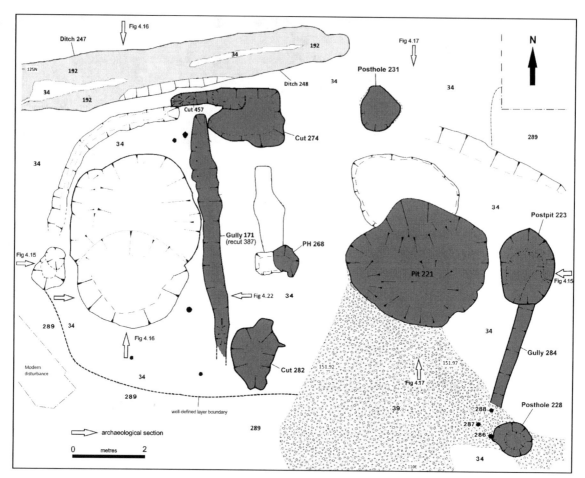

FIGURE 4.40
Area A – Period III Structure 467 with Period III.3 features highlighted

and 3233). The fills of each ditch recut produced pottery of CP3, whilst in section Ditch 3105 cut a pit (Figure 4.3 and 4.36; Pit 3107) of earlier Period III date, the function of which was unclear. All the later ditch recuts had broad U-shaped profiles that were of comparable scale to the earliest enclosure ditch [3023].

A further group of four linear cut features of probable early medieval origin were revealed in section (Figure 4.30) at the southeastern end of Cutting 1 (Figure 4.3), where the trench revealed a series of intercut linear features [Features 3194, 3196, 3197 and 3198]. The southernmost feature (3198) was cut from the same horizon, but on a converging alignment and produced pottery of CP3. The alignment of the intercutting group [Features 3194-3197] was interpreted to reflect a succession of linear structural features defining the south side of timber Structure 479 (Figure 4.29).

A group of stone post-settings of similar size (Figure 4.3 and 4.29, Features 3130, 3158, 3036, 3264 and 3265) replaced the enclosure ditch, some of which were cut into its uppermost fill [3022]. The relationship between the post-settings and the latest ditch recut [3038 and 3103] was not entirely clear and it is at least possible that the enclosure surrounding Building 477 was defined by both a fence

and a ditch in its latest form during CP3. A further short section of the enclosure ditch was examined in section (Figure 4.9) to the south of Building 477. Here, the boundary was represented by a shallow flat bottomed ditch (Ditch 3023 – the southern side of which was very unclear in the excavated section) and a charcoal-rich posthole [3265] located just inside the line of the ditch cut.

The stratigraphic evidence from Area H, combined with the ceramic phasing, indicates that, with the exception of Structure 475, which did not produce any direct dating evidence and was therefore at least possibly of a later date, all the structures and activity in Area H had been abandoned by the end of ceramic phase 3, before the end of the 11th century and possibly somewhat earlier.

Period III.3 (Ceramic Phase 4, cAD 1100–1200)

INTRODUCTION
The principal evidence for structural activity during Period III.3, broadly the first half of the 12th century, was confined to Area A where Building 467 appears to have been substantially modified or possibly largely rebuilt. Although the overall size and internal layout of the building remained essentially unchanged, the phase of reconstruction

EXCAVATIONS

FIGURE 4.41
Area A showing period IV and V walls overlying the fill of Period III pits 221 and 234. Facing E. Scales 2m

was distinguished by the recutting of the internal partition (Figure 4.40, Gully 387) and the ceramic phasing (CP4) of other associated structural features which, for the first time on the site, produced small quantities of glazed Bristol Ham Green wares along with other new and distinctive pottery fabrics, in particular 'Westcountry Dishes' in FT75. Other activity associated with Period III.3 was confined to the continued cutting of pits and postholes along the southern boundary of the farmstead in Area A (Figures 4.19 and 4.20).

STRUCTURE 467 (FIGURES 4.15, 4.22 AND 4.40)
The eastern gable-post of the earlier building was replaced with a new timber that was erected in a pit 400mm deep (Figure 4.15, Cut 223). In the process, it is presumed to have entirely destroyed an earlier, original, east gable posthole. The basal socket for the replacement timber was significantly larger than that of the western gable posthole (Posthole 195) and could have accommodated a timber in the round of 750mm diameter.

Two irregular shallow pits (Figure 4.40; Features 274 and 282) were dug at either end of Gully 387, a direct recutting of Gully 171. Both features respected the line of the gully and were separated from it by very thin ridges of natural clay. The fill of Feature 282 [281] contained scorched limestone cobbles and a large amount of fragmentary heat-affected daub, but no evidence of any post-packing or timber socket. Cut 274 was irregular and cut an earlier short section of foundation trench [Cut 457] although both features shared a single homogeneous fill [273] which provided no clear expression of their relative sequence. Cut 274 had a flat base and became shallower towards the south; both it and Feature 282 appeared too shallow to have supported an upright principal-post, but deep enough to have

held a shallower sleeper. Posthole 231 was deeper (350mm deep). Its position in relation to Feature 274 and Terrace 429 suggested that it formed part of Building 467 from the outset, although its fill [123] had been disturbed and contained intrusive later pottery of CP5. The inclusion of the feature in Period III.3 is therefore tentative, but strongly supported by the overall spatial arrangement of Building 467.

Gully 171 was recut (Figure 4.22, Cut 387) whilst Layer 185 was accumulating (Figure 4.15) and maintained the position of the internal division precisely. The primary fill of the recut [170] contained large amounts of carbonised material (Section 5.14) and very faint sinuous lines of charcoal, which appeared to represent the remains of timber wattle that had been burnt in-situ. The deposit also produced the earliest sherds of glazed Bristol Ham Green pottery from the site, a regional type which was first produced at Ham Green, Bristol during the early to mid 12th century (R. Burchill pers comm). A radiocarbon determination (Section 6.1, *UB3206*) obtained from carbonised material recovered from Deposit 170 provided a calibrated 1-sigma date range of AD 1168–1254, broadly consistent with the intra-site ceramic dating.

By Period III.3, the earlier sunken floor features (Figures 4.13, 4.16 and 4.17; Features 179 and 234) appear to have been partially or largely filled, since neither contained pottery any later than CP3. However, the bulk of the fill [252] of Pit 385 contained pottery of CP4, which suggests this sunken floor area remained a feature of the building into the 12th century (Period III.3). Pit 221 cut Pit 234 inside the eastern end of the building. It [221] was cut to a maximum depth of 450mm and contained an aceramic primary fill [246] and a charcoal-rich lens (Figure 4.17 Deposit 237) that produced pottery of CP4. A radiocarbon determination (Section 6.1, *UB3298*) from deposit 237 provided a calibrated mean date of AD 1021 and a 1-sigma date range of AD 988–1152. This date appears rather too early, although the 1-sigma distribution just about overlaps with the ceramic dating for Period III.3. The secondary fill of Pit 221 [220] was homogeneous and produced pottery of CP5, although the dating evidence from Fills 246 and 237 (Figure 4.17) indicates that the pit relates to the Period III.3 occupation of the building. By inference this suggests that a significant proportion of the lower pit fill [220] was of a similar date. With the benefit of hindsight, it is clear the homogeneous fill of Pit 221 would have benefited from 'planum' excavation and regular vertical segregation of pottery.

At the eastern end of the building, the northern end of Gully 284 (Figure 4.40) was slightly cut into the upper fill of Post-pit 223. Its southern end appeared to run as far as a large single posthole [228] and a group of three stakeholes [286, 287 and 288]. The gully [284] was sealed beneath a thin layer of later yardsoil (65) and contained the remnants of a shallow V-shaped stone packing [224]. Posthole 228 cut cobbled Layer 39 and was also sealed by the thin yardsoil [65]. The fills of both the gully [224] and the posthole [229] produced pottery of CP4, plus small quantities of CP5 material. The CP5 pottery was considered to be intrusive in these contexts, a consequence of gradual erosion and mixing during the later use of the yard.

BUILDING 467: THE LONGITUDINAL SECTION (FIGURE 4.15)

An axial running section (Figure 4.15) was recorded from west to east through Building 467 and during the preceding excavation of later medieval deposits and structures that overlay the Period III features. The section highlights the spatial organisation and vertical stratigraphy of the Period III features and their relationship to the later Period IV and V features. Gully 171 was recut (Figure 4.22; Cut 387) from an undefined occupation horizon within Layer 185 and was filled by a charcoal-rich soil (170) which had a greater concentration (>50%) of carbonised material towards the base of the fill. The feature was finally filled by a second charcoal-rich soil [155], which extended over the upper fill [252] of sunken-floor feature 179. The upper surface of the pit fill had been disturbed by a group of foundation stones (Figure 4.15; Feature 116), some of which were set edge-on, for Period V Wall 10; this event also introduced intrusive (CP5) pottery into the upper part of Deposit 252. The construction of Wall 10 also appeared to have truncated the Period III west gable posthole [195]. To the west of Wall 10, no evidence of Period III occupation was preserved. Here, the demolition rubble [3] from the walls of the Period V building (Building 460) lay directly above weathered natural clay [34].

Area A – Period III.3: Other Evidence

The boundary ditches (Figure 4.13; Ditches 248 and 247) to the north of Building 467, which were cut during Periods III.1 and III.2, do not appear to have been recut during Period III.3. The upper fills of both produced pottery of CP4. This suggests these ditched boundaries were either a feature of the farmstead until the construction of stone Building 462, when they were deliberately filled, or they were gradually filled and levelled during the occupation of Building 467. No discreet horizon within the trackway cobbling (Figure 4.16, 174) could be attributed to this period, although the fills of Ditch 258 [127 and 128] in Trench D (Figure 4.42), both of which produced pottery of CP4, indicate that the trackway continued in use during this phase.

In the yard to the south of the building, a layer of loam soil [65] continued to accumulate and be reworked, gradually sealing earlier features (eg Layer 39, Pit 416, Features 298 and 299). Other than two lenticular layers [293 and 313], no stratified and sealed deposits definitely relating to Period III.3 activity were identified. Two small postholes (Figure 4.19; Features 409 and 411) were cut into the upper fill of Pit 416. These and Features 298, 299 and 228 were broadly contemporary and, on the basis of their spatial arrangement alone, may have formed elements of a single oval or subrectangular timber structure (Figure 4.19, Structure 480).

At the southern edge of Area A, further pits and postholes (Figures 4.19 and 4.20, Features 327, 346, 336 and 329) were dug into the natural clay terrace. Two shallow, flat-bottomed pits [327 and 346] cut the earlier boundary ditch [348]. Pit 327 had an asymmetric profile and was roughly 600mm deep although, because of the natural slope, its southern lip was less than 100mm high. Pit 346 was larger, but also asymmetric from north to south. Both pits were heavily undercut on their northern face, possibly due to erosion by water during their use, or as a result of general weathering whilst open, and contained pottery of CP4. The pit fills [347 and 340] also contained quantities of domestic refuse, although not enough to suggest they had been deliberately dug for rubbish. A narrow channel linking Pits 327 and 346 probably represented a remnant of earlier Ditch 348 although it contained no distinctive fill. Postholes 336, 329 and 424 were also filled during CP4 but were not all contemporary, as Feature 336 cut Feature 329, whilst Feature 424 was cut into the fill [347] of Pit 346.

A shallow pit or posthole (Figure 4.21; 424) was cut into the northern edge of Pit 346 and located adjacent to a large limestone boulder [459]. The feature contained a concentration of limestone rubble and a possible padstone. Layer 345 extended over the margins of Posthole 424, partially sealing pit Fills 347 and 355 and butting the boulder. The

EXCAVATIONS

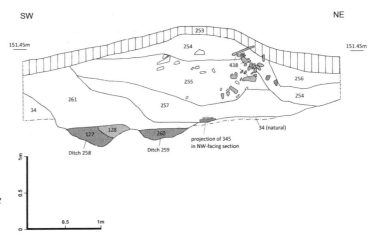

FIGURE 4.42
Trench D – SE-facing section showing Period III ditches overlain by Period IV-V earth bank and rubble revetment [438]

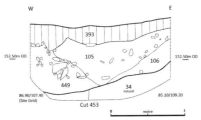

FIGURE 4.43
Trench C – South-facing section

posthole contained no evidence of either a stone packing or lining.

Area A – Period III: Evidence Not Attributed to Any Particular Subphase

STAKEHOLES
A number of small stakeholes were recorded inside Building 467, in the yard (Structure 464) and adjacent to Pit Group 469. All the features were aceramic and can only be assigned to Period III activity in general on the basis of their spatial arrangement or stratigraphy.

Five stakeholes (Figure 4.13; Features 275, 276, 277, 278 and 279) were located inside the western bay of Building 467. Two, Features 278 and 279, may have formed part of a wooden framework for the south wall, although the arrangement of the others provided no indication as to their function.

The position of Stakeholes 337 and 423 (Figure 4.20) appeared to be related to the digging or use of Pits 327 and 346. The function of others (Figure 4.19; Features 314 and 399–402), which were cut into the natural clay in the yard, could not be determined and their inclusion in Period III must be considered tentative.

Trench D (Figures 1.6 and 4.42)

A cutting excavated through the trackway (Structure 474) and the earthwork bank along the western side of the yard area revealed two Period III boundary ditches (Figure 4.42; Ditches 259 and 258), the fills [260 and 127] of which produced pottery of CP2 and CP4 respectively (Periods III.2 and III.3). No contemporary trackway surface was revealed in the section, but both ditches were sealed by an accumulation of yardsoil [261] which contained pottery of CP5. Ditch 258 therefore provided a *terminus post quem* of CP4 for the development of the boundary bank [Deposits 261–255]. The pottery from ditch fill 260 (CP2) suggests that it related to the early occupation (Phase III.2) of Building 467. It may therefore have represented a continuation of Ditch 363 recorded in Area A (Figures 4.13 and 4.16).

Ditch 258 was cut into the base of a slight terrace in the natural clay [34], to the west of Ditch 259. The primary fill [127] and an upper gravelly lens [128], produced pottery of CP4 reflecting activity during the later Period III occupation of the farmstead.

Trench C (Figures 1.6 and 4.43)

Trench C was opened across a narrow ditch and bank earthwork, which ran from Area A to the southwest. The ditch (Figure 4.43, Cut 453) was cut into the natural subsoil [34] and its primary fill [449] contained consolidated limestone rubble and pottery of CP4 (including Featured Pot Number 79, a virtually complete Westcountry Dish). The uppermost ditch fill [105] also produced pottery of CP4.

Trench E (Figures 1.6 and 4.44)

Trench E was opened across the trackway (Structure 474), where it consisted of a hollow-way at its widest point between Areas A and B. The majority of the layers revealed were aceramic, although the earliest stratigraphic features (Figure 4.44; Ditches 433 and 434) were considered to represent Period III features. Both ditches were shallow and cut into the natural clay [34] and, as with Ditches 258 and 259 in Trench D, both were sealed by a thick wedge of soil [120] that formed the later earthwork bank. The stratigraphic evidence suggested that Ditch 434 was the later of the two and that a layer of sporadic cobbles [Layer 121] that sealed Ditch 433 represented the remnants of a Period III trackway surface. Other

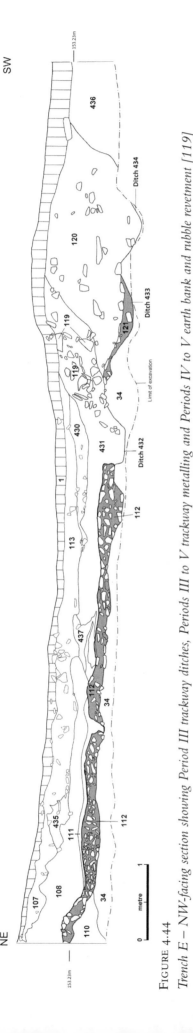

FIGURE 4.44
Trench E – NW-facing section showing Period III trackway ditches, Periods III to V trackway metalling and Periods IV to V earth bank and rubble revetment [119]

deposits revealed in the trench section, in particular metalling Layer 112, related to later surfacing and use of the trackway during Periods IV and V.

Periods III.2 and III.3 Structures: Discussion of the 11th-Century Structures

AREA A: PERIODS III.2 AND III.3

It is not possible to be certain about the original form of Building 467, although the later refurbishment or rebuilding during Period III.3 seems to have altered little in terms of its original footprint and plan-form. The rebuilding certainly entailed replacing the east gable-post, which by inference, would probably also have necessitated fairly substantial reconstruction of the walls, at least at the eastern end, and perhaps an entire re-roofing – the replacing of the smaller central post (Figure 4.13; Posthole 268) may support this. Gully 284 is likely to have served as the foundation for a fence or partition attached at the southeast corner, but may also have aided the drainage of the new east gable-post (perhaps the original post was replaced due to waterlogging and rotting). An alternative interpretation is that the southeast corner of the building was extended to the south, by means of a new timber structure or wall set up between the east gable-post and Postholes 224/228 (Figure 4.19).

The position of the walls of the building was only directly observed from Foundation Trenches 251 and 457, which define the northwest corner of the building, and the boundary of Layer 289 and Layer 34, which described a mirror image of the two foundation trenches. Unfortunately, the fill of Gully 251 provided no clear indication as to the nature of the construction it may have held (a series of vertical staves seems more practical than a curved timber sleeper). The curve of Terrace 429 and the extent of Soil Layer 289 provide additional evidence that at least three of the corners of the building were very likely rounded. A pair of opposing doorways in the north and south walls, linked by a cross passage, is indicated by the arrangement and position of Features 171, 265, 274 and 282, the latter two denoting the position of wear immediately inside the door thresholds. As noted above, it is possible that the rebuilt south wall was extended and enlarged along a line between Postpit 223 and Postholes 224/228. Such a modification would explain the spatial relationship and identical ceramic phasing for Gully 284, the east gable-post [223], Feature 224 and Posthole 228, as well as the extent of the intervening layer of metalling [Layer 39].

Inside the building, Gully 171 appears to have served as the foundation for an internal partition wall that separated the floor space into a smaller west bay and a larger east bay. However, if this was the case, the floor space in the west bay during the later phase of occupation would have been virtually entirely taken up by the pits, assuming that they were open and not covered by some means. The pits were clearly intercut, but their common primary fill [149] indicates they were open as a single entity during CP3, when they would have formed a large single sunken-floored area. At the same time Pit 234 provided a further sunken-floor space within the east bay. No direct evidence was recovered to indicate whether these sunken-floor features were indeed covered, for example with wooden planking, or open, or indeed whether the sunken space was used for storage or insulation or provided the actual interior floor space, the latter at least considered unlikely by the writer.

The various pits and postholes outside Building 467 indicate associated agricultural structures inside a small attached yard or enclosure (Figure 4.2, Structure 464). The function of Pit 416 (Figure 4.19) remains unclear, as does the reason why a large earthenware vessel (FPN 490) was buried complete and inverted within it. The four surrounding stakeholes indicate it may have been enclosed or perhaps covered by a lightweight timber structure. Postholes 298 and 299 provide further evidence that other, more substantial, timber structures were sited in this central area of the yard. These may also have related to the use of Pit 416, although their spatial arrangement provided no clear indication one way or the other. The overall sequence of pits and ditches cut along the southern boundary of the enclosure (Figures 4.19 and 4.20) indicate that an earlier boundary [Ditch 348] may have been superseded by more general pit-digging [Pit 319 etc], possibly in part for the extraction of Fullers Earth clay (although see Section 8 below). The presence of Posthole 339 does no more than suggest that other Period III.2 timber structures were probably located immediately to the south of the farmstead, outside the excavation area.

AREA H: PERIODS III.2 AND III.3

The main timber building (Figures 4.14 and 4.45; Building 477) recorded in Area H was slightly larger in plan than that built in Area A (Building 467), although here, apart from the principal earthfast foundations, there was little supporting evidence to indicate the precise outline of the intervening walls. However, the size, number and organisation of its earthfast foundations indicate that, overall, it was probably a more substantial structure, whose earthfast foundations alone indicate a difference in construction between the southwestern and northeastern ends of the building. The principal foundations of the building were, with the exception of the southwestern post-pit, set out fairly symmetrically along an axial line drawn between Posthole 3088 and Post-pit 3013. The distinction between the use of similarly-sized postholes at the northeastern end of the building and larger, but also similarly sized post-pits at the southwestern end is considered significant – the implication being that the post-pits were dug to hold larger timbers that were required to support greater weight.

No direct structural or stratigraphic relationship was preserved between Pit Group 476 (Figure 4.45) and the principal foundations of the building, although the pottery phasing for the two groups is very similar and only distinguished by minor variations. Similarly, the spatial organisation of the two groups, particularly the location of Pit 3017 and its relationship to Posthole 3080, seems highly unlikely to be one of chance. Pit 3017 (Figure 4.14) was located close to the centre of Building 477. The four adjacent postholes [3068 etc] were organised roughly symmetrically around the edge of the pit. This arrangement could conceivably have formed part of a central internal roof support or perhaps, a structure surrounding a central hearth (although the pit contained no evidence of burning). However, in view of the clear and apparently deliberate difference between the post-pits and postholes that supported either end of the building, it is suggested that the structure is more likely to represent the location of a central wooden turriform structure, possibly one that provided access to an upper storey. The two pits [3049 and 3019] located immediately to the south of the central pit group were, in comparison with the central pit, relatively shallow and also separated by a very narrow ridge of natural clay. A smaller posthole [3074] was cut into the shoulder of Pit 3019, immediately adjacent to the ridge of natural clay. This arrangement is interpreted to reflect erosion and wear of the natural clay to either side of the threshold of a south-facing entrance or doorway, where the narrow ridge of clay reflected the location of a timber sill that protected the underlying clay. On that basis, Posthole 3074 may have held an earthfast post and jamb for a door.

The inclusion of Structure 475 as a contemporary element of Building 477 is certainly arguable and not conclusively proven by the excavated evidence. In another location it would happily conform to the range of simple four-posted structures often interpreted as raised grain stores and, since carbonised cereals were certainly recovered from many of the Period III postholes and post-pits around and about it (Section 5.14), such an interpretation is possible here. The suggestion here that the structure formed a contemporary element of Building 477 rests largely on the spatial relationships and the virtual absence of evidence for settlement-related activity in Area H as a whole after CP3.

The southwestern side of Structure 475, indicated by Postholes 3190 and 3189 (the latter seeming to respect the gable-post, 3088) could possibly have followed the interpolated line of a curved section of wall (of similar plan-form to the corners of Building 467 in Area A) that ran between Postholes 3005 and 3088. If so, the position of Posthole 3189, sited inside the east gable-post [3088] remains problematic, as its construction would seem to have entailed

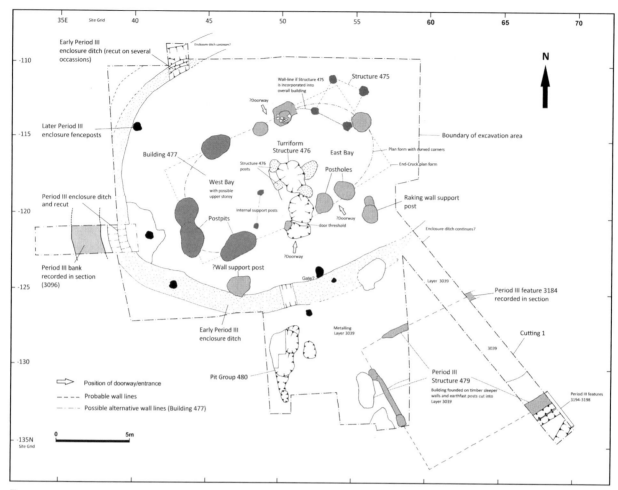

FIGURE 4.45

Area H – arrangement and interpretation of Period III features

demolishing a section of the wall of the building. If one excludes this possibility and interprets Posthole 3088 as having held a standard single end-cruck timber, then the likelihood that Structure 475 was contemporary with Structure 477 is less likely still and the fact that Posthole 3189 appears to respect the gable-post, 3088, may therefore be one of chance and not an indicator that they were contemporary structures.

In its earliest form, Building 477 was set inside a small semicircular enclosure formed, at least to the west and south, by a sequence of shallow curving ditches, which were recut on a number of occasions, located immediately inside an earth bank, as indicated by Layer 3096/3097 (Figure 4.36). Whether the ditches continued to the east of the building to confine it within a complete oval or possibly D-shaped enclosure, was not confirmed by excavation, although the geophysical survey data, specifically geophysical features m9 and m10 (Section 3.2), indicate that this probably was the case. The group of stone post-settings located just inside the line of the boundary ditches to the west and south of the building, interpreted to represent the foundations for some form of timber fence, were added at a slightly later stage during CP3. Most were located just inside the line of the latest of the ditch cuts, although Posthole 3036 was cut into the fill of Ditch 3023 and clearly post-dated this part of the earlier enclosure ditch.

A second timber building (Structure 479) is suggested by an associated group of features located immediately to the southeast of Building 477, in the southeastern corner of excavation Area H (Figures 4.29 and 4.45, Structure 479). The group appeared to represent the southwestern end of a rectangular timber structure founded upon smaller earthfast posts and intervening sill-beams or foundation slots. Little else by way of interpretation can be offered concerning the structure, other than that it seems to have been rectangular in plan and somewhat less substantial than Building 477 and possibly of slightly later date, as indicated by its relationship with Ditch 3023 in section. It was considered likely that the series of shallow recut linear features (Figures 4.29 and 4.45, Features 3194–3197) revealed at the southeastern end of Cutting 1, incorporated a series of recut foundation slots for the southeast wall of this same building. If so, the collective evidence suggests a structure that was approximately 5m wide and in excess of 8m long.

It is difficult to provide any clear interpretation for a third group of pits and postholes (Figure 4.45; Pit Group 480) located immediately to the west of

EXCAVATIONS

Structure 479. They may have represented part of a third, separate, timber structure that was only partially exposed, as two of the postholes were of the right size, but the overall arrangement of the group provided no clear indication one way or the other.

Period IV (Ceramic Phases 4–5; cAD 1200–1275)

Introduction

Evidence of 13th-century (Period IV) structures was confined to the farmstead in Area A, where two new stone buildings (Figures 4.2 and 4.4; Structures 462 and 465) were constructed during ceramic phase 4, the early 13th century. Both buildings appear to have continued in use until the later 13th century (CP5), when they were replaced by Period V Buildings 460 and 463 (Figure 4.2). Period IV marks an important transition from the use of timber to stone as the main building material on the site and also seems to mark a general cessation of ditch and pit digging throughout the settlement as a whole. Building 462 was built directly above the filled pits, ditches, and postholes of the Period III timber building (Structure 467). Building 465 appeared to have been slightly larger than Building 462 overall, although it was less fully preserved and its interpretation relies upon fragments of drystone masonry and soil features that were of fairly limited extent.

The boundary of the farmstead in Area A defined in Period III was maintained, although it was redefined by earth banks and stone revetments that replaced the earlier ditch boundaries. Despite this, the earlier boundaries were maintained very precisely, for example the north wall of Building 462 followed the exact line of Period III Ditch 363 (Figure 4.16). This continuity in the layout of the settlement boundaries across a period of extensive reorganisation is important, as it implies the continuity of established land ownership. Elsewhere, evidence of Period IV activity was limited. Layers sealed beneath Period V Building 460 indicated that a yardsoil [185/193] continued to accumulate whilst a distinctive soil horizon (Figure 4.46, Layer 346) accumulated at the southern end of the

FIGURE 4.46A
Area A – Period IV Wall 13 overlying fill of Period III Pit 234. Facing N. Scales 2m

FIGURE 4.46B
Area A – masonry forming th SE corner of Period IV Building 462. Facing W. Scale 2m

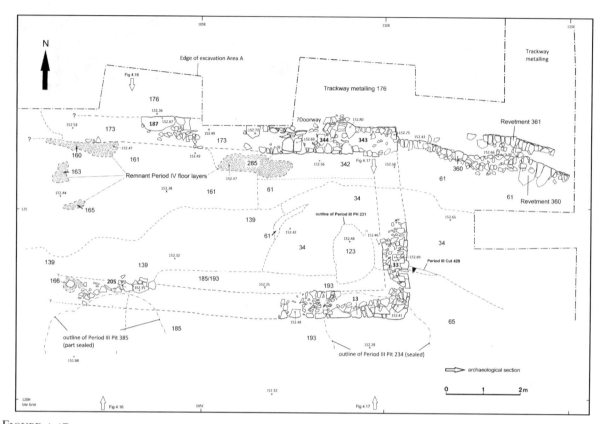

FIGURE 4.47
Area A – Period IV Building 462 and associated features and deposits

yard (Structure 464), sealing the earlier Period III pits and boundary ditches.

Building 462 (Figures 4.2, 4.4, 4.41, 4.46A, 4.46B, 4.47 and 4.53)

Only the eastern part of the building was substantially preserved (Figure 4.47, Walls 13, 33, 187, 205 and 343). The walls were built above Period III pit and ditch fills (Figures 4.16 and 4.17) and were formed of roughly coursed and faced limestone rubble bonded with natural clay and smaller stones (Figure 4.48). The western end of the building had been destroyed. The remains of a north-facing doorway [344] were preserved at the northeastern corner, where the masonry [343] survived to five courses. Fragments of internal floor layers (Figure 4.47; Layers 160, 285 and 342) were only preserved where they had been sealed and protected beneath the walls of the subsequent Period V building (Building 460).

The surviving section of the north wall [343/187] was 7m long, although the extent of Layer 160 (Figure 4.47) indicated that it was originally at least 9.5m long. The southern half of the east wall [33] was preserved for 2.5m, although its junction with Wall 343 had been cut by a later (Period V) drain (66). At the eastern end, a short section of the south wall [13] was bonded with Wall 33, whilst to the west a heavily disturbed 2m section of the south wall (205) indicated its overall length was at least 9m. Collectively, this evidence indicates the building was 5m wide and at least 9.5m long.

The walls were built above Period III ditch and pit fills (Figures 4.16 and 4.17) that contained pottery of CP4 or earlier. The relationship of Wall 187/343 (CP4) to Ditch Fill 362 (CP2) suggested that the northern side of the building plot may have been levelled prior to construction. The south wall (Walls 13 and 205) was built along the northern edge of Period III Pit 221, above the fill of Pit 234 (Figure 4.17) and at the edge of Pit 385 (Figure 4.16). This precise layout, coupled with the ceramic dating (CP5) from Pit Fill 220 (Figure 4.17), suggests that both the earlier Period III pits were at least evident as surface features and possibly still partially open at the time of construction, and were therefore a factor in the positioning and construction of the wall. Wall 187 lay above a distinctive sandy layer [173] which produced pottery of CP4. This arrangement, combined with the fact that the walls did not seal any pottery later than CP4, suggests a construction date for the building around the turn of the 13th century (late CP4).

FLOOR LAYERS
A group of texturally similar charcoal-rich soil layers and patches (Figure 4.47, Layers 160, 163, 165, 166 and 285) containing pottery of CP5 were preserved inside the building. All were of limited extent, having been preserved beneath either the walls [11] or floor layers [46] of the subsequent Period V building.

EXCAVATIONS

FIGURE 4.48

Area A – the SE corner of Period IV Building 465 as indicated by wall fragments 55 and 391, the former reused as the entrance threshold of Period V Building 463. Facing N. Scale 2m

Layers 285 and 160 represented remnants of a floor layer, which accumulated immediately inside the north wall [187/343]. This relationship indicated that the wall [187] originally extended at least as far as the westernmost extent of Layer 160. Layer 342 sealed Period III Ditches 247 and 248 and butted the internal face of Wall 343. This indicated that it also represented the remains of an earlier floor layer preserved in the northeastern corner of the building. Pottery from that part of the layer [342] which was sealed and not subject to later reworking (as Deposit 61 was), was dated no later than CP5. Other remnants of floor layers [163 and 165] were preserved in shallow depressions in the upper surface of Layer 161 and sealed beneath Period V Floor Layer 46. Deposit 166 was preserved adjacent to an area of highly disturbed remnant masonry [Wall 205] and above a redeposited natural clay [139] that sealed Period III Ditch 251 (Figure 4.16).

Building 465 (Figures 4.4 and 4.56)

Features relating to the second Period IV building in Area A (Building 465) were preserved, either beneath, or incorporated into later (Period V) Building 463. Again, the structural remains were poorly preserved and consisted of short sections of limestone masonry and a fragment of an internal floor layer [315] preserved beneath a later (Period V) wall. Remnants of the north [115], east [391] and south [55 and 324] walls were preserved, as was part of the outer face of the north wall [210], which had been incorporated as a revetment in the Period V building. The building clearly appeared to extend beyond the excavation area to the west.

WALLS (FIGURES 4.4, 4.48 AND 4.56)

All the wall fragments were formed of drystone limestone rubble and, with the exception of Wall 115,

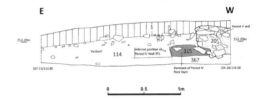

FIGURE 4.49

Area A – North facing section through Wall 20 of Period V Building 463 showing remnant Period IV floor layer 315 and inferred line of Period IV wall 391

only a single course of masonry survived. Walls 391 and 55 were bonded to form the southeastern corner of the building, although only Wall 391 retained both an internal and external face. Wall 324 was represented by just two stones (Figure 4.56) whose southern edge formed a line with the southern edge of Wall 55. Further evidence that this represented a fragment of the south wall was indicated by Period III Feature 322 (Figure 4.12), whose limited extent indicated that it represented a part of a once more extensive deposit that had been preserved beneath a later linear feature. The external face of Wall 210 was in line with the external face of Wall 115 (Figure 4.56) and reflected a further part of the same. This, albeit limited, structural evidence indicated a building that was originally 6m wide and at least 10m long, slightly larger than Building 462.

FLOOR LAYER 315 (FIGURES 4.4 AND 4.49)

This fragment of an internal floor layer, Layer 315, was roughly rectangular in plan and contained pods of reworked natural clay and gravel. It was preserved beneath Period V Wall 20 (Figure 4.49) and butted the internal face of Wall 391. The layer produced pottery of CP5 and sealed a layer of early yardsoil [367] containing pottery of CP2.

The pottery from Layer 315 indicated that Building 465 was in use during CP5 (*c*AD 1250–1300)

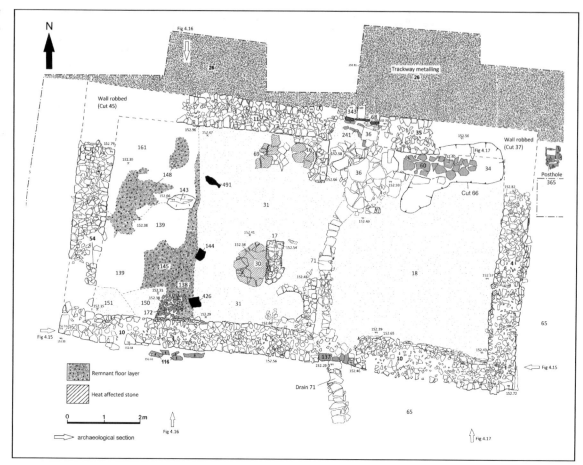

FIGURE 4.50

Area A – Period V Building 460 showing remnant Period V.1 floor layers and deposits preserved in the western bay

and may have continued in use until the end of that period. The date of construction seems slightly earlier, as none of the walls sealed material any later than CP4. On that basis, it seems likely that the building was constructed later in CP4, during the early 13th century.

Period IV: Other Evidence

THE TRACKWAY (FEATURE 474)
The trackway continued in use during Period IV. The surface was metalled with a layer of small rounded stones and cobbles (Figures 4.16 and 4.47, Layer 176) that butted the north wall [187] of Building 462.

REVETMENTS 360 AND 361
These drystone revetments (Figure 4.47) flanked the southern side of the trackway and butted the northeast corner of Building 462. They were formed of roughly coursed limestone rubble and built directly above the fill of Period III Ditch 363 (Figure 4.13) and followed the line of that earlier boundary precisely. Revetment 360 butted the eastern end of Wall 343 and was the later of the two features, as Revetment 361 was sealed by a layer of later trackway cobbles [26].

PIT 221
The bulk of the Period III pit was filled during CP5 (Figure 4.17, Fill 220), whilst Building 462 was either being built or was in use. Much of the fill was homogeneous and appeared to have been deposited rapidly, as it was sealed by a significant accumulation of yardsoil [193], a deposit that also accumulated during the occupation of Building 462.

THE YARD – STRUCTURE 464: YARDSOIL 193 AND 185
This homogeneous soil layer (Figures 4.16 and 4.17, Layers 193 and 185) accumulated immediately south of Building 462 and sealed pit fill 220. The layer was texturally indistinguishable from the latest (Period V) yardsoil [65], but, where it was sealed beneath Period V Wall 10 (Figures 4.16 and 4.17, Layer 193), the pottery was no later than CP5. Evidence that certain areas of the yard were also being eroded during this phase was indicated by the contaminated fills of Period III Feature 284 [224] and Posthole 228, both of which contained intrusive CP5 pottery.

LAYERS 316, 346 AND 330
These irregular layers (Figure 4.4) accumulated along the southern edge of the yard and produced pottery of CP5, plus significant amounts of occupation debris. The deposits reduced the slope of

EXCAVATIONS

FIGURE 4.51
Area A showing Period V Building 460 during excavation with the south wall [10] overlying Period III cut features. Facing N. Scales 2m

the natural terrace that had been a feature of the Period III farmstead and sealed the complex of Period III ditches and pits (Figures 4.19 and 4.20) cut into it. A patch of limestone rubble [332] was impressed into the upper surface of Layer 346. The bulk of the rubble was situated at the crest of the slope and, although it was not coursed, possibly represented the remains of a simple stone revetment or wall. The layer also filled Period III Ditches 350 and 404, and Posthole 422. It is therefore possible that the earlier features continued to form the southern boundary of the farmstead during the earliest part of Period IV.

The latest Period IV activity was represented by an oval soil layer [330], which accumulated around a large limestone boulder [459] of uncertain function, but possibly used either as an anvil or craft block, or as a simple step up to a sleeping loft.

Period V (Ceramic Phases 5–6; Late 13th and 14th Century)

Introduction

During Period V, a series of new stone buildings, including a farmhouse and byre or barn, were constructed in Area A (Figures 4.2 and 4.5, Structures 460, 463 and 466). They were built during CP5 (Period V.1a), although the earliest evidence relating to their occupation and use dates to CP6 (Period V.1b). The great majority of the evidence associated with their occupation relates to their latest use and abandonment during the second half of the 14th century (Periods V.2 and V.3).

The buildings were abandoned during CP6 (Period V.3), although there is evidence to suggest that some sections of masonry remained standing after *c*AD 1400 (CP7, Period VI.1).

All of the Period V buildings in Area A were constructed in roughly coursed and faced limestone rubble using drystone technique, although certain sections of the masonry, in particular the northwestern and northeastern corners of the farmhouse (Building 460), had been destroyed by later robber pits (Figure 4.62). Structures associated with the farmhouse and the byre (Building 463) included a square kiln or oven house (Structure 466) and a stone hayrick base (Structure 473). Many of the internal features and associated fittings, particularly those inside the main farmhouse (Building 460), were well preserved and included hearths, ovens, drains and walls. The position of postpads also provided evidence of internal partitions. Outside the buildings, soil and domestic refuse continued to accumulate in the area of the yard (Figure 4.5, Structure 464).

At about the same time as the farmhouse (Building 460) was constructed in Area A (Period V.1a) a further new stone building was built on a levelled platform adjacent to the trackway in Area B (Figures 4.64 and 4.65, Structure 461). The building had been substantially destroyed by later stone-robbing, although some of its masonry foundations and a flight of entrance steps (Figure 4.65) were preserved, plus a ground level hearth that was located at the eastern end of the building.

Building 460: Period V.1a (Figures 4.5 and 4.50)

The farmhouse was built above the remains of Period IV Building 462 and the infilled Period III features (Figures 4.15, 4.16 and 4.17). Its construction is dated to the second half of the 13th century (CP5; *c*AD 1275), as none of its walls [4, 10, 11, 54 and 35] or internal features [16, 30, 42, 143, 60 and 71] sealed pottery later than CP5. The building was rectangular with its long axis aligned west to east

FIGURE 4.52

Area A showing Period V Building 460 during excavation and fully excavated Period III features 251 and 385 of Building 467 in the foreground. Facing N. Scales 2m

and measured 12.4m × 6m in plan. The roughly coursed and faced rubble walls were preserved for a maximum of eight courses and to a height of 800mm (Figures 4.51 and 4.52).

WALL 54 (FIGURES 4.5, 4.15 AND 4.50)

The west wall of the building was preserved to a maximum height of eight courses of masonry and 300mm and was built above Deposit 161, the upper fill of Period III boundary ditches dated to CP4 (Figure 4.16) and a layer of reworked natural clay (Figure 4.15, Deposit 139). At the northern end, it was cut and completely robbed out by a post-medieval pit [Cut 45]. Part of the southern end had also been robbed, although a single course of masonry remained indicating that it was originally bonded with the south wall [10].

WALL 10 (FIGURES 4.15, 4.16, 4.17 AND 4.51)

The south wall was preserved to a maximum of nine thin courses of standing masonry and up to 700mm in height, although the eastern end leaned outwards (Figure 4.16). The masonry at the western end was constructed above the fill [156/252] of Period III Pit 179 (Figure 4.15). To accommodate the depression over the earlier pit, the masonry was stepped down and deeper at this point (Figure 4.51) and tabular limestone rubble [116] was rammed end-on against the external face as support, possibly in an attempt to halt the development of the perilous lean outwards. It is during this process that pottery of CP5 appears to have contaminated the upper (Period III) pit fill [156]. The centre and eastern end of the wall sealed a deposit of yardsoil that had accumulated during Period IV (Figures 4.16 and 4.17, Layers 185 and 193), which produced pottery sherds of CP5.

WALL 4 (FIGURES 4.5, 4.15, 4.50 AND 4.62)

The east wall [4] sealed an earlier yardsoil [193], although at its northern end it was laid directly above the natural clay [34]. The northern end was also cut by a robber pit (Figure 4.62, Cut 37) whose fill [14] contained early post-medieval pottery of CP7.

WALLS 11 AND 35 (FIGURES 4.16 AND 4.50)

The north wall consisted of two sections of masonry [Walls 11 and 35], both of which were essentially of drystone construction although possibly also incorporating some deliberate clay infill. The wall was butted by stones forming the threshold of a north doorway [68 and 343]. The doorway was 1.2m wide and incorporated a raised stone sill [68] that was some 100mm high along the outer edge, and formed by three limestone slabs set edge-on and side by side. Wall 35 sealed Period IV floor Layer 342 and overlay Period IV Wall 343. The eastern end and junction with Wall 4 was cut by a post-medieval robber pit [37]. Wall 11 overlay the north wall (Figure 4.16, Wall 187) of Period IV Building 462 and sealed a remnant of a Period IV floor layer [160]. The western corner and junction with Wall 54 had also been destroyed by a second post-medieval robber pit [45].

TROUGH 66 (FIGURES 4.17 AND 4.50)

This sunken stone feature was built into the floor in the northeastern corner of the building and cut

EXCAVATIONS

FIGURE 4.53
Area A showing the eastern end of Period V Building 460 as excavated and the southeast corner of Period IV Building 462, revealed by the excavation of Period V floor layer 18. Facing S. Scales 2m

the west wall [33] of Period IV Building 462. The base of the trough was lower than the bottom course of Wall 35, although, as preserved, the cut for the trough was less than 100mm deep. The base and southern face were lined with limestone slabs and rubble [60], which joined the northern end of a narrow stone-lined drain [71]. The eastern end was disturbed by a robber pit [37] and filled with loose rubble [58] which sealed a thin silty primary fill [59].

DRAINS 71 AND 241 (FIGURES 4.50 AND 4.53)
Drain 71 (Figure 4.53) curved through the eastern half of the building; its level running from northeast to south, from the trough [60/66] in the east bay, beneath the cross passage and out below the south doorway [137] into the yard. The drain channel was cut into Layer 193 and was carefully lined along its sides and base with small limestone slabs and rubble. The internal channel was capped with larger limestone slabs, several of which appeared to be fragments of reused limestone roof tiles. The cover slabs were in turn partly sealed by the latest floor layer [18]. At the junction with the trough [60/66], it was connected with a shorter section of covered stone drain [241] that ran beneath a group of larger threshold slabs [36] laid immediately inside the northern doorway.

OVENS 16 AND 42 (FIGURES 4.50 AND 4.54)
Two identical circular stone structures, both either ovens or bases for boiling furnaces, were located centrally, on opposing sides of the middle bay. The north oven [16] was 800mm in diameter and butted the internal face of Wall 11. It was built above ditch Fill 161 (CP4) and was formed of rough drystone masonry preserved to a maximum of three courses. The base of the oven was lined with four scorched limestone slabs. Similar scorched slabs [69] were set in the floor immediately outside the entrance. Oven 42 was constructed against the opposing wall [10], above Layer 185 (CP5) and was also preserved to between one and three courses of rubble masonry. The feature also overlay the edging stones of the drain [71]. It was built in precisely the same fashion as the northern oven, but did not contain base slabs and had a slightly smaller diameter (750 mm). When excavated, the feature contained a complete medieval iron sickle (SF569; Figure 5.46, 68).

HEARTH 30 AND HEARTH WALL 17 (FIGURES 4.50 AND 4.55)
The hearth was formed of a closely-packed group of very heavily scorched limestone slabs set at floor level, which butted a low rubble wall [17]. Both features were constructed above Layer 185 (CP5) and slightly to the southwest of the centre of the building, inside the middle bay. The hearthstones were about 100mm thick and a rectangular patch at the centre had weathered to a fine grey powder as a result of continual scorching. The back wall of the hearth, Wall 17, was preserved to a height of just 250mm. The stonework forming the western face was heavily scorched and carefully curved at the southern end. The stonework on the east face was also scorched, although far less intensely.

FIGURE 4.54
Area A – Period V Building 460 during excavation showing Period III trackway metalling and ditches partly exposed in the left foreground. Facing E. Scales 500mm and 2m

FIGURE 4.55

Area A – the western part of Period V Building 460 during excavation with Feature numbers added. Showing Period III trackway metalling [174] and Period IV wall fragment [187] in the foreground. Facing S. Scales 1m and 2m

EXCAVATIONS

PACKING 172 (FIGURES 4.50 AND 4.55)
A tightly-packed square of limestone cobbles [172] butted the internal face of Wall 10. The feature was laid above pit Fill 186 (CP4) and sealed by floor Layer 46 (CP6). The cobbles were not scorched and their purpose was not clear, although they may have formed a foundation for an internal structural feature, possibly a timber cruck-base, or have been related to the attempt to support the outward leaning of the wall.

BOULDER 143 (FIGURES 4.16, 4.50, 4.55 AND 4.61)
The large irregular limestone boulder was set into the floor in the west bay of the building, where it stood to a height of 250mm above the soil floor. A dense concentration of finds were recovered from the latest floor layers that surrounded the boulder (Figure 4.61, Layers 135 and 46). The collection included a complete glazed jug (Figure 5.19, 167 and 5.22), a large glazed cistern decorated with a stylised stag head (Figures 5.20 and 5.21) and a group of four bronze cauldron feet (Figures 5.50 and 5.51). The finds appeared to reflect objects broken in-situ and therefore possibly related to the function of the boulder. Nonetheless, the purpose of the boulder was unclear and a range of interpretations is possible. These include its use as an anvil or as a makeshift trestle or table base, or perhaps as a step that allowed access to a loft sleeping space, a crude *solar* built over the northern part of the bay in the space of the roof rafters.

THRESHOLD SLABS 36 (FIGURE 4.50)
A group of large and medium sized limestone slabs [36] were laid immediately inside the north doorway [68], over Drain 241. The slabs butted the rear of the northern oven [16] and the edge-on stones that formed the threshold sill [68]. The surface was approximately 100mm higher than the soil floor inside the building and 200mm lower than the top of the threshold sill [68].

Building 460: Period V.1b (Figure 4.50)

The earliest evidence of occupation and activity inside the building was represented by a series of remnant floor layers (Figure 4.50; Layers 138, 145, 148, 150 and 151) preserved in the west bay. The layers were sealed beneath later floor layers (Figure 4.61, Layers 46, 31 and 72) and contained pottery of CP6.

FLOOR LAYERS 138, 145 AND 148 (FIGURE 4.50)
These remnant floor layers were texturally similar and contained reworked natural clay and small limestone fragments. They filled shallow depressions in the underlying layers [139 and 186] and were all less than 50mm thick. Their distribution suggested that at this early stage the west bay was already subdivided into two rooms along a line indicated by the eastern edge of Layer 138.

LAYERS 150 AND 151 (FIGURE 4.50)
Two discrete layers [150 and 151] were preserved inside the southwestern corner of the building, both approximately 50mm thick. Layer 150 partially overlay a squared stone packing [172] and merged with Layers 138 and 151 with no clearly defined boundary. The deposit contained an unusually high concentration of animal bones, very likely domestic rubbish (Section 5.13). Layer 151 contained significant amounts of reworked natural clay and brash. Both layers overlay pit Fill 186 (CP5).

LAYERS 31 AND 18 (FIGURES 4.17, 4.50 AND 4.55)
Floor layers 31 and 18 were extensive and texturally indistinguishable. They appeared to have accumulated gradually throughout the occupation of the building (Period V.2), although the earliest material seems to have been laid down at the same time as Floor Layers 138, 145, and 148 (Figure 4.16). Because of their homogeneous nature, it was not possible to identify a discrete horizon associated with the earlier (Period V.1b) use of the building.

Structure 463: Period V.1 (Figures 4.5, 4.56 and 4.57)

Structure 463 replaced Period IV Building 465. This new stone building was rectangular in plan and also formed of roughly coursed and faced drystone limestone rubble. The western end of the building was not exposed, although the part that was excavated indicated that it was originally 8m wide and at least 9.8m long. The south and east walls [242 and 20] were well preserved, but the southeastern corner [81, 82 and 243] had suffered considerable later disturbance. The northern face of the building was open and formed by a low stone revetment [210], a reuse of masonry that formed the north wall of Period IV Building 465. A narrow doorway was located in the east wall; its stone threshold [55] formed by the foundation masonry of Period IV Wall 55. Inside the building a complex arrangement of rubble soakaways was set into the floor (Figure 4.57). Pottery indicates a construction date during CP5, broadly contemporary with the construction of Building 460, as none of the walls or internal features sealed pottery of CP6, although the east wall [20] did preserve the remains of an earlier floor layer (Figure 4.49, Layer 315) containing pottery of CP5. This ceramic dating indicates a period of use contemporary with the occupation of Building 460 during the late 13th and 14th centuries.

WALLS 20 AND 22 (FIGURES 4.49 AND 4.56)
Wall 20 formed the eastern end of the building and was preserved to a maximum height of 700mm and up to five courses of roughly coursed and faced

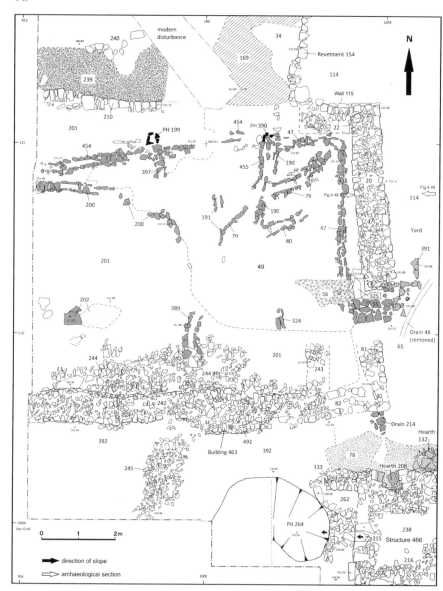

FIGURE 4.56

Area A – plan showing Period V Building 463 and part of Structure 466 as excavated with remnants of Period IV Building 465

FIGURE 4.57
Area A showing Period V Building 463 during excavation. Facing SE. Scale 2m

limestone rubble masonry. It was built at the edge of a low terrace formed by an earlier yard soil [367] and sealed a fragment of Period IV floor Layer 315 (Figure 4.49), both of which contained pottery of CP5. At the northern end it was bonded with a short section of the north wall [22] and butted the remains of Period IV Wall 115. The southern end of the wall was supported on a foundation of larger limestone blocks [325] that had been placed quite precisely, immediately inside the southeast corner of the earlier Period IV stone building (Building 465).

WALL 242 (FIGURES 4.56 AND 4.58)
The south wall [242] was preserved to a maximum of five courses of drystone masonry and a height of 450mm. The western end was not exposed, although its full extent is indicated by the preliminary earthwork survey (Figure 1.7) and contour surveys (archive). The wall was built along the edge of a slight terrace in the underlying layers. To compensate for the uneven surface, the base of the outer stonework was stepped down approximately 200mm and, in the middle section, was supported by a short foundation layer (Figure 4.56, Wall 492) that extended outside the outer edge of the wall by as much as 400mm. The eastern end of the wall was poorly preserved and difficult to interpret. It probably originally continued, as indicated by two wall fragments [81 and 82], to form the southeastern corner of the building, although that relationship was complicated by a short section of stone-lined drain [214], which ran through, although not clearly beneath, the junction of the two. Wall 243 was represented by a single course of masonry and appeared to represent a short return wall inside the building. It is therefore possible that Walls 81, 82 and 243 enclosed a small drained chamber situated inside the southeast corner of the building.

REVETMENT WALL 210 (FIGURE 4.56)
The north face of the building was delineated by a low revetment wall [210] that was formed by the bottom two or three courses of masonry of the north wall of Period IV Building 465. The gap between the eastern end of the revetment and Wall 22 corresponded with the location of two stone post-settings [199 and 390], which may have flanked a wide north-facing doorway. Alternatively, they may have represented two of a larger number of small posts that supported a wooden lintel which crossed the open north front.

POSTHOLES 199 AND 390 (FIGURE 4.56)
These rubble post-packings were roughly squared in plan and set about 1m inside the north face of the building. Both of the internal sockets would have held a timber of up to 200mm in diameter and each was formed from small flat stones that were set edge-on into a shallow cut in the natural clay [201]. Only three of the vertical stones relating to Feature 390 remained, perhaps because it was located at the junction of a group of rubble soakaways.

FIGURE 4.58
Area A showing the south wall [242] of Period V Building 463 with demolition rubble and small cobbled path immediately outside. Structure 466 and the southern part of the Yard beyond. Facing E. Scales 2m

SOAKAWAYS 47, 79, 80, 190, 191, 200, 397, 389, 454 AND 455 (FIGURES 4.56 AND 4.57)
This complex of small rubble drains was set into the floor of the building and cut Period III.1 Layer 189. All were constructed in the same fashion, whereby a narrow channel cut in the clay was edged with vertical or slanting stones and covered with small flat slabs. The width of the internal channels varied between 50mm and 200mm, although none contained any distinctive fill. Some, for example Features 79, 190 and 455, were clearly intercut, although their generally poor state of preservation made the determination of any sequence impossible. Overall the features would have drained the building from north to south and were most commonly replaced between post packings 198 and 390, most likely as a result of heavy erosion and damage inside the north entrance of the building. Soakaway 389 butted Wall 242 and would have allowed groundwater to filter out through the masonry voids. Soakaway 47 ran into a shallow patch of coarse gravel and small stones [56] which also seems to have been designed to assist drainage.

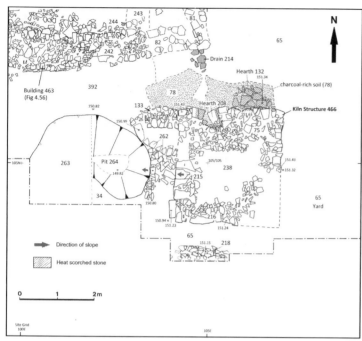

FIGURE 4.59
Area A – plan showing Period V Kiln 466 and associated features as excavated

LAYER 244 (FIGURE 4.56)
This layer consisted of densely packed limestone stones and cobbles that butted Wall 242 and overlay Soakaway 389. Although it was not fully excavated, it appeared to represent a general floor levelling layer at the rear of the building, perhaps also laid to assist drainage.

Structure 466: Period V.1 (Figures 4.56, 4.59 and 4.60)

This small square structure located in the southwestern corner of the yard (Figure 4.60) was formed of roughly coursed limestone rubble that was faced externally. A small oven (Hearth 208) built into the north wall contained large quantities of woody charcoal and some carbonised cereal grains (Section 5.14). Other features associated with the structure included a stone hearth [132] laid at floor level just to the side of the oven and a pit [264], possibly used for raking-out spent fuel or produce. The walls sealed a fragment of yardsoil containing pottery of CP5. This indicated that it was also built during that phase and was contemporary with the construction of Buildings 460 and 463.

WALLS 75, 133, 215 AND 216 (FIGURE 4.59)
The walls [75, 215 and 216] forming the structure were of drystone and built in roughly coursed and faced limestone rubble that was preserved to a maximum height of 300mm. Together, they

FIGURE 4.60
Area A showing Period V Kiln 466 during excavation. Facing S. Scales 1m and 2m

appeared to have formed the solid base of a small structure that was roughly 3m square in plan. All the masonry was coursed and faced on the outside, although the space within the walls contained only loose limestone rubble. This suggested that the structure was originally a solid pedestal with no internal chamber or void at ground level. Several large flat stones on the upper surface of the west wall [215] were angled and smoothed, possibly to form part of a simple sluice, flue or rake-hole associated with an adjacent pit [264]. Wall 133 butted Walls 75 and 215 and joined a short section of stone revetment [262] laid at the eastern edge of the pit.

HEARTH CHAMBER 208 (FIGURE 4.59)
The hearth chamber opened to the north and was 400m deep, 500mm wide, and preserved to a height of 450mm. It was bonded with the north wall [75]. The sides and back were formed by vertical limestone slabs that were all heavily scorched; the slab forming the west side had been disturbed and sloped at c45 degrees. The base of the recess was formed by a single limestone slab which, surprisingly, was not scorched.

HEARTH 132 (FIGURES 4.59 AND 4.60)
The hearth base consisted of a roughly rectangular arrangement of heavily scorched limestone slabs set into the surface of the yardsoil [65]. The exterior face of Wall 75 was also heavily scorched directly above the hearth stones.

PIT 264 AND REVETMENT 262 (FIGURE 4.59)
The pit was approximately 1m deep and had an asymmetric V-shaped profile. It was cut into the natural clay [34] from a horizon within Layer 392 (CP6); a layer indistinguishable from the general yardsoil [65]. The eastern face of the pit was roughly lined with rubble, which was pressed into the clay from the lower edge of Wall 215 to the base of the pit. A single course of stone revetment at the shoulder of the pit butted Walls 133 and 215. The position of the pit, its lining and the smoothed stones in Wall 215, suggests it was dug to receive material from Structure 466. The pit was filled in the main by random limestone rubble and had a thin primary clay fill [263] which produced pottery of CP6.

Period V.1: Other Features

REVETMENT 154 (FIGURE 4.56)
The revetment was formed of tabular limestone rubble that was faced on the west side and extended between the south wall [10] of Building 460 and the north face [22] of Building 463. In doing so, it would have separated the main yard [114] from the north entrance of Building 463. The north end of the feature overlay the upper fill [156] of Period III Pit 179, although its southern end lay directly above the natural clay [34].

POSTHOLE 365 (FIGURE 4.50)
The posthole measured 600mm × 400mm in plan and enclosed a rectangular socket that was 200mm deep. It was set into Layer 61 (CP5) and formed of a solid packing of edge-on limestone slabs. Its position, immediately adjacent to the outer face of Wall 4, suggested it represented the northern end of a timber fenceline that separated the north side of the yard from the trackway.

Period V: Phase V.2 Area A

This phase relates to the latest use and abandonment of the farmstead in Area A during the second half of the 14th century (CP6). Most of the evidence was represented by occupation layers, although a number of minor structural features, for example the hayrick base (Structure 473), also appear to have been added.

Building 460: Period V.2 (Figure 4.61)

During the latest phase of occupation of the building, floor Layers 31 and 18 appear to have continued to variously accumulate and erode, whilst very similar material (Layer 46) sealed the earlier (Period V.1b) floor layers at the western end of the building. The soils accumulated throughout the building; against the walls, the boulder, the entrance slabs, the hearth and both ovens, and completely covered the stone drain [71]. A series of more restricted occupation layers (Figure 4.61; Layers 64, 67, 73, 72, 135, 136 and 142) also accumulated in the western half of the building, whilst a group of postpads [144, 426, 491, and possibly 427] were set into the soil floor, indicating the maintenance (and presumably the repair) of a timber partition structure that subdivided the west half of the building into two smaller rooms, the middle and west bays.

FLOOR LAYER 18 (FIGURES 4.17 AND 4.61)
The layer was generally around 100mm thick and sealed an earlier yard soil [185] (Figure 4.17), pit Fill 123, and the natural clay [34]. It also sealed the stone drain [71] and partially overlay Period IV Walls 13 and 33, although its surface was only slightly higher than the lowest course of Wall 10. The quantity of finds recovered from the layer was very small and significantly less than that recovered from equivalent floor layers [31 and 46] in the western half of the building.

LAYER 64 (FIGURE 4.61)
A thin rectangular patch of charcoal-rich soil overlay Layer 18 and butted Wall 4. The wall adjacent was heavily scorched.

FLOOR LAYERS 31 AND 46 (FIGURES 4.16 AND 4.61)
These layers were texturally indistinguishable and their division was based on their relationship to earlier floor layers and the group of probable

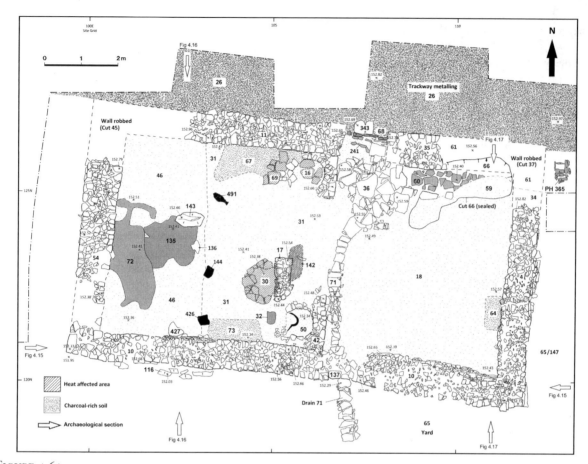

FIGURE 4.61

Area A – plan showing Period V Building 460 as excavated with latest CP5 features and floor layers

postpads [491, 144, 426 and 427] that appeared to have divided the western half of the building into two smaller rooms; a chamber or inner room and a kitchen/hall. Layer 31 sealed ditch Fill 161 (CP4), yardsoil 185 (CP5) and reworked natural clay 139. It was less than 50mm thick and butted the hearth and both stone ovens. The deposit contained a greater concentration of small stones and gravel between the north oven and the hearth.

Layer 46 (Figure 4.16) butted Walls 11, 54 and 10, and sealed Period V.1b floor layers 138, 145, 148, 150 and 151. The deposit produced a very large assemblage of structural, personal and household objects (Figures 7.11 to 7.21) including a silver Groat of Edward III dated AD 1351–1352 (Section 5.4). The character and distribution of finds of various classes recovered from the interior of the building is examined in detail in Section 7.

LAYER 67 (FIGURE 4.61)

The layer was roughly rectangular in plan and less than 50mm deep. It butted a group of scorched limestone slabs (69) and consisted of loose charcoal-rich sandy clay, which filled a shallow depression in the surface of floor Layer 31. Large amounts of domestic pottery, including a complete dripping dish (Figure 5.17, 140) were recovered from the layer. The western edge of the deposit respected the line of the suggested partition wall indicated by the group of stone postpads.

DEPOSITS 32 AND 73 (FIGURE 4.61)

Layer 73 filled a shallow depression in Layer 31, adjacent to the south oven [50]. Texturally, the deposit was very similar to Layer 67, although it contained far fewer pottery sherds. Separating it and the oven was a small heap of burnt red clay [32] which may have represented the final cleanings from the oven chamber [50].

LAYERS 72 AND 135 (FIGURE 4.61)

These layers were situated at the western end of the building, to the west of the line of internal postpads suggested to reflect an internal partition wall. Layer 135 filled a shallow scour in Layer 46, which had also eroded earlier floor layers [138 and 148]. The deposit butted the limestone boulder [143] and contained an extremely dense concentration of artefacts (Figures 7.11 to 7.21) that included a group of copper alloy cauldron feet (Figure 5.50) as well as a complete glazed jug (Figure 5.19, 167), and the elaborately-decorated Stag's Head cistern (Figure 5.20). Layer 72 was less than 50mm thick and composed of a mixture of scorched clay, charcoal, small stones and fragments of reworked natural clay. It sealed Layer 135 and an earlier floor layer [138] and also contained a rich group of domestic and household objects (Section 7) including iron fittings and knife blades, an iron lock, worked bone objects and a single jet bead, the latter possibly from a rosary.

EXCAVATIONS

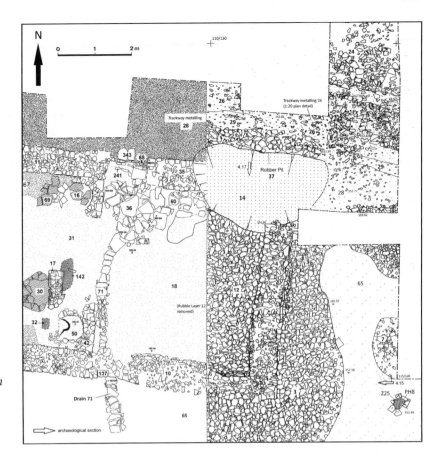

FIGURE 4.62A

Area A – plan showing the eastern end of Period V Building 460 with demolition rubble [3 and 12] yet to be excavated and post-medieval Robber Pit 37

POSTPADS 427, 426, 144 AND 491 (FIGURE 4.61)
These four postpads were set into the surface of Layers 31 and 46 in the western half of the building.

Three of the four [426, 144 and 491] formed an irregularly spaced line across its width which corresponded with the extent of Layers 67, 73 and 135.

FIGURE 4.62B
Area A showing the eastern end of Period V Building 460 with demolition rubble [3 and 12] in situ and cut of post-medieval Robber Pit 37 in the foreground. Facing S. Scale 2m

FIGURE 4.63
Area A – detail of Period V haystack base (Structure 473) as excavated. Facing NE. Scale 2m

The stones appeared to represent the foundations for a simple internal timber partition or wall that divided the west half of the building into two small rooms or bays; the chamber or inner room to the west and the kitchen/hall located centrally.

THE TRACKWAY

The trackway continued in use during Period V at which time it ran directly outside the north wall and doorway of Building 460 (Figure 4.50 and 4.61). It was no more than 3m wide overall and the surface incorporated various discrete patches of differently-sized stones and small rubble [26] indicating some periodic repair, some of which used clinker-rich material (Figure 4.44, Layer 111). A series of more defined and linear spreads of soil (Figure 4.69, Layer 29) appeared to represent wheel ruts spaced approximately 1.5m apart preserved in the surface of the trackway.

Detailed cleaning of the trackway surface (Figure 4.69) and the demolition rubble covering the remains of Building 460 (Figure 4.69) also defined the edges of two separate post-medieval robber pits [45 and 37], dug to rob stone from the western end and northeastern corner of the building.

Structure 463: Period V.2 (Figure 4.56)

LAYER 49

This occupation layer was preserved at the eastern end of Building 463, immediately beneath the destruction rubble [19], where it sealed Period III Layers 189 and 322 and a posthole, [295]. The layer was no more than 100mm thick and contained variable amounts of small stone and gravel; towards the centre of the building it thinned and only occasionally sealed the rubble soakaways. It produced a relatively small amount of pottery dating to CP6. Elsewhere inside the building the floor level was formed by weathered natural red clay [201].

COBBLING 239 (FIGURE 4.56)

This very well consolidated layer of small stones, rubble and clay was laid outside and immediately to the north of Building 463. The layer produced pottery of CP6 and butted the lowest course of masonry forming the revetment wall [210]. It [239] was partly overlain by a thin charcoal-rich layer [240] that produced pottery of CP7. Elsewhere it was sealed by a thick layer of mixed natural clay and limestone rubble.

Other Evidence: Period V.2

STRUCTURE 473: HAYRICK/FODDER BASE
(FIGURES 4.5, 4.19 AND 4.63)

This semicircular packing of limestone cobbles and small rubble [9] was laid on the east side of the yard, directly onto the yardsoil (Layer 65, CP6). The foundation (Figure 4.63) was well consolidated and appeared to represent a dry-standing, possibly for a hay or fodder stack. The diameter of the packing measured approximately 4m overall.

EXCAVATIONS

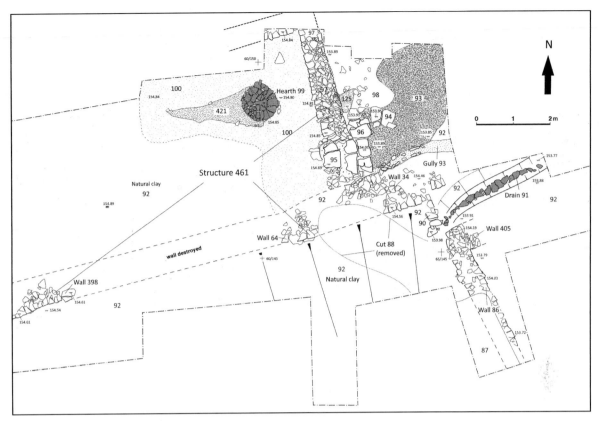

FIGURE 4.64
Plan showing Area B and Period V Building 461 as excavated

THE YARD (FIGURE 4.5)
The stony soil [65] forming the latest surface of the yard continued to be variously reworked. The only discrete deposit attributed to this latest phase was represented by centrally-located Deposit 41. The deposit appeared to represent a dump of domestic refuse and contained a collection of artefacts including a single sherd from the decorated 'Stag's Head' cistern (Figures 5.20 and 5.21), the remainder of which was located as a single group in the west bay of Building 460.

Area B: Periods V.1 and V.2

Building 461 (Figures 1.6, 1.7, 4.64, 4.65 and 4.70)

During the later 13th century, and around the same time as the construction of Building 460 in Area A, a large new stone building, Building 461, was constructed in Area B (Figure 4.64) on a prepared platform on the west side of the trackway (Figure 4.70). In general, the remains of the building were poorly preserved, although the east wall [97] and a flight of three entrance steps (95) were preserved, the latter essentially complete (Figure 4.65). The south wall [Walls 34, 64 and 398] had been almost entirely robbed, although, between the remnant masonry that was preserved, the original line of the wall was clearly defined by a ghost-line of pale clay.

The overall dimensions of the building were difficult to determine with certainty, although the extent of the levelled platform and the boundary formed by the trackway suggest it was around 5m wide and 8m to 10m long. Other structural features included a stone hearth [99] laid at floor level (Figure 4.64) and the remnants of internal soil floor layers [100 and 421] which produced pottery of CP6. A crude stone drain [91] appeared to have been laid to carry water away from the entrance steps, a function supported by the edges of the steps, which were heavily pock-marked with solution-holes caused by dripping water.

Further sections of drystone masonry including part of a possible trackway boundary wall [86/405] and a roughly metalled surface or yard were recorded immediately to the south of the building during the final watching brief on the site (Section 4.4). The ceramic phasing (CP6) for the final occupation of the building is supported by a coin of Edward I dated to *c*AD 1300–1302 (Section 5.4) recovered from the internal floor layers.

Period V: Concluding Comments

During Period V, the settlement was substantially redeveloped as new buildings were laid out in Area B and the earlier (Period IV) stone buildings in Area A were demolished and replaced with more substantial structures comprising a farmhouse [Building 460], a barn or animal shed [Building 463] and a kiln or corn-dryer [466]. The material assemblage relating to this latest phase of medieval settlement is rich,

FIGURE 4.65
Area B showing detail of the entrance steps to Period V Building 461. Facing W. Scale 2m

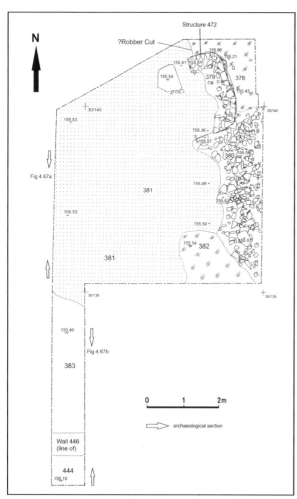

FIGURE 4.66
Area G – plan as excavated showing Structure 472

varied and extensive, and was particularly well preserved inside the farmhouse [460].

The ceramic evidence indicates abandonment of the farmhouses in Areas A and B by AD 1400 at the latest, and possibly soon after AD 1352. The physical and material evidence alone provides no direct explanation for this event, although the quality and range of portable objects which remained completely undisturbed inside the farmhouse in Area A suggest the departure of the occupants may have been unexpected and rapid – the archaeology confirms that it was certainly permanent.

Other Areas Investigated

Area G (Figures 4.66 and 4.67A and B)

A further small area, designated Area G (Figures 1.6 and 1.7), was opened by machine to investigate an irregular earthwork located to the west of Area B, adjacent to the boundary with the modern cemetery. The cutting (Figure 4.66) was approximately 5m square with a deeper trench extending to the south from the southwest corner.

The majority of the trench revealed a layer of sandy tan soil [381] up to 200mm deep directly below the topsoil [377]. The deposit contained common fragments of lime-based mortar and later post-medieval ceramic building material. The extent of the deposit appeared to reflect a large irregular area of disturbance, probably a robber pit,

EXCAVATIONS

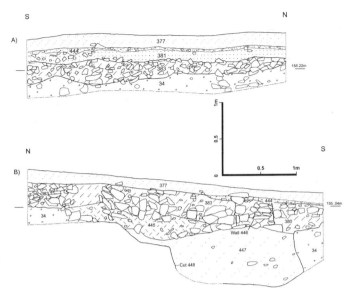

FIGURE 4.67 A AND B

Area G – Section drawings showing possible Period III sunken-floor feature (Cut 448) overlain by later medieval wall foundation (446)

which had largely destroyed a former building, the remains of which were represented by a fragment of curved drystone masonry (Figure 4.66, Wall 379). The masonry was formed of roughly coursed and faced small limestone rubble and was preserved to a maximum height of 600mm. The small portion that was revealed in the excavation area was insufficient to allow any precise interpretation, although the structure could have represented part of an east-facing entrance of a building aligned west to east, congruent with the alignment of Building 461 in Area B just to the east. Features associated with this building included part of a worn cobbled surface [380] and a charcoal and clinker-rich soil layer [378]. The latter produced sherds of post-medieval (CP7) pottery and an assemblage of 17th-century clay tobacco pipes, the latter including marked pipe-bowls from makers in Bristol, Marlborough and Mendip (Section 5.9).

The deeper cutting opened to the south from the main excavation area revealed a sequence of deposits and a possible structure, all of which were recorded in section (Figures 4.67A and B). The east-facing section (Figure 4.67A) revealed little more than a deposit of soil and demolition rubble [383] directly below the sandy layer [381], which produced a few sherds of later medieval (CP6) pottery. This in turn overlay undisturbed natural clay at a depth of approximately 500mm.

The west-facing section (Figure 4.67B) revealed the rubbly soil [383] directly below the topsoil [377]. The deposit [383] also appeared to include the remains of a drystone wall [446], which was also preserved directly below the topsoil. Unfortunately, the wall was not recognised in plan during excavation. The wall was built over the fill [447] of a pit [448] cut into the natural clay. The pit was up to 800mm deep and had a broad asymmetrical profile that appeared to incorporate a shallower shelf or step on the north side and a steep to undercut face to the south. The base was fairly flat and the single

FIGURE 4.68

Testpit Area K showing Period V Wall 3155. Facing E. Scale 200mm graduations

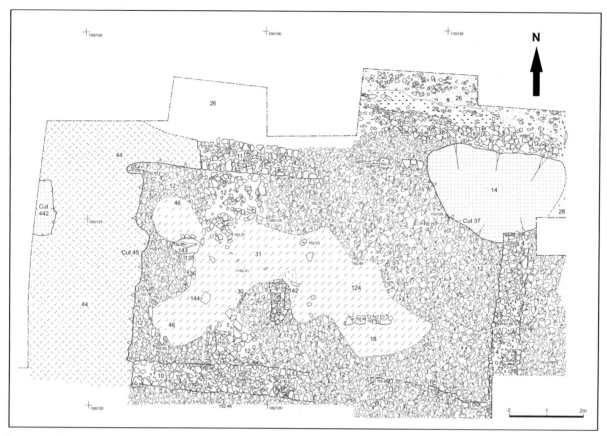

FIGURE 4.69

Area A – Plan showing the Period V Building 460 after the removal of topsoil only with demolition rubble [3 and 12] yet to be excavated. Also showing post medieval robber pits [37 and 45]

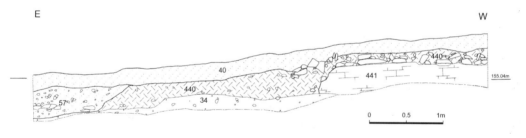

FIGURE 4.70

Area B – section drawing showing rock-cut platform prepared for period V Building 461. Facing N

fill consisted of homogeneous and relatively stone-free silt-clay. The pit did not produce any stratified dating evidence, although, on the basis of its general morphology and the relationship between it and the wall built directly over the fill, it closely resembled the general stratigraphic sequence recorded in Area A, where sunken-floor features forming part of Period III Structure 468 underlay subsequent Period IV and V walls. If correct, this suggests further sunken-floored timber structures of Period III date were also constructed in this part of the site.

Evaluation Testpits: Areas J and K (Figures 1.6 and 1.7)

Two small testpits (Figures 1.6 and 1.7, Areas J and K, not illustrated in detail) were opened by hand in the area of earthworks immediately north of Eckweek House Farm. Testpit Area K measured just 3.4m by 1m in plan and was opened by hand at site grid coordinate 20E/37N. The cutting revealed the remnants of a drystone wall [3155] (Figure 4.68) formed of limestone rubble and aligned north to south. The masonry was preserved to just two courses and was butted by large amounts of demolition rubble [3156]. The trench was cleaned by hand but no further excavation was undertaken, although the presence of a soil deposit [3154] below the wall indicated that the base of archaeological stratigraphy had not been reached. The wall appeared broadly to coincide with a series of high-resistance anomalies detected by the geophysical survey (Section 3.2) and interpreted to reflect buried wall footings. Pottery from Area K was mostly of CP6 (Period V), but also contained a few sherds of CP7, as well as some

EXCAVATIONS

earlier residual material of CP3 and CP4. Evidence of later disturbance, probably due to stone-robbing, was also indicated by the condition of Wall 3155, which would account for the presence of the early post-medieval (CP7) ceramics.

Testpit Area J measured just 2m by 1m in plan and was opened by hand at site grid coordinate 22E/25N. The cutting revealed a simple sequence of topsoil overlying sterile natural clay.

This, albeit very limited, evidence indicated the presence of a further, separate, later medieval farmstead group at Eckweek. Furthermore, the presence of earlier pottery of ceramic phases 3 and 4 recovered from the testpits suggests the likelihood that, here as in Area G, the later masonry buildings may have been preceded by an earthfast timber phase. Collectively, the evidence indicates that in its latest form this farmstead group was likely to have incorporated two, and possibly three, stone buildings, and if so, reflected a farmstead site of equal potential and importance to that examined in detail in Area A. It is therefore to be regretted that no detailed archaeological work of any kind was undertaken in this area prior to housing development.

4.4 WATCHING BRIEF

No formal watching brief was undertaken after the completion of the detailed excavation work in Area H, either to monitor the construction stages of the new road carriageway or, perhaps more regrettably, the subsequent residential housing scheme. Monitoring of minor works associated with the extension of the cemetery burial ground that took in excavation Areas B and G (Figure 4.71) was undertaken by Alexander Kidd and the writer. These works included the excavation of foundation trenches for a new cemetery boundary wall and some associated topsoil stripping. Further monitoring was undertaken by Alexander Kidd during earthmoving and the excavation of a new service trench for a construction compound just to the south of Eckweek House Farm in OS Field 2756 (Figures 1.7, 4.71 and 4.73). Despite this ad-hoc work, the overwhelming majority of the development area, which took in the site of at least one further well preserved medieval farmstead (centred on the testpits, Areas J and K), was not examined, monitored or recorded in any way. In 2015, such a lack of oversight would be astonishing, but in 1990, only very shortly after the publication of PPG16 (DoE 1990), it should be remembered that the provision of archaeological monitoring was still largely in the gift of the developer and not yet a standard statutory requirement. This does not however, excuse the fact that the opportunity to characterise and record a further important and extensive body of evidence relating to the late Saxon and medieval settlement, acutely demonstrated by the discovery of mid-Saxon burials and activity just to the south of the site in 2004–2005 (Rowe and Alexander 2011), was entirely and irrevocably lost.

The limited evidence that was recorded by the watching brief in the area of the cemetery extension and construction compound is summarised below. Further detailed information relating to these features can be found in the project archive.

The Cemetery Extension (Figures 4.71 and 4.72)

Topsoil stripping revealed a series of wall foundations [3258, 3259, 3261, 3262 and 3255], the majority of which appeared originally to have extended beyond the areas that were opened by machine. All were drystone and formed of roughly coursed and faced limestone rubble that was preserved to a maximum of four or five courses and up to 750mm wide (Figure 4.74). In this respect they were all very similar to the 14th-century drystone walls previously recorded in Areas A and B. Walls 3258 and 3259 (Figure 4.72) appeared to form the southeastern corner of a building or yard area immediately to the west of, and behind, Building 461 in Area B. The area contained by the walls was surfaced with a layer of well consolidated rounded stones and small cobbles [3260] that appeared more likely to indicate use as a yard as opposed to the interior of a building. The course of Wall 3258 continued to the east where it was recorded as Wall 3261. This foundation in turn appeared originally to have joined Wall 3262, which demarcated the western side of the track and hollow-way. These structures, in combination with Wall 3259, indicated that Building 461 recorded in Area B was originally constructed on a level terraced platform (Figure 4.70) and set in a rectangular building plot which was defined on the south and west sides by a boundary wall. Areas of metalling [3260 and 3263] located immediately outside these walls indicated an associated agricultural or animal yard was laid out immediately to the south of the building, as Layer 3263 produced a collection of later medieval (Period V) pottery sherds including fragments of strap-handled jugs and glazed table wares. The surface of Layer 3260 produced a collection of earlier post-medieval pottery sherds including sherds of tin-glazed earthenware and South Somerset glazed red wares, indicating that this enclosure probably was associated with the building identified in Area G immediately to the west. A further short stretch of wall foundation (Figure 4.75, Feature 3255) revealed on the east side of the hollow-way indicated that at this location the later medieval trackway was defined by boundary or retaining walls on both sides.

A series of widely spaced cut soil features (Figure 4.72, Cuts 3243, 3245, 3247, 3250 and 3254), all representing ditches, were revealed in a narrow foundation trench excavated by machine for a new cemetery wall. Cuts 3250 and 3254 were both cut into the natural clay and were some 500–600mm deep. Both were sealed beneath a layer of

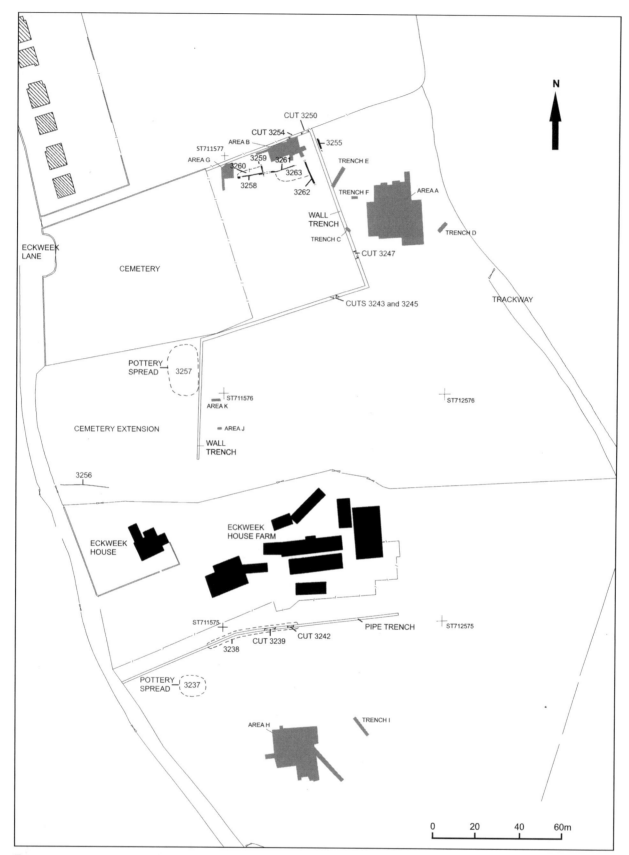

FIGURE 4.71
Plan showing location of features recorded during the watching brief stage

approximately 150mm of consolidated stones and small cobbles that represented the latest trackway surface (Figure 4.64, Deposits 93/98). No finds or dating evidence were recovered from the ditches, although their stratigraphic position indicated that they probably represented Period III activity. A further shallow ditch [3247] was revealed in the trench just to the southwest of excavation Area A.

EXCAVATIONS

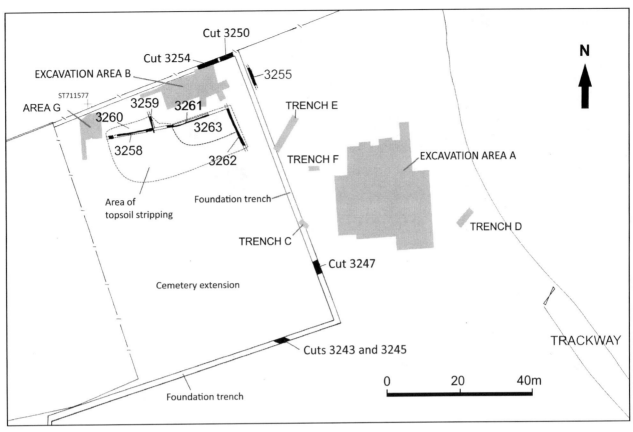

FIGURE 4.72
Detail showing features recorded during the watching brief adjacent to Excavation Areas A, B and G

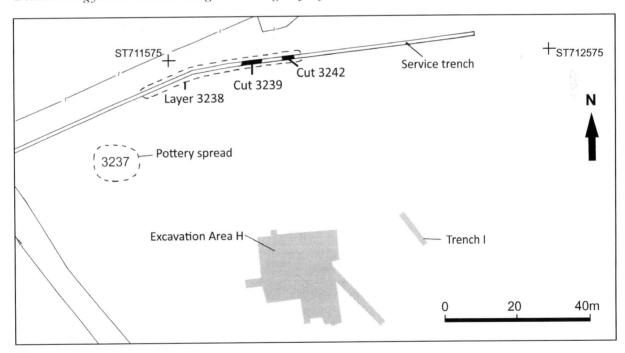

FIGURE 4.73
Detail showing features recorded during the watching brief adjacent to Excavation Area H

The feature was approximately 1.2m wide and 600mm deep and aligned broadly west to east. In this respect it bore no obvious relationship with the surface earthworks in this part of the site and, despite an absence of finds, was interpreted to reflect further evidence of Period III activity. Cuts 3243 and 3245 were intercut, 3245 being the later of the two, and in combination were 2.5m wide and up to 700mm deep. They coincided with a low earthwork interpreted to reflect a post-medieval field boundary.

A spread of later post-medieval and modern pottery, along with metalwork, vessel glass and brick

FIGURE 4.74
Walls 3258 and 3259 revealed during the watching brief immediately west of Area B. Facing W. Scales 2m

FIGURE 4.75
Wall 3255 recorded during the watching brief defining the east side of the medieval trackway. Facing E. Scale 2m

(Figure 4.71, 3257), was revealed immediately to the west of the wall trench in OS field 2470 (Figure 1.7) to the northwest of the testpits, Areas J and K. Part of a stone land drain [3256] was revealed in the extreme southwestern corner of the same field.

The Construction Compound (Figures 4.71 and 4.73)

A narrow service trench was excavated by machine and a small area was stripped of topsoil in OS Field 2756. The central part of the trench revealed a charcoal-rich occupation deposit containing sparse stones [3238] that produced a handful of plain medieval pottery sherds. This deposit sealed two substantial ditches [3239 and 3242], both of which were cut into the natural clay. Each appeared to be aligned broadly north to south and the fill [3240] of the former produced three sherds of 12th- to 14th-century earthenware including one sherd of FT5.

A spread of medieval pottery sherds [3237] was revealed by machine below the topsoil close to the northwestern corner of the field. The assemblage was restricted to body sherds of plain and undecorated earthenware that included examples of Fabric Types 3, 4, 5, 69, 75 and 103. The majority of the fabrics identified are consistent with the date range of Saxo-Norman activity recorded in Area H, although the presence of a small number of sherds in FT75 indicates that the activity represented by the assemblage may date as late as the early 12th century. The spread also produced a complete lead spindle whorl that has unfortunately since been lost.

5
ARTEFACTS AND ENVIRONMENTAL EVIDENCE

5.1 PREHISTORIC CERAMICS – POTTERY, BRIQUETAGE AND A BRONZE-WORKING CRUCIBLE
by Dr Elaine Morris (1992, updated 2015)

A total of 78 sherds of prehistoric ceramic material (374g; Figure 5.1) was submitted for analysis. This collection includes one sherd of Bronze Age pottery, 73 sherds of Iron Age pottery, three sherds from Droitwich salt containers or briquetage, and one fragment from a possible bronze-working crucible. The fabric types referred to below are described in detail in Figure 5.5.

Bronze Age Pottery

The single undecorated body sherd of Bronze Age pottery is made from the only grog-tempered fabric in the collection (FT162). It is moderately thick-walled (10mm), oxidised on the exterior only and very soft-fired. It is likely to be from an earlier Bronze Age vessel dating to the first half of the second millennium BC based on the fabric and firing condition. Grog-tempered fabrics are typical of late Neolithic–early Bronze Age beakers, early Bronze Age biconical vessels and some middle Bronze Age pottery in the local and wider region (Cleal 1995; Williams 1990; Woodward 1990; Morris 2009, 37; Woodward 2007, 43). However, this fabric is not unknown amongst later prehistoric pottery from Ham Hill (Morris 1987, 34–35), Ilchester (Ellison 1982, 125) and Meare Village West (Orme et al 1981, 48), but in such cases it is usually harder fired.

Iron Age Pottery

The Iron Age pottery is characterised by a range of calcareous-gritted fabrics, a fine sandy fabric and one with flint temper: FT158A – coarse, platy fossil shell, FT158B – coarse fossiliferous limestone and fossil shell, FT158C – fine fossil shell and fossiliferous limestone, FT160 – oolitic limestone, FT164 – calcite, FT165 – very fine quartz sand, and FT166 – flint-tempered with round quartz sand (Figure 5.2). All of these fabrics could have been produced from local resources. The site lies in an area of the Jurassic system containing a range of Lias and Inferior Oolite deposits (Kellaway and Welch 1948, fig. 1) which may have provided the fossil shell and oolitic limestone inclusions present in four of these seven pottery fabrics (FT158A, FT158B, FT158C, FT160). Several different locations in the area to the north, west and south of Eckweek contain Palaeozoic strata which can include deposits of calcite in the Carboniferous Limestone and which are potential sources for the calcite in fabric FT164.

Fabric type	Date	Fabric description	Number of sherds	Weight of sherds (g)
FT158A	IA	coarse fossil shell	29	113
FT158B	IA	shelly limestone	10	59
FT158C	IA	fine fossil shell and limestone	2	4
FT160	IA	oolitic limestone	18	69
FT162	BA	grog-tempered	1	5
FT163	IA	vitrified fabric – crucible	1	1
FT164	IA	calcite-gritted	11	92
FT165	IA	fine quartz and mica	2	6
FT166	IA	flint-tempered, sandy	1	2
FT167	IA	Droitwich salt container	3	23
Total			78	374

FIGURE 5.1

Quantification of the prehistoric ceramics by fabric type

Fabric type	Date	Fabric description	Percentage by number	Percentage by weight
FT158A	IA	coarse fossil shell	38.2	30.7
FT158B	IA	shelly limestone	13.2	16.0
FT158C	IA	fine fossil shell and limestone	2.6	1.1
FT160	IA	oolitic limestone	23.7	18.8
FT164	IA	calcite-gritted	14.5	25.0
FT165	IA	fine quartz and mica	2.6	1.6
FT166	IA	flint-tempered, sandy	1.3	0.5
FT167	IA	Droitwich salt container	3.9	6.3
Total			100%	100%

FIGURE 5.2

Relative frequency of Iron Age pottery and briquetage by fabric type

Context/ CAR	Feature or layer	Fabric types										Total
		FT158A	FT158B	FT158C	FT160	FT162	FT163	FT164	FT165	FT166	FT167	
No = count, Wt = weight (g)		No Wt	No Wt	No Wt	No Wt	No Wt	No Wt	No Wt	No Wt	No Wt	No Wt	No Wt
3162/1998	Ditch 3161	2 12	- -	- -	- -	- -	- -	- -	- -	- -	- -	2 12
3177/1997	Ditch 3176	- -	1 3	1 2	3 12	- -	- -	9 81	2 6	- -	- -	16 104
3075/1981	Ditch 3076	14 47	8 46	1 2	13 48	- -	1 1	2 11	- -	- -	3 23	42 178
3125/1927	Posthole 3126	2 7	- -	- -	- -	- -	- -	- -	- -	- -	- -	2 7
3123/1928	Posthole 3124	1 3	- -	- -	- -	1 5	- -	- -	- -	- -	- -	2 8
3109/1914	Posthole 3110	1 5	- -	- -	- -	- -	- -	- -	- -	- -	- -	1 5
3064/1862	Period III Pit 3029	1 1	- -	- -	- -	- -	- -	- -	- -	- -	- -	1 1
3039/1982	Layer	6 26	- -	- -	- -	- -	- -	- -	- -	- -	- -	6 26
3020/1897	Period III Posthole (unexc)	1 6	- -	- -	- -	- -	- -	- -	- -	- -	- -	1 6
3006/1844	Period III Posthole 3005	- -	- -	- -	- -	- -	- -	- -	- -	1 2	- -	1 2
3001/1876	Topsoil	- -	- -	- -	1 2	- -	- -	- -	- -	- -	- -	1 2
US/1985	Unstratified	1 6	1 10	- -	1 7	- -	- -	- -	- -	- -	- -	3 23
	Total	29 113	10 59	2 4	18 69	1 5	1 1	11 92	2 6	1 2	3 23	78 374

FIGURE 5.3

The prehistoric pottery

The closest possibility would be the area between Paulton and Pensford in a southwest/northwest running band 5–10km from the site which could be considered as locally accessible. Further afield there are similar deposits west of Pensford and others stretching north of Bristol and across into south Wales, while the Mendip Hills which are located approximately 10–15km to the south of Eckweek have been recommended as the source for Southwestern decorated Glastonbury ware Group 3 calcite-tempered fabric (Peacock 1969, 48). There are various river terraces in the Eckweek vicinity where sandy clays bearing round quartz grains may occur and where gravel-type flint could be crushed and added as temper to make FT166. Silty clays could also be resourced from locations along river beds.

This is not to say, however, that it is possible to prove that these fabrics were made from these locally available resources but rather that, based on a model of pottery production and resource procurement derived from a study of pottery-making agricultural communities around the world, these fabrics were most likely (87% probability) to have been made from naturally-gritted clays and any added inclusions found within 7–10km of their home base (Arnold 1985; Morris and Woodward 2003, 289–290) as they are available in most cases up to this distance in the immediately local area. The single pot made from FT166, for example, may have been made 15–20km to the east with flint derived from the Upper Chalk on Salisbury Plain (Melville and Freshney 1982, fig. 1, 88–89). If that were the case, then this vessel was not locally-made.

The use of the term 'gritted' rather than 'tempered' to describe calcite-bearing fabric FT164 (Figure 5.5) is due to the texture and condition of the calcite itself which is not crisp with sharply edged pieces of angular crystalline calcite but rather has weathered calcite fragments present which are subangular to subround in shape. These shapes suggest that the calcite may have been naturally-occurring in the clay matrix used to make the pots rather than crushed and added as temper. This fabric is very different from the calcite-tempered ones used to make the majority of late Bronze Age vessels found at Field Farm, Shepton Mallet (Morris 2009, 36–37) and Group 3 calcite-tempered fabric Southwestern Glastonbury Ware pottery (Peacock 1969, 48, fig. 5, 1–8), for example. Peacock specifically notes the condition of the Group 3 calcite fragments as 'rhombs with sharp angles showing no sign of rounding' and interprets these as added temper (1969, 48) which contrasts distinctively with the weathered calcite in the Eckweek fabric. Therefore, the more rounded nature of the calcite suggests that it was naturally-occurring in the clay rather than added as temper and that the source for the Eckweek fabric is not the same as that for Field Farm or Group 3 calcite-tempered fabrics. Two samples of fabric FT164, thought to derive from different vessels found in ditch 3176, were selected for thin sectioning and petrological analysis to characterise this fabric in detail. Examination of these using a polarizing microscope confirmed that there was a slight variation in the frequency of calcite fragments between them, which can be interpreted as representing different vessels, but that the actual character of the calcite was similar.

The variety of fabrics identified in the Eckweek assemblage is typical of the later prehistoric period in Somerset and Gloucestershire. Shelly and oolitic limestone-bearing fabrics were the dominant types identified in the late Bronze Age material from Combe Hay (Barrett 1980) located just a couple of kilometres north of Peasdown. More significant, however, for comparison with the Eckweek material in terms of likely date range are the fabrics from the Cadbury Castle sequence. Although mixtures of calcite and shell are the main fabric types for Iron Age Cadbury 5 ceramic phase (Woodward and Bevan 2000, 27) dated to the eighth to seventh century cal BC (Bayliss, Freeman and Woodward

ARTEFACTS AND ENVIRONMENTAL EVIDENCE

Fabric Type	Evidence of use Pitting on interior	Charred matter/soot
FT158A	15 sherds	3 sherds
FT158B	1 sherd	6 sherds
FT160	12 sherds	
FT164		9 sherds
FT165		2 sherds

FIGURE 5.4

Correlation of Iron Age fabric types to visible evidence of use

2000, fig. 175), there are also fabrics from that phase bearing quartz and flint and fine sand with a micaceous sparkle (Alcock 1980, 690–691), as is also reported for the Iron Age pottery from Ham Hill (Morris 1987, 34; 1998, 93, table 2). However, Cadbury 6 is dominated by shelly wares specifically (Woodward and Bevan 2000, 27) and has been dated from the seventh to fifth century cal BC (Bayliss, Freeman and Woodward 2000, fig. 175). The sizeable Iron Age assemblage of fifth- to fourth-century date from Cannards Grave near Shepton Mallet was identified as having 96% shell-predominant fabrics (Mepham 2000). During the middle to late Iron Age Cadbury 6–7 phase, shell fabrics continue to dominate that site. Fossil shell fabrics are the principal types in the Ham Hill assemblage reported in the 1994 and 1998 early to late Iron Age assemblage from Ham Hill (Morris 1998, 92–94, table 2). Closer to Eckweek, shell-bearing fabrics dominate the earliest Iron Age assemblage of large sherds dated to the seventh to sixth century from recent work at Bathampton Down, Bath with 82% of fabrics bearing predominantly fossil shell inclusions and 13% made from oolitic limestone fabric pottery (Brown 2012). At Eckweek shell-bearing fabrics FT158A–158C represent 48% to 54% of all the non-Bronze Age pottery fabrics whether by number or weight of sherds, while the oolitic limestone fabric pottery represents 19–24% of the Eckweek assemblage (Figure 5.2).

Calcite-gritted fabrics dominate the Post-Deverel Rimbury late Bronze Age assemblages of Brean Down Unit 4 (Williams and Woodward 1990, 122, table 7; Woodward 1990, 133–140) and Field Farm-Sites 2–3, Shepton Mallet (Morris 2009, 36–37 and table 2), as well as being a significant component of the otherwise shell fabric-dominated late Bronze Age South Cadbury 4 assemblage (Williams and Woodward 2000, 259; Woodward and Bevan 2000, 27, fig. 10 – fabric a/calcite and fabric c/shell). This is not surprising for Brean Down as the closest source of this type of rock is located just east in the Mendips but this source is *c*20km to the north of Cadbury and therefore not local to that site. Iron-rich dolomite limestone (calcite) fabrics were used to make at least 90% of vessels recovered from the early-middle Iron Age site at Dibbles Farm, Christon immediately east of Weston-super-Mare (Morris 1988, 29, table 1), while 68% of the

FT158A – *coarse, fossil shell-rich fabric*
Common to very common (20–30% concentration), poorly-sorted, subangular, platy fossil shell with very rare (up to 1% concentration) fossiliferous limestone, measuring 6mm or less across, in a clay matrix which may be quartz sand-free; any grains of quartz present are likely to be silt-grade in size and only visible microscopically

FT158B – *coarse, fossiliferous limestone and fossil shell fabric*
Abundant (40–50%), poorly-sorted, subround, shell-bearing limestone and platy fossil shell, 7mm or less with the majority less than 4mm across, which are evenly distributed throughout an apparently quartz-free clay matrix

FT158C – *fine, fossil shell and fossiliferous limestone fabric*
Moderate (10–15%), very well-sorted, subround, platy fossil shell and fossiliferous limestone with rare (1–2%) ooliths up to 2mm across, which are evenly distributed throughout an apparently quartz-free clay matrix

FT160 – *oolitic limestone fabric*
Abundant (40–50%), very well-sorted, round ooliths, usually 1mm or less across, with rare to sparse (2–5%), moderately sorted, subangular, platy fossil shell and limestone, 3mm or less, evenly distributed throughout an apparently quartz-free clay matrix

FT162 – *grog-tempered fabric*
Very common (30–35%), moderately well-sorted, angular grog, 4mm or less, evenly distributed throughout an apparently quartz sand-free clay matrix

FT163 – *vitrified, vesicular fabric*
Common (20–25%), subrounded vesicles or holes, 1.5mm or less across, in a lightweight, overfired and vitrified, very porous, clay matrix; probably a crucible fabric

FT164 – *calcite-gritted fabric*
Common to abundant (25–40%), subangular to subrounded, weathered calcite, 3mm or less, in a clay matrix with rare to sparse (1–3%), naturally-occurring, fine to silt-grade, subangular to subrounded quartz, 0.2mm or less; two samples submitted for thin sectioning and petrological analysis

FT165 – *very fine, silty fabric*
Very common to abundant (30–40%), very well-sorted, very fine to silt-grade quartz and possible mica flecks, less than 0.1mm

FT166 – *flint-tempered, sandy fabric*
Moderate (10–15%), well-sorted, angular to subangular, calcined flint, 2mm or less, in a clay matrix which also contains sparse to moderate (3–10%), round to subrounded quartz, 2mm or less; the difference in shape between these two types of inclusions indicates that the flint is temper that was added to a naturally-occurring sandy clay matrix

FT167 – *Droitwich briquetage fabric Ia (clay pellet-rich) (Morris 1985, 342–343)*

FIGURE 5.5

Prehistoric pottery fabric descriptions

pottery from middle-late Iron Age Blaise Castle Hill, Bristol is calcite-tempered (ApSimon 1959, 160; Morris 1983a, 142–144). Nearly all of the burnished middle-late Iron Age pottery assemblage found at 45–53 West St., Bedminster, Bristol (BSMR 22276) is calcite-tempered including both bowls and jars which had been used as cookpots and to hold acidic foodstuffs (Morris 2007). During the later Iron Age period in Somerset, many examples

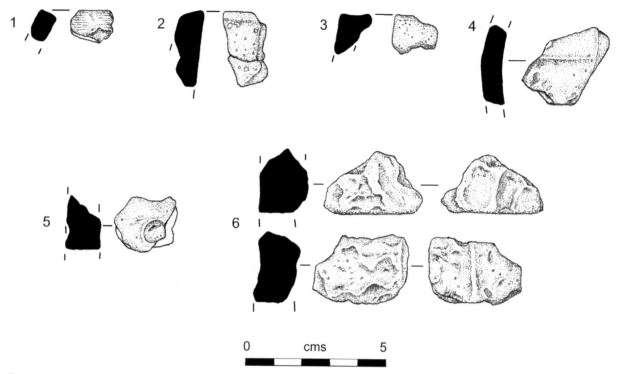

FIGURE 5.6

Illustrated prehistoric pottery and briquetage
1. R1; fabric 164; burnished on exterior and top of rim; PRN 11, context 3075, ditch cut 3076, CAR 1981
2. R2; fabric 158A; PRN 13, context 3075, ditch cut 3076, CAR 1981
3. R3; fabric 160; PRN 21, context 3075, ditch cut 3076, CAR 1981
4. A1; fabric 158A; PRN 28, context 3109, posthole 3110, CAR 1914
5. D1; fabric 158A; PRN 25, context 3125, posthole 3126, CAR 1927
6. Droitwich briquetage body sherds; fabric 167; PRN 24, context 3075, ditch cut 3076, CAR 1981

of Southwestern Glastonbury ware decorated vessels are also made from a distinctively calcite-tempered fabric that was argued to be from a Mendips source (Peacock 1969, 48, fig. 5, 1–8). In Gloucestershire, ceramic phase I activity at the early-middle Iron Age hillfort of Uley Bury, which is located 35km north of Eckweek, has no calcite fabric pottery, which does not appear until ceramic phase II (2–4% of that period assemblage), and this increases significantly after that from 21–93% in the final ceramic phase III (Morris 1983b, 14–17, fig. 11). Shell and oolitic limestone fabrics may dominate the early occupation (ceramic phases I–II) at Uley Bury as they dominate at Eckweek but at the same time calcite-gritted fabric FT164 represents 15% to 25% of the Eckweek assemblage (Figure 5.2).

Therefore, while fabrics are very useful for differentiating between earlier prehistoric (grog-tempered) and later prehistoric (shell, calcite, oolitic limestone) pottery in Somerset, the common use of one or more calcareous-type fabrics throughout most of the first millennium BC makes the dating of assemblages more reliant on the presence of specific vessel forms, decoration and surface treatments. The major challenge with determining the actual date for the Eckweek assemblage, however, lies in the limited number of the rims available for comparative analysis within a small assemblage of less than 100 potsherds characterised by a high fragmentation rate with a mean sherd weight of 5 grammes and visibly small sherd sizes which together restrict a confident understanding of the vessel forms recovered. A similar problem was encountered by Woodward in her analysis and assignment of date to the 528 prehistoric potsherds with a mean sherd weight of 6g from Whitegate Farm, Bleadon (Young 2007) south of Weston-super-Mare due to the infrequency of diagnostic items (2007, 45). Only three rim fragments were identified in the Eckweek collection (Figure 5.6, 1–3): one from a flat-topped vessel with an uncertain vessel profile (database type R1), one from an ovoid jar with bevelled edge (R2) and one rim with a slight recess to the upper rim surface created by the potter pressing down onto the top edge during manufacture (R3). In addition, there is one slightly angled body sherd (type A1) from the shoulder of a jar and one small sherd from a different vessel which is decorated (type D1) with a finger-tip/nail impression (Figure 5.6, 4–5). These remnants of rims suggest that they may derive from neckless, ovoid or convex-profile jars which are found in assemblages from the late Bronze Age to middle Iron Age, while the decorated sherd and the shoulder sherd would normally be assigned to the late Bronze Age/early Iron Age period. This range of forms and decorations would not be out of place in the late Bronze Age/early Iron Age assemblages from Sherborne House, (Timby 2003) and Allcourt (Timby 2013) at Lechlade in Gloucestershire, Early Iron Age Cadbury 6 and 7 assemblages (Alcock 1980, 691–694, fig. 14; Woodward and Bevan 2000, 28–30, fig. 12), and ceramic phase 1 pottery from Ham Hill (Morris 1998, 97–101, fig. 6, 3–8) for example, which are broadly dated to the 7th to 5th century BC. Sherds from the early Iron Age occupation at the enclosure site of Little Solsbury Hill Camp near Bath suggest that the Eckweek rim type R3 may have broken along the joint between the rim and vessel body at its neck and that the recess may have been created by deliberate finger-tipped impressions along the rim top (Dowden 1962, fig. 40, 109a–b); four sherds were illustrated with finger-tip impressions including one which may be a flat wall sherd similar to that from Eckweek (Dowden 1962, fig. 40, 412). The Eckweek rims are also similar to the upper rim parts of many examples from the early to middle Iron Age hillfort at Uley Bury in south Gloucestershire where two examples of angled or shoulder sherds were also identified including one decorated with finger-tip impressions (Saville and Ellison 1983, figs. 9–10). There are at least two phases of activity at Uley Bury (Saville and Ellison 1983, 22–23): one which has finger-tip decoration present and the other which included a linear-tooled decorated sherd from a Group B1 Palaeozoic limestone fabric vessel sourced from either May Hill (Glos.), the Malvern Hills (Worcs.) or the Woolhope Hills (Heref.) (c.f. Peacock 1968). Seriation analysis of the Uley Bury pottery, independently of stratigraphical phasing on that site, revealed that fossil shell and oolitic limestone fabrics, probably made from local sources, were the only types found in the earlier phases of the site but that calcite fabric vessels probably from a source in the Mendips (Morris 1983b, 17) and other non-local pottery such as the Group B1 sherds appear to have replaced the use of locally made vessels during the later activity at the site (Morris 1983b, fig. 11).

The presence of body sherds from a burnished, fineware vessel (FT165 in ditch 3176), which is likely to have been a bowl, would support this date range from the late Bronze Age to early Iron Age period as well. However, at both Eckweek and Uley Bury, no examples were found of early Iron Age red-slipped sherds or vessels displaying linear decoration similar to those found at Pagans Hill, Chew Stoke, located 18km to the west of Eckweek (ApSimon, et al 1957–1958). Therefore, the weight of evidence is pointing to an early Iron Age date for the Eckweek assemblage due to several aspects of similarity to the ceramic phases 1–2 of the multi-period early and middle Iron Age assemblage found at Uley Bury: a dominance of fossil shell fabric sherds with a significant percentage of sherds made from a calcite-gritted fabric, rim subtleties suggesting simple vessel profiles especially ovoid jars with the rare occurrence of an angled or shouldered profile, the absence of any red-slipped sherds, but the rare presence of a flat sherd with finger-tip impressed decoration. These characteristics of the pottery from Eckweek, the earliest phase at Uley Bury and most of the activity at Little Solsbury Camp correspond well to the pottery from the first Iron Age ceramic phase at Ham Hill and Cadbury 6–7. One further aspect pushes that date towards the end of the early Iron Age period.

Droitwich Salt Containers

It is the presence of other ceramic material recovered from context 3075 of ditch cut 3076 which provides the strongest clue as to the date of this assemblage, namely three body sherds from two different Droitwich salt containers (Morris 1985, 338–352). The original vessels had been made from fabric Ia of that distinctive material which is a blocky-structured, apparently unwedged, clay pellet and quartz sand fabric which would normally be oxidised throughout during firing as is the case with these three sherds. Two of the sherds from one of the vessels display the typical exterior surface fingering in vertical grooves with edge spurs or ridges used to seal the coil or collar joints in contrast to the highly irregularly bulbous interior surface displaying no attempt at having been smoothed (Figure 5.6, 6). The source for this fabric type is the Keuper Marls located in and around the area of Droitwich in Worcestershire (Morris 1985, 344–345). These very distinctive flared-profile, flat-based saltmaking containers were used as ceramic packs first to dry brine from the salt springs at Droitwich and then transport the crystals to settlements and hillforts in western Britain. The enclosed site at Eckweek is the furthest distance from the source that these specialised containers have been identified, ie c100km to the south of Droitwich (Morris 1985, figs 5–6).

The identification of Droitwich salt container sherds at Eckweek is quite significant because it is this fabric which has been identified as the earliest example of this material having been found at Chasleton hillfort, Crickley hillfort and Shenberrow Camp in Gloucestershire (Morris 1985, 346–350, table 1, fig. 5). Identifying the earliest type of Droitwich salt container at Eckweek indicates that it was likely to have been contemporary with ceramic phase 2 activity at Uley Bury where 33 sherds (410g) of Droitwich salt container material was also identified (Morris 1983b), a period diagnostic of the end of the early Iron Age and the beginning of the middle Iron Age. The arrival of an early type of Droitwich salt container at the Eckweek enclosure and a significant number (not assigned to fabric type) at Uley Bury hillfort presaged the dramatic development in the production and regional exchange of ceramics (and their content of salt in the case of briquetage) that dominated the later Iron

Age in the wider region and elsewhere in many parts of Britain with the production and wide distribution of many types of pottery and brine-drying and salt-transportation containers (Allen *et al* 1994; Morris 1994; Lane and Morris 2001; Knight et al 2003; Morris 2012).

A Possible Bronze-working Crucible

A single small sherd of pottery had been overfired to the point of bloating the clay matrix and evaporating any inclusions in the clay thus leaving holes where the inclusions had once been and creating a vesicular fabric (FT163). The piece is not simply amorphous fired clay but rather has two parallel, curved surfaces just like a potsherd. The sherd is likely to derive from a crucible used to melt copper and tin to create bronze or to recycle a bronze object to make a new one.

Discussion

The earliest stratified pottery is from Ditch 3161 in Area H, comprising two sherds of fabric FT158A from context 3162. Most of the same pottery fabrics occur in the stratified sequence of deposits in ditch cut 3176 (see this report, Figure. 4.6), part of the same ditch revealed during area excavation as ditch cut 3076 exposed in Cutting 2 of Area H (Figure 5.3). Ditch 3176 contained 16 sherds from five different fabrics, including FT158B, 158C, 160, 164, and 165. The larger excavated section of ditch 3076 in Cutting 2 revealed 41 sherds consisting of four main pottery fabrics, including FT158A, 158B, 158C, 160, 163, and 164 as well as the Droitwich salt container material (FT167). Therefore, the infilling of the different ditch sections 3176 and 3076 were likely to have occurred during the same period, and not long after the infilling of ditch cut 3161. The pottery from several other features in Area H including postholes, a scoop and a pit contain small quantities of the same fabrics as identified in these ditch cuts (Figure 5.3), and it would not be inappropriate to consider these as contemporary or later features.

Some indication of the use of these vessels was observed on several sherds. The range of usewear evidence includes interior pitting of calcareous fabric sherds, charred matter on the interior surfaces and sooting on the exterior. The former indicates the use of a vessel as container of acidic material, probably a liquid, while the latter two residues indicate cooking vessels. Figure 5.4 correlates this evidence with the various fabrics.

The significance of the range of materials from this unexpected later prehistoric site lies in the nature of the activities present and the trading contacts evidenced by these materials. Although the majority of the pottery could have been made locally, it belongs to a wider Somerset and Wessex coarseware tradition. The salt container sherds indicate the need for this commodity and the extent of contacts much further north into the Severn valley via an extended exchange system. The presence of possible evidence for bronze-working at Eckweek in the Somerset-Avon area would add another occurrence of bronze metalworking at early-middle Iron Age non-hillfort settlement sites noted previously nearby at Camerton enclosure (Wedlake 1958, 39), at the Dibbles Farm, Christon (Morris 1988, 68, fig. 14, 3), and at Glastonbury and the Meare Lake Villages (Bulleid and Grey 1911, 300–309; 1953, 414–427). The loss of a simple bronze bracelet (see this report Section 5.6) supports on the site bronze-working. Therefore, the range of activities and contacts evidenced from such a small amount of area at the Iron Age site at Eckweek has added significantly to our knowledge of this period and the nature of these sites in this area during the less well-known period just prior to the classic middle Iron Age of the 4th to 1st century BC.

5.2 ROMANO-BRITISH POTTERY
by Dr Jane Timby (2015)

Summary

A small assemblage of just 12 sherds of Roman pottery weighing 104.5g and four fragments of Roman ceramic building material (CBM) weighing 657g were found. The material was sorted into fabrics and quantified by sherd count and weight for each recorded context. Known, named regional traded wares are coded using the National Roman fabric reference series (Tomber and Dore 1998) (codes in brackets). Other wares are coded more generically on the basis of firing colour, inclusion type and texture. The data has been summarised in Figure 5.7.

The assemblage is heavily biased towards samian ware which accounts for seven sherds suggesting this is a selected group of material. The sherds are generally quite small with an overall sherd weight of just 7.7g, which is slightly on the low side for generally more robust Roman pottery.

Roman

The Roman assemblage comprised seven sherds of samian; one sherd of unidentified amphora; three reduced sandy wares and one sherd of South-west oxidised (SOW OX) ware.

The samian appears to comprise one possible sherd (burnt) of Martres-de-Veyre (MDV SA); five sherds of Central Gaulish ware (Lezoux) (LEZ SA) and one probable sherd of British Pulborough samian (PUL SA). There are two decorated sherds, probably from Dragendorff 37-type bowls, along with the base from the same bowl form and one rim from a dish Dragendorff 18/31. This latter vessel is

Context	Fabric	Type/form	Wt (g)	No	Refs	Comment	Date
2	CBM	box-flue	122	1	/736\ 97.55/113.20		Roman
2	CBM	pila	441	1	/559\, 106.85/111.50		Roman
2	MDVSA?		0.5	1	[1015], FT25	slightly burnt	early C2
2	LEZSA	Dr 37	2	1	[1004], FT25	decorated	C2
2	LEZSA		4	1	[1004], FT25		C2
2	PULSA?	18/31	4	1	CAR1129, FT25		C2
2	LEZSA	Dr 37?	0.5	1	CAR1101, FT25	v small décor	C2
2	GY		11	2	Area A, FT150		Roman
2	BW	?bowl	7	1	Area A, FT150		Roman
65	AMP	body	42	1	FT150		Roman
114	LEZSA	Dr 37 base	25	1	CAR1124		C2
114	SOWOX		8	1			C2/C3
160	CBM	box-flue	55	1	/716\, 102.65/126.85		Roman
161	CBM	box-flue	39	1	/738\, 102.95/125.15		Roman
318	LEZSA		0.5	1	[1392] CAR, FT25, WAKE 11		C2
Total			761.5	16			

FIGURE 5.7

Summary of Romano-British pottery and ceramic material

the Pulborough example. All these wares would be current in the early-mid 2nd century. Other wares include one sherd of imported amphora, possibly shouldered, in pale oxidised ware with sparse lime voids and quartz sand. The coarsewares include one rim, probably from a bowl in black sandy ware; two slightly sandy local grey wares and one bodysherd in South-west oxidised ware (SOW OX). The latter suggests a 2nd or 3rd century date.

Ceramic Building Material (CBM)

The CBM includes three fragments of box flue with combed exteriors and one fragment of flat tile (*pila*). These all indicate the presence of a moderately well-appointed Roman building furnished with underfloor heating.

Conclusion

This is a very small group of material which indicates activity from the locality in the 2nd century AD. The dominance of samian with at least two decorated vessels indicates an assemblage from an establishment of some status but may also reflect, in part, deliberate selection. The CBM also confirms the proximity of a higher status Roman building, Wellow villa.

5.3 THE LATE SAXON, SAXO-NORMAN, MEDIEVAL AND POST-MEDIEVAL POTTERY

by Andrew Young and Alexander Kidd (1990–1991, reviewed by Andrew Young 2015)

5.3.1 Introduction

Excavation at Eckweek yielded a large assemblage of stratified late Saxon, Saxo-Norman and medieval pottery. Over twenty-one thousand sherds, weighing slightly less than 220kgs, were recorded, catalogued, and analysed during the post-excavation programme, the overwhelming majority of which was recovered from stratified deposits associated with the late Saxon, Saxo-Norman and medieval settlement recorded in Areas A, B and H (Figures 1.6 and 1.7). The post-excavation programme focused on this material to formulate a detailed medieval ceramic sequence by means of a comprehensive and thorough examination and description of the fabrics represented and a subsequent detailed seriation of those fabrics by context and vessel forms represented (the seriation done entirely by hand by the writer and Alexander Kidd on paper under the guidance of Varian Denham of English Heritage). Although the fabric identification, seriation and analysis work was done in 1991, well before the publication of the guidelines for such work published by the Medieval Pottery Research Group (MPRG 2001), it was nonetheless undertaken broadly in accordance with those guidelines, as well as the broader guidelines for assessment and post-excavation analysis set out in Management of Archaeological Projects 2 (English Heritage 1991). In conjunction with the structural data, the ceramic phasing (CP) provides the basis for dating the sequence of activity recorded on the site. The post-excavation research design for the project, along with the ceramic assemblage itself, the portable Fabric-Type series and all other tables and extended comments not included here are to be found in the project archive.

The post-excavation research aims for the pottery, in particular the medieval assemblage, were set out in the post-excavation research design (archive), which recognised its central role in interpreting the chronology, development and character of the late Saxon and medieval settlement, both in site specific and wider terms. Key aims in the analysis stage included the definition of an intra-site ceramic sequence and both a relative and absolute chronology of such, the latter initially achieved through the integration of recognised and well-dated regional ceramics such as Bristol Ham Green ware, NW Wiltshire (Minety) ware and South Somerset wares, and thereafter supported by the series of independent radiocarbon determinations (Section 6.1). Particular attention was paid during the process of seriation to identify residuality in the ceramic assemblage, as a means of defining an accurate ceramic sequence, whilst functional indicators including vessel form, surface treatments, sooting and other vessel concretions were recorded in detail as a means of establishing how individual vessel types were used and, thereby, the character and development of domestic and associated settlement related activity through time. In order to address these questions every individual sherd of pottery was initially examined in hand specimen and under low magnification using a binocular (×20) microscope by the writer and Alexander Kidd to define its general fabric characteristics, principal fabric inclusions and mineralogy and vessel form or, where it represented a recognised regional type, its source and external chronology.

A total of 96 separate late Saxon, Saxo-Norman and medieval pottery fabrics were identified and defined petrologically (Figure 5.8). Selected examples were subsequently further defined by means of thin-section petrological descriptions undertaken by the writer (who studied geological mineralogy at Bristol University as a Geology undergraduate) with the grateful assistance and facilities of the University of Bristol, Department of Geology. Further thin-section analysis was undertaken of 51 selected sherds by Dr David Williams (Section 5.3.4) in order to establish whether their petrological characteristics indicated any particular geological provenance or similarity with other petrological studies undertaken for medieval ceramics in the region.

This process led to the refinement and characterisation of the final 96 pottery fabric types, 86 of which related to activity during successive phases of late Saxon, Saxo-Norman and medieval settlement during Period III. Each context-based body of ceramic data was entered onto an early 1990s computerised *Superfile* database with individual data fields included for context, count, weight, fabric types, ware and vessel forms, along with aspects of decoration and characteristics potentially relating to vessel function, in particular sooting, wiping, and other vessel concretions. A small number of selected sherds were examined by Dr Richard Evershed at the University of Liverpool, Department of Biochemistry as part of a wider study of the function and use of selected medieval vessels through analysis of Lipid residues. The study was designed to identify what types of foodstuff vessels originally contained although, unfortunately, the analysis technique was at the earliest stages of development at that time and in 2015 the preliminary results obtained are now considered by Dr Evershed to be unreliable (V Straker pers comm).

The following catalogue and discussion of the pottery is period based and outlines the characteristics and, where appropriate, the development, of ceramics dated between the late Saxon and earlier post-medieval periods. The report focuses upon the late Saxon, Saxo-Norman and medieval ceramic wares, amalgamations of individual ceramic fabrics that have similar fabric and vessel form characteristics. These are described and discussed in particular detail, whilst the post-medieval pottery, which constitutes only a very small proportion of the assemblage as a whole, is summarised here and detailed more fully in the project archive. Wares, as for individual fabrics, were initially classified on the basis of similar ranges of inclusions and/or overall fabric and reflect related groups of pottery containing broadly similar fabrics, both from known and unrecognised production centres. As such, an individual ware can usefully be thought of as the product of an associated production centre, in some cases this might represent no more than a single kiln but in others a series of kilns operating out of a number of separate but associated workshops, all of which utilised broadly similar raw materials and technology to produce a similar range of fabrics and vessel types. Ceramic forms, relatively restricted in the Eckweek assemblage (for details of ceramic forms see the project archive), fulfilled a subordinate role in refining the characteristics of ceramic wares, but were recorded in detail in an attempt to define broad chronological trends which may have related to functional attributes alone.

Comparanda

During the cataloguing and analysis of the medieval ceramics the following excavation archive and reference collections were visited by the author for direct comparison of sherds:

1   Barrow Mead, Bath (Woodhouse 1976 at Roman Baths Museum, Bath)
2   Beckery Chapel, Glastonbury (Taunton Museum)
3   Bristol Type Series (Bristol City Museum)
4   Castle Neroche, Somerset (Taunton Museum)
5   Cheddar Palace, Cheddar (Rahtz 1979 at Taunton Museum)
6   Citizen House, Bath (Roman Baths Museum)
7   Clarendon Palace, Wiltshire (Salisbury Museum)
8   Ilchester, Somerset 1980–1981 (Pearson 1982 at Taunton Museum)
9   Ilchester (1985) Somerset (Taunton Museum)
10 Lacock, Nash Hill, Wiltshire (McCarthy 1974 held at Devizes Museum)
11 Langley Burrell, Chippenham, Wilts (Devizes Museum)
12 Laverstock Kilns, Wilts (Musty, J, Algar, D and Ewence, P 1969 at Salisbury Museum)
13 Nether Stowey, West Somerset (Coleman-Smith and Pearson 1970 at Taunton Museum)
14 Old Sarum, Salisbury (Salisbury Museum)

ARTEFACTS AND ENVIRONMENTAL EVIDENCE

FT	Ware	Count (% of assemblage)	Weight g (% of assemblage)	Eckweek ceramic phases	Core date range	Made by	External parallels	Glazed (%)	Wiped (%)	Sooted (%)	Typical colour ext/int surfaces	Fabric hardness feel, fracture	Major inclusions	Minor inclusions	Common vessel forms	Rare vessel forms	Comments
1	1	181 (0.75%)	2388g (1.12%)	CP3	AD 1050–1100	wheel	none	0%	38%	50%	7.5YR 6/4 (ext) 7.5YR 8/0 (int)	Hard, sandy, hackly	Quartz, mica	Limestone, organics, FeO	2, 4	33, 35, 48	Possibly a subdivision of FT5. Type I cooking pots only
2	6	40 (0.16%)	288g (0.13%)	CP2	AD 1000–1050	hand	Bristol BPT3	0%	8%	10%	7.5YR 6/4 (ext) 7.5YR 4/0 (int)	Soft, soapy hackly	Limestone, quartz, voids	Sandstone, shell, flint, calcite, FeO	–	4, 31	Bristol BPT3 dated AD1000–1070 at Bristol Castle
3	2	749 (3.12%)	7886g (3.71%)	CP2, 3, ?4	AD 1000–1250	wheel	none	0%	7%	2%	7.5YR 6/4 (ext) 7.5YR 6/6 (int)	Soft sandy	Quartz, limestone	FeO	32, 33, 35, 37, 1, 3, 4	31, 34, 39, 40, 41, 48, 49, 54, 2, 73, 74	Forms and FT similar to FT15. Low sooting indicates rarely used for cooking pots
4	1	662 (2.75%)	5185g (2.44%)	CP?1, 2, 3, ?4	AD 1000–1100	hand and wheel	none	0%	11%	25%	5YR 4/2 (int) 10YR 4/2 (ext)	Soft sandy hackly	Quartz, mica	Flint, limestone, FeO	32, 35, 4	2, 31, 33, 34, 37, 40, 48, 49, 51	Type I cooking pots only. Usually reduced throughout
5	1	2635 (10.97%)	32263g (15.20%)	CP2-4 and ?5	AD 1000–1250	wheel	none	0%	22%	35%	5YR 7/6 (int) 5YR 5/4 (ext)	Hard sandy hackly	Quartz, mica	Flint, limestone, FeO, organics	2, 4, 32, 33, 35, 37	1, 3, 22, 23, 25, 72, 31, 34, 39, 40, 41, 48-51, 53-56, 60, 63, 65	Rare paired finger-tip decoration on cooking pot rims. Very rare slash/comb decorated pitchers. Mainly Type I cooking pots
6	2	50 (0.20%)	902g (0.42%)	CP2	AD 1000–1050	wheel	none	0%	20%	36%	10YR 3/2 (ext) 2.5YR 6/2(int)	Hard sandy hackly	Quartz, mica, FeO	Limestone, shell, calcite, ?coal		2, 3, 4	Mostly Type I cooking pots plus very rare Westcountry Dishes
7	–																Withdrawn as group
8	–																Withdrawn – as FT40
9	–																Withdrawn – as FT3
10	4	94 (0.39%)	1459g (0.68%)	CP4	AD 1100–1250	hand	none	0%	1%	5%	10YR 8/2 (ext) 10YR 4/1 (int)	Soft sandy	Quartz, flint, limestone	Mica, FeO, ?mudstone	4, 32	2, 31, 33, 39, 41, 59	Type II cooking pots only with very rare applied decoration
11	2	1380 (5.75%)	13752g (6.48%)	CPs 3, 4 and 5	AD 1050–1300	wheel	none	0%	18%	25%	10YR 8/2 (ext) 10YR 4/1 (int)	Hard sandy hackly	Quartz, mica	Organics, clay relicts, FeO	2, 4, 32, 33, 35, 37	3, 21, 73, 31, 34, 39, 40, 41, 47-51, 53, 54, 56, 60, 63	Mainly Type I cooking pots. Rare jugs and very rare Westcountry Dishes. Oxidised firing of low iron clays
12	–																Withdrawn – as FT94
13	7	456 (1.90%)	3281g (1.54%)	CP1	AD 930–1000	hand	Great Som'ford ware, OXAC	0%	4%	9%	2.5YR 6/6 (ext and int)	Soft soapy	Limestone shell	Quartz, flint, FeO, voids	4, 31, 32	2, 33, 35, 49, 53	Distinctive shell and limestone tempered fabric with wheel-stamp body decoration and rare paired finger-tip decoration to rim. Type II cooking pots with 12–20cm diameter

FIGURE 5.8

Description of late Saxon and medieval pottery fabrics

FT	Ware	Count (% of assemblage)	Weight g (% of assemblage)	Eckweek ceramic phases	Core date range	Made by	External parallels	Glazed (%)	Wiped (%)	Sooted (%)	Typical colour ext/int surfaces	Fabric hardness feel, fracture	Major inclusions	Minor inclusions	Common vessel forms	Rare vessel forms	Comments
14	1	336 (1.4%)	3284g (1.54%)	CP2	AD 1000–1050	hand	none	0%	27%	40%	5YR 6/3 (ext) 5YR 6/4 (int)	Soft sandy hackly	Quartz, organics, FeO	Flint, limestone, mica, voids	2, 4, 32	33, 41, 51, 53, 72	Mainly Type I cooking pots with rare finger tip decoration on rim. Very rare pitchers
15	1	500 (2.08%)	6274g (2.95%)	CP2–4	AD 1000–1250	wheel	none	0%	11%	5%	7.5YR 5/2 (ext and int)	Hard smooth hackly	Quartz	Limestone, mica, FeO, ?slag	1–4, 32, 33, 35	31, 34, 37, 40, 41, 47–49, 73–74	Mainly Westcountry Dish forms with some Type II cooking pots with rare finger-tip decoration to rims. Flat bases prior to CP4
16	2	464 (1.93%)	4557g (2.14%)	CP2–5	AD 1000–1300	wheel	none	0%	30%	27%	5YR 5/2 (ext) 5YR 7/1 (int)	Hard smooth hackly	Quartz, mica, limestone	Organics, FeO	2, 4, 33, 37, 51	31, 32, 34, 35, 40, 41, 48, 52, 53, 56	Type I cooking pots only with very rare applied strips and combing. Predominantly reduced fabric
17	2	297 (1.23%)	3312g (1.56%)	CP4–5	AD 1100–1300	?wheel	none	0%	40%	30%	2.5YR 3/2 (ext) 2.5YR 5/1 (int)	Hard smooth hackly	Quartz, mica, limestone	Organics, flint, ?mudstone	1, 4, 32, 41	2, 33, 35, 37, 56, 61	Mainly Type I cooking pots with very rare applied strip decoration plus rare Westcountry Dishes. Over 13% with internal calcareous concretions
18	-																Withdrawn as group – part of FT16
19	-																Withdrawn as group
20	-																Withdrawn as group
21	14	222 (0.92%)	2031g (0.95%)	CP5	AD 1250–1300	wheel	none	23%	2%	3%	7.5YR 6/6 (ext) 10YR 7/4 (int)	Soft smooth	Quartz, mica, FeO	organics	4, 41	2, 21, 31, 37, 45, 51, 64, 71	Type II cooking pots and rare jugs with significant number containing calcareous concretions
22	4	82 (0.34%)	821g (0.38%)	CP2	AD 1000–1050	hand	none	0%	29%	27%	7.5YR 5/4 (ext) 5YR 6/6 (int)	Soft smooth	Quartz, limestone flint	Calcite, mica, clay relicts, FeO	-	2–4, 32, 35, 37, 40, 49, 50, 56	Type I cooking pots only in predominantly oxidised fabric with characteristic flint inclusions
23	7	10 (0.04%)	55g (0.02%)	CP5	AD 1250–1300	wheel	NW Wilts and BPT18	80%	0%	0%	10YR 5/1 (ext) 10YR 6/1 (int)	Hard sandy hackly	limestone	Quartz, shell, FeO	-	-	Sherds often have thin external glaze often decorated with simple combing. Mainly representing small number of ?jugs. Similar to FT58
24	13	11 (0.04%)	54g (0.02%)	CP2	AD 1000–1050	wheel	SE Wilts wares	73%	0%	0%	2.5YR 5/8 (ext and int)	Hard sandy hackly	Quartz	none	-	-	Common external greenish glaze with wavy combed decoration. Representing a few tableware pitchers
25	51	10 (0.04%)	36g (0.01%)	residual	Roman		Samian										Residual Roman Samian ware
26	-																Withdrawn as group
27	-																Withdrawn as group – part of FT17
28	-																Withdrawn as group – part of FT75
29	5	18 (0.07%)	245g (0.11%)	CP4–5	AD 1100–1300	hand	none	0%	22%	6%	5YR 5/4 (ext) 5YR 6/6 (int)	Soft sandy hackly	Calcite, quartz, limestone	Mica, clay relicts, FeO	36	4, 32	Type II cooking pots with characteristic Calcite temper
30	8	3 (0.01%)	11g (0.005%)	CP2–3	AD 1000–1100	wheel	Stamford Ware, Lincs	100%	0%	0%	10YR 8/2 (ext and int)	Hard smooth concoidal	Quartz	FeO	-	-	Imported Stamford ware glazed pitcher fabric

FIGURE 5.8 CONT.

ARTEFACTS AND ENVIRONMENTAL EVIDENCE

FT	Ware	Count (% of assemblage)	Weight g (% of assemblage)	Eckweek ceramic phases	Core date range	Made by	External parallels	Glazed (%)	Wiped (%)	Sooted (%)	Typical colour ext/int surfaces	Fabric hardness feel, fracture	Major inclusions	Minor inclusions	Common vessel forms	Rare vessel forms	Comments
31	–															Withdrawn as group – part of FT23
32	–															Withdrawn as group – part of FT108
33	15	110 (0.45%)	824g (0.38%)	CP5–6	AD 1250–1375	wheel	Naish Hill, Lacock, Wilts	78%	4%	4%	5YR 7/4 (ext and int)	Hard sandy hackly	Quartz	Mica, FeO, limestone	–	4, 8, 23, 48, 56	Glazed tableware representing small number of jugs decorated with applied strips, combing, dot-and-circle, painted slip and finger-tips
34	12	72 (0.30%)	596g (0.28%)	CP5–6	AD 1250–1375	wheel	none	85%	3%	1%	7.5YR 7/4 (ext and int)	Hard sandy hackly	Quartz, chalk	Mica, FeO, opaques	–	4, 8, 45, 48, 62	Type II cooking pots and jugs. 6% with external calcareous concretions
35	–															Withdrawn as group – part of FT91
36	–															Withdrawn as group – part of FT11
37	2	47 (0.19%)	642g (0.30%)	CP2–3	AD 1000–1100	wheel	none	0%	9%	2%	5YR 4/3 (ext) 5YR 6/6 (int)	Soft sandy hackly	Quartz, FeO, limestone	mica	35	2, 3, 32	Type II cooking pots and Westcountry Dishes
38	–															Withdrawn as group – part of FT3
39	–															Withdrawn as group – part of FT5
40	2	176 (0.73%)	2571g (1.21%)	CP2–3	AD 1000–1100	wheel	none	0%	28%	49%	5YR 5/2 (ext) 5YR 6/3 (int)	Soft smooth hackly	Quartz, mica, limestone	FeO	2, 4, 31, 35	3, 32, 33, 37, 40, 48, 65	Mainly Type I cooking pots with rare finger-tip decoration to rim and very rare Westcountry Dishes
41	–															Withdrawn as group – part of FT29
42	–															Withdrawn as group – part of FT29
43	–															Withdrawn as group – part of FT40
44	–															Withdrawn as group – part of FT51
45	–															Withdrawn as group – part of FT50
46	2	110 (0.45%)	735g (0.34%)	CP4	AD 1100–1250	wheel	none	44%	6%	9%	5YR 6/6 (ext and int)	Hard sandy hackly	Quartz, mica, organic matter	Limestone, flint, FeO, clay relicts	–	21, 23, 35, 40, 51, 55, 56	Type II cooking pots and rarer jugs. Common horizontal and hatched combing. Possibly a development from FT69 and the only glazed and commonly decorated fabric in Wares 1 and 2
47	14	85 (0.35%)	244g (0.11%)	CP5	AD 1250–1300	wheel	South Somerset ware	73%	0%	1%	5YR 7/7 (ext and int)	Soft smooth	none	Quartz, mica, FeO	–	2, 23, 38	Fine oxidised fabric representing a small number of jugs decorated with combing, applied strips and painted slip
48	17	43 (0.17%)	322g (0.15%)	CP4–5	AD 1100–1300	hand	Ham Green A (BPT 26)	98%	0%	0%	2.5YR 8/2 (ext and int)	Hard sandy hackly	Quartz	Mica, opaques	–	73	Common applied strips on decorated jugs. Bristol Ham Green dated AD1150–1300 in Bristol
49	14	138 (0.57%)	963g (0.45%)	CP5	AD 1250–1300	wheel	none	8%	7%	12%	5YR 6/4 (ext) 5YR 5/1 (int)	Soft smooth hackly	Mica, quartz, organic	Limestone, FeO	51	1, 2, 4, 31, 32, 37, 40, 41	Type II cooking pots and rare Westcountry Dishes. Usually in a reduced fabric with rare finger-tip and combed decoration

FIGURE 5.8 CONT.

FT	Ware	Count (% of assemblage)	Weight g (% of assemblage)	Eckwork ceramic phases	Core date range	Made by	External parallels	Glazed (%)	Wiped (%)	Sooted (%)	Typical colour ext/int surfaces	Fabric hardness feel, fracture	Major inclusions	Minor inclusions	Common vessel forms	Rare vessel forms	Comments
50	6	222 (0.92%)	1318g (0.62g)	CP1	AD 930–1000	hand	Cheddar FTE and Cheddar FT8	0%	16%	10%	5YR 5/6 (ext and int)	Soft sandy hackly	Quartz, limestone and voids	Sandstone mica, FeO flint	4, 31, 32, 35	2, 33, 34, 39, 40, 53	Well defined fabric with characteristic voids and rare paired finger-tip decoration on rim. Dated cAD945–1000 by coin at Cheddar Palace (FTE and FT8)
51	16	170 (0.70%)	1181g (0.55%)	CP5-6	AD 1250–1375	wheel	Naish Hill, Lacock, Wilts	85%	1%	0%	10YR 8/3 (ext and int)	Hard sandy hackly	Quartz, FeO	Clay relicts, opaques	–	2, 4, 5, 8, 21, 31, 48, 55–57	Type II cooking pots and rarer jugs in oxidised low Fe clay with very common ext. green glaze. Rare applied, combed and incised decoration to body with finger-tip bases and slashed handles. Dated at kiln site to cAD1275–1325
52	2	186 (0.77%)	2632g (1.24%)	CP2–?3	AD 1000–1050	hand	none	0%	26%	39%	7.5YR 6/4 (ext and int)	Hard sandy hackly	Quartz, chalk	Flint, mica, FeO	4, 33	31–35, 37, 39, 45, 48	Type I cooking pots only with very rare finger-tip decoration to rims. Distinctive 'biscuity' fabric
53	–																Withdrawn
54	2	60 (0.25%)	776g (0.36%)	CP2	AD 1000–1050	wheel	none	0%	17%	27%	5YR 5/4 (ext) 2.5YR 6/6 (int)	Soft sandy laminated	Quartz, limestone	Flint, FeO	–	4, 31, 33, 35	Type I cooking pots only with distinctive black laminated core. Analogous to Bath 'A' fabrics
55	15	244 (1.01%)	1765g (0.83%)	CP5–?6	AD 1250–1300	wheel	Naish Hill, Lacock, Wilts	67%	1%	7%	7.5YR 8/2 (ext) 7.5YR 7/2 (int)	Hard sandy hackly	Quartz	FeO, opaques, mica	2, 52	4, 6, 8, 32, 37–39, 41, 51, 56	Mainly Type II cooking pots. Rare applied ornament with combing, painted slip and finger-tip decoration of bases. Well-sorted quartz temper.
56	10	30 (0.12%)	201g (0.09%)	CP5–?6	AD 1250–1300	wheel	Laverstock, Wilts	90%	10%	0%	7.5YR 7/4 (ext and int)	Very hard, smooth, concoidal	Quartz	Limestone, mica	–	6, 21	Glazed jug fabric with rare applied strips and combing and some painted slip
57	18	84 (0.35%)	1402g (0.66%)	CP6	AD 1300–1375	wheel	none	99%	0%	0%	10YR 7/4 (ext and int)	V. hard sandy hackly	Quartz	Mica, opaques	6, 56	21, 51, 71	Fabric represented by a single reconstructed jug (FPN 74)
58	7	268 (1.11%)	3267g (1.53%)	CP6	AD 1300–1375	wheel	NW Wilts, Minety ware	35%	1%	3%	10YR 7/3 (ext) 10YR 8/3 (int)	Hard smooth hackly	Limestone quartz	Shell, FeO	2	4, 8, 9, 21, 32, 33, 37, 44, 51, 54, 64, 71	NW Wilts Minety ware – Type II cooking pots and glazed jugs decorated with rare combing and applied strips. Strap handles slashed.
59	4	72 (0.30%)	582g (0.27%)	CP1	AD 930–1000	hand	none	0%	13%	22%	2.5YR 6/4 (ext and int)	Soft grainy hackly	Quartz, flint, limestone	Mica, FeO, voids	4	1, 31–33, 35, 50, 51	Type I cooking pots with rare finger-tip decoration to rim and rare Westcountry Dishes. Distinctive oxidised fabric with coarse inclusions
60	14	518 (2.15%)	3466g (1.63%)	CP5–?6	AD 1250–1300	wheel	?Donyatt, South Somerset	10%	1%	5%	5YR 7/6 (ext and int)	Soft smooth	Mica, clay relicts, FeO	Quartz, organics	1–4, 40, 41, 51, 56	21, 23, 31, 32, 37, 39, 43, 54, 55	Type II cooking pots, Westcountry Dishes and rare jugs. Decoration includes geometric combing, painted slip and applied strips. Slashed handles. No deliberate temper
61	–																Withdrawn – as FT58

FIGURE 5.8 CONT.

ARTEFACTS AND ENVIRONMENTAL EVIDENCE

FT	Ware	Count (% of assemblage)	Weight g (% of assemblage)	Eckweek ceramic phases	Core date range	Made by	External parallels	Glazed (%)	Wiped (%)	Sooted (%)	Typical colour ext/int surfaces	Fabric hardness feel, fracture	Major inclusions	Minor inclusions	Common vessel forms	Rare vessel forms	Comments
62	9	14 (0.05%)	23g (0.01%)	CP6	AD 1300–1375	wheel	Surrey White ware	93%	0%	0%	5YR 8/2 (ext and int)	Hard smooth	Quartz	–	2, 5, 46		Surrey White ware representing two small bowls at most
63	14	285 (1.18%)	4786g (2.25%)	CP6	AD 1300–1375	wheel	?Donyatt, South Somerset	64%	1%	7%	7.5YR 7/4 (ext) 7.5YR 6/4 (int)	Soft sandy	Quartz, FeO, clay relicts	mica	2, 5, 38, 42, 56	4, 7, 8, 21, 22, 24, 32, 37, 58, 60, 71, 72	Includes 'Stag Head' Cistern FPN62, dripping dishes (FPN 48 and 52) and a bowl (FPN44)
64	–																Withdrawn – same as FT130
65	4	85 (0.35%)	875g (0.41%)	CP1–?2	AD 930–1000	hand	none	0%	0%	27%	2.5YR 6/1 (ext) 7.5YR 6/4 (int)	Soft v sandy hackly	Quartz, limestone, flint	FeO, voids	–	2, 4, 31, 32, 34	Type I cooking pots never decorated
66	–																Withdrawn – as FT80
67	6	465 (0.68%)	1525g (0.71%)	CP1	AD 930–1000	wheel	none	0%	10%	11%	7.5YR 7/1 (ext) 7.5YR 7/0 (int)	Soft sandy laminated	Quartz, limestone, sandst.	Flint, FeO, voids	4, 35	31, 55	Type II cooking pots only. Well defined fabric with distinctive reduced and laminated core
68	1	382 (1.59%)	3743g (1.76%)	CP2–?3	AD 1000–1050	hand	none	0%	11%	33%	10YR 4/2 (ext and int)	Soft granular hackly	Quartz	Organics, flint, opaques, FeO	4	2, 25, 32, 33, 35, 37, 41, 48, 49, 51	Predominantly Type I cooking pots plus very rare pitchers in reduced fabric
69	2	1020 (4.25%)	11627g (5.47%)	CP1, 2 and ?3	AD 930–1050	wheel and hand	none	0%	18%	35%	7.5YR 5/2 (ext) 7.5YR 6/2 (int)	Soft sandy	Quartz, organic limestone	Mica, FeO	2, 4, 32, 35	1, 3, 31, 33, 34, 37, 39, 40, 48, 49, 51, 53, 55, 71	The only Ware 2 fabric present in CP1. Common organic temper component and mainly Type I cooking pots plus very rare pitchers
70	4	253 (1.05%)	2556g (1.20%)	CP4	AD 1100–1250	wheel	none	0%	11%	6%	10YR 6/2 (ext) 10YR 4/1 (int)	Hard smooth hackly	Quartz, flint, limestone	Mica, clay relicts, FeO	1, 2, 4, 32, 39, 40	3, 33, 37, 41, 50, 51, 52, 54	Type II cooking pots and Westcountry Dishes. Similar to FT75 but does not contain shell
71	15	486 (2.02%)	2841g (1.33%)	CP5–6	AD 1250–1375	wheel	Naish Hill, Lacock Fabric A	45%	3%	5%	2.5YR 6/6 (ext and int)	Hard v sandy	Quartz, FeO, opaques	Clay relicts ?slag	2, 52, 56	4, 8, 31, 35, 37, 40, 43, 48, 50, 51, 53–55, 60, 21, 23, 71	Predominantly Type II cooking pots and rare jugs with rod handles. Decoration rare applied strips, painted slip on body and neck and finger-tips around base
72	–																Withdrawn – as Minety NW Wilts ware
73	–																Withdrawn – as FT89
74	1	107 (0.44%)	869g (0.40%)	CP4–?5	AD 1100–1250	hand	none	0%	1%	2%	10YR 6/3 (ext) 10YR 5/1 (int)	Soft sandy hackly	Quartz, mica, organics	Clay relicts	4	2, 22	Highly micaceous reduced fabric with patchy darker ?organic streaks. Type II cooking pots and ?rare skillets. Rare decoration using applied strips

FIGURE 5.8 CONT.

FT	Ware	Count (% of assemblage)	Weight g (% of assemblage)	Eckweek ceramic phases	Core date range	Made by	External parallels	Glazed (%)	Wiped (%)	Sooted (%)	Typical colour ext/int surfaces	Fabric hardness feel, fracture	Major inclusions	Minor inclusions	Common vessel forms	Rare vessel forms	Comments
75	4	509 (2.12%)	5633g (2.65%)	CP4-?5	AD 1100–1250	hand (earlier) and wheel	none	2%	5%	9%	10YR 7/4 (ext and int)	Soft sandy hackly	Flint, limestone, quartz, shell	Organics, mica, FeO, clay relicts	1–4, 37, 39, 40, 41	32–34, 47, 48, 51, 53, 62, 74	Predominantly Westcountry Dishes plus rare Type II cooking pots and possibly very rare pancheons. Rim form 40 is characteristic of the flint-shell tempered reduced fabric. Decoration restricted to very rare finger-tips on rim and around base.
76	–																Withdrawn – as FT106
77	14	300 (1.25%)	2186g (1.03%)	CP5-?6	AD 1250–1300	wheel	?South Somerset	1%	5%	10%	10YR 4/2 (ext and int)	Soft sandy	Quartz, mica, limestone	Organics	2, 4, 32, 41, 51	1, 3, 33, 34, 37, 40, 45, 55, 56, 71	Predominantly Type II cooking pots plus very rare Westcountry Dishes. Very rare applied strips and simple comb decoration. Well-defined reduced fabric
78	–																Withdrawn – as FT11
79	15	33 (0.13%)	87g (0.04%)	CP5-?6	AD 1250–1300	wheel	none	100%	0%	0%	10YR 8/1 (ext and int)	Hard smooth	Quartz	FeO	–	45, 48, 54	Glazed jugs only with rare applied strips and very rare roulette to body. Low Fe content clay
80	16	266 (1.10%)	2134g (1.00%)	CP5-?6	AD 1250–1300	wheel	Naish Hill, Lacock Fabric B or D	90%	0%	0%	5YR 7/6 (ext) 5YR5/1 (int)	V hard sandy hackly	Quartz, opaques	FeO, calcite, black 'spherules'	–	–	Mainly jugs plus rare Type II cooking pots with common applied strips, painted slip designs and rare combing to body. Handles commonly stabbed and bases usually have finger-tip decoration. Dated AD1275–1325 at Naish Hill
81	–																Withdrawn – as FT51
82	4	43 (0.17%)	437g (0.20%)	CP5	AD 1250–1300	wheel	none	3%	31%	10%	7.5YR 6/2 (ext and int)	Soft smooth	Quartz, chalk, flint	Mica, clay relicts, FeO	2	1, 3, 4, 32, 34, 41, 73	Mainly Type II cooking pots plus rare Westcountry Dishes. No decoration
83	10	9 (0.03%)	44g (0.02%)	CP5	AD 1250–1300	wheel	Laverstock, Wilts	100%	0%	0%	7.5YR 7/2 (ext and int)	V hard smooth conchoidal	Quartz	?Limestone, ?slag	–	–	Jug fabric with all-over green glaze. Common ornamented applied strips, combing and painted slip decoration. Dated AD1230–1275 at kiln site
84	12	22 (0.09%)	109g (0.05%)	CP5-?6	AD 1250–1300	wheel	none	91%	0%	0%	2.5YR 6/6 (ext and int)	Hard sandy hackly	Quartz, limestone, FeO	–	–	21, 37, 49, 56	Well defined oxidised fabric represented by jugs only. Common applied ornament, combing and painted slip with slashed handles
85	–																Withdrawn – as FT67
86	–																Withdrawn – as FT96
87	15	37 (0.15%)	477g (0.22%)	CP6–7	AD 1300–1375+	wheel	Bristol BPT254	81%	0%	0%	10YR 8/4 (ext and int)	Hard sandy hackly	Quartz, FeO,	Clay relicts	–	2, 4, 8, 45, 71	Represented by jugs and a single costrel (FPN121) with patchy green glaze. Rare applied ornamented strips, rare combing and painted slip on body. Oxidised low Fe clay
88	15	7 (0.02%)	55g (0.02%)	CP7	AD 1375+	wheel	none	71%	0%	0%	5YR 6/6 (ext and int)	Hard sandy hackly	Quartz, FeO	Limestone, opaques	–	–	Probably representing a single jug decorated with ornamented applied strips

FIGURE 5.8 CONT.

ARTEFACTS AND ENVIRONMENTAL EVIDENCE

FT	Ware	Count (% of assemblage)	Weight g (% of assemblage)	Eckweek ceramic phases	Core date range	Made by	External parallels	Glazed (%)	Wiped (%)	Sooted (%)	Typical colour ext/int surfaces	Fabric hardness feel, fracture	Major inclusions	Minor inclusions	Common vessel forms	Rare vessel forms	Comments
89	3	110 (0.45%)	1010g (0.47%)	CP5–26	AD 1250–1300	wheel	none	14%	1%	7%	10YR 6/2 (ext and int)	Soft sandy	Quartz, limestone organics	Mica, FeO	1, 2, 4	21, 22, 32, 41, 43, 51, 55	Type II cooking pots and Westcountry Dishes plus rare jugs and skillets. Common wavy and linear combing to body plus slash and finger-tip decoration to strap handles. Some 6% have calcareous concretions
90	–																Withdrawn
91	19	113 (0.47%)	936g (0.44%)	CP5–6	AD 1250–1375	wheel	Bristol Redcliffe BPT118	99%	3%	1%	7.5YR 4/0 (ext and int)	V hard sandy hackly	Quartz, mica	Limestone, FeO	–	8, 43	Glazed Redcliffe jugs decorated with common elaborate applied strip ornament, rare combing, incised lines and painted slip. Flashed strap handles. Dated 1300–1350 at Bristol Castle
92	–																Withdrawn – as FT60
93	18	2 (0.00%)	45g (0.02%)	CP7	AD 1375+	wheel	none	100%	0%	0%	7.5YR 7/6 (ext and int)	Hard smooth hackly	Quartz	Mica, opaques	–	23, 41	Probably representing a single jug from Area G. Oxidised skin and reduced core with stabbed rod handle
94	3	100 (0.41%)	946g (0.44%)	CP2–5	AD 1000–1300	wheel	none	0%	14%	23%	5YR 6/3 (ext) 5YR 7/3 (int)	Soft smooth	Quartz, limestone	–	–	2, 4, 21, 32, 34, 35, 55, 65	Type I and II cooking pots with very rare paired finger-tip decoration to rim. One slashed handle
95	–																Withdrawn
96	4	151 (0.62%)	1047g (0.49%)	CP5–26	AD 1250–1300	wheel	none	1%	2%	1%	7.5YR 6/4 (ext) 7.5YR 6/6 (int)	Soft sandy	Quartz, flint, limestone	Mica, FeO, organics	32, 37, 39, 41, 51	1, 31, 33, 35, 40, 63, 73	Oxidised fabric represented by Type II cooking pots and Westcountry Dishes
97	–																Withdrawn – as FT55
98	–																Withdrawn
99	–																Withdrawn – as FT117
100	–																Withdrawn – as FT55
101	–																Withdrawn
102	–																Withdrawn – as FT71
103	3	47 (0.19%)	480g (0.22%)	CP2–3	AD 1000–1100	wheel	none	0%	26%	17%	2.5YR 5/8 (ext and int)	Soft sandy laminated	Quartz, chalk	Mica, FeO	–	4, 31, 32, 35	Type I cooking pots only with distinctive oxidised skin. Similar fabric at Beckery Chapel, Glastonbury
104	–																Withdrawn
105	–																Withdrawn – as FT80
106	14	236 (0.98%)	1586g (0.74%)	CP6	AD 1300–1375	wheel	?South Somerset ?Donyatt	20%	3%	13%	7.5YR 4/2 (ext and int)	Soft smooth	Mica, FeO	–	1, 2, 41	4, 8, 23, 32, 35, 37, 38, 42, 51, 56	Mainly Type II cooking pots and Westcountry Dishes plus rare jugs and a single dripping dish. 8% have calcareous concretions internally. Rare finger-tip decoration to applied strips and combing. Slashed rod-shaped handle. Distinctive smooth micaceous surfaces

FIGURE 5.8 CONT.

FT	Ware	Count (% of assemblage)	Weight g (% of assemblage)	Eckweek ceramic phases	Core date range	Made by	External parallels	Glazed (%)	Wiped (%)	Sooted (%)	Typical colour ext/int surfaces	Fabric hardness feel, fracture	Major inclusions	Minor inclusions	Common vessel forms	Rare vessel forms	Comments
107	18	20 (0.08%)	262g (0.12%)	CP7	AD 1375+	wheel	none	95%	0%	0%	10YR 7/1 (ext and int)	Hard sandy hackly	Quartz	FeO		49, 71	Possibly from a single glazed vessel with pale surfaces and strong throwing rings
108	14	86 (0.35%)	1008g (0.47%)	CP5–6	AD 1250–1375	wheel	Taunton Castle FT 4.2	93%	2%	4%	7.5YR 7/6 (ext and int)	Hard smooth	Quartz, organic FeO	Mica	–	4, 5, 21, 37, 38, 46, 55	Type II cooking pots and jugs with common applied strip, dot-and-circle, combed and painted slip decoration. Slashed strap handles. Probable Donyatt kilns product
109	–																Withdrawn – as FT3
110	–																Withdrawn
111	–																Withdrawn – as FT15
112	14	66 (0.27%)	716g (0.33%)	CP5–?6	AD 1250–1300	wheel	South Somerset (Rod Burchill pers. comm.)	20%	2%	15%	10YR 5/4 (ext and int)	Soft sandy	Quartz, mica,	Opaques, FeO		2, 4, 8, 73	Represented by Type I cooking pots, jugs and rare dripping dishes. Jugs decorated with finger-tips around base
113	15	58 (0.24%)	438g (0.20%)	CP5–?6	AD 1250–1300	wheel	none	62%	3%	9%	7.5YR 7/2 (ext) 7.5YR 7/6 (int)	Hard smooth hackly	Quartz, FeO	Mica, organics	–	2, 8, 32	Type II cooking pots and rare jugs decorated with rare applied strips, combing and painted slip. Finger-tip decoration to jug bases
114	–																Withdrawn
115	–																Withdrawn
116	1	469 (1.95%)	3848g (1.81%)	CP2–4	AD 1000–1250	wheel	none	0%	10%	16%	7.5YR 6/2 (ext) 5YR 6/4 (int)	Soft sandy hackly	Quartz, mica	Limestone	4, 32, 35, 37	2, 31, 33, 39, 40, 41, 48, 49, 51–53, 58, 65	Type I cooking pots only with rare paired finger-tip decoration to rim and rare incised lines to body
117	3	98 (0.40%)	910g (0.42%)	CP?1–2	AD 1000–1050	?hand	none	0%	11%	16%	10YR 6/3 (ext) 10YR 5/2 (int)	Soft granular	Quartz, limestone, mica	Sandstone, flint, FeO, clay relicts	2, 4	31–33, 37	Coarse fabric in Type II cooking pots with a single paired finger-tip decoration to rim. CP1 date rests on a single sherd
118	–																Withdrawn – as FT113
119	–																Withdrawn
120	–																Withdrawn
121	–																Withdrawn
122	–																Withdrawn
123	–																Withdrawn
124	–																Withdrawn – as FT40
125	2	70 (0.29%)	616g (0.29%)	CP2–4	AD 1000–1250	?hand	none	0%	16%	34%	Light brown (ext) light grey (int)	Soft granular	Quartz, mica, limestone	Organics, FeO	–	1, 2, 4, 31, 32	Type I cooking pots and possibly very rare Westcountry Dishes. No decoration

FIGURE 5.8 CONT.

ARTEFACTS AND ENVIRONMENTAL EVIDENCE

FT	Ware	Count (% of assemblage)	Weight g (% of assemblage)	Eckweek ceramic phases	Core date range	Made by	External parallels	Glazed (%)	Wiped (%)	Sooted (%)	Typical colour ext/int surfaces	Fabric hardness feel, fracture	Major inclusions	Minor inclusions	Common vessel forms	Rare vessel forms	Comments
126	14	46 (0.19%)	785g (0.36%)	CP7	AD 1375+	wheel	Donyatt South Somerset	87%	2%	4%	5YR 7/8 (ext and int)	Soft smooth	Quartz	Mica, FeO	–	2, 5, 21, 32, 41, 45, 48, 49, 51, 55, 56, 71	Type II cooking pots, jugs and very rare ?tiles. Decoration includes rare applied strips, incised lines and painted slip. Finger-tip decoration to jug base. An oxidised fabric probably without any deliberate temper
127	–																Withdrawn
128	–																Withdrawn – as FT82
129	–																Withdrawn – as FT71
130	2	347 (1.44%)	3748g (1.76%)	CP2–4	AD 1000–1250	hand	none	0%	16%	22%	10YR 4/2 (ext) 10YR 7/3 (int)	Soft sandy	Quartz organic limestone	Mica, FeO, flint	2, 4, 32, 33, 37, 49	1, 3, 31, 35, 40, 48, 51, 53, 63, 21, 23	Predominantly Type I cooking pots with rare jugs and possibly rare Westcountry Dishes
131	1	135 (0.56%)	950g (0.44%)	CP3–24	AD 1050–1100	wheel	none	0%	19%	19%	7.5YR 6/2 (ext) 5YR 6/6 (int)	Hard sandy hackly	Quartz	Limestone, mica, FeO	2	4, 32, 33, 39	Type I cooking pots only with distinctive oxidised skin and pale core. Rare decoration of applied strips and a single paired finger-tip to rim
132	4	60 (0.25%)	509g (0.23%)	CP3–24	AD 1050–1100	wheel	none	0%	10%	22%	10YR 7/2 (ext) 10YR 7/3 (int)	Soft sandy smooth	Quartz flint chalk	Mica, FeO, organics	32, 34, 51	2, 4	Type I cooking pots only. Rim form 34 is characteristic of this fabric
133	15	28 (0.11%)	251g (0.11%)	CP5–26	AD 1250–1300	wheel	?Naish Hill, Lacock	89%	0%	4%	10YR 7/3 (ext) 10YR 8/1 (int)	Hard sandy hackly	Quartz, mica	Organics, clay relicts, ?sandstone	–	2, 21	Represented by small number of patchy glazed jugs with common applied ornament and combing to body. Slashed rod handles
134	–																Withdrawn – as FT126
135	–																Withdrawn – as FT107
136	4	40 (0.16%)	498g (0.23%)	CP3+	AD 1050–1100	?hand	none	0%	43%	5%	7.5YR 6/2 (ext) 7.5YR 3/0 (int)	Hard smooth hackly	Quartz flint, mica	Limestone, voids	–	4, 31, 32, 39, 42	Type II cooking pots only in a reduced fabric similar to FT10. End date uncertain.
137	3	205 (0.85%)	1972g (0.92%)	CP2–24	AD 1000–1250	wheel	none	0%	14%	27%	7.5YR 6/4 (ext and int)	Hard sandy hackly	Quartz chalk	Mica, FeO	4, 32	2, 35–37, 39, 50, 51, 53	Type I cooking pots only. Similar to FT5 but with significantly greater calcareous inclusions
138	1	2730 (11.37%)	13449g (6.33%)	CP1–5	AD 930–1300	hand and wheel	none	0%	5%	20%	variable	variable	N/A	N/A	4	1–3, 32, 35, 37, 39–41, 48, 49, 51, 53, 54, 56, 59, 72	Predominantly Type I cooking pots and rare Westcountry Dishes. Variable group of mainly quartz tempered fabrics belonging to Ware 1
139	2	75 (0.31%)	790g (0.37%)	CP4–25	AD 1100–1250	wheel	none	0%	33%	29%	10YR 7/3 (ext) 10YR 8/1 (int)	Hard sandy hackly	Quartz	Limestone, mica, FeO	37	4, 32, 33, 51	Type I and II cooking pots with rare paired finger-tip decoration to rim and very rare incised lines to body

FIGURE 5.8 CONT.

FT	Ware	Count (% of assemblage)	Weight g (% of assemblage)	Eckweek ceramic phases	Core date range	Made by	External parallels	Glazed (%)	Wiped (%)	Sooted (%)	Typical colour ext/int surfaces	Fabric hardness feel, fracture	Major inclusions	Minor inclusions	Common vessel forms	Rare vessel forms	Comments
140	2	1709 (7.12%)	8708g (4.10%)	CP1–5	AD 930–1300	hand and wheel	none	0%	7%	13%	N/A	N/A	N/A	N/A	2, 4	1, 3, 6, 31–33, 35, 37, 39–41, 48, 50–54, 56	Predominantly Type I cooking pots plus rare Westcountry Dishes and very rare jugs. A variable group of fabrics belonging to Ware 2 but not assignable to a well-defined fabric. Rare applied strips, combing to body and paired finger-tip decoration to rims
141	–																Withdrawn – as FT50
142	3	4 (0.01%)	36g (0.01%)	CP6+	AD 1300+	wheel	none	0%	0%	0%	5YR 7/6 (ext) 7.5YR 6/0 (int)	Hard sandy hackly	Quartz limestone FeO	Mica, organics	–	–	Fabric characterised by large soft FeO inclusions and distinctive yellowish-red oxidation skin
143	14	155 (0.64%)	1236g (0.58%)	CP5–?6	AD 1250–1300	wheel	none	0%	3%	10%	7.5YR 5/2 (ext) 7.5YR 4/2 (int)	Soft sandy hackly	Quartz FeO	Mica, ?sandstone ?limestone	2, 4	37, 39, 41, 47, 51, 53, 54, 57	Predominantly Type II cooking pots and possibly very rare pancheons. A distinctive range of rim forms, particularly Form 57
144	3	793 (3.30%)	3629g (1.71%)	CP2–5	AD 1000–1300	wheel and hand	none	0%	5%	9%	N/A	N/A	Quartz limestone	–	32	31, 33, 35, 37, 39, 40, 41, 49, 51, 60	A variable group of quartz and limestone tempered fabrics belonging to Ware 3 but not assignable to a well-defined fabric. Rare applied strips, and paired finger-tip decoration to rims
145	4	783 (3.26%)	4120g (1.94%)	CP2–5	AD 1000–1300	wheel and hand	none	0%	8%	14%	N/A	N/A	Quartz flint, limestone	–	2, 4	1, 3, 31–33, 35, 37, 39–41, 43, 48, 50, 51, 53–55	Predominantly Type I cooking pots and rare Westcountry Dishes. A variable group of flint tempered fabrics belonging to Ware 4 but not assignable to a well-defined fabric. Very rare applied strips to body
146	52	20 (0.08%)	127g (0.05%)	N/A	cAD 1700–1900	wheel	Delft	–	–	–	N/A	N/A	N/A	–	–	–	Miscellaneous Tin-glazed earthenwares. Late 17th to 20th century – identified by Rod Burchill
147	51	2 (0.00%)	23g (0.01%)	residual	Roman	–	New Forest ware	–	–	–	–	–	–	–	–	–	Roman New Forest ware sherds from medieval contexts
148	4	30 (0.14%)	257g (0.12%)	CP4	AD 1100–1250	?wheel	?Bath A	0%	5%	0%	10YR 6/2 (ext) 5YR 4/1 (int)	Hard sandy hackly	Flint, quartz	Mica, FeO, voids	–	3, 4, 32, 34, 37, 53	Type II cooking pots and Westcountry Dishes in well defined flint-tempered fabric
149	–																Withdrawn
150	51	5 (0.02%)	22g (0.01%)	residual	Roman	–	Samian	–	–	–	–	–	–	–	–	–	Residual Roman fine ware sherds from medieval contexts
151	–																Withdrawn
152	52	11 (0.04%)	109g (0.05%)	CP7+	cAD 1600–1700	wheel	Somerset Wanstrow	–	–	–	2.5YR 6/8 (ext and int)	–	–	–	–	–	Glazed post-medieval Wanstrow sherds from Area G – identified by Rod Burchill

FIGURE 5.8 CONT.

ARTEFACTS AND ENVIRONMENTAL EVIDENCE

FT	Ware	Count (% of assemblage)	Weight g (% of assemblage)	Eckweek ceramic phases	Core date range	Made by	External parallels	Glazed (%)	Wiped (%)	Sooted (%)	Typical colour ext/int surfaces	Fabric hardness feel, fracture	Major inclusions	Minor inclusions	Common vessel forms	Rare vessel forms	Comments
153	52	8 (0.03%)	40g (0.01%)	CP7+	AD 1690–1800	wheel	Bristol/Staffs slipware	–	–	–	–	–	–	–	–	–	Combed Bristol/Staffs post-medieval slipware from Area G – identified by Rod Burchill
154	52	11 (0.04%)	95g (0.04%)	CP7+	cAD 1600–1700	wheel	Spanish earthenware	–	–	–	–	–	–	–	–	–	Imported post-medieval Spanish earthenware from Area G – identified by Rod Burchill
155	52	66 (0.27%)	572g (0.26%)	CP7+	cAD 1580–1800	wheel	South Somerset	–	–	–	–	–	–	–	–	–	Post-medieval South Somerset (Wanstrow/Donyatt) glazed wares from Area G – identified by Rod Burchill
156	52	162 (0.67%)	3320g (1.56%)	CP7+	cAD 1500–1700	wheel	Donyatt	–	–	–	–	–	–	–	–	–	Post-medieval Wanstrow glazed wares from Area G – identified by Rod Burchill
157	52	12 (0.05%)	261g (0.12%)	CP7+	P-med	wheel	South Somerset	–	–	–	–	–	–	–	–	–	Post-medieval South Somerset glazed wares from Area G – identified by Rod Burchill
158	50	49 (0.20%)	141g (0.06%)		Iron Age			–	–	–	–	–	–	–	–	–	Late prehistoric – see report by Elaine Morris
159	51	7 (0.02%)	883g (0.41%)		Roman	–	–	–	–	–	–	–	–	–	–	–	Roman tile fragments
160	50	16 (0.06%)	58g (0.02%)		Iron Age	–	–	–	–	–	–	–	–	–	–	–	Late prehistoric – see report by Elaine Morris
161	1	2 (0.00%)	17g (0.00%)	CP2–3	AD 1000–1100	wheel	none	100%	0%	0%	7.5YR 6/6 (ext and int)	Hard sandy hackly	quartz	Opaques, FeO	–	–	Two sherds of 11th-century glazed fabric from Area H.
162	50	3 (0.01%)	10g (0.00%)		Prehistoric	–	–	–	–	–	–	–	–	–	–	–	Late prehistoric – see report by Elaine Morris
163	50	1 (0.00%)	1g (0.00%)		Prehistoric	–	–	–	–	–	–	–	–	–	–	–	Late prehistoric – see report by Elaine Morris
164	50	9 (0.03%)	83g (0.03%)		Prehistoric	–	–	–	–	–	–	–	–	–	–	–	Late prehistoric – see report by Elaine Morris
165	50	2 (0.00%)	5g (0.00%)		Prehistoric	–	–	–	–	–	–	–	–	–	–	–	Late prehistoric – see report by Elaine Morris

FIGURE 5.8 CONT.

Summary of the Ceramic Assemblage by Period

Period III *Late Saxon, Saxo-Norman and Medieval*: Ceramic Wares 1 to 19

A total of 96 coarse and fine ware pottery fabric types (Figure 5.8) dated to between the later 10th and early 15th centuries. Assigned to seven ceramic phases (CP):
Ceramic phase 1: cAD 950–1000
Ceramic phase 2: AD 1000–1050
Ceramic phase 3: AD 1050–1100
Ceramic phase 4: AD 1100–1250
Ceramic phase 5: AD 1250–1300
Ceramic phase 6: AD 1300–1400
Ceramic phase 7: AD 1400–c1500.

Period IV *Post-medieval*: Ceramic Ware 52
Six pottery fabrics broadly dated between the 16th and 19th centuries.

5.3.2 Classification of the Late Saxon, Saxo-Norman and Medieval Pottery (Ceramic Wares 1–19)

Introduction

The pottery catalogue describes and characterises the medieval ceramic wares, fabrics (Figure 5.8) and vessel forms recovered during the excavations at Eckweek. The illustrated vessel forms for each ceramic ware are drawn from featured sherds (FPN followed by the number) and the relevant ceramic ware and fabric for each illustrated form is indicated. The illustrated pottery as a whole is representative of all late Saxon and medieval forms identified on the site. A separate complete description of medieval vessel forms can be found in the project archive, although as noted above, here the individual forms described below are illustrated by means of individual illustrated sherds or vessels.

Evidence of the functional properties of the pottery are discussed in Section 5.3.5 and the discussion and conclusion draws together the data presented in the descriptive catalogue and assesses the late Saxon and medieval fabrics, forms, and functional data within a chronological framework.

Vessel Forms

Details of the illustrated forms for each ceramic ware are described below with details for each vessel listed in the following order:

Fabric type (FT); vessel form; description; featured pot number (FPN); context (CT); ceramic phase (CP); comments including residuality (R)

Other abbreviations used in the illustrated catalogue for each of the ceramic wares described below are as follows:

FT	fabric type
FPN	featured pot number
CP	ceramic phase
CT	context
gl	glaze
R	residual in this context
CC	calcareous concretions
P	pitcher
Fr	fragment
ext	external
int	internal
HM	handmade
WHF	wet hand finish
CPT	cookpot
DD	dripping dish
WCD	Westcountry Dish
CS	cistern
JR	jar

Classification of Late Saxon and Medieval Pottery Forms

The pottery forms represented at Eckweek were classified as follows.

Form	Description	Illustrated example (Figure)
1	Simple flat base. Internal angle <90	5.13, 80
2	Simple flat base. Internal angle >90	5.10, 25
3	Sagging base. Internal angle <90	5.11, 47
4	Sagging base. Internal angle >90	5.9, 4
5	Heeled flat base	5.19, 168
6	Heeled footring base	5.19, 167
7	Solid pedestal base	5.20, 149
8	Heeled, frilled, and sagging base	5.18, 161
9	Simple foot	5.15, 110
21	Strap handle	5.19, 167
22	Projecting strap handle	5.17, 144
23	Rod handle	5.18, 159
24	Unperforated lug	5.16, 136
25	Perforated lug	5.9, 2
31	Everted neck, rounded rim	5.13, 76
32	Everted neck, rolled or beaded rim	5.10, 23
33	Everted concave neck, rounded or internally hooked rim	5.10, 17
34	Everted concave neck, rolled or beaded rim	5.12, 56
35	Upright or slightly everted neck, rounded or flattened rim	5.9, 13
36	Everted curved neck, flat internally ledged or beaded rim	5.14, 93
37	Everted neck, channelled rim	5.9, 14
38	Neckless, channelled, rolled, or ledged rim	5.17, 145
39	Everted neck, clubbed rim	5.13, 71

40	Everted wedged neck, rounded or flattened rim	5.13, 79
41	Everted neck, internally bevelled rim.	5.15, 119
42	Neckless, flat rim	5.17, 141
43	Upright collared rim	5.19, 171
44	Highly everted neck, rounded rim	5.14, 103
45	Tall upright or slightly everted neck and rolled rim	5.16, 126
46	Neckless, slightly rolled rim	5.15, 112
47	Everted neck, flanged rim	5.11, 41
48	Upright neck, channelled rim	5.12, 64
49	Upright neck, beaded rim	5.12, 62
50	Upright neck, clubbed rim	5.14, 89
51	Everted neck, broad flat rim	5.12, 65
52	Everted neck, externally chamfered rim	5.11, 40
53	Everted concave neck, flat rim	5.16, 133
54	Upright neck, flat ledged rim	5.16, 132
55	Simple upright neck, flat rim	5.18, 158
56	Everted neck, flattened rim	5.20, 149
57	Everted collared neck, internally hooked rim	5.15, 121
58	Collared neck, beaded rim	5.15, 120
59	WITHDRAWN	
60	Everted, neckless, flattened rim	5.11, 38
61	Inverted neck, rolled rim	5.12, 63
62	Upright or slightly everted neck, beaded/channelled rim	5.13, 86
63	Neckless, inverted, beaded rim	5.13, 85
64	Upright neck, beaded and internally bevelled rim	5.15, 109
65	Neckless, inverted rim, internal bead	5.13, 75
71	Simple pulled spout	5.17, 140
72	Tubular spout	5.20, 149
73	Body perforation	5.13, 80
74	Basal perforation	5.10, 37

Description of Pottery Wares and Illustrated Forms

A total of 96 late Saxon, Saxo-Norman, medieval and post-medieval fabrics (Figure 5.8) were identified by means of the examination of sherds in hand specimen, under low binocular magnification and in a series of petrological thin-sections prepared and examined by the author (for details see the project archive). Further thin-section analysis of 51 selected sherds was undertaken independently by Dr David Williams (Section 5.3.4) of the University of Southampton, Department of Archaeology, as part of a wider study of ceramic petrology commissioned by English Heritage (AML Report 7/1991). These two separate studies of the ceramic fabrics present at Eckweek produced results that certainly differ in detail, but broadly agree in terms of the general mineralogical groups represented.

The combined results of these studies led to the classification of 19 separate late Saxon, Saxo-Norman and medieval Ceramic Wares, each ware an amalgamation of separate fabrics with similar general characteristics. The wares are described and illustrated below and the principal characteristics of individual fabrics are presented in Figure 5.8.

WARE 1

Fabric Types (FT): 1, 4, 5, 14, 15, 68, 74, 116, 131, 138 and 161.
Source: Unknown.
Description and development: Fabrics that are overwhelmingly quartz-tempered, have either none or very rare calcareous inclusions and are characterised overall by coarse to very coarse sand to granule-sized inclusions (0.5–2mm). Quartz grains are commonly rounded to well-rounded and set within a fine grained quartz rich matrix. Fabrics are variably micaceous, although this is not a diagnostic characteristic. Other minor inclusions are variable and include iron oxides, clay relicts, opaques and rare flint. Fabrics are predominantly oxidised, although can exhibit pale grey surfaces (for example FT131) possibly suggesting iron-deficient clay sources, or, less commonly, be reduced throughout (FT4), again possibly a consequence of source material, but alternatively due to variable kiln-control.

With the possible exception of FT4 the ware first appears in quantity during the earlier 11th century (CP2) and immediately constitutes a large proportion (some 50%) of the overall medieval coarseware assemblage. During the 12th century, proportions of the ware appear to decline (Figure 5.34) but it is not until the mid 13th century (CP5) that the latest products (FTs 5, 74, and 116) appear to have been replaced.

The most common vessel types are cooking pots, the majority with sagging bases, with the earlier varieties sometimes squat. The vessel rim forms are relatively restricted and include vessel forms 31, 32, 33, 35 and 37. Rare pitchers with lug handles and tubular spouts are present in 11th-century contexts, which are later replaced by equally rare jugs and possibly skillets. Other forms represented include Westcountry Dishes, significantly exclusive to FT15 with rare basal perforations and very rarely sooted, and rare 13th- to 14th-century pancheons and small bowls. Most vessels are wheel thrown although some earlier examples (ie FPN13) are handmade. External wiping and heavy sooting, particularly of the external lower body, is very common throughout the ware (Figure 5.9, 1 and 16), whilst decoration is rare generally and mostly confined to paired finger-tip impressions on rims (Figures 5.9, 11 and 5.10, 24). Body decoration is confined to very rare, crude, applied strips. Only FT161, represented by just two sherds, is glazed, suggesting very rare prestige vessels confined to the 11th century.

Fabrics from Ware 1 are generically similar to those classified as Bath A (Vince 1979), which are widely distributed throughout the region (after Gerrard 1987). Fabrics very similar to FT4 and FT5 were recognised in the pottery assemblages recovered from Beckery Chapel, Glastonbury (Rahtz and Hirst 1974), Cheddar Palace (Rahtz 1979: Type J (10a)), Taunton Castle (Pearson 1984, Taunton type III.3) and Barrow Mead, Bath (Woodhouse 1976). Some fabrics common and distinctive at Eckweek, for example FT15, were not recognised at all in any of the local and regional collections examined as part of the project.

Illustrated Pottery (Figures 5.9 to 5.11, 1–41 and Figure 5.23)

1. FT5; CPT; FORM 35; HM; Rough FT impressions from construction, Heavy ext sooting, ext/int wiping, CC int; FPN6, context 326 CP5 ?R
2. FT5; ?P; FORM 25; HM; Lug handle, rectangular section. Vertical tooled decoration; FPN235, context 3047, CP2
3. FT68; ?P; FORM 25; HM; Lug handle positioned at rim, black smoothed granular surfaces; FPN248, context 3091, CP2
4. FT1; CPT; FORM 4; pale grey surfaces, hard, int sooting; FPN8, context 338, CP2
5. FT14; ?P; FORM 72; Fr. of tubular spout, heavy ext sooting; FPN223, context 3030, CP2
6. FT68; ?P; FORM 25; HM; Lug handle, as no 3; FPN224, context 3064, CP2
7. FT15; CPT; FORM 4; Slightly sagging base, unsooted; FPN220, context 3048, CP2
8. FT116; CPT; FORM 48; Smaller CPT, slight ext sooting; FPN228, context 3082, CP2
9. FT15; WCD; FORM 3; Rare example of this form, that has ext sooting and CC concretions, Fr removed for lipid analysis; FPN249, context 3142, CP2
10. FT14; ?CPT; FORM 32; Small CPT or bowl, single finger-tip impression on rim, ext. sooting; FPN221, context 3048, CP2
11. FT5; CPT; FORM 32; Paired finger-tip decoration on rim; FPN9, context 338, CP2
12. FT68; CPT; FORM 33; Large globular cookpot, reduced throughout, heavy ext sooting; FPN225, context 3042, CP2
13. FT5; CPT; FORMS 35 and 4; Complete, reconstructed, cookpot. Ext and int sooting; FPN251, context 413, CP3 (Figure 5.23)
14. FT5; CPT; FORM 37; Deeply channelled rim; FPN183, context 236, CP3
15. WITHDRAWN
16. FT5; CPT; FORM 4; ?HM; Smooth, uneven surfaces and heavy ext sooting; FPN219, context 3040, CP3
17. FT4; CPT; FORM 33; HM; Small, squat, CPT. Uneven body, wiped ext/int, heavy ext sooting, light int sooting; FPN13, context 318, CP3
18. FT15; ?WCD; FORM 3; Basal angle 90 degrees; FPN234, context 3087, CP3
19. FT15; ?WCD; FORM 74; Base sherds with two narrow, pre-firing, perforations; FPN233, context 3112, CP3
20. FT5; ?JUG; FORM 23; Rod handle, vertical ridges and pulled thumb impressions; FPN183, context 155, CP4
21. FT15; WCD; FORM 3; Thickened basal angle, wiped ext; FPN10, context 347, CP4
22. FT5; CPT; FORM 37; Channelled rim, thin wavy bead. Wiped ext/int, light ext sooting; FPN71, context 293, CP4
23. FT5; CPT; FORM 32; ?HM; Unusual pale grey surfaces, int WHF, light ext sooting; FPN17, context 313, CP4
24. FT5; CPT; FORM 32; Paired finger-tip impressions on rim, light ext sooting; FPN68, context 293, CP4
25. FT5; CPT; FORM 2; Simple flat base, light int sooting; FPN168, context 340, CP4
26. FT5; CPT; FORM 31; Heavy ext sooting; FPN180, context 355, CP4
27. FT74; ?CPT; Crude applied body strips, heavy ext sooting; FPN212, context 185, CP5 R
28. FTI5; FORM 47; Rimsherd from ?pancheon; FPN186, context 235, CP5
29. FT5; CPT; FORM 63; Heavy ext sooting; FPN176, context 316, CP5
30. WITHDRAWN
31. FT5; CPT; FORM 37; Deep channelled rim with paired finger-tip decoration. Hard and thin walled, light grey surfaces, light ext sooting; FPN21, context 316, CP5
32. FT5; CPT; FORM 61; Ext sooting and wiping; FPN173, context 331, CP5
33. FT5; CPT; FORM 39; Rimsherd, unsooted; FPN20, context 316, CP5
34. FT131; CPT; HM; Body sherd decorated with crude applied strips; FPN191, context 65, CP6 R
35. FT5; FORM 72; Fr of tubular spout, heavy ext and int sooting, FPN99, context 2, CP6 R
36. FT5; CPT; FORM 33; Unusually exaggerated hooked rim; FPN25, context 1, CP6 R
37. FT15; WCD; FORMS 1 and 74; Roughly rectangular pre-firing basal perforation; FPN154, context 65, CP6 R
38. FT5; ?CUP; FORM 60; Rimsherd of small cup or bowl; FPN137, context 65, CP6 R
39. FT5; CPT; FORM 54; Rimsherd, ledged and channelled, light ext sooting; FPN136, context 65, CP6 R
40. FT116; CPT; FORM 52; Light ext sooting; FPN158, context 65, CP6 R
41. FT15; FORM 47; Pancheon, unsooted; FPN75, context 1, CP6 R

ARTEFACTS AND ENVIRONMENTAL EVIDENCE

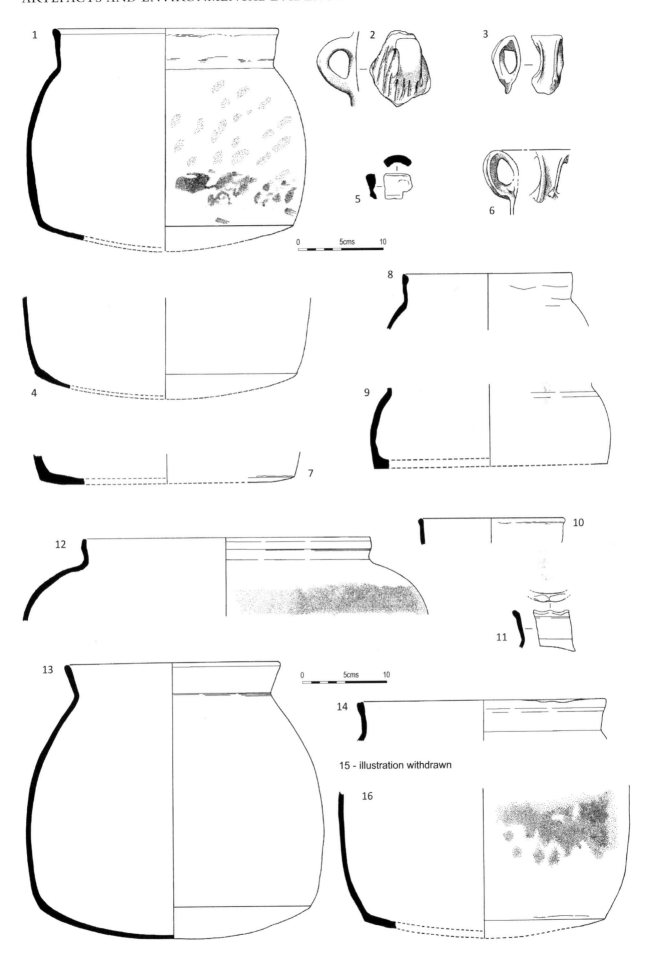

FIGURE 5.9
Medieval pottery illustrations Nos 1–16

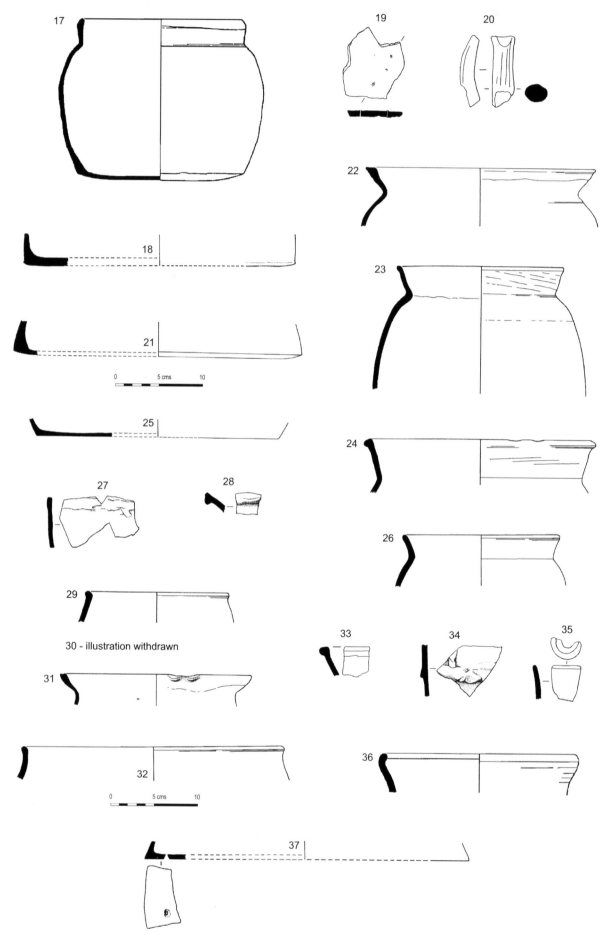

FIGURE 5.10
Medieval pottery illustrations Nos 17–37

WARE 2

Fabric Types (FT): 3, 6, 11, 16, 17, 37, 40, 46, 52, 54, 69, 125, 130, 139 and 140.
Source: Unknown.
Description and development: Fabrics with a similar range of quartz inclusions as Ware 1, although more commonly containing subrounded varieties and distinguished from Ware 1 fabrics by consistently higher, although still subordinate, proportions of calcareous inclusions. Calcareous inclusions are moderate, commonly subround, chalky and coarse sand to granule-sized (0.5–3mm). Micaceous surfaces are common where wiped (exceptions being FTs 52 and 54), although mica content is never abundant or a diagnostic characteristic. Other inclusions recognised in subordinate quantities include iron oxides, organics (FTs 69 and 130), clay relicts and flint. Fabrics are predominantly oxidised though surface colours vary widely. Fabrics produced from iron deficient clays, for example FT11, represent a significant proportion of the ware. Only FTs 6 and 16 are thoroughly reduced throughout.

The ware is first recognised during the later 10th century (CP1) although here it is restricted to a single fabric, FT69. During the 11th and 12th centuries varied new fabrics emerge in large quantities that amount to some 40% of the total ceramic assemblage during ceramic phases 2 and 3. As with Ware 1, many of the fabrics are confined to the 11th and 12th centuries and only a small range of fabrics (FTs 11, 16 and 17) appear to survive beyond the 12th century – those that do continue to be represented until the mid 13th century (Figure 5.34).

Vessel forms are broadly similar to those recognised for Ware 1 with cooking pots most common, which show an even greater preponderance for sagging bases. Simple everted, concave, channelled and upright rim forms occur in similar proportions to Ware 1, although distinctive concave and rolled forms (Form 34) do appear to be more common. Other forms include Westcountry Dishes (mostly confined to FT3) very rare jugs and small upright jars or bowls. The majority of vessels appear wheel thrown, although Fabric Types 3, 52, 69 and 125 are occasionally handmade. External wiping and sooting of the girth is common (Section 5.3.5), although it is not as dominant a characteristic as it is for Ware 1.

Decoration is mostly confined to single and paired finger-tipping on rims (eg Figure 5.11, 42 and 46), and body sherds are decorated very rarely with simple slashes, wavy combing and stabs. Only FT 46 (CP3) is glazed (Figure 5.11, 48), the glaze often decorated with simple body combing or stabs.

Ware 2 fabrics share some common characteristics with Ware 1 and appear to fall within the range of inclusions ascribed to Bath A. Vince (1979) has suggested that earlier Bath A fabrics tend to be coarser and have more limestone inclusions and at Eckweek one of the earliest fabrics analogous to Bath A, Eckweek FT69, has significant calcareous inclusions although they are rarely coarse. Fabrics very similar to FT11 were recognised in assemblages from nearby Barrow Mead (Woodhouse 1976, no fabric series) and Ilchester (Pearson 1982, Fabric 14 dated to the 11th century), and were present in some quantity in the assemblage from Cheddar Palace (Rahtz 1979).

Illustrated Pottery (Figures 5.11 and 5.12, 42–69 and Figure 5.26)

42 FT69; CPT; FORM 33; HM; Squat cookpot, internally hooked rim, with single pair of finger-tip impressions. Heavy lower body sooting, ext uneven wiping; FPN236, context 3134, CP2

43 FT69; CPT; FORM 35; Flattened rim, single finger-tip impression on rim, ext wiping; FPN216, context 3091, CP2

44 FT11; CPT; FORM 33; HM; Uneven wiped surfaces, possibly coil built, SWF, ext sooting; FPN12, context 318, CP3

45 FT3; CPT; FORM 35; HM; Wiped ext and int, pinkish-buff throughout, slight ext sooting; FPN11, context 318, CP3

46 FT69; CPT; FORM 32; ?HM; Squat bulbous body, paired finger-tip decoration on rim, heavy external sooting; FPN246, context 3018, CP3 (Figure 5.26)

47 FT3; WCD; FORM 3; Rare example with basal perforation, ext. wiping; FPN232, context 3112 CP3

48 FT46; ?JUG; FORM 21; Fr of strap handle, raised margins and central rib, yellowish green glaze, sparse CC; FPN210, context 192, CP3

49 FT69; ?CPT; Body sherd decorated with oblique slashes; FPN226, context 3077, CP3

50 FT11; ?CPT; Body sherd decorated with wavy combing; FPN218, context 3040, CP3

51 FT11; ?CPT; Body sherd decorated with en-echelon slashes, light ext sooting; FPN217, context 3040, CP3

52 FT46; ?CPT; Bodysherd decorated with stab decoration; FPN187, context 252, CP4

53 FT130; CPT; FORM 63; ?HM; Patchy int and ext sooting, smooth ext surfaces; FPN138, context 128, CP4

54 FT11; JUG; FORMS 39 and 21; ?HM; Hard, light grey surfaces; FPN214, context 185, CP5 ?R

55 FT11; CPT; FORM 34; Rim decorated with single finger-tip decoration, heavy ext sooting; FPN5, context 347, CP4

56 FT11; ?CPT; FORM 34; FPN171, context 326, CP5 ?R

57 FT37; CPT; FORM 35; Cookpot with flat base, ext wiping; FPN72, context 330, CP5 ?R

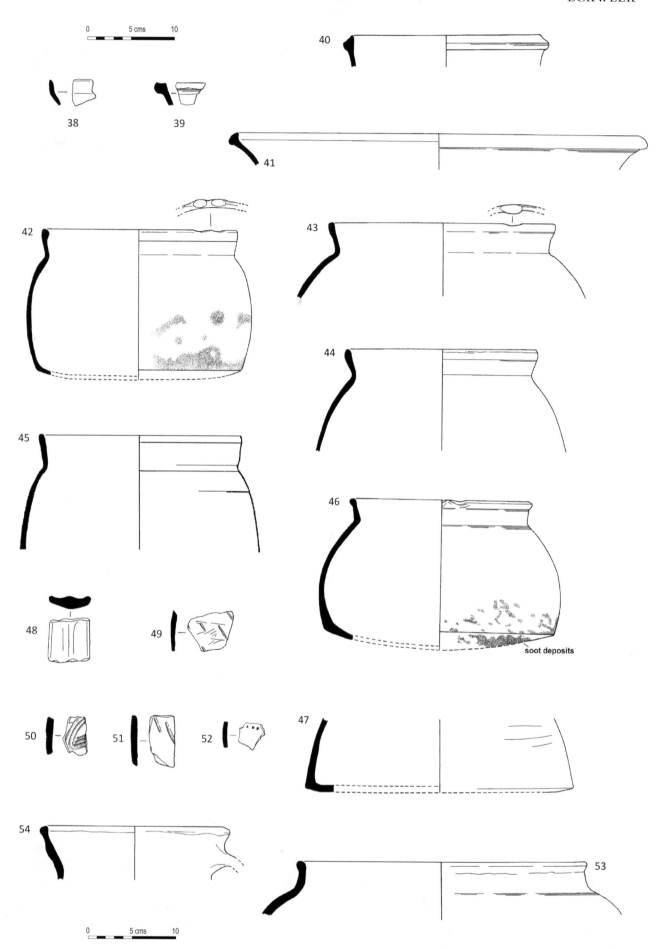

FIGURE 5.11
Medieval pottery illustrations Nos 38–54

ARTEFACTS AND ENVIRONMENTAL EVIDENCE

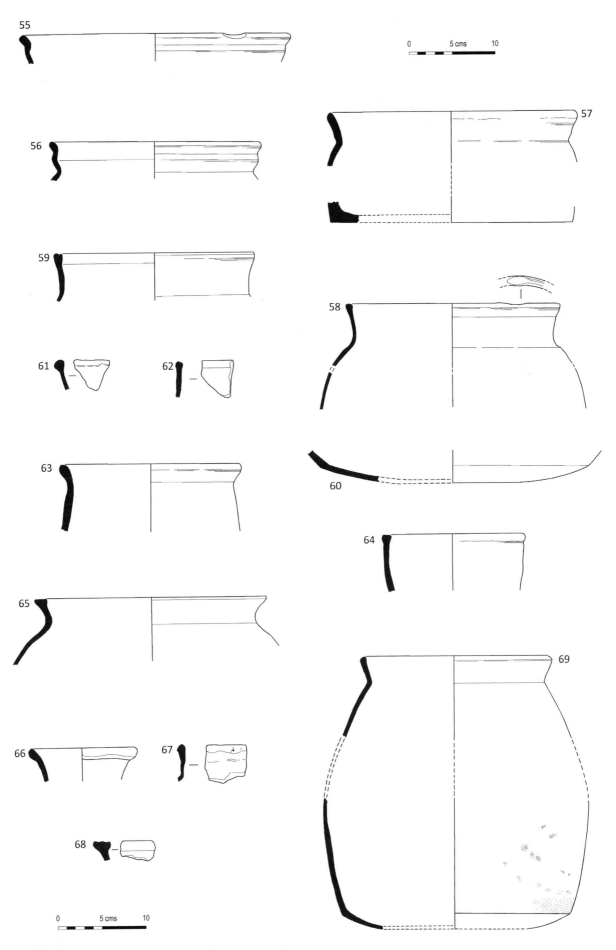

FIGURE 5.12
Medieval pottery illustrations Nos 55–69

58　FT52; CPT; FORM 37; HM; Rim decorated with single finger-tip impression, thin walled, biscuity texture, light ext sooting; FPN208, context 224, CP5
59　FT11; CPT; FORM 48; Slight ext sooting; FPN177, context 316, CP5
60　FT17; CPT; FORM 4; ?HM; Heavy ext sooting, heavy int CC, wiped ext; FPN85, context 316, CP5
61　FT17; ?CPT; FORM 39; FPN78, context 316, CP5
62　FT130; ?CPT; FORM 49; FPN77, context 316, CP5
63　FT3; ?CPT; FORM 61, FPN169, context 2, CP2
64　FT16; ?CPT; FORM 48; HM; Small cookpot or bowl, flattened and channelled rim; FPN133, context 65, CP6
65　FT11; CPT; FORM 51; Broad flattened rim, smooth, light ext sooting; FPN84, context 114, CP6
66　FT140; ?JUG; FORM 32; Possible jug rim sherd; FPN242, context 3153, CP6
67　FT3; CPT; FORM 35; ?HM; FPN141, context 65, CP6
68　FT69; ?CPT; FORM 37; Flat double channelled rim; FPN243, context 3153, CP6
69　FT69; CPT; FORM 31; HM; Deep cookpot, patchy ext sooting; FPN250, context 3001, CP6

WARE 3

Fabric Types (FT): 89, 94, 103, 137 and 144.
Source: Unknown.
Description and development: A variable group of fabrics characterised by common, often granular-sized, calcareous inclusions between 1mm and 4mm that are variably subangular to subrounded, chalky or hard and matt. Quartz inclusions are abundant, rounded or subround and medium to very coarse sand sized (0.25–2mm). Minor inclusions are confined to iron oxides, organics (FT89) and mica. Surfaces are commonly oxidised with the exception of FT89. The ware forms a minor component of the total assemblage throughout the medieval period, never more than around 5% (Figure 5.34). Vessel forms and decoration fall within the range recognised for Wares 1 and 2 with a few exceptions, including a small number of jugs, for example, Figure 5.13, 73. Although fabrics generally contain a significantly higher proportion of calcareous inclusions than Ware 2, and whilst these were considered distinct during sorting, the incidence of the ware suggests it may possibly reflect end members within the overall range of Ware 2 rather than a distinct, separate, product source.

A fabric very similar to FT103 is present in the pottery assemblage from Ilchester (Pearson 1982, fabric 14) where it is dated to the 11th century.

Illustrated Pottery (Figure 5.13, 70–75)

70　FT103; CPT; FORM 32; Simple rolled neck; FPN157, context 65, CP6
71　FT137; CPT; FORM 39; White/buff surfaces, heavy ext sooting; FPN215, context 185, CP5 ?R
72　FT89; ?DD: FORM 22; HM; Terminal of projecting strap handle; FPN155, context 65, CP6 ?R
73　FT94; JUG; FORM 55; Strap handle decorated with incised slashes; FPN59, context 211, CP6+
74　WITHDRAWN
75　FT94; CPT; FORM 64; FPN201, context 220, CP5

WARE 4

Fabric Types (FT): 10, 22, 65, 70, 75, 96, 132, 145 and 148.
Source: Unknown.
Description and development: Fabrics characterised by sparse to common, often very coarse (fine gravel occasionally sized up to 8mm), flint inclusions, variable coarse sand-sized (0.5–2mm) subrounded quartz and chalky limestone (up to 4mm). Other inclusions vary and include shell (FT75), minor calcite, mica, organics, iron oxides and clay relicts. Surfaces are commonly reduced and usually grey or dark grey although they can be variably oxidised (FTs 96 and 132). The ware is present within the ceramic phase 1 (10th-century) assemblage at Eckweek where it is represented by a single coarse fabric, FT65. New fabrics in small quantities are produced during the 11th century (FTs 22 and 132). These conform to the simple range of rim forms recognised from the earlier varieties of Wares 1 and 2, although concave and rolled rims (Form 34) are a characteristic of FT132. During the earlier 12th century large numbers of Westcountry Dishes, now with perforations around the body, rather than in the base, are produced in new fabrics (FTs 70 and 75). At the same time several coarse, sometimes handmade, cooking pot fabrics occur (FTs 10 and 148). These new fabrics comprise approximately 20% of the 12th-century assemblage, although proportions of the ware decrease during the 13th century and, with the possible exception of FT96, do not appear to continue in use beyond around AD 1250 (Figure 5.34).

Vessels are variably handmade or wheel thrown and rarely sooted (Section 5.3.5), whilst cooking pot Fabrics 10 and 148 are often wet-hand finished. Decoration is very rare and confined to a few sherds with simple incised lines and patchy yellowish-green glaze.

Fabrics with significant flint temper from the Bath area are sometimes suggested to represent early variants of Bath A ware. At Eckweek, if anything,

ARTEFACTS AND ENVIRONMENTAL EVIDENCE

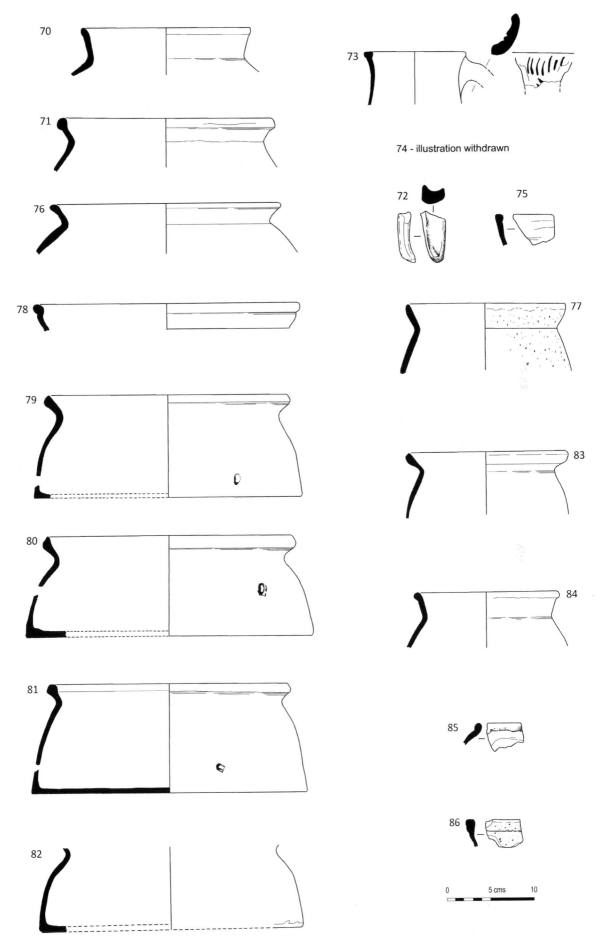

FIGURE 5.13
Medieval pottery illustrations Nos 70–86

the opposite would appear to be the case since the bulk of Ware 4 products do not appear at Eckweek until the 12th century, when they appear to partially replace established quartz-tempered fabrics.

Very similar fabrics, that occasionally include Westcountry Dish forms, were recognised in assemblages from Barrow Mead (Eckweek FTs 75 and 96) and Beckery Chapel (Eckweek FTs 65 and 75).

Illustrated Pottery (Figures 5.13 and 5.14, 76–92 and Figure 5.27)

76 FT65; ?CPT; FORM 32; Harsh granular surfaces, int WHF; FPN205, context 139, CP2
77 FT65; ?CPT; FORM 31; Granular surfaces; FPN2, context 139, CP2
78 FT132; ?CPT; FORM 34; FPN209, context 192, CP3
79 FT75; WCD; FORMS 40, 73 and 1; HM; Three lower body perforations, one rounded, two subrectangular. Perforations arranged at c45 degrees to each other. Thin walled and fragile; FPN35, context 449, CP4 (Figure 5.27)
80 FT75; WCD; FORMS 40, 73 and 1; Rectangular, mid body, perforation. Hard. Ext wiping; FPN33, context 155, CP4
81 FT75; WCD; FORMS 40, 73 and 1; Rectangular lower body perforation; FPN34, context 155, CP4
82 FT75; WCD; FORM 1; Ext/int wiping; FPN247, context 185, CP5
83 FT75; CPT; FORM 37; Concave, channelled, and externally chamfered rim. Ext sooting; FPN167, context 316, CP5
84 FT22; CPT; FORM 32; Int sooting; FPN132, context 104, CP5
85 FT96; CPT; FORM 63; Rim sherd, slight ext sooting; FPN150, context 114, CP6
86 FT75; CPT; FORM 62; Rim sherd, beaded and channelled; FPN149, context 65, CP6
87 FT70; ?CPT; FORM 39; Cookpot or ?bowl; FPN102, context 2, CP6
88 FT70; ?WCD; FORM 1; Base with footring; FPN103, context 2, CP6
89 FT10; ?CPT; FORM 50; Rare angular clubbed rim; FPN111, context 2, CP6
90 FT10; ?CPT; FORM 33; FPN105, context 2, CP6
91 FT70; ?CPT; FORM 39; External wavy bead; FPN143, context 65, CP6
92 FT10; ?CPT; FORM 32; HM; Irregular surfaces, ext WHF; FPN1, context 114, CP6

WARE 5

Fabric Type (FT): 29.
Source: Unknown.
Description and development: A single fabric characterised by common, angular, coarse sand-sized (0.5–1mm), calcite inclusions; common subrounded chalky limestone (up to 2mm) and moderate to common, coarse sand-sized, rounded quartz grains. Minor inclusions include mica, clay relicts and iron oxides. Surfaces are soft, oxidised, and variably black to buff. This fabric is found in very small quantities and can only be broadly dated between the early 12th and late 13th centuries, ceramic phases 4 to 5. Vessels appear handmade and are confined to smaller cooking pots or jars in a single, diagnostic, rim form (Form 36). Decoration is restricted to common finger-nail impressions on rims.

This fabric was not recognised in any of the local or regional collections consulted for comparison.

Illustrated Pottery (Figure 5.14, 93 and 94)

93 FT29; CPT; FORM 36; Incised finger-nail impressions on rim, black surfaces; FPN14, context 330, CP5
94 FT29; CPT; FORM 36; FPN175, context 316, CP5

WARE 6

Fabric Types (FT): 2, 50, 67 and 117.
Source: Unknown (but includes fabric analogous to Cheddar 'E').
Description and development: Fabrics characterised by very coarse sand to granule-sized (1–4mm), rounded, quartz inclusions, in conjunction with rare but significant, subangular, sandstone inclusions (up to 3mm).

Limestone is common, sometimes subangular and coarse (up to 4mm) and can be chalky or matt and hard. Other variable minor inclusions include flint, shell, mica, calcite, and iron oxides; large irregular voids are characteristic of some fabrics, in part possibly where surface inclusions have burnt out during firing (FTs 2 and 50). Fabrics are variably oxidised and reduced, and mostly handmade (with the exception of FT 67 which has a strongly laminated core). Dr Alan Vince (pers comm) has confirmed that Fabric Type 50 is closely analogous to fabric 'E' from Cheddar Palace (Rahtz 1979).

Ware 6 fabric types 2 and 117 occur in the well preserved 11th-century assemblage at Eckweek, although, on the basis of the close similarity between FT50 and Cheddar 'E', they are suggested to first occur in the later 10th century (Figure 5.34). Rims are rounded and restricted to simple everted and upright forms (Forms 31, 32 and 35). Bases are usually sagging, although rare flat bases do occur. Overall, vessels appear to be confined to simple, often small, cooking pot types, although sooting is surprisingly rare generally (Section 5.3.5) and suggests they were utilitarian vessels. A distinctive, white, external wet hand finish, almost a slip, characterises FT67. Decoration is rare generally and confined to single finger-tip impressions on rims.

ARTEFACTS AND ENVIRONMENTAL EVIDENCE

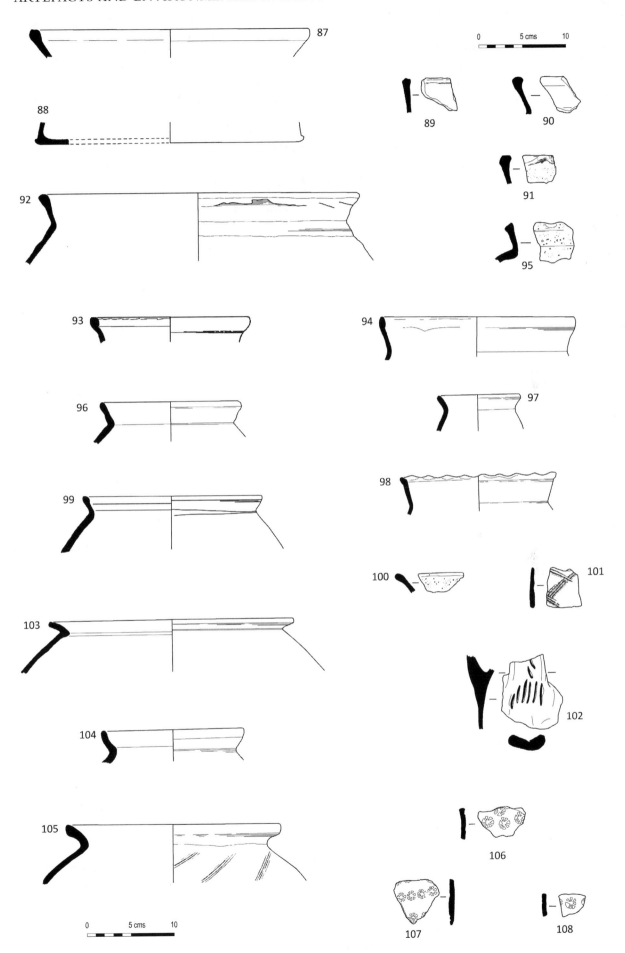

FIGURE 5.14
Medieval pottery illustrations Nos 87–108

Excluding Cheddar 'E', whose distribution appears widespread in the Somerset region (after Gerrard 1987), fabrics similar to those in Ware 6, specifically FT67, were recognised, in small quantities, at Beckery Chapel (FT117), and Cheddar Palace, whilst Eckweek FT2 appears similar to Bristol Pottery Type 3, dated AD 1000–1070 by the excavator, (Ponsford 1974). A similar fabric was also recognised at Ilchester, both as tubular spouts and body sherds decorated with round rosette stamps (for example, Ilchester 81, Pot 17).

Illustrated Pottery (Figure 5.14, 95–98)

95 FT50; CPT; FORM 40; Everted, wedged and flattened rim, coarse corky texture, thick orange oxidation skin, single finger-tip decoration on rim; FPN239, context 362, CP2
96 FT67; CPT; FORM 31; Harsh texture, white ext WHF, black laminated core; FPN182, context 322, CP1
97 FT50; CPT; FORM 31; HM; Unusually small. Corky texture, sooted ext and thickly just inside rim; FPN185, context 206, CP1
98 FT117; CPT; FORM 33; HM; Heavy ext sooting; FPN192, context 65, CP6 R

WARE 7

Fabric Types (FT): 13, 23 and 58.
Source: NW Wiltshire/Cotswold tradition (includes Minety ware).
Description and development: A group of fabrics characterised by rounded calcareous inclusions that appear variously micritic or fossiliferous (FT13) or chalky (FT58) in hand specimen, and are of variable size (between 0.5–3mm). The sphericity of calcareous inclusions is generally low. Medium sand-sized (0.25–0.5mm) quartz is sparse or rare and subround. Shell, flint, opaques and iron oxides occur as minor inclusions. Chronologically the ware appears to be split between a single late Saxon product (FT13) and two later medieval fabrics (FTs 23 and 58) and could therefore reflect two wholly separate sources.

Fabric Type 13 is closely similar to wares from Great Somerford (Thompson 1970 and A Vince pers comm), although the suggested late 10th-century date at Eckweek appears to be significantly earlier than at the type site (McCarthy and Brooks 1988) where it is dated to the 12th century. Similar fabrics from Bristol Castle (Ponsford 1974, BPT 2) are dated to the earlier 11th century, although they may well be significantly earlier (Rod Burchill pers comm). Vessels are generally handmade and commonly have a distinctively soapy texture with predominantly oxidised surfaces. Cooking pot forms are rarely sooted and have a restricted range of forms, most commonly simple everted necks with rounded or rolled rims. Small numbers of sherds are decorated with rounded wheel stamps; one (Figure 5.14, 106) has the slight remnant of a simple rounded pouring-hole or spout, similar to vessels identified from 11th-century contexts at Bristol (Ponsford 1974) and, in particular, at Mary Le Port, Bristol (Watts and Rahtz 1985). At Cheddar similar pouring-hole vessels were suggested to have been associated with some industrial process. In addition, cooking pots in a similar calcareous fabric recovered from pre-Conquest contexts at the Mary-Le-Port site are also decorated with rounded 7-spoked wheel-stamps (Figure 5.14, 106–108) that are sometimes termed 'rosettes'.

The later medieval fabrics at Eckweek, in particular FTs 23 and 58, are closely analogous to NW Wiltshire Minety-type, a source recognised widely throughout the region that is often characterised by fossil limestone, which is often leached-out at the surface. The ware is identified throughout the south west region and described in detail elsewhere (McCarthy and Brooks 1988). At Eckweek, the Minety-type products include cooking pots and externally glazed strap handled jugs; a single foot suggests rare tripod pitchers may also have been used.

Pottery very similar to FT13 was recognised in collections from excavations at Barrow Mead, Beckery Chapel, Glastonbury (Rahtz and Hirst 1974), Cheddar Palace, Citizen House, Bath (Cunliffe 1979), and Preston, Cirencester (Jan Roberts pers comm).

Illustrated Pottery (Figures 5.14 and 5.15, 99–111 and Figure 5.25)

99 FT13; ?CPT; FORM 31; FPN27, context 139, CP1
100 FT13; CPT; FORM 32; Sandy rather than soapy surface, heavy ext sooting; FPN184, context 206, CP1
101 FT23; ?JUG; Body sherd decorated with cross hatched combing and thin, ext greenish-yellow glaze; FPN166, context 316, CP5
102 FT58; JUG; FORM 21; Slash decorated handle, unglazed; FPN245, context 211, CP6+
103 FT58; CPT; FORM 44; Minety-type, thin int green glaze confined to rim; FPN53, context 67, CP6
104 FT58; CPT; FORM 33; Thin, ext yellowish-green glaze extends inside rim; FPN51, context 41, CP6
105 FT58; CPT; FORM 44; Dark grey throughout, soapy. Ext diagonal combing and thin yellowish-green glaze inside rim; FPN76, context 83, CP6
106 FT13; ?P; HM; Body sherd with offset round wheel stamps and Fr of pouring hole rim; FPN3, context 2, CP6 R
107 FT13; Body sherd with horizontal lines of round wheel stamps; FPN28, context 114, CP6 R

108 FT13; Worn body sherd with rounded wheel stamps; FPN148, context 2, CP6 R
109 FT58; JUG; FORM 64; Rim sherd of jug with simple pulled spout, thin ext yellowish-green glaze; FPN64, context 263, CP6
110 FT58; FORM 9; Simple triangular ?foot; FPN64, context 252, CP6
111 FT58; JUG; FORM 51; Reconstructed, strap handle decorated with slashes, ext yellowish-green glaze; FPN50, contexts 12, 73, and 41, CP6 (Figure 5.25)

WARE 8

Fabric Type (FT): 30 (not illustrated).
Source: Lincolnshire (Stamford Ware). Industrially-produced wheel-thrown cooking and table ware pottery from the town of Stamford, Lincolnshire, which is produced between the later 9th and 12th centuries. External yellowish to pale green glaze. Common from the 10th century onwards with main distribution initially within the area of the Danelaw and thereafter common in eastern England generally (Kilmurry 1980).
Description and development: A single fabric characterised by abundant fine sand sized (0.12–0.25mm) quartz inclusions and identified as 11th-century Stamford Ware (Paul Miles pers comm), which is fully discussed elsewhere (Mahany et al 1982). Just two body sherds in a white to cream fabric throughout were recovered at Eckweek, both with a thin, greenish-yellow, external glaze and pronounced internal throwing rings. Both are considered to be residual in context and it is not possible to suggest what vessel forms are represented, although the sherds suggest at least one fine item of tableware, perhaps a jar or pitcher.

WARE 9

Fabric Type (FT): 62.
Source: Surrey White Wares. A generic term describing products from a number of workshops operating in the Farnham and Kingston-upon-Thames area of Surrey whose products first appear in London around the middle of the 13th century and which are widespread by the mid 14th century (McCarthy and Brooks 1988).
Description and development: A single fabric characterised by fine sand-sized (0.12–0.25mm) quartz inclusions within an oxidised, iron-deficient, matrix. Identified as Surrey White Ware (R Burchill pers comm). Represented at Eckweek by a single late medieval bowl from a later 13th-century context.

Illustrated Pottery (Figure 5.15, 112)

112 FT62; BOWL; FORM 46; Neckless bowl with rolled rim and heeled base, thick greenish-yellow glaze all over; FPN73, context 161, CP5

WARE 10

Fabric Types: 56 and 83 (not illustrated).
Source: ?Laverstock, SE Wiltshire.
Description and development: Hard fabrics characterised by fine sand-sized (0.125mm to 0.25mm) quartz inclusions and a distinctive sub-conchoidal fracture. Surfaces are pale and suggest oxidised iron-deficient clays. Less than 40 sherds were recovered at Eckweek, some with patchy reddish-yellow or apple green external glaze, from later medieval contexts (CP5 and CP6).

At Eckweek these appear to represent a small number of fine tableware jugs. Similar fabrics were recognised from the kiln site assemblage at Laverstock (Musty et al 1969), although they also appeared to be present within the kiln site assemblage from Langley Burrell (unpublished), Wiltshire. As such, the suggested provenance of the fabrics at Eckweek remains uncertain.

WARE 11

Withdrawn: formerly Roman Wares

WARE 12

Fabric Types (FT): 34 and 84.
Source: Unknown.
Description and development: A group of rare later medieval fabrics at Eckweek characterised by abundant, medium to coarse sand-sized (0.25–1mm) quartz and sparse, large, chalky calcareous inclusions (up to 3mm). Quartz grains are commonly subrounded and set within a fine quartz matrix. Surfaces are hard and variably grey to buff. Minor inclusions include iron oxides, mica and opaques. Forms indicate that most sherds are from jugs, though rare cooking pot types do occur. External glazing is common, yellowish-green in the case of FT34, and brownish-red for FT84. Decoration for FT84 includes cream painted slip and applied pellets (not illustrated).

These fabrics appear to represent rare imported products and are not found at Eckweek before the mid 13th century (ceramic phases 5 and 6), although they do not appear to be represented during the latest medieval occupation in Area A.

Illustrated Pottery (Figure 5.15, 113–116)

113 FT34; ?CPT; FORM 62; Unglazed; FPN203, context 220, CP5
114 FT34; ?JUG; FORM 51; Rim decorated with an applied pellet in what is possibly a stylised face. Thick patchy, ext bronzish-green glaze; FPN58, context 204, CP5
115 FT34; ?JUG; FORM 8; Frilled base with patchy ext green glaze; FPN174, context 364, CP5

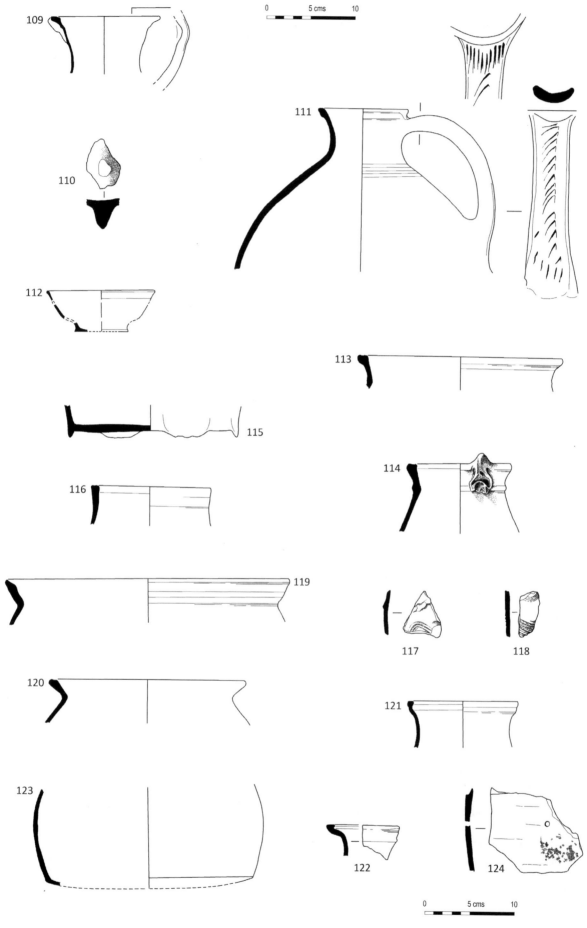

FIGURE 5.15
Medieval pottery illustrations Nos 109–124

116 FT34; ?JUG; FORM 48; Rim sherd, patchy ext yellowish-green glaze; FPN86, context 2, CP6

WARE 13

Fabric Type (FT): 24.
Source: ?SE Wiltshire.
Description and development: Rare earlier medieval glazed ware characterised by abundant, coarse sand-sized (0.5–1mm) rounded, quartz inclusions. No other significant inclusions appear present. Surfaces are sandy, oxidised and commonly brownish-red. The fabric has been identified by Dr Alan Vince as South-East Wiltshire Ware. Although no definite forms were identified, the small number of decorated body sherds at Eckweek probably represents a handful of tableware jugs.

The earliest unglazed sherds are dated to the 11th century (CP3) at Eckweek, although glazed sherds are not recognised until the early 12th century (ceramic phase 4). External surfaces commonly have a brownish-green glaze that is often decorated with wavy combing.

Illustrated Pottery (Figure 5.15, 117–118)

117 FT24; Ext brownish-green glaze, wavy combing, possible remnant of applied strip; FPN23, context 316, CP4
118 FT24; Ext brownish-green glaze, wavy combing; FPN22, context 316, CP4

WARE 14

Fabric Types (FT): 21, 47, 49, 60, 63, 77, 106, 108, 112, 126 and 143.
Source: South Somerset wares.
Description and development: A range of later medieval fabrics characterised by medium to fine sand sized (0.5–0.1mm) quartz inclusions. Fabrics commonly contain no deliberate temper and exhibit very smooth micaceous surfaces with rare visible quartz grains (FTs 47, 49, 60, 106 and 126). Slightly coarser fabrics are tempered with moderate to abundant medium sand-sized quartz (0.25–0.5mm). Fabric Type 21 is unusual in that it contains sparse, rounded and granular (up to 3mm), pink quartz grains whose proportions within the fabric suggest they may have been present in source material and not a deliberate addition. Iron oxides, often soft and subrounded, pale clay relicts, and opaques are common in finer fabrics; coarser varieties often contain these as minor inclusions in conjunction with mica and, rarely, organics. Surfaces are usually soft and always oxidised although Fabric Type 108 suggests the rare use of iron-deficient clay sources.

These fabrics do not occur at Eckweek until the second half of the 13th century (CP5) and are initially found in small quantities (around 5% see Figure 5.34). During the 14th century the ware is found in increasing quantities and commonly in specialised domestic forms. Vessel types are varied and include wheel thrown cooking pots, commonly with everted necks and internally bevelled rims, Westcountry Dishes, bowls, decorated jugs and slab-built dripping dishes. There is also a single example of a spectacularly decorated cistern (Figures 5.20 and 5.21), the 'Stag's Head' cistern, for which no close parallel has to date been found (Dr Alejandra Gutiérrez pers comm). Bases are variably flat or sagging, though jugs are often heeled and frilled. Decoration is varied and includes use of applied strips, combing, finger impressions, slashes and painted slip. External glaze is common and usually yellowish or brownish-green.

South Somerset wares from a number of separate sources seem to be generically similar and are often difficult to differentiate in hand specimen. The range of forms at Eckweek, in particular the handmade dripping dishes and Westcountry Dishes, are not present in the assemblage from the Donyatt kilns (Coleman-Smith and Pearson 1988), or those from Nether Stowey and Wrangway. The precise source of these vessels and therefore the ware as a whole at Eckweek, remains uncertain.

Illustrated Pottery (Figures 5.15 to 5.18, 119–149; Figure 5.20; Figure 5.21; Figure 5.24)

119 FT21; CPT; FORM 41; Smooth, unsooted; FPN61, context 169, CP6
120 FT49; CPT; FORM 51; Smooth, micaceous; FPN41, context 2, CP6
121 FT63; JUG; FORM 58; Dribbles of ext yellowish-green glaze; FPN109, context 2, CP6
122 FT143; ?CPT; FORM 57; Rare rim form, dark brown throughout; FPN97, context 2, CP6
123 FT49; CPT; FORM 4; Ext sooting and wiping, thick int CC, highly micaceous; FPN40, context 204, CP5
124 FT112; CPT; Body sherd with two rounded perforations, ext and int sooting, patchy thin ext green glaze; FPN123, context 44, CP6
125 FT112; DD; Profile of dripping dish, int dribbled green glaze, heavy int and ext sooting; FPN110, context 2, CP6
126 FT60; JUG; FORM 41; Applied strip with deep rounded finger-tip impressions, thin ext brownish-green glaze; FPN120, context 2, CP6
127 FT21; JUG; FORM 45; Large full bodied, simple pulled spout and crenulated, thumb impressed, strap handle. Smooth buff surfaces and very thin walled. Decayed brown glaze on handle, ext CC; FPN54, context 169, CP6 ?R
128 FT108; ?JUG; FORM 21; Short strap handle, vertical slashes, hexagonal section; FPN38, context 2, CP6
129 FT112; JUG; FORM 8; Ext dribbled cream slip into thumb impressions; FPN36, context 2, CP6

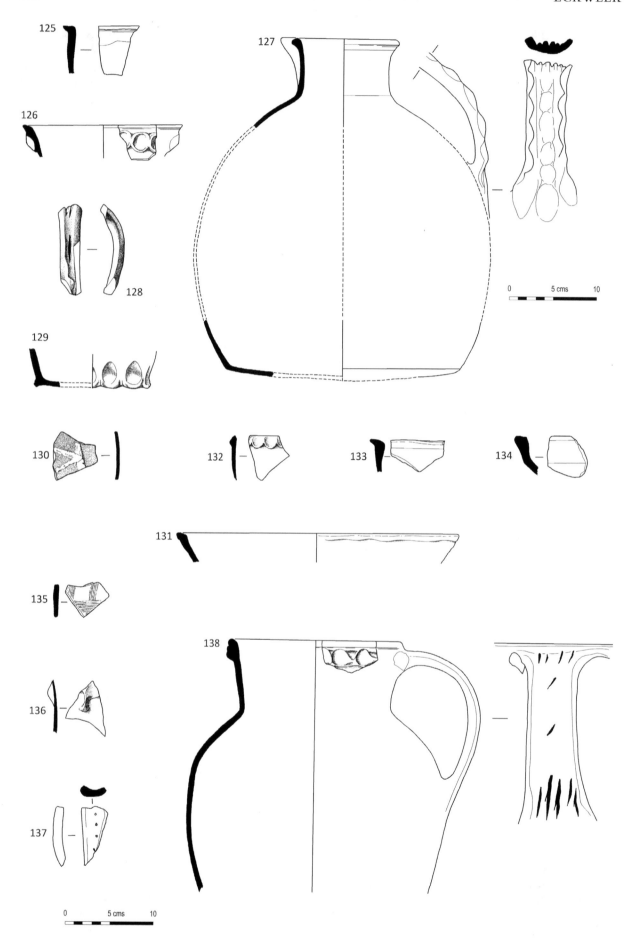

FIGURE 5.16
Medieval pottery illustrations Nos 125–138

ARTEFACTS AND ENVIRONMENTAL EVIDENCE

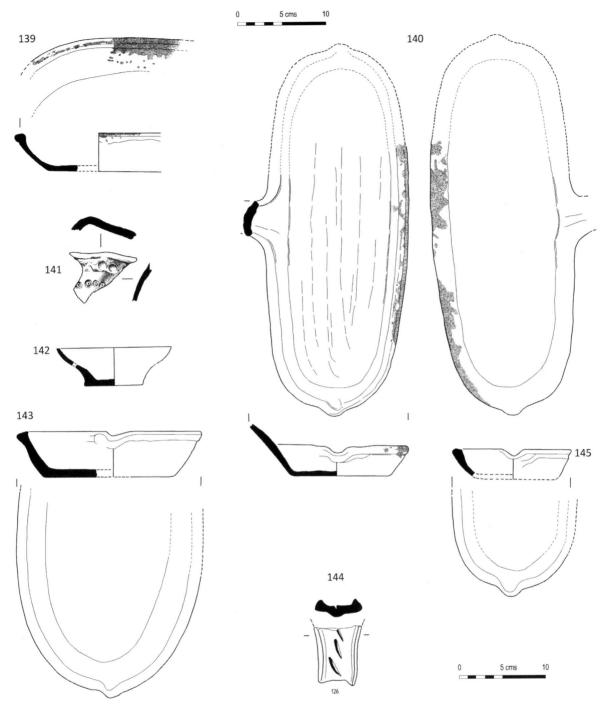

FIGURE 5.17
Medieval pottery illustrations Nos 139–145

130 FT60; Body sherd, ext cream geometric painted slip; FPN43 context 46, CP6

131 FT77; ?CPT; FORM 41; Black, micaceous; FPN113, context 2, CP6

132 FT106; Bodysherd, applied thumb impressed strip; FPN206, context 114, CP6

133 FT143; ?CPT; FORM 54; FPN89, context 2, CP6

134 FT143; ?CPT; FORM 53; FPN112, context 2, CP6

135 FT60; Bodysherd with geometric combing, thin ext yellowish green glaze; FPN94, context 2, CP6

136 FT63; Bodysherd with unperforated lug, thin ext green glaze; FPN108, context 2, CP6

137 FT108; ?JUG; Fr of strap handle with small vertical punctures, FPN197, context 74, CP6

138 FT108; JUG; FORM 51; Large wide rimmed jug, applied strip with finger-tip impressions around rim, slashed strap handle, patchy ext yellowish-green glaze; FPN45, contexts 2, 19, 57, 135, and 147, CP6

139 FT106; DD; FORM 38; HM; Dripping dish, patchy int green glaze, heavy rim and int sooting, int CC; FPN47, context 146, CP6

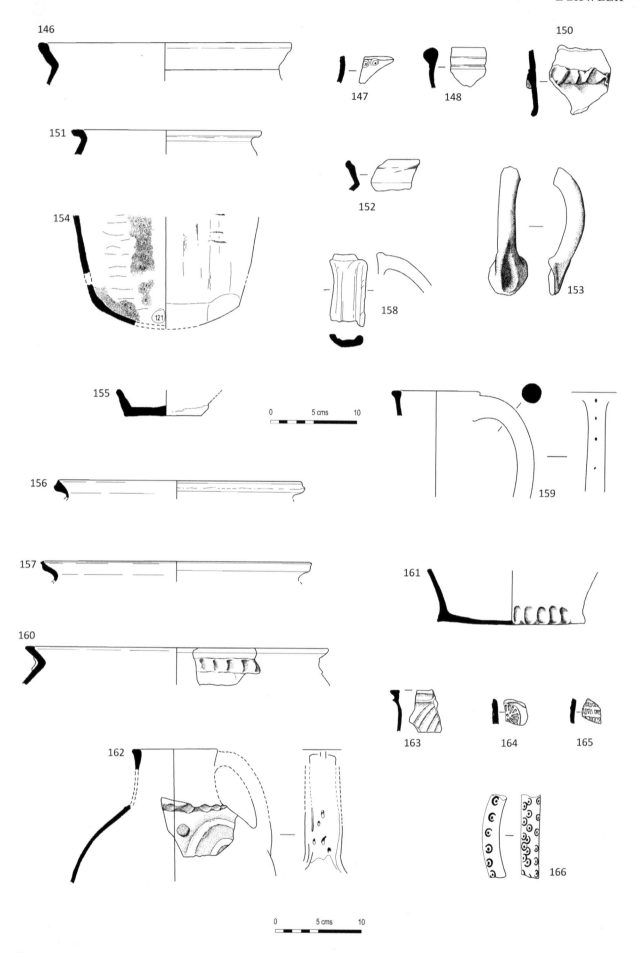

FIGURE 5.18
Medieval pottery illustrations Nos 146–166

140 FT63; DD; FORM 38; HM; Reconstructed dripping dish, projecting strap handle, simple pulled spout, slightly channelled rim, int yellowish-green glaze, heavy ext sooting opposite handle, spouted end sags; FPN48, context 67, CP6 (Figure 5.24)

141 FT108; ?CPT; FORM 38; Rimsherd, impressed applied strip and dot and circle decoration, yellowish-green ext glaze, red slip on applied strip. ?pouring lip or possibly Fr from base of firedamp; FPN83, context 2, CP6.

142 FT63; BOWL; FORM 42; Smooth, buff throughout; FPN44, context 31, CP6

143 FT63; DD; FORM 42; HM; Large dripping dish, pulled spout, remnants of int yellowish-green glaze, heavy ext and int sooting on one side only, int CC; FPN52, contexts 31 and 41, CP6

144 FT63; ?DD; FORM 22; HM; Terminal of projecting strap handle with slash decoration, smooth, buff; FPN126, context 41, CP6 Possibly part of FPN52 above

145 FT63; DD; FORM 38; HM; Spouted terminal of dripping dish, as 140 above; FPN49, context 41, CP6 Almost certainly the other end of FPN48 (140 above)

146 FT106; CPT; FORM 51; Smooth, micaceous; FPN211, context 88, CP7

147 FT108; Body sherd with dot and circle decoration, ext green glaze; FPN98, context 2, CP6

148 FT126; ?CPT; FORM 32 (Variant); FPN124, context 44, CP7

149 FT63; CS; FORMS 56, 7 and 21; Fully reconstructed single-spigoted cistern, complex zoomorphic decoration in form of stag's head and antlers styled with incised lines, green glaze, white painted slip, and white ?mica-like? slip. Thin walled; FPN62, contexts 2, 12, 15, 38, 44, 46, 72, 124 and 135, CP6 (Figures 5.20 and 5.21)

WARE 15

Fabric Types (FT): 33, 55, 71, 87, 88, 113 and 133.
Source: Wiltshire ?Lacock (Nash Hill). A range of very hard and mainly oxidised sandy fabrics from kilns close to the medieval abbey and village at Lacock (McCarthy 1974). Dating is based upon typological aspects to between the later 13th century and c1325.
Description and development: Later medieval fabrics distinguished by abundant, medium to very coarse sand-sized (0.3–1.5mm), rounded quartz inclusions. Other significant inclusions comprise soft subrounded iron oxides, and rounded opaques. Mica and pale clay relicts are minor inclusions. Surfaces are always oxidised, although commonly pale (eg FTs 55, 87, 88) suggesting significant use of iron-deficient clays and can be sandy or smooth. The ware first appears at Eckweek during the second half of the 13th century (CP5) although some fabrics (FTs 87, 88) are confined to the 14th century (CP6). Fabric types 55 and 71 are found in significantly greater quantities than other fabrics. Cooking pot forms predominate, the majority with distinctive externally chamfered rim forms (Form 52), although they are only very rarely sooted. Jugs do occur and a single costrel is recognised. Glazing is common (some 50%) and can be equally external or internal and is usually yellowish-green. Decoration is rare and mostly confined to white painted slips, and finger impressions although combing, incised lines and applied strips do occur.

Fabric Types 55 and 71 are present in the kiln site assemblage from Lacock, Wiltshire (McCarthy 1974) where products are dated between cAD 1275–1325. Fabric type 71 was also present in the assemblage from Barrow Mead, Bath. These fabrics are considered closely related to those of Ware 16 (see comments for Ware 16).

Illustrated Pottery (Figures 5.18, 150–157)

150 FT87; ?JUG; FORM 45; Rim sherd, pinkish-buff throughout, wavy applied strip around neck; FPN122, context 2, CP6

151 FT71; CPT; FORM 54; Painted yellowish slip inside rim, slight ext sooting; FPN196, context 65, CP6

152 FT55; ?CPT; FORM 37; Rimsherd, patchy int green glaze; FPN194, context 65, CP6

153 FT71; ?JUG; FORM 23; Short rod handle, remnants of yellowish green glaze; FPN55, context 38, CP6

154 FT87; FORM 4; HM; Rounded bag-like base of costrel, thick dribbled int green glaze, angular knife trimmed ext surfaces. FPN121, context 65, CP6

155 FT87; ?JUG; FORM 2; Common int voids, patchy ext yellowish-green glaze; FPN42, context 31, CP6

156 FT71; ?CPT; FORM 52; Pinkish-buff surfaces, thin yellow glaze inside rim; FPN100, context 2, CP6

157 FT55; CPT; FORM 52; Light brown throughout, light ext sooting ; FPN87, context 2, CP6

WARE 16

Fabric Types (FT): 51 and 80.
Source: Lacock (Nash Hill), Wiltshire (See comments for Ware 15).
Description and development: Later medieval fabrics characterised by abundant, medium sand-sized (0.25–0.5 mm) subrounded quartz inclusions and common well-rounded opaques. Large subrounded iron oxides are variable. No other inclusions are present. Surfaces are hard and oxidised, although FT51 is usually pale suggesting iron-deficient clays.

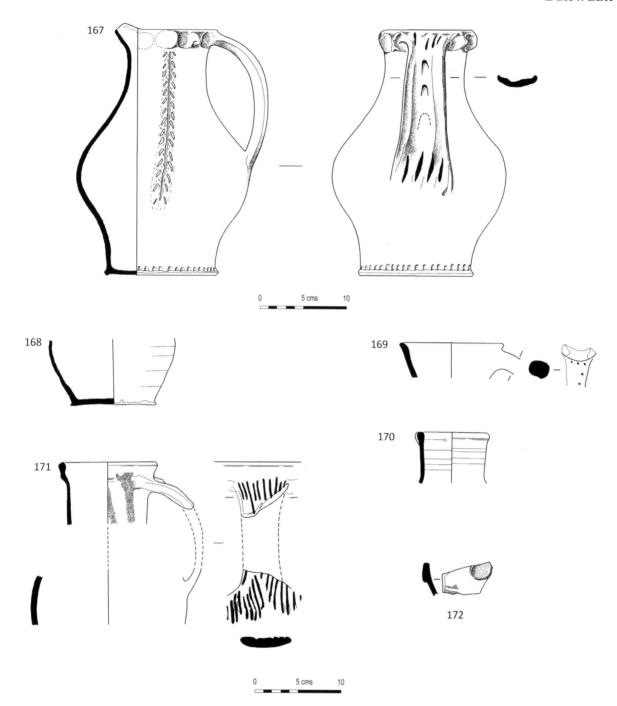

FIGURE 5.19
Medieval pottery illustrations Nos 167–172

Fabric 80 invariably has a distinctive reddish oxidation skin and blue-grey core. These fabrics do not occur before the second half of the 13th century (CP5) and although they occur in greater proportions during the 14th century (CP6) they are not found in any quantity within the latest medieval abandonment assemblage inside Building 460. The majority of vessels appear to be jugs, particularly for FT80, many with upright necks and simple flat rims. Cooking pot forms are rare and, perhaps significantly, never sooted. There are also a small number of possible tile, floor or roof, fragments. Glaze as a whole is very common (c90%) and usually green although internal glazing is surprisingly rare (c10%). Decoration is varied and common and includes ornamented applied strips, painted slip, combing, slashes and stabbing.

These distinctive fabrics are present in large quantities in the kiln site assemblage from Nash Hill, Lacock (McCarthy 1974). There seems little doubt that the examples at Eckweek represent products from that centre. It is likely that Wares 15 and 16 were both produced at the Lacock kilns and that Ware 15 represents coarser cooking wares and Ware 16 primarily finer tableware, mainly jug fabrics.

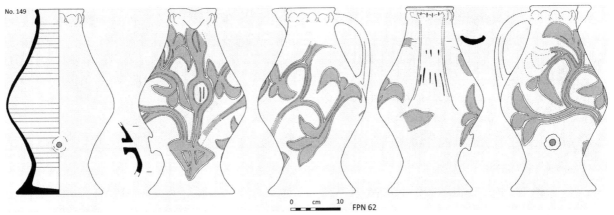

FIGURE 5.20
Medieval pottery illustration No. 149. FPN62

Illustrated Pottery (Figure 5.18, 158–166)

158 FT80; JUG; FORM 55; Rim and strap handle, variable orange to green ext glaze; FPN90, context 2, CP6

159 FT80; JUG; FORM 55; Rod handle with vertical stabs, patchy olive green ext glaze; FPN128, context 114, CP6

160 FT51; ?CPT; FORM 57; Brownish-green glaze inside rim; FPN145, context 114, CP6

161 FT80; JUG; FORM 8; Pulled finger-tip impressions around base, thin patchy ext olive glaze; FPN82, context 65, CP6

162 FT80; JUG; FORM 55; Jug decorated with applied strip and pellets in brown slip and curvilinear cream painted slip. Thick ext brownish-green glaze, stabbed strap handle; FPN63, context 392, CP6

163 FT80; JUG; FORM 54; Rimsherd with incised lines across neck, thick ext dark green glaze; FPN152, context 65, CP6

164 FT51; Bodysherd with dense triangular rouletting, thin ext brownish-green glaze; FPN101, context 2, CP6

165 FT51; Bodysherd with applied pellet in wheel design, green ext glaze and brown painted slip; FPN153, context 65, CP6

166 FT80; ?JUG; FORM 23; Rod handle, thick green glaze, dot and circle decoration; FPN244, context 3153, CP6

WARE 17

Fabric Type: 48 (not illustrated).

Source: Bristol, Ham Green ware. A group of hard and generally reduced handmade fabrics from the kiln site at Ham Green near Bristol dated at Bristol Castle and Chepstow between the 12th century and *c*1300. Forms are varied but include common glazed and decorated jugs as well as cooking pots (McCarthy and Brooks 1988).

Description and development: Fabric characterised by fine sand-sized (0.1–0.25 mm) subrounded quartz inclusions. Minor inclusions include mica and opaques. Pale oxidised surfaces suggest iron-deficient clays and cores are usually bluish-grey. The fabric is hard and appears handmade. This is Ham Green A (Rod Burchill pers comm), which is typified by tripod pitchers at Bristol and first occurs at Eckweek in small quantities during CP4. The fabric is dated at Bristol between the mid 12th and early 14th centuries (Barton 1963), but the ware is mainly confined to the 12th century at Chepstow.

A small number of glazed body sherds with remnants of applied strip and roulette decoration, plus a single spout fragment, indicates a handful of tableware jugs are represented at Eckweek associated with the later use of Period III timber building, Building 467. Ham Green ware sherds provide an

FIGURE 5.21
No. 149. The Stag's Head Cistern. FPN62

FIGURE 5.22
No. 167. Leaf Jug. FPN74

FIGURE 5.23
No. 13. Reconstructed cooking pot. FPN251

important external link for the intra-site dating of ceramic phase 4 at Eckweek.

WARE 18

Fabric Types: 57, 93 and 107.
Source: unknown – possibly South Somerset, Donyatt.
Description and development: Later medieval fabrics characterised by medium sand sized (0.2–0.5 mm) subrounded to subangular quartz inclusions. Other inclusions are rare and are confined to mica, opaques and iron oxides (FT107 only). Fabrics are commonly very hard and appear predominantly oxidised; surface colours are usually pale brown or grey suggesting moderately iron-rich clays. Cores are variably pale grey (FT57) to black (FT93). These fabrics appear to represent a small number of late 14th- and possibly 15th-century jugs and no cooking pots are represented.

Fabric 57 is almost entirely represented by a single, complete, jug (Figures 5.19 and 5.22) recovered from the latest medieval abandonment floor and is considered to be well-dated to the mid to late 14th century. External glaze is very common and usually lustrous green; decoration appears to be similarly common and includes use of applied strips, incised patterns, thumb impressions, painted slip, slashing, and stabbing.

Ware 18 fabrics were not recognised in any of the local or regional collections visited for comparison, although very similar decoration of vertical painted slip leaves (Figure 5.22) are found in the Period 4, very late medieval to 16th-century, assemblage at the Donyatt kilns (Coleman-Smith and Pearson 1988, 143).

Illustrated Pottery (Figure 5.19, 167–170 and Figure 5.22)

167 FT57; JUG; FORM 56; Complete, reconstructed. Simple pulled spout, neck decorated with applied strip and finger impressions, body with three vertical incised leaf designs highlighted in white slip, slashed strap handle, pulled finger-tip around base. Deep green ext glaze; FPN74, contexts 41, 46 and 135, CP6 (Figures 5.19, 167 and 5.22)
168 FT107; JUG; FORM 5; Ext and int patchy yellowish-green glaze; FPN46, context 44, CP6
169 FT93; JUG; FORM 41; Buff surfaces, unglazed, rod handle; FPN241, context 383, CP7
170 FT107; JUG; FORM 49; Remnant of pulled spout, strong throwing rings, patchy ext yellowish-green glaze; FPN172, context 2, CP6

WARE 19

Fabric Type (FT): 91.
Source: Bristol Redcliffe ware. Fabrics described from wasters from Redcliffe Hill in Bristol dated to between the mid 13th to late 15th centuries. A range of wheel thrown buff sandy fabrics that can be reduced pale bluish-grey. Forms include common

ARTEFACTS AND ENVIRONMENTAL EVIDENCE

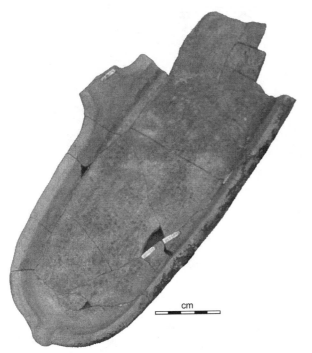

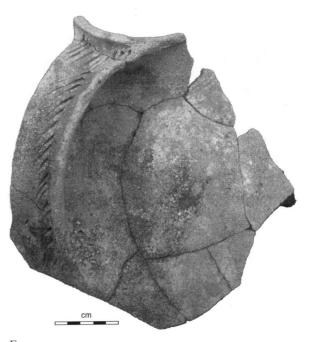

FIGURE 5.24
No. 140. Reconstructed Period V fish dish. FPN48

FIGURE 5.25
No. 111. Reconstructed Period V jug. FPN50

cooking pots, skillets and glazed and decorated jugs (Good and Russett 1987).

Description and development: Fabric characterised by medium sand-sized (0.25–0.5mm) subrounded quartz inclusions. Described from sherds identified in hand specimen as Redcliffe Ware (Michael Ponsford pers comm) although, based on the descriptions of fabrics described by Chris Gerrard (1987), the range of inclusions recognised at Eckweek, in particular rare chalky limestone and common mica, suggests this is a variant of the ware. The fabric occurs at Eckweek in small quantities during ceramic phase 5 (1250–1300) and similar products are dated at Bristol between cAD 1280–1350. The total number of sherds at Eckweek probably only represents a small number of table ware jugs. Almost all the sherds are glazed externally, usually dark green and decoration includes applied pellets, slashes, and painted brown slip.

Illustrated Pottery (Figure 5.19, 171–172)

171 FT91; JUG; FORM 43; Ext green glaze, slashed strap handle, vertical, dark brown, painted slip; FPN39, context 154, CP5
172 FT91; Body sherd, applied pellet in brown slip, ext green glaze; FPN119, context 19, CP6

5.3.3 Period IV: Post-medieval

WARE 52

Fabric Types: 152, 153, 154, 155, 156 and 157 (not illustrated).

Description and development: A small collection of widely recognised post-medieval fabrics was recovered from evaluation pits opened in Area G (Figure 1.7) where associated artefacts including clay tobacco pipe (Section 5.9) indicates a phase of activity during the 17th century.

The post-medieval sherds were not examined in detail or reclassified due to their widely recognised and published characteristics, but included small quantities of tin glazed products (FT153) and a few fragments of possible Spanish origin (FT154). The remainder and bulk of the collection is of South Somerset origin, the majority from the Donyatt kilns (Rod Burchill pers comm).

Post-medieval fabrics represent less than 1% of the total ceramic assemblage recovered during the Eckweek project.

5.3.4 The Petrology of Medieval Pottery
by D F Williams PhD FSA, Department of Archaeology, University of Southampton (Undertaken as part of the HBMC Ceramic Petrology Project – Ancient Monuments Laboratory Report 7/1991)

Summary

A total of 51 samples of late Saxon to later medieval pottery from Eckweek was thin-sectioned for fabric characterisation. This showed nine broad fabric groupings:

Quartz/sedimentary iron ore group
Chert/sedimentary iron ore group
Fossil limestone/sedimentary iron ore group
Chert/quartz group

FIGURE 5.26

No. 46. Reconstructed Period III cookpot. FPN246

FIGURE 5.27

No. 79. Reconstructed Period IV Westcountry Dish. FPN35

Sphaerosiderate group
Ironstone group
Fossil limestone group
Calcite group
Quartz group.

It was difficult to match these fabrics with previous petrological work done on pottery in the area, although the Ironstone group may be connected with late Saxon Cheddar Fabric E. The majority of the pottery could well have been made at no great distance from the Eckweek site.

Introduction

The pottery samples were submitted for detailed examination in thin-section under the petrological microscope. The main aims of the analysis were twofold: firstly, to try to characterise the various fabrics involved, comparing the sherds with one another, and, secondly, if possible to suggest likely source areas for the pottery. Eckweek is situated some six miles south west of Bath and lies on Fullers Earth, very close to Inferior Oolite Limestone, near to outcrops of Great Oolite and not far from Keuper Marl (Mercia Mudstone) deposits (Geological Survey 1" Map of England Sheet 281).

Petrology

On the basis of the range and texture of the non-plastic inclusions present in the sherd samples submitted, a number of broad fabric divisions are suggested here. The original fabric numbering of the sherds has been retained.

Quartz/Sedimentary Iron Ore Group

The sherds in this group contain frequent subangular quartz grains of variable size and frequency, flecks of mica and iron ore. Also present in all the samples are a scatter of disaggregated minerals that appear to be a natural constituent of the clay. These minerals tend to be irregular to rounded in shape, with an average size below 0.30mm. They are often cracked in appearance, have moderate relief, and vary in colour in plain light from light green to shades of brown and red, with little or no birefringence. It is difficult to be certain of the identification, as the condition of many of the grains is not good. Nevertheless, it seems likely that we are dealing with a sedimentary iron ore mineral, possibly the hydrated iron silicate Chamosite (the colour and condition may have been affected to some degree by the firing of the pottery vessels, see for example Hallimond 1939).

Many iron ore minerals occur as synergetic sedimentary beds in Jurassic rocks, which are common in the Eckweek region (Kellaway and Welch 1948). The size and frequency of the quartz grains in these samples tends to be somewhat variable, which would seem to argue against a single source for this material. However, previous petrological analysis of medieval wares from nearby Bath by Vince (1979), which also includes descriptions of the fabrics from the kilns at Ham Green, near Bristol, and Lacock, Wiltshire, makes no mention of inclusions of sedimentary iron ore minerals in the pottery, such as those described above.

It is interesting to note that a number of other fabric groups listed below also contain these sedimentary iron ores, although the range of accompanying non-plastic inclusions differs; with chert, cherty-sandstone and fossil limestone also present. Altogether, well over half of the samples examined from Eckweek, 33 out of a total of 51 sherds, contain conspicuous sedimentary iron ores. Bearing this in mind, it is difficult not to think in terms of a fairly local origin or origins for the majority of this material, much of which is made up of utilitarian cooking pots and jugs. However, it has not been possible in this current study to engage in a geological sampling programme in the region, to see if these sedimentary iron ore materials might have found their way into local clays.

(Note – FT and ware numbers below are those proposed by Andrew Young)

1. FPN313 (context 316, CAR1358). Rim sherd from a cooking pot. Eckweek FT11 and Ware 2
2. FPN337 (context 2, CAR1042). Rim sherd from a decorated jug. Eckweek FT60 and Ware 14
3. FPN336 (context 65, CAR1169). Body sherd from glazed and decorated non-cooking pot. Eckweek FT63 and Ware 14
4. FPN329 (context 169, CAR1125). Body sherd from ?glazed jug. Eckweek FT21 and Ware 14
5. FPN341 (context 65, CAR1170). Handle from glazed jug. Eckweek FT57 and Ware 18
6. FPN339 (context 114, CAR1091). Body sherd from glazed non-cooking pot. Eckweek FT76 (same as FT106) and Ware 14
7. FPN338 (context 19, CAR1025). Body sherd from glazed pitcher. Eckweek FT108 and Ware 14
8. FPN303 (context 185, CAR1694). Body sherd from wiped cooking pot. Eckweek FT74 and Ware 1

Chert/Sedimentary Iron Ore Group

The sherds in this group, besides quartz and discrete sedimentary iron ore grains, similar to those sampled in the previous group, also have present moderate to sparse inclusions of irregular shaped pieces of chert and cherty-sandstone. Flecks of mica and a little iron oxide are normally also present, and occasionally flint, especially in sample 26 (below). The texture of the quartz grains, and to some extent the frequency of the sedimentary iron ore grains, is again variable between many of the samples. Chert is commonly found in the Eckweek area.

9. FPN334 (context 2, CAR1004). Body sherd from cooking pot. Eckweek FT143 and Ware 14
10. FPN306 (context 114, CAR1124). Body sherd from cooking pot. Eckweek FT52 and Ware 2
11. FPN349 (context 330, CAR1481). Body sherd from sooted/wiped cooking pot. Eckweek FT40 and Ware 2
12. FPN348 (context 2, CAR1016). Rim sherd from glazed non-cooking pot. Eckweek FT89 and Ware 3
13. FPN319 (context 296, CAR1553). Body sherd from sooted cooking pot. Eckweek FT117 and Ware 6
14. FPN309 (context 128, CAR1109). Body sherd from sooted/wiped cooking pot. Eckweek FT130 and Ware 2
15. FPN300 (context 355, CAR1420). Body sherd from sooted/wiped cooking pot. Eckweek FT5 and Ware 1
16. FPN310 (context 128, CAR1109). Body sherd from sooted/wiped cooking pot. Eckweek FT65 and Ware 4.
17. FPN320 (context 296, CAR1553). Body sherd from cooking pot. Eckweek FT59 and Ware 4
18. FPN301 (context 173, CAR1649). Body sherd from sooted/wiped cooking pot. Eckweek FT14 and Ware 1
19. FPN317 (context 161, CAR1291). Base sherd from sooted cooking pot. Eckweek FT125 and Ware 2

20 FPN307 (context 340, CAR1361). Body sherd from sooted/wiped cooking pot. Eckweek FT16 and Ware 2
21 FPN312 (context 330, CAR913). Base sherd from cooking pot. Eckweek FT17 and Ware 2
22 FPN304 (context 347, CAR1364). Body sherd from Westcountry Dish. Eckweek FT3 and Ware 2.
23 FPN333 (context 2, CAR1018). Body sherd from glazed non-cooking pot. Eckweek FT33 and Ware 14
24 FPN302 (context 347, CAR1364). Body sherd from Westcountry Dish. Eckweek FT15 and Ware 1
25 FPN305 (context 21, CAR1075). Body sherd from cooking pot. Eckweek FT68 and Ware 1
26 FPN322 (context 347, CAR1364). Body sherd from sooted/wiped cooking pot. Eckweek FT136 and Ware 4

Fossil Limestone and Sedimentary Iron Ore Group

The sherds in this group also contain sedimentary iron ore grains scattered throughout the fabric, this time with moderate to sparse irregular-shaped cryptocrystalline limestone and occasional pieces of curved fossil shell. Also present are the odd piece of chert and flint, (especially in samples 29, 30 and 33), a little calcite, flecks of mica and some iron oxide. Sherds 31 and 33 contain only a few pieces of limestone and otherwise might be placed in the preceding group. It has not been possible to tie down the limestone inclusions to any particular source.

27 FPN318 (context 65, CAR1170). Rim sherd from cooking pot. Eckweek FT77 and Ware 14
28 FPN324 (context 44, CAR1039). Base sherd from Westcountry Dish. Eckweek FT75 and Ware 4
29 FPN342 (context 252, CAR1579). Body sherd from cooking pot. Eckweek FT148 and Ware 4
30 FPN347 (context 238, CAR1579). Base sherd from non-cooking pot. Eckweek FT28 and Ware 4
31 FPN315 (context 114, CAR1124). Base sherd from cooking pot. Eckweek FT10 and Ware 4
32 FPN321 (context 158, CAR1690). Rim sherd from cooking pot. Eckweek FT132 and Ware 4
33 FPN343 (context 65, CAR1142). Rim sherd from non-cooking pot. Eckweek FT96 and Ware 4

Chert and Quartz Group

A reasonably clean clay matrix containing irregular pieces of chert, a few pieces of cherty sandstone and a moderate amount of ill-sorted subangular quartz grains ranging to over 1mm in size. Also present are some flecks of mica and a little iron oxide. Sample 37 is slightly coarser-textured than the others. These sherds appear to lack the sedimentary iron ore grains present in the preceding samples.

34 FPN350 (context 3136, CAR1973). Body sherd from sooted cooking pot. Eckweek FT103 and Ware 3
35 FPN346 (context 2, CAR1018). Body sherd from glazed and decorated non-cooking pot. Eckweek FT84 and Ware 12
36 FPN308 (context 290, CAR1453). Body sherd from sooted/wiped cooking pot. Eckweek FT54 and Ware 2
37 FPN314 (context 114, CAR1124). Body sherd from cooking pot. Eckweek FT67 and Ware 6

Sphaerosiderate Group

Under the microscope a number of black circular discs, some over 1mm in size (especially in sample 38) can be seen scattered throughout a reasonably fine-textured fabric. These distinctively shaped grains can probably be identified as sphaerosiderate. Also present are fairly frequent ill-sorted subangular grains of quartz and some iron oxide. Sphaerosiderate is a mineral commonly found in Wealden formations (Peacock 1977), but it also occurs in the Upper Carboniferous (Spencer 1925), of which the nearest deposits to Eckweek lie a few miles to the south in the Mendip region. In thin-section, this is a very distinctive fabric not noted before by the writer.

38 FPN332 (context 2, CAR1042). Body sherd from internally glazed cooking pot. Eckweek FT71 and Ware 15
39 FPN330 (context 114, CAR1110). Base sherd from glazed decorated jug. Eckweek FT80 and Ware 16

Ironstone Group

All three samples listed below appear in a fairly fine-textured fabric, in which the most noticeable non-plastic inclusions are sparse fragments of ironstone (or ferruginous sandstone) ranging up to 1.7mm in size. A scatter of quartz grains, flecks of mica and the odd piece of chert, flint and cryptocrystalline limestone are also present. Sample 42 is slightly coarser than the other two sherds. Origin unknown although not too different from Cheddar Fabric E (Peacock 1979), which also contains some ironstone.

40 FPN325 (context 201, CAR1531). Rim sherd from cooking pot. Eckweek FT50 and Ware 6
41 FPN335 (context 238, CAR1579). Body sherd from sooted and glazed cooking pot. Eckweek FT55 and Ware 15
42 FPN311 (context 3016, CAR1814). Body sherd from cooking pot. Eckweek FT69 and Ware 2

ARTEFACTS AND ENVIRONMENTAL EVIDENCE

Fossil Limestone Group

The most prominent inclusions in all three samples are plentiful fragments of limestone that in the main are reasonably rounded. Some of these are clearly fossiliferous, and coral was noted in Sample 45. Also present in the samples is a little calcite and some quartz. It is difficult to identify the exact type of fossils in order to suggest a particular geological formation.

43 FPN326 (context 65, CAR1565). Body sherd from cooking pot. Eckweek FT2 and Ware 6
44 FPN327 (context 2, CAR1017). Body sherd from glazed non-cooking pot. Eckweek FT23 and Ware 7
45 FPN316 (context 114, CAR1455). Body sherd from cooking pot. Eckweek FT13 and Ware 7

Calcite Group

A group identified by a fairly clean clay matrix containing a moderate amount of calcite, mostly irregular in shape, together with frequent ill-sorted subangular grains of quartz, some of them polycrystalline, ranging in size to over 1mm. Also flecks of mica, a little cryptocrystalline limestone, quartz sandstone, argillaceous material and some iron oxide and flint.

The calcite grains present in this sample are relatively few compared with the frequent pieces, some of them quite large and of good rhombic shape, that characterise Cheddar Fabric G pottery for example (Peacock 1979). Bearing this in mind, it seems unlikely that the Eckweek vessel shares a common source with Cheddar Fabric G, particularly when it was suggested that the calcite in the latter was probably deliberately crushed and added as temper. It appears more likely that the comparatively small amount of calcite in the Eckweek vessel was a natural inclusion in the clay. As Eckweek is situated in an area where limestone rocks are common, it is quite possible for this vessel to have a fairly local origin.

46 FPN323 (context 330, CAR1481). Body sherd from sooted cooking pot. Eckweek FT29 and Ware 5

Quartz Group

The samples included in this very broad fabric category contain little else but grains of quartz, and are accordingly difficult to characterise sufficiently to enable meaningful suggestions about their source to be made without recourse to comparable material of known origins. The variety of textures exhibited amongst the sherds suggests several different sources.

47 FPN328 (context 338, CAR1475). Body sherd from glazed and decorated non-cooking pot. Eckweek FT24 and Ware 13

Contains frequent subangular quartz grains, some of them polycrystalline, between 0.3 and 0.6mm in size, but with a few grains over 1mm in size. Inclusions are set in a very clean reddish-brown clay matrix. Also present is the odd small piece of chert and a few flakes of mica.

48 FPN331 (context 147, CAR1119). Base sherd from glazed non-cooking pot. Eckweek FT51 and Ware 16
Contains moderately frequent subangular quartz grains, between 0.2 and 0.4mm in size, but with a few larger grains, some iron oxide, flecks of mica and a little argillaceous material.

49 FPN340 (context 83, CAR1558). Body sherd from glazed costrel. Eckweek FT87 and Ware 15
Contains frequent subangular quartz grains, some of them polycrystalline, up to 0.8mm in size, with flecks of mica and a little iron oxide.

50 FPN344 (context 114, CAR1091). Body sherd from glazed jug. Eckweek FT34 and Ware 12
Contains a scatter of ill-sorted, subangular quartz grains, some of them polycrystalline, up to 1mm in size. The inclusions are set in a dark brown clay matrix of silt-sized quartz grains and small flecks of mica. A few pieces of cryptocrystalline limestone are also present.

51 FPN345 (context 65, CAR1142). Body sherd from glazed non-cooking pot. Eckweek FT133 and Ware 15
Contains a groundmass of small quartz grains under 0.1mm in size, and a few flecks of mica. Inclusions are set in a very clean reddish-brown clay matrix. Also present are a sparse scatter of larger quartz grains and some argillaceous material and iron oxide.

5.3.5 Vessel Function

Functional indicators including sooting, calcareous concretions, wiping and glazing were recorded in detail as part of the pottery catalogue. The data derived from this recording enables some general statements to be made regarding the predominant function of particular types of vessel, as well as some individual fabrics and particular ceramic wares more generally. The data provides an opportunity to suggest some broad chronological trends in the use of the medieval domestic pottery recovered from the site.

Sooting (Figure 5.28)

The incidence of sooting on vessels, both internally and externally, was recorded on the premise that, in the majority of cases, where present it indicated heating very close to, or directly on, an open fire. The incidence of internal to external sooting (Figure 5.28) suggests there are two, and possibly three, distinct subgroups within the assemblage. Fabrics with common external sooting (> 15% of the total number of sherds) are, as might be expected, considered 'classic' cooking pot fabrics (Type I); most of the vessels from these fabrics were probably placed directly on the fire during use. Fabrics in cooking pot forms, where external sooting is rare or absent (<15%), are considered to have more commonly fulfilled utilitarian roles (Type II); they may well have been used for cooking, but not in the same way as Type I vessels. Small numbers of fabrics with unusually high proportions of both internal and external sooting (Type III) may have used for specifically 'heavy duty' purposes, for example when used over a boiling furnace, although this distinction is more tentative. In general external sooting is a feature of earlier medieval fabrics and vessels at Eckweek, and is much less common after the mid 13th century.

Calcareous Concretions (Figure 5.29)

Calcareous concretions were considered to represent either the specific function of a vessel, usually as a kettle when the concretions were internal, or, when external, to reflect the means of heating through poaching inside a larger vessel. The relationship between sooting in general and the incidence of calcareous concretions (Figure 5.29) appears to broadly confirm the divisions identified from the incidence of sooting alone, as the greater incidence of calcareous concretion is mainly associated with utilitarian (Type II) vessels. Concretions do occur on Type I cooking pots, but they are almost entirely confined to the interior. When found on Type II vessels, both cookpot and jugs, it is variously internal and external. From this, it appears that Type II vessels, when used for cooking, were more commonly heated indirectly, possibly 'poached' in larger metal or ceramic boiling cauldrons (fragments of several copper alloy cauldrons were present in the kitchen/hall bay of Building 460).

Wiping (Figure 5.30)

Cookpot fabrics commonly appear to have been wiped or smoothed during production. Vessels are most commonly wiped around the external girth and base. Some are wiped internally, although this is less common. There appears to be a significant correlation between the incidence of sooting and wiping (Figure 5.30); fabrics that are most commonly sooted (Type I) are invariably externally wiped. Wiping may be related to vessel production (it is most commonly associated with sagging based cookpots), although it may also have been a desirable functional attribute (perhaps to reduce porosity or an attempt to distribute heat more evenly around the base). Chronologically, wiped finishing is particularly prevalent in earlier medieval fabrics and vessels.

Glazing (Figures 5.31–5.33)

Glazed sherds comprise 9% of the total medieval assemblage and less than 1% occur prior to ceramic phase 5 (*c*AD 1250). The small number of early medieval glazed sherds appear to represent isolated vessels from specialised regional or national centres, for example SE Wiltshire and Stamford wares. Within the later medieval assemblage, they are relatively common (17%), although in particular instances, for example the abandoned domestic assemblage within Building 460, they are more common than coarsewares.

Fabrics that are glazed are rarely sooted (Figure 5.33) or wiped (Figure 5.32), and are more likely to display calcareous concretions (Figure 5.31). This suggests, as might have been expected, that glazed fabrics are predominantly associated with jugs and utilitarian cooking vessels.

Other Vessel Types

Westcountry Dishes occur throughout the medieval assemblage. With a distinctive squat form and small side-wall perforations they appear to have been produced for a specific function. Earlier examples are rarely perforated, when they are the hole is in the base; those from the 12th and 13th centuries are mostly perforated in the body, usually with four opposing holes. Later examples are rarely perforated at all. Sooting or any other concretion is, with the exception of one or two sherds, never a significant feature. Previous interpretations suggest they may have been used as honey pots or 'bee skeps' (after Good and Russett 1987), although the perforations have yet to be explained. Samples of these vessels from Eckweek were submitted to Dr Richard Evershed at the University of Liverpool (Biochemistry Dept.) for Lipid profile analysis in 1990. In the main the analyses were negative (Dr Evershed pers comm), although at the time Dr Evershed felt that the vessels are unlikely to have been used in dairying processes and there is no evidence of any waxy or honey based residues (*It should be clearly noted that in 2015, having reviewed the 1990s lipid analyses, Dr Evershed indicated that the results and his comment cannot now be considered reliable*).

5.3.6 A Summary of the Development of Late Saxon and Medieval Pottery at Eckweek

Figure 5.34 outlines the chronological incidence of late Saxon and medieval ceramic wares at Eckweek as a proportion of the total assemblage. It identifies four broad periods where the emphasis of the ceramic assemblage differs. The characteristics of these periods are summarised below.

Late Saxon: Ceramic Phase 1 – cAD 950–1000

Ceramic wares (Wares 1 and 2) ascribed to the second half of the 10th century include a restricted number of fabrics that appear most likely to represent a local ceramic tradition. Other, again possibly

ARTEFACTS AND ENVIRONMENTAL EVIDENCE

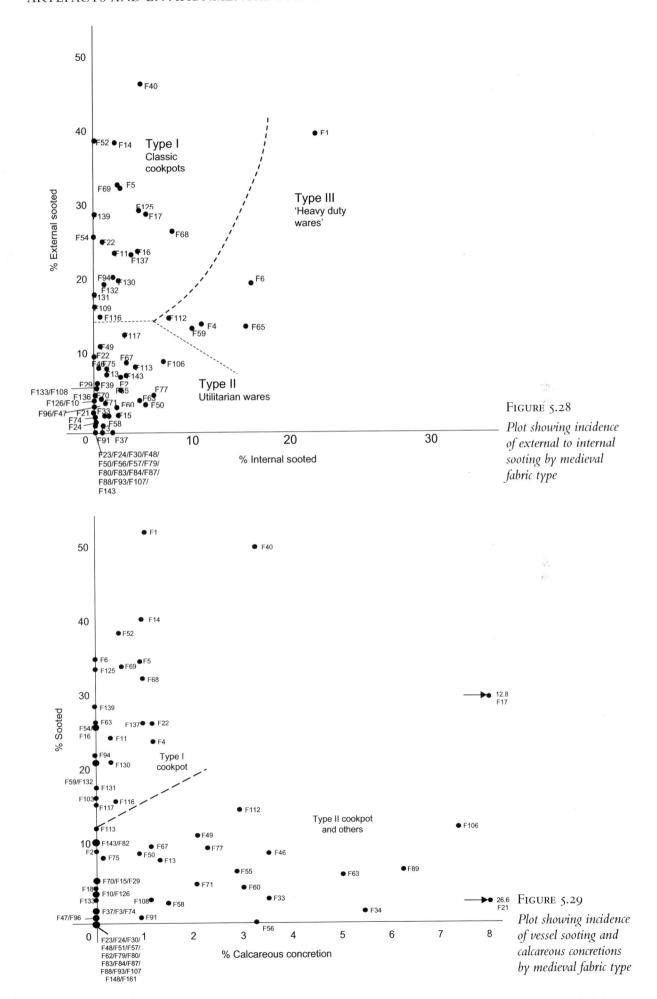

FIGURE 5.28
Plot showing incidence of external to internal sooting by medieval fabric type

FIGURE 5.29
Plot showing incidence of vessel sooting and calcareous concretions by medieval fabric type

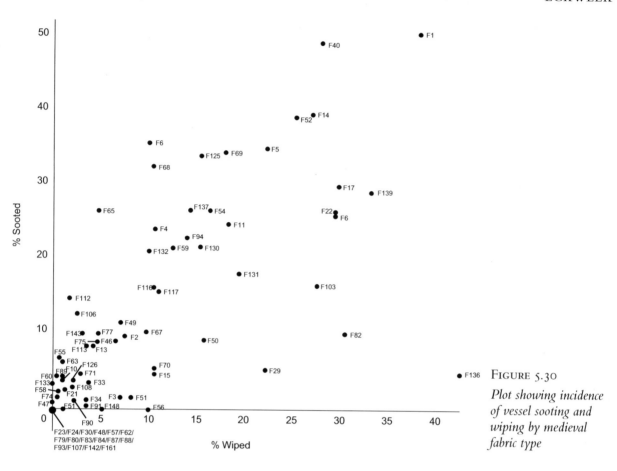

FIGURE 5.30
Plot showing incidence of vessel sooting and wiping by medieval fabric type

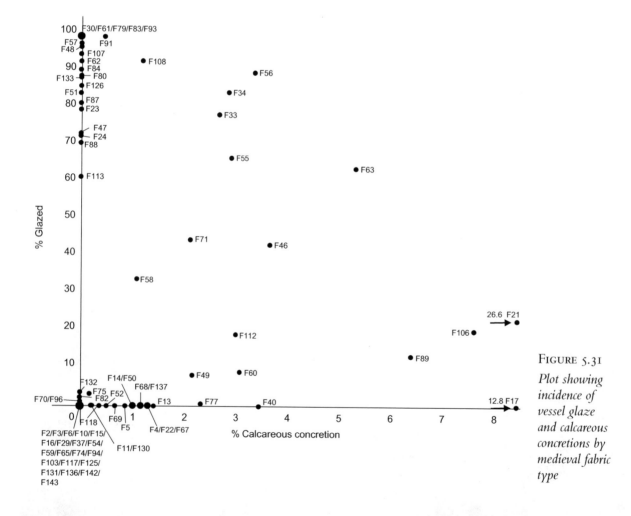

FIGURE 5.31
Plot showing incidence of vessel glaze and calcareous concretions by medieval fabric type

ARTEFACTS AND ENVIRONMENTAL EVIDENCE

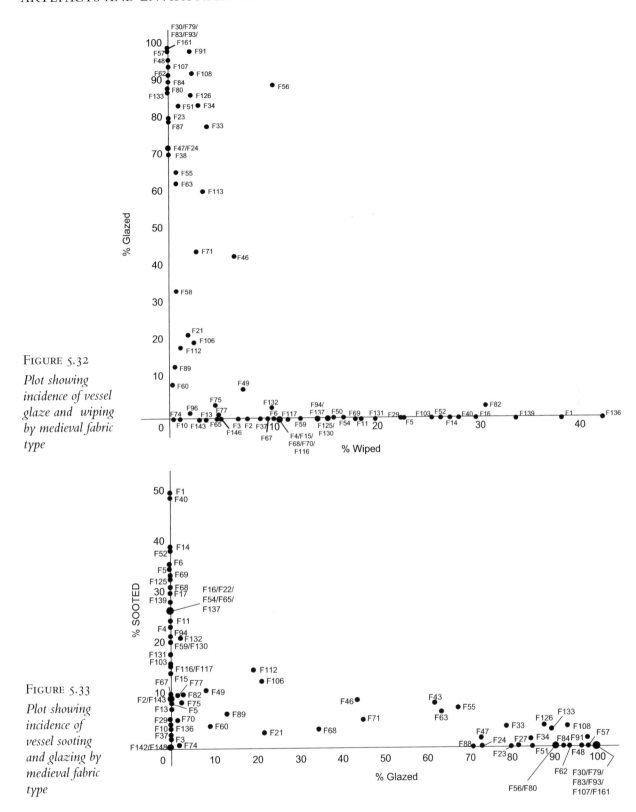

FIGURE 5.32
Plot showing incidence of vessel glaze and wiping by medieval fabric type

FIGURE 5.33
Plot showing incidence of vessel sooting and glazing by medieval fabric type

local, products are suggested by small quantities of a single, coarse flint-tempered, fabric (FT59, Ware 4). Associated with these products, and present in similar proportions, are fabrics very similar to the widely recognised fabric type, Cheddar E (Eckweek Ware 6). Given the wide regional distribution of Cheddar E, these fabrics possibly represent numbers of non-local products. Further regional links are suggested by the presence of a few stamp-decorated sherds in a fabric that is very similar to Great Somerford ware, although the presence of very similar fabrics at a number of other locations (eg Citizen House Bath, Beckery Chapel Glastonbury, and Cheddar), suggests a more widespread distribution for this particular fabric than was perhaps thought.

In general vessels appear to be restricted to a range of small cooking pots (rims commonly less than 20cms), usually with sagging or flat bases and simple everted and rounded rims. One stamped sherd

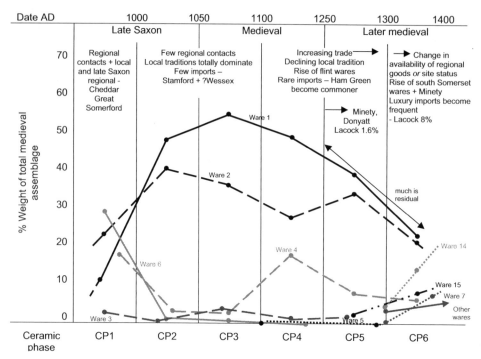

FIGURE 5.34
Plot showing relative proportions of medieval ceramic wares by ceramic phase and date

of Fabric Type 13, with the remnant of a simple pouring hole, suggests other rare vessel forms. Most vessels appear to be handmade, although those in FT67 are always wheel thrown. Decoration is rare in all fabrics and usually confined to single finger-tipping of rims, with the exception of FT13. Sooting is surprisingly rare on these early fabrics, possibly suggesting the vessels were not primarily used as classic 'cookpots'.

Saxo-Norman: Ceramic Phases 2 and 3 – cAD 1000–1100

The 11th-century pottery is dominated by a range of varied, and mostly new, fabrics of Wares 1 and 2 (together they comprise 90% of the assemblage) which could well represent the development of a new relatively local production centre. A considerable number of individual fabrics are first recognised overall, although only a small range dominate the later assemblage. Fabric Type 69, first recognised in CP1, becomes increasingly common. Other 10th-century fabrics occur in small quantities, although most are probably residual. In terms of quantity, Fabric Types 3, 5, 15, and 69 are the most commonly occurring fabrics during CP2. During CP3 significant quantities of FT11, mainly produced from iron deficient clays, appear. It is noticeable that flint tempered fabrics are rare throughout the period.

Cooking pots (Type I), usually sagging, are the most commonly occurring vessel type. Earlier examples are usually small and squat, though deeper forms occur throughout the period. Many vessels are handmade, although some fabrics, in particular Fabric Type 5, are usually wheel thrown. Rim forms are restricted to the range recognised for Wares 1 and 2, usually consisting of simple everted and upright or occasionally deeply channelled forms. Rare lugged pitchers appear to be confined to CP2. Westcountry Dishes, confined to FTs 3 and 15, first occur in CP2 and have sagging and rare perforated bases. Very rare strap handled jugs, in local fabrics, first occur in CP3 (Figure 5.11, 48 and 54), one of which provides the earliest example of a possibly local, glazed fabric. Products from outside the region are confined to a few sherds of Stamford ware and Southeast Wiltshire ware that may only represent just two vessels.

Decoration is rare and mostly confined to the finger-tipping of rims, commonly as a single pair (possibly they served as a simple pouring lip). Only a single decorated body sherd is recognised from CP2, a lug handle with incised tooling (Figure 5.9, 2). During CP3 instances of body slashing, combing and stabbing first occur although they remain very rare, and are mostly confined to FT11.

Medieval: Ceramic Phase 4 – cAD 1100–1250

During the 12th and earlier 13th centuries established products from Wares 1 and 2 continue to dominate the assemblage, although in a reduced number of fabrics, and reducing quantities. Some fabrics first produced in the 11th century (notably FTs 5, 11, and 15) remain common and occur alongside new variants of the same ware, in particular FTs 17, 16 and 74. A range of significant 11th-century fabrics (in Particular FTs 69, 3, 68, 4 and 103) only occur in small quantities.

A new range of flint tempered fabrics (the bulk of Ware 4) appear (c20% of the assemblage in CP4), primarily as a result of the introduction of new Westcountry Dish forms. Cookpots (Type I) remain the dominant vessel type, though everted and deeply channelled forms (Form 37) are significantly more common in the 13th century. A range of handmade and often crude cooking pots form an element of these new flint tempered wares. Sagging Westcountry Dishes continue to be used (FT15), although new flint tempered varieties are always flat based. Small numbers of jugs, now with strap or rod handles, occur, as do rare projecting strap handles, possibly representing a small number of skillets.

Decoration is as rare, if not rarer where cookpots are concerned, as in the later 11th century. Small numbers of rims are still decorated with finger-tipping, although only a very small number of body sherds are decorated, mostly with crude applied strips (Figure 5.10, 34). Glazed sherds are remarkably rare and confined to a few Ham Green sherds that possibly represent just a single traded jug.

Later Medieval: Ceramic Phases 5 and 6 – cAD 1250–1400

Around the middle of the 13th century the emphasis of the ceramic assemblage changes significantly. The majority of the earlier medieval cookpot and Westcountry Dish fabrics disappear, and are replaced by new ranges of utilitarian cookpots and jugs from emerging pottery centres in Wiltshire and south Somerset. A small number of existing coarseware fabrics (FTs 11, 17, and possibly FT5) do appear to continue in use, and a few new variants first occur (FTs 96 and 77). Many of these appear to be from the kilns at Lacock, although the source of the generic south Somerset products has yet to be identified. Many new glazed fabrics appear to continue in use well into the 14th century although the latest abandonment assemblage suggests that many products, including those from Lacock, were less common, or had disappeared, by c1400. They appear to have been replaced, at least within the domestic environment, by a small range of south Somerset fabrics (FTs 63, 106, and 108) and Minety-type products from north Wiltshire. Products from the Bristol area remain surprisingly rare and are confined to a few Redcliffe jugs.

Utilitarian cookpots (Figure 5.12, Type II) appear to replace classic coarseware types, although this is largely based on the assessment of the domestic assemblage and may not reflect activities throughout the settlement. Jugs occur far more commonly than had previously been the case but the numbers of Westcountry Dishes appear to decline and those that do occur are rarely perforated. The later 14th-century assemblage is characterised by a new range of specialised and sophisticated domestic vessels that includes dripping dishes, bowls and highly decorated jugs – a trend that culminates in the elaborately decorated cistern (Figures 5.20 and 5.21).

5.4 COINS
by Sarah Newns (2015)

A small assemblage of coins was recovered, comprising five Roman and four medieval coins (Figure 5.35). The Roman coins are residual, of copper alloy or bronze, and are of 3rd- or 4th-century AD date (Figure 5.36). All the coins were initially identified and catalogued in 1990 by Dr David Dawson of Taunton Museum (Figure 5.37).

The medieval coins are of a relatively restricted date range, from the early 13th to the mid 14th centuries AD. The coins comprise two silver pennies, one denier and one groat (of the value of four pennies). Most are worn, but in good condition (Figures 5.38 and 5.39), with the exception of the French denier, of which only one third survives, probably as a result of clipping (Figure 5.38, 3).

The earliest coin recovered is the French denier tournois, which dates to between 1205 and 1285. The denier tournois was first minted at Tours in the late 12th to early 13th centuries, and it was most commonly used as currency in England during this early period, when parts of western France were ruled by the Angevin dynasty, thus coming under the jurisdiction of Henry II of England up until 1203 (Williams, PAS no. LEIC-892AF6). Four deniers tournois were equivalent to one English penny and the coin thus met the need for small change, which was keenly felt amongst the poorer parts of the population due to the lack of copper coinage, and the dearth of halfpennies and farthings (Spufford 1963, 132). Research based on coin hoards of largely early 14th-century and later date has suggested that foreign sterling equivalents made up some 1% of coins in general circulation at that time (Spufford 1963, 127), and that the actual coins themselves had a lengthy circulation period, one example having remained in use for over one hundred years (Spufford 1963, 128).

From the late 14th century onwards, legislation was introduced to try to curb the introduction of foreign gold and silver coins, particularly targeting money from the Low Countries. A plea from the Commons of 1402 on behalf of the poor, highlighting the need for small change, refers to their use of clipped deniers and half deniers, amongst other foreign currencies:

> la Monnoie d'estranges Terres…es aucuns parties Demy-deniers coupes… (Spufford 1963, 133).

The king replied, saying that henceforward one third of the silver minted should be in denominations of halfpennies and farthings, and by the early to mid 15th century, such imitative continental sterlings had virtually disappeared from circulation (Spufford 1963, 139).

The denier tournois is thus not an unknown find on English archaeological sites, numerous examples

Coin	Date	SF Number	Context
?Roman AE	?Roman	900	318
?Roman AE4	?324–330	547	2
Roman AE4	330–335	903	332
?Roman AE3	4th century AD	888	114
?Roman AE4	4th–5th century AD	504	2
Denier tournois	c1205–85	791	88
Edward I penny	1278–1307	548	2
Edward I penny	c1300–1302	938	98
Edward III groat	1351–1352	586	46

FIGURE 5.35

Coins in chronological order

Context	Coin	Date	SF Number
2	?Roman	4th–5th centuries AD	504
2	?Roman	?324–335	547
2	Edward I penny	1278–1307	548
46	Edward III groat	1351–1352	586
88	Denier tournois	c1205–1285	791
98	Edward I penny	c1300–1302	938
114	?Roman	4th century AD	888
318	?Roman	?Roman	900
332	Roman	330–335 AD	903

FIGURE 5.36

Coins in context number order

SF	Context	Description
504	2	Probable Roman AE 4, fragmentary, very worn and corroded, dated 4th–5th century AD
547	2	Probable Roman AE 4, possibly 'PROVIDENTIAE AUGG/CAES' type, dated AD 324–330
548	2	Edward I penny, minted in Canterbury, dated 1278–1307. **Figures 5.38, 1 and 5.39, 3**
586	46	Edward III groat, series C, dated 1351–52. **Figures 5.38, 2 and 5.39, 2**
791	88	French silver denier tournois, one third surviving; obverse: short cross, '…O REX', reverse: chastel tournois, '…SCIV'; dated c1205–1285. **Figure 5.38, 3**
888	114	Roman, 4th century copy, very worn
900	318	Copper flan, possibly Roman, irregular, 19–22mm diameter, very worn
903	332	Roman AE 4, 'URBS ROMA' type, 'PTR', minted in Trier, dated AD 330–335. **Figure 5.38, 4**
938	98	Edward I penny, type IXb, minted in Kingston-Upon-Hull, dated c1300–1302. **Figure 5.39, 1**

FIGURE 5.37

Catalogue of coins

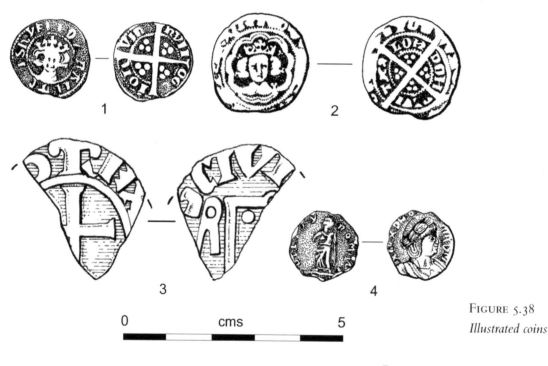

FIGURE 5.38

Illustrated coins

FIGURE 5.39

1) Edward I penny SF938, 2) Edward III groat SF586, 3) Edward I penny SF548

existing on the Portable Antiquities Database and in museum collections (the Fitzwilliam Museum, Cambridge, amongst others). The denier is of the 'short cross' type, but pennies and deniers of this type were liable to be clipped (to provide small denominations), so a 'long cross' type was introduced, in which the arms of the cross extended right up to the edge of the coin (Spink 2000, 149).

In Britain, the silver penny had become common currency under the reign of King Edgar in AD 959, and by the mid 12th century was minted under five main types, issued by over sixty mints. Indeed, up until the reign of Henry III (1133–1189), the penny was the only denomination to be minted in England (Clayton 2015). The two examples recovered from Eckweek were minted at Canterbury and Hull, in the reign of Edward I.

With the exception of the groat, the majority of the coins are thus of the lower denominations, but would have represented not inconsiderable sums of money, at a period in which the average rate of pay for a master thatcher ran to two pence per day (1261–1270; Dyer 1989, 209), rising to three pence per day by 1350.

In terms of context, it is worth noting that all four coins were recovered from the areas of buildings towards the northern end of the site. The Edward I penny (SF548, Figures 5.38, 1 and 5.39, 3) and the Edward III groat (SF586, Figures 5.38, 2 and 5.39, 2) were both recovered from Area A, the penny from a cleaning layer associated with Phase 4 or 5 occupation within Buildings 462 and/or 460, and the groat from one of the latest floor layers inside Building 460. The latter is significant, in that the presence of the groat, amongst a range of personal and domestic items, provides a useful terminus post quem of the mid 14th century for the abandonment of the latter building, and thus excludes the possibility that the building was abandoned due to the first major outbreak of epidemic in 1348.

The denier tournois and the second Edward I penny (Figures 5.38, 3 and 5.39, 1) were both recovered from Area B. The denier was recovered from the fill of a robber pit, and is thus residual, but its presence suggests that a building was in existence in this area by the late 13th century, or possibly later, due to the longevity of these foreign sterling equivalents (above). The Edward I penny was recovered from the latest floor layer within Building 461, and thus provides a terminus post quem of 1300–1302 for the latest phase of occupation within this building.

It is also worth noting that no coins were recovered from the earlier, 11th-century occupation (Phases 2 and 3) in Area H, even though Building 477 may have been of seignorial status.

Comparison with other rural medieval sites indicates that the low numbers of coins recovered at Eckweek is not unusual and consistent with other excavated assemblages. The site at Goltho, Yorkshire, for example, yielded only six coins in total, three of which, two pennies and one halfpenny, dated to the reign of King Stephen (1135–1154; Archibald 1987, 188). The rural medieval site at Shapwick, Somerset, yielded one William I penny, a farthing of John (1204–1205), two coins of Edward I (one penny and one halfpenny) and one Edward III penny (Minitt 2007, 1159–1160). Only eight coins of medieval date were recorded at the rural settlement of West Cotton, Raunds, and of these, half were Long Cross issues, falling within the reign of Henry III (Archibald 2010, 394–395).

5.5 IRON AND LEAD OBJECTS
by Ann Thompson (1991)

Introduction

The iron and lead finds are grouped in this report according to function and are manufactured from iron unless stated otherwise. All the ironwork has been X-radiographed at the Ancient Monuments Laboratory, London and Bristol. Selected items were further examined using X-ray Fluorescence (XRF) to analyse the non-ferrous metal plating and decoration. Although much of the material was not badly corroded, the X-radiographs aided the identification and illustration of the objects.

Following the use on site of the Central Excavation Unit (CEU) finds recording system, the catalogue of the iron and lead finds was prepared on the corresponding computer database, DELILAH (copyright of English Heritage, the Central Excavation Unit).

This report lists the objects by type using the small find (SF) or Common Artefact number (CAR). The context number (given in brackets), allocated ceramic phase and a measurement, usually length or diameter, of each object are also given. Full measurements and descriptions, together with references of comparative objects can be found in the catalogue. Illustrated objects for each category are listed followed by objects that are not.

The iron and lead objects, X-radiographs, XRF results, the catalogue and report form part of the site archive.

Knives and Shears

The collection of knives forms the largest category of object at Eckweek, apart from binding and sheet fragments and structural nails. Of the 25 knives identified, 12 had whittle tangs, for insertion into handles of bone, horn or wood and eight had scale tangs for riveted handles. Five blades and one tang were too incomplete to classify.

The earliest dated knife in the collection is SF963, from the 11th century, which has a distinctive blade with elongated s-shaped cutting edge, straight back and a shoulder that falls away to meet the tang. Generally regarded as a characteristic Viking knife type, it has been identified at the Anglo-Scandinavian sites in York (Waterman 1959, 73, fig 7.4, 11 and Tweddle 1986, 192) and in 10th- to 11th-century deposits at Goltho (Beresford 1987, 181).

All the knives from pre-1300 contexts (SFs 849; 880; 920; 963; 1685 and 1789) were associated with the occupation of an 11th- to 12th-century timber building (Structure 467) in Area A and the 11th-century timber building (Structure 477) recorded in Area H and are of whittle tang form. This supports the dating for the development of the scale tang form in the 13th century and the change to its common use by the 14th century (Cowgill et al 1987, 51). Further confirmation of this dating is provided by the contexts of the Eckweek scale tang knives, five are from ceramic phase CP6 (1300 to 1380+), one is from ceramic phase CP7 (post-medieval) and the remaining two were unstratified and recovered from the topsoil.

At the beginning of the medieval period the knife was a basic implement that could serve any use that required a blade with a cutting edge. Whilst different uses cannot be attributed to a blade having a whittle tang as opposed to a scale tang handle, there does seem to have been an overall development in specialised knife forms, such as the table knife. In London this development has been linked to the preference for the scale tang form (Cowgill et al 1987, 51).

Specific uses can be suggested for some of the Eckweek knives. The parallel-sided rectangular-sectioned blade of SF579 is of common form, particularly in the 12th and 13th centuries, but can be found throughout the medieval period. The large size of SF579, together with SF551, a large blade of triangular-section with straight back and cutting edge that widens before tapering at the tip, suggests that these are probably carving knives. SFs 623, 666 and 800 are recognisable as table knives with triangular-sectioned blades, straight backs and a tapering cutting edge, which date to the 14th century. At the junction of the scale tang handle and blade are two protective shoulder plates of copper alloy, one riveted to each side of the handle. The handles were attached by copper alloy rivets placed centrally along the length of the tang. Metallurgical analysis of the shoulder plates on SFs 623 and 800 show a low-zinc brass with a trace of silver on SF623, which also had the remains of leather between the rivet and the guard of the shoulder plate.

SF519 (not illustrated) is an example of a post-medieval table knife. The blade is rectangular in section and the straight back and cutting edge taper to a rounded tip.

One knife, SF573, has apparently served a secondary function as a chisel. The blade, with cutler's mark, has a parallel straight back and cutting edge that both taper to a rounded tip. The tang is short and hammer spread at the broken end, which together with the mineral replaced wood present on both sides of the blade, suggests that the knife blade has been hammered into wood. Only the tang fragment of SF592, which is encased in wood, provides any evidence of an original handle.

Of the four cutlers' marks examined at AML only two were inlaid, SF666, a low-zinc brass with traces of lead and tin and SF573 with copper, lead and tin. Inlays of non-ferrous metal were often simply hammered into place and so were easily lost. The cutlers' marks on blades SF766 and SF551 may well have been inlaid originally. All the knives with cutlers' marks were recovered from contexts dating from 1300, which supports the mid 14th-century date for the practice of marking knives (Ward-Perkins 1940).

Three pairs of shears were recovered from the site. Two are very fragmentary, SFs 694 and 879, whilst one pair (SFs 501/554) is almost complete. SFs 501/554 is a small pair of shears with long triangular-sectioned blades and parallel straight back and cutting edges. The plain blade tops and looped bow are characteristic of the post-Conquest form. Although recovered from the topsoil, the rectangular section of the handle of SFs 501/554 dates this pair of shears to the 14th century (Cowgill et al 1987, 58). Long slender blades have been identified with a requirement for accuracy and continuity in cutting (Cowgill et al 1987, 59). Shears, like knives, will probably have had a variety of uses and the Eckweek examples could have been used to cut hair and cloth, as well as for shearing sheep.

Illustrated Knives (Figures 5.40 and 5.41)

1   SF551 (context 41) CP6, length 290mm. The only whittle tang knife with a cutler's mark. Large blade of triangular section with a straight back and a cutting edge that broadens before tapering to the broken tip
2   SF579 (31) CP6, length 225mm. Large blade of rectangular section and parallel sides
3   SF531 (2) Topsoil, length 98mm
4   SF963 (3043) CP2, length 72mm. The earliest dated knife from Eckweek, from the 11th century, with a distinctive triangular-sectioned blade with elongated s-shaped cutting edge, straight back and shoulder that falls away to meet the tang. Generally regarded as a characteristic Viking knife type it has been identified at Anglo-Scandinavian sites in York (Waterman 1959, 73, fig. 7.4–11 and Tweddle 1986, 192) and in 10th-century deposits at Goltho (Beresford 1987, 181)
5   SF 573 (73) CP6, length 87mm. This scale tang knife has apparently served a secondary function as a chisel. The blade, with cutler's mark, has a parallel straight back and cutting edge that both taper to a rounded tip. The tang is short and hammer-spread at the broken end, which, together with the mineral replaced wood present on both sides of the blade, suggests that the knife blade was hammered into wood
6   SF623 (72) CP6, length 160mm. Scale tang knife with triangular sectioned blade that has a straight back and tapering cutting edge. At the junction of the scale tang handle and blade are two protective shoulder plates of copper alloy, one riveted to each side of the handle. The handle was attached by copper alloy rivets placed centrally along the length of the tang. Metallurgical analysis by the Ancient Monuments Laboratory of the shoulder plates on this knife and knives SF666 and SF800 show a

low-zinc brass with a trace of silver on SF623, which also had the remains of leather between the rivet and the guard of the shoulder plate

7   SF666 (3) CP6, length 178mm. As SF623 above. Cutler's mark
8   SF800 (2) Topsoil, length 282mm. As SF623 above
9   SF501 (1) and SF554 (2) Topsoil, maximum length 198mm. Small pair of shears with long triangular-sectioned blades which have parallel straight back and cutting edges. The plain blade tops and looped bow are characteristic of the post-Conquest form. Although recovered from the topsoil, the rectangular section of the handle of both further dates this pair of shears to the 14th century (Cowgill *et al* 1987, 58)
10 SF766 (65) CP6, length 132mm. Description as SF666 above

Other Knives, Unidentified Blades and Shears (not illustrated)

SF849 (139) CP2, length 90mm
SF880 (313) CP4, length 89mm
CAR1685 (183) CP1, length 43mm
CAR1789 (3091) CP2, length 57.5mm
CAR1667 (340) CP4, length 59mm. As SF579, but smaller
SF507 (2) Topsoil, length 93mm. As SF531
SF708 (3) CP6, length 104mm. As SF531
CAR1 572 (212) CP7, length 74mm
SF876 (21) CP6, length 73.5mm. As SF666
SF595 (44) CP7, length 78mm. As SF666
SF566 (31) CP6, length 54mm. As SF666
SF519 (2) Topsoil, length 121mm. As SF666
SF694 (1470) CP6, length 181mm. As SF501/554
SF879 (313) CP4, length 59mm. As SF501/554
SF668 (78) CP6, length 132mm
SF665 (3) CP6, length 105mm
SF536 (12) CP6, length 94mm
CAR1321 (150) CP6, length 32mm
SF630 (2) Topsoil, length 80mm
SF592 (46) CP6, length 37mm. Only tang remains

Household Items

The category of household objects includes utensils – three vessel fragments and two spoons – three rings, a perforated weight, a ferrule, a swivel ring, three hinges for boxes or chests and a variety of fittings and mounts and numerous small fragments of binding. The fittings and mounts would have originally belonged to domestic items, especially furniture and often combine a functional purpose with decoration. The fragments of plain and perforated sheet would have served as binding, supporting and covering a variety of household objects. Many of the objects in this category have a form that can be found throughout the medieval period and indeed were recovered from ceramic phases CP2–CP7, ranging from the late 10th to the 15th centuries.

Illustrated Household Items (Figures 5.41 and 5.42)

11 SF718 (38) CP7, length 70mm. Vessel rim fragment from a plain rimmed bowl or dish that was decorated with two parallel incised lines below the internal rim edge. Post-medieval
12 CAR1618 (333) CP4, length 50mm. Handle from a small bowl
13 SF511 (2) Topsoil, length 168mm. Spoon fragment, the broken bowl probably of ball-spoon form
14 SF939 (114) CP7, internal diameter 10mm. Lead ring of ovoid shape and section
15 SF622 (72) CP6, diameter 42mm. Solid lead disc with central circular perforation which has an hourglass-shaped section. This perforated weight was roughly finished as indicated by the irregular edges
16 SF633 (2) Topsoil, diameter 41mm. Ferrule consisting of a cylinder of subcircular shape with overlapping ends
17 SF533 (2) Topsoil, length 128mm. Swivel fitting comprising a ring with a supporting interlocking tear-shaped loop
18 SF761 (114) CP6, length 48mm. Box hinge consisting of a leaf-shaped terminal with a central rivet hole that appears in the X-radiograph to have lines of plating radiating from it, although cleaning revealed no visible plating material
19 SF735 (2) Topsoil, length 42mm. Tear-drop shaped box hinge with rivets at both ends and a loop at the narrow end
20 SF581 (31) CP6, length 90mm. Dumbbell-shaped fitting.
    One of three very similar dumbbell-shaped fittings which have disc terminals ornamented with inlaid grooves radiating from a central rivet. Analysis by AML showed that the grooves contained tin with traces of lead. Probably a decorative fitting from a chest or box. Similar fittings, but manufactured in copper alloy, are identified at Colchester (Crummy 1988, 18, 1789) and Goltho (Goodall in Beresford 1987, fig 154, 17)
21 SF540 (2) Topsoil, length 77mm. As SF581
22 SF917 (316) CP5, length 54mm. Decorative hooked fitting with spiral terminals and a central fixing rivet
23 SF822 (2) Topsoil, length 31.5mm. Triangular-shaped fitting with a broken protrusion at the apex and a rivet hole along the break on the base edge
24 SF990 (3142) CP2, diameter 19mm. Solid subcircular lead terminal that tapers to a flat base, with a square recess cut into it. Possibly part of a spigot

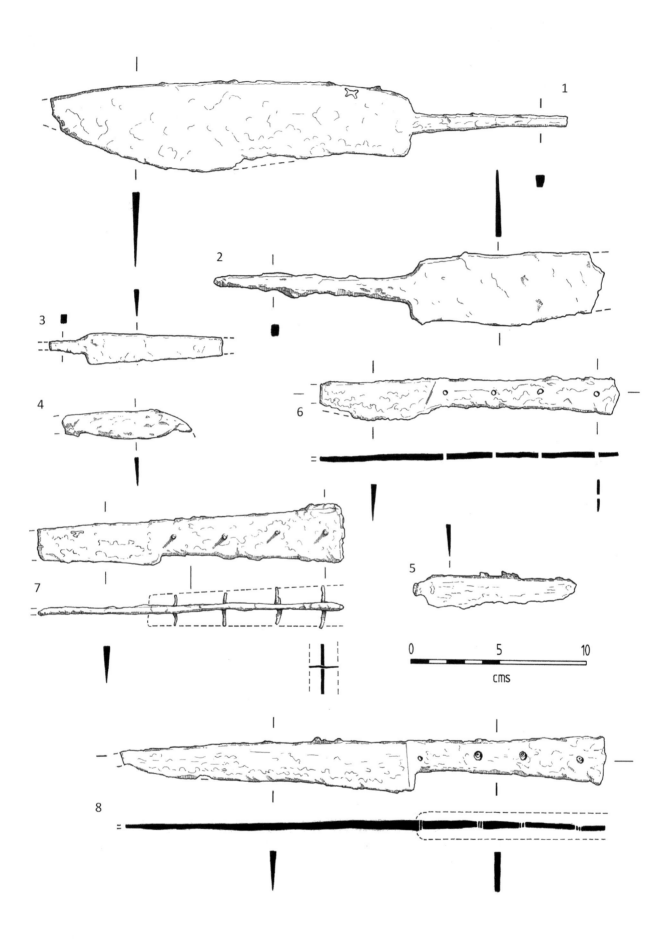

FIGURE 5.40
Metalwork illustrations Nos 1–8. Knives

ARTEFACTS AND ENVIRONMENTAL EVIDENCE

25 SF680 (31) CP6, diameter 21mm. As SF990 but with a subcircular recess
26 SF731 (161) CP5, length 85mm. Fragment of binding sheet with curving edges and rivets for attachment

Other Household Items (not illustrated)

SF790 (2) Topsoil, length 40mm. Drop handle
CAR (362) CP2, length 41mm. Spoon
SF781 (211) CP6, internal diameter 11mm. Lead ring
1752 (378) CP7, diameter 29mm. Ring
SF761 (114) CP6, length 48mm. Box hinge
SF530 (2) Topsoil, length 138mm. Box hinge
SF557 (46) CP6, length 105mm. As SF581
SF979 (3057) CP2, length 35mm. Bar fitting with rounded terminal
SF971 (3048) CP2, length 42mm. Mount consisting of a rectangular-shaped strip with a disc-headed terminal on the underside of the one remaining edge

Buckles

Although representing a small collection overall, the range of buckles used in personal dress or on sword belts throughout the medieval period is represented at Eckweek. The most common is the D-shaped buckle, as it is on many other sites in the 11th to 15th centuries.

Illustrated Buckles (Figure 5.42)

27 SF683 (145) CP6, length 52mm. D-shaped buckle. Pin missing
28 SF987 (3077) CP3, length 53mm. D-shaped buckle of typical harness form. Square-sectioned except for the revolving upright circular-sectioned bar, which would have made it easier to thread leather straps through the buckle and prevent them from chafing (Goodall 1987, 184)
29 SF697 (151) CP6, length 27mm. Rectangular buckle, pin missing except for its attachment loop
30 SF707 (114) CP6, length 46mm. Double buckle of figure-of-eight form, pin missing. Tinned
31 SF867 (293) CP4, length 22mm. Strap end buckle. Tinned
32 SF642 (2) Topsoil, length 24mm. As SF683

Other Buckles (not illustrated)

SF560 (2) Topsoil, length 62mm. As SF683
SF578 (31) CP6, length 47mm. As SF683
SF758 (114) CP6, length 32.5mm. As SF697
CAR 1975 (3136) CP3, length 35mm. Buckle pin
CAR 1978 (3046) CP2, length 34mm. Buckle pin

Horse Equipment and Cattleshoes

A large collection of horseshoes and horseshoe nails was recovered from all phases. Four of the five cattle shoes were from the topsoil, the fifth from ceramic phase CP6, and are all of later medieval date. Two bridle pieces and four spurs complete the items of horse equipment.

Whilst only horseshoe SF911 is sufficiently complete to be identified as of 'Norman' type, with the distinctive lobate outer edge created by deep countersunk nailholes forcing the edge outwards, six other horseshoe fragments (SFs 919, 899, 833, 884, 850, 981), by their circular countersunk nailholes and general thickness, probably also belong to the same type. The 'Norman' type dates from the late 11th century through to the 13th century. Three 'transitional' type horseshoes (SFs 724, 989 and 689) were recovered, dating from the late 13th to early 14th century. This type is distinguished by the presence of countersunk rectangular nailholes with no lobate edge.

Six later medieval type horseshoes were found in the 14th-century farmhouse and yard area (SFs 508, 542, 577, 629, 649 and CAR 1179). The later medieval horseshoe dates from the mid 14th century, has rectangular nail holes, no longer countersunk, a hemispherical section and sometimes calkins. Often there is a fold at the toe to help shape the shoe, perhaps to the narrower rear hoof.

A total of 70 horseshoe nails was recovered from ceramic phases CP2–CP7, the majority, 25, are from CP6, although 26 were also found in the topsoil. The earlier fiddle-key form, which has a flat hemispherical-shaped head in profile that is no thicker than the shank, dates from the 12th to mid 13th century (Goodall type A, 1980, 182). This nail type was suited to horseshoes with countersunk nail holes and the points of shanks are often found bent over (double-clenched). A total of 21 of these early fiddle-key nails was found, two from the topsoil, nine from CP6 and three each from CP2, CP3 and CP5, with the remaining one from CP4. The later type of horseshoe nail, dating from the late 13th century, is better represented at Eckweek. The head is trapezoidal and expands in profile to a flat top (Goodall type B, 1980, 182). A total of 49 examples of this type are recorded, of which 23 are from the topsoil and 16 are from CP6, four each from CP5 and CP7 and one each from CP1 and CP2, these latter possibly therefore intrusive in those contexts.

Illustrated Horse Equipment and Cattleshoes
(Figures 5.42 and 5.43)

33 SF911 (330) CP5, length 102mm. 'Norman' type horseshoe. Rectangular in section, four countersunk nailholes on each branch, one with a nail in situ, forming the characteristic lobate outer edge. One calkin remaining

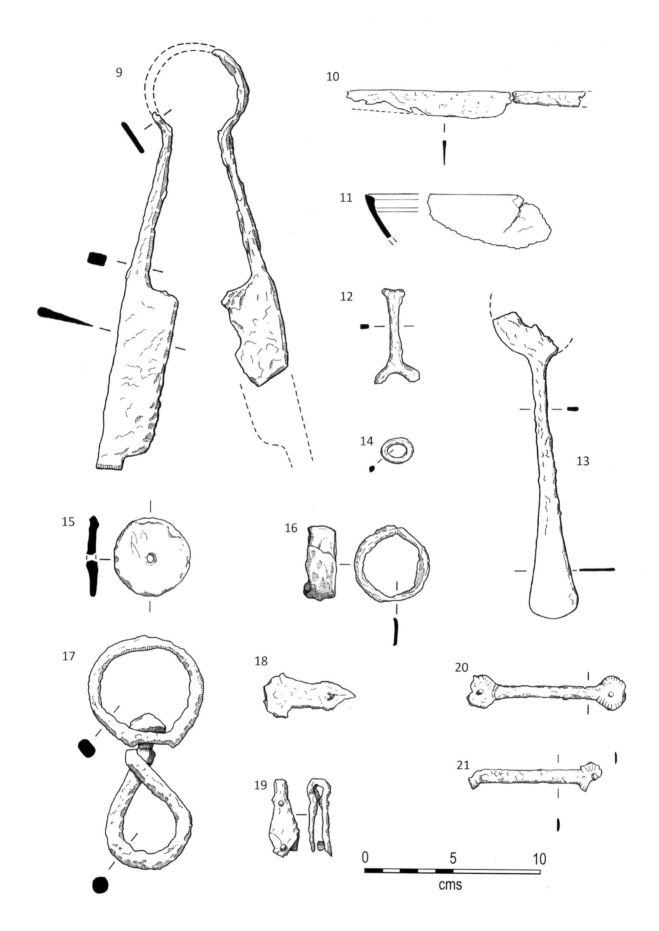

FIGURE 5.41
Metalwork illustrations Nos 9–21

ARTEFACTS AND ENVIRONMENTAL EVIDENCE

34 SF724 (161) CP5, length 117mm. Transitional type of horseshoe with three rectangular countersunk nailholes on one branch remaining together with a calkin
35 SF577 (67) CP6, length 105mm. Later medieval type of horseshoe
36 SF751 (207) CP2, length 30mm. Early type of fiddle-key nail
37 CAR1182 (114) CP6, length 39mm. Later type of fiddle-key nail
38 SF509 (2) Topsoil, length 120mm. An almost complete rowel spur with only one leg slightly damaged. The sides of the spur are curved to fit under the wearer's ankles. There is a single pierced terminal on each leg through which is a ring with a hooked attachment for a leather strap. Mineralised leather is visible round the buckle. The rowel has five points. A projecting ornamental point or crest at the junction of the body and shank dates this spur to the end of the 14th to the mid 15th century. The spur was probably plated originally, although tin was only detected on loose fragments
39 SF841 (265) CP3, length 87mm. Leg from a prick spur that ends in a flattened plate which would have been riveted onto a leather strap. Plating is evidenced by traces of tin. A type of spur that was introduced into England by Vikings/Normans and this example does come from an 11th-century context, although a second prick spur leg fragment from Eckweek (below not illustrated) was recovered from a 15th-century context
40 SF722 (169) CP5, length 104mm. Possible bridle piece. Circular-sectioned shank with a rectangular perforated D-shaped terminal that has a flat side, possibly to take a strap. Tinned
41 SF974 (3063) CP2, length 74mm. Bridle piece. Leaf-shaped shank with a rectangular perforated terminal
42 SF512 (2) Topsoil, length 111mm. Cattleshoe with four rectangular nailholes and one nail still in-situ
43 SF882 (114) CP6, length 56mm. Prick spur leg fragment
44 SF608 (40) Topsoil, length 75mm. Cattleshoe. As SF512

Other Horse Equipment and Cattleshoes (not illustrated)

SF919 (318) CP3, length 44mm. As SF911
SF899 (332) CP5, length 70mm. As SF911
SF833 (20) CP6, length 62mm. As SF911
SF884 (114) CP6, length 45mm. As SF911
SF850 (139) CP2, length 32mm. As SF911
SF981 (3064) CP2, length 60mm. As SF911
SF989 (3142) CP2, length 39mm. As SF724
SF689 (148) CP6, length 37mm. As SF724
SF649 (46) CP6, length 95mm. As SF577
SF629 (104) CP5, length 50mm. As SF577
SF542 (12) CP6, length 74mm. As SF577
CAR1179 (41) CP6, length 110mm. As SF577
SF508 (2) Topsoil, length 52mm. As SF577
CAR1598 (260) CP2, length 36mm. Unidentified horseshoe
CAR1996 (3077) CP3, length 32.5mm. As CAR1598
CAR1739 (127) CP4, length 33mm. As CAR1598
SF146 (149) CP3, length 35mm. Spur leg terminal with double perforation
SF974 (3063) CP2, length 74mm. Bridle piece
SF613 (40) Topsoil, length 87mm. As SF512
SF516 (26) Topsoil, length 95mm. As SF512
CAR1098 (57) CP6, length 90mm. As SF512

Structural Objects and Fittings

The building and structural ironwork consists of various structural fittings and objects. Staples were used to hold fittings in place such as door and gate hasps and can be found throughout the medieval period. At Eckweek the 17 U-shaped staples recovered come from ceramic phases CP2, CP3, CP5 and CP6, with one from the topsoil. Of the staples, 12 have square-sectioned shanks, the remainder are rectangular-sectioned. The split end loop, SF808, was probably also used as a form of staple.

The 10 hinge pivots and 16 strap hinges were all recovered from the 14th-century deposits, primarily associated with the stone farmhouse. The hinge pivots have a circular-sectioned short guide arm and square or rectangular-sectioned long tang, which tapers to a point for insertion into wood or walls. The largest is 125mm long and the smallest is 30mm, variations in size that reflect variety in the sizes of the doors and shutters of which they formed part. The strap hinges similarly vary in size with the largest 300mm long and the smallest 112mm. Where the evidence survives, these hinges have a supporting eye of U-shaped hanging form, through which the hinge pivot guide arm will have slotted. Although most of the strap hinge terminals are simply rounded in shape, SF640 is split into two curving branches, an example of a more decorative form that may have belonged to a piece of furniture, such as a box or chest, rather than a shutter or door.

One large wall hook, SF952, was recovered from the topsoil and seven smaller hooks from the 14th-century building. A large spike, SF513, with a double flanged head, in which each flange was perforated, was also found in 14th-century deposits.

A total of 236 timber nails were recovered at Eckweek, of which 77 were from the topsoil and the remainder from ceramic phases CP1–CP7. There is a predominance in the number of nails, of all types, recovered from CP6 (85 in total). The nails have been classified into nine types based on the shape of the nail head as follows:

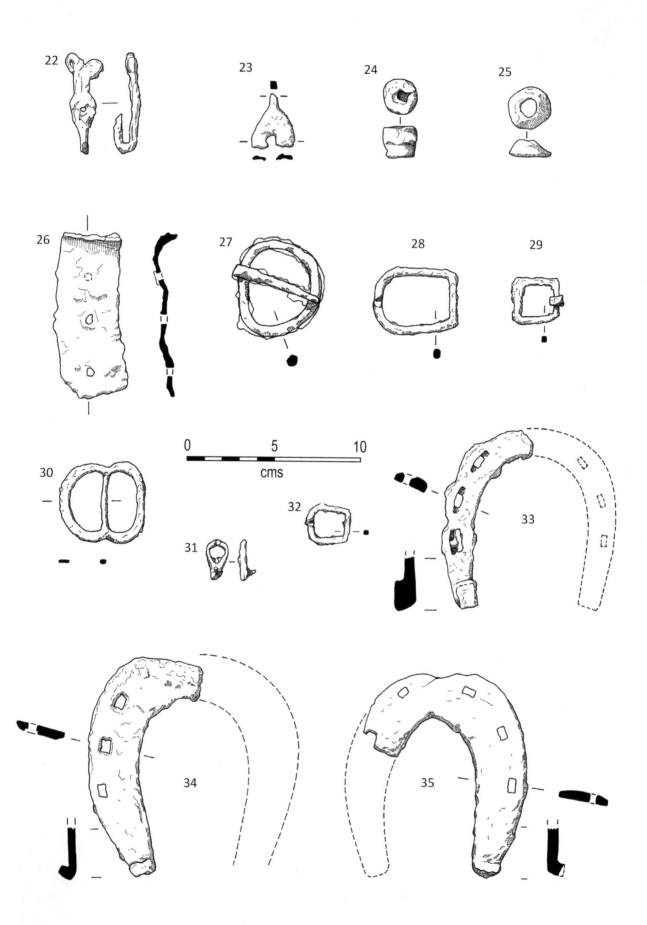

FIGURE 5.42
Metalwork illustrations Nos 22–35

ARTEFACTS AND ENVIRONMENTAL EVIDENCE

Nails

Type 1: nail with circular, sub-circular, or oval flat head. Shank centrally applied. The most common form of timber nail at Eckweek, 75 found in CP2, CP3 and CP5–CP7 and another 51 from the topsoil

Type 2: nail with rectangular flat head. Shank centrally applied. Second most common form of nail at Eckweek, 36 found in CP1–CP3 and CP5–CP7 and 17 from the topsoil

Type 3: nail with flat square head and centrally applied shank. 23 found in CP2, CP5–CP7 and six from the topsoil

Type 4: nail with flat figure-of-eight head. Two from CP6, one from CP7 and one from the topsoil

Type 5: nail with flat trefoil head. One from CP6

Type 6: nail with head extending from the edge of the shank. Three were found, one each from CP2, CP4 and CP5

Type 7: nail with circular concave head and shank centrally applied. One from CP6

Type 8: nail with triangular head and centrally applied shank. Eight from CP2, CP4 and CP6 and one from the topsoil

Type 9: stud with domed head and centrally applied shank. Some of these are very large. Nine from CP2, CP4 and CP6 and one from the topsoil.

Illustrated Structural Objects and Fittings (Figures 5.43 and 5.44)

45 SF852 (237) CP5, length 63mm. Square-sectioned staple
46 SF808 (2) Topsoil, length 78mm. Split end loop, rectangular section
47 SF583 (31) CP6, length 94mm. Hinge pivot
48 SF648 (31) CP6, length 112mm. Strap hinge
49 SF658 (3) CP6, length 142mm. Strap hinge with u-shaped hanging eye
50 SF640 (2) Topsoil, length 120mm. Strap hinge with one split terminal
51 SF952 (3001) Topsoil, length 78mm. Wall hook with rectangular section
52 SF927 (331) CP5, length 50mm. Hook with a pointed end for easier insertion into a wall or wood
53 SF513 (9) CP6, length 212mm. Large spike with double flanged head, each flange perforated. Square-sectioned tapering shank
54 CAR1904 (3142) CP2, length 21mm. Type 2 nail with rectangular flat head and shank centrally applied
55 SF754 (65) CP6, length 44mm. Type 4 nail with flat figure-of-eight head
56 SF545 (12) CP6, length 98mm. Type 9 nail. Stud with domed head and centrally applied shank
57 SF557 (46) CP6, length 160mm. Strap hinge with hinged pivot
58 SF696 (150) CP6, length 170mm. Formed strap hinge with five nails remaining

Other Structural Objects and Fittings (not illustrated)

Staples – Square-sectioned

CAR1810 (3040) CP3, length 47mm
CAR1885 (3042) CP2, length 44.5mm
CAR1269 (145) CP6, length 46mm
SF755 (65) CP6, length 58mm
SF853 (237) CP5, length 57mm
SF961 (3010) CP2, length 43mm
SF995 (3087) CP3, length 51mm
SF964 (3042) CP2, length 32.5mm
SF820 (2) Topsoil, length 45mm
SF954 (3010) CP2, length 34mm
SF659 (3) CP6, length 65mm

Staples – Rectangular-sectioned

SF662 (3) CP6, length 95mm
SF740 (194) CP2, length 31mm
CAR1699 (185) CP5, length 26mm
CAR1996 (3077) CP3, length 35mm
CAR1072 (44) CP7, length 53mm

Hinge Pivots

SF538 (14) CP7, length 125mm
SF895 (65) CP6, length 46mm
SF543 (12) CP6, length 49mm
SF588 (72) CP6, length 30mm
SF597 (65) CP6, length 34mm
SF610 (40) CP6, length 22mm
SF522 (2) Topsoil, length 100mm
CAR1176 (3) CP6, length 64mm
CAR1176 (3) CP6, length 63mm

Strap Hinges

SF713 (83) CP7, length 11mm
SF661 (3) CP6, length 135mm
SF558 (43) CP6, length 172mm
SF565 (31) CP6, length 300mm
SF660 (3) CP6, length 134mm
SF797 (238) CP5, length 55mm
SF678 (18) CP6, length 104mm
CAR1139 (21) CP6, length 95.5mm
CAR1176 (3) CP6, length 135mm
CAR1189 (235) CP5, length 21mm

Hooks

SF787 (2) Topsoil, length 42mm. As SF927
CAR1419 (340) CP4, length 30mm
SF890 (201) CP6, length 36.5mm
SF639 (67) CP6, length 35mm
SF804 (2) Topsoil, length 40mm
SF786 (2) Topsoil, length 40mm

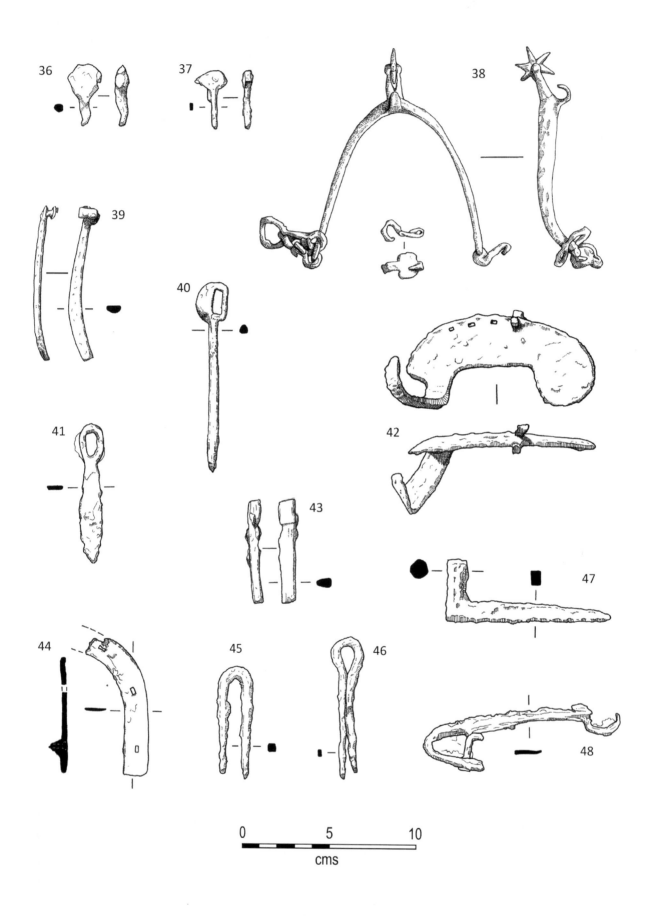

FIGURE 5.43
Metalwork illustrations Nos 36–48

Locks and Keys

Several types of key were found on the site. SF776 is a rotary key with a solid rectangular-sectioned stem, plain bit and a perforated terminal for a handle. This type of key is usually found in copper alloy and decorated with mouldings, as at Colchester (Crummy 1988, fig 87, 3228–3229) where it was probably a key for a small box or chest.

SF628 is a door key with solid circular-sectioned stem, D-shaped bow and rolled-in-one bit with toothing on the fore edge. This type of key is found from the 13th century (Ward-Perkins 1940, 139) and at Eckweek SFs 628 and 860 were recovered from ceramic phase CP6, whilst SF614 was from the topsoil.

SFs 865 and 957 are incomplete barrel padlock bolts with part of the circular heads, spines and leaf springs surviving. This type of bolt was used with box or barrel padlocks and is to be found throughout the medieval period from the 10th century. SF865 is from CP6, whilst SF957 is from CP3. SFs 728 and 941 are padlock keys for use with barrel padlocks with end keyholes. SF728 has a simple circular bit with rectangular slot set laterally to the rectangular-sectioned stem, and a hook terminal, which is the most common handle form dated in York (Tweddle 1986, 963) and London (Ward-Perkins 1940, 3–6) from AD 1100. SF941 is the same as SF728, except for a rectangular-shaped bit which has notched edges.

SF621 is probably a fragment of a plate lock only identifiable in X-radiograph. A complete example comes from Oxford Castle (Hassall 1976, fig 28, 59). SF643 is a sliding-bolt from a fixed lock with a single lower edge projection. SF523 is a possible latch lifter which was found at the base of the topsoil in association with a hinge pivot (SF522) next to a recess in a wall.

Illustrated Locks and Keys (Figure 5.45)

59 SF776 (2) Topsoil, length 42.5mm. Rotary key with a solid rectangular-sectioned stem, plain bit and a perforated circular terminal for a handle
60 SF628 (46) CP6, length 129mm. Door key with solid circular sectioned stem, D-shaped bow and rolled-in-one bit with toothing on the fore-edge
61 SF865 (65) CP6, length 57mm. Barrel padlock bolt fragment. Only part of the casing survives with two of the supporting rods
62 SF728 (170) CP4, length 169mm. Padlock key with simple circular bit with rectangular slot set laterally to the rectangular-sectioned stem and a hook terminal
63 SF941 (57) CP6, length 122mm. Padlock key. As SF728 except for a rectangular-shaped bit which has notched edges
64 SF643 (a and b) (114) CP6, length 77mm. Sliding bolt in two parts from a fixed lock with a single lower edge projection

Other Locks and Keys (not illustrated)

SF614 (40) Topsoil, length 68mm. Door/chest key fragment
SF860 (65) CP6, length 72mm. As SF865
SF957 (3037) CP3. As SF865
SF523 (2) Topsoil, length 97mm. Possible latch lifter
SF621 (72) CP6, length 70mm. Plate lock, very fragmentary. Probably from a box or chest

Weapons

Seven arrowheads were identified with various shaped blades. SFs 988 and 747 have broad flat leaf-shaped blades that date from the 11th century, whilst SF982 is a barbed arrowhead of pre-Conquest form that did not continue in use beyond the 13th century. The most numerous arrowhead at Eckweek however is the bullet-shaped form that dates from the 14th century, with CARs 1311, 1254, 1098 and SF685 all from ceramic phase CP6. These arrowheads were probably used for both hunting and as a weapon.

The only other item of weaponry is a chape, SF620, a simple U-shaped binding to protect the lower edge of a leather sword or dagger scabbard.

Illustrated Weapons (Figure 5.45)

65 SF988 (3134) CP2, length 73mm. Arrowhead with broad flat leaf-shaped blade
66 CAR1311 (135) ceramic phase 6, length 33mm. Bullet-shaped arrowhead
67 SF620 (98) CP6, length 37mm. Chape

Other Weapons (not illustrated)

SF747 (204) CP5, length 45mm. As SF988
SF982 (3064) CP2, length 32mm. Barbed arrowhead
CAR1254 (31) CP6, length 32mm. As CAR1311
CAR1098 (570) CP6, length 33mm. As CAR1311
SF685 (145) CP6, length 35mm. As CAR1311

Agricultural Tools

Apart from two ox goads (SFs 771 and 706), the only agricultural tool is a complete sickle (SF569) with a long slender triangular-sectioned blade, which has a cutler's mark. Although impossible to date an object form that has not changed from the 12th century to the present day, this tool was recovered in a ceramic phase CP6 deposit (inside the base of an oven) inside Building 460 and the presence of the cutler's mark suggests a pre-1600 date, probably 14th-century.

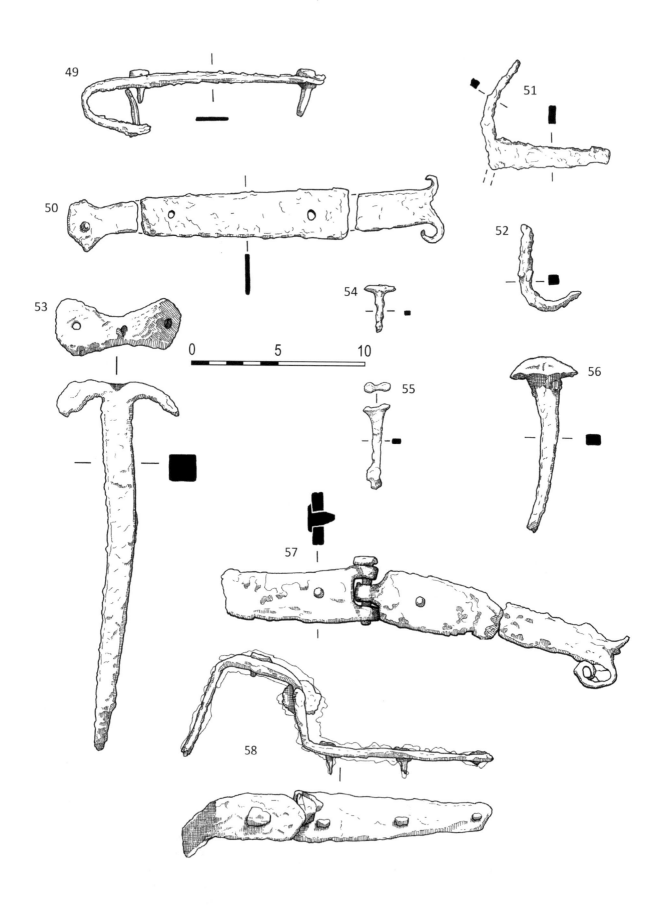

FIGURE 5.44
Metalwork illustrations Nos 49–58

ARTEFACTS AND ENVIRONMENTAL EVIDENCE

Illustrated Agricultural Tools (Figures 5.45 and 5.46)

68 SF569 (50) CP6, length 448mm. Complete sickle
69 SF771 (193) CP5, length 54mm. Ox goad

Other agricultural tools (not illustrated)

SF706 (114) CP6, length 75mm. Ox goad

Woodworking Tools

The collection consists of two spoonbits (SFs 734 and 685), a tool used in wood turning and for drilling holes in timber, which changed little in form from the Roman to medieval period. Both spoonbits have a circular-sectioned shank with one end rounded and hollowed out on one side and the other terminal widening before tapering to a rounded point. This point, with a rectangular section, would have fitted into the transverse of a wooden handle.

Illustrated Woodworking Tools (Figure 5.45)

70 SF734 (2) Topsoil, length 137mm. Spoonbit with a circular sectioned shank with one end rounded and hollowed out on one side and the other terminal widening before tapering to a rounded point. This point, with a rectangular section, would have fitted transverse into a wooden handle

Other Woodworking Tools (not illustrated)

SF685 (145) CP6, length 50mm. Spoonbit

Textile Working Tools

Only one needle fragment was identified from context 169 (CAR1144) although some other fine fragments of iron rod may also represent the stems of needles. Also these fragments could be teeth from wool or flax combs, used to prepare wool or flax for spinning. The teeth of circular and rectangular section would have been set in blocks of wood with a handle.

Textile Working Tools (not illustrated)

CAR1144 (169) CP5, length 48.5mm. Needle with ovoid section and circular eye

Leatherworking Tools

Several awls were found. These tools for piercing leather change little from the Roman to medieval periods. They vary in size, reflecting the need for different sized perforations. A total of 14 awls were found in contexts ranging from the 12th to the 14th centuries.

Illustrated Leatherworking Tools (Figure 5.45)

71 SF534 (2) Topsoil, length 135mm. Awl
72 SF929 (331) CP5, length 59mm. Awl
73 SF568 (31) CP6, length 63mm. Awl

Other Leatherworking Tools (not illustrated)

SF708 (3) CP6, length 52mm
SF703 (161) CP5, length 50mm
SF580 (31) CP6, length 138mm
CAR1651 (173) CP4, length 63mm
SF916 (316) CP5, length 84.5mm
SF924 (340) CP4, length 78mm
CAR1236 (31) CP6, length 60mm
SF765 (114) CP6, length 92mm
CAR1188 (114) CP6, length 62mm
SF732 (2) Topsoil, length 112mm
SF780 (2) Topsoil, length 66mm

Iron-working Tools

Punches, all six of which either date to the 14th century or were recovered unstratified from the topsoil, are the only indication of iron working on the site.

Illustrated Iron-working Tools (Figure 5.45)

74 SF591 (46) CP6, length 89mm. Punch with angled head

Other Iron-working Tools (not illustrated)

SF857 (65) CP6, length 66mm
CAR1060 (19) CP6, length 52mm
CAR1157 (146) CP6, length 43mm
SF571 (73) CP6, length 128mm
SF794 (2) Topsoil, length 66mm
SF812 (28) CP7, length 80mm

Miscellaneous Objects

Illustrated Miscellaneous Objects (Figure 5.46)

75 SF567 (67) CP6, length 40mm. Rectangular-sectioned shank, the one terminal remaining is in a crescent shape with an inner squared edge
76 SF908 (332) CP5, length 32mm. P-shaped object, a spiral terminal created by the lozenge-sectioned shank looping over
77 SF743 (201) CP6, length 187mm. Rectangular bar broken one short end, rounded at the other. On one long side there is a broken protrusion with a rectangular notch cut into it
78 SF817 (83) CP7, length 158mm. Long thin rod, slightly curving along its length, with the rectangular section becoming circular
79 SF631 (78) CP6, length 87mm. Tapering rectangular-sectioned rod, fractured at one end

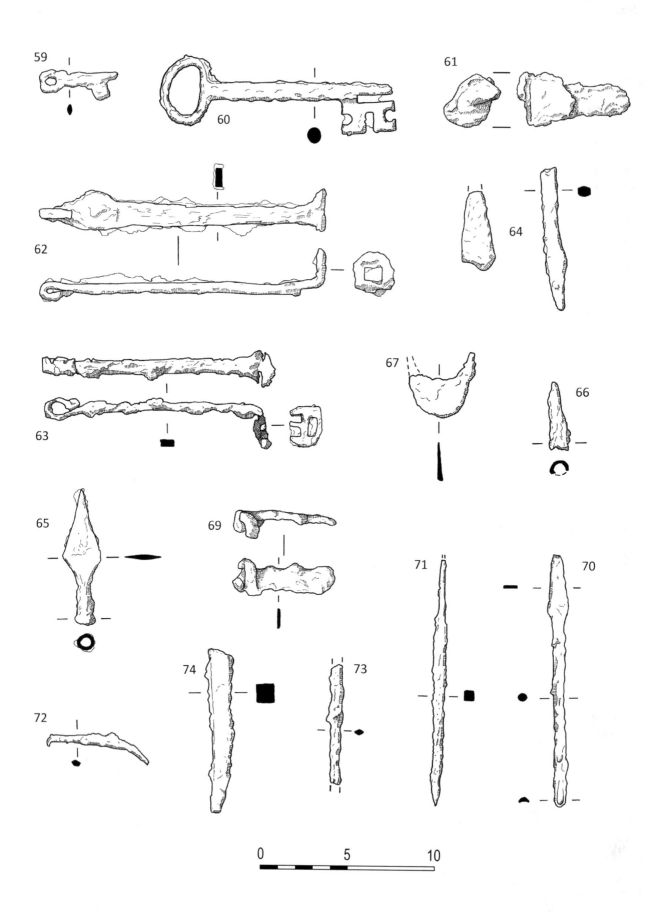

FIGURE 5.45
Metalwork illustrations Nos 59–74

ARTEFACTS AND ENVIRONMENTAL EVIDENCE

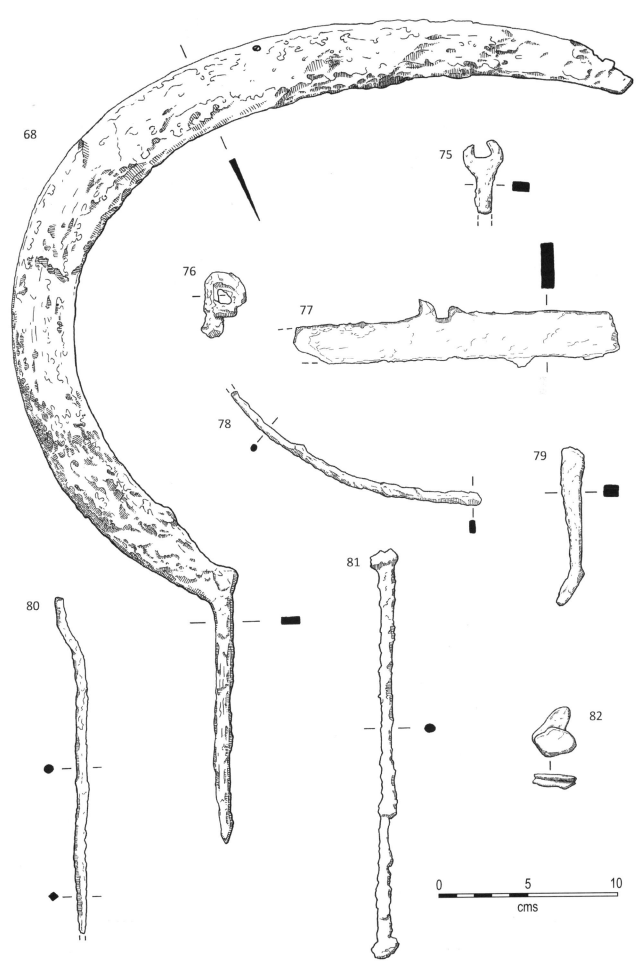

FIGURE 5.46
Metalwork illustrations Nos 68 and 75–82

80 SF514 (2) Topsoil, length 188mm. Rod of lozenge section that becomes circular
81 SF593 (18) CP6, length 225mm. Square-sectioned rod with rounded terminals
82 SF609 (40) Topsoil, length 29mm. Oval-shaped disc of lead that surmounts an irregular-shaped strip, a groove between the two

Other Miscellaneous Objects (not illustrated)

SF773 (230) CP4, length 21.5mm. Lead strip of sub-square section, L-shaped

CAR1775 (413) CP3, length 34mm. Lead strip of triangular section, broken at both ends and slightly curving along its length

SF710 (149) CP3, length 52.5mm. Solid cylindrical object of D-shaped section, rounded at one end and broken at the other

CAR1733 (250) CP2, length 33mm. Two thin rectangular-sectioned shanks with rounded terminals which are each centrally perforated for a rivet

CAR1736 (294) CP2, length 38mm. Rectangular-sectioned rod that tapers to a point, the other end folds under twice

SF641 (2) Topsoil, length 90mm. Rectangular-sectioned bar that curves slightly along its length. Broken both ends with one end thickening into a triangular section

SF549 (25) Post-medieval, length 75mm. Flat thin strip of rectangular-section that has a trefoil terminal, the other end is broken

Summary and Discussion

The assemblage of iron and lead finds reflect a site of rural occupation with associated craft industries that would have ensured a measure of self-sufficiency for the small rural community.

Agricultural activity at Eckweek is indicated by the presence of a sickle, animal husbandry by the cattleshoes, ox goads and shears. The practice of rearing and keeping stock, as well as arable farming, often leaves little evidence in the archaeological record and so whilst the finds recovered date largely to the 14th century, it is likely that the earlier inhabitants of the site undertook a similar range of land and animal management.

The use of horses for riding and transport is evidenced by the many horseshoes and several harness fittings, bridle pieces and spurs found on the site. Indeed the spurs suggest some wealth and therefore may indicate the status for the inhabitants of the 14th-century farmhouse, Building 460.

Craft industries on the site include wood, leather and textile working, with some possible late iron-working. Evidence for these activities include spoonbits, textile working tools (needle and wool/flax comb teeth/heckles), awls for leatherworking and possibly some punches used as part of iron-working. The evidence for these activities, from the iron objects alone, dates largely to the 14th century when the inhabitants of the settlement are likely to have been largely self-sufficient.

A small range of personal possessions including buckles, knives, a rim from a metal vessel, several vessel handles, spoons and box fittings were recovered from the site. For both these types of object the date range extends throughout the medieval period, from the 11th to the 15th century. It is likely that alternative materials to iron for cooking, tableware and storage vessels, in the form of ceramics, glass, copper alloy, wood and even basket-work were preferred, due to their relatively modest expense and the norm throughout the life of the settlement. However, with regard to structural domestic equipment, the range of ironwork is extensive and includes staples, hinges, pivots, straps, binding, hooks and numerous nails and studs, as well as keys and lock fittings. These structural-type objects are associated in particular with the 14th-century stone farmhouse (Building 460) and its associated yard area, in part perhaps due to the seemingly very rapid abandonment of the farmhouse and the apparently limited disturbance it underwent thereafter.

There is some evidence for the presence of weaponry on the site, namely a few arrowheads and a sword/dagger chape. The arrowheads however could have just as easily been used for hunting. Three of the arrowheads date to the 10th to 11th centuries, which may be significant for the status of the occupants and broader social obligations, whilst the remaining four date to the 14th century. Whilst activity on the site as a whole can be traced from the 10th century, the period which produces the greatest quantity and variety of iron and lead artefacts relates to the later phase of occupation during Period V, ceramic phases CP5–CP7 dated to the 14th to 15th centuries.

Acknowledgements

Thanks for help received in the preparation of this report go to Colin Slack, Ancient Monuments Laboratories, London, who completed the X-radiography and metallurgical analysis at short notice, to Davina Ware for illustrating the finds and to Andrew Young for provision of site and contextual data.

5.6 COPPER ALLOY OBJECTS
by Sarah Newns (2015)

A small assemblage of copper alloy objects was recovered (Figure 5.47), comprising 17 personal/dress items and 35 which have been classed as fittings or household items. The overwhelming majority of the items date to the later medieval phases of the site (c1200 to 1400 or later). A single object (SF984), a curved length of wire, was retrieved from an Iron Age ditch in Area H, and two further items are likely to be of modern date. All the objects were examined, identified and catalogued in 1991 by Dr Alison Goodall, but not reported further.

Personal and Dress Items

The majority of the personal and dress items date to the post-Conquest period of the site's occupation and three items only are likely to be of late Saxon date. These comprise two dress hooks/fasteners and one penannular earring. The dress hooks (Figures 5.48, 1 and 5.48, 2; SFs 863 and 978) are small, with rivet holes for attaching to clothing. The earring (Figure 5.48, 3; SF962) is a simple ring of wire with overlapping, tapered ends. Examples of both items have been recovered during excavations of the late Saxon settlement at Thetford, Norfolk (Goodall 1984, 69 fig. 110.20 and 133 fig.111.31–40).

Buckles

Buckles comprise the most numerous dress item recovered from post-Conquest period deposits. Seven buckles and one probable buckle plate were recovered, ranging in date from 13th century to post-Dissolution. The three 13th-century buckles comprise a complete single loop oval example, and a small fragment of rectilinear buckle frame, both decorated with transverse grooves (Figure 5.48, 6; SF596 and, Figure 5.48, 4; CAR1182), and part of a double-looped buckle with decorative knops (SF704). It is possible that the latter example is, in fact, of post-medieval date, as, although the moulding resembles that on 13th-century buckles, the form of the pin bar, extending beyond the frame, suggests a date range of c1575–1700 (Whitehead 1996, 92).

Of slightly later date is an oval buckle (Figure 5.48, 5; SF556) with attached forked spacer, cast integrally with the frame, onto which a pair of buckle plates would have been soldered. A similar buckle was found in the grave of a young man at the Austin Friars, Leicester, and dated to the early to mid 14th century (Clay 1981, 133, fig. 48.25). The position of the buckle suggested that it had been part of a waist belt.

One of the most complete early buckles is SF991 (Figure 5.49, 40), a probable spur buckle, dating to between 1250 and 1400 (Whitehead 1996, 32–34) recovered from an unstratified context. The buckle is composed of a single small loop, with tapering plate, ending in a decorative, pointed knop. The rear of the plate has two rivets for securing to a leather strap.

The remaining two buckles and buckle plate (Figure 5.48, 7–9; SFs 656, 873 and CAR1069) are less closely datable. SF 656 is a plain rectangular buckle, SF873 is a double-looped rectangular buckle, and CAR1069 a square, undecorated buckle plate. All three may range in date between the 14th and the early 18th centuries (Whitehead 1996, 15; 26–27; 74–75).

Strap Ends/Belt Chapes

Three medieval strap ends/belt chapes were recovered during the excavation. Two are highly decorated, one (Figure 5.48, 10; SF768) with white metal plating and alternating plain and textured stripes, and the second ((Figure 5.48, 11a and b; SF885) with a repoussé stylised floral and geometric design. Both are similar in form to an unstratified example from excavations at the medieval settlement of Goltho (Goodall 1975, 91, 5). The third example (Figure 5.48, 12; SF772) is fragmentary and without diagnostic features.

Other Personal Items

Three further personal or dress items were recovered, all of medieval date. These consisted of a subcircular ring/brooch (Figure 5.48, 13; SF709), a narrow, tapering lace end (Figure 5.48, 14; SF695) and a pair of tweezers ((Figure 5.48, 15; SF830). The tweezers are made from a single narrow strip, folded in half and twisted to give a handle and looped terminal, with splayed ends. Similar examples have been recovered from medieval deposits at Shifnal (Barker 1964, 204 fig. 44), Waterbech Abbey (Cra'ster 1966, 83 fig. 4(b)) and Lyveden (Steane and Bryant 1975, 114 fig. 43.50).

A necklace (SF741, not illustrated) formed of modern graduated links was also recovered from the fill (44) of a post-medieval robber pit in Area A.

Fittings and Household Items

Mounts and Pendants

Three pendants or probable pendant mounts were recovered during the excavation, all of probable medieval date. These comprise a complete pendant bell (SF935), similar to one of 12th- to 13th-century date recovered during excavations in Oxford (Goodall 1980, fiche 2B13 note 6 fig. 24.7), a small, gilded hemispherical pendant (Figure 5.48, 16; SF912), similar to one recovered from York (Goodall 1980, note 5) and a triangular openwork mount/pendant with lobed corners (Figure 5.48, 17; SF767), similar to examples on the PAS database (CUPL-5DB651; SOM-4BCE71). It is likely that these objects formed part of horse harness decoration, and are not uncommon finds on agricultural land (Griffiths 2014, 1). Traditionally dated to the 14th century, openwork examples, such as the triangular mount, may have a 12th-century origin, and it is possible that smaller examples, such as the hemispherical mount, may have been worn as a dress accessory (Griffiths 2014, 2).

A small decorative mount fragment (Figure 5.48, 18; SF816), showing two large circular perforations,

SF/CAR	Context	Description
505	2	Small key with irregular pierced bow. Stem has been hollowed at distal end. Overall length: 32mm. **Figure 5.49, 39**
526	2	Large, subsquare sheet fragment with one circular pierced perforation. One side has been folded. Two sides have been roughly trimmed square. Dimensions: 92mm × 78mm × 1mm maximum thickness. **Figure 5.49, 26**
529	2	Square sheet fragment, possibly originally from a vessel, with rivet hole and cut mark indicating possible re-use. Dimensions: 41mm × 64mm.
552	2	Large, irregular, semicircular sheet fragment. Maximum dimensions: 118mm × 53mm. **Figure 5.49, 23**
556	46	Buckle with oval, lipped and notched frame and fractured copper alloy pin. Buckle includes forked spacer, cast integrally with the frame, onto which a pair of buckle plates would have been soldered. Probable date: early to mid 14th century (Clay 1981, 133). Maximum dimensions: 70mm × 31mm × 3.5mm. **Figure 5.48, 5**
563	15	Probable foot from cast copper alloy vessel. Wedge-shaped, with flattish base, curved inner face and concave outer face with pronounced midrib (Dunning 1962, 98–100). See also SFs 587, 626, 652 and 669. Metallic analysis suggests that the copper ore is likely to have been of continental origin, and that the finished product was produced as cheaply as possible (Section 5.10, Blades this report). The feet would have been retained for their scrap value after breakage. Dimensions: 55mm × 29.5mm × 45mm. Weight: 194g. **Figure 5.50, 28**
582	31	Concave irregular sheet fragment with two rivet holes. Dimensions: 79mm × 70mm. **Figure 5.49, 24**
587	46	Probable foot from cast copper alloy cooking vessel. Wedge-shaped, with flattish base, curved inner face and sloping outer face with pronounced vertical midrib (Dunning 1962, 98–100). See also SFs 563, 626, 652 and 669. Dimensions: 58mm × 37mm × 39mm. Weight: 242g. **Figure 5.50, 29**
596	65	Cast copper alloy single loop oval buckle with narrowed and offset pin bar. Outer edge of frame decorated with five transverse grooves. Dated to late 13th century. Maximum dimensions: 22mm × 18mm × 2mm.
598	65	Fragment of flat-backed binding strip, bent down at each end through 90°. **Figure 5.49, 22** Length: 24mm.
626	72	Probable foot from cast copper alloy cooking vessel. Irregular, wedge-shaped, with suggestion of midrib on sloping outer face. See also SFs 563, 587, 652 and 669. Dimensions: 62mm × 37mm × 33mm. Weight: 226g. **Figure 5.50, 31**
652	46	Probable foot from cast copper alloy cooking vessel. Wedge-shaped, with flattish base, curved inner face and sloping outer face with break in slope and pronounced vertical midrib (Dunning 1962, 98–100). See also SFs 563, 587, 626 and 669. Dimensions: 55mm × 32mm × 47mm. Weight: 200g. **Figure 5.50, 32**
656	12	Plain rectangular buckle with bevelled edges. Similar examples span 14th–17th centuries (Whitehead 1996, 26). Dimensions: 34mm × 21mm × 2mm. **Figure 5.48, 7**
664	3	Length of decorative strip, decorated with pierced roundels. Part of decorative binding, or possibly tweezers.
669	135	Probable foot from cast copper alloy cooking vessel. Wedge-shaped, with flattish base, facetted inner face and sloping outer face with pronounced midrib (Dunning 1962, 98–100). See also SFs 563, 587, 626 and 652. Dimensions: 51mm × 27.5mm × 31.5mm. Weight: 154g. **Figure 5.50, 30**
691	148	Four concave pieces of copper alloy sheet, three of which have been broken off from main piece. Three rivet holes present, two of which have been torn open. Fragments probably represent patch/repair to vessel such as cauldron/skillet. **Figure 5.49, 25**
695	147	Narrow, tapering lace end, made from rolled sheet and probably riveted at the top. Length: 25.5mm. **Figure 5.48, 14**
704	31	Part of double-looped buckle, with rounded loop with moulded outer edge. Narrowed pin bar with decorative knops extending beyond frame. Fractured iron pin. Maximum external dimensions: 23mm × 30mm. Although moulding suggests 13th-century date, pin bar is of post-medieval type.
709	49	Sub-circular ring, max. 400mm external diameter, with circular perforation in the frame. Possibly used as simple brooch. **Figure 5.48, 13**
737	2	Small sheet fragment, subrectangular, with two rectilinear edges. Circular perforation at one end. Dimensions: 16mm × 9mm. **Figure 5.49, 37**
741	44	Curb chain of graduated links, becoming larger towards the centre, probably modern. Length: 290mm.
760	65	Subrectangular folded fragment of copper alloy sheet. Dimensions: 38mm × 34.5mm.
767	65	Triangular openwork mount, with lobed and perforated corners, one of which contains a rivet. Similar to medieval examples on PAS database (CUPL-5DB651; SOM-4BCE71, pendant loop). **Figure 5.48, 17**
768	65	Decorated rectangular strap end, plated with white metal and decorated with alternate plain and textured stripes. Similar in form to belt chape from Goltho (Goodall 1975, 91, no.5) (and see also SF885). Dimensions: 29mm × 21mm. **Figure 5.48, 10**
769	65	Small folded scrap of copper alloy sheet. Dimensions: 9mm × 5mm.
772	193	Small subrectangular fragment of copper alloy sheet, with two pierced rivet holes. Probable undecorated fragment of strap end or buckle plate. Dimensions: 17mm × 15mm. **Figure 5.48, 12**
789	2	Fragment of rod or wire, approximately rectangular in section, partly twisted and bent into an approximate right-angle. Length: 27mm long. **Figure 5.49, 38**
803	2	Small curved fragment and smaller fragment of copper alloy sheet, larger fragment possibly gilded, with tapered edges. Dimensions: 12.5mm × 8.5mm.
816	65	Small decorative mount with two large circular perforations and grooved decoration between. Similar to examples from Oxford (Goodall 1980 fig.25.75, fiche 2 B13) and Acton Court (Courtney 2004, 368, 2 or 390, 175, 176, book clasps), 15th-/16th-century contexts. Dimensions: 14.5mm × 11mm. **Figure 5.48, 18**

FIGURE 5.47

Catalogue of copper alloy objects (No. denotes illustration number)

ARTEFACTS AND ENVIRONMENTAL EVIDENCE

SF/CAR	Context	Description
830	114	Tweezers with splayed ends, made from single narrow strip, folded in half and twisted, to give handle and attachment loop. Similar tweezers have been found in medieval deposits (Barker 1964, 204; Cra'ster 1966, 83; Steane and Bryant 1975, 114). **Figure 5.48, 15**
863	65	Small hook with circular head, with two rivet holes, probably used as clothes fastener (see SF978). Similar examples found at Thetford, Norfolk, in late Saxon contexts (Goodall 1984, 133). Overall length: 13mm; maximum diameter of head: 9.5mm. **Figure 5.48, 1**
873	65	Double looped rectangular buckle, with bevelled internal edge and iron pin. Examples span period 1350–1700, but more prevalent from 1570s onwards (Whitehead 1996, 74–75, 464). Dimensions: 47mm × 41mm. **Figure 5.48, 8**
885	131	Two subrectangular fragments of strap end/belt chape, one of which has repoussé stylised floral/geometric decoration. The second fragment is plain, with a curved edge, perforated with a rivet hole. Similar to belt chape found at Goltho, Croft A, unstratified (Goodall 1975, 91 no.5). Dimensions of larger fragment: 25mm × 19mm. **Figure 5.48, 11a and 11b**
906	316	Small, clamped strip fragment, rectilinear. Dimensions: 16mm × 3mm. **Figure 5.49, 36**
912	330	Small undecorated medieval pendant with gilded surface. Hemispherical, hollow, with circular attachment loop. Similar example found at York (Goodall, The Archaeology of York, forthcoming). Dimensions: 19.5mm by 13mm. **Figure 5.48, 16**
937	240	Small subrectangular copper alloy sheet fragment with rivet hole, probable vessel repair. Dimensions: 32mm × 25mm. **Figure 5.49, 27**
935	349	Pendant bell with attachment loop. Bell itself is made from a single sheet, with flaps folded inwards to close the bottom of the bell. The inside is filled with corrosion products from an iron pea. Bells of this type have been found at York and Oxford (the latter from a late 12th-/early 13th-century context (Goodall 1980, fiche 2 B13, notes 5 and 6). Overall length: 28mm; maximum diameter of bell: 17mm.
942	98	Small rectangular mount with rivet hole at either end. Dimensions: 14mm × 5mm. **Figure 5.49, 19**
962	3042	Penannular earring with overlapping tapered ends, of a type found on sites of late Saxon period such as Thetford, Norfolk (Goodall 1984, 69). Diameter: 16mm. **Figure 5.48, 3**
978	3057	Small hook with perforated head, probably used as clothes fastener, similar to those found in late Saxon contexts at Thetford (Goodall 1984, 133). Dimensions: 13mm × 9mm. **Figure 5.48, 2**
984	3075	Length of wire of uneven thickness, sub-circular in section, bent at either end. Length: 40mm. Diameter: 1–2mm. Recovered from iron age ditch fill. **Figure 5.49, 33**
991	u/s	Probable spur buckle of cast copper alloy, with single loop and integral decorative plate. Oval frame with tapering plate, ending in decorative pointed terminal. Rear of plate has two rivets for securing to leather strap (Whitehead 1996, 32–34). Dated c1250–1400. Dimensions: 48mm × 15mm maximum width. **Figure 5.49, 40**
1069	2	Undecorated buckle plate with associated iron pin. Unrecessed plate is square, with two small rivet holes. Examples span 14th–17th centuries (Whitehead 1996, 15, 27). Dimensions of plate: 22mm × 22m. Length of pin: 27mm. **Figure 5.48, 9**
1182 (4003)	114	Small fragment of buckle frame, rectilinear, with bevelled upper face and three transverse grooves. Dated to later 13th century. Dimensions: 12mm × 5mm × 3mm. **Figure 5.48, 4**
1203 (4004)	65	Folded length of copper alloy strip. Dimensions: 27mm × 12mm maximum width.
1351 (4001)	18	Small fragment of very thin sheet, attached to ferrous corrosion, possibly from a rivet. Dimensions: 23mm × 4mm × 5mm maximum breadth.
1724	57	One small fragment of copper alloy sheet with rivet hole, with two smaller fragments. Dimensions of largest fragment: 31mm × 17mm maximum width.
1744 (4005)	u/s Area A	Small folded fragment of copper alloy strip. Dimensions: 9.5mm × 7mm.
1744 (4006)	u/s Area A	Small copper alloy wheel, probably machine-made, with three spokes and central perforated hub. Probable post-medieval date. Diameter: 17mm.
1744 (4007)	u/s Area A	Sub-rectangular copper alloy strip, one end bent. Dimensions: 51mm × 19mm.
1756 (4002)	383 Area G	Cast foot from skillet/ewer, probably post-medieval. Angular, facetted appearance, with raised horizontal collar in internal angle. Height: 32mm. **Figure 5.50, 34**
1759	377 Area G	Probable mount, cut from copper alloy sheet, with pierced attachment lugs at either end. Mount is sub-rectangular, with lugs located off-centre. Rear of mount has frequent peck marks. Dimensions: 32mm × 18mm. **Figure 5.49, 20**

FIGURE 5.47 CONT.

with grooved decoration between, is similar to examples from Oxford (Goodall 1980, fig. 25.75, fiche 2B13) and Acton Court (Courtney 2004, 368 no.2; 390 nos.175, 176), dating to the 15th to 16th centuries, the latter examples identified as book clasps. Two further plain subrectangular mounts were recovered, (Figures 5.49, 19 and 20; SF942 and CAR1759).

Decorative/Binding Strips

Two small decorative strips were recovered, one (Figure 5.49, 21; SF664) possibly part of a pair of tweezers, decorated with roundels, and the second, a plain flat-backed and clamped binding strip (Figure 5.49, 22; SF 598), both of probable medieval date.

Cauldron Repairs and Cast Feet

Seven fragments of copper alloy sheet (SFs 526, 529, 552, 582, 691, 937 and CAR1724), two of which are concave, have been identified by Dr Goodall as vessel repairs. The fragments (Figures 5.49, 23–27) show rivet holes, and would have been used to repair bronze vessels such as the medieval skillet

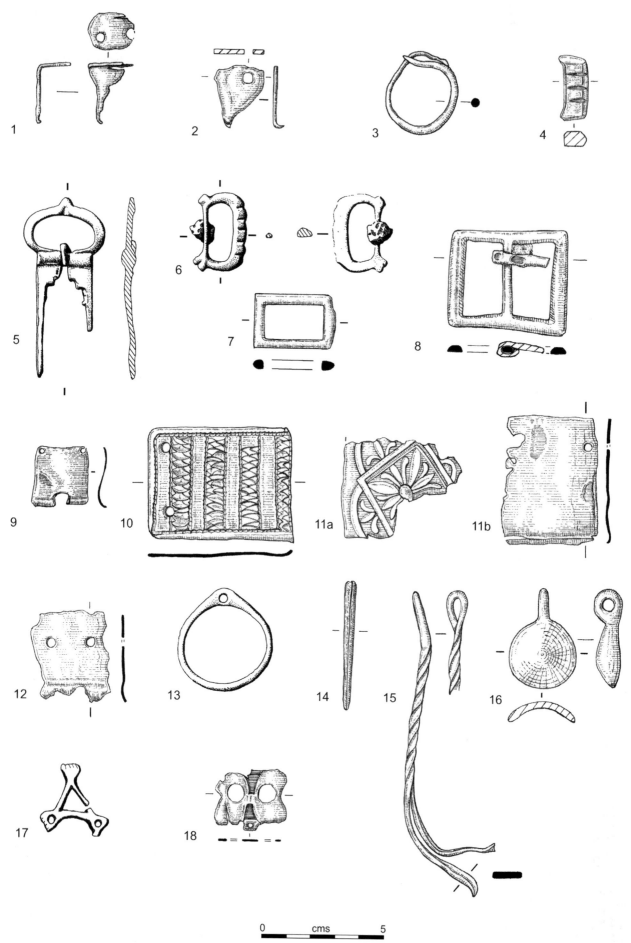

FIGURE 5.48
Copper alloy illustrations Nos 1–18

recovered from Stanford-in-the-Vale, Berkshire, which showed six patches, secured in place by no less than forty bronze rivets (Dunning 1962, 98–100). Fragments of similar vessels have been recovered from Acton Court, South Gloucestershire, from levels dating to the Tudor period (Courtney 2004, 369, 370). Metal vessels such as these would have been highly valued possessions, and it would have been considered important to repair, rather than to replace them.

A group of five small, roughly triangular to wedge-shaped objects (Figures 5.50, 28–32 and 5.51; SFs 563, 587, 626, 652 and 669) was recovered from the floor of the 14th-century farmhouse (Building 460) in Area A during the excavation. These have been identified as feet from cast cooking vessels, such as those referred to above. The objects are all of similar form, more or less wedge-shaped, usually with a pronounced vertical mid-rib on the outer face, which may be concave, and a curved vertical inner face. Identical examples are present on the PAS database (CORN-B2B042; CORN-E75F85; CORN-0C2D27), where they are identified as cauldron feet. Two very similar vessel feet were recovered from Croft A at Goltho, Lincolnshire (Beresford 1975, fig. 45), albeit from unstratified contexts. Metallurgical analysis of the composition of the Eckweek feet undertaken by Nigel Blades (Section 5.10) indicates that their main copper component may have a continental origin, and that the objects were produced relatively cheaply, and may have been relatively short-lived. This analysis corresponds almost exactly to that of a similar vessel foot recovered from Cornwall (CORN-B2B2042), where a date range of 14th to early 16th centuries is suggested. An alternative suggestion, that the objects are, in fact, copper alloy ingots, is discussed and largely dismissed in the analysis by Blades. It seems that the feet were retained after the vessel was broken up, possibly with the intention of their being sold for scrap or being reused on site.

A later vessel foot (Figure 5.50, 34; CAR1756), similar in form to a 17th-century example from Sandwich, Kent (Dunning 1962, 211–212) was also recovered from excavation Area G and a deposit that also produced 17th-century clay tobacco pipes.

Keys

A small key (Figure 5.49, 39; SF505) with irregular pierced bow and hollowed terminal to the stem was recovered from the topsoil/rubble over Building 460 in Area A. The key is likely to have been a casket key, and the hollowed stem represents an additional level of security and sophistication, as the bore has to fit over a corresponding pin in the lock. A similar example was recovered from excavation of the medieval settlement at Raunds (Hylton 2010, 373 fig. 11.20).

Wire

Two short lengths of wire were recovered, one (Figure 5.49, 33; SF984, now lost), of uneven thickness but possibly part of an armlet, from an Iron Age ditch within Area H, and the second (Figure 5.49, 38; SF789), approximately rectangular in section, of probable medieval date.

Miscellaneous Sheet and Strip fragments

Ten miscellaneous fragments of copper alloy sheet and strips were recovered during the excavation, the majority from medieval contexts, including one with possible gilding (SF803) from the topsoil in Area A, one with attached ferrous corrosion (Figure 5.49, 35; CAR1351), one small clamped strip (Figure 5.49, 36; SF906) and a fragment of sheet with rivet hole (Figure 5.49, 37; SF737).

Other

A small copper alloy wheel, 17mm diameter, probably a machine-made mechanical component of modern origin, was also recovered.

Site Phasing/Distribution

The majority of the copper alloy items fall within site phasing Period V (*c*AD 1275 to 1400). One item only (SF984, since lost) is of prehistoric date (Period I), and was recovered from the Iron Age ditch within Area H in the south of the site. Three items fall within site Period III (*c*AD 950 to 1200), and these comprise the penannular earring, one of the two probable late Saxon dress hooks and the pendant bell (SFs 962, 978 and 935). The second dress hook (SF863) was possibly residual within context 65, the yard surface in Area A.

The second of the three pendants recovered on the site is dated to Period IV (*c*AD 1200 to 1275), as are the pair of tweezers and one of the miscellaneous copper alloy sheet fragments. One of the cauldron repair fragments falls within Periods IV to V (*c*AD 1200 to 1400), as does the more fragmentary of the strap end/buckle plates, which was retrieved from a deposit associated with the occupation of Building 468 during the late 12th to 13th century.

A relatively high proportion of the items, both personal and fittings, was retrieved from context 65, the yard soil within Area A, dated to CP6 (AD 1325 to 1400) and it is possible that many of these may be residual. Possible residual items in this deposit include the highly decorative buckle plate (SF768), and the dress hook. Other items retrieved from this deposit include the possible book clasp (SF816), the triangular mount (SF767) and two of the buckles (SFs 596 and 873). The same context also yielded several of the plain copper alloy sheet fragments.

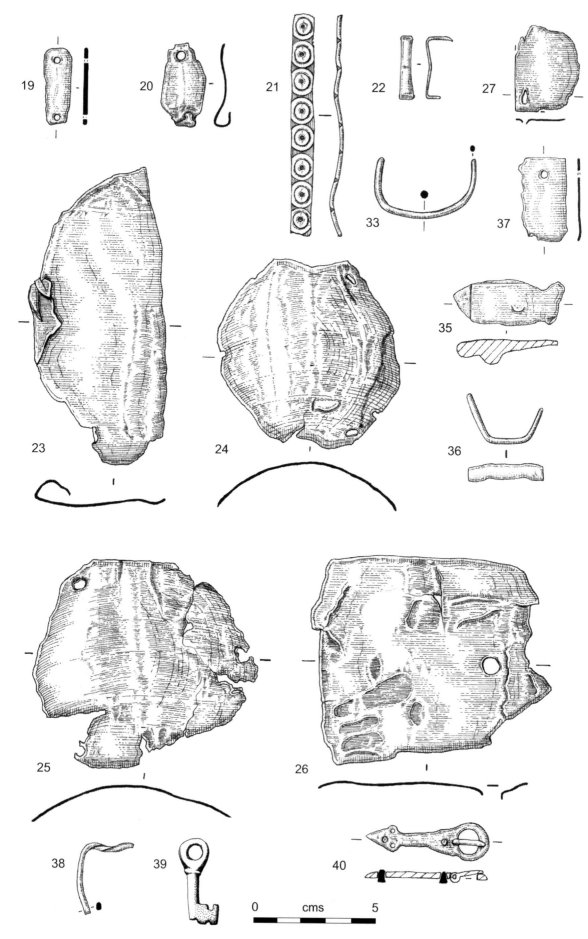

FIGURE 5.49
Copper alloy illustrations Nos 19–27, 33 and 35–40

ARTEFACTS AND ENVIRONMENTAL EVIDENCE

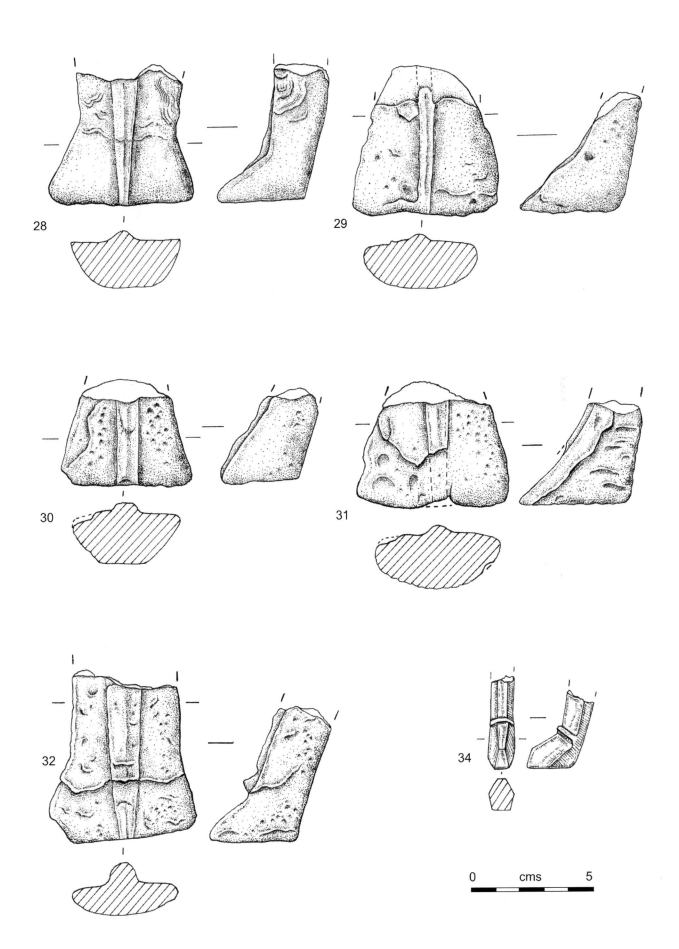

FIGURE 5.50
Copper alloy illustrations Nos 28–32 and 34. Vessel feet

FIGURE 5.51
Copper alloy vessel feet from Period V Building 460

A similarly high proportion of the items were retrieved from context 2, a topsoil residue cleaning layer, also within Area A. These items are almost exclusively residual, and include the buckle plate (SF69), one of the cauldron repair fragments (SF529), the small key (SF505) and, as above, several of the copper alloy sheet fragments. Whilst from secondary contexts, all of these items are very likely associated with the occupation of Building 460 during the 14th century.

Discussion

The majority of the personal items are clearly paralleled from medieval rural sites of similar date, such as Raunds (Chapman 2010), Shapwick (Gerrard and Aston 2007) and Goltho (Beresford 1987). The proportionately large number of buckles compared with other find types is common to all three sites. At Raunds, for example, a total of 23 buckles, 13 of which are of copper alloy, was retrieved out of a total of 114 costume/jewellery items (Hylton 2010, 343). Similarly, eight copper alloy strap ends, largely of 14th-century date, were retrieved from Raunds (Hylton 2010, 345–346) and six strap ends/buckle plates from Goltho (Goodall 1975, 91–92).

Tweezers of a similar type have been paralleled from medieval deposits at Shifnal, Waterbech Abbey and Lyveden. The two probable dress hooks are probably more unusual, but are paralleled from excavation at Thetford, Norfolk, in late Saxon contexts (Goodall 1984, 133).

Mounts of various types are common finds in medieval contexts. The examples from Goltho date to no earlier than the early 13th century (Hylton 2010, 346–347). The pendant mounts are not uncommon finds, and may have been worn as a dress item, or may have formed part of horse harness decoration (Griffiths 2014, 1–2).

Probably the more unusual of the domestic items are the objects relating to bronze cooking vessels, in particular the vessel feet. Bronze vessels themselves are recorded widely and may be paralleled from Acton Court (Courtney 2004, 369–370) and from Stanford-in-the-Vale (Dunning 1962, 98–100). The latter vessel shows evidence of frequent repair, a practice suggested by the perforated vessel fragments from the present site. Perhaps the most unusual of the copper alloy finds, however, are the probable vessel feet, of medieval date. Comparison with the small number of similar items on the PAS database, relative both to their form and their metallurgical composition, indicates that their identification as vessel feet is correct.

5.7 FLINT
by Vince Russett (1991)

Summary

The excavations at Eckweek produced a total of 283 pieces of flint (Figures 5.52 and 5.53), all from secondary, mainly medieval, contexts. These included the surprisingly large number of 21 cores and 44 other tools, totalling 22.96% of the total flint recovered. This compares with the 24.05% from the Harcombe site at Marshfield (Russett 1985), but very few other flint industries or sites recorded in the region appear to have such high percentages of tools, more typical figures being 10% or less.

The source of the flint is almost entirely the chalk of the Wessex Downs, only a few kilometres to the east. Two river gravel pebbles also occurred, as well as two pieces of a honey-brown flint of unknown origin, and one fragment each of Blackdown and Portland cherts.

Patination

There is a spread of patination classes throughout the range. This, along with the tool studies, indicates clearly that the flint recovered from the site is not a homogeneous industry.

The damage to many tools by recent activity of some kind is also clear. Many of the patinated tools and flakes (probably c60%) have some unpatinated areas where chips have been detached, this damage being evident on all types of flints, including the medieval strike-a-lights. When this damage happened is not clear from the flints themselves. Few trends emerge from a study of the patination of various tools types. The clearest is the correlation of strike-a-lights with no patination (class 5). Five of the six are of this class, a sixth of class 3. This is to be expected, as this type of implement is generally thought to be of medieval or later date.

A second trend is the association of a group of very highly patinated cores with weathered edges, generally of class A type (one striking platform), and slightly larger than average (32g as opposed to 28g). This group (cores 10, 12, 13, 14, 19 and 22) may also include the only non-discoid scraper, S6, which also has the same thick white weathered patina, and a number of the flakes listed above. This is very likely an early industry represented in the collection, perhaps early Neolithic, and one core, (19), has a definite Mesolithic influence, with its very long thin shallow flake scars detached from either end of the core.

As might be expected, of the datable arrowheads; two leaf-shaped of broadly Neolithic date and one of the three barbed and tanged, of early Bronze Age date; are of patination class 1, while the other two barbed and tanged arrowheads are of classes 2 and 4. The two polished flint axe fragments, generally dated to the early Neolithic, are class 1, both on their original polished surfaces, and on the subsequent scars from reworking. The majority of the rest of the finds show no particular patination trends.

Tools

Strike-a-Lights

This class of tool is frequently dismissed on medieval sites as intrusive prehistoric material.

The implements are characterised by three features:

1. They have a blocky shape, with edge angles usually over 90 degrees, and broad, shallow flake scars.
2. They are totally unpatinated.
3. They have edges which have been crushed to a characteristic crackled finish, often with iron-staining.

In use the flint was struck with an iron or steel implement to generate sparks. The implement in the post-medieval period generally took the form of a blade, similar to a thick knife blade, with a long or curved handle to keep the hand away from the area where the sparks were generated. The sparks were struck onto a small heap of 'tinder', usually very dry moss or lichen, which would smoulder and then burn when gently blown on, the whole process generally taking only a few seconds.

Five implements of this type were found in the excavations, one on a floor associated with a 14th-century hearth, and about 1m from it, and two more in an 11th- to 12th-century pit. These were presumably contemporary with the pit contents, and if so, indicate that patination in this type of environment takes at least 800 years to significantly affect flint. Four of the five strike-a-lights were incomplete, presumably broken in normal use by the stress fractures induced by striking.

Other Flint Tools

The assemblage lacks the smallest components that would be expected of a prehistoric occupation site (pieces under c10mm long and c5mm wide) indicating that the sample obtained from the excavation is almost certainly biased. Overall, the flint is a multi-period assemblage, ranging from a blade and core industry of possible Mesolithic character, through a clearly recognisable group of early Neolithic character, including cores, scrapers and arrowheads (Figure 5.54), a group of discoid scrapers of Beaker/early Bronze Age type, an assemblage of various artefacts only broadly datable as Neolithic/early Bronze Age, and a group of crushed-edge tools, almost certainly strike-a-lights of medieval date.

The spread and number of flint tools on the site indicate some presence on or near the site during parts of the Neolithic and Bronze Ages, although it does not indicate that there was any major occupation.

Tool number	Context	Weight (g)	Class	Patination	Date
CORES					
1	1118/44	37.0	B3	1	Neolithic
2	1753/378	32.5	B2	3	Neo/Bronze Age
3	1154/49	31.5	-	2	
4	1458/65	26.5	B3	3	
5	1988 U/S	24.5	-	4	
6	Original number reassigned				
7	1988 U/S	25.5	B3	4	
8	Original number reassigned				
9	1499/1	21.5	-	3	
10	1499/1	36.5	A1	1	
11	1832/30	31.0	C	3	
12	1147/149	43.5	A2	1	
13★	1400/331	21.0	A1	2	
14	1706/192	15.0	A2	1	
15★	1201/65	34.5	A2	2	
16	1360/316	39.5	C	2	
17	Original number reassigned				
18	1328/18	27.0	B2	2	
19	1467/217	38.0	B2	1	
20★	1215/2	16.0	-	5	Recent?
21	1183/113	19.5	B2	2	
22	1394/318	33.0	A2	1	
23SF	564 U/S	101.0	E	4	
24SF	572/31	110.0	E	4	

Tool number	Context	Weight (g)	Class	Patination	Scraping angle
SCRAPERS					
S1	Original number reassigned				
S2 SF	854/192	3.3	C	2	40-60
S3 SF	874/21	9.7	C	5	30-70
S4★	1771/414	5.5	C	3	40-60
S5★	1418/351	11.0	C	4	50-90
S6	1360/316	12.4	D1	1	60-90
S7★	1195/65	5.4	-	4	30-90
S8	1521/265	6.2	-	1	50-60
S9★	1819/3025	2.7	-	3	?
S10	1147/149	10.7	C	3	40-60
S11	1147/149	7.9	C	4	50-70
S12	1211/2	11.0	C	5	50-70
S13	1561/83	9.4	C	1	40-60
S14★	1370/2	7.0	-	5	Steep
S15	1214/2	4.9	C	5	50-70
S16	1988 U/S	18.5	C	5	70-90

Tool Number	Context	Weight (g)	Class	Patination
HAMMER STONES				
H1	1753/378	183.0		2

Tool number	Context	Weight (g)	Class	Patination
BARBED AND TANGED ARROWHEADS				
B&T1★	770/193	2.4	-	2
B&T2★	1503/2	2.8	Green Low?	4
B7T3★	1084/2	3.0	-	1
LEAF SHAPED ARROWHEADS				
L1 SF	532/2	1.3	Green 3Ah	1
L2 SF	965/3044	1.3	Green 4 Cr	1
POLISHED FLINT AXE FRAGMENTS				
PA1★	1988 U/S	-	-	1
PA1★	1988 U/S	-	-	1
KNIVES				
K1	1976/3136	3.0	-	2
K2★	1912/3087	22.7	-	2
K3	1611/114	5.6	-	3
BLADES				
B1	1623/139	-	-	4
AWLS				
A1	1357/345	7.5	-	3
A2	1470/291	4.6	-	5
A3SF	889/114	1.5	-	2
CRUSHED EDGE TOOL				
CE1	1870/3028	38.2	-	1
OTHER				
SAW 1	1934/3131	15.9	-	5

Tool number	Context	Weight (g)	Class	Patination
UTILISED FLAKES				
U1	1147/149	6.7		5
U2	1096/57	7.2	-	1
RETOUCHED FRAGS (OTHER)				
R1	1926/3118	-	-	3
R2	1400/331	-	-	2
R3SF	936/349	-	-	5
R4	1864/3064	-	-	1
STRIKE-A-LIGHTS				
SL1	1753/378	18.5	-	3
SL2★	1437/230	10.5	-	5
SL3★	1437/230	4.7	-	5
SL4	1214/2	27.9	-	5
SL5★	1246/31	3.7	-	5
SL6★	1446/235	4.2	-	5

Tools labelled with an asterisk (★) are broken or otherwise incomplete. In many cases, this has rendered the weighing of the tools unnecessary, but occasionally it has been carried out to indicate the minimum weight of the tool type.

FIGURE 5.52

Catalogue of flint cores and other flint tools (Classes of scrapers and cores are after Wainright 1972. Classification of arrowheads is after Green 1984.)

ARTEFACTS AND ENVIRONMENTAL EVIDENCE

CAR & Context number	Description	Patination
1601/229	Heavily battered fragment, no retouch.	2
1363/340	Core trimming flake, one edge utilised.	1
	Core trimming flake with edge damage; resembles scraper but no retouch.	1
1437/230	Small thick fragment, all edges heavily crushed. Strike-a-light.	5
	Pointed, keeled object, with light crushing around edges. Strike-a-light.	5
1782/381	Squared-off fragment long blade, unused.	3
	Secondary flake, with two areas of thin cortex.	5
1779/407	Secondary cortical flake, honey-coloured flint, much recent damage.	3
1154/49	Small core with remaining area of cortex at one end. Severely heat-crackled.	2
1749/382	Poorly-struck cortical flake with hinge fracture and ill-defined bulb. Poor quality flint, chalky cortex.	5
1463/211	Minute cortical fragment.	2
	Large, flat, thick flake with steeply retouched edges and one cortical end. Unused strike-a-light?	5
1725/57	Small trimming flake, traces of platform remaining; end recently lost.	1
1535/161	Core trimming flake.	1
1766/332	Thick, keeled cortical flake, no util.	2
1753/378	Globular flint pebble in light honey-coloured flint, mostly complete with intact cortex, but with some areas of battering, and one where a V-shaped deep notch has been struck out. Edges of this area are heavily crushed.	Hammer-stone 2
	Core, with thick cortex down one edge, and later crushing of apices.	3
	Thick core preparation flake, with thick cortex around edges.	2
	Slug-shaped fragment, steep-edged, with some edge-crushing. Strike-a-light?	3
	Two small flakes, one recently broken.	1,1
1488/193	Thin flake of Portland chert, with some retouch along one edge.	5
	Core rejuvenation flake, some recent damage at one end.	2
1118/44	Core, long with cortical patches. Subsequent use as strike-a-light.	1
1513/65	Struck keeled flake with cortical patch opposite bulb. Battered edges.	1
	Small cortical fragment.	2
1894/3039	Struck flake with hinge fracture. Util. on edge next to bulb. ?Used for whittling.	2
1044/25	Mottled tertiary flake, with most of an original hinge fracture removed by a patch retouch/damage.	4
1198/2	Thick cortical fragment, triangular section with flat ends.	5
1440/236	2 thick fragments, one recently damaged.	1,2
1541/65	Struck broad flake with hinge fracture.	1
1771/414	Round scraper with extensive edge damage.	3
1359	Struck cortical flake, with a small portion of core platform.	1
1096/57	Secondary flake with thick cortex on one edge. Utilised notch flake.	1

CAR & Context number	Description	Patination
1847/3006	Two small fragments.	M & 2,2
	Triangular fragment, with small area retouch on one face. Mottled.	4
	Large cortical flake of honey-coloured chert.	4
1394/318	Triangular flake, patch of cortex on one edge.	1
	Long flake, recent edge damage.	2
	Small fragment, recent damage.	3
	Core, recent damage.	1
1434/322	Large thick fragment no cortex.	3
1446/235	Small cortical flake.	5
	Thick small flake, with crushed edges. Strike-a-light.	5
1418/351	Damaged and crazed fragment (prob. heat-crackled) with potlid fractures. Possible fragment of a strike-a-light.	5
	Heavy round-nosed scraper, with patch cortex on top.	4
1474/341	Two cortical fragments, no retouch.	5,5
1078/2	Fragment of blade, end snapped off.	2
1514/2	Cortical fragment, no retouch, recent damage to one end.	2
	Thick blade/core fragment, utilised one end.	1
1470/291	Awl/borer, with a retouched notch and hollow end.	5
1555/296	Tertiary flake.	2
1534/201	Secondary flake, strongly curved and small, some recent damage to end.	2
	Flake, no retouch.	4
	Flake in honey-coloured flint.	5
1152/128	Thick cortical fragment.	2
1183/114	Long keeled flake.	1
	Small core, with cortical face.	2
	Secondary flake.	M & 2
1450/252	Heavily heat-crackled flake.	2
1594/362	Thick heat-crackled flake.	2
1215/2	Thick cortical flake with several flake scars. Core on flake.	5
1586/220	Three crushed and burnt fragments (?From lime/chalk spreading.)	3,3,3
	Blade fragment, with recent damage.	2
1192/2	Small fragment.	5
1467/217	Long multi-platform core.	1
1404/331	Thick core-trimming flake.	2
1328/18	Small core.	2
1525/271	Small recently damaged fragment.	2
1166/2	Tiny cortical fragment.	5
1161/2	Three thickly patinated flake fragments, one with end damage.	1,1,1
	Cortical flake.	2
	Hinge fractured fragment.	4
1084/2	Fragment of a barbed-and-tanged arrowhead.	1
1714/24	Thick cortical fragment of split pebble.	2
1051/2	Small broken flake fragment.	3
1387/330	Heavy fragment.	1
1391/313	Small fragment.	2
	Large fragment with patches of cortex, with possible flake scars at one end.	1

FIGURE 5.53
Description of flint objects

CAR & Context number	Description	Patination
1366/347	Thick fragment, with possible flake scars.	1
	Two small fragments.	M & 2,3
	Thickly patinated flake with a patch of cortex on one edge, some recent damage.	2
	Thick, poorly struck flake, with triangular section and some crushing on both acute-angled edges.	5
	Cortical boss-shaped flake, with crush damage on the boss, and the rest of the flake with damaged edges.	4
	Thick core-type fragment, with small areas of crushing on edges. Strike-a-light.	5
1408/316	Thick flake, with part of edge of core platform. Small area of cortex, some later damage.	2
1360/316	Small core.	2
	Thickly patinated scraper on crude flake. Small areas cortex.	1
	Two fragments.	2,2
	Crudely struck flake.	1
	One thick struck flake.	3
1037/2	Thick triangular section flake with one utilised edge.	2
1201/65	Core, with much modern damage.	2
	Thick flake with modern damage.	2
1498/39	Cortical secondary flake.	3
1506/65	Section of a secondary flake, one face cortex, with its end recently snapped. Small amount of original retouch on non cortical face.	1
1312/135	Small flake fragment with hinge fracture.	1
1706/192	Core, with some cortical areas.	1
1357/345	Awl/borer. Flake with rounded, blunted back and with worked notch and point.	3
1373/65	Two cortical flakes.	2,3
1195/65	Fragment, with cortical patches, recent edge damage.	2
	Thick cortical flake.	5
	Scraper fragment, made from earlier tool, and recently broken.	M & 5 on 4
1521/265	Scraper fragment with much wear and later damage. Patches of remaining cortex.	5 on 1
1665/195	Fragment of triangular-section flake, with recent crushed edge.	2
1626/224	Thick struck flake with hinge fracture.	2
	Long thin flake, with hinge fracture.	2
1400/331	Core fragment, with cortical edge. End recently damaged.	2
	Retouched flake, with a scraper-type retouch along two edges.	2
1576/269	Lump of naturally fractured flint.	1
1458/65	Fractured flake.	M & 3
	Small multi-platform core.	3
1740/127	Cortical flake on honey-coloured flint.	5
1370/2	Heavily broken scraper fragment.	5
	Cortical secondary flake.	4
	Heavily battered fragment. (Fragment shell of O. edulis)	3
1064/2	Small fragment.	5
1211/2	Small fragment.	5
	Scraper fragment, with cortical back, broken on the non-scraping edge.	5
1615/65	Irregular blocky flake.	2
	Small hinge-fractured flake.	3

CAR & Context number	Description	Patination
1214/2	Large flake, with thick cortex on dorsal surface, and crushing of opposite edge.	5
	Strike-a-light.	5
	Scraper, very lightly patinated.	5
	Small lightly patinated flake, with possible retouch on one edge.	5
	Four small flakes.	1,1,1,1
1158	Large cortical flake.	4
1140/21	Two long irregular small flakes.	3,3
1246/31	Broken fragment of a non-patinated flint object, with crushed edges. Strike-a-light.	5
1204/65	Long, very fractured fragment, one end with cortex. Possible recent artefact.	5
	Small flat flake.	4
	Small flake, recent damage.	2
1623/139	Small section flat blade, ends both snapped off square. One side extensively damaged, the other with very fine nibbled working. Mesolithic. Blade?	4
1709/249	Blocky irregular fragment, end broken.	1
1008/2	Hinge fractured corticated flake.	2
	Irregular flake.	M&2
	Blade fragment, tip snapped off. Edge damage, probably recent.	M&1
	Secondary flake, recent edge damage.	5
1378/83	Small flake.	4
	Heavy cortical flake, with concave area of cortex.	2
1499/1	Large secondary flake, some cortex around bulb.	2
	Small secondary flake.	3
	Heat-crackled fragment.	2
	Core, with edges crushed before patination. Possible prehistoric re-use as strike-a-light.	1
	Heat-crackled core fragment.	3
1745 U/S	Angular fragment.	4
1803/3001	Cortical flake, recently heavily damaged.	3
	Flake with end recently snapped off.	2
1796/3001	Broken triangular section of blade.	4
1912/3087	(Apex of shell of O. edulis)	
1875/3001	Small fragment.	4
1972/3135	Small blade fragment, with hinge fracture.	2
1926/3118	Snapped flake.	5
	Irregular, recently damaged flake.	4
	Large irregular flake.	1
	Irregular fragment.	1
	Retouched fragment, with low-angle working.	H&3
1864/3064	Retouched fragment, blocky with thick patination. Possible fabricator fragment.	1
	Flake fragment.	4
	Three small secondary flakes.	2,2,2
1841/3001	Steeply keeled flake, with a blunted end, possibly from use as a crude borer.	3
	Flat secondary flake.	5
1561/83	Cortical-backed scraper, with some contemporary damage to side. (h)	1
1920/3112	Three secondary flakes.	2,2,4
	Blocky lump.	1
1912/3087	Small, broken flake.	4
	Stout blade frag, with heavy wear down both edges. End snapped off. Knife?	4
1552/289	Small secondary flake.	2

FIGURE 5.53 CONT.

ARTEFACTS AND ENVIRONMENTAL EVIDENCE

CAR & Context number	Description	Patination
1836/3010	Stout cortical flake.	2
	Secondary flake, cortical tip.	2
1909/3050	Heavily fractured fragment.	4
1830/3073	Blocky, broken fragment.	5
1899/3081	Primary flake, heavily corticated.	2
	Heat-crackled flake, with edges broken away as a result.	2
1886/3042	Small flake.	2
	Large, thick flake.	2
1943/3146	Small fragment, cortex one end.	2
1892/3052	Speck.	5
1913/3083	Flake fragment.	2
1832/3016	Thick irregular flake.	4
	Five small broken fragments.	2,2,3,4,4
	Very irregular core on poor quality flint, heavy subsequent damage, perhaps due to use as hammer stone.	3
1955/3060	Flake.	4
	Broken secondary flake.	2
	Broken fragment.	2
1923/3116	Thick flake, with some cortex.	3
	Small fragment.	5
1958/3067	Thick struck flake, with cortex on one side. Probably primary flake.	1
1882/3018	Small hinge fractured flake.	3
1870/3028	Three long, broken flakes.	2,2,2
	Two irregular fragments, one possibly a core-trimming flake.	3,3
	Four broken irregular fragments.	4,4,4
	One cracked corticated flake.	5
	Crushed-edge tool, on large heavily corticated flake, possibly used as hammer stone or in food preparation.	1
1811/3040	Secondary flake with damaged edge.	4
1934/3131	Large flat flake, with two shallow notches in one edge, both with denticulate retouch. Saw?	5
1980/3075	Fragment fractured pebble.	2
	Two small fragments.	M&4,4
1792/3144	Blocky fragment with two smooth edges – not from polished tool. (h)	2
1857/3057	Blocky fragment.	2
	Thick, broken flake.	3
1147/149	Large, single-platform core.	1
	Round scraper.	3
	Keeled, thick scraper.	4
	Utilised flake, with a notch worn on one side.	5
1976/3136	Thick secondary flake, with one heavily utilised sharp edge, and retouched blunted back. Small knife.	2
1990/3151	Corticated flake.	5
1819/3025	Scraper fragment.	3

FIGURE 5.53 CONT.

CAR & Context number	Description	Patination
1988 U/S	Two small fragments polished axe.	1,1
	Small scraper, made on original single-platform core.	5
	Two small cores.	M&4,4
	Three heavily corticated flakes.	4,4,4
	Two secondary flakes, both with small patches of cortex.	?
	Large fragment, with one corticated face.	2
	Small fragment.	2
	Necked fragment.	3
1611/114	Flake, retouched to blunt-backed knife.	3
194	Speck.	?
1995/3153	Primary flake, from the corner of a rectangular pebble.	5
1964/3062	Thick corticated fragment, with faces so heavily patinated that it is probably a naturally broken fragment of geological age.	1
1760/377	Eight irregularly fractured fragments of flint, possibly from recent agricultural activity (chalk-marling?).	4,4,4,4
	Irregular blocky fragment.	3
	Thick flake, with corticated back and contemporary edge damage.	3
	Small thick flake, with edge damage.	5
	Irregular fragment.	1
	Two large irregular secondary flakes.	1,1
1940/3135	Secondary flake.	M&2
	Irregular fragment.	2
1872/3037	Irregular damaged flake, corticated one end.	3

FLINT SMALL FINDS

CAR & Context number	Description	Patination
SF503 (context 2)	Barbed-and-tanged arrowhead.	4
SF528 (2)	Hinge fractured tertiary flake.	2
SF564 U/S	Large core.	4
SF572 (31)	Nodule of flint, with few flakes struck from surface, then ends used for hammering or crushing. Wear at both ends.	4
SF632 (2)	Broad, fine thin leaf arrowhead. Figure 5.54, No 1	1
SF770 (193)	Barbed-and-tanged arrowhead, tip missing. Figure 5.54, No 2	1
SF854 (192)	Scraper, with a small patch cortex.	2
SF874 (21)	Secondary flake, retouched to scraper, with the scraping edge carried onto an area of cortex.	5
SF889 (114)	Awl/borer on a hinge-fractured flake.	2
SF926 (331)	Flat-keeled secondary flake, cortex at one end, other end damaged, no retouch.	1
SF936 (349)	Retouched flake.	M&5
SF965 (3044)	Small leaf arrowhead, long in relation to width. Complete.	1

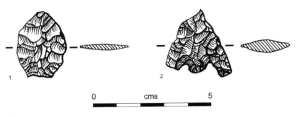

FIGURE 5.54
Illustrated flint arrowheads

5.8 WORKED STONE OBJECTS

by Alexander Kidd and Andrew Young (1991) with contributions by Professor Gilbert Kelling and Dr David Moore (1991)

Introduction

Eckweek lies towards the southern end of the Cotswold Hills in a region of complex geology consisting of rocks ranging from Silurian to Recent. The site itself is situated upon Fullers Earth of the Jurassic Great Oolite Series, however within the environs of the hamlet's field system there are also extensive outcrops of Great and Inferior Oolite Limestone. Due to the variety of local rock types, identifying the source of stone artefacts from hand specimen is difficult and, of course, the nearest possible source need not be the actual production site. The local Oolitic limestone was most commonly used for structural work and certain domestic artefacts, whilst Pennant Grit was often used for whetstones and querns. Unfortunately, there is some doubt as to the provenance of the objects of Pennant Grit since, 5km southwest of Eckweek around Radstock, it has been shown that whetstones of this material were being traded from Hanham, near Bristol, to medieval Winchester (Moore 1983). A total of 165 worked stone artefacts was recovered during the excavations, five of which were functionally unidentifiable. Figure 5.55 (A and B) summarise the incidence of stone and artefact types by ceramic phase as well as detailing the total site assemblage; including finds which, although from post-medieval contexts (eg topsoil), are nevertheless probably of medieval date in view of the very limited post-medieval activity on the site.

A small sample of five of the sandstone stone objects (SFs 690, 856, 922, 934 and 980) were thin sectioned at the University of Bristol, Department of Geology by the writers and examined petrologically by Professor Gilbert Kelling of Keele University Department of Geology in an attempt to clarify the provenance of objects made of 'Pennant Grit' type sandstone. A summary of his examination of the petrology of this small sample group is included below. In addition, the typology of the worked stone objects formulated by the writers and detailed below was reviewed by Dr David Moore of the Natural History Museum and where appropriate his comments are included below.

Structural Worked Stone

The earliest stone buildings were constructed in CP4–5 (*c*AD 1200–1250), however no structural worked stone may be attributed to this phase. The final medieval stone buildings utilised the local Oolite Limestone for timber padstones (Figures 5.56, 2, 3 and 4), door pivot stones (Figure 5.56, 1) and window sills (Figure 5.56, 5). None of these items require any great sophistication and would have been made locally as part of the construction process. Building stone could have been quarried within several hundred metres of the site, indeed a quarry is marked on the 1843 Wellow Tithe Map approximately 350m northeast of the modern Eckweek Farm, whilst another is shown *c*400m east of the farm on the 1886 OS 25" map. Further evidence is provided by a lease of 1386 which mentions a furlong named 'la Quere', which lay in the East Field, possibly to the southeast of Eckweek Farm (Shorrocks 1974, 292/469).

Also associated with the final medieval farmhouse were four limestone roof slates, two of which had been used to cap a drain (71). The numbers are too few to postulate a fully slated roof, however these few may have been used around the smoke-hole or along the eaves.

Illustrated Structural Worked Stone (Figure 5.56)

1 Pivot stone with heavily worn socket cut into its side. Opposed sinkings suggest a failed attempt to bore through the piece. The surfaces are extensively scorched and this, together with its location, suggests that it held the door to oven 50 within building 460. Shelly limestone. Context 31. CP6

2 Dressed padstone with rectangular sinking for an upright timber. Its location at the southeast corner of the destruction rubble of building 460 suggests that it could have mortised a roof timber into the top of the wall. Oolitic limestone. Context 3. CP6

3 Dressed and chamfered padstone with rectangular sinking for an upright timber. Opposed circular sinkings indicate a failed attempt to bore through the slab or could reflect reused pivot-holes. Shelly limestone. Context 57. CP6

4 Dressed padstone with rectangular sinking for an upright timber. Its location suggests that it could have mortised a roof timber into the top of the south wall of building 460. Oolitic limestone. Context 21. CP6

5 Sill of an unglazed loop with sinking for a central saddle-bar. Oolitic limestone. Context 212. CP7

Domestic Worked Stone

The range of domestic worked stone objects is not great, the main items represented being whetstones, rotary querns and several crude stone weights, possibly used in weaving. Minor items include spindle whorls, rubbers, pot lids, hammer stones, possible counters and single examples each of a saddle quern, a bead, a mortar and a possible food mould. Rotary querns were made from Pennant Grit or Mendip Old Red Sandstone, apart from a single unstratified example in Millstone Grit, probably from north Avon. The

ARTEFACTS AND ENVIRONMENTAL EVIDENCE

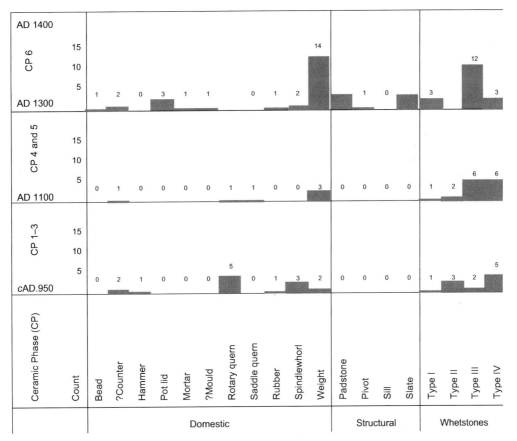

FIGURE 5.55A

Worked stone by ceramic phase and function

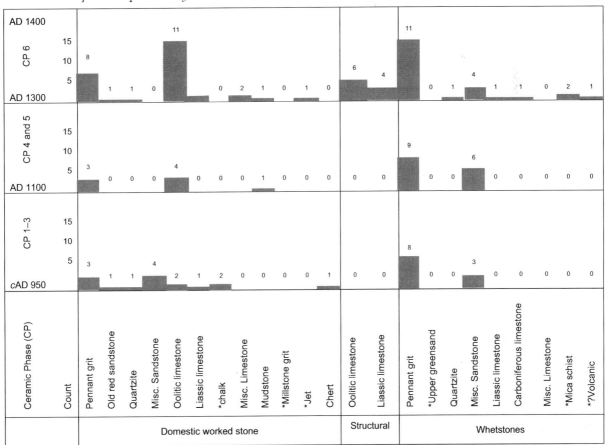

*=non-local stone

FIGURE 5.55B

Worked stone by ceramic phase and source geology

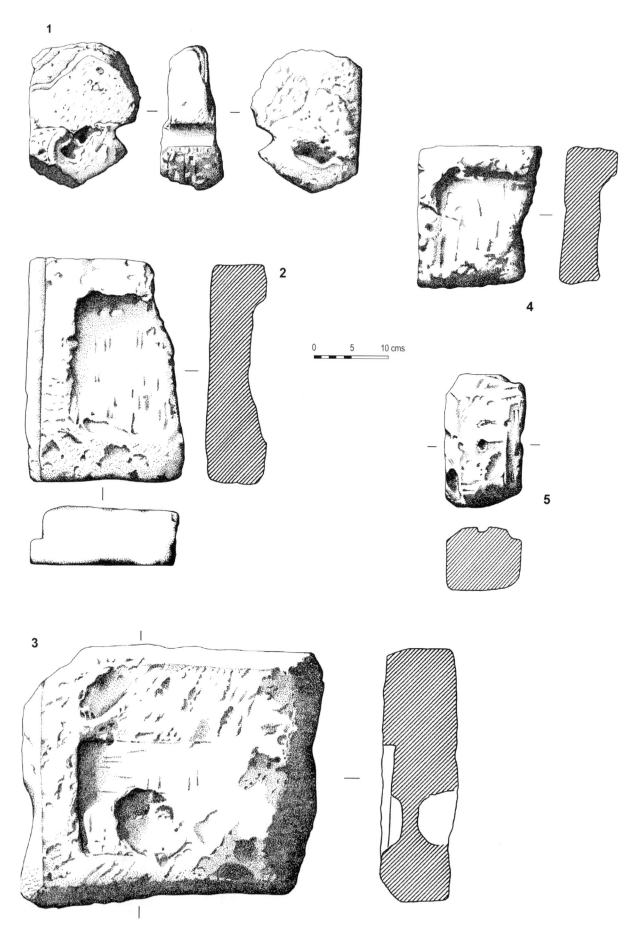

FIGURE 5.56
Worked stone illustrations Nos 1–5

stone weights (Figure 5.58, 21–26) are made of the local Oolitic limestone, except for a single example in sandstone. Typologically these objects could be interpreted as loom weights; however they are very variable both in shape and weight, the latter ranging between 57g and 2547g, whilst their occurrence is mainly within later medieval (CP6) features where they were often reused as building stone. Warp-weighted vertical looms are believed to have become obsolete by the 12th century (Clarke 1984) and larger stones may have been used as thatch or rick-weights.

Spindle whorls (Figure 5.57, 10–15) were made from a wide variety of rock types which are mainly represented in the local region, but include two examples in chalk, possibly from the Wiltshire Downs. Of the remaining minor items little need be said except to note that all the stone could be obtained in the local region, except for the jet bead (Figure 5.58, 27, SF627), which may well have come from the northeast of England.

Illustrated Domestic Worked Stone (Figures 5.57 and 5.58)

6 Hollowed stone trough. Possibly a fragment of a butter or some other food mould. Similar objects from Cheddar Palace have been described as lamps (Rahtz 1979, 228), However, the absence of any sooting would seem to preclude such an interpretation of this object. Oolitic limestone. Context 67. CP6. 406. SF637
7 Rim of a mortar with external rib. Liassic limestone. Context 19. CP6
8 Rubber stone with opposing struck facets. Pennant Grit. Context 31. CP6
9 Rubber stone with opposing facets. Coarse-grained sandstone. Context 180. CP2
10 Fossil echinoid with central perforation: possibly used as a makeshift spindle whorl. Shelly limestone. Context 2. Topsoil
11 Trace fossil with central hole: possibly used as a makeshift spindle whorl. Shelly limestone. Context 65. CP6
12 Conical spindle whorl with circular grooves suggesting that it was lathe-turned. Mudstone. Context 65. CP6
13 Conical spindle whorl with circular grooves suggesting that it was lathe-turned. Mudstone. Context 3001. Topsoil
14 Dome-shaped spindle whorl with incised lattice decoration. Liassic limestone. Context 3037. CP3
15 Conical spindle whorl with circular grooves suggesting that it was lathe-turned. Chalk. Context 3079. CP2
16 Pot lid with bevelled rim. Its diameter of 20cm would fit many of the ceramic cooking pots. Liassic limestone. Context 12. CP6
17 Rotary quern upper stone. Old Red Sandstone. Context 67. CP6 (419)
18 Crude hammer stone. Well-cemented coarse sandstone. Context 420. CP1 (422)
19 Crude hammer stone on pebble. Quartzitic sandstone. Context 3001. Topsoil
20 Corner of a saddle quern. Pennant Grit. Context 252. CP4
21 Perforated stone weight (57g). Oolitic limestone. Context 2. Topsoil
22 Perforated stone weight (608g). Oolitic limestone. Context 146. CP6
23 Perforated stone weight (1840g). Shelly limestone. Context 65. CP6
24 Perforated stone weight (1304g). Oolitic limestone. Context 83. CP7
25 Perforated stone weight (765g). Shelly limestone. Context 12. CP6
26 Perforated stone weight (526g). Oolitic limestone. Context 12. CP6
27 Highly polished and perforated jet bead. Possibly from a rosary. Jet. Context 46. CP6 SF627

Whetstones

Whetstones were by far the most common stone object recovered comprising 79 out of 165 objects. The group is subdivided into five distinct types on the basis of wear patterns and morphology (examples of three of the groups are shown in Figure 5.63).

Throughout the occupation of the site most whetstones were made of Pennant Grit. Unfortunately, it is unclear whether this stone came from the North Somerset or Bristol Coalfields. Coal Measures Sandstones were much exploited for whetstones throughout the Middle Ages and have been identified at Cheddar Palace (Rahtz 1979), Taunton, Bristol, Winchester (Ellis and Moore 1990) and at the nearby deserted hamlet of Barrow Mead (Moore 1978). Of the other rocks only Norwegian Ragstone (a mica schist from the Telemark area of southern Norway) is recognised as having been extensively traded, which occurs mainly in towns in southern and eastern England, although examples are known from Bristol (Moore 1978), and possibly also from Cheddar Palace (Rahtz 1979). A single, unstratified, Upper Greensand whetstone is also of interest since the Blackdown Hills on the Somerset–Devon border were a well known source of whetstones in the 19th century, and their exploitation may have begun by the 16th century (Moore 1978).

Whetstone Categories

TYPE I (8 EXAMPLES AT ECKWEEK)

Definition: Rod-shaped with rectangular to oval cross-section, over 2cm thick, and often with a tapered end. No complete examples were found but original lengths were probably over 20cm.

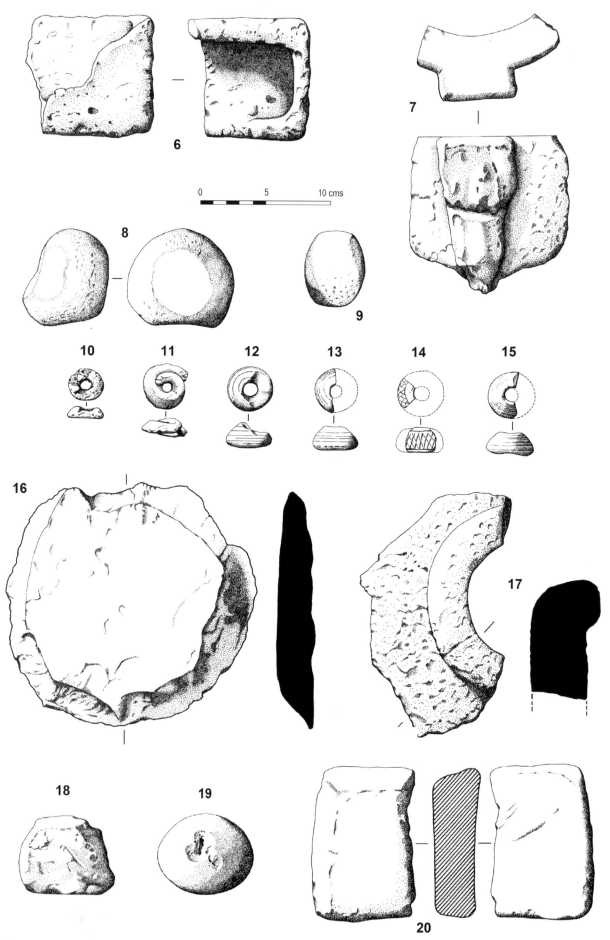

FIGURE 5.57
Worked stone illustrations Nos 6–20

ARTEFACTS AND ENVIRONMENTAL EVIDENCE

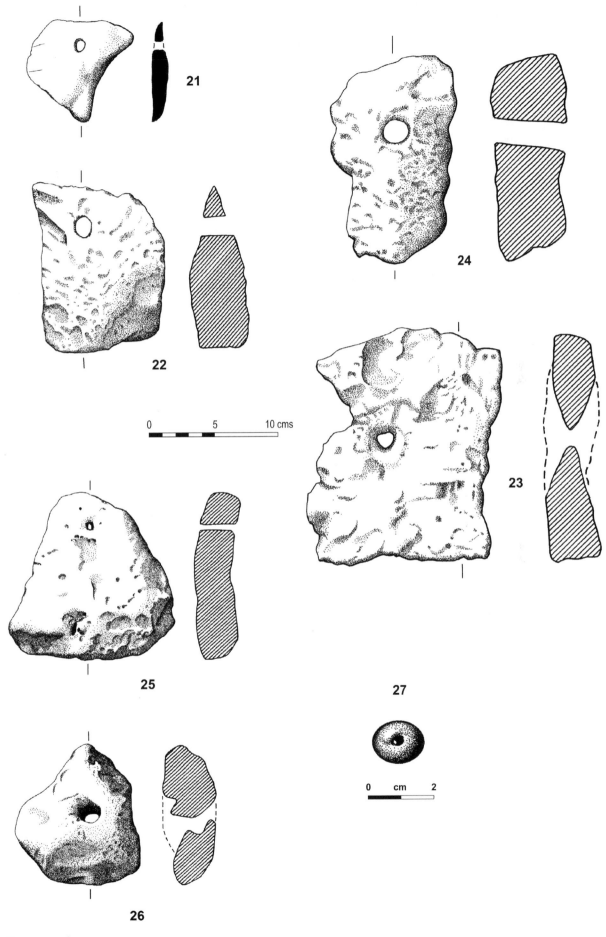

FIGURE 5.58
Worked stone illustrations Nos 21–27

Observations: All appeared to be plain, unadorned rods generally worn smooth all over. Five had one or more sharpening groove (eg Figure 5.59, 30). The majority were made of Pennant Grit, however there was one example each of carboniferous limestone and of a fine-grained, possibly volcanic, rock.

Function: Long rod-shaped whetstones similar to these are known as 'scythe stones' which were used for sharpening large agricultural blades. Sharpening grooves indicate that they were also used on pointed objects such as augers, however it is possible that this was a secondary use. Pure limestone is too soft to effectively whet a blade and so this whetstone may in fact be a 'strop' for smoothing the burr after initial sharpening.

Whetstone Type I Illustrations (Figure 5.59)

28 Tapered end of a whetstone Type I with slight sharpening grooves. Pennant Grit. Context 135. CP6
29 Tapered end of a whetstone Type I. Fine-grained ?volcanic rock of non-local origin. Context 49. CP6
30 Whetstone Type I with multiple deep sharpening grooves on one face. Pennant Grit. Context 83. CP7
31 Whetstone Type I. Pennant Grit. Context 355. CP4
32 Whetstone Type I. Pennant Grit. Context 3077. CP3

TYPE II (18 EXAMPLES AT ECKWEEK)

Definition: Rod-shaped generally with rectangular or sub-rectangular cross-section less than 2cm thick. The length rarely exceeds 15cm and both blunt and tapering ends are represented. It is distinguished from Type I on the basis of size and from Type III by the absence of the concave wear pattern which is characteristic of that group.

Observations: Most are unadorned, however there are five with partial or complete perforations for belt attachment. Sharpening grooves are absent, however slight scratch marks on the otherwise smooth surfaces indicate that the stone has been wiped across a blade (or vice versa). The majority, eight, were made of Pennant Grit or other local sandstone (four); whilst four utilised mica schist (probably imported Norwegian Ragstone – D T Moore, pers comm) and there were also two in limestone which may be regarded as 'strops' as noted above. This is the only whetstone type to show clear signs of development since no examples either of belt attachments or of mica schist occurred prior to CP6 (AD 1300–1400).

Function: Small whetstones similar to this are sometimes described as 'slipstones', the distinctive feature being the application of stone to blade rather than vice versa. The absence of sharpening grooves is remarkable considering that approximately half the whetstones of Types I, III and IV display them: this suggests that they were not used on pointed objects. This selective use combined with the presence of belt attachments, almost unique to this type, and of exotic mica schist stones suggests that these may have been valued possessions carried on the person rather than tools kept around the house or farmyard.

Whetstone Type II Illustrations (Figure 5.60)

33 Whetstone Type II with slight rib and incomplete perforation for belt attachment. Pennant Grit. Context 2. Topsoil
34 Whetstone Type II with neck and incomplete perforation for belt attachment. Mica schist (probably Norwegian Ragstone – Dr D T Moore, pers comm). Context 114. CP6
35 Whetstone Type II with perforation for belt attachment. Pennant Grit. Context 148. CP6
36 Whetstone Type II. Mica schist (probably Norwegian Ragstone – Dr D T Moore, pers comm). Context 49. CP6
37 Whetstone Type II. Pennant Grit. Context 146. CP6
38 Whetstone Type II. Fine-grained sandstone. Context 330. CP5
39 Whetstone Type II. Pennant Grit. Context 31. CP6
40 Whetstone Type II. Mica schist (probably Norwegian Ragstone – Dr D T Moore, pers comm). Context 2. Topsoil
41 A very small whetstone Type II with perforation for belt attachment. Pennant Grit. Context 65. CP6
42 Whetstone Type II. Well-cemented sandstone. Context 3134. CP2

TYPE III (28 EXAMPLES AT ECKWEEK)

Definition: Rod or slab-shaped generally with rectangular or sub-rectangular cross-section. Length is typically 10 to 20cm with blunt ends. The distinctive characteristic of this type is a concave wear pattern which may occur on one or more sides.

Observations: This type is unadorned except for one with a belt attachment (Figure 5.62, 50). Most stones are worn smooth all over and sharpening grooves are common (13 cases). There seems to be a 'classic' form consisting of a rectangular cross-section slab about 2cm thick, 6cm wide and 10 to 20cm long with one thin side worn concave and with sharpening grooves on either face. Stone is predominantly Pennant Grit (19) or other sandstone (7) with a single example in Upper Greensand.

Function: These may be 'oilstones' or 'bench stones' which are described as rectangular stone blocks to

ARTEFACTS AND ENVIRONMENTAL EVIDENCE

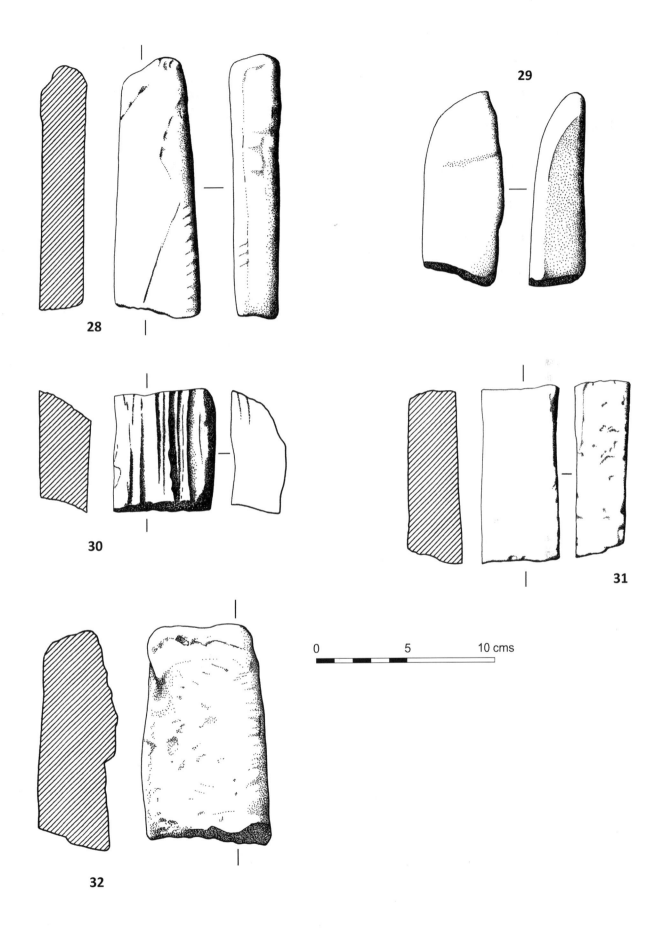

FIGURE 5.59
Worked stone illustrations Nos 28–32

which a blade is applied, often with a stropping motion which may account for the concave wear pattern. The frequency of sharpening grooves indicates their use on pointed objects such as augers and awls. Overall the impression is of a general purpose tool used to sharpen knives and other small implements.

Whetstone Type III Illustrations (Figures 5.61 and 5.62)

43 Whetstone Type III with concave wear on all four sides. Fine-grained sandstone. Context 145. CP6
44 Whetstone Type III with concave wear on three sides. Pennant Grit. Context 347. CP4
45 Whetstone Type III with concave wear on one side and sharpening grooves on each face. Pennant Grit. Context 201. CP6
46 Whetstone Type III with concave wear on one side and scratch marks on three sides. Pennant Grit. Context 114. CP6
47 Whetstone Type III with concave wear on one side and a sharpening groove on one face. Pennant Grit. Context 65. CP6
48 Whetstone Type III with concave wear on one side and a sharpening groove on another. Pennant Grit. Context 293. CP4
49 Whetstone Type III with concave wear on all four sides. Fine-grained sandstone. Context 316. CP5
50 Whetstone Type III with, uniquely for this type, an incomplete perforation for belt attachment. Concave wear and a sharpening groove on one side. Pennant Grit. Unstratified
51 Whetstone Type III with concave wear on one side. Micaceous sandstone. Context 290. CP2

TYPE IV (24 EXAMPLES AT ECKWEEK)

Definition: These are makeshift whetstones without classifiable form.

Observations: They occur only in local sandstones (five) and Pennant Grit (19). Sharpening grooves are present in eleven cases. In the earlier medieval period (CP1–CP3) this was the most common whetstone type but by the 14th century (CP6) they had been largely superseded by the regular types.

Whetstone Type IV Illustrations (Figure 5.62)

52 Whetstone Type IV with intermittent smoothed facets on all faces and deep sharpening grooves on two sides. Pennant Grit. Context 2. Topsoil
53 Whetstone Type IV with very shallow concave wear on one surface. Fine grained sandstone. Context 65. CP6

TYPE V (1 EXAMPLE AT ECKWEEK)

Definition: Slab-shaped with a distinctive circular concave wear pattern on a face.

Observations: A single example in Pennant Grit. It is worn smooth on both sides and faces.

Function: The wear on the sides indicates normal whetstone use, however the circular concave wear is unusual and may have been caused by finishing gouges or chisels (V Russett, pers comm).

Whetstone Type V Illustrations (Fig 5.62)

54 Whetstone Type V with circular concave wear on one face. Pennant Grit. Context 2. Topsoil

Discussion and Conclusions

The use of stone objects at Eckweek shows only limited evidence of chronological development in terms of the artefacts and of the rock types represented. Whetstones are the most commonly occurring object in Periods III–V, although this may be explained partly by their limited useful life. The main whetstone types were present throughout the site's medieval occupation, suggesting perhaps that there was no dramatic change in sharpening requirements during this time. The suite changes little, either typologically or petrologically, throughout the period cAD 950–1300 (CP1–CP5) with only Pennant Grit and other, probably local, sandstones being represented. A change occurs in the 14th century (CP6) with the decline of the makeshift Type IV whetstones, the appearance of belt attachments on Type II whetstones and the presence of a wider variety of rocks, including some of traded continental origin.

Other stone objects show a very limited range in the earlier, pre-Conquest, period (CP1–CP3), consisting mainly of rotary querns, spindle whorls and weights made from locally occurring stone. Very few of these domestic objects were recovered from 12th- to 13th-century (CP4–CP5) contexts, despite the fact that the quantity of pottery present increased by over 50% and that of whetstones by 36%. If this apparent decline is correct then it may indicate a significant decline in the domestic use of stone with implications such as reduction of hand-milling of corn and even the spinning of wool by distaff and spindle. The 14th century (CP6) saw the reversal of this decline with an increase in the range of domestic objects and also the adoption of structural worked stone. Again the use of local stone remained predominant.

Overall, the range of objects remained restricted until at least the end of the 13th century when there appears to have been access to a wider range of goods, presumably via a local market, than was hitherto the case (Figure 5.55). Comparison with other sites in the region is hampered either by the limited extent of excavations or by the lack of adequately quantified data. However the 13th- to 14th-century peasant house at Barrow Mead (Woodhouse 1976)

ARTEFACTS AND ENVIRONMENTAL EVIDENCE

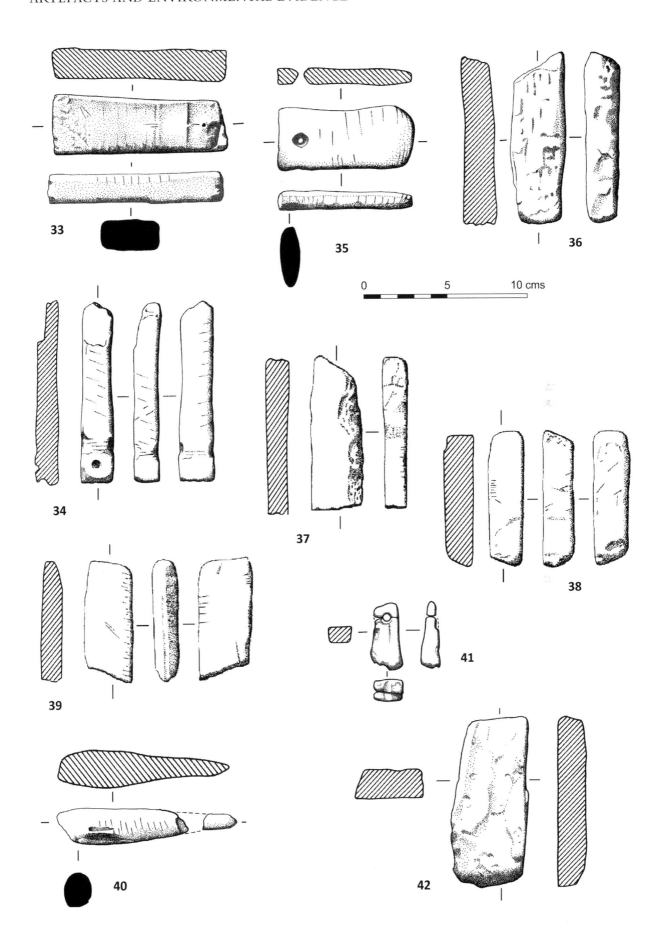

FIGURE 5.60
Worked stone illustrations Nos 33–42

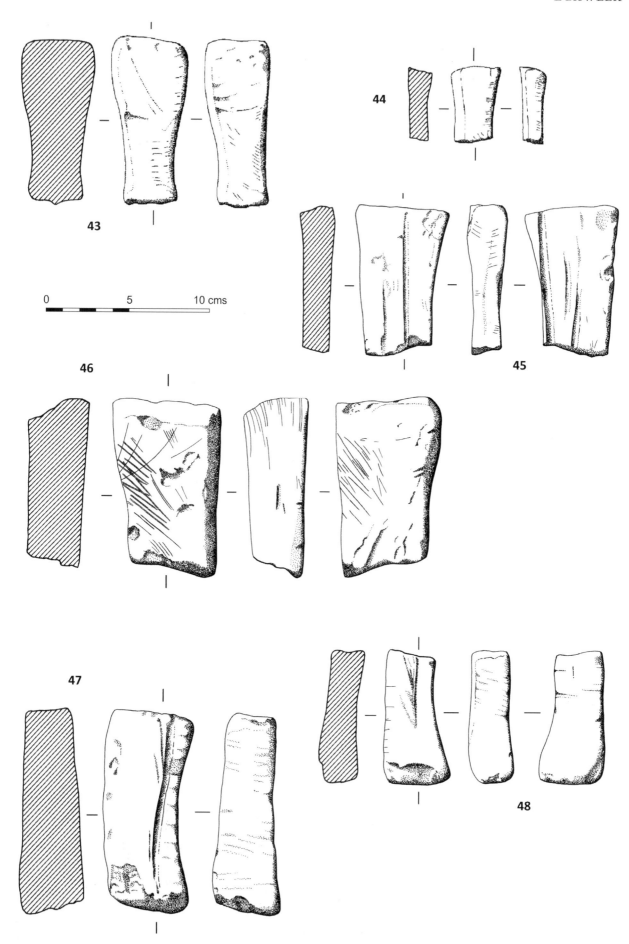

FIGURE 5.61
Worked stone illustrations Nos 43–48

ARTEFACTS AND ENVIRONMENTAL EVIDENCE

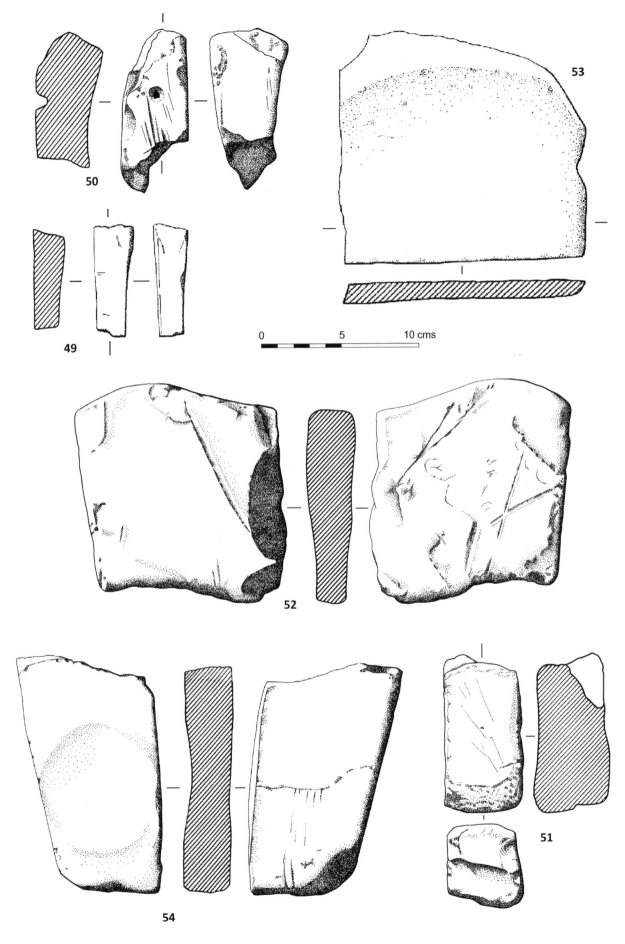

FIGURE 5.62
Worked stone illustrations Nos 49–54

FIGURE 5.63
Examples of whetstone types I, III and II

produced a similar assemblage of whetstones and spindle whorls, as well as a reused fossil echinoid spindle whorl (Figure 5.57, 10), and a single jet bead. Not surprisingly the Royal palace at Cheddar had a wider range of imported stone and architectural fragments, however the domestic assemblage was no more varied than at Eckweek comprising whetstones, querns and lamps (Rahtz 1979).

5.8.1 The Petrology of Medieval Whetstones of Sandstone from Eckweek
by Professor Gilbert Kelling, Department of Geology, University of Keele (1991)

Petrographic examination of a sample of five thin-sections taken from SF objects 690, 856, 922, 934 and 980, all of which appear broadly similar in hand specimen, reveals the presence of two groups.

The first group comprises the thin sections taken from SFs 690, 922, 934 and 980, which vary only slightly in mean grain-size and degree of post depositional weathering (with conspicuous ferruginous staining in SF980, for example). Nevertheless, all these sections display similar petrographic characteristics, being essentially lithic arenites, with a rock fragment content dominated by sedimentary intraclasts of silt and fine sand grade, and subordinate low grade metamorphic clasts. In addition, variably altered plagioclase feldspar and detrital muscovite are significant minor constituents of all these samples. Thin section SF922 is slightly more lithic than the others but shares the same essential petrography.

All four samples are typical of the Bristol and Somerset Pennant Group, probably from the lower part of the Formation. However, it is not possible to ascribe these thin sections to particular outcrops of the Pennant since both the Radstock and the Bristol (eg Hanham) outcrops of the Pennant Group are composed of petrographically similar sandstones.

The second 'group' comprises a single sample, SF856. It is distinguished from those above by its more quartzose, less lithic character, better sorting and a distinctive late-diagenetic cement of fine grained sericite that is arranged in fringes around the tightly packed grains. The provenance of this material is less easy to determine, but it does resemble some examples of the Quartzitic Sandstone Group of the Millstone Grit Series from the Bristol-Somerset area. If this very tentative ascription is correct then it tends to favour the Radstock region as a source for the material, since the outcrops of the Quartzitic Sandstone in this area are more extensive (and have been more thoroughly quarried) than in the Bristol area.

5.9 CLAY TOBACCO PIPE
by Sarah Newns (2014)

A small assemblage of clay tobacco pipe fragments, comprising 48 stems and 16 bowls, weighing a total of 284g, was recovered during the excavations. The majority of the assemblage was recovered from Area G, a small area containing earthworks investigated in the northwest corner of the site. The assemblage contains a high proportion of

ARTEFACTS AND ENVIRONMENTAL EVIDENCE

CAR no.	Context no.	Weight (g)	Description
1107	2	6g	1 × stem fragment, with fractured pedestal heel.
1118	44	2g	1 × plain stem fragment.
1749	382	4g	2 × plain stem fragments.
1753	378	96g	5 × complete/near-complete bowls, comprising:
			2 with maker's stamp: 'RG', Figure 5.65, No. 1, with fleur de lys above: Richard Greenland, working in Devizes/Marlborough *c*1688–1736 (Price 2014, 1904–5).
			1 × Gloucestershire Type 2b bowl, overhung, with pedestal heel, not burnished. Type favoured by Bristol and Wiltshire makers, dated 1630–60 (Peacey 1979, 46, fig. 1).
			1 × Gloucestershire Type 4 bowl, elongated, with 2nd waist before milled rim (ibid.).
			1 × plain overhung bowl with pedestal heel, Marlborough Type B/C, Bristol Type 6, dated *c*1650–80 (Atkinson 1965, 89, fig. 1; Jarrett 2013, 219, fig. 4.18).
			1 × undiagnostic bowl fragment.
			1 × stem fragment with pedestal heel marked, 'RICH/GREN/LAND' (above).
			15 × stem fragments, including 3 with soot-blackening.
1760	377	168g	10 × complete/near-complete bowls, comprising:
			2 with maker's stamp, 'RICH/GREN/LAND' (see above). Figure 5.65, Nos 2 and 5.
			2 with maker's stamp, 'JEF/FRY/H'. Figure 5.65, No. 7: one of two possible makers, working in Norton St Philip (*c*1640–52) (Price 2014, 2280–1).
			1 with maker's stamp, 'JOHN/HUN(T)'. Figure 5.65, No. 3: one of two possible makers, working in Bristol *c*1651–1714 (ibid.).
			1 with maker's stamp, 'TH'. Figure 5.65, No. 6: Thomas Hunt, one of three possible makers with this name, working in Norton St Philip and Marlborough *c*1637–1691 (ibid.).
			3 × plain overhung bowls with pedestal heels (incl. 2 with milled rims), Bristol Type 6, dated *c*1650–80 (Jarrett 2013, 219, fig. 4.18).
			1 plain overhung bowl with pedestal heel and unevenly milled rim, Marlborough Type C, Bristol Type 7, dated *c*1650–80 (Atkinson 1965, 89, fig. 1; Jarrett 2013, 219, fig. 4.18).
			1 × stem fragment with marked pedestal heel, bearing maker's mark: '..D../UNDE/HIL', Figure 5.65, No. 4: Edward Underhill, working in Leigh-upon-Mendip *c*1650–95 (Price 2014, 4193).
			26 × plain stem fragments, including 4 with partial soot-blackening.
1782	381	6g	1 × plain stem fragment.

FIGURE 5.64
Catalogue of clay tobacco pipes

marked fragments, which have been correlated with five or six known pipe makers, most of whom were working in the local area between 1637 and 1736 (Figure 5.64).

Four of the marked bowls were produced by members of the Hunt family, an important pipe making family (Price 2014, 2280–2281) who were based around the village of Norton St Philip, some 6km east of the settlement at Eckweek. The first pipe maker of the family was Jeffery Hunt I, who established a manufactory in Norton, and was working between *c*1620 and his death in 1690. It is thought that the pipes marked 'JEF/FRY/H' are likely to be the work of his son, Jeffery II (Figure 5.65, 7), who established his own manufactory in the same village, where he was working from *c*1640 to *c*1652. A further Jeffery Hunt (III), from the same family, is thought to have been working as a pipe maker in Devizes in the later 17th century.

One of the bowls is marked, 'TH' (Figure 5.65, 6), and is likely to be the product of one of three Thomas Hunts, all pipe makers working in the area in the mid 17th century. Jeffery Hunt I's half-brother, Thomas Hunt I, is thought to have set up his own manufactory, probably in Norton St Philip or Rode, and to have been working between *c*1639 and 1652 (Price 2014, 2280–2281). One of two further pipe makers of the same name from the same family (Thomas Hunt II or III) is thought to have established a pipe manufactory at Marlborough, where he was working up until his death in 1692 (Price 2014, 2281, 2286).

John Hunt I was the brother of Thomas Hunt I, and moved to Bristol, where he became one of the founder members of the Bristol Pipemakers' Guild in 1652 (Price 2014, 2281). One of his nephews, also called John, is also known to have been working in Bristol up until *c*1714. It is not known which of these Bristol makers produced the 'JOHN/HUN(T)' pipe (CAR1760, Figure 5.65, 3) retrieved during the excavations at Eckweek.

The remaining marked pipe fragments are local products, one having been produced by Edward Underhill (Figure 5.65, 4), who was working in Leigh-upon-Mendip (around 10km south of Eckweek) between *c*1654 and 1695 (Lewcun in Price 2014, 4193), and the others being the products of Richard Greenland (Figures 5.65, 1, 2 and 5), a pipe maker of Devizes (30km east of Eckweek), who was working between *c*1688 and 1736 (Price 2014, 1904–1905).

The unmarked bowls predominantly conform to local typologies, Gloucestershire Types 2b and 4, Bristol Types 6 and 7, and Marlborough Types B and C (Peacey 1979, 46, fig.1; Jarrett 2013, 219, fig. 4.18 and Atkinson 1965, 89, fig. 1). These

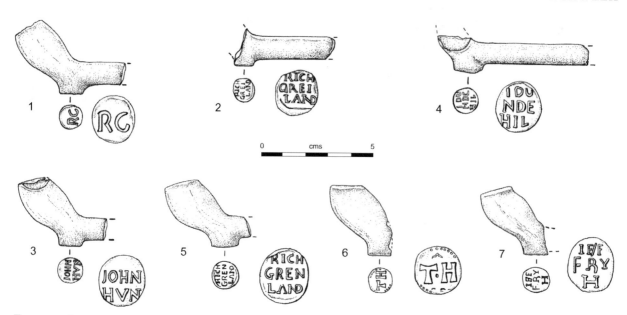

FIGURE 5.65
Illustrated clay tobacco pipes

unmarked bowls fall within the same broad date range as the marked fragments, and span the mid to late 17th century (c1630 to c1700). Stylistically, it is significant that all the bowls are of the small overhung type, with pedestal heels, which prevailed until the gradual introduction of the larger, more open bowl types with spur heels, which were introduced from the late 17th/early 18th centuries onwards (Jarrett 2013, 218–221).

Pipes of the Hunt family are commonly found in the West Country, and those of John Hunt, and other members who migrated to Bristol, were exported as far afield as America (Price 2014, 2281). Pipes of Edward Underhill are less widely distributed, but are occasionally recovered from excavations in Somerset (Lewcun in Price 2014, 4193). Those of Richard Greenland are known from Salisbury, Bath, Marlborough, Taunton etc; all towns within a 50 mile radius of their place of manufacture (Atkinson 1965, 88).

Comparison with the excavated medieval settlements of Raunds and Goltho would suggest that the presence of a relatively tightly dated assemblage of clay tobacco pipe, from a restricted area, such as that recovered from Eckweek, is likely to be of some significance. Goltho, for example, yielded no recorded pipe material whatsoever, and it is thought that the specific area of settlement under excavation at Goltho was abandoned during the late 15th/early 16th centuries (although the homesteads may have been relocated elsewhere, out in the fields; Beresford 1987, 5).

At the medieval settlement of Raunds, a very small assemblage of clay tobacco pipe was retrieved from specific features of post-medieval date, such as banks, ditches and a stream course that were still in use into the 18th century (Hylton 2010, 414).

By contrast, the small but significant pipe assemblage from Eckweek, dating largely to the mid to late 17th century and recovered from one specific area of the site, suggests at least some continuity of settlement into the post-medieval period, one focus of which was around the building located in Area G. The total absence of clay tobacco pipe from other areas of the site investigated during the project supports the impression that settlement activity had diminished very substantially by the early post-medieval period.

5.10 THE COMPOSITION OF A GROUP OF LATER MEDIEVAL COPPER ALLOY 'INGOTS' AND OTHER OBJECTS

by Nigel Blades, Department of Geology, Royal Holloway and Bedford New College, University of London (April 1991)

Introduction

A group of 15 copper alloy objects, all recovered from later medieval contexts, were examined as part of a wider study into the chemical composition of copper alloy artefacts from the UK in the period cAD 350–1600 using Inductively Coupled Plasma Emission Spectrometry (ICPS). The analyses were undertaken to establish the chemical composition of the objects individually and feed that information into the wider research project, but also in particular to shed light on the original function of a group of closely related objects (SFs 563, 587, 626, 652 and 669) initially described as 'ingots', which were recovered from the interior of Structure 460, the 14th-century farmhouse. The objects that underwent ICPS analysis and their chemical signatures are detailed in Figure 5.66.

Object No.	Description	Context	Cu %	Zn %	Pb %	Sn %	Fe %	As %	Bi %	Cd %	Sb %	Co %	Ni %	Cr %	P %	S %	Mn %	Ag %	Au %	V %	Total %
563	'ingot'	15	66.55	0.07	11.03	0.45	0.44	2.27	0.10	0.00	6.25	0.04	0.68	0.00	0.00	0.83	0.00	0.05	0.00	0.00	88.76
563	'ingot'	15	61.40	0.04	11.62	0.24	0.21	2.85	0.10	0.00	5.52	0.04	0.63	0.00	0.00	0.56	0.00	0.05	0.00	0.00	83.26
587	'ingot'	46	66.77	0.24	13.71	0.98	0.16	0.74	0.03	0.00	4.37	0.00	0.07	0.00	0.00	0.57	0.00	0.06	0.00	0.00	87.70
626	'ingot'	72	60.64	0.18	13.45	0.87	0.17	0.81	0.03	0.00	4.87	0.00	0.07	0.00	0.09	0.62	0.00	0.07	0.00	0.00	81.87
652	'ingot'	46	69.74	0.06	6.74	0.21	0.34	2.73	0.09	0.00	6.11	0.04	0.67	0.00	0.00	0.56	0.00	0.07	0.00	0.00	87.36
669	'ingot'	135	65.77	0.07	16.55	3.24	0.09	1.71	0.03	0.00	2.38	0.08	0.19	0.00	0.02	0.49	0.00	0.09	0.00	0.00	90.71
582	Sheet	31	86.49	6.02	0.63	4.56	0.28	0.05	0.00	0.00	0.14	0.02	0.03	0.00	0.00	0.08	0.00	0.05	0.00	0.00	98.35
691	Sheet	148	86.92	5.93	0.57	4.63	0.27	0.04	0.01	0.00	0.17	0.01	0.03	0.00	0.00	0.08	0.00	0.09	0.00	0.00	98.75
873	Buckle	65	77.95	6.20	2.80	6.26	1.63	0.10	0.02	0.00	0.24	0.01	0.04	0.00	0.03	0.07	0.00	0.04	0.00	0.00	95.39
789	Wire	2	79.18	0.02	1.09	9.67	0.44	0.10	0.01	0.00	0.21	0.01	0.09	0.00	0.03	0.05	0.00	0.06	0.00	0.00	90.96
767	Decorative object	65	81.67	4.34	3.78	6.66	0.61	0.02	0.01	0.00	0.32	0.00	0.03	0.00	0.01	0.04	0.00	0.08	0.00	0.00	97.57
529	Sheet	2	89.61	3.27	0.46	3.63	0.09	0.13	0.02	0.00	0.32	0.01	0.04	0.00	0.00	0.02	0.00	0.12	0.00	0.00	97.72
552	Sheet	2	92.75	3.29	0.49	3.99	0.09	0.16	0.02	0.00	0.31	0.02	0.03	0.00	0.00	0.04	0.00	0.07	0.00	0.00	101.26
556	Buckle	46	81.42	5.42	2.37	4.76	1.37	0.14	0.02	0.00	0.34	0.01	0.03	0.00	0.01	0.09	0.00	0.10	0.00	0.00	96.08
704	Buckle	31	84.97	5.01	0.42	2.95	1.25	0.71	0.00	0.00	0.19	0.00	0.22	0.00	0.01	0.05	0.00	0.09	0.00	0.00	95.87

FIGURE 5.66
Results of ICPS analysis of copper alloy objects

Methodology

The copper alloy objects from Eckweek that were chosen for ICPS analysis were selected on the basis of the reliability of either their typological or stratigraphic dating, since secure dating was central to the validity of the research project as a whole. Very small samples (5–10mg) were taken from each of the objects by Nigel Blades, either by clipping (the sheet objects) or 1mm diameter drilling (other objects).

Results

The Vessel Feet

The analysis data for this group of five very similar objects (Figure 5.50, 28–32; SFs 563, 587, 626, 652 and 669), initially identified as 'ingots', indicated an unusual composition containing large amounts of arsenic, antimony and lead with very little tin or zinc. This, coupled with their very slaggy and inhomogeneous textures, (a feature demonstrated by the variations evident in the data from two separate samples taken from SF563) was initially taken as evidence that they were indeed associated with some intermediate stage of copper production – at some point after initial smelting but before final purification. Beyond this the analyses also indicate that at least two of the objects, SFs 587 and 626, were produced from the same batch of cast metal.

Subsequent comparison of the objects with the typological identifications of identical medieval objects found in Worcester, London, Hull and Gloucester and with chemical compositions of similar objects obtained by Roger Brownsword at Coventry Polytechnic (Brownsword et al 1983–1984) confirm that they represent cast feet from at least two copper alloy cauldrons or skillets.

Nonetheless, their chemical composition is of interest, as the distinctively high levels of lead, antimony and sometimes arsenic appears to be restricted to alloys of the medieval and post-medieval periods, where it is quite commonly used to make large cast objects such as vessels. The nature of the alloy is such that it would be too hard and brittle to work in any other way other than casting, and even in casting it is a poor metal, being prone to corrosion and lacking in strength. The high levels of antimony and arsenic in the samples indicate a *Fahlerz* or 'grey' copper ore source, rich in the minerals tetrahedrite, Cu_3SbS_3. Such an ore is likely to have been of continental European origin, as very little copper mining of any kind appears to have been carried out in this country during the medieval period, and there is no record of 'grey' ores being mined here at this time.

The overall impression from the analysis of the vessel feet is of objects made as cheaply as possible where an attempt was made to extract the maximum amount of metal from the ore, with no purification of the product – hence the large amounts of arsenic and antimony carried over. With the addition of lead, the result was an alloy which could be used for casting but would be fairly weak as the large amounts of soluble lead would segregate at grain boundaries on cooling. Such grain boundaries are known to be prone to fracturing (hence the brittleness of the alloy) and also provide pathways along which corrosion may penetrate.

Other Copper Alloy Objects

Of the other copper alloy objects analysed, points to note are that, within the limits of analytical precision, the pieces of sheet metal (SFs 582 and 691) can be considered identical, as can SF objects 529 and 552.

Small find CAR no.	Context	Description
692	147	Worked bone needle, fractured. Flattened head with large circular eye. Worn/polished shaft is flattened at either end, lozenge-shaped in section in centre, tapering to oval-sectioned point. Overall length: 138mm. Figure 5.68, No. 5
847	220	Worked fragment of sheep/goat scapula with large perforation at proximal end. Transverse grooves adjacent to perforation on upper face; bone has been shaved smooth around perforation on lower face. Possible tool fragment. Dimensions: 90mm × 45mm × 18mm. Figure 5.68, No. 6
848	220	Pointed terminal of pin beater of very highly polished bone/antler. Sub-rectangular in section. Length: 27mm. Figure 5.68, No. 13
933	347	Complete pin beater, fashioned from a long bone fragment, with pointed, tapering terminals. Shaft is D-shaped in section and highly polished/worn. Length: 79mm. Figure 5.68, No. 1 and Figure 5.69, No. 3
959	3010	Near complete pin beater of very highly polished bone, probably from cattle rib or long bone. Pointed terminal has worn grooves to either side. Sub-rectangular-sectioned shaft. Length: 77mm. Figure 5.68, No. 3 and Figure 5.69, No. 1
955	3004	Near complete pin beater of polished bone, probably from cattle rib or long bone. Pointed terminal with faint worn grooves on either face. Oval-sectioned shaft. Length: 69mm. Figure 5.68, No. 2 and Figure 5.69, No. 2
CAR1541	65	Near complete pin beater of highly polished bone. Pointed terminal with broken end. Oval-sectioned shaft. Length: 90mm. Figure 5.68, No. 4 and Figure 5.69, No. 6
CAR1037	2	Pointed terminal of pin beater with sub-rectangular sectioned shaft. Surfaces are slightly polished/worn. Length: 32mm. Figure 5.68, No. 7
CAR1217	2	Probable terminal of pin beater. Pointed, sub-rectangular in section, worn/polished. Length: 27mm. Figure 5.68, No. 8
CAR1373	65	Shaft of bird long-bone, fractured at either end. Small, sub-circular perforation on upper face and similar perforation on lower face, slightly staggered. Possibly part of bone whistle. Dimensions: 60mm × 7mm × 4mm. Figure 5.68, No. 9
CAR1394	318	Small fragment of worked bone, rectangular in section, with irregular scored grooves on upper and lower faces. Bone is worn/polished. Fractured at either end. Possible pin beater fragment. Length: 44mm. Figure 5.68, No. 10
CAR1498	39	Two fragments of worked bone inlay, decorated with turned ring and dot decoration. Dimensions of fragment a): 22mm × 9mm × 1mm. Dimensions of fragment b): 19mm × 8mm × 1mm. Figure 5.68, No. 11 and Figure 5.69, No. 4
CAR1530	201	Probable terminal of pin beater. Pointed, sub-oval in section, worn/polished. Length: 29mm. Figure 5.68, No. 12
CAR 784	2	Antler horn core worked to a point. 122mm. Figure 5.68, No. 15
624	72	Bone knife guard. Highly polished finish with a chamfered rectangular-shaped opening for blade tang and a pair of shallow rounded depressions on upper surface. Possibly originally part of scale tang knife SF623 (this report, Section 5.5, No. 6) recovered from the same deposit, 57mm × 13mm. Figure 5.68, No. 14 and Figure 5.69, No. 5

FIGURE 5.67

Catalogue of worked bone objects

5.11 WORKED BONE OBJECTS
by Sarah Newns (2015)

A small group of worked bone objects (Figure 5.67) was recovered, comprising eight probable pin beaters, one needle, one possible bone tool and one possible bone whistle. It is likely that all these objects date from the Period III Saxo-Norman phase of occupation.

The majority of the worked bone items, the pin beaters and needle, are linked to textile production. Pin beaters, of the double-pointed variety, of which four complete or near complete examples (Figure 5.68, 1–4) were recovered from Eckweek, are common on settlement sites of the early and middle Anglo-Saxon period. The tool would have been used to separate coarse threads, which have a tendency to catch on each other during the weaving process (Hylton 2010, 385). One example (SF959; Figure 5.68, 3) shows worn irregular grooves, which may have been formed by friction against the warp threads. It is thought that a further fragment of worked bone (CAR1394; Figure 5.68, 10), which is more slender than the rest, but of a similar form, and with similar irregular grooves, may be a smaller and more worn example of the same tool.

The needle (SF692; Figure 5.68, 5) is of faceted bone, with pointed tip and flattened, spatulate head with large circular eye. Similar examples are known from medieval contexts, often fashioned from pig fibulae (Hylton 2010, 387, no 32).

Two of the objects (recorded jointly under CAR1498) are small fragments of decorative bone inlay, with characteristic ring and dot decoration (Figure 5.68, 11). These may have formed part of a composite bone comb, or may have formed a decorative inlay to a larger object, such as a casket.

The remaining two objects are less easily identified. One, a fragment of sheep/goat scapula (SF847; Figure 5.68, 6), has a circular perforation at its proximal end, with cut marks and a smoothed, shaved area around the perforation. The object bears a resemblance to an antler tool recovered during excavations at Shapwick, which is thought to have been fitted with a wooden haft, and used as a rake, hoe or hammer (Gutierrez 2007, 795–796, fig. 18.10). Similar examples have been recovered from both Britain and the Low Countries, all of Roman date (Macgregor in Gutierrez 2007). The example from Eckweek, being similar in form, but of a smaller size, may well have also been part of a composite tool with a wooden haft, probably for less heavy-duty tasks.

ARTEFACTS AND ENVIRONMENTAL EVIDENCE

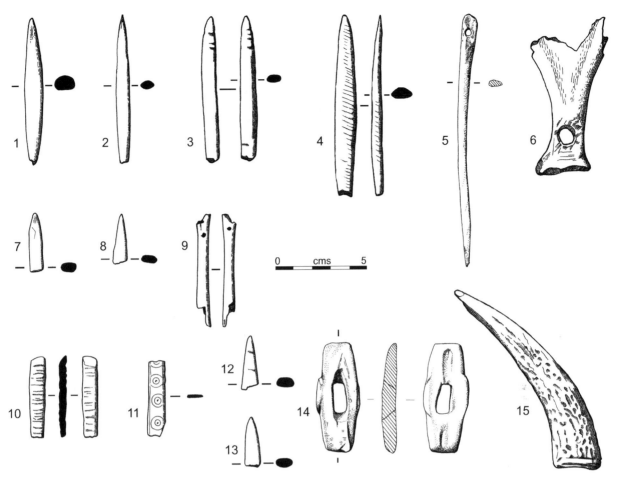

FIGURE 5.68
Illustrated medieval worked bone objects

The second less easily identified object is a fragment of bird long bone (CAR1373; Figure 5.68, 9), hollow, with two circular incised perforations, one on the upper face and one on the lower. It is at least possible that this object is part of a bone whistle, similar to an example recovered during excavations at Acton Court, South Gloucestershire (Courtney 2004, 368–369, fig. 9.32.6). A similar whistle, from Southampton, came from a context of early 14th-century date (Megaw in Courtney 2004).

Discussion

Textile working finds are common on sites of medieval date, and may be associated with either hand-spinning (spindle whorls etc), sewing (bone pins) or weaving (Hylton 2010, 384–386). The significant number of probable pin beaters amongst the Eckweek bone assemblage suggests that textile weaving would have been undertaken on the site, probably on a vertical warp-weighted two-beam loom, a type of loom probably introduced in the 9th century. Numbers of pin beaters have also been recovered from the medieval settlement at Raunds, in contexts which suggest that their use was confined to the 12th century or earlier (Hylton 2010, 384–386). It is thought that the double-pointed type of pin beater (as SF933) was more common in the early medieval period. Examples from Goltho are possibly later Saxon, as they are double-ended with both a pointed and a spatulate terminal (MacGregor 1987, 190). A number of 7th-century examples

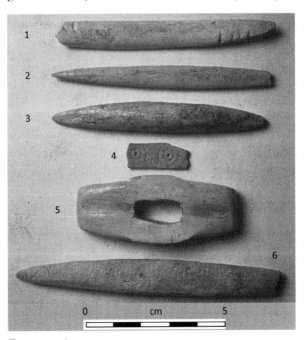

FIGURE 5.69
Medieval worked bone objects including pin-beaters, a decorated fragment and a knife guard

of double-pointed pin beaters have been recovered from Shakenoak, Oxfordshire (Brodribb in Gutierrez 2007, 790), but later examples may span the 9th to the early 13th centuries (Gutierrez 2007, 790–792).

Ring and dot bone mounts such as CAR1498 have an extremely long lifespan, and are common from the late Roman to the later medieval period. Examples from caskets are rare – two local examples being those from South Cadbury, of 11th-century date (Alcock in Gutierrez 2007, 795) and Ludgershall Castle, Wiltshire, of 12th century date (Macgregor in Gutierrez 2007, 795). A small fragment of ring and dot decorated mount was recovered from amongst an assemblage of residual medieval finds from a modern context during excavations at Shapwick, Somerset (Gutierrez 2007, 795, fig. 18.9.7).

Composite combs have a similar longevity to the ring and dot mounts, and are known from contexts spanning the Roman period to the 15th century (Ashby 1999, 1–5, Types 1b to 13). The above motif was a common form of decoration throughout this extended period, present on the decorative plates which would have been attached to the body of the comb.

Excavations at the medieval settlement at Goltho yielded examples of both a ring and dot decorated mount, and a composite bone comb with incised line decoration, both of probable early medieval date (MacGregor 1987, 191, fig. 161, 2). Excavations at Raunds yielded a complete composite bone comb, with ring and dot decoration, dated 1150 to 1250, and a small ring and dot decorated mount (Hylton 2010, 349, fig. 11.7.42–43). It is likely that the examples from Eckweek, being small and fragmentary, derive from a composite bone comb, on which they would have formed decorative sideplates, similar to those present on the example recovered from Raunds.

5.12 THE JET BEAD SF627
by Sarah Newns (2015)

A large spherical jet bead (SF627) some 15mm in diameter was recovered from context [46], a floor layer dated to the 14th century and located inside Period V.2 Building 460 (CP6). The bead (Figure 5.58, 27) was perforated at the centre and was in reasonable condition with only minor surface spalling.

Jet beads such as SF627 are traditionally identified as rosary beads, and are relatively common finds in medieval contexts (McSloy 2013, 241, fig. 4.29.3). Two undecorated examples, such as SF627, are known from Bristol, one from a 14th-/15th-century context (Good in McSloy 2013) and a further example, probably residual, from a post-medieval deposit (McSloy 2013, 241). Similar examples have been retrieved from 16th-century contexts from the Tudor courtier's house of Acton Court, South Gloucestershire (Courtney 2004, 366, fig. 9.43). No examples of such beads were retrieved from the early medieval phases at either Raunds or Goltho, which may indicate that their use was confined to the later medieval period.

5.13 FAUNAL REMAINS
by Dr Simon J M Davis, Ancient Monuments Laboratory, English Heritage (1992, slightly updated 2015)

Introduction

A particular interest of the animal bones from Eckweek (Figure 5.70) is that they comprise a reasonably well-dated sequence from a rural settlement. The aim of this report is to describe the animal bones from Eckweek and provide tables of their measurements.

Methods

Most of the bones were hand-recovered. In addition, some bones were retrieved by wet sieving (with a mesh of 500 microns) a small volume of deposit from certain contexts. Due to the small size of the faunal assemblage, and at the suggestion of Andrew Young, the data have been pooled into two main phases, an early one (ceramic phases 1–4 dated cAD 950–1250) and a late one (ceramic phases 5 and 6 dated cAD 1250–1400).

For a full description of the methods used see Davis (1992a). In brief, all mandibular teeth and a restricted suite of '*parts of the skeleton always recorded*' (ie a predetermined set of articular ends/epiphyses and metaphyses of girdle, limb and foot bones; listed in Figures 5.71 and 5.72) were recorded and used in the counts. In order to avoid multiple counting of very fragmented bones, at least 50% of a given part had to be present for it to be included (broken, and therefore single, caprine and cattle metapodial condyles were counted as halves). An epiphysis is described as 'fused' once spicules of bone have formed across the epiphysial plate joining metaphysis to epiphysis.

Sheep/goat teeth were assigned to the eruption and wear stages of Payne (1987 and Figure 5.75), pig and cattle teeth were assigned to the eruption and wear stages of Grant (1982). Measurements taken on the cattle metapodials are illustrated in Davis (1988 and Figures 5.76 and 5.77). In general, other measurements taken follow those suggested by Driesch (1976).

The sample of wet sieved bones included mandibles of *Apodemus*. The two British species of this genus, *A. sylvaticus* the woodmouse, and *A. flavicollis* the yellow-necked mouse, are difficult to distinguish. Recent specimens in the AM Lab comparative collection (now in the Centre for Archaeology, Portsmouth) were measured and, notwithstanding age-related variation, the height of the mandibular ramus measured up the external side opposite the

Animal	Period AD 950–1250 n	%	Period AD 1250–1400 n	%
Horse	13	4	14	3
Pig	24	8	54	10
Cattle	71.5	25	112.5	22
Sheep/Goat	182.5	62	333	65
(Sheep)	(47)		(72)	
(Goat)	(-)		(-)	
Total domestic ungulates	**291**		**513.5**	
Rabbit	-		2	
Hedgehog	-		9	
Dog	-		3	
Cat	-		7	
Galliform	8		24	
(Chicken)	(5)		(6)	
(Pheasant)	(-)		(-)	
Goose	2		11	
cf Mallard	-		1	
Woodcock	-		1	
Partridge	1		-	
Rook	-		1	
Corvid	1		1	
?Hooded Crow	1		-	

Galliform = probable chicken or pheasant

FIGURE 5.70

Medieval animal fauna by period

middle of M_2 seems to provide a reasonably good separation of the two species – *A. flavicollis* are generally larger than *A. sylvaticus* (Figure 5.78).

Results and Discussion

Condition and Recovery

Certain smaller parts of the skeleton such as sheep carpals, incisors, premolars and phalanges (Figures 5.71, 5.72 and 5.73 and 5.79) are notably scarce. These may have been missed during excavation. Species retrieved by sieving are recorded in Figure 5.74. With such a small volume put through this operation at Eckweek it is impossible to estimate the original proportion of smaller parts of the skeleton and smaller species such as mice and small birds. Most of the bones are fairly well preserved. The scarcity of some of the later-fusing skeletal parts such as distal radius and distal metapodials, suggests that differential preservation has had some effect too.

Several bones with gnaw marks were found throughout the sequence at Eckweek as were several bones displaying the characteristic features which Payne and Munson (1985) describe for bones partially digested by dogs. These gnawed and 'semi-digested' bones corroborate the suggestion that extensive dog activity at Eckweek has influenced the pattern of preservation of the bone assemblage.

Species Present and their Frequencies

Some 878 hand-recovered mammal and bird bones have been recorded (Figures 5.70 to 5.72). Most of them belonged to sheep (no goat remains were recognised), cattle, and some pig. Several equid bones and teeth probably belonged to horse – the lower molars have a 'U' shaped lingual (internal) fold, with buccal (external) fold partially penetrating between the flexids. Rabbit bones could be distinguished from those of hare on the basis of their small size.

Most of the galliform bones probably belonged to either chicken or pheasant; bones of these two species being difficult to distinguish. However two exceptions are a) the proximal femur and b) the tarso-metatarsus. None of the chicken/pheasant tarso-metatarsi and femora found at Eckweek could be identified as pheasant. It is quite likely then, that all the galliform bones belonged to chickens.

No deer and remarkably few remains of game species were found. The absence of deer may have some significance. In medieval England commoners were not allowed to hunt large game such as deer which were reserved for the aristocracy. This may have a bearing on the status of the inhabitants. Presumably Eckweek was not inhabited by the aristocracy.

Sheep bones comprise 60–65% of the assemblage, far outnumbering the remains of cattle (20–25%), and pig (8–10%). However, given the larger size of an ox, the inhabitants of Eckweek probably ate more beef than mutton. Comparison of the early (950–1250) with the late (1250–1400) assemblages shows (Figure 5.70) that very little change occurred in the relative frequencies of different species. The high proportion of sheep compared to cattle is of some interest and puts Eckweek in a similar category, in terms of large mammal remains, to the post-10th-century levels in Lincoln (O'Connor 1982), when sheep had increased in frequency from *c*30% to over 40%. O'Connor correlates the contemporary fall in the number of cattle bones with the gradual change from the use of oxen to horses for ploughing. By this time the rigid breast harness which enabled horses to be used for ploughing had reached England from the continent (Lefebvre des Noettes 1931, 122). In addition, the increase of sheep numbers may well reflect the growth of the wool industry. In their reviews of animal remains from Saxon and medieval archaeological sites in southern and central England, Matilda Holmes (Holmes, in press) and Umberto Albarella (Albarella, in press) respectively found that the majority of sites in Saxon southern England comprise mainly cattle and sheep with rather fewer pigs. Moreover there was, in terms of faunal frequencies, little difference between rural, urban, ecclesiastical and high status sites. At Eckweek the tooth-wear data show that a substantial proportion of the sheep belonged to the older age groups (*c*4–6 years) which had undoubtedly been shorn of several fleeces (and ewes may have been milked too) prior to slaughter.

The significant, though admittedly small, number of equid remains is worth noting, and may typify rural sites, such as Raunds in Northamptonshire (Albarella and Davis 1994), rather than urban

cAD 950–1250 Ceramic phases 1–4	Sheep/Goat	Cattle	Pig	Horse	Dog	Other
Mandible	13Sh + 17	5	4	–	–	
Mandibular tooth: i	1 (-)	- (-)	3 (-)	- (-)	–	
Mandibular tooth: I	13 (-)	10 (-)	3 (-)	3 (-)	- (-)	
Mandibular tooth: dp2	- (8)	- (1)	- (-)	- (-)	–	
Mandibular tooth: dp3	1 (10Sh)	3 (1)	- (-)	- (-)	–	
Mandibular tooth: dp4	2Sh + 1 (11Sh)	3 (2)	- (1)	- (-)	–	
Mandibular tooth: P1			- (-)		- (-)	
Mandibular tooth: P2	- (1)	1 (1)	1 (-)	1 (-)	- (-)	
Mandibular tooth: P3	1 (8)	6 (2)	- (-)	- (-)	- (-)	
Mandibular tooth: P3/4				- (-)		
Mandibular tooth: P4	5 (9)	1 (1)	1 (1)	1 (-)	- (-)	
Mandibular tooth: M1	5 (21)	1 (3)	- (1)	- (-)	- (-)	
Mandibular tooth: M2	5 (19)	1 (-)	- (2)	- (-)	- (-)	
Mandibular tooth: M3	20 (11)	3 (1)	1 (1)	- (-)	- (-)	
Mandibular tooth: M1/2	31 (-)	11 (1)	3 (-)	–		
Mandibular tooth: C			3 (1)	1 (-)	- (-)	
Scapula – Coracold U	2	–	–	–	–	
Scapula – Coracold F	2	1	1	–	–	
Scapula – Coracold ?	2	–	–	–	–	
Humerus – dist metaph U	3	–	–	–	–	
Humerus – dist epiph U	–	–	–	–	–	
Humerus – dist F	7	1	1	–	–	?Hooded crow:1 Rook:1
Radius – dist metaph U	2	–	1	–	–	
Radius – dist epiph U	–	–	–	–	–	
Radius – dist F	1	1	–	2	–	
Radiale	–	–	–	–	–	
C2 + 3	–	1	–	–	–	
Metacarpal – dist metaph U	2	–	–	–	–	
Metacarpal – dist epiph U	–	–	–	–	–	
Metacarpal – dist F	2.5Sh	1	–	–	–	Goose:1
Ischium	12	3	–	1	–	
Femur – dist metaph U	–	–	–	–	–	
Femur – dist epiph U	1	–	–	–	–	
Femur – dist F	–	–	–	–	–	Chicken:2 Partridge:1
Tibia – dist metaph U	2	–	–	–	–	
Tibia – dist epiph U	–	–	–	–	–	
Tibia – dist F	5	1	1	–	–	Gall:2
Astragalus	1Sh + 2	6	–	2	–	
Calcaneum – tuber calcis U	1Sh	–	–	–	–	
Calcaneum – tuber calcis F	4Sh	–	–	–	–	
Calcaneum – tuber calcis ?	–	2	–	–	–	
Metatarsal – dist metaph U	2	2	–	–	–	
Metatarsal – dist epiph U	1Sh	–	–	–	–	
Metatarsal – dist F	1.5Sh	2.5	–	–	–	Goose:1 Chicken:3 Gall:1
Metapoidial – dist metaph U	–	–	–	–	–	
Metapoidial – dist epiph U	1	–	–	–	–	
Metapoidial – dist F	0.5	1	–	–	–	
Phalanx – prox metaph U	1	–	1	–	–	
Phalanx – prox epiph U	–	–	–	–	–	
Phalanx – prox F	9	4	–	2	–	
Phalanx 3	–	–	–	–	–	
Totals	**182.5**	**71.5**	**24**	**13**	**–**	

FIGURE 5.71

Medieval animal fauna and body parts in ceramic phases 1–4 (Periods III–IV)

Counts of trench-recovered mammal bones and teeth from Eckweek. A mandible fragment with one or more teeth is counted as a mandible. Counts for loose teeth and for teeth in mandibles are given separately, the count for teeth in mandibles being in parentheses.
Note: 'Horse incisors' includes both upper and lower teeth.
Some sheep and goat teeth and bones could be identified to species. For example SHEEP/GOAT astragalus '7Sh+2' refers to the presence of 7 astragali which could be identified as definitely sheep and 2 which are either sheep or goat.
Key: Rab – Rabbit   Gall – Galliform   F – epiphysis fused (adult)   U – epiphysis unfused (juvenile).
(for a detailed breakdown of the counts of rabbit, cat and hedgehog teeth see archive)

ARTEFACTS AND ENVIRONMENTAL EVIDENCE

AD 1250–1400 Ceramic phases 5–6	Sheep/Goat	Cattle	Pig	Horse	Dog	Other
Mandible	15Sh + 20	7	11	–	–	Rab:2 Cat:3 Hedgehog:7
Mandibular tooth: i	2 (-)	-(-)	2 (-)	- (-)	–	
Mandibular tooth: I	7 (-)	16 (-)	13 (-)	2 (-)	- (-)	
Mandibular tooth: dp2	- (9)	- (2)	1 (2)	- (-)	–	
Mandibular tooth: dp3	2sh (12sh)	1 (2)	- (4)	- (-)	–	
Mandibular tooth: dp4	12Sh (14Sh)	3 (1)	1 (4)	- (-)	–	
Mandibular tooth: P1			- (-)		- (-)	
Mandibular tooth: P2	- (1)	1 (-)	- (1)	- (-)	- (-)	
Mandibular tooth: P3	1 (3)	3 (-)	- (2)	- (-)	- (-)	
Mandibular tooth: P3/4						
Mandibular tooth: P4	4 (6)	4 (2)	- (3)	- (-)	- (-)	
Mandibular tooth: M1	3 (17)	- (2)	- (4)	- (-)	1 (-)	
Mandibular tooth: M2	7 (17)	- (4)	- (2)	- (-)	- (-)	
Mandibular tooth: M3	44 (13)	10 (5)	1 (-)	1 (-)	- (-)	
Mandibular tooth: M1/2	85 (1)	13	5 (2)	4		
Mandibular tooth: C			1 (1)	- (-)	1 (-)	
Scapula – Coracold U	–	–	1	–	–	
Scapula – Coracold F	6	2	–	–	–	Goose:1 Corvid:1
Scapula – Coracold ?	8	–	2	–	–	
Humerus – dist metaph U	3	–	–	–	–	
Humerus – dist epiph U	–	–	–			
Humerus – dist F	32	1	1	–	1	Cat:4 Hedgehog:2 Gall:3 Goose:1 Woodcock:1
Radius – dist metaph U	1	1	1	–	–	
Radius – dist epiph U	1	–	–	–	–	
Radius – dist F	2	2	–	–	–	?Gall:1
Radiale	–	3	–	–	–	
C2 + 3	–	1	–	–	–	
Metacarpal – dist metaph U	1	–	0.5	–	–	
Metacarpal – dist epiph U	–	–	–	–	–	
Metacarpal – dist F	1.5Sh	3	–	–	–	Gall:3 Goose:8 ?Mallard:1 Rook:1
Ischium	9	2	2	2	–	?Goose:1
Femur – dist metaph U	–	–	–	–	–	
Femur – dist epiph U	–	–	1	–	–	
Femur – dist F	–	1	–	–	–	Chicken:1 Gall:1
Tibia – dist metaph U	4	–	–	–	–	
Tibia – dist epiph U	1	–	–	–	–	
Tibia – dist F	20	4	–	–	–	Gall:7
Astragalus	7Sh + 2	1	2	–	–	
Calcaneum – tuber calcis U	5	–	2	–	–	
Calcaneum – tuber calcis F	3	1	–	–	–	
Calcaneum – tuber calcis ?	–	3	2	–	–	
Metatarsal – dist metaph U	1	1	–	–	–	
Metatarsal – dist epiph U	–	–	–	–	–	
Metatarsal – dist F	6.5Sh + 0.5	2.5	–	–	–	Chicken:5 Gall:3
Metapoidial – dist metaph U	4.5	–	1	–	–	
Metapoidial – dist epiph U	–	2	0.5	–	–	
Metapoidial – dist F	–	–	–	1	–	
Phalanx – prox metaph U	–	–	2	–	–	
Phalanx – prox epiph U	1	–	–	–	–	
Phalanx – prox F	9	18	1	1	–	
Phalanx 3	2Sh	6	–	2	–	
Totals	**333**	**112.5**	**54**	**14**	**3**	

Figure 5.72

Medieval animal fauna and body parts in ceramic phases 5–6 (Period V)

Counts of trench-recovered mammal bones and teeth from Eckweek. A mandible fragment with one or more teeth is counted as a mandible. Counts for loose teeth and for teeth in mandibles are given separately, the count for teeth in mandibles being in parentheses.
Note: 'Horse incisors' includes both upper and lower teeth.
Some sheep and goat teeth and bones could be identified to species. For example SHEEP/GOAT astragalus '7Sh+2' refers to the presence of 7 astragali which could be identified as definitely sheep and 2 which are either sheep or goat.
Key: Rab - Rabbit   Gall - Galliform   F - epiphysis fused (adult)   U - epiphysis unfused (juvenile).
(for a detailed breakdown of the counts of rabbit, cat and hedgehog teeth see archive)

Body part	Sh/G 950–1250	Mn	Sh/G 1250–1400	Mn	Cattle 1250–1400	Mn
Mandible	30	15	35	18	7	4
i + I	14	3	9	5	16	3
dp+P	49	9	64	11	19	4
Molars	112	19	187	32	34	6
Scapula	6	3	14	7	2	1
humerus dist	10	5	35	18	1	1
Radius dist	3	2	3	2	3	2
radiale	0	0	0	0	3	2
C2 + 3	0	0	0	0	1	1
Metacarpal – dist	5+2	4	3+3	3	3+1	2
Ischium	12	6	9	5	2	1
Femur – dist	1	1	0	0	1	1
Tibia – dist	7	4	24	12	5	3
Astragalus	3	2	9	5	1	1
Calcaneum	5	3	8	4	4	2
Metatarsal – dist	4+2	3	8+3	6	4+1	3
Phalanx 1 – prox	10	2	10	2	18	3
Phalanx 3	0	0	2	1	6	1

Body-part frequencies. Counts of the different parts of the skeleton of Sheep/Goat and Cattle in the period AD 1250–1400 and Sheep/Goat in the period AD 950–1250 at Eckweek. Data are from Figures 5.71 and 5.72. The Mn column provides an approximate guide to the relative occurrences of the different elements taking into account their anatomical frequency i.e. 2 'Humeri', 8 'i+I', 6 'Molars', 2 'Radii', 8 'Phalanx 1' etc. The numbers of metapoidials have been apportioned equally to metacarpals and metatarsals. (These MN numbers would therefore be equal if whole carcasses had originally been buried and if recovery and preservational biases had had an equal effect on all parts of the skeleton.) Fractions have been rounded up. For example 3 radii must have come from at least 2 (=3/2) individuals, 110 molar teeth must have come from at least 19 (=110/6) individuals, and 6 phalanges must have come from 1 (=6/8) individual

FIGURE 5.73

Medieval sheep/goat and cattle body parts

ones. In her review, Holmes (in press) found horse remains comprise on average less than 2% of the large mammals in late Saxon rural sites.

Body Part Frequency (Figures 5.73 and 5.79)

The relative abundance of different parts of the skeleton shows that, allowing for recovery bias (this would account for the low count of sheep incisors, carpals and third phalanges), there is a large discrepancy between the numbers of teeth and the numbers of limb bones. A similar discrepancy was noted at the Saxon-medieval rural site of Burystead/Langham Road (Davis 1992b) which was probably caused by extensive activity of dogs. Dogs tend to avoid jaws with their sharp teeth, and so this part of the anatomy is preferentially preserved.

An unusually high frequency of sheep molars, distal humeri and distal tibiae in the later period is difficult to explain. It may be due to a combination of preservation and recovery factors.

Measurements (Figure 5.80)

Bone measurements are an important source of information in zooarchaeology. It is probably safe

Context number	213		273	
Nature of fill	drain		pit	
Ceramic phase	6		4	
Description	n	%	n	%
Pygmy shrew mandibles	–		1	1
Common shrew mandibles	2	4	6	6
Mole mandibles	1	2	1	1
House mouse				
Estimated total number of mandibles	4	9	2	2
Wood mouse				
Estimated total number of mandibles	32	68	57	54
Field vole M1	2	4	20	19
Bank vole M1	6	13	19	18
Rabbit tibia shaft			+	
cf turdidae distal tarso-metatarsus			+	
cf Chaffinch distal humerus			+	
Small songbird phalanx 3	+			
cf Galliform phalanx 2			+	
Amphibian long-bone shaft	+			
Totals	**47**		**106**	

Eckweek sieved samples. Numbers of mandibles/lower first molar teeth and other bones from small animals recovered from sieving contexts 213 and 273. In context 213 there were 28 isolated wood mouse M1s, 4 mandibles with M1, and no edentate murine mandibles, giving an estimated total of 32 wood mouse mandibles. In context 273 there were 11 isolated wood mouse M1s and 28 wood mouse mandibles with their M1s in place. However, there were also 10 edentate mandibles belonging to either house mouse or wood mouse, and therefore the original number of wood mouse mandibles was estimated as c57 (allowing the possibility of 1 edentate mandible belonging to a house mouse)

FIGURE 5.74

Medieval small mammal, bird and amphibian fauna from sieved samples

to assume that within a lineage of domesticated animals an increase in size over time signifies their improvement. John Burke (1834, 20) in volume I of his 'British Husbandry' attributed the dawn of general improvement in this country to the reign of Edward III (1327–1377). While osteometric studies of sheep from archaeological sites in various parts of England showed that by post-medieval times sheep had become considerably larger than in earlier times, subsequent studies indicate that improvement of sheep as well as other livestock in Britain probably began as early as the 14th or 15th centuries. Improvements were also probably gradual (Albarella and Davis 1996; Davis and Beckett 1999; Thomas 2005).

The 10th- to 14th-century sheep bones at Eckweek are rather small, smaller than a sample of modern unimproved Shetland sheep as shown in Figure 5.80. This figure also shows measurements of sheep bones from medieval and post-medieval Launceston Castle in Cornwall. The small size of the Eckweek sheep is clear. Moreover they appear to have been no different from the small medieval ones at Launceston indicating that they were unimproved. It is likely that they represent the kind of sheep commonly found in England before improvements began in the 14th and subsequent centuries.

The chicken bones too are small and little different from those of present-day bantams. In terms of

ARTEFACTS AND ENVIRONMENTAL EVIDENCE

Payne wear stage	0	1	2	3	4	5	6	7	8	9	10	11	12	13	14	15	16	17	18	19	20	21	22	23	?
Ceramic phases 5–6 (AD 1250–1400)																									
dP4	1	.	.	1	.	.	.	3	2	1	.	.	2	6	.	6	.	1	1	.	1	.	.	.	1
P4	1	2	.	.	.	.	.	.	2	1	.	.	3	.	1	.	.	.	.	.	.	.	.	.	.
M1	.	.	.	.	.	1	.	.	1	10	.	1	2	.	.	4	.	.	.	.	.	.	.	.	1
M1/2	2	.	4	.	2	5	5	17	16	24	2	3	1	.	.	1	.	.	.	.	.	.	.	.	4
M2	.	.	1	.	1	1	1	4	.	13	.	3	.	.	.	.	.	.	.	.	.	.	.	.	.
M3	8	.	4	.	.	2	1	2	3	3	2	27	.	.	.	.	.	.	.	.	.	.	.	.	5
Ceramic phases 1–4 (*c*AD 950–1250)																									
dP4	.	.	.	.	1	1	.	.	.	1	.	1	2	6	.	2	.	.	.	1	.	.	.	.	1
P4	4	.	.	.	.	.	.	2	3	.	.	.	2	.	1	.	.	.	.	.	.	.	.	.	.
M1	.	.	2	.	.	.	.	3	1	13	.	.	3	.	.	3	.	.	.	.	.	.	.	.	1
M1/2	4	1	.	.	1	4	2	3	15	1	.	.	.	.	.	.	.	.	.	.	.	.	.	.	.
M2	.	.	.	.	1	4	1	5	7	1	.	.	1	1	.	.	.	.	.	.	.	.	.	.	3
M3	4	.	1	.	1	3	.	1	4	2	2	8	1	.	.	.	.	.	.	.	.	.	.	.	4

FIGURE 5.75

Payne large mammal tooth wear stages by ceramic phase

Grant wear stage	a	b	c	c/d	d	e	e/f	f	g	h	i	j	j/k	k	l	m	n	o	p	?
Ceramic phases 5–6 (AD 1250–1400)																				
dP4	.	.	1	.	.	.	.	.	.	.	.	.	.	1	1	.	1	.	.	.
P4	.	.	1	.	1	.	.	3	.	.	.	.	.	1	.	.	.	.	.	1
M1	.	.	.	.	.	.	.	.	1	.	.	.	.	1	.	.	.	.	.	.
M1/2	.	2	.	.	2	.	.	1	.	.	1	.	3	2	2	.	.	.	.	.
M2	.	.	.	.	.	.	.	.	1	.	.	.	.	2	1	.	.	.	.	.
M3	.	1	1	1	.	.	.	.	7	.	.	2	.	1	1	1	.	.	.	.
Ceramic phases 1–4 (*c*AD 950–1250)																				
dP4	.	.	.	.	.	.	.	.	1	.	.	1	.	3	.	.	.	.	.	.
P4	.	.	.	.	.	.	.	1	1	.	.	.	.	.	.	.	.	.	.	.
M1	1	.	.	.	.	.	.	.	1	.	.	.	.	2	.	.	.	.	.	.
M1/2	.	2	.	1	.	.	2	2	.	.	1	.	2	1	.	.	.	.	.	1
M2	.	.	.	.	.	.	.	.	.	.	.	.	.	1	.	.	.	.	.	.
M3	.	.	.	.	.	.	1	.	1	1	.	.	.	.	1	.	.	.	.	.

FIGURE 5.76

Eckweek medieval cattle mandibular wear stages (after Grant 1982)

Grant wear stage	a	b	c	d	e	f	g	h	i	j	k	l	m	n	?
Ceramic phases 5–6 (AD 1250–1400)															
dP4	.	.	1	1	1	1	.	.	1	.	.	.	.	.	.
P4	.	2	.	.	1	.	.	.	.	.	.	.	.	.	.
M1	.	.	1	.	2	1	.	.	.	.	.	.	.	.	.
M1/2	3	1	1	.	1	1	.	.	.	.	.	.	.	.	.
M2	1	1	.	.	.	.	.	.	.	.	.	.	.	.	.
M3	1	.	.	.	.	.	.	.	.	.	.	.	.	.	.
Ceramic phases 1–4 (*c*AD 950–1250)															
dP4	.	.	.	.	1	.	.	.	.	.	.	.	.	.	.
P4	.	.	1	1	.	.	.	.	.	.	.	.	.	.	.
M1	.	.	.	.	.	.	.	.	.	.	1	.	.	.	.
M1/2	.	3	.	.	.	.	.	.	.	.	.	.	.	.	.
M2	.	.	.	.	.	.	1	.	1	.	.	.	.	.	.
M3	1	1	.	.	.	.	.	.	.	.	.	.	.	.	.

FIGURE 5.77

Eckweek medieval pig mandibular wear stages (after Grant 1982)

their size, the few cattle bones at Eckweek resemble those from other sites of this period.

Ageing

(For translations of tooth-wear stage in sheep to actual age in years I refer to Deniz and Payne 1982)

The deciduous and permanent teeth of sheep and their assignment to wear stages (Figure 5.75) suggest that a fairly wide range of ages was selected for slaughter, and in this respect there is little evidence for any difference between early and late periods at Eckweek. A ratio of 40 dP$_4$s:24 P$_4$s suggests that over half the sheep consumed at Eckweek

Minimum height of mandible (mm)	Apodemus flavicollis	Apodemus sylvaticus	Apodemus (Eckweek)
3.8	O		
3.7			
3.6	o		
3.5	o		
3.4	oaAO		
3.3	ayyA		A
3.2	yy	O	AAAA
3.1	yyyy	AAAAOOO	YAA
3.0	yy	YAAAOOO	YYAAO
2.9		YYAAAAAAOO	YAAAAA
2.8	y	YA	YAAO
2.7		YAA	A

Distinction between mandibles of *Apodemus sylvaticus* and *A. Flavicollis* and the identity of the Eckweek Apodemus from contexts 273 and 213. The minimum height of the mandibles in millimetres measured up the external side adjacent to M2 is plotted. Modern *flavicollis* and *sylvaticus* from the AM laboratory comparative collection are compared with mandibles from Eckweek.

Key: Lower case letters refer to laboratory bred animals, upper case letters refer to wild caught animals. Mandibles were assigned to one of three 'age' groups 'Young', 'Adult', and 'Old', according to the amount of wear on the lower first molar tooth (see Miller, 1912: 802) as follows:

Y – dentine of 1 or more of the tubercles t1–t4 is separate – t3–t4 are distinct from t5–t6

A – dentine of t1–t4 is confluent

O – dentine of t5–t6 is also confluent with the median posterior tubercle

Note that the mandible appears to increase in size with age. Despite this age-dependent variation, the Eckweek Apodemus can be identified as *A. sylvaticus*

FIGURE 5.78

Distinction between mandibles of Apodemus sylvaticus and A. flavicollis and the identity of the Eckweek Apodemus from contexts 273 and 213

were less than 2 years old (the approximate age when dP_4 is shed and replaced by P_4) however the real proportion of juveniles was probably a little lower since isolated dP_4s are more easily recovered than isolated P_4s. Of the 217 M1s and M2s assigned to wear stage, 49% are in wear stages 0–8 (ie less than 2 years old). The majority of the dP_4s are in wear stages 14–16 which probably belonged to lambs aged 5–14 months. The peaks of M₁s in wear stage 9 (1–3 years), M₂s in wear stage 9 (2.5–c7 years) and M₃s in wear stage 11 (3.5–c9 years) suggests that many of the adult sheep were slaughtered between the ages of 2–5 years. Thus both lambs and prime-mutton animals were slaughtered for local consumption.

A high proportion of cattle dP_4s compared to P_4s (Figure 5.76) may have come from surplus calves slaughtered locally. Wear-data of the other teeth suggest that cattle of a wide range of ages were slaughtered – perhaps these were lame animals not fit for droving into town for sale. Most of the pigs (Figure 5.77) were slaughtered fairly young which is the usual situation in zooarchaeological assemblages and is not surprising for an animal usually only reared for its meat and fat.

	Sheep/Goat cAD 950–1250	Sheep/Goat AD 1250–1400	Cattle AD 1250–1400
Mandible	++++	++++++	++
I + I	+	++	+
dp + P	+++	++++	++
Molars	+++++++	+++++++++++	++
Scapula	+	+++	+
Humerus – dist	++	++++++	+
Radius – dist	+	+	+
Radiale			+
C2 + 3			+
Metacarpal – dist	++	+	+
Ischium	++	++	+
Femur – dist	+		+
Tibia – dist	++	++++	+
Astragalus	+	++	+
Calcaneum	+	++	+
Metatarsal – dist	+	++	+
Phalanx – prox	+	+	+
Phalanx 3		+	+

FIGURE 5.79

Display of the data in Figure 5.73. Each cross represents a MN of 3

The Sieved Small Animal Remains – Origin and Environmental Considerations

Eight small fish vertebrae were found among the sieved material. Andrew Jones (Archaeological Resources Centre, York) has identified them as belonging to marine fish. Seven belong to the Clupeidae (herring family) and one to the Apodes (eels/conger eels).

Two contexts, 213 and 273, provided large samples of small bones retrieved by wet sieving (Figures 5.74 and 5.78). Context 213 represented a drain in ceramic phase 6 and context 273, a pit in ceramic phase 4. Under microscopic inspection the small animal bones and teeth retrieved by the wet-sieving operation are etched in a manner reminiscent of bones consumed and subsequently regurgitated by owls (ie from 'owl pellets'). All the small bird and mammal bones have this sheen and etching. These small animal remains from contexts 213 and 273 are probably derived from owl pellets. Owls probably roosted in the roofs of the buildings in which these contexts were found.

The abundant remains of common shrew, bank vole, field vole and woodmouse in the sieved samples is not surprising in view of the rural location of Eckweek. Owls will forage over an area of some 2–3 square miles, and this spectrum of small mammal species characterises a local environment consisting of open deciduous woodland, some ungrazed grassland, and perhaps fields with hedgerows. The amphibian bones may evidence the presence of semi-permanent bodies of water in the vicinity.

Pathology

Few bones exhibited signs of disease or injury. Three of the cattle incisors, one in the later phase and two

ARTEFACTS AND ENVIRONMENTAL EVIDENCE

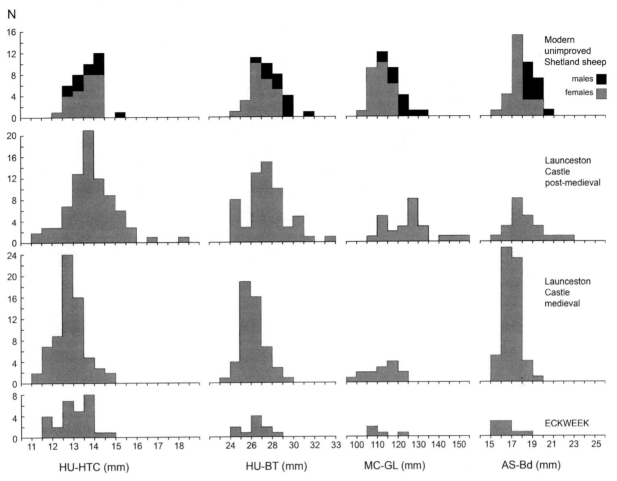

FIGURE 5.80

Measurements, in millimetres, of sheep bones from Eckweek compared to modern unimproved Shetland sheep in the Ancient Monuments Laboratory (Davis, 2000; now in Portsmouth; above), and sheep from medieval and post-medieval levels at Launceston Castle, Cornwall (Albarella and Davis 1996)

The increase in size of the Launceston sheep between medieval and post-medieval times probably reflects agricultural improvements in England at that time (Albarella and Davis 1996; Davis and Beckett 1999). Each small rectangle represents a single specimen. The plots are the minimum diameter of the humerus trochlea (HU-HTC), the humerus trochlea width (HU-BT), the length of the metacarpal (fused specimens only; MC-GL) and the distal width of the astragalus (AS-Bd). These stacked histograms show that the Eckweek sheep were small in comparison to the modern unimproved Shetland sheep – a small breed – and were of similar size to the sheep from medieval Launceston, and of course smaller than those from post-medieval times. The Eckweek sheep were presumably an unimproved variety.

in the earlier phase, exhibit small 'v' shaped notches on the lateral sides at the base of their crowns.

This abnormal pattern of wear is said to be due to long grass, perhaps associated with abrasive soil, being drawn between the teeth during grazing (Miles and Grigson 1990, 494–495). A single case (out of 19) was observed of a cattle M_3 with absent third pillar (hypoconulid).

Conclusions and Summary

Most of the large mammal remains found at Eckweek derive from animals killed locally. Beef and mutton were the main sources of meat during the 10th to 15th centuries. The remains of sheep and cattle suggest a 'producer' rather than a 'consumer' economy. Some pork, rabbit, chicken and goose were also eaten. The absence of wild game such as deer may reflect the low status of the people who inhabited Eckweek.

In terms of their dimensions, the sheep bones from Eckweek are probably typical Saxon/medieval sheep and slightly smaller than modern unimproved Shetland sheep – a small traditional breed. They were also very similar in size to the medieval ones from Launceston Castle in Cornwall and smaller than those from the post-medieval ones there. Clearly they were unimproved sheep and perhaps typical in terms of their size to the sheep found in England before the agricultural improvements that probably began in the 14th and subsequent centuries (Albarella and Davis 1996; Davis and Becket 1999; Thomas 2005).

Acknowledgements

I am grateful to Sebastian Payne and Caroline Grigson who both offered advice, and to Andrew Jones for identifying the fish bones. Both Matilda Holmes and Umberto Albarella kindly sent me copies of their unpublished regional reviews.

5.14 CHARRED PLANT REMAINS
by Wendy Carruthers (1995, updated 2015)

Introduction

Relatively few rural medieval sites in Britain have been studied in detail for charred plant remains. Although more rural sites have been investigated in recent years, there are still very few sites where an extensive sampling programme has been put in place and a high percentage of the samples has been fully analysed. The well-preserved site at Eckweek provided a valuable opportunity to examine charred plant remains from several centuries of rural occupation.

Methodology

Bulk soil samples were taken for analysis from selected features including ditches, drains, floor surfaces, pits, postholes and hearths. The samples were wet-sieved by Eckweek project staff using a 250 micron meshed sieve to recover the flot. Residues were sieved to 500 microns and stored dry.

The residues were sorted by eye by Eckweek project staff for environmental remains and artefacts. Further soil samples from the 1990 season of excavation were processed and sorted by A. al Azm at the Ancient Monuments Laboratory. In some cases it was necessary to use hydrogen peroxide to assist in the disaggregation. The flots were sorted by the author using a binocular microscope at ×10 to ×50 magnifications.

A total of 57 samples were analysed for this report. Identification and analysis were carried out by the author using the Ancient Monuments Laboratory and the author's own reference collections. On the recovery of a few calcium phosphate replaced (Green 1979) plant remains from one of the drains, further microscopic sorting of residues from drain samples was carried out. This produced virtually no additional plant remains but numerous small mammal bones which are discussed (Section 5.13, Davis this volume).

Results

Figure 5.81 lists the percentage compositions of the 24 richest charred plant assemblages (>80 fragments). Figure 5.82 presents a summarised species list by ceramic period. Figure 5.84 illustrates the proportions of charred medieval plant remains by type and ceramic phase. Full details for each sample (including sample sizes) are presented in the archive report (Carruthers 1995). Nomenclature and habitat information follows Stace (2010) for wild plants and Zohary and Hopf (2000) for cereals.

The large grain deposit, context 359, was sorted in its entirety for weed seeds, chaff fragments and cereals other than wheat. Small fragments of wheat were sieved off and poorly preserved indeterminate grains were separated out. The various categories of cereal and indeterminate cereal were then counted using a seed counter.

Cereal fragments were roughly quantified as approximate numbers of whole grains by adding fragments together in order to make data analysis as accurate as possible. This will have produced a minimum number of grains, as many fragments were too small to sort and count.

Some Notes on Identification

a) Wheat

Both free-threshing tetraploid (*Triticum turgidum* s.l.) and hexaploid (*T. aestivum* s.l.) wheats were identified using criteria outlined by Moffet (1991) for rachis fragments. It is more difficult to distinguish between the grains of the two types of wheat as they can vary greatly in shape (Jacomet 2006). The morphology of the Eckweek wheat ranged from short and round hexaploid-type grains to more oval, narrow but 'hump-backed' tetraploid-types. The best preserved wheat grains were initially recorded as *Triticum* c.f. *turgidum/durum* or *T.* cf. *aestivocompactum* in the full species list in the archive report (Carruthers 1995, table 3) but the information has not been presented in this publication as grain identification is unreliable (Jacomet 2006) and it is not known whether one of the two types is more prone to distortion than the other, making the counts of well-preserved grains unrepresentative. Considering the difference in breadmaking qualities for the wheats (rivet wheat is a soft, mealy grain whilst bread wheat has a high gluten content and so is more suitable for making bread), differential distortion and fragmentation of grains is a distinct possibility. Identification of the grain has, therefore, been left at the level of genus for this report. In addition, as figure 1 in the archive report (Carruthers 1995, fig. 1) shows (y axis = breadth/length; x axis = thickness/length for 100 wheat grains), a complete range of intermediate forms between the two extremes occurs (Jacomet 2006). The dimensions used for archive figure 1 were taken from the best preserved, least distorted caryopses. It is unfortunate that the numbers of rachis fragments recovered was not greater over the six phases sampled, as these would have provided much more secure estimates as to the relative proportions of wheats grown.

Although rivet (*T. turgidum* L.) and hard wheat (*T. durum* Desf.) cannot be separated morphologically, it is most likely that rivet wheat was the species present, since it is the hardier of the two and is known to have been cultivated in Britain from documentary evidence (eg Tusser 1580).

The separation of bread wheat (*T. aestivum* L.) from club wheat (*T. compactum* Host.) by differences

Context	Feature	% Cereals	% Chaff	% Weed seeds	% Legumes	% Other	Total frags
PHASE 2							
338	pit 339	72	0	25	2	0	464
3042	pit 3009	86	4	7	3	0	216
3062	pit 3061	85	7	6	1	1	1175
3108	pit 3080	94	<1	2	4	0	547
3140	pit 3082	89	4	1	6	0	94
PHASE 3							
149	pit 179	81	0	12	4	3	182
236	pit 234	82	0	13	4	1	360
265	pit 266	92	0	2	5	1	88
291	pit 299	89	2	2	7	<1	272
318	pit 319	43	1	52★	4	0	653
341	pit 319	78	<1	16	4	2	275
354	pit 319	70	0	14	12	4	121
359	pit 357	87	6	5	2	<1	10305
3087	pit 3088	83	0	10	7	0	91
3135	pit 3088	91	3	5	1	0	156
3143	pit 3094	83	2	6	9	0	882
PHASE 4							
127	ditch 258	93	0	2	4	1	225
170	gully 387	77	1	15	5	2	1850
230	pit 223	88	<1	8	3	1	450
340	pit 327	85	<1	5	9	1	1014
347	pit 346	95	<1	<1	3	2	301
PHASE 5							
220	pit 221	89	1	5	3	2	180
237	pit 221	88	6	2	2	2	1579
285	occupation layer	85	1	10	3	1	363

FIGURE 5.81

The percentage compositions of the 24 richest medieval charred plant assemblages (> 80 fragments)

in rachis internode length is not always possible (Jacomet 2006), so the identification of free-threshing hexaploid wheat has been has been left at *T. aestivum* s.l. which includes club wheat. As most of the grains were large and rounded and there were no very short grains or very short wheat rachis internodes present bread wheat was most likely to have been cultivated at Eckweek.

b) Barley

From the small quantity of barley grains recovered it is clear that six-row hulled barley (*Hordeum vulgare* ssp. *vulgare*) was present, as some twisted lateral grains were recovered. It is possible that some of the barley was two-rowed, but this could not be confirmed. Some of the grains were notably large and straight.

c) Oats

It is not possible to be certain that oats were grown as a crop at Eckweek, as the few remains still possessing identifiable floret bases were of the wild oat type (*Avena fatua* L.) with 'suckermouth' scars. However, a couple of samples produced oats in high enough numbers to suggest that they may have been grown as a crop (context 359 CP3 and context 170 CP4).

d) Rye

Grains of rye (*Secale cereale*) can be difficult to distinguish from distorted wheat grains, but rye was positively identified from a few rachis fragments and well preserved grains. However, as the quantities were very low it is likely that this cereal was growing as a minor crop or weed. Rye is a useful fodder catch-crop, so it may have been grazed off whilst still green in spring. It can also be used as a green manure if ploughed back into the soil in spring.

e) Vetches

In the species table (Figure 5.82), leguminous taxa have only been identified to species level where hila were present, apart from field bean (*Vicia faba*) which can often be identified even when an incomplete bean is found due to its large size and distinctive morphology.

Leguminous seeds were frequent in the medieval assemblages, but they rarely possessed well-preserved hila which are needed in order to identify them to species level. For the archive report the diameters of the best preserved legumes by phase were plotted with seeds identified to species level shaded on the graph (Carruthers 1995, fig. 2). Most of the legumes retaining hila were identified as common vetch (*Vicia sativa* L.) and at least some are likely to have been the cultivated subspecies, *V. sativa* subsp. *Sativa*, as the diameters ranged from 2.7–4.2mm. Allowing at least 10% for shrinkage due to charring several seeds fall within the 4.5–7mm size range given for cultivated vetch in Zohary and Hopf (2000, 118). For example, in ceramic phase 3 16% of the measured seeds were over 4mm in diameter (4.5mm minimum reduced by 10% to take into account shrinkage following charring). Almost all of the vetch-rich samples came from ceramic phases 3 and 4.

Where 'legumes' are discussed in the report, and listed in Figure 5.81, only *Vicia/Lathyrus* sp., *Vicia/Lathyrus/Pisum* sp. fragments and peas and beans are included (i.e. items most likely to be cultivated crops) and not small-seeded weeds such as clovers and medick.

Discussion

Iron Age

As only a small amount of charred material was recovered from the two Iron Age ditch samples, the remains are of little interpretive value. Indeterminate wheat (*Triticum* sp.) and hulled barley (*Hordeum* sp.) were the cereals represented, and a few typical arable and disturbed ground weed seeds were present; (fat hen (*Chenopodium album*), clover-type (*Trifolium/Medicago/Lotus* sp.), knotgrass (*Polygonum aviculare*), dock (*Rumex* sp.) and black bindweed (*Fallopia convolvulus*). All of the Iron Age weed taxa were also found in the medieval samples, with the exception of fat hen, which is a common nitrophilous weed of disturbed and cultivated soils.

Medieval (Figure 5.84)

Preservation and Distribution Across the Site

The relatively undisturbed nature of the site at Eckweek meant that fairly large assemblages of charred plant remains were recovered from the samples, which were less likely to have been affected by post-depositional differential preservation. Only two of the 60 samples originally examined contained no charred plant remains at all. The fact that the remains were not always well-preserved is more likely to be a reflection on the conditions under which they became charred and moisture content of the grain, rather than weathering. Many of the cereal grains were puffed and distorted, indicating high temperature charring. However, damage due to redeposition and trampling at the time of occupation needs to be taken into account when considering the composition of the assemblages. In addition, differential preservation may have occurred at the time of burning, ie some of the more delicate plant remains may have been destroyed, as will be discussed later.

A single buttercup (*Ranunculus acris/bulbosus/repens*) achene was found to be mineralised by calcium phosphate replacement. Calcium phosphate mineralisation occurs in deposits which are highly organic and contain high concentrations of minerals, for example cess pits and middens (Green 1979), particularly in calcareous areas. The recovery of the seed from the fill of drain 71 which ran below the farmhouse (structure 460) indicates the organic nature of the waste present in the drain and the damp conditions. Davis (Section 5.13) identified large numbers of small mammal bones from this feature which he suggested probably originated in owl pellets from birds roosting in the roofs; these would have been a further source of phosphates.

AREA A

Most of the samples examined for this report came from Area A (42 out of 55). In this area several timber structures were identified dating from the 10th and 11th centuries, including a small possible 10th-century dwelling and a substantial 11th-century timber farmhouse (Building 467; Period III). Samples related to these periods of occupation are recorded in the summarised species table (Figure 5.82) under ceramic phases 2 to 4. The following phases of activity involved the replacement of the timber farmhouse with new stone buildings (Period IV; *c*AD 1200–1275), and in the later medieval period (Period V; *c*AD 1275–1400) major rebuilding of the stone buildings took place. Samples from these later medieval activities are listed in the table under ceramic phases 5 and 6.

For the archive report (Carruthers 1995) distribution maps were drawn in an attempt to determine whether specific activity areas could be observed. Cereal grains were mapped separately from chaff fragments and weed seeds, and from legumes, using standardised data consisting of 'seeds (or chaff fragments) per litre of soil processed'.

The main findings with regard to distribution were as follows:

– In the earlier ceramic phases (CP2 and CP3) the richest samples were recovered from a group

FIGURE 5.82 (OPPOSITE)

Charred plant species list by period and medieval ceramic phase
[ ] = mineralised; no brackets = charred: HABITAT / SOILS KEY: A=arable; C=cultivated; D=disturbed; E=heath; F=fen; G=grassland; H=hedgerow; M=marsh; P=pond; S=scrub; W=woods; Y=wayside; a=acidic; b=shady; c=calcareous; d=dry; h=heavy; l=light; o=open; s=sandy; w=wet/damp

	Habitat preferences	IA	CP1	CP2	CP3	CP4	CP5	CP6
GRAIN								
Triticum aestivum/turgidum (free-threshing wheat grain)		.	1	1233	6880	1967	1638	81
Triticum sp. (indeterminate wheat grain)		2	.	.	.	.	.	.
Hordeum vulgare L. (six row hulled barley grain)		.	.	17	34	7	.	.
Hordeum sp. (barley grain)		5	.	71	378	46	9	4
Avena fatua L. (wild oat floret)		.	.	.	3	1	.	.
Avena sp. (wild/cultivated oat grain)		.	.	43	225	135	10	7
Avena/Bromus sp. (oat/brome grassgrain)		.	.	81	219	120	.	.
Secale cereale L. (rye grain)		.	.	.	7	.	.	.
Secale cereale/Triticum sp. (rye/wheat grain)		.	.	.	5	.	.	.
Indeterminate cereal grains		2	4	990	3860	901	332	79
CHAFF								
Triticum aestivum-type (bread-type wheat rachis frag.)		.	.	3	27	1	10	.
Triticum turgium-type (rivet-type wheat rachis frag.)		.	.	2	20	1	53	.
Triticum aestivum/turgidum (free-threshing wheat rachis frag.)		.	.	55	300	10	23	.
Hordeum sp. (barley rachis frag.)		.	.	5	45	.	.	.
Avena sp. (oat awn frags)		.	.	.	+	+	.	.
Secale cereale L. (rye rachis frag.)		.	.	.	5	.	.	.
indeterminate rachis frag.		.	.	.	125	.	.	.
cereal-sized culm node		.	.	32	84	9	9	1
cereal-sized culm base		.	.	4	8	.	.	.
LEGUMES, FRUITS & NUTS								
cf. *Lens esculenta* Moench. (cf. lentil)		.	.	.	2	.	.	.
Pisum sativum L. (pea)		.	.	.	1	.	.	.
Vicia faba (field bean)		.	.	1	.	4	.	.
Vicia sativa cf. subsp. *sativa* (cf. cultivated vetch seed)		.	.	.	15	9	.	.
Vicia/Lathyrus/Pisum sp. (vetch/tare/pea)		.	.	83	423	212	49	3
Prunus spinosa (sloe stone) HSW		.	.	.	2	.	.	6
Prunus domestica subsp. *domestica* (plum stone)		.	.	1	.	.	.	.
Prunus sp. (sloe/cherry/plum stone frag)		.	.	.	.	2	.	1
Crataegus monogyna Jacq. (hawthorn fruit stone) HSW		.	.	.	.	.	.	3
Rubus sect. *Glandulosus* (bramble seed) DHSW★		.	.	.	.	.	.	1
Corylus avellana L. (hazelnut shell frag.) HSW		.	.	10	33	62	37	4
Sambucus nigra L. (elder seed) DHSW		.	.	1	.	.	.	.
WEEDS & WILD PLANTS								
Fumaria sp. (fumitory achene)	CD	.	.	.	1	.	.	1[1]
Ranunculus acris/bulbosus/repens (buttercup achene)	DG	.	.	.	1	.	.	.
Medicago lupulina L. (black medick fruit)	DG	.	.	.	.	.	.	6
Medicago/Trifolium/Lotus sp. (medick/clover/trefoil seed)	GD	.	.	.	.	8	2	3
Lathyrus nissolia L. (grass vetchling seed)	G	.	.	.	.	1	.	.
cf. *Sorbus* sp. (whitebeam seed)		.	.	.	.	2	.	.
Potentilla anserina L. (silverweed achene)	DGYo	.	.	.	.	.	1	.
Potentilla sp. (cinquefoil achene)	DGY	.	.	.	.	1	.	.
Aphanes arvensis L. (parsley piert achene)	Co	.	.	.	.	1	.	.
Viola sp. (violet seed)	GEWSH	.	.	.	5	1	1	1
Linum catharticum L. (fairy flax seed)	Gdcs	.	.	1	.	.	.	.
Brassica/Sinapis sp. (mustard, turnip, charlock etc.)	CD	.	.	.	7	14	2	.
Brassica/Sinapis sp. (charlock etc. siliqua frag.)	CD	.	.	.	2	.	.	.
Alliaria petiolata (M. Bieb.) Cavara & Grande	DHb	.	.	1	.	.	.	.
Polygonum aviculare (knotgrass achene)	CD	1	.	2	9	4	1	.
Fallopia convolvulus (L.) A. Love (black bindweed achene)	CD	1	.	3	9	.	.	.
Rumex acetosella L. (sheep's sorrel achene)	EoGCas	.	.	.	.	3	.	.
Rumex sp. (dock achene)	CDG	1	.	20	38	7	2	.
Stellaria media (L.) Vill. (common chickweed seed)	Cno	.	.	.	1	.	.	.
Silene cf. *vulgaris* Garke (cf. bladder campion seed)	Gdo	.	.	.	.	.	1	.
Silene dioica (L.) Clairv. (red campion seed)	HWb	.	.	.	3	.	.	.
Silene latifolia Poir. (white campion seed)	CDYol	.	.	.	1	.	.	.
Agrostemma githago L. (corn cockle seed)	A	.	.	.	8	.	.	.
Chenopodium album L. (fat-hen seed)	CDn	.	.	.	.	.	.	.
Atriplex patula/prostrata (orache seed)	CDn	.	.	.	.	.	.	.
Chenopodiaceae embryo	CD	2	.	.	.	.	.	.
Anagallis arvensis L. (scarlet pimpernel)	Ado	.	.	.	2	1	.	1
Sherardia arvensis L. (field madder nutlet)	AD	.	.	1	6	1	.	.
Galium cf. *verum* L. (cf. lady's bedstraw nutlet)	Gcd	.	.	.	.	1	.	.
Galium aparine L. (cleavers nutlet)	CDSH	.	.	1	19	2	1	.
Galium sp. (cleavers nutlet frag.)	CDGH	.	.	.	1	1	.	1
Plantago lanceolata L. (ribwort plantain seed)	Go	.	.	.	.	.	.	.
Odontites vernus/Euphrasia sp. (red bartsia/eyebright seed)	ADG	.	.	60	347	15	13	.
Rhinanthus sp. (yellow-rattle seed)	G	.	.	1	.	13	.	2
Carduus/Cirsium sp. (thistle achene)	GDY	.	.	.	.	.	1	.
Centaurea cf. *nigra* L. (cf. lesser knapweed achene)	GY	.	.	.	3	1	1	.
Lapsana communis L. (nipplewort achene)	DHWo	.	.	2	4	.	.	.
Crepis capillaris (L.) Wallr. (smooth hawk's beard achene)	DG	.	.	.	1	.	.	.
Anthemis cotula L. (stinking chamomile achene)	Ahw	.	.	12	55	32	20	8
Valerianella dentata (L.) Pollich. (narrow-fruited corn-salad fruit)	AD	.	.	.	1	12	.	.
Knautia arvensis (L.) Coult. (field scabious achene)	Gdl	.	.	1	10	4	1	.
Scandix pecten-veneris L. (shepherd's needle mericarp)	AD	.	.	4	10	2	.	.
Berula erecta (Huds.) Coville (lesser water-parsnip mericarp)	FMc	.	.	.	1	.	.	.
Aethusa cynapium L. (fool's parsley mericarp)	CD	.	.	.	.	1	.	.
Bupleurum rotundifolium L. (thorow-wax mericarp)	Ac	.	.	6	10	17	1	.
Daucus carota L. (carrot mericarp)	Gc	.	.	.	.	1	.	.
Carex sp. (trigonous sedge nutlet)	MPw	.	.	1	1	1	.	.
Cladium mariscus (L.) Pohl (great fen-sedge)	FP	.	.	.	.	.	1	.
Lolium temulentum L. (darnel)	AD	.	.	.	20	21	1	.
Lolium perenne/rigidum (rye-grass caryopsis)	GD	.	.	12	78	16	6	1
Arrhenatherum elatius var. *bulbosum* (Willd.) St-Amans (onion couch tuber)	G	.	.	.	.	1	.	.
Bromus sect. *Bromus* (brome grass caryopsis)	AD	.	.	25	61	5	11	5
Poaceae (indeterminate grass seed)	CDG	.	.	14	77	42	15	6
TOTAL		18	5	2718	13521	3723	2254	237
total number of samples		2	1	15	14	7	8	13
volume of soil processed		8.6	6	146	207.3	116	50	138.25
charred fragments per litre (all samples)		2	1	19	65	32	45	2

of pits located towards the southern end of the Area A trench.
- In the later ceramic phases (CP4 and CP5) the few rich samples came from pits, a spread and a gully within or next to the stone farmhouse in the north of the trench. No rich samples were dated to CP6, even though nine samples from this phase were examined.

The three rich CP2 and CP3 pits in a group consisted of Pit 339 (CP2) containing primarily free-threshing wheat grains (*Triticum aestivum/turgidum*-type) with some barley (*Hordeum* sp.), oat grains (*Avena* sp.) and a range of weed seeds; Pit 357 (CP3) containing nearly 9000 grains (mainly free-threshing wheat with barley and oats), the highest number of chaff fragments from the site and a wide range of weed taxa, and Pit 319 (CP3) which produced fairly clean deposits of free-threshing wheat with some barley, very little chaff and few weed seeds. In ceramic phases 4 and 5 the large Pit 221 at the eastern end of building 460, an occupation deposit under the wall of the building (context 285, 308 grains) and the primary fill of Gully 171 (context 170, CP4) produced large quantities of free-threshing wheat with quite a few oats (only *Avena fatua* confirmed from one complete floret) and some barley. It is unlikely that all of the 117 unidentified oats were wild oats as the percentage composition of this sample was 85% wheat, 13% oats and 2% barley. It is possible that grain for both human and livestock consumption was represented in this sample, as well as some hay, as yellow rattle seeds (*Rhinanthus* sp.) were common. Samples from ceramic phase 6 generally contained much smaller amounts of charred cereal remains (Figure 5.83).

None of the samples produced high concentrations of chaff fragments or weed seeds to indicate that cereal processing waste had been deposited. Chaff fragments (primarily rachis fragments with occasional straw 'joints' (culm nodes) and culm bases never made up more than 7% of the assemblage and weed seeds only reached an 'abundant' level in one sample that contained many small seeds of red bartsia/eyebright (*Odontites verna/Euphrasia* sp.). Very small seeds such as this can accumulate in the deposit by trickling down through the soil. A moderate range of common weeds of cultivated and disturbed soils was present (such as brome (*Bromus* sp.), vetch/tare (*Vicia/Lathyrus* sp., corn cockle (*Agrostemma githago*) and stinking chamomile (*Anthemis cotula*)), in addition to some taxa more characteristic of grasslands and hay meadows (such as purging flax (*Linum catharticum*) and yellow rattle (*Rhinanthus* sp.)). The latter suggest that waste hay may have been present amongst the assemblages, as described below. Vetches comprised 1%–12% of the assemblages, but were generally around 4% in most of the samples.

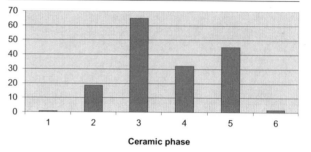

No. of samples	Ceramic phase	Average charred frags per litre by ceramic phase
1	1	0.8
15	2	18.6
15	3	65.2
6	4	32.1
7	5	45.1
9	6	1.7

FIGURE 5.83
Charred plant remains count by medieval ceramic phase

No obvious distribution pattern for these waste components emerged from the spatial analysis undertaken for the archive report (Carruthers 1995).

AREA H

During the early 11th century a substantial timber building was erected in Area H, although the building was only occupied in Period III, ceramic phases 2 and 3. The samples from features in Area H were as uniform in content as those in Area A, and as in Area A, cereals were the principal component, with larger quantities of chaff, weed seeds and legumes mainly occurring where the total assemblages were large (Figure 5.84). No obvious pattern emerged from the 1995 distribution plots but two CP2 pits and one CP3 pit contained high concentrations of charred plant remains. Pits 3061 (CP2; 47 frags per litre (fpl)), 3080 (CP2; 182 fpl) and 3049 (CP3; 220.5 fpl) in Area H contained fairly large assemblages, the latter including a relatively high concentration of cultivated vetch seeds.

Distribution Through the Phases

Although there is some variation in the numbers of samples analysed per ceramic phase and in the sizes of soil samples (Figure 5.82), the standardised data in Figure 5.83 shows that significant differences occurred in the levels of activity through time, if concentrations of charred cereal remains are accepted as a valid measure of arable activity. As only ceramic phases 2 to 5 are reasonably well represented, the main change is the drop off in activity in CP6. As noted above, there are a number of possible reasons for changes in concentrations of charred plant remains, but as the settlement in Area A was abandoned around this time the reduced evidence from charred plant remains presumably demonstrates a drop off in arable production. The dip in

ARTEFACTS AND ENVIRONMENTAL EVIDENCE

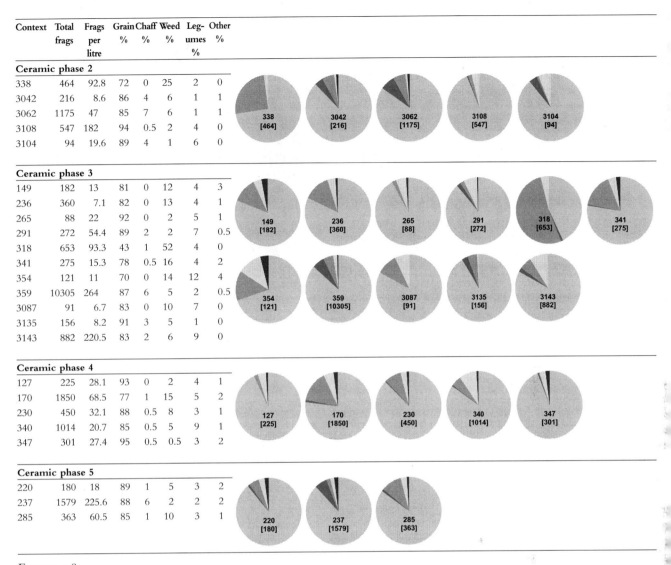

Context	Total frags	Frags per litre	Grain %	Chaff %	Weed %	Legumes %	Other %
Ceramic phase 2							
338	464	92.8	72	0	25	2	0
3042	216	8.6	86	4	6	1	1
3062	1175	47	85	7	6	1	1
3108	547	182	94	0.5	2	4	0
3104	94	19.6	89	4	1	6	0
Ceramic phase 3							
149	182	13	81	0	12	4	3
236	360	7.1	82	0	13	4	1
265	88	22	92	0	2	5	1
291	272	54.4	89	2	2	7	0.5
318	653	93.3	43	1	52	4	0
341	275	15.3	78	0.5	16	4	2
354	121	11	70	0	14	12	4
359	10305	264	87	6	5	2	0.5
3087	91	6.7	83	0	10	7	0
3135	156	8.2	91	3	5	1	0
3143	882	220.5	83	2	6	9	0
Ceramic phase 4							
127	225	28.1	93	0	2	4	1
170	1850	68.5	77	1	15	5	2
230	450	32.1	88	0.5	8	3	1
340	1014	20.7	85	0.5	5	9	1
347	301	27.4	95	0.5	0.5	3	2
Ceramic phase 5							
220	180	18	89	1	5	3	2
237	1579	225.6	88	6	2	2	2
285	363	60.5	85	1	10	3	1

FIGURE 5.84

The proportions of charred medieval plant remains by type and ceramic phase

concentrations of charred cereal remains in CP4 could indicate a slight change in the arable/pastoral balance towards increased livestock rearing, since the percentage of oats increased and a wider range of grassland taxa was found in the samples, including meadow vetchling (*Lathyrus nissolia*), cf. lady's bedstraw (*Galium* cf. *verum*), cinquefoil (*Potentilla* sp.), yellow rattle (*Rhinanthus* sp.), carrot (*Daucus carota*), onion couch (*Arrhenatherum elatius* var. *bulbosum*) and sheep's sorrel (*Rumex acetosella*). Onion couch often grows in abandoned arable fields that have been returned to pasture. Sheep's sorrel and several of the cinquefoil species are more characteristic of heaths and acid pastures than calcareous soils, so it would appear that hay was being brought in from further afield.

The record for Eckweek in the Domesday Book states that the settlement lacked both pasture and meadow (Welldon Finn 1973). This may have continued to be the case in later years, since in the 14th century the residents rented a meadow at Oxenham some 2km southeast of Eckweek (Shorrocks 1974, 189). As the soils for several miles around Eckweek are primarily well-drained and calcareous it is not possible to determine how far the occupants had to go to find hay and grazing. Davis (Section 5.13) notes the high occurrence of sheep, particularly older animals, so it may be that the renting of extra grazing related to an increase in wool production.

The increase in grassland taxa amongst the cereal remains in CP4 could also be due to the adoption of crop rotation involving long periods of fallow. In addition, increases in the cultivation of oats as a fodder crop at the expense of barley are sometimes seen as an indicator of the change from using oxen to using horses for ploughing. These suggestions remain very tentative as there was no evidence of such changes from the bone assemblage (Section 5.13, Davis this volume).

Crop Plants

A) CEREALS

Tetraploid (probably rivet) and hexaploid (bread wheat-type) free-threshing wheats were the predominant cereals in all of the samples examined. Wheat grains were also the most numerous component of almost all of the assemblages, with only one or two having a few more weed seeds or indeterminate grains. These facts are unusual on a site, but even more so considering that the occupation spans three centuries. It is interesting to note that the faunal remains indicated that there was also very little change in the species and the relative proportions of animals consumed over the periods studied (Section 5.13).

As discussed earlier, it was not possible to determine what the relative proportions of the two wheats were, although where identifiable rachis fragments were present roughly equal amounts of rivet wheat-type and bread wheat-type were recorded in ceramic phases 2 to 4. One ceramic phase 5 sample (context 237) contained a large quantity of rachis fragments which were predominately rivet-type, but as the other samples in this phase contained little, if any, chaff it is not possible to know whether this sample was representative of the phase as a whole.

It is unfortunate that wheat grains cannot be identified to species level (Jacomet 2006), as changes in the cultivation of the two cereals would be informative because they have different growing requirements, growth forms and baking qualities. From the archaeobotanical evidence, bread wheat has previously been considered to have been the major wheat grown from the Saxon period onwards across much of the British Isles. However, over the past two decades increasing evidence for the cultivation of rivet-type wheat has been recovered from medieval sites in Britain (Moffet 1991).

Documentary sources suggest that rivet wheat was at one time the primary wheat grown in southern England (Woodward & Luff 1983). It is a late maturing cereal which grows on a long straw ideal for thatching. Being an awned wheat it is not so readily attacked by sparrows, and according to Percival (1948) it is also 'highly resistant to rust, smut and bunt diseases'. The grain is soft and mealy and so would produce a rather dense bread in comparison with bread wheat. Percival (1948) suggests that rivet wheat is suitable for biscuit making but can also be mixed with the flour of bread wheats for baking. It is possible that by growing both wheats farmers would have been 'hedging their bets' against pests and diseases. If grown as separate crops the different grains could be kept for the specific culinary purposes to which they are best suited, or if grown as a maslin the flour would be of mixed quality.

Barley, oats and rye were recovered in small quantities from most of the samples. It is likely, therefore, that these cereals were only growing as minor crops, or as relict crops or weeds amongst the wheat, particularly in the case of oats where the only identifiable florets were of wild oat. However, as noted earlier, slightly larger amounts of oats were recovered from the CP3 samples which may indicate cultivation as a minor crop. Rye was only recovered as a few grains in two CP3 samples so was probably a contaminant or was maybe grown as a forage crop, ie grazed from the field when young.

There is no evidence to suggest that barley was a major crop at any point, as the quantities recovered were of similar magnitude to those of oats and no samples were dominated by barley. This is unexpected as the local calcareous soils would have been well-suited to growing barley, but taphonomy could be one explanation. If barley was primarily used for fodder it would not have undergone parching to remove the husk and so would have been less likely to have become charred. Vetch seeds (*Vicia/Lathyrus* sp. including *Vicia sativa*) occurred at a similar or slightly higher rate than barley grains in most of the samples. Vetch was almost certainly a fodder crop, although it may have been used for human consumption in times of famine. Vetches also do not require exposure to fire during the processing, but (as with barley used for fodder) charring may have occurred through the burning of waste bedding and spoilt crops. The vetches may also have been growing as a relict crop amongst cereals under a crop rotation system. Being legumes, vetches are particularly valued in crop rotations or as a green manure, since they possess root nodules containing nitrogen-fixing bacteria which help to restore fertility to impoverished soils. However, it is difficult to determine from archaeobotanical evidence whether crop rotation was being practised at Eckweek. Documentary evidence can be more helpful. 14th century title deeds (Shorrocks 1974) describe a two field system at Eckweek, West field and East field. One of the furlongs was called Langebrech, a name that suggests newly cleared ground. Unfortunately, there was insufficient data from the CP6 samples to investigate the suggestion of expansion, but no new weed taxa were present in the CP6 samples to indicate the ploughing up of a different soil type.

It is likely that small amounts of barley, vetches and forage crops provided all of the fodder required, in addition to being of value in a crop rotation system. Barley and vetch could have been grown as a maslin (mixed crop), although there was no clear evidence for this suggestion. Wheat would have been the preferred cereal for human consumption, and by growing two types of wheat all of the culinary and thatching requirements were met. There is documentary evidence to support the cultivation of barley at Eckweek in the later medieval period. Three title deeds of the 14th century (Shorrocks 1974) describe a two field system which includes a furlong named as *berforlong* (barley furlong). Perhaps the cultivation of barley was limited enough to warrant this specific naming. Unfortunately, the quantity of charred plant macrofossil data was low in the 14th century samples (CP6), so it is uncertain whether the remains are truly representative of the range of crops grown at this time.

B) LEGUMES

The recovery of leguminous seeds from 75% of the samples, amounting to *c*4% of the total remains indicates that legumes were an important crop for the medieval settlement. There was evidence for common vetch (*Vicia sativa*), pea (*Pisum sativum*) and field bean (*Vicia faba*), and two possible lentils (cf. *Lens esculenta*) were present in a CP3 sample. There is little firm evidence for the cultivation of lentils as a crop in this country during the medieval period. However, one or two seeds have been recovered from a number of medieval sites, for example Higham Ferrers, Northants (Moffett 2007), Dean Court Farm, Oxon (Moffett 1987) and Newbury, Berks (Carruthers 1997a). A 19th-century reference from Oxfordshire (Young 1813) mentions the growing of a small acreage of this pulse as hay for ewes, so lentils appear to have been grown on a small scale in medieval times.

Vetch was recovered from all ceramic phases, although it was only identified to species level in ceramic phases 3 and 4. A single pea was identified in a ceramic phase 3 sample, but is likely that many of the less well preserved large legume fragments from other phases were also peas. A few field beans were present in ceramic phase 2 and 4 samples. As mentioned earlier, it should be remembered that legumes are likely to be under-represented in a charred assemblage through their lack of contact with fire. Peas and beans may have been grown on a garden scale, although there is a documentary record for Eckweek from the 13th century of a grant of corn and beans to the hospital of St. John the Baptist in Bath (A. Young pers comm) which suggests that beans were a major crop.

Documentary records for the cultivation of vetches are frequent from the 13th century onwards (Currie 1988). Archaeobotanical evidence for cultivated vetch has been recovered from several rural sites including a peasant village at Burton Dassett (Moffett unpublished 1991), a grange farm at Dean Court Farm (Moffett unpublished 1987) and a 13th-century farmstead at Roundwood, Stansted (Murphy 2004). In an urban context, two deposits of charred vetch seeds were recovered from the waterfront at Reading Abbey (Carruthers 1997b). Considering the preservation biases mentioned earlier, it is clear that vetches were an important component of the medieval rural economy.

C) OTHER POSSIBLE FOOD PLANTS

Charred seed assemblages are largely derived from the processing and use of cereals and so are not often a good source of evidence for other dietary components, such as herbs, spices, fruit and vegetables. However, burnt domestic refuse may contain the remains of fruit and nuts. In the case of wild taxa it is not possible to be certain that they had been deliberately gathered and consumed, rather than accidentally burnt amongst firewood, but it seems likely that all of the local natural resources would have been fully exploited, particularly as there was no evidence that the occupants could afford to buy imported exotic fruits such as are common in urban assemblages of the same period.

The remains of wild fruits such as elderberry (*Sambucus nigra*), hawthorn (*Crataegus monogyna*), sloe (*Prunus spinosa*) and blackberry (*Rubus* sect *Glandulosus*) were recovered in small quantities from a few of the samples. These fruits can be used for dyeing as well as for culinary purposes. The hawthorn and blackberry seeds, however, had probably been burnt amongst fuel in the ?kiln (structure 466), as they were recovered from charcoal spreads within and alongside this structure. Hazel nut shell fragments (*Corylus avellana*) were present in low numbers in a high proportion of the samples (27 out of 57 samples) indicating that nuts were commonly consumed. A possible fruit of cf. *Sorbus* sp. (includes rowan, whitebeam, service tree) was recovered from a large pit of ceramic phase 3 (feature 324). Mabey (1972) notes that some *Sorbus* fruits are edible if they are first allowed to blet' (rot) and Mears and Hillman (2007) suggest that it is safer to eat wild service fruits (*Sorbus torminalis*) if they are pounded to a pulp, left to dry and roasted. All of these fruits and nuts are likely to have been readily available in hedgerows and open woodlands.

The only evidence for cultivated fruits was a single large plum stone (*Prunus domestica* subsp. *domestica*) which was recovered from a CP2 pit (feature 3115). It is possible that the farmstead had its own plum tree, or the fruits may have been bought at market as an occasional treat. It is difficult to assess the importance and range of non-cereal foodstuffs from a charred assemblage, but as primarily wild fruit and nut remains were recovered, it appears that imported luxury goods, such as grapes, were not a regular part of the occupants' diet. Grape pips are very common in waterlogged urban waste deposits and are quite often preserved by charring. It is interesting to note that Davis (Section 5.13) recorded surprisingly few remains of game animals and no deer bones. He suggests that this may point to the low status of the settlement at Eckweek.

It is not possible to know whether the brassica (*Brassica/Sinapis* sp.; CP3 to CP5) and carrot (*Daucus carota*; CP4) seeds were from cultivated or wild plants. As with fruits, the likelihood of evidence for vegetables being preserved by charring is remote, and even more so for plants harvested before they set seed, such as the leafy brassicas and root vegetables.

Evidence for herbs and spices is rarely preserved by charring, although urban anaerobic deposits have produced a wide range of taxa for the medieval period (Greig 1991). One record of interest in a 14th-century title deed (Shorrocks 1974) refers to the lease of Eckweek tenements and payment for one pound of cumin. Although there is no suggestion that the farmstead at Eckweek is connected with the cumin, this reference does demonstrate that imported herbs and spices were available locally to those who could afford them. Cumin seeds have not yet been recovered achaeobotanically from medieval deposits in this country to the author's knowledge, but are mentioned in medieval records from the Port of Southampton (Green 1984).

Origins of the Charred Plant Remains and Crop Processing Activities

The Eckweek charred plant assemblages are notable in their uniformity (Figure 5.85). Species composition and proportion of crop to crop processing waste (ie grains to chaff fragments and arable weed seed ratios) were remarkably constant across the site and through the phases. The fact that, for example, no samples were dominated by any cereal other than wheat and yet other cereals were present in most of the samples in small numbers, is unusual. Similarly, all of the samples were dominated by cereal grains rather than crop processing waste. This suggests that the charred remains probably represent mixed domestic waste swept up from floors and cleaned out of hearths and ovens, and that these types of debris were not subject to change through the phases of occupation. The main points to note are that the bulk of the charred waste was being purposefully deposited in the pits, rather than blowing about the site, being washed into gullies or accumulating in occupation layers. There was no evidence of large scale accidental burnings of a processed or unprocessed crop, or the deliberate burning of quantities of crop processing waste. It could be argued that rich samples such as context 359 from Pit 357 could represent an accidentally burnt processed crop that had not been completely cleaned of contaminants (c37 : 3 : 2 : 1, grain : chaff : weed seeds : legumes) but if so very similar ratios were also found in most of the other, less productive samples.

A number of factors could account for the absence of deposits rich in cereal processing waste:

1) Waste products may have been produced and stored (for the purpose of being fed to livestock) away from the dwellings and not transported to the sampled area.
2) Cereal processing waste was likely to have been a valuable asset that was not often burnt as waste or for fuel.
3) The farmsteads were well-organised and well-maintained such that charred waste did not accumulate in features other than rubbish pits.
4) Some differential preservation may have taken place during charring and burial.

1) It is likely that the initial stages of removing the grain from the straw would have occurred under

Cereal	CP2(%)	CP3(%)	CP4(%)	CP5(%)	CP6(%)	Average (%)
Wheat	90	91	91	98	88	92
Barley	7	5	3	1	4	4
Oat	3	3	6	1	8	4
Rye	0	1	0	0	0	<1
total grains	1364	7527	2156	1657	92	overall total grains =12,796

FIGURE 5.85

Cereals by percentage across the medieval ceramic phases

cover on account of the unpredictable British weather. No samples were taken from within the proposed beast house (Structure 463) which might have served as a threshing floor, but samples from the general area did not produce any greater quantities of crop processing waste.

2) and 3) For the remains to have been preserved by charring some contact with fire is required. It is unlikely that bonfires would be lit close to any of the buildings, and as no large ashy areas were observed or sampled, it is possible that burning occurred outside the area excavated. The ash would also have been a useful source of potash, so it may well have been routinely spread on the fields. However, what is more likely is that unburnt crop processing waste was a useful commodity which could be fed to livestock, used as a temper in building materials and used as tinder in household fires and ovens. Evidence for use in the farmhouse hearths and ovens is slight, with only a few cereal grains having been recovered from these structures in the latest phase of Building 460. It is likely that such features would have been regularly cleaned out. Redeposited ash from these sources may have ended up in any of the features sampled or been deposited on fields.

The proposed kiln, Structure 466, produced slightly greater concentrations of charred plant remains but these assemblages (contexts 78 and 209) were composed primarily of grain and contained no chaff fragments. The presence of hawthorn and blackberry seeds, as noted earlier, indicates that fuel is represented, but if crop processing waste was used for this purpose, very little evidence has survived. Most of the weed seeds present were grassland taxa, such as clover (*Medicago/Trifolium/Lotus* sp.), grasses (indeterminate Poaceae) and yellow rattle (*Rhinanthus* sp.). This may indicate the use of waste hay for tinder. Although some cereals were recovered from the ?kiln the quantity was not great and the material may have been burnt as waste. The charred plant remains, therefore, provide no clear evidence for use of Structure 466 as a corn drier.

4) Experimental work by Boardman and Jones (1990) has demonstrated that differential preservation of cereal remains may take place under different regimes of charring. Cereal grains are more likely to survive burning than rachis fragments, and this should be taken into account when examining the

relative proportions of each component. In addition, material cleaned out from hearths and ovens may have suffered further effects of differential preservation through the destruction of more delicate chaff fragments during redeposition. This may partially explain why arable weed seeds are often more numerous than might be expected, since many are more likely to survive redeposition than delicate chaff fragments. However, differential preservation is not likely to have caused the total destruction of chaff fragments if reasonable quantities had originally been present.

The chaff fragments recorded included rachis fragments, which are small and relatively heavy and would mostly be removed as fine sieving waste towards the end of the processing (Hillman 1981), and large, heavy culm nodes and culm bases. These latter fragments would have mostly been removed in the early stages of processing along with the straw. The fact that they were relatively frequent suggests that a mixed type of waste is present which may be partially derived from animal fodder, but could also represent burnt bedding and thatch. This suggestion is supported by the presence of hay meadow taxa such as yellow rattle and purging flax which were most likely deposited amongst burnt animal bedding or fodder. The weed seeds included both large and small seeds. The small seeds may have been sieved from the crop along with the rachis fragments in a late stage in the processing, but many of the larger weed seeds such as wild oat, brome grass and shepherd's needle, are of a similar size to the grain and would have to have been hand-picked from the crop. They may, therefore, have been charred as hand-picked waste, or as contaminants amongst the grain.

Medieval urban charred assemblages usually contain few chaff fragments although some weed seeds may be present. It is likely that free-threshing cereals would have been processed close to their point of production and transported into towns as clean grain. Some final cleaning might have been carried out in the towns, producing small quantities of chaff and weed seeds. A rural settlement, therefore, might be expected to produce more evidence of crop processing activities, particularly a farmstead. What is notable about the Eckweek assemblages, however, is their uniformity, both in species composition and wheat to chaff and weed seed ratios. None of the samples produced large quantities of chaff and arable weed seeds, but most had small quantities of both amongst the predominant component, the cereal grains. This type of charred assemblage is typical of most samples from any medieval site, urban or rural, representing the general background rubbish that is generated by settlements.

The Weed Seeds

Most of the weed and wild seeds recovered in the charred assemblages were weeds of arable and cultivated land. An examination of the arable weed assemblage can provide information concerning the types of soils cultivated and can also give an insight into crop husbandry methods.

Several of the weed taxa were characteristic of the local calcareous soils, for example thorowax (*Bupleurum rotundifolium*) and field madder (*Sherardia arvensis*). Others grow on a wider range of soil types and are common in medieval assemblages, eg corn cockle (*Agrostemma githago*), shepherd's needle (*Scandix pecten-veneris*), brome grass (*Bromus* sect. *Bromus*) and narrow-fruited cornsalad (*Valerianella dentata*). Some of the remaining taxa grow in a wider range of habitats which may include waste ground and grassland as well as cultivated fields. This group includes red bartsia/eyebright (*Odontites verna/Euphrasia* sp.), a small seed which was numerous in Pit 339 (ceramic phase 2) and the upper fill of the adjacent Pit 319 (ceramic phase 3). Red bartsia and eyebright are semi-parasitic on grasses and because of this can grow on nutrient-poor soils either as arable or grassland weeds. They occurred in samples from CP2 to CP5.

Stinking mayweed (*Anthemis cotula*) shows a preference for heavy, damp soils, such as might occur alongside the tributaries of the Avon to the north and south of the site. Other plants of moist soils, such as sedges (*Carex* sp.) and great sedge (*Cladium mariscus*), may have been growing amongst hay on damp meadows along local watercourses. Grassland species may indicate the presence of burnt hay within the assemblages, or may be evidence of crop rotation where fallow is included every two or three years. Campbell (1994) suggests that tenacious perennials such as field scabious (*Knautia arvensis*; CP2 to CP5) may be indicative of fallow, as they may be able to regenerate after periodic ploughing. Along with purging flax (*Linum catharticum*; CP2), it is characteristically found in dry, calcareous grassland. It is not possible to determine whether a year of fallow was employed within a crop rotation system at Eckweek. Brenchley and Warrington (1993) have shown that with some, but not all, weed species fallowing can have beneficial effects in lowering the weed seed population. Of the Eckweek taxa, this is true for cleavers and black medick, but fallowing has little benefit over continuous cropping for shepherd's needle and red bartsia. The absence of pasture and meadow at Eckweek suggests that there may have been a certain amount of pressure on the land such that cropping was fairly continuous. The growing of large quantities of legumes would have helped to maintain fertility, as would the spreading of domestic and animal waste on the fields. It is notable that no mineralised cess-pit deposits were excavated, even though the mineralisation in drain 71 demonstrates that this type of preservation can occur on the local calcareous soils. Perhaps 'night soil' was being spread on the land to help maintain soil fertility.

Indeterminate and Lolium-type grass seeds were frequent in many of the samples. Grassland taxa accounted for 1% or 2% of the total assemblages where seed numbers were high, with artificially raised percentages for the smaller assemblages in the Iron Age and ceramic phase 6 samples. Some taxa, such as silverweed (*Potentilla anserina*) and ribwort plantain (*Plantago lanceolata*) are more typical of open, grazed and trampled grassland.

Comparisons Between 11th-century Samples from Area A and Area H

Comparison of the assemblages from Area A and Area H can only be done for ceramic phases 2 and 3 (11th century), as the building on Area H was occupied for only a short time. Although the cereal remains appear to be very similar for both farmsteads, small differences in the weed assemblages can be seen. Adjusting the data to account for differences in sampling, the occurrences of two small-seeded weeds were found to be much greater in Area A than Area H. Red bartsia/eyebright (*Odontites verna/Euphrasia* sp.) was found to be eight times more frequent in the charred waste in rubbish pits from Area A than the waste from pits in Area H (2.32 per litre of soil processed as opposed to 0.3pls). Stinking chamomile seeds (*Anthemis cotula*) were 35 times more frequent in samples from Area A than Area H, suggesting that there were some differences in the types of soils being cultivated at each site. As previously noted, stinking chamomile is an indicator of heavy, damp clay soils. The alternative explanation is that some differences in crop processing methods had been used, for example perhaps a larger meshed sieve mesh was used by the Area H farmstead to remove fine waste from the crop. Chaff fragments and weed seeds were present in some of the Area H samples but these were mainly larger, heavier items. Wheat rachis fragments were frequent in one Area H sample but in general weed seeds were less frequent and diverse, perhaps due to more efficient crop cleaning methods. The interpretation of this difference is inconclusive but does suggest that the two properties were operating as separate entities.

Comparison With Other Sites

Rural sites at Burton Dassett, Warwickshire (Moffett, unpublished 1991), Dean Court Farm, Oxon (Moffett, unpublished 1987) and Roundwood, Stansted, Essex (Murphy 2004) bear close resemblance to Eckweek in the cultivation of rivet-type and bread wheat-type cereals as well as vetch. As at Eckweek, the quantity of barley recovered from Burton Dassett was low, perhaps because there were specific obligations to grow certain crops. Closer to Eckweek, other sites in Somerset that have produced very similar assemblages dominated by both types of free-threshing wheat include West Wick near Weston-super-Mare (11th–12th centuries; Pelling 2009), Whitegate Farm, Bleadon (Smith 2007), Church Field, Puxton (12th–13th centuries; Jones 2009), Shapwick House Moat (Smith and Campbell 2007) and Shapwick Parish (13th–14th centuries; Straker, Campbell and Smith 2007). In all cases barley was present in low quantities with some oats, although the oats were often thought to have been weedy contaminants. Rye was sometimes present in very small amounts. Grains were almost always dominant in the samples and the levels of chaff fragments were low except for in the Shapwick House Moat where there appeared to have been some dumping of cereal processing waste. Waterlogging in this feature (which protects delicate items from frost damage) and the absence of trampling in a water-filled moat may also have helped chaff to survive. Pea, field bean and vetches (with Vicia sativa confirmed in some cases and some tentative suggestions of cultivation as a crop) were present at each site and there was very little evidence for the consumption of luxury foods. One exception to this was at Bridewell Lane, Shapwick Parish, where two peach stone fragments were recovered from a 13th-/14th-century ditch fill, demonstrating that occasional treats could be afforded by some residents. A basal ditch fill at Church Field, Puxton contained some flax seeds, capsule fragments and stem fragments.

The 14th- to 16th-century rural settlement at Barton Bendish, Norfolk (Murphy and Locker unpublished 1988) produced fewer charred plant remains, which included bread wheat-type grain and peas but no tetraploid wheats or cultivated vetch. In other locations where the poor quality of the soils would have been a limiting factor, a range of arable crops better suited to infertile acidic soils have dominated, for example assemblages from the 13th-century farmstead at Cefn Graeanog, Gywnedd, Wales (Hillman 1982) were dominated by oats with some evidence for peas, and a 12th-century granary at Lydford, Devon, produced mainly rye and cultivated oat (Green 1980).

All of these charred assemblages from rural settlements produced evidence of mixed cereals and legumes with only the occasional indication of luxury goods, such as walnut at Barton Bendish, fennel at Dean Court Farm, peach at Puxton and a plum at Eckweek. It is possible that the presence of waterlogged or mineralised faecal deposits might have provided more evidence of imported fruits and spices, although the mineralised and waterlogged remains from the market town of Newbury only produced the additional taxon apple, which might have been picked from the wild (Carruthers 1997a). Waterlogged remains from a medieval rural settlement at Hungerford included cultivated flax and opium poppy, but no cultivated fruits. Of the charred remains, hexaploid free-threshing wheat was dominant with some evidence for peas (Carruthers, unpublished).

This contrasts strongly with the wide range of cultivated and imported fruits, nuts, herbs and spices from larger urban, high status and ecclesiastical sites such as the moated manor at Cowick (Hayfield and Greig 1988) and Reading Abbey (Carruthers 1997b). Admittedly, most of these remains were preserved anaerobically rather than charred, but in general there is little evidence that rural communities could afford to supplement their diet with many imported goods.

It is not possible to link the documentary records precisely to the buildings excavated in Area A, but a 14th-century record referring to a middle ranking peasant household with 17 acres appears to fit the evidence. The plant remains support this suggestion, in that the ability to grow predominantly wheat on the local well-drained calcareous soils would have provided a reasonable income. Although there was no evidence for imported foods the occupants may have had their own fruit trees. Fruits and nuts were gathered from the wild and legumes such as peas, beans and maybe lentils were grown.

Summary and Conclusions

The main findings of the study were as follows:

- The main crops being grown throughout the late Saxon to later medieval periods of occupation were rivet wheat- and bread wheat-type free-threshing wheats. Barley (including six-row hulled barley) and possibly oats (status as a crop not confirmed) were minor crops throughout these periods. Rye was scarce and probably growing as a weed.
- Cereal grains were by far the most frequent items in all but one of the samples (context 318 which produced a very high count of a small weed taxon, *Odontites verna/Euphrasia* sp.; 236 seeds).
- Chaff fragments and weed seeds were poorly represented in all except three samples (context 3062, Pit 3061 Area H; context 359, Pit 357, Area A; context 237, Pit 221, Area A). Pie charts (Figure 5.84) drawn for the 24 richest samples illustrate this finding.
- Almost all of the rich samples derived from pits (21 out of 24 samples; Figure 5.81).
- In the earlier ceramic phases (CP2 and CP3) the richest samples were recovered from pits in a group of four located towards the southern end of Area A.
- In the later ceramic phases (CP4 and CP5) in Area A the few rich samples came from pits, a spread and a gully within or next to the stone farmhouse in the north of the trench. No rich samples were dated to CP6, though nine samples from this phase were examined.
- The periods producing the highest concentrations of charred cereal remains (deriving primarily from domestic activities) were *c*AD 1000–1100, Period III, in particular ceramic phase 3, and *c*AD 1275–1325, Period V, specifically ceramic phase 5 (Figure 5.83).
- Almost all of the vetch-rich (*Vicia sativa*) samples came from ceramic phases 3 and 4, particularly samples containing seeds large enough to have been cultivated vetch, *Vicia sativa* subsp. *sativa*. Peas and field beans were present in low numbers in ceramic phases 2 to 4. Leguminous crops appear to have been much less common in the later medieval period, Period V.
- Differences were found between the 11th-century samples from Areas A and H with regard to the occurrence of two small-seeded weed taxa. This could relate to differences in crop processing or to the cultivation of crops on different soils.

Acknowledgements

I would like to thank Cat (A. al Azm) for sorting many of the flots. I am especially grateful to Vanessa Straker for her help in organising the environmental sampling and post-excavation work and her useful comments on the report. I would also like to thank Lisa Moffett and Gill Campbell for providing me with comments, references and information about their unpublished sites and am very grateful to Ruth Pelling for providing me with references for more recent publications from Somerset.

5.15 MOLLUSCS
by Dr Matthew Law (2014)

Introduction and Methods

Sediment samples taken from excavated features at Eckweek in 1989 were presented for examination by the writer in 2014.

Shells were identified to at least genus level. Comparisons were made to the author's own reference collection. All identifications were carried out under a low power binocular microscope. Ecological information is taken from Evans (1972), Kerney and Cameron (1979), and Davies (2008). Nomenclature follows Anderson (2008).

For each gastropod taxon within a sample, the most commonly represented non-repetitive element (usually the shell apex, umbilicus, or body whorl with mouth) was counted to determine the minimum number of individuals (MNI) present. This avoids the underestimation reported when only shell apices are counted (Giovas 2009). Diversity indices were calculated using PAST (http://folk.uio.no/ohammer/past/).

As an aid to interpretation, taxa were arranged into groups, broadly following those of Evans (1972) and Evans (1991). These are:

Context	Ecological Group	32	59	67	72	78	149	185	194	207	213	217	220	227	230	236	241	249	250	261	263
Sample			V	V	V	V	III	IV		III	V			IV/V	III		V	III			V
				Farmhouse 460	Farmhouse 460												Farmhouse 460				
Taxon																					
Aegopinella spp.	1a	.	1	.	1	.	.	.	.	.	5	.	.	1	.	.	.	.	1	.	.
Nesovitrea hammonis (Ström 1765)	1a	.	5	.	.	.	.	.	.	1	3	.	.	.	.	.	.	.	.	.	.
Oxychilus spp.	1a	.	28	.	1	.	3	.	1	.	11	5	.	.	3	1	5	1	.	.	9
Vitrea spp.	1a	.	6	.	.	.	1	1	1	.	31	.	.	.	3	1	.	.	.	.	.
Discus rotundatus (O F Müller 1774)	1c	1	106	.	4	3	.	1	.	1	98	26	1	8	.	.	1	.	3	.	9
Acanthinula aculeata (O F Müller 1774)	1d	.	.	.	.	.	.	.	.	.	3	1	.	.	.	.	.	2	.	.	1
Clausilia bidentata (Ström 1765)	1d	.	16	.	.	.	.	.	.	.	15	.	.	.	2	.	.	.	.	.	.
Clausilia sp.	1d	.	.	.	1	.	.	.	.	.	6	6	.	.	.	.	.	.	.	.	1
Ena montana (Draparnaud 1801)	1d	.	.	.	.	.	.	.	.	.	.	.	.	.	.	1	.	.	.	.	.
Lauria cylindracea (Draparnaud 1801)	1d	.	.	.	.	.	1	.	.	.	2	.	1	.	.	.	.	.	.	.	.
Punctum pygmaeum (Draparnaud 1801)	1d	.	.	.	.	.	.	.	.	.	3	.	1	.	.	.	.	.	.	.	2
Trochulus striolatus (C Pfeiffer 1828)	1d	.	53	2	3	13	14	.	2	3	25	23	2	5	24	14	5	3	3	12	28
Cepaea spp.	3	.	4	.	1	.	1	.	.	2	.	3	.	.	.	.	.	.	.	.	.
Cochlicopa lubrica (O F Müller 1774)	3	.	5	.	.	1	.	.	.	.	8	5	.	1	2	.	.	.	.	1	1
Limacidae	3	.	.	.	.	.	.	.	.	.	1	.	.	.	.	.	.	.	.	.	.
Candidula intersecta (Poiret 1801)	4	.	.	.	.	.	.	.	.	.	.	.	.	1	.	.	.	.	.	.	.
Helicella itala (Linnaeus 1758)	4	.	.	.	.	.	.	.	.	.	.	3	.	.	.	.	.	.	.	.	.
Pupilla muscorum (Linnaeus 1758)	4	.	.	.	.	.	.	.	.	.	.	.	.	.	1	1	.	.	.	.	.
Vallonia costata (O F Müller 1774)	4	.	1	.	.	2	5	2	.	1	5	6	.	3	2	3	2	2	4	3	5
Vallonia cf. *excentrica* (Sterki 1893)	4	.	.	.	1	4	.	.	.	.	7	11	.	.	.	.	1	.	2	.	1
Vertigo pygmaea (Draparnaud 1801)	4	.	.	.	1	.	4	1	.	1	7	1	1	1	.	1	.	.	2	.	1
Galba truncatula (O F Müller 1774)	5a	.	.	.	.	.	.	.	.	.	.	.	.	.	.	.	.	.	.	.	1
Cecilioides acicula (O F Müller 1774)	7	.	2	.	1	5	.	2	.	.	107	6	.	.	2	5	3	2	.	1	3
Carychium spp.	.	.	4	.	.	.	.	2	.	.	42	5	.	.	3	1	.	.	9	.	6
Total		1	231	2	14	28	29	9	4	9	379	101	6	20	42	28	17	8	26	17	68

	32	59	67	72	78	149	185	194	207	213	217	220	227	230	236	241	249	250	261	263
Marine shell frags	.	.	.	.	.	.	.	.	✓	.	.	.	.	✓	.	.	.	.	.	.
Fossil bivalve frags	.	.	.	.	.	.	.	.	.	.	.	.	.	.	.	.	.	.	.	.
Earthworm granules	.	.	.	.	.	.	.	.	✓	.	✓	.	✓	✓	.	.	.	.	.	✓
Heterodera capsules	.	✓	.	.	.	.	.	.	.	.	.	.	.	.	.	.	.	.	.	.
Animal bone frags	.	.	.	.	.	✓	.	.	.	.	.	.	.	✓	.	.	.	.	.	.
Fish bone	.	.	.	.	.	.	.	.	✓	.	.	.	1	.	.	.	.	.	.	.
Fish scale	.	.	.	.	.	.	.	.	.	.	.	.	.	✓	.	.	.	.	.	.
Charcoal	.	.	.	.	.	✓	.	.	✓	✓	.	.	✓	✓	.	.	.	.	.	.
Sambucus nigra (elder) seed	.	.	.	.	.	.	.	.	.	.	.	.	.	.	.	.	.	.	.	.
Taraxacum officinalis (dandelion) seed	.	.	.	.	.	.	.	.	.	.	.	.	.	.	.	.	.	.	.	.
Other seeds	.	.	.	.	.	.	.	.	.	.	.	.	.	✓	.	.	.	.	.	.
Fired clay frags	.	.	.	.	.	.	.	.	.	.	.	.	.	✓	.	.	.	.	.	.
Crinoid	.	.	.	.	.	.	.	.	.	1	.	.	1	.	.	.	.	.	.	.
Snail egg	.	.	.	.	.	.	.	.	.	2	.	.	.	.	.	.	.	.	.	.
Woodlouse	.	.	.	.	.	.	.	.	.	.	.	.	.	.	.	.	.	.	.	.
Millipede	.	✓	.	.	.	.	.	.	.	.	.	.	.	.	.	.	.	.	.	.
Oribatid mites	.	✓	.	.	.	.	.	.	.	.	.	.	.	.	.	.	.	.	.	.

Key: ✓ = present   ★ = Sambucus ID via Tom Roland

FIGURE 5.86

Minimum number of snail (MNI) values for the vertical sequence of samples. (Numbers in parentheses are snails that are most likely modern intrusions, judging by their preservation.)

1a Gastrodontoidea (Zontidae of earlier authors), comprising *Aegopinella spp.*, *Nesovitrea hammonis*, *Oxychilus spp.*, and *Vitrea spp*. These are broadly woodland species, present in damp shaded ground

1c *Discus rotundatus*. Typical of shaded habitats

1d Other shade-loving species, comprising *Acanthinula aculeata*, *Clausilia bidentata*, *Ena montana*, *Lauria cylindracea*, *Punctum pygmaeum* and *Trochulus striolatus*. This group contains a broad range of tolerances, but usually avoid dry, open conditions

265	267	269	273	285	290	291	296	318	340	340	341	347	358	388	3062	3064	3075	3077	3087	3108	3109	3116	3123	3135	3140	3143	3162
															2556	2557	2567	2561	2560	2567	2567	2565	2566	2555	2558	2563	2573
		III				III	III	III	3	III	III	III	III	III													
																	Ditch fill										
.	.	.	.	.	.	.	.	.	.	.	.	.	.	.	.	.	.	.	.	.	.	.	.	.	.	.	.
.	.	.	.	.	1	.	.	.	.	.	.	.	.	.	.	.	.	.	.	.	.	.	.	.	.	.	1
1	.	1	1	.	.	.	2	2	5	3	12	.	1	2	.	1	29	.	.	1	.	.	.	.	.	.	.
.	.	1	.	.	.	.	.	.	.	.	1	1	1	.	.	.	1	.	.	1	.	.	.	.	.	.	1
.	.	.	1	.	.	.	1	.	.	.	.	.	.	.	.	3	28	.	.	.	.	1	.	.	.	.	12
.	.	.	.	.	.	.	.	.	.	.	.	.	.	.	.	.	1	.	.	.	.	.	.	.	.	1	.
.	.	.	.	.	.	.	.	.	.	.	.	.	.	.	.	.	8	.	1	.	.	.	.	.	.	.	3
.	.	.	.	.	.	.	.	.	.	.	.	.	.	.	.	.	.	.	.	.	.	.	.	1	.	.	.
.	.	.	.	.	.	.	.	.	.	.	.	.	.	.	.	.	1	.	.	.	.	.	.	.	.	.	.
.	.	.	.	.	.	.	.	.	.	.	2	.	.	.	.	.	.	.	.	.	.	.	.	.	.	.	.
.	.	.	2	.	1	.	1	.	.	.	.	.	.	.	.	.	.	.	.	.	.	.	.	.	.	.	.
2	4	2	6	2	1	6	6	15	41	9(2)	16	14	4	2	13	2	51	3	1	1	8	6	4	.	6	4	16
.	.	.	.	.	.	.	1	.	.	.	.	.	.	1	.	.	.	.	.	.	.	.	.	.	.	.	.
.	.	1	.	.	.	2	.	1	1	3	6	2	.	1	1	.	2	1	.	.	.	.	.	.	1	.	.
.	.	.	.	.	.	.	.	.	.	.	.	.	.	.	.	.	.	.	.	.	.	.	.	.	.	.	.
.	.	.	.	.	.	.	.	.	.	.	.	.	.	.	.	.	.	.	.	.	.	.	.	.	.	.	.
.	.	.	.	.	.	.	.	.	.	.	.	1	.	.	.	.	.	.	.	.	.	.	.	.	.	.	.
.	.	.	.	.	.	.	.	.	.	.	.	.	.	.	.	.	7	.	.	.	.	1	.	.	.	.	.
1	1	.	.	.	2	4	1	1	.	.	13	1	.	1	1	1	9	.	.	.	.	.	.	.	2	.	.
4	.	2	.	1	1	.	17	1	.	.	10	3	.	14	3	.	8	.	.	.	5	1	1	.	2	2	.
.	1	.	2	1	1	2	8	1	.	1	4(1)	.	.	3(1)	.	.	2	.	.	1	.	.	.	.	.	.	.
.	.	.	.	.	.	.	.	.	.	.	1	.	.	.	.	.	.	.	.	.	.	.	.	.	.	.	.
1	3	.	2	.	.	.	.	3	2	.	9	.	3	1	1	.	1	.	.	.	1	.	.	.	1	17	.
.	.	.	1	.	.	.	.	.	.	.	1	.	.	.	1	.	62	.	.	.	.	.	.	.	.	.	.
9	9	7	15	4	7	14	37	24	49	16	75	22	9	25	20	7	210	4	2	4	14	9	5	1	12	24	33
														.													
.	.	.	.	.	.	.	.	.	.	.	.	✓	.	.	.	.	.	.	.	.	.	.	.	.	.	.	.
.	.	.	.	.	.	.	.	.	.	.	.	.	.	✓	.	.	.	.	.	.	.	.	.	.	.	.	.
.	.	.	.	.	.	.	.	.	✓	.	✓	.	.	✓	.	✓	.	.	✓	.	.	.	.	.	✓	.	.
.	.	.	.	.	.	.	✓	.	.	.	✓	.	.	.	.	.	.	.	.	.	.	.	.	.	.	.	.
.	.	.	.	.	.	.	.	.	.	✓	.	.	.	.	.	.	.	.	✓	.	.	.	.	.	.	.	.
.	.	.	.	.	.	.	.	.	.	.	.	.	.	.	.	.	.	.	.	.	.	.	.	.	.	.	.
.	.	.	.	.	.	.	.	.	.	.	.	.	.	✓	.	.	.	.	.	.	.	.	.	.	.	.	.
.	.	.	.	.	.	.	✓	.	.	.	.	.	.	✓	.	.	.	.	.	.	.	.	.	.	.	✓	.
.	.	.	.	.	.	.	.	.	.	.	1*	.	.	.	.	.	.	.	✓	.	.	.	.	.	.	.	.
.	.	.	.	.	.	.	.	.	.	.	.	.	.	✓	.	.	.	.	.	.	.	.	.	.	.	.	.
.	.	.	.	.	.	.	.	.	.	.	.	.	.	.	.	.	.	.	.	.	.	.	.	.	.	.	.
.	.	.	.	.	.	.	.	.	.	.	.	.	.	.	.	.	.	.	.	.	.	.	.	.	.	.	.
.	.	.	.	.	.	.	.	.	.	.	.	.	.	.	.	.	.	.	.	.	.	.	.	.	.	.	.
.	.	.	.	.	.	.	.	.	.	.	.	.	.	.	.	.	.	.	.	.	.	.	.	.	.	✓	.
.	.	.	.	.	.	.	1	.	.	.	.	.	.	.	.	.	.	.	.	.	.	.	.	.	.	.	.
.	.	.	.	.	.	.	.	.	.	.	.	.	.	.	.	.	.	.	.	.	.	.	.	.	.	.	.
.	.	.	.	.	.	.	.	.	.	.	.	.	.	.	.	.	.	.	.	.	.	.	.	.	.	.	.

3 Catholic/intermediate, comprising *Cepaea spp.*, *Cochlicopa lubrica*, and Limacidae sp.
4 Open country, comprising *Candidula intersecta*, *Helicella itala*, *Pupilla muscorum*, *Vallonia costata*, *Vallonia cf. excentrica* and *Vertigo pygmaea*
5a *Galba truncatula*. An amphibious species found in wet grassland and poor freshwater habitats
7 *Cecilioides acicula*. A subterranean species.

The groupings broadly represent a progression from woodland conditions through more open environments to gradually wetter conditions. *Cecilioides acicula*, as a burrowing species, is usually judged to be intrusive in archaeological samples.

Note that not all taxa within a group are present in all samples. Although useful as a broad guide, the use of ecological groups may mask fine details, therefore consideration is also made of the tables of species counts.

Results

Minimum number of individuals (MNI) values for the vertical sequence of samples are presented in Figure 5.86. Numbers in parentheses are snails that are most likely modern intrusions, judging by their preservation.

Discussion

In general, the sampling revealed fluctuations in the abundance of a few dominant taxa (especially *Discus rotundatus*, *Trochulus striolatus* and *Vallonia cf. excentrica*) and the changing presence or absence of other species. Molluscan abundance was highly variable, but seldom reached high numbers. Many of the samples contained too few snails to draw meaningful conclusions about the local environment. The number of snails in a sample may be related to the rate of deposition, in general slower deposition favours more shells being incorporated into the sample. Relatively slow deposition is therefore suggested for contexts 59, 213, 217, 230, 263, 340, and 3075, the latter the fill of an early to middle Iron Age ditch.

The general picture is one of more or less shaded conditions at different points and times on the site. Especially shaded conditions are suggested for contexts 59, 213, and 3075. Small numbers of open country snails, especially *Vallonia costata*, are to be expected even in wooded conditions (Evans 1972, 158). Peaks in *Vallonia cf. excentrica*, however, especially when linked to low numbers of group 1 snails, would suggest relatively open conditions. This may be the case with contexts 75, 265, 3109, and especially 296 and 388. Context 3075 was an Iron Age ditch fill, and although slow deposition in a shaded environment is suggested, there was nothing in the sample to suggest wet conditions.

Where *Carychium* spp. coincide with relatively high numbers of Gastrodontoidea, it seems likely that many will be *Carychium tridentatum*. This occurs in context 213 and the ditch fill 3075, and suggests abundant leaf litter. *Acanthinula aculeata* and *Clausilia bidentata* are both rupestral species which prefer slightly drier conditions above ground level. Where they occur together, such as contexts 213, 217, 263 and 3075, the presence of fallen branches, walls or standing tree trunks is suggested. *Galba truncatula* is an amphibious snail, associated with damp ground and water margins. Its presence in contexts 263 and 341 may relate to seasonal flooding, or possibly material being imported to the site from a wet environment. *Ena Montana* is scarce in the British Isles today. Its decline has been linked to climatic deterioration since the Mesolithic (Evans 1972), specifically a decrease in temperature. *Candidula intersecta* is a late arrival in the British fauna, thought to have been introduced in medieval times (Davies 2010, 176), the specimen here preserves its proteinaceous periostracum, and so is very likely to be intrusive in this context.

As a subterranean species, *Cecilioides acicula* is problematic for archaeologists. It can occur in quite large numbers in samples, but is usually regarded as intrusive. Evans (1972, 186) reports that they have been seen 2 metres below the ground surface. They are usually described as a medieval introduction to Britain from Europe (eg Davies 2010, 176) and Evans (1972, 186) notes that they 'are common in areas which have been cultivated recently but often absent from longstanding grassland which would appear to provide suitable habitats'.

Conclusions

The Eckweek assemblage is one of very few land snail assemblages to have been analysed from the north east Somerset area, and so represents a valuable addition to understanding of environmental change in the area. Many of the samples yielded assemblages that were too small to carry much interpretative value however. Nonetheless it is recommended that the entire collection be retained in the site archive for future study and reference.

6
INDEPENDENT DATING

6.1 RADIOCARBON DATING
by Dr Peter Marshall of Historic England (^{14}C dates 1991, report updated 2015)

Five samples of charred plant material from medieval deposits were submitted to the Queen's University Belfast, Radiocarbon Dating Laboratory in 1989–1990 for radiocarbon dating. All five were pre-treated using an acid-alkali-acid protocol (Mook and Waterbolk 1985), combusted to carbon dioxide in positive pressure stream of oxygen, converted to benzene using a chromium-base catalyst as described by Noakes *et al* (1965) and dated by liquid scintillation spectrometry (Pearson 1979; 1984).

The laboratory maintained a continual programme of quality assurance procedures, in addition to participating in international inter-comparisons (Scott *et al* 1990) during the period during which the measurements were made and these tests indicate no significant offsets and demonstrate the validity of the precision quoted.

Radiocarbon Results

The results (Figure 6.1) are conventional radiocarbon ages (Stuiver and Polach 1977), and are quoted in accordance with the international standard known as the Trondheim convention (Stuiver and Kra 1986).

Radiocarbon Calibration

The calibrations of these results, which relate the radiocarbon measurements directly to the calendrical time scale, are given in Figure 6.1 and in Figure 6.2. All have been calculated using the datasets published by Reimer *et al* (2013) and the computer program OxCal v4.2 (Bronk Ramsey 1995; 1998; 2001; 2009). The calibrated date ranges cited are quoted in the form recommended by Mook (1986), with the end points rounded outward to 10 years. The ranges in Figure 6.1 have been calculated according to the maximum intercept method (Stuiver and Reimer 1986); the probability distributions shown in Figure 6.2 are derived from the probability method (Stuiver and Reimer 1993).

Sample Selection

Sample selection for the material submitted in the 1980s was limited by the amount of carbon required for liquid scintillation counting, however, the majority of samples all have excellent taphonomic

Laboratory Code	Sample	Material and context	δ13C (‰)	Radiocarbon Age (BP)	Calibrated Date (95% confidence)
UB-3203	340	Charred cereal grain; wheat, barley, weed seeds, small charcoal and shell fragments (V Straker) from the charcoal-rich lower fill of a pit cut into natural: one of a group of cascading pits linked by gullies	−24.4	1019±58	cal AD 890–1160
UB-3204	359A	Charred cereal grain; free threshing wheat, oats, chaff, hulled barley, corn cockle seeds (V Straker) from a dense loam/charcoal mix forming the primary fill of a pit	−23.3	891±42	cal AD 1020–1250
UB-3205	359B	As UB-3204	−23.3	962±53	cal AD 980–1210
UB-3206	170	Charred cereal grain: a few charcoal fragments, weed seeds, free threshing wheat, rachis fragments, oats and a few peas, (V Straker) from along the secondary fill of a gully, which partially underlay a late medieval limestone walled farmhouse	−23.9	830±41	cal AD 1050–1270
UB-3298	237	Charred cereal grains; free threshing wheat, rachis fragments and weed seeds, (V Straker) from a charcoal layer forming the lowest fill of a pit	−23.3	990±64	cal AD 890–1190

FIGURE 6.1

Radiocarbon dating results

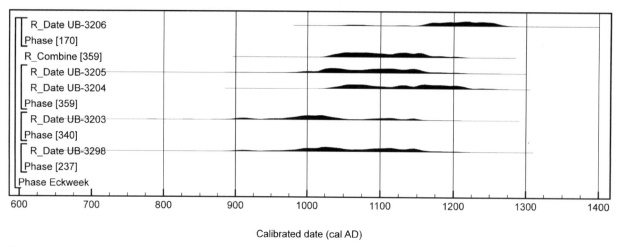

FIGURE 6.2

Probability distributions of radiocarbon dates. The distributions are the result of simple radiocarbon calibration (Stuiver and Reimer 1993)

integrity; a number of the 'bulk' samples of carbonised material came from 'single event' deposits.

Discussion

The two measurements on short-life bulk samples from context [359] are statistically consistent (T'=1.1; ν=1; T' (1%)=3.8; Ward and Wilson 1978) and so a weighted mean (919±33 BP) has been taken as providing the best estimate for the age (cal AD 1020–1210) of the deposit.

6.2 COMMENT ON THE 1991 RADIOCARBON DATES

by Andrew Young (1991, revised 2015)

A comparison is made below between the independent scientific dates obtained from the series of radiocarbon determinations (Section 6.1) and the chronology of the late Saxon and medieval activity derived from the intra-site ceramic phasing (Section 5.3) and stratigraphy (Section 4).

Sample 359a (UB3204) and Sample 359b (UB3205)

These two samples were taken from the same charred grain deposit and yet show a difference of 132 years in their basic calibrated ages at one sigma probability. However, in his 2015 review, Peter Marshall notes that the two measurements are statistically consistent and therefore present a weighted mean (919±33 BP) as providing the best estimate for the age (cal AD 1020–1210) for the deposit. On the basis of the ceramic phasing (CP4 or earlier) and stratigraphy alone, it is considered unlikely that the deposit is later than the early 12th century AD, whilst the most likely overlap of the one sigma ^{14}C probability distributions (1σ overlap is between AD 1042 and 1157) would seem to place the formation of the deposit in the later 11th century.

Sample 170 (UB3206)

The one sigma radiocarbon probability range (1σ range is AD 1168–1264 with a mean of AD 1221) is acceptable in view of the ceramic dating of CP4 (AD 1100–1250). It is likely that the deposit sampled was associated with the destruction of Period III Building 467 and the transition from timber to stone construction.

Sample 340 (UB3203)

The calibrated radiocarbon age of AD 1012 is too early based of the ceramic dating of CP4 (AD 1100–1250), although the two sigma probability distribution (2σ date range AD 890–1159) would just allow an early 12th-century date. It is at least possible that the earlier than expected radiocarbon age is a consequence of a sample that contained significant amounts of residual charcoal.

Sample 237 (UB3298)

Again, the calibrated radiocarbon age of AD 1021 of this secondary fill of a sunken floor feature appears too early based of the ceramic dating of CP4 (AD 1100–1250), although the two sigma probability distribution (the 2σ range is AD 900–1180) would also just about allow an early 12th-century date.

7

RECONSTRUCTING LATE SAXON AND MEDIEVAL ECKWEEK

(2015)

This section presents a discussion and interpretation of the various strands of evidence recovered from the site associated with the extended period of rural medieval settlement and related activity. The underlying theme is concerned with continuity and dynamic change: how that is, or is not, apparent in the archaeological record.

It begins in Section 7.1 with a detailed examination of the various late Saxon and medieval buildings and associated structures described in Section 4, leading to a reconstruction of their individual form, function, structural affinities and inferred status. The structural reconstructions are followed in Section 7.2 by an examination of the character and spatial arrangement of associated artefacts, which is used to illuminate the organisation, function and use of the principal structures and how that does or does not change through time.

The discussion turns to the evidence of the rural medieval economy in Sections 7.3, 7.4 and 7.5 in order to characterise the fundamentals of the medieval settlement; how its economic profile, agriculture and husbandry is expressed in the archaeological record and the extent to which the community was connected to the wider world.

The strands developed in this chapter (7) are drawn together and evaluated in Chapter 8 in a concluding overview of the late Saxon and medieval settlement. This situates evidence from Eckweek in its wider context and considers how it adds to our understanding of rural medieval settlement, both in the South West region and nationally.

7.1 THE MEDIEVAL BUILDINGS AND STRUCTURES

Period III – The Late Saxon and Saxo-Norman Timber Structures

Examples of large earthfast rural timber buildings of the late Saxon and Saxo-Norman period are rare in the Somerset region and equally so nationally. As a result, examples closely comparable to those recorded at Eckweek in Areas A and H are, more than 25 years after the project fieldwork, still very rare in the archaeological record.

The earliest Period III structure, Structure 468, is dated to the second half of the 10th century (ceramic phase 1) and is in most respects unremarkable, save for the fact that its long axis is, somewhat unusually, aligned north to south (Hamerow 2012). In all other respects the structure appears to conform to a recognised mid to later Anglo-Saxon building type that was founded upon a rectilinear arrangement of small earthfast posts that supported load-bearing walls, where the numbers of individual wall posts used seems to diminish by the later Anglo-Saxon period (Hamerow 2012). Buildings 467 and 477 represent far more substantial and complex earthfast timber buildings, both of which were constructed in the first half of the 11th century during ceramic phase 2. Building 477 in Area H was abandoned by around AD 1100, the end of ceramic phase 3, whilst Building 467 appears to have continued in use well into the first half of the 12th century, ceramic phase 4, and perhaps as late as AD 1200. As such, it seems reasonable to conclude that Building 467 at least, represents a 'multi-generational' dwelling (Hamerow 2012). The plan-forms of both 11th-century structures exhibit some similar general characteristics, as both are aligned broadly west to east with suggested entrances in the side walls and earthfast superstructures founded upon a relatively small number of large principal posts, in both cases without corner posts. In other respects they differ significantly. The organisation of the principal features and their structural logic indicate that each building was founded upon pairs of principal roof trusses combined with a single (but see below) large gablepost that in at least one case incorporated curved corner walls. This plan-form and structural arrangement is extremely rare, not only in the South West region, but nationally, and has particular implications in respect of the specific character and social status of both buildings and, by inference, their inhabitants.

Period III.1, Structure 468 – Area A

This earliest late Saxon structure was identified in Area A (Figures 42 and 4.12; Structure 468) and is interpreted to reflect the remains of a rectangular earthfast timber structure, possibly, but not certainly, a dwelling. The structure was aligned north to south and measured approximately 10m by 5.5m in plan (c590 square feet), although the position of the north end was not ascertained with any certainty and potentially the building could have extended as far as a boundary ditch (248), and therefore have been up to 12.5m long. The presence of the boundary ditch is considered significant as it suggests that both the adjacent trackway and the farmstead plot, all more fully defined archaeologically in later periods, was already established by this date. The structure itself was defined by a group of shallow 'tadpole-shaped' and irregular postholes, the former a posthole morphology that has been interpreted to reflect 'prop-sockets' and thereby an indicator of the direction in which principal trusses were raised. These were accompanied by a shallow linear gully [322], possibly the foundation for a sill-beam, and remnants of a compacted internal floor layer [189]. Collectively, these features were characterised by a similar morphology and pottery of ceramic phase 1, which is dated to the second half of the 10th century, although the use of the structure may have extended into the early part of the 11th century.

Taken as a whole, the excavated features indicate that the structure had at least one west-facing entrance, represented by a pair of elongated postholes and an area of erosion [233] just inside the threshold. In addition, it appears to have had a small enclosed yard or pen attached to the southeastern corner, as indicated by a shallow curved gully [300], although it is at least conceivable that this feature represented a further element of the main building, for example the remains of an eavesdrip gully. If so, its structural logic and original form remains very unclear indeed.

In terms of its size and suggested plan-form alone, combined with an absence of all but the barest traces of internal features and deposits, the structure is consistent with the range of mid to later Saxon 'houses' that have been recorded archaeologically (Gardiner 2013 and Hamerow 2012, 17–66), where the principal structural elements appear to have developed gradually and as a continuum from closely-spaced arrangements of post-in-trench along load-bearing walls to small numbers of larger and more widely spaced principal posts by the 11th century.

What is clear from subsequent activity recorded in Area A, is that the structure was entirely replaced by a far more substantial earthfast dwelling, Building 467, during the early 11th century (ceramic phase 2).

Periods III.2–III.3, Building 467 – Area A

The building was 13m long and 7m wide in its final form (Figure 4.13) although its development appears to have involved at least one phase of rebuilding or repair, as indicated by the enlarged and deepened east gable postpit [223] that produced stratified pottery of CP3, the later 11th century. In addition, Features 274 and 282 also produced pottery of CP3, although an earlier plan-form that is restricted to features dated by pottery to CP2 alone (Figure 4.40) displays little structural logic. As such, a coherent structural interpretation of the building is most possible in its latest form, although an entirely separate early plan-form that is associated solely with features dated by pottery to CP2 cannot be discounted.

The overall shape of the building is defined by the west and east gableposts in conjunction with a curved gully [251], which represented a structural element (and clearly not an eavesdrip trench as it ran up to the west gablepost [195]), a curved terrace [429] cut into the natural substrate, and an extremely well defined soil boundary that separated Deposits 34 and 289 and demarcated the southwestern corner of the building. In combination, these features delineate a rectangular building with at least three rounded corners that was founded upon a small number of large earthfast principal posts, a plan-form that is rare in the archaeological record but not unique (Cunliffe 1976, Building S15, dated to the later 10th century). The fourth corner of the building, the southeastern, appears to have incorporated a different arrangement, where foundations included a gully [284] attached to the east gablepost, a group of three stakeholes [286–288] and a posthole [228]. These earthfast features possibly represented a development of the structure contemporary with the rebuilding or repair of the east gablepost [223], as both the gully and the posthole also produced pottery of CP3. As a group of related features they appear to have extended the south wall of the building rather awkwardly to the south, into the adjacent yard. An associated layer of rough metalling [39] extended across the south wall-line (as indicated by Layers 34/289) and inside the eastern end of the building, as far as Pit 221. Where the line of the south wall was indicated by the boundary separating Layers 34 and 289, no trace of any substantial earthfast foundation equivalent to Gully 251 was present. This difference might be explained by comparing the OD levels of the natural substrate [34] alongside the gully, where they measured 152.20m and 152.23m, and those at the boundary of Layers 34 and 289, where the surface was at 151.67m, some 500mm lower. There was no clear evidence that this evident fall across the surface of the natural from north to south was a result of subsequent erosion and it is therefore possible that the absence of any earthfast foundations defining the south side of the building are due to the wall-line on that side having been raised, possibly by the use of a timber ground-sill or a series of wall plates, in order to achieve a level interior floor (see below). Such an arrangement might also explain why internal Gully 171 was somewhat shallower at the southern end and indeed faded out altogether before reaching the boundary of Layers 34/289. An obvious weakness of this argument is the complexity of constructing a curved timber ground-sill, whether as a single piece or in a series of sections. Other means of non-earthfast wall foundation are possible, for example a formation using plain earth or cob, although in each case there would have been obvious drawbacks in building in such material directly over the natural substrate.

At least one internal division is indicated inside the building by Gully 171, a feature that was recut [387] on at least one occasion; the upper fill [155] of the recut overlying the upper fill of the adjacent sunken-floor feature, Pit 179. The position of the gully cut [171] indicated that it either respected, or was respected by, the edge of the pit, whilst the absence of any clear post-in-trench features (other than a single very shallow feature located at the extreme southern end), combined with traces of charred wattle-like material preserved in the latest fill [155], suggested that the structure it contained was fairly lightweight and probably not major load-bearing. The recovery of an iron padlock key (SF728, Figures 5.45, 62 and 7.1) from the secondary fill [170] of the gully, close to the southern end, provides tentative evidence for the position of an internal door in the partition, one that could be secured if necessary.

The partition gully respected, or was respected by, the position of Features 274 and 282, both of which were represented by somewhat irregular and shallow cut features approximately 250mm deep, located on opposing sides of the building. On morphology alone, they appear to have served a different function to either the end gable postholes or Posthole 231. The symmetry of the features suggests that they could have represented the foundations for principal posts, although, if so, their shallow broad form raises the possibility (at least) that they held a timber sill-beam to support a base-cruck truss. However, the possible use of a base-cruck truss in this building is highly problematic on the grounds of dating alone since the earliest confirmed examples of such date to the mid 13th century (Alcock and Miles 2013, table 2.2). The position of Features 274 and 282 and their relationship to the suggested partition gully [171] is also problematic as, if they did indeed represent the foundations for a principal truss, whatever its precise form, the position of the internal partition would have been far more sensibly (and presumably both more securely and easily) located directly below and in line with the truss, as opposed to offset from it. On balance, it is therefore considered more likely that Features 274 and 282 represent areas of wear inside a pair of opposing doorways and that the position of the principal truss would have been located in line with Gully 171 (Figures 4.13 and 7.1), albeit, this implies that the truss was founded at either end on a raised timber sill or sleeper as opposed to an earthfast setting (again, a method seemingly more suited to a cruck-truss as opposed to a principal post). This interpretation would also explain why the wall-line gully [Cut 457] was offset and extended slightly to the north at this point (Figure 4.18d), thereby outside the position of a postulated truss-post or cruck-base located adjacent to the northern end of Gully 171. It is perhaps worth noting here that cruck construction in its earliest and simplest form is the only type of roof construction placed immediately inside a timber or other form of wall-line.

A smaller posthole [268], which was replaced on at least one occasion [492], was located equidistant between the gableposts and precisely on the centre-line of the building. On the basis of its position alone the post could have provided additional support for a central ridge timber, although, if so, such an arrangement seems incongruous with a roof structure founded upon principal posts and rafters or indeed cruck-trusses.

Posthole 231 was located on the projected line of the north wall, as indicated by Gully 457 and Cut 429, and is interpreted to have represented one of an opposing pair of principal post foundations for a further principal roof truss. Unfortunately, no evidence for an equivalent opposing foundation was located along the south side of the building, where Layer 39 regrettably was not excavated. In view of this, it is at least possible that an equivalent post or truss-base was laid directly on Layer 39, or a timber sill laid above it, or that Layer 39 sealed and masked an earlier earthfast timber setting.

The interior space of the building was, as excavated, taken up in large part by two sets of sunken-floor features (Figures 4.13 and 7.1). The floor space in the smaller west bay, defined by the partition gully [171], was almost entirely occupied by intercutting Pits 179 and 385, plus a narrower contemporary cut [386], and that in the larger east bay also was substantially taken up, by intercutting Pits 221 and 234. Although the plan-form of Features 179, 385 and 386 suggests they were opened on separate occasions, their profile and sequence of fills (Figure 4.16) indicates that in their final form they were contemporary and formed a single large sunken-floor feature. This was partially filled [149] during ceramic phase 3, when the primary fill reduced the overall footprint of the sunken area but did not fill it altogether. Pits 221 and 234 were located towards the eastern end of the building and, on the basis of their plan-form alone, also appear to have been opened on separate occasions. Their profile and sequence of fill deposits (Figure 4.17) seem to support the view that Pit 221 was the later

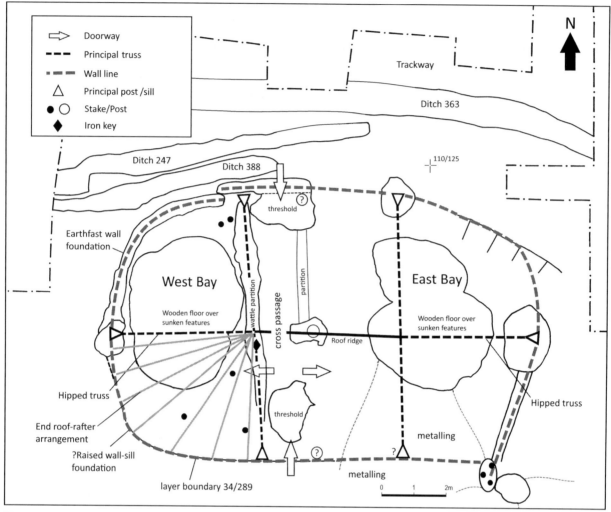

FIGURE 7.1

Structural interpretation of Period III Building 467 in Area A

of the two, having been dug into the fill [236] of Pit 234. Alternatively, in view of the sequence of events suggested for Pits 179/385 above, it is possible that both features were initially open together to form a single figure of eight-shaped depression, the northern part of which [Pit 234] was subsequently partially filled by Deposit 236 during CP3, leaving a smaller sunken area formed by Pit 221 and the southern half of Pit 234. A radiocarbon determination from charred material in Layer 237 (Figure 4.17) produced a calibrated radiocarbon date of AD 900–1180 at 95% confidence (UB3298; Section 6.1). This, and the ceramic phasing (CP4) indicate that this sunken-floored feature, albeit of reduced size, remained open inside the building into the 12th century.

The plan-form of the principal structural features provides no definite evidence concerning the position of the entrance or entrances to the building, although, as noted above, a cross-entry located in the north and south walls where Features 274 and 282 indicate areas of erosion directly inside the entrance threshold is plausible, particularly given the curved nature of the corner walls. An alternative interpretation could have involved an entrance in the line of the north wall between Posthole 231 and Feature 274, although the gap of more than 2m between these features seems overly large. The proposed reconstruction ground plan (Figure 7.1) incorporates a narrow (little more than 1m wide) cross-passage defined by the position of Gully 171 and linear Feature 266/265, the latter also incorporating Posthole 492/268 as part of the partition structure. The building was entered via a pair of opposing doorways located in the north and south walls, each coinciding with the position of Features 274 and 282. The position of a further pair of opposing internal doorways in each partition, into the west and east bay respectively, is suggested to be slightly off-centre along the cross passage, south of Posthole 492/268 and at approximately the position an iron padlock key was recovered from the secondary fill of Gully 171. A further layer of complexity is added when the nature of the interior floor space of the building is considered.

Neither pair of sunken-floor features located towards either end of the building provided any substantial evidence to suggest that they were either significantly eroded by wear or originally lined with vertical timber revetments whilst in use. In addition, their primary deposits were not really consistent with occupation or domestic activity occurring directly inside them. This evidence, combined with the absence of in-situ floor deposits inside the building generally and the suggestion that the level of the south wall was raised by means of a timber ground-sill or some alternative construction, leads to the conclusion that the floor was, at least in part, formed of wooden planks that were raised and laid over the sunken areas. Criteria applied to the identification of suspected wooden floors in Saxon Grubenhauser have been defined by Tipper (Tipper in Hamerow 2012, 56–58) and support eight categories of evidence designed to establish whether a building contained a suspended wooden floor, albeit for the much earlier Saxon Grubenhauser structures excavated at West Stow. These same criteria support the interpretation for the use of suspended wooden floors in Building 467 at Eckweek, possibly across the entire floor area. It should be noted, however, that the use of floorboards at ground level is virtually unknown in the earliest surviving vernacular buildings and, as a result, their use during the late Anglo-Saxon period remains entirely hypothetical. Irrespective of the type of floor that was employed, the combined interior space of the building, taking account of the suggested curved corners, would have measured approximately 70 square metres (c750 square feet), as large as the internal footprint of many recorded later medieval domestic buildings (Gardiner 2000).

No clear evidence was identified to indicate the position of an internal hearth and the only possible candidate for such was provided by Feature 266, the shallow cut feature interpreted above to represent the remains of a partition wall. The feature was, however, located on the central axis of the building, a characteristic of late Saxon buildings (Hamerow 2012), and filled by a charcoal-rich soil [265] that produced pottery of CP2. Nonetheless, the elongated rectangular form of the feature, combined with its position directly alongside Posthole 492/268, seems on balance to argue against it reflecting the position of a hearth.

A reconstruction of the building's roof structure (Figure 7.1) is entirely speculative and envisages a superstructure founded upon two pairs of principal post trusses, each probably joined with a heavy tie-beam, which were in turn attached to the gable or hip-posts (in order to restrict 'racking' of the central trusses) by means of at least one principal hipped roof truss at either end of the building. In order to fit the suggested rounded corners of the building, this arrangement would also require a curved hip roof structure formed by a semi-circle of radiating timber rafters that saxen attached at the junction of the principal hip-rafter and the ridge apex and carried at the eaves by the curved wall structure. Such a structure, indicated on Figure 7.1, whilst certainly complex, is not entirely fanciful, as a similar arrangement is described by Hewett and others (Hewett 1982, fig 8; Alcock and Miles 2013, 203), albeit in relation to 12th-century church roof structures. An alternative interpretation of the roof end structures could, hypothetically, have involved the use of a principal end-cruck truss (Brunskill 2007, fig d.66), again with an arrangement of radiating and hipped roof-rafters as described by Hewett (1982), carried at the eaves by the curved end walls. A problem with this method of construction, highlighted to the writer by Dr Gardiner (and leaving aside the chronology of cruck-truss building techniques as they are currently understood and noted above), is that for Building 467 the distance between the base of an end-cruck (ie the gable posthole) and the point at which it would have joined the apex of the first lateral principal truss would have measured in the region of 4m; a distance that would seem large to be carried by either a single or a scarf-jointed cruck-blade.

Whatever the detailed form of the roof structure, we can be far surer that it was covered with thatch, a material that would have been suitable to model and sweep to the suggested curved and hipped ends of the building. Thatched roofs were the norm in the rural vernacular architecture of Somerset and the wider South West region and are also indicated at Eckweek by a virtual absence of stone roof tiles from the site as a whole: that is apart from a stone roof tile complete with nail hole reused in a stone drain [Feature 71] in 14th-century Building 460, possibly indicating that at least one of the earlier (Period III or IV) buildings may have incorporated a partly-tiled smoke opening or louvre.

Comparable earthfast buildings of the 11th century are rare in the archaeological record for the South West region and indeed nationally. The characteristic features of Building 467, the rounded form of at least three of its corners and large internal sunken-floor features, is nowhere mirrored directly, although there is some indication that similar building forms were in use elsewhere in the region, for example at Bickley, Cleeve (Ponsford 2001, figs 8 and 9), where the general plan-form of Building 2 of the mid to late 12th century excavated by Michael Ponsford appears to have incorporated a rounded western end. A further earthfast timber building of the 11th century, which incorporated a floor-level hearth and a large sunken-floor feature at the southeastern end, along with a curved gable end, was identified by Donna Young at Brent Knoll (Young 2009). A less certain parallel was recorded in 1964 close to Eckweek, at Barrowmead, Bath, by Jayne Woodhouse (Woodhouse 1976, Period II structures F11, F14 and F29). Here the Period II features dated to the 12th to 13th centuries hint at an earthfast timber structure that had a curved and subrectangular plan-form. Further afield, Building S15 at Porchester Castle (Cunliffe 1976), Hants, had similar curved corners or apsidal ends, although these were interpreted to reflect elements of a 10th-century aisled building.

Periods III.2–III.3, Structure 471 – Area A

The original purpose of this deep elongated pit (416, Figure 4.19) located in the 'yard' area was not evident from the deposits that filled it (Figure 4.23), although a group of three stakeholes, two at the southern end and one at the northwest corner, indicated that it may have either been fenced or covered when open. Use as a latrine, sited alongside but set back from the dwelling (Building 467), is a possibility, although no significant cess-like material was present in the primary [415] or secondary [414] fills.

The secondary fill of the pit contained a complete cooking pot (Figure 4.23; FPN490) that was buried upside-down and filled with small stones. The reason for this act is unclear, although the deposition of similar special or votive deposits in late Anglo-Saxon contexts has been recognised elsewhere, in particular the placement of complete ceramic vessels as a deliberate means of signifying a 'termination deposit' (Hamerow 2006, 27). Whether the burial of the pottery vessel in Pit 416 represents an example of such a practice remains unknown.

Period III.3, Structure 480 – Area A

Elements of a subsequent earthfast structure (Figure 4.19, Structure 480), which possibly was attached to the southeastern corner of Building 467, was constructed over the fill of Pit 416, as indicated by a group of postholes, Features 228, 298, 299, 409 and 411 and a rubble and soil layer [292 and 293]. The combined plan-form of these features may indicate a subcircular or oval structure of fairly lightweight construction, although, if so, it is ill-defined and seemingly incomplete. The purpose of such a structure was not indicated by the associated archaeology.

Period III, Pit Group 469 – Area A

This group of intercutting pits and gullies (Figures 4.19 and 4.20) appeared to define the southern side of the farmstead plot, although the pottery recovered from them indicates that activity associated with two ceramic phases was represented. All the features were cut into the underlying stone-free Fullers Earth clay.

The three central pits, Features 319, 327 and 346, were each shallow and the latter two might be more accurately described as pans rather than pits. These features [327 and 346] were intercut with a pair of narrow and mostly straight-sided gullies that extended beyond the excavation area to the east, in the direction of a modern pond located at the field edge. The absence of any stratigraphic relationship between the features and the homogeneous nature of the deposit that filled them suggests that in their final form they formed a contemporary group. Finds recovered from them (Figures 7.30–7.33) were mixed and provide no clear indication as to use and, despite the close ceramic phasing provided by the pottery, it is therefore certainly possible that they formed simply as a result of intermittent pit and ditch digging along the southern boundary over an extended period.

A possible alternative explanation is that the group represents a cascade of shallow features that originally were dug to hold still or slowly running water, which was fed into them by the narrow gullies from the pond located just to the east (this of course assumes that a pond was present in the 11th century). A similar explanation is proposed for a group of features of late Saxon date identified at Lawn Farm, Shapwick (Gerrard with Aston 2007, 974), where a group of shallow troughs linked by straight-sided channels is suggested to relate to either the retting of flax (Blair and Ramsay 1991, 324) or the fulling of woollen cloth by trampling it in water to remove grease and speed the matting process (Blair and Ramsay 1991, 330). In view of the nature of the natural substrate the features were cut into at Eckweek, the latter is considered the more likely of the two. As at the Shapwick site, the presence of a number of associated stakeholes located alongside and close to the pit group at Eckweek raises the possibility that they relate to the subsequent drying and stretching of woollen cloth on wooden tenters. Alternative explanations, wholly unrelated to cloth processing, are also suggested for the Shapwick features, including the keeping of freshwater eels and the growing of watercress (Gerrard with Aston 2007).

Period III, Building 477 – Area H

The building was approximately 14m long and 7m wide in its final form (Figures 4.3 and 4.14); this compares with 8.9m × 4m for House 1 at Goltho and 11.4 × 7.2m for the Period 5 late Saxon Hall at the same site, both of which are dated by the excavator to the 11th century (Beresford 1987). It [477] incorporated a range of large earthfast timber features, all of which produced pottery of ceramic phases 2 and 3 (pottery of CP4 and later was entirely absent from stratified contexts), a ceramic phasing that dates its construction, occupation and abandonment to the 11th century.

The development of the building appears to have involved at least one phase of major repair or rebuilding, as indicated by the second of two large gable postpits at the western end of the building and an intermediate stone foundation or underpinning revealed in Postpit 3009 (Figure 4.14, 3041) that produced pottery of CP3. The structural logic of the building is complex and further complicated

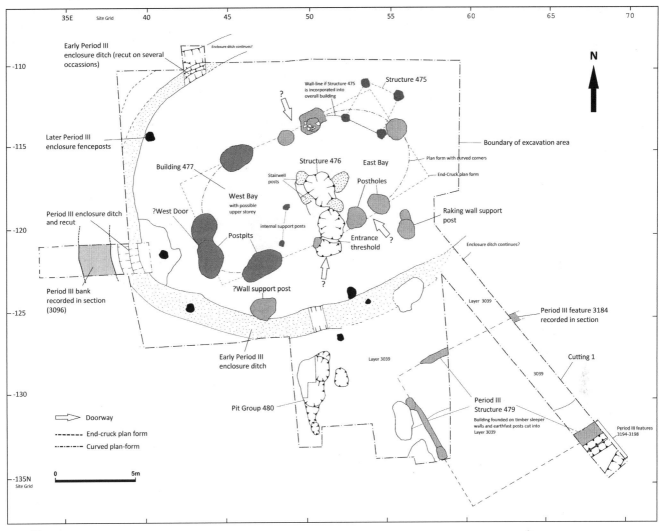

FIGURE 7.2

General structural interpretation of Period III features in Area H

by a separate, but seemingly contemporary four-posted pit structure [Structure 476] centrally located inside the building, and a second four-post structure [Structure 475], all features of which were aceramic, located adjacent and to the north of the east gable-post. As a result, it is possible to suggest at least two coherent structural interpretations for the building in both an initial and final, as excavated, form (Figure 4.45), along with different interpretations that either incorporate or exclude Structures 476 and 475.

The overall shape of the building is defined by the western and eastern gableposts and further groups of three and four earthfast postpits or postholes located along the north and south sides, with those defining the eastern end of the building seemingly paired across its width. Unlike Building 467 in Area A, there are no intervening features or floor deposits that directly indicate the precise plan-form of the building, although differences in the morphology of the principal post foundations are considered significant in relation to the overall superstructure (below). At face value, these and associated features appear to delineate a large rectangular or subrectangular, earthfast building that was set inside an oval enclosure defined by a very shallow ditch. Immediately to the west of the building the ditch was set just inside an earth bank (Figure 4.45), but to the south it separated off the building from an adjacent compound that contained at least one further timber building.

The absence of any evidence for corner posts, combined with the curved nature of the surrounding enclosure ditch [3023] and the suggested rounded-end form of contemporary Period III Building 467, indicate that this building may also have had a subrectangular plan-form that incorporated rounded corners (Figure 7.2) of a closely similar type to those suggested for Building 467 in Area A. Whether it was of strictly rectangular plan or had rounded corners, it would have had an internal area in the region of 90 square metres (*c*960 square feet).

The suggested layout and symmetry of the building in its final form is indicated on Figure 7.2 where the principal earthfast foundations at the northeastern end of the structure are represented by a set of five postholes (Figure 4.14, 3005, 3007, 3078, 3080 and 3088) of broadly similar size, whilst the

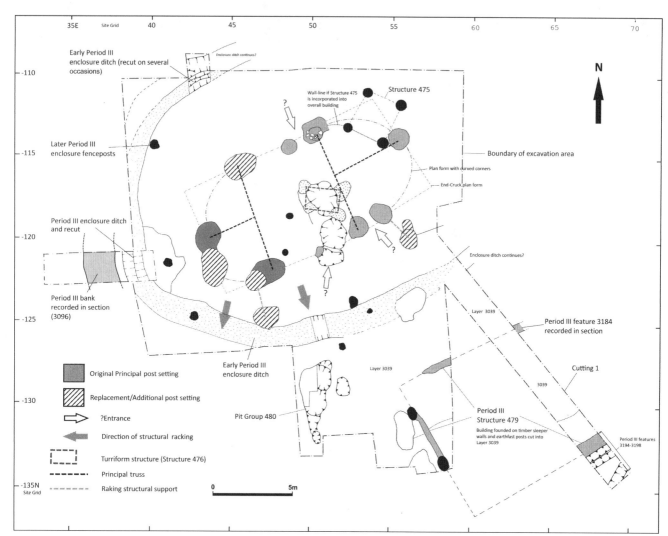

FIGURE 7.3A

Structural interpretation of Period III Building 477 in Area H – Option 1

southwestern end is delineated by a single smaller posthole (3074) and three larger postpits, Features 3009, 3013 and 3137. In combination, the planform of these features suggests three opposing pairs of principal post trusses with a heavy tie-beam roof structure, although, if so, their spatial arrangement (Figure 7.2) indicates that none of the trusses would have been even close to perpendicular to a centre line drawn between the end gableposts. A pair of opposing entrances are indicated approximately midway along the building by opposing Postholes 3078/3080 in the south wall and 3005/3007 in the north, although this standard (Hamerow 2012, 37–45) cross-entry interpretation is complicated by pit Features 3019 and 3049. These, in combination with Posthole 3074, could reflect an alternative entrance, where the pits represent erosion to either side of a slightly skewed doorway, the threshold of which was represented by a narrow ridge of natural clay that separated the two pits. This interpretation, favoured by the writer, remains open to question, in particular (but not solely) because, if so, the line of the suggested doorway would appear to have been oblique to the line of the south wall.

The various points considered above relating to the possible roof structure of Building 467 apply equally to this building if a similar rounded planform is adopted, although here the morphology of the postpits and postholes indicate that the structure potentially could have incorporated either two (Figure 7.3A) or three (Figure 7.3B) sets of load-bearing principal posts and trusses (plus a further principal post at the gable end). In this respect, the superstructure is consistent with the interior footprint, which would have been significantly larger than that of Building 467. In addition, the difference in size alone of the larger postpits at the southwestern end of the building indicates that they were dug to accommodate substantially larger earthfast posts than those that supported the northeastern half of the structure. The smaller postholes delineating the northeastern half of the building would have accommodated a timber in the region of 400mm in the round, whilst the larger postpits in the southwestern half could have held a timber of approximately 650mm diameter. This apparent difference carries implications for the structural interpretation of the building, both as it was originally

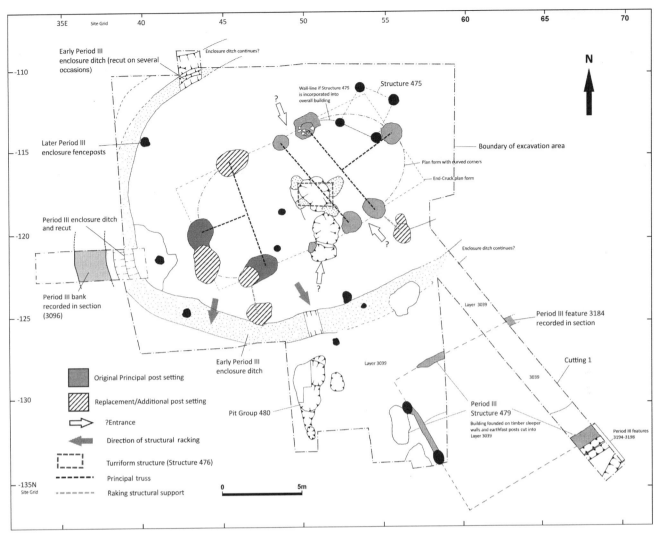

FIGURE 7.3B

Structural interpretation of Period III Building 477 in Area H – Option 2

built and for its subsequent (Period III, Phase 1b) structural modification (Figures 7.3A and B), the latter more accurately reflecting largescale and perhaps emergency structural support rather than normal and expected earthfast repairs.

A second large principal post [3015] was erected at the southwestern gable end, immediately adjacent to and alongside Post-pit 3013. Just like the deposits that filled the original post-pit [3013], both the primary [3072] and secondary [3071] fills of Feature 3015 produced pottery of CP2, an indication at least that only a relatively short period of time separated the two events and that in the building's final phase the two posts may well have stood alongside one another. At approximately the same time (CP2), the principal post in Postpit 3009 appears to have been either replaced or, perhaps more likely, underpinned, as indicated by a well-consolidated rubble packing [3041] that formed an intermediate fill. The stone packing was essentially circular in plan and was laid slightly off-centre, tight against the southwestern edge of the pit cut.

Further repair or reinforcement of the foundations at the southwestern end of the structure is also indicated by the elongated plan-form of Postpit 3137, a feature which suggests that it may have been recut or enlarged, again conceivably for a second post inserted alongside the first. Unfortunately, the cutting excavated through the feature was opened laterally as opposed to longitudinally, had it been the latter the possibility that a second post was indeed introduced might have been confirmed. Only the uppermost fill of the pit, Deposit 3136, produced pottery of CP3. Further evidence for the reinforcement or support of the building was provided by Features 3082/3139 and 3020, both of which were located a similar distance outside and to the south of the south wall-line and slightly oblique to the nearest principal post. Only one of the features [3082/3139] was fully excavated, the primary fill of which, stone packing [3134], produced pottery of CP2 and was set off-centre, alongside the southeastern edge of the cut. This arrangement suggests that the posthole was dug to hold a raking timber and, if so, one that could have provided additional support to principal posts 3078 and/or 3080. Feature 3020 was sadly only part-excavated and produced pottery of CP2: on the basis of its position alone it is also

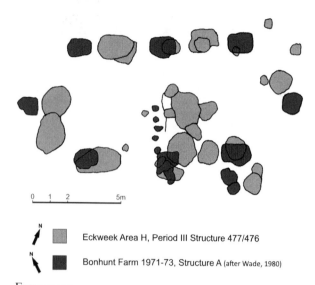

FIGURE 7.4

Comparison of Building 477/476 at Eckweek and Structure A at Bonhunt Farm, Essex

likely to have held a similar raking support timber, attached either to an original, a replacement, or a second principal post founded in Postpit 3137.

The reason for this apparently largescale rebuilding and/or reinforcement work is not immediately evident, although the emphasis of the work appears to have been focused on the southwestern end of the building and the south wall (Figures 7.3A and B). The excavated evidence indicates two possible aspects to the work. Firstly, the introduction of an intermediate layer of the stone reinforcement [3041] in Postpit 3009 suggests that the original timber had rotted in the base and was either, trimmed and underpinned in-situ, or replaced entirely. Secondly, the original posts set in Postpits 3013 and 3137 may have suffered similar decay, although here it appears that the preferred response was to add one and possibly two new principal posts (3015, and a second located in the western extension of Postpit 3137). If this was indeed so, the position of these additional principal posts suggests an urgent need to oppose a movement of the structure outwards at the southwestern corner (shown on Figure 7.3A and B) and indeed outwards along the south wall as a whole. Reinforcement of the latter is also indicated by the position of the pair of suggested raking supports, Features 3082 and 3021. This suggested sequence of events does not however explain why the principal posts that were set in larger postpits, which by inference were therefore of larger scantling, needed replacing and/or reinforcing, whilst the smaller principal posts supporting the northeastern end of the building did not.

One possible explanation is that the posts at the southwestern end of the building were originally larger because they were required to support a greater load; a load that was concentrated principally over the southwestern end of the building. This increased load either led directly to an outward force on the building to the south and southwest or magnified the effects of rotted principal posts generally. Either way, it would have led to a potentially disastrous lateral racking of the superstructure that required additional and largescale support. Evidence for similar reinforcement of a major building was recorded at Springfield Lyons, Essex (Tyler and Major 2005), where a series of postholes set approximately one metre outside the south wall of Building 3 are interpreted to represent later structural supports. In addition, Mark Gardiner (2013) notes that the Springfield Lyons building appears to have formed part of a manorial centre and that the occupants are unlikely to have undertaken such reinforcement work unless the building reflected their status.

The plan-form of the building's [477] principal earthfast features, excluding those associated with Structure 476 (discussed below), has (in 2015) remarkably few direct parallels in the published literature, save for a building excavated at Wicken Bonhunt, Essex, by Keith Wade (Wade 1980, 96–103) in the early 1970s. Structure A on that site (dated to the period AD 1100–1300) bears close similarity with Building 477 at Eckweek, both in terms of its form and overall dimensions. To illustrate their remarkable similarity, the two structures are shown superimposed on Figure 7.4. The excavator interpreted Structure A at Bonhunt Farm as representing elements of a larger, aisled building, evidence of whose exterior structural envelope had entirely failed to survive. In addition, it was also suggested that the structure was of higher social status with seigniorial connections.

The structural logic of the larger principal post settings at the southwestern end of Building 477 implies that they were required to accommodate timber of larger scantling and thereby support a greater load, although the use of postpits that are substantially larger than the scantling of the timbers they held has been interpreted to reflect a need to be able to precisely position principal timbers in-situ during the construction process. If the timbers were indeed larger, the structural implications that flow from this are that the western end of the building incorporated some form of larger superstructure, perhaps the most obvious being a partial upper storey. Two-storey buildings are virtually absent from the archaeological record of late Anglo-Saxon England, albeit with the possible exception of the Long Hall at Cheddar Palace (Rahtz 1979) which, along with a handful of possible wooden turriform structures (see below), have been interpreted to corroborate a 10th-century entry in the *Anglo Saxon Chronicle*, which describes how a group of important nobles and councillors fell from the first floor of a building in Calne, Wiltshire:

In this year the leading councillors of England fell down from an upper storey [in uno solario] at Calne... (ASC 978).

Structure 476

The morphology and character of Structure 476 (Figure 4.14), an earthfast structure located approximately centrally and seemingly inside Building 477, is problematic. The structure was founded upon a roughly squared arrangement of four smaller post settings, all of which were cut at the shoulder of a shallow pit [3017] and all of which, the pit and the postholes, produced a pottery assemblage of ceramic phase 2; an assemblage that is indistinguishable from that recovered from the fills of the various principal postholes and postpits of Building 477. This, combined with the close spatial arrangement between the southernmost posthole [3047] and Pit 3049 (and thereby in turn with Feature 3033 and Posthole 3074), appears to support the hypothesis that the structure [476] constituted a contemporary element of Building 477, as opposed to an entirely separate earthfast structure. This interpretation is supported by the shallowness of at least three of the four post-settings, which appear insufficient to have supported a free-standing timber structure. The morphology of the postholes (Figures 4.14 and 4.33, profiles A and B), or more specifically of the three that were fully excavated, whilst not entirely consistent, indicates that at least two [3047 and 3070] of the three held timbers of rectangular scantling that, if they closely fitted the posthole cuts, would have measured in the region of 300mm x 150mm (12" × 6"). The elongate plan-form of the unexcavated posthole [3051] indicates that it also probably held a similar, elongate timber. The spatial arrangement of the postholes is neither entirely regular nor squared, although as a group they represent an approximately squared timber structure that would have measured roughly 2m east to west and 1.5m north to south.

Determining what type of structure the four-post and pit arrangement may have supported is more problematic still. A number of possible interpretations arise that, in no particular order, include:

1. a free standing smoke-hood for a hearth;
2. a free standing four-posted open hearth structure, for example one that could have been used to suspend cooking vessels;
3. a simple stairwell or ladder structure;
4. the principal foundations for a bell or observation turret (see Hewett 1982, 62–69);
5. a combination of iii and iv above;
6. an entirely separate sunken-floored Grubenhauser-type structure of the 11th century, akin to the sunken-floored features present in Building 467 in Area A. The shallowness of the post settings would seem, however, to argue against this.

Putting the spatial arrangement of the structure to one side for the moment, the possibility that the group reflects the position of a hearth structure of some sort, where Feature 3017 represents a hearth pit, is plausible but is not supported by the excavated evidence, which failed to detect any significant trace of burning, hearth-fuel residue or hearth structure, either in the pit or posthole fills, or in the area of the structure as a whole. In view of the suggestion made above that the building may have incorporated at least a partial upper storey, some form of straight and open ladder-flight or companionway (Brunskill 2000, 124–125) formed by wooden treads alone to provide access to an upper level is possible. However, this latter interpretation stands very much alone and cannot escape the fact that firm evidence for late Saxon two-storey timber buildings of any variety is lacking in the archaeological record.

In 1990, and indeed up until as recently as 2008, the possibility that the structure represented the foundations of a wooden turret-like structure or tower would have been considered the least probable interpretation. However, excavation undertaken by Gabor Thomas at the late Saxon settlement site at Bishopstone (Thomas 2008 and 2010), East Sussex, has produced new and persuasive evidence with which to support such an interpretation. The Bishopstone site revealed the remains of a cellared timber structure (Structure W), which incorporated four canted or oval earthfast posts, each of which was set into a curved recess at the four corners of the cellar pit. The excavator suggests that these represented the principal foundations of a timber tower or turret, which incorporated a cellared store or strongroom. The structure was of more than one storey in height and was surrounded, and possibly supported at the base, by a lightweight lean-to structure with a rounded ground plan. The dimensions of the four post settings indicated that the suggested tower measured approximately 3m by 2.6m with a footprint of some 8.1 square metres. The principal elements of Structure 476 at Eckweek, a group of four posts set in a roughly squared arrangement around a shallow pit, whilst of smaller plan-form overall and certainly not incorporating a deliberate cellar, have some distinct similarities with those of Structure W at Bishopstone. There is other, earlier, excavated evidence for late Saxon timber turriform structures, notably the suggested two-cell tower building at Springfield Lyons in Essex (Tyler and Major 2005).

Finally, in view of the sunken-floor features that were incorporated inside Building 467 in Area A, it is possible that Structure 476 represents an entirely separate, small sunken-floored structure, although, if so, the indistinguishable ceramic phasing for it and Building 477 provides precious little time for both structures, in whatever order, to have been separately built, abandoned and replaced.

The apparent similarities between Structure 476 and Structure W recorded at Bishopstone, combined with contemporary documentary references to turriform structures associated with buildings of 'burhgeat' or 'thegnly' status in the late Saxon period, a class defined in the 11th-century text of the *Promotion Law*, supports the suggestion that Building 477 incorporated a small timber turriform structure that was integrated into the overall structure of the larger building in its latest form when it was accessed directly via a separate side entrance. This, in combination with the overall character of Building 477, a large and imposing structure that was set inside a small 'protected' enclosure (Hamerow 2012, 109–119) defined by a bank set outside a ditch, would seem, to the writer at least, to meet a number of the key requirements of a *thegnly* residence as described in the *Promotion Law*.

Structure 475

This small regular structure measuring approximately 2.5m squared was indicated by a group of four postholes (Figures 4.3 and 4.14, Postholes 3187, 3188, 3189 and 3190), each of very similar size and distinctive morphology. None of the features produced any stratified dating evidence and their inclusion in Period III is based upon the absence of stratified pottery any later than CP3 from excavation Area H as a whole, plus the seemingly deliberate and precise relationship between Posthole 3189 and the gable posthole of Building 477, Posthole 3088. Nonetheless, it remains possible that the structure reflects medieval activity in Area H very late in ceramic phase 3, directly after Building 477 had been demolished. Alternatively, it may reflect a structure of later medieval date and a phase of activity that left no associated artefacts or dating evidence of any kind.

If the structure does reflect activity contemporary with Building 477 during Period III, then its interpretation, as has already been noted above, is problematic, as it would have crossed the wall-line of Building 477, whether the building had a standard rectangular plan-form or rounded corners (Figure 7.2). This relationship alone argues against the two structures being contemporary, although a note made during the excavation of Posthole 3088, which states its very 'cess-like' texture and colour, raises the possibility at least that the structure was attached to Building 477 as a chamber for some form of latrine, one that on occasion drained into the posthole.

If the structure post-dates the 11th century, then the standard interpretation would be that it represents the foundations of a raised grain store (Gardiner 2011) although such structures are invariably located at a settlement focus and not sited in isolation. In addition, no evidence to suggest the substantial processing or storage of cereals, specifically charred grain or chaff, was recovered from either the foundation postholes or the footprint of the structure.

Periods III.2 and III.3, Structure 479 – Area H

Features relating to this rectangular earthfast structure (Figures 4.3 and 7.2) aligned southwest to northeast, parallel to Building 477, indicated that it was in excess of 8m long and approximately 8m wide. Although only a small part of the structure was revealed during the fieldwork, those features that were indicate a structure founded upon intermittent post-in-trench or post and earthfast sill-beam walls, construction methods that become increasingly common during the later Anglo-Saxon and early post-Conquest periods and which invariably indicate a roof structure carried directly on load-bearing walls, often with less substantial end walls (Hamerow 2012, 22–31). No internal features were identified and too little of the structure was revealed to say with any certainty whether it represented a dwelling, although, on the basis of its size alone, this is considered likely.

The structure was constructed slightly later than Building 477 on stratigraphic grounds, as its principal features were cut into Deposit 3039, a layer of coarse gravelly metalling whose characteristics are consistent with deliberately prepared ground recorded on a number of higher status late Saxon sites (Hamerow 2012). The metalling layer filled the curved enclosure ditch [3023] that had been opened in CP2 around Building 477 and appeared to have been laid down in CP3 at the same time as the boundary was subsequently defined by a fence, indicated by a series of small posts [3158/3264 etc].

The absence of any pottery later than CP3 from Area H as a whole indicated that during the latest stage of CP3 both buildings were in use at the same time. In addition, the ceramic phasing indicates that both were also abandoned by the end of the 11th century, if not somewhat earlier.

Period IV, Buildings 462 and 465 – Area A

The construction of Buildings 462 and 465 in Area A (Figure 4.2) during ceramic phase 4, broadly the period between AD 1200 and 1275, marks a major transition in the built environment of the settlement that is signified by a change from the use of earthfast timber structures to the adoption of stone sill or load bearing walls. By implication, the change is also likely to have involved a transition from the use of principal posts and rafters to that of cruck-built or timber-framed superstructures. This shift in building tradition evident at Eckweek is consistent with a widespread and pivotal change in rural building tradition that is recognised elsewhere across large parts of England during the 12th century (Gardiner 2014), a change that, at Eckweek at least, also appears to mark an end of ditch and pit digging and the earthfast tradition generally throughout the settlement. The reason for this widespread transition from building in the ground in timber to building on it in stone is suggested to have its roots at least in part in the emergence of a new class of specialist artisan carpenters and the subsequent development of new techniques in joinery (Gardiner 2014 and Dyer 2000, section 8), in particular the use of tightly cut mortice and tenon joints. Other reasons suggested to have influenced the change include a diminishing availability of substantial mature timber and the emergence of the cruck building technique, the latter a factor favoured by Christopher Dyer (2000, 156).

Building 462 replaced Building 467 and was constructed after the principal earthfast features of the latter had been wholly or largely backfilled with deposits containing pottery of CP4, which indicates a date of construction around the turn of the 13th century. The relationship between the two structures was direct and demonstrated by stratigraphic relationships. Although the plan of Building 462 as excavated was incomplete, it was clearly founded upon at least three bonded drystone walls, each around 700–800mm wide that appear to have defined slightly less internal space (at least 34 square metres) than the earlier timber building (Building 467). The foundations were preserved to just a couple of courses of intermittent stonework (Figures 4.47 and 4.48) and there was no direct evidence to indicate their original height. This is in part because the masonry appeared to have been deliberately cleared (no trace of Period IV demolition rubble was identified in Area A) before the construction of Period V Building 460, rather than simply having collapsed. Mark Gardiner (2014, 20) suggests that clay-bonded walls exceeding 500mm in width could conceivably have been built to the height of the eaves, although the absence of any significant Period IV demolition rubble makes this very unlikely for this building.

Too little of the structure was preserved to determine its original layout in any detail, although those parts that were intact indicate that it probably did not incorporate the standard cross passage arrangement as suggested for the preceding timber building, but included an entrance [344] in the north wall at the northeastern corner of the building that gave access directly to and from the metalled trackway. This arrangement appears unusual at a time when cross passage doorways were increasingly the norm in domestic houses (Grenville 1997). In siting the building, the builders also appeared concerned to maximise the use of the land available in the farmstead tenement and to do so built the north wall precisely over the backfilled Period III boundary ditch [363], which had previously separated the plot from the trackway. This decision may, at least in part, also have been influenced by the need to avoid building the south wall directly over the filled (and possibly less well consolidated) Period III sunken-floor features. Associated deposits were restricted to scraps of a floor layer [Layer 285 etc], none of which provide any information beyond that the floors were very likely of earth. Two separate phases of stone revetment [Features 360 and 361] built against the northeast corner of the building indicate that the boundaries of the farmstead yard were now defined by a series of low earth banks whose exterior face was often revetted in drystone work.

The remains of Building 465 (Figures 4.4 and 4.56) located just to the south were, if anything, even less well preserved than Building 462. Overall, it appears to have been slightly larger than Building 462, although this is based upon a few short sections of clay bonded masonry and just a single soil feature, probably a remnant of floor layer [315], which was preserved beneath a later, Period V, wall and produced pottery of CP4–5. Again, the absence of any significant amounts of associated rubble suggests the masonry as excavated reflected the remains of a building founded upon a series of low dwarf walls. Neither the arrangement of the few structural features nor the finds associated with them provide any clear indication concerning the original function of the building, although the fact that it was replaced in Period V with an open-fronted byre suggests it was likely not a dwelling.

Period V, Building 460 – Area A

The remains of the 14th-century stone farmhouse in Area A (Figures 4.2 and 7.5) represented by far the best preserved structure recorded by excavation on the site and provided the greatest range of evidence to elucidate its original form, organisation and associated domestic activity.

Walls

The building was essentially rectangular in plan with overall dimensions of 11m east to west and 5m north to south. In terms of overall size, this is very consistent with the size of other recorded later medieval so-called peasant dwellings (Dyer 2000, 153–155).

The masonry forming the walls (Figure 4.50; Walls 4, 10, 11, 35 and 54) consisted of roughly faced and coursed oolitic limestone rubble between 730mm and 880mm wide that was bonded sporadically with a clay matrix (Figure 4.51). The northeastern and northwestern corners of the building, those nearest to the metalled trackway, had been completely robbed out during the post-medieval period, although where best preserved the masonry survived for eight irregular courses and some 400mm above the level of the internal floor. The walls were built directly over earlier deposits (Figure 4.52) without any significant buried foundation. Whilst there is no direct evidence with which to determine their full original height, the amount of limestone rubble that overlay and butted the intact and remaining foundations (Figures 4.62 and 4.69) suggests construction to eaves height in stone appears at least possible (Gardiner 2014). However,

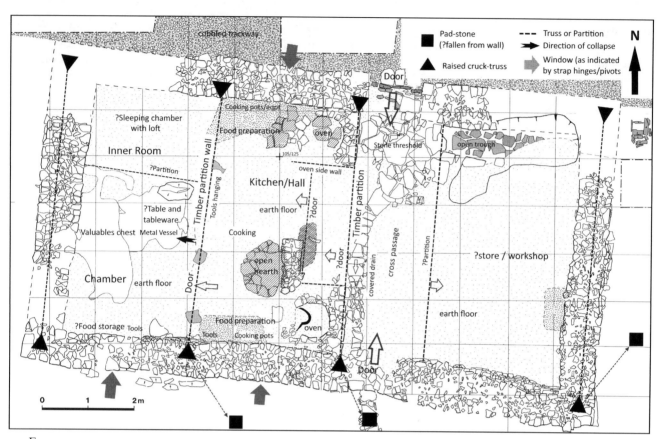

FIGURE 7.5
Structural interpretation of Period V Building 460 in Area A

a series of lower ground-sill or dwarf walls, at least 400mm high (and quite possibly nearer 1m), could have supported wooden sole plates and protected the raised timber crucks, and is considered more likely.

Roof Structure

Little can be deduced with certainty concerning the original roof structure. Two principal types of later medieval roof structure are recognised in the region: the straight principal cruck and the raised cruck (Brunskill 1994, 40–49; Alcock et al 2014, figs F6 and F7), although simple roof trusses attached to timber wall plates were also used. A principal cruck consists of single curved timbers rising from floor level to the top of, or close to, the ridge, each pair of which were often linked by a tie-beam. The alternative raised-cruck method involved pairs of curved timbers morticed into the top of a low masonry sill-wall. Either of these methods could have been utilised in Farmhouse 460, most likely along with simple mud-and-stud or wattle gable ends that were attached to the gable end truss. Alternatively, the gable ends of the building could have been hipped. The recovery of three simple padstones (Figure 7.5) from in amongst the rubble just outside the south and east walls supports the suggestion that the building incorporated a series of raised crucks that sat above the ground sill-walls.

The size of the building and its internal three-bay layout suggests a pair of open crucks or principal rafters were located roughly centrally (Figure 7.5) with two further, possibly closed, pairs either close to or at each gable end. On that basis, it seems likely that the interior was probably open to the rafters throughout, whilst the position of the hearth at floor-level in front of a low fireback wall, indicates it vented through a simple smokehole or holes, these possibly located centrally or, more likely, at the apex of the gable ends. The roof was almost certainly thatched over less substantial common rafters in the local tradition.

Doors and Windows

The building had two opposing doorways (Figure 7.5), both of which were located slightly off-centre, one each in the north and south walls. The south doorway had a simple stone threshold (137, Figure 4.50), whilst the northern entrance, directly off the trackway, was defined by a kerb of tabular slabs set edge-on [68] and a small area of paved flooring [36], the entrance threshold proper. Finds including iron strap hinges, hinge-pivots, locks and keys (Figures 7.6 and 7.7) from the building during this phase indicate that both these main entrances probably had substantial wooden doors complete with locks.

The location of windows is not evident from the remains of the masonry foundations alone, although the associated artefacts imply unglazed and louvred openings or shuttered 'lights' with wooden lintels and vertical wooden spars (Alcock *et al* 2014, fig. 25). Whilst there is no evidence as to their size, it seems likely that there was at least one opposing pair in the middle Kitchen/Hall bay that provided light from both sides of the building with a third in the south wall of the west bay, the chamber and inner room (Figure 7.5).

Internal Space and Structures

The interior space of the building was subdivided into three distinct bays (Figure 7.5) and thereby conformed to the main elements of the later medieval 'tripartite' domestic plan, whose principal divisions of internal space were invariably articulated by a building's main structural elements – the principal post and tie beam or cruck-trusses (Dyer 2013, 19–27; Gardiner 2000, 159–179).

The opposing entrances were located slightly off-centre in the long walls and define the position of a cross passage, the eastern side of which is suggested to have been separated from the east bay by means of a wooden screen or similar, as indicated by the extent of both the threshold slabs [36] inside the north door and the drain-point of the open trough [60/66] in the east bay. The north door opened directly onto the trackway, an arrangement that evidently required a deliberate raised sill [68] in order to restrict the amount of muck entering the house. Evidence that this represented the main entrance to the building was provided by a threshold of irregular flagstones [36] laid immediately inside the doorway, this in turn overlay a short section of stone drain [241] that fed into the channel [71] that drained the stone trough [66]. The presence of a lateral screen or wooden partition located at the point where the threshold stones end and both the base masonry and cut for the open trough began is therefore likely and would have provided a simple means to separate and define the two areas.

The function of the east bay, an internal division that might conventionally be termed the service area, remains unclear, as neither the artefacts it contained (Section 7.2), nor the structural features it incorporated, provide any conclusive evidence of what it was used for. The open stone-lined trough [60/66] located at the northeastern corner of the bay fed into a carefully constructed and covered drain [71] that was sealed below the latest floor layer [18]. It ran through the cross passage and beneath the south doorway and beyond into the yard. Unfortunately, the trough had been disturbed by a post-medieval robber pit [37] dug to remove the building's corner masonry, an event that may also have effectively enlarged the original cut [66] for the trough, as its plan-form as excavated indicates that it was constructed before the masonry of the north wall [35]. Whether the trough was also originally either fully or partially covered was unclear, although its presence, along with the drain, could conceivably indicate that the bay was used to house livestock of one sort or another, a feature often attributed to rural medieval dwellings generally, but more specifically associated with the true later medieval long house (Grenville 1997, 134–141). However, the position of the trough alone, which was positioned on the slightly higher side of the room, indicates that it would simply not have worked to drain livestock effluent. An alternative function could have involved using the trough for washing or fulling woollen cloth, where the exit to the drain was temporarily plugged and cloth would have been trampled underfoot along with Fullers Earth clay to remove grease and speed the matting process (Walton 1991). The presence of Fullers Earth clay and silts (BGS online) beneath the farmstead in Area A adds some support to this interpretation, although the trough could equally have been used for retting flax (Walton 1991, 324).

The central bay represented the main communal living space of the house and was accessed from the cross passage via an entrance, almost certainly a door or doors, located in the space between the stone fireback [17] and the side walls of the two small domestic ovens or kilns [16 and 42]. The room appears to have combined the functions of both kitchen and hall in a remarkably small space (just 5m by 3m) and as such can usefully be described as the main '*housespace*' (Grenville 2008, 107). No direct evidence for door jambs was identified, although the likelihood of a timber-framed partition or screen separating this area from the cross passage, with a door attached, seems high and is supported by the location of a latch lifter and hinge pivots immediately to the rear of the stone fireback [17]. The room contained a stone hearth [30] at floor level that was intensely heat-affected and retained by the low fireback [17], which, judging by the absence of masonry rubble around it, appeared unlikely to have been more than a foot or so high when complete. The two small ovens/furnaces were located symmetrically in the corners of the room and built of limestone rubble bonded with clay. This evident symmetry was maintained by deposits of charcoal-rich soil [67 and 73] that were located just outside the entrance of each oven. Only one, the northern, had a stone base and exterior slabs, all of which were sooted and deeply heat-affected. Both possibly could have originally had a dome-like clay superstructure that covered an internal oven chamber, although medieval domestic ovens either fired or accessed from floor level are extremely rare. Furthermore, no significant amounts of heat-affected clay lining, consistent with a formed clay roof structure, were recovered from either structure. In view of this, it is equally likely that each structure represented the base of a cooking or boiling kiln, where a floor level fire-chamber heated a raised pot or metal cauldron, similar to examples recorded at Wharram Percy (Wrathmell 2012, fig. 114 and plate 37).

A group of small stone slabs (Figure 4.50, Features 144, 426 and 491) are interpreted to represent postpads for a timber partition-wall that separated off the western end of the building, a chamber or inner room measuring approximately 5m by 2.5m overall, from the kitchen/housespace. A fourth postpad [427], of similar size but slightly offset, may also have formed part of this group. This suggested partition wall coincides with the inferred position of a principal cruck-truss (Figure 7.5) and is further supported by the extent of Deposits 67 and 73 and contemporary floor layers (31 and 46). The room incorporated a large limestone boulder [143], which was set into the soil floor immediately to the west of the partition wall and to the north of a doorway suggested by the arrangement of Padstones 144 and 426 and the distribution of structural objects (Figure 7.6). The position of the boulder, combined with the extent of floor deposits [72 and 135] (Figure 4.61), indicated that the room may have been further subdivided to incorporate a tiny cell at the northern end that would have measured no more than 2m by 2.5m (Figure 7.5). The suggestion that this room represented the inner, private chamber and that it was further subdivided is supported by the distribution and range of artefacts recovered from the floor layers inside it.

Internal Floors

The interior floors throughout the building were entirely of trodden or rammed earth except for the small area of threshold paving [36] laid just inside the north door. Several patches of charcoal-rich soil (Figure 4.61, Layers 67 and 73) appeared to represent the latest rakings from the ovens, although the reason for others, for example Deposits 64 and 142, was not clear. A layer of deeply reddened soil [72], possibly the result of scorching, on the floor in the west bay may have indicated where a wooden chest was burnt, the remnants overlying traces of an earlier (Period V.2) soil floor formed of reworked clay subsoil (Figure 4.50, Layers 138, 145 and 148).

It is possible that at least some of the interior floor areas would have been covered with straw or some other disposable dried vegetation such as dried *Juncus* grass (Wrathmell 2012, 349). However, this would seem less likely in the central bay, the main communal and domestic area, where the cooking or boiling ovens and floor level hearth with just a low stone fireback, and perhaps also some form of suspended fire-canopy, examples of which are recorded in medieval buildings on Dartmoor (Wilson and Hurst 1965, 210–212), would have presented a constant and very real fire hazard.

Period V, Building 463 – Area A

The remains of this 14th-century stone building (Figure 4.2) were moderately well preserved and produced a modest assemblage of finds. Nonetheless, these, in combination with the layout and form of the structural remains, indicate that the building was not primarily for habitation or associated domestic activity, but agricultural, most probably either an animal byre or a cartshed, or possibly a building that combined both functions. Stratified pottery dates the construction of the building to ceramic phase 5, as none of the walls or internal features sealed pottery of ceramic phase 6. The east wall [20] did preserve the remains of an earlier floor layer (Figure 4.49, Layer 315) that produced pottery of CP5.

Although the western end of the building was not excavated, the building clearly had a broadly rectangular plan with overall dimensions of approximately 10m east to west and 8m north to south. The masonry forming the walls (Figure 4.56; Walls 20, 22, 81, 82, 210, 242 and 243) consisted of roughly faced and coursed small limestone rubble that was mostly in the region of 800mm wide, other than in the south wall where it was up to 1m wide in places. The masonry was bonded sporadically throughout with a clay-rich soil matrix. These were built directly over earlier deposits without any significant buried foundation and, whilst there was no direct evidence with which to determine their original full height, the relatively small amount of limestone rubble that overlay and butted the foundations indicated that they formed a series of low ground-sill or dwarf walls that were originally in the region of at least 600–700mm high. Like the suggested structure of Building 460, these could also have supported wooden sole-plates and protected raised timber crucks. The northern face of the building was defined by a low stone revetment [210], a reuse of masonry that formed the north wall of the earlier Period IV building [Building 465] and it is this feature, combined with the group of small post settings [199 and 390], which indicates the building was open-fronted to the north where it was entered from a cobbled track or yard [239].

Aside from the open front, the building had a narrow doorway in the east wall, the stone threshold [55] of which was formed by the remaining foundations of Period IV Wall 55, and a further entrance in the south wall, as indicated by the remains of a narrow metalled path [245] located just outside. The arrangement of small rubble soakaways set into the floor points to the building having been used at least in part to house animals, although the construction of the drains was at best rudimentary (and fragile) and it is hard to see them having provided any substantial drainage of the interior or lasting very long under hoof. This, coupled with the small collection of tools and equipment found towards the rear wall of the building (Figure 7.22) and the corresponding area of rubble (Figure 4.56, Layer 244) seemingly laid as a hardstanding for a work area, suggests the building probably was not used primarily to house animals, but more likely provided a multi-purpose building for both storage and for undertaking general agricultural and craft work. In addition, it may well have included space for housing a most important and valuable wooden cart (Dyer 2000, 276).

Period V, Structure 466 – Area A

This small masonry structure (Figures 4.5 and 4.59) measured approximately 3m squared and incorporated a small hearth or fire box (208) plus an exterior hearth (132) at floor level. Only the exterior sides of the masonry were faced, a feature that suggests it originally formed a solid pedestal base for an elevated structure. It is interpreted to represent the base for a detached curing chamber, or a corn-drying (Williams 1990, 232–242) or malting kiln. Malting and corn drying kilns are often similar and may have been used interchangeably, although malt kilns often show greater evidence of scorching due to the greater heat required, whereas corn can be damaged by over-heating (Beresford 1979, 98–142).

Period V, Structure 473 – Area A

This subcircular rubble structure (Figure 4.63) was formed of a thin layer of compacted limestone rubble of some 3.5m diameter. It was located (Figures 4.2 and 4.19) at the east side of the Period V farmyard and is interpreted to represent the simple stone base for an open-air hay or straw stack used for the storage of fodder crops.

Based upon its stratigraphy the structure may well have been one of the very last agricultural features built in Area A, as it overlay the latest yard soil (65, CP6) and was sealed by turf and topsoil alone. The rubble forming the base, whilst irregular, was closely packed and of fairly consistent size overall, but did not appear to incorporate space for a central wooden post.

The surprising rarity of this type of agricultural structure is noted in a recent review of late Saxon and medieval crop storage features by Mark Gardiner (2011, 23–38), who sets out the general characteristics of such fodder storage features, although all those he cites are distinguished by earthfast and ditched features and none are formed of stone.

7.2 ARTEFACTS: THE CHARACTER AND DISTRIBUTION OF LATE SAXON AND MEDIEVAL FINDS

Introduction

The position of each non-ceramic artefact was for the most part recorded three-dimensionally as a small find (SF) throughout the course of the fieldwork. Pottery was either recorded three-dimensionally as a small find, where the characteristics of the sherd(s) or vessel justified such, or by context. In the case of the latter, further subdivision was made in Area A using either 5m or 1m site grid squares that were laid out OS-style from a site baseline (Figure 1.6). In order to gain maximum definition of the distribution of pottery and other Common Artefacts (those not recorded as small finds) inside the later (Period V) medieval buildings, finds were recorded and segregated on a 1m by 1m grid. Externally, in the adjacent 'yard' area, finds were recorded and segregated by a 5m grid square. The subsequent examination of artefact distributions involved three stages as follows:

1. Plotting the distribution of structural artefacts and their relationship with structural features in order to enable a physical reconstruction of the various buildings, so far as the quality of preservation would allow.
2. Plotting the distribution of non-structural artefacts by material type and/or artefact class in order to examine the spatial organisation and use of the various late Saxon and medieval buildings and structures recorded on the site, in particular the organisation, use and abandonment of the Period V farmhouse and byre in Area A, Buildings 460 and 463, for which the quality of preservation was most complete.
3. Analysis of artefact distributions as a means to elucidate site-formation processes, in particular the circumstances of the abandonment of the latest farmstead in Area A, Buildings 460, 463 and 466.

As a consequence of the quality of preservation, combined with the seemingly rapid nature of abandonment, the distribution of artefacts for the Period V farmstead in Area A, broadly dating to the 14th century, is the most complete and illuminating. The distribution of artefacts associated with earlier phases of occupation, in particular the 11th-century earthfast timber buildings, is also examined.

Artefact Distributions

Stage 1 – Structural Objects

Period V, Building 460 – Area A

Structural artefacts associated with Building 460, including hinge-pivots, strap hinges, latch lifter, bolts, padstones, pivot-stones, nails and staples, were plotted three-dimensionally or on a 1m excavation grid (Figures 7.6 and 7.7). These, combined with the physical remains of the walls and internal features, indicate that the building was subdivided into three internal bays or rooms that were arranged in a classic 'through passage' plan (Figure 7.5). The bay divisions are defined mainly on the basis of the internal structural features, particularly the opposed doors and rear walls of the two ovens, which define

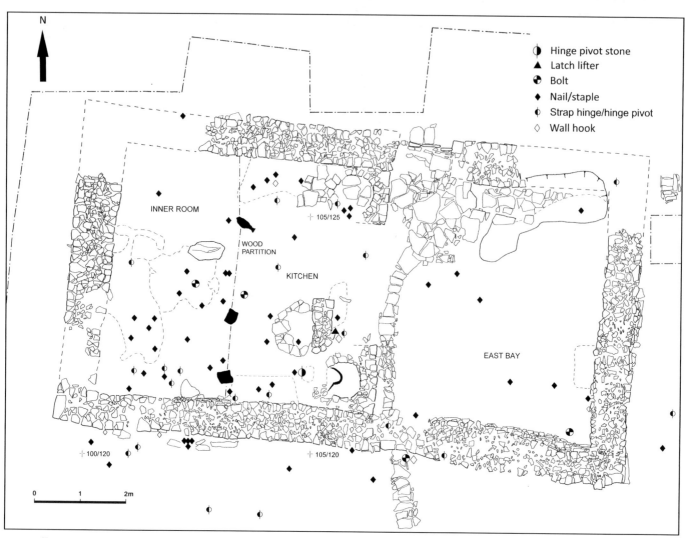

FIGURE 7.6

Period V Building 460 – distribution of structural metalwork

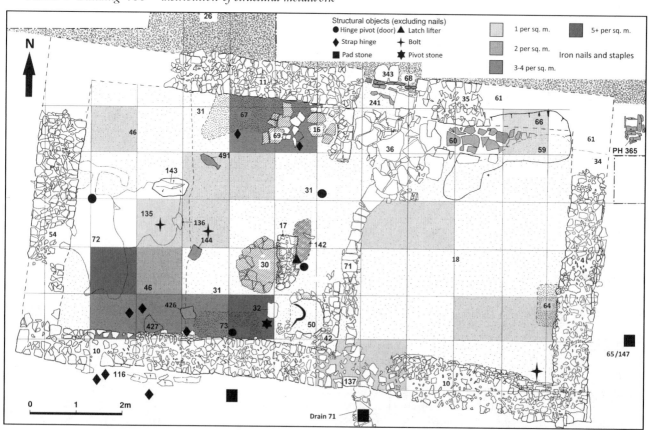

FIGURE 7.7

Period V Building 460 – distribution of structural objects including nails and staples

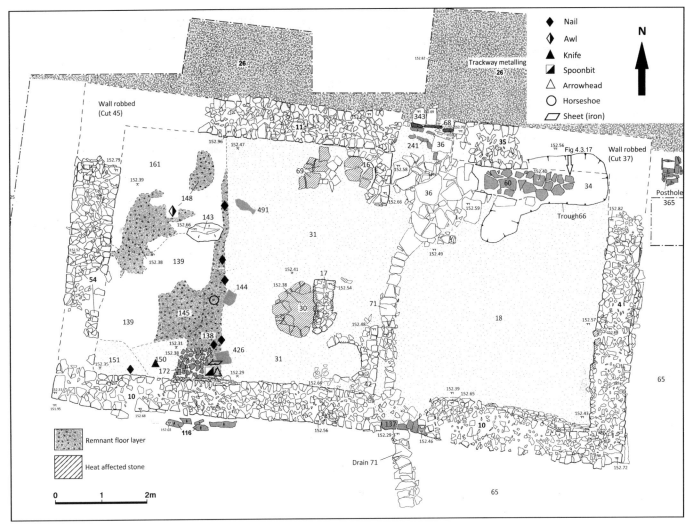

FIGURE 7.8

Period V Building 460 – distribution of Phase V.1 objects

the division between middle and east bays. The group of simple padstones [Features 144, 426 and 491] set at floor level, in conjunction with various context boundaries, define the division between the west and middle bays. This reconstruction is supported by the fact that the south wall [10] kinks markedly towards the south in the east bay; similarly irregular wall-lines are associated with cruck construction at Wharram Percy (Wrathmell 2012). Also of relevance are three padstones located near the edge of the external destruction rubble to the south and east of the building (Figure 7.7). Their location suggests that they may have fallen from the south wall and could have served as templates for a raised cruck roof structure. Templates of timber were the norm in the local late medieval vernacular tradition of the South West region (Hall 1983), however, similar 'basyng' stones are documented in North East England (Wrathmell 2012). In addition, the raised cruck method is common in late medieval and early post-medieval buildings, particularly those of lower status, in rural Somerset and the wider Bristol region. Finally, the building may have been laid out, like many slightly later buildings, using the medieval rod, pole or perch (16.5 feet) since its internal width of 16.8 feet and internal length of 35.4 feet may reflect the use of a 4-foot standard unit as is documented elsewhere in the South West regional vernacular tradition (*op cit*).

The distribution of iron nails (Figures 7.6 and 7.8) shows a slight concentration running along and to the west of the western internal partition, a feature that appears to have subdivided the interior of the building from its earliest phase. The later of the two distributions (Figure 7.6) suggests that the partition collapsed to the west, into the inner room. This interpretation is supported by the breakage patterns of both the leaf-decorated jug (Figure 5.22) and the 'Stag's Head' cistern (Figure 5.21), which were constrained by the line of the partition, although the location of sherds from these vessels in the sump of the yard (Figure 7.28) indicates that they could have been broken before it collapsed. Two iron bolts located just to the south of the stone boulder [143] indicate that there was very probably a lockable door to the inner room.

The locations of strap hinges along with nail concentrations and possibly hinge-pivots (Figure 7.6)

– although all the hinge-pivots from the house are described by Thompson as being for doors – suggest two or possibly three shuttered windows (Figure 7.5); one in the north wall in the centre of the middle bay and two in the south wall – one in the centre of the west bay and one towards the west end of the middle bay.

Finally, although at least one of the external doors may have been removed prior to collapse (no trace of the fittings for the north door were found), the presence of a large door key suggests that they are both likely to have been pretty solid constructions fitted with a lock.

Period V, Building 463 – Area A

Structural and other objects recovered from the interior of the open-fronted byre or cart shed building and areas adjacent (Figure 7.9) provide little direct additional evidence concerning its structural form, although, since it was contemporary with the farmhouse (Building 460) and preserved in the main as low drystone walls, it was quite possibly of a similar raised cruck construction generally, with the north side of two internal crucks carried over the open front by a wide timber beam that was in turn supported by at least two small timber posts [Postholes 199 and 390]. A single padstone located in the yard just to the east of the east wall represented the only supporting evidence for such an arrangement.

A doorway in the south wall is indicated by an external cobbled pathway (Figure 4.56, Feature 245) and a layer of stone [244] laid immediately inside the threshold, although fittings for such, for example hinge-pivots, are absent and associated structural items are restricted to a single strap hinge and an iron key (Figure 7.9). The number of structural nails, staples and alike appears low generally, although a concentration located directly inside the suggested south doorway conceivably could reflect the remains of a collapsed wooden door.

Periods V–VI, Building 461 – Area B

On the basis of its ceramic dating and the character of its stone foundations alone, this building appears to have shared many of the structural characteristics recorded in Period V Buildings 460 and 463 in Area A, in particular the series of dwarf walls that probably provided foundations for an arrangement of raised timber crucks. Despite its poor preservation, the physical remains of the building indicate a different internal layout to that of Building 460 in Area A, where the floor level hearth [99] was located close to the eastern end of the building, probably in the east bay, adjacent to the east (and probably the main) entrance. However, unlike Building 460, the structural artefacts recovered by excavation were far more limited, both in terms of their range and number (Figure 7.29).

The assemblage is restricted to a small number of nails and/or bolts along with a single hinge-pivot and two iron keys. As a group they add little to the interpretation, since the majority were recovered from secondary contexts, whose distribution reflects post-depositional action, as opposed to primary location. Nonetheless, they indicate that the building probably had at least one shuttered window in the south wall and two doors that could be securely fastened.

Period V, Structure 466 – Area A

Structural objects associated with the small malting or drying kiln (Figures 4.59 and 7.9) were restricted to a handful of iron nails, none of which provide any meaningful pattern or arrangement.

Period IV, Building 462 – Area A

The number of artefacts that could be attributed with any certainty to the occupation and use of this building were few (Figure 7.10), with those of a structural nature restricted to a handful of iron nails. These provide no additional information concerning the original form and nature of the building.

Period III, Building 467 – Area A

The range of structural objects recovered from features relating to this large earthfast timber building was also limited (Figure 7.30). Furthermore, the majority of the objects were recovered from secondary contexts, for example the fills of the sunken-floor pit features, and their archaeological distribution in most cases does not therefore provide direct information relating to the form and layout of the building. Nonetheless, the numbers of objects represented, along with their nature, provides some useful information concerning the general character of the building, how it was constructed and how it was organised internally.

The overwhelming impression provided by the assemblage (Figure 7.30) is that the building was not reliant to any great extent upon structural ironwork or fittings. The only significant exception appears to have been the iron padlock key (and by inference padlock) recovered from the secondary fill of the partition gully.

This apparent dependence upon carefully carpentered structural timberwork at Eckweek during the 11th century (albeit without the benefit of tight mortice and tenon joints, which are not recorded until the early 12th century) is consistent with the still surprisingly limited archaeological evidence for late Saxon timber buildings recorded elsewhere. In his recent review of the sophistication of late Saxon timber buildings Mark Gardiner (2013) notes the present limitations in making an accurate reconstruction of a building based upon excavated evidence

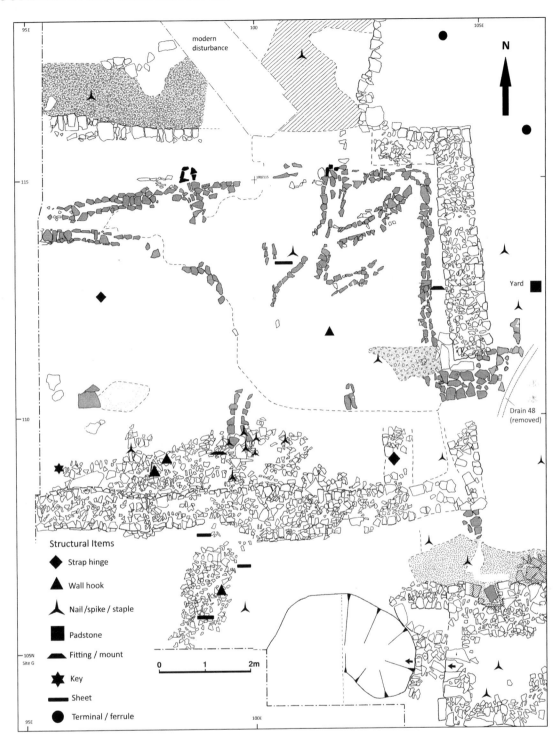

FIGURE 7.9

Period V Building 463 – distribution of structural objects

alone, but instead emphasises the importance of recognising the precision of plan-form and layout as a likely signature of a building's original complexity and sophistication. In this respect at least, both of the major 11th-century timber buildings recorded at Eckweek, Building 467 and Building 477, appear to share a similar concern for structural symmetry and precision.

Whilst accepting the limitations of reconstruction from excavated evidence noted by Gardiner and, indeed, his subsequent warning about the danger of *'essays of imagination'*, the tentative structural reconstruction shown in Figure 7.1 cannot reasonably be avoided – it is presented in expectation that it may well be tested by future studies.

Period III, Building 477 – Area H

The range of structural objects recovered from the negative cut soil features associated with this 11th-century earthfast building (Figures 4.3 and 7.2) were remarkably few and entirely restricted to a small collection of iron nails (Figure 7.34). In addition, and as noted for Period III Building 467,

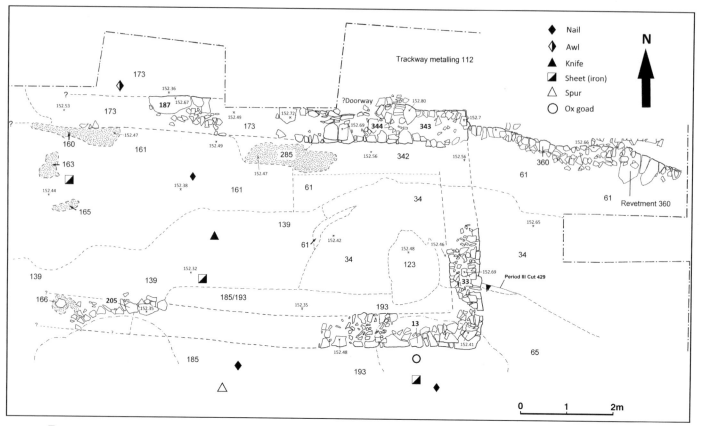

FIGURE 7.10
Period IV Building 462 – distribution of structural and other objects

their archaeological context must be considered secondary.

The numbers and distribution of structural nails provide no obvious indication concerning the form of the building's superstructure, other than to emphasise that, as for Building 467, the structural integrity of the building was not reliant to any great extent upon structural ironwork or fittings, but once again upon jointed and pegged timber. One possible exception is indicated by the greater number of nails present in the shallow central pit of Structure 476, the base of the suggested turriform structure, where the construction of an uncommon timber form may have required additional ad-hoc bracing.

The limitations of reconstruction noted above for Building 467 apply to an equal or greater extent for this building – nonetheless, the tentative structural reconstructions shown in Figures 7.2, 7.3A and 7.3B are not avoided and also presented in the expectation that they will be tested by future studies.

Stage 2 – The Organisation and Use of Buildings as Indicated by Domestic Artefacts and Other Finds

Period V, Phase V.3, Building 460 – Area A

The proposed structural reconstruction of Building 460 (Figure 7.5) identifies three principal internal rooms or bays. The eastern bay contains a stone-lined trough and drain that was separated from the cross passage by a wooden partition wall of some kind. This in turn led to the middle bay, the most important housespace, which housed a floor level hearth and two corner ovens or boiling furnaces. The middle bay was divided from the western bay, the inner room or chamber, by a timber partition wall with door. Two opposing external doors gave entry to the eastern bay, whilst the middle bay probably had a shuttered window in each wall; the west bay appears to have had at least a single window in the south wall.

The East Bay

The number and range of non-structural artefacts recovered from Floor Layer 18 was very low indeed, with only a light scatter of fragmentary pottery and bone (Figures 7.11 and 7.12) and a few metal objects, the latter including a rod, a punch and a piece of iron sheet (Figures 7.13 and 7.14). This suggests the room was not used principally for habitation or the main domestic activities of the household, but for some other activity. As noted above, possible options include simply an area for storage or wholly perishable craft work, especially since the trough vat could have been used for cleaning wool. If not, then the reason for the trough and drain is unclear, although conceivably it could have simply drained a room that was used on occasion to house animals.

The Middle Bay (The Kitchen/Hall)

This room represented the main living space of the house and was accessed from the cross passage, and in turn provided access to the chamber or inner room.

The assemblage of finds recovered from the latest floor layers (Figures 7.11 to 7.21) included a wide range of domestic artefacts including awls for leatherworking, a punch for ironworking, horseshoes and a sickle. Personal items appear to be largely absent. Alongside the northern oven [16] were two dripping dishes (Figure 7.11), a quern and a small stone trough or mould (Figure 7.15) that were associated with a slight concentration of fragmentary animal bone. The southern of the two ovens/boilers [42] contained a complete (and entirely unrelated to its use) iron sickle (Figures 5.46, 68 and 7.13) but, unlike Oven 16, lacked any associated ceramic cooking equipment. One possible explanation for this difference is that the latter was used for general food preparation, whilst Oven 42 was reserved for some specific activity such as baking. Beyond these artefact patterns, the bay produced little evidence for other spatial organisation except that a number of the knives (Figure 7.13) seem to follow the line of the east side of the partition, possibly because they were stored on a shelf or hung from pegs. The generally low incidence of fragmentary pottery and animal bone suggests the floor was swept clean, especially around the hearth, although this was not uniform throughout (Figures 7.11 and 7.12).

Furnishings and fittings (Figures 7.14 and 7.21) consisted of a single wall hook, presumably once attached to either the partition or the north wall, a wooden box indicated by a hinge, and perhaps a small 'cupboard' set into the recess to the north of Oven 42 and to the rear of the hearth wall [17]. The cupboard is suggested by the presence of a hinge-pivot, a latch lifter, two fragments of iron sheet and an iron terminal, as well as a slight concentration of animal bone (Figure 7.12). The general structural arrangement adds to the suggestion that this small area was enclosed since the masonry forming the south end of Wall 17 was carefully faced to form a curve that projected slightly beyond the line of the main masonry. The close association of the hearth and oven masonry at this point could indicate the location of some form of drying or curing chamber.

This bay represents the combined peasant kitchen and hall, the main '*housespace*' (Grenville 1997) that served the functions of kitchen, living room and workshop. The frequency of awls in the bay (Figure 7.13) suggests leatherworking was one of the crafts undertaken here, in addition to a variety of day-to-day household food preparation tasks using both the floor level hearth and the pair of small ovens or boiling kilns. The knives and whetstones (Figures 7.16 and 7.17), ostensibly of utilitarian domestic function, may also have been used in leatherworking.

THE WEST BAY (THE CHAMBER/INNER ROOM)

The assemblage of finds recovered from the floor of the room (Figures 7.11 to 7.21) was rich and varied and included a number of ornate and essentially complete ceramic tableware vessels and personal items, the latter indicating the presence of a wooden chest. The range and distribution of finds recovered possibly could indicate a further threefold division of activities undertaken inside this small space (Figure 7.5), whilst the concentration of valuables and personal items indicates that one of its functions was for the safe storage of valuables.

Finds included the most elaborate domestic objects from the 14th-century farmstead including the decorated 'Stag's Head' cistern (Figure 5.20), glazed tableware jugs and pitchers, metal vessels, decorated knives and whetstones, plus a variety of personal items including a collection of buckles, a coin, a key, the jet bead, possibly from a rosary, and an arrowhead. Craft work is also represented (Figure 7.13) by a leatherworking awl, two ironworking punches, horseshoes and a carpenter's spoonbit. Furniture is indicated by a collection of fittings (Figure 7.14) including a lock plate and decorative mounts, these possibly from a wooden valuables chest, and fragments of iron sheet.

A group of ceramic tableware and metal vessels (Figures 7.11, 7.16 and 7.18) were located in close association immediately to the south of the large stone block [143] and adjacent to the partition wall. Some of the objects, particularly the buckles, whetstones, horseshoes, awls, the spoonbit and the arrowhead, are concentrated in a line parallel to the partition, suggesting that they were most likely either hung or shelved on it. The presence of the lock plate and the mounts indicate a casket or wooden chest, a safe store for the most important household valuables such as cash, represented by the silver groat, and jewellery, by the jet bead. There is a slight concentration of bone refuse in the southeast corner of the bay (Figure 7.12), the presence of which, in association with the stone block and several whetstones and knives, raises the possibility that the room could have been used on occasion for butchery: a more straightforward explanation of course is that these items, perhaps along with joints of meat, were hung from or shelved on either the partition or south wall. Two ironworking punches were located along the west wall [54] and also could have been hung from it. Their concentration in this bay, in association with an area of heat-affected soil [72] and the stone block, raises the possibility at least that it was used for household smithing or craft tasks, although if for the former, no substantial traces of metalworking residue were recovered.

The north end of the bay, to the north of the stone block [143] and Layer 72, was largely devoid of finds of any kind. However, the corner wall

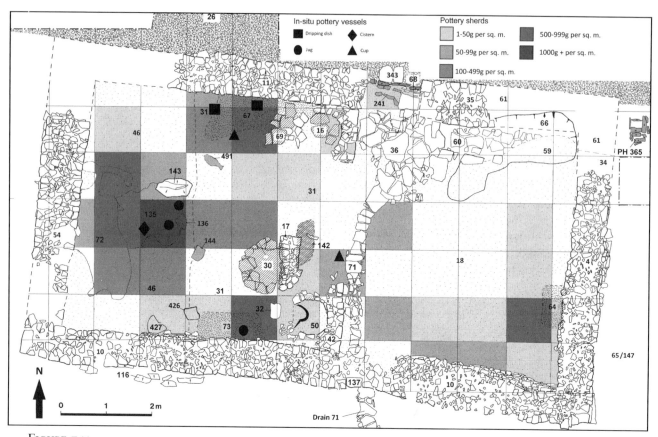

FIGURE 7.11

Period V.3 Building 460 – distribution of pottery vessels and sherds

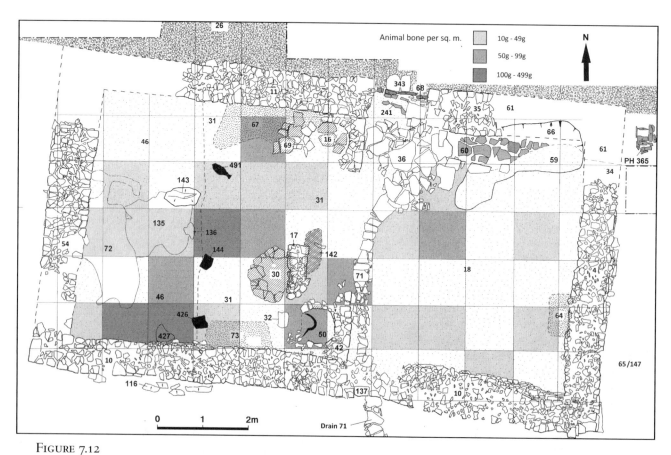

FIGURE 7.12

Period V.3 Building 460 – distribution of animal bone

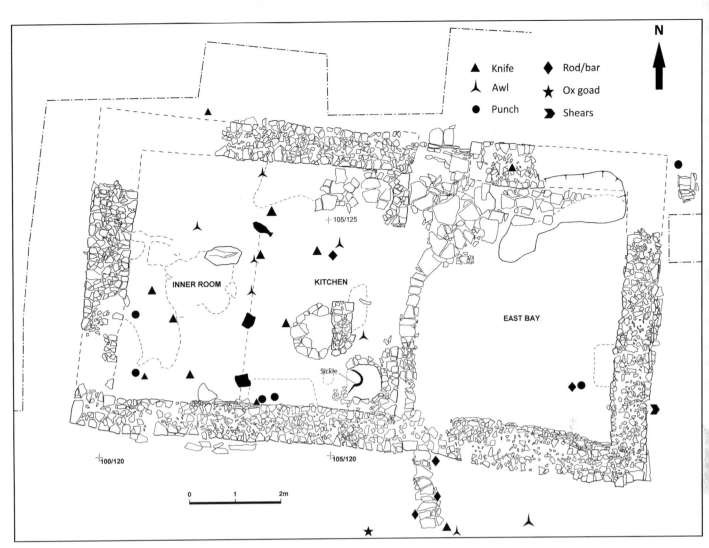

FIGURE 7.13
Period V Building 460 – distribution of tools

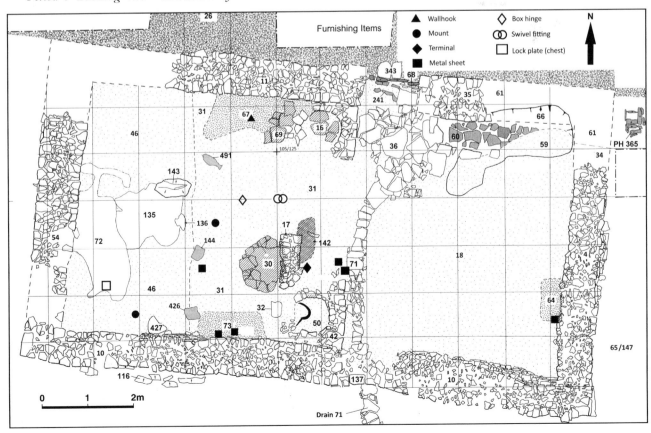

FIGURE 7.14
Period V Building 460 – distribution of furnishings

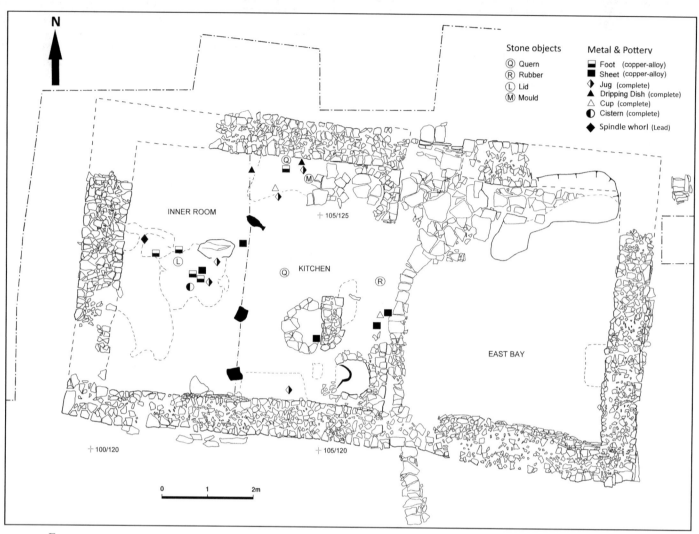

FIGURE 7.15
Period V Building 460 – distribution of domestic objects

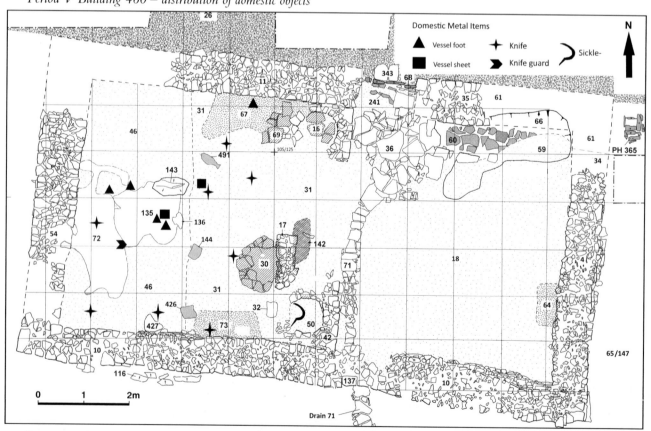

FIGURE 7.16
Period V Building 460 – distribution of domestic metalwork

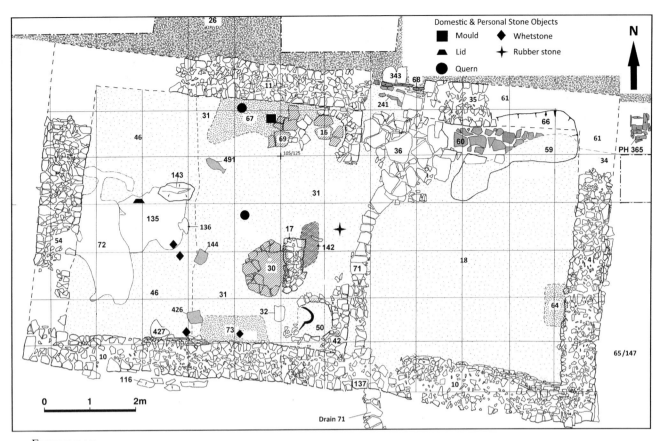

FIGURE 7.17
Period V Building 460 – distribution of personal and domestic stone objects

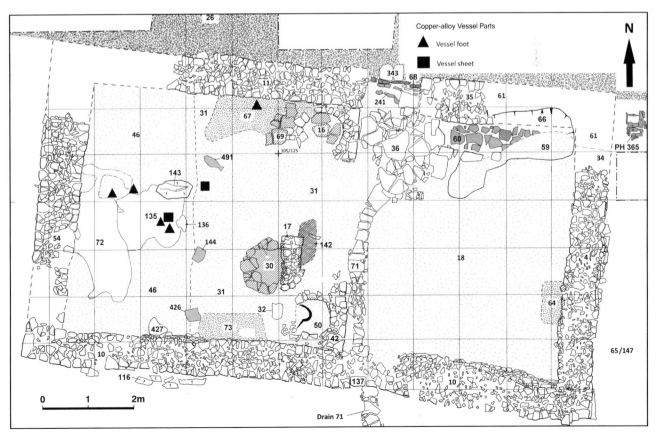

FIGURE 7.18
Period V Building 460 – distribution of metal vessel parts

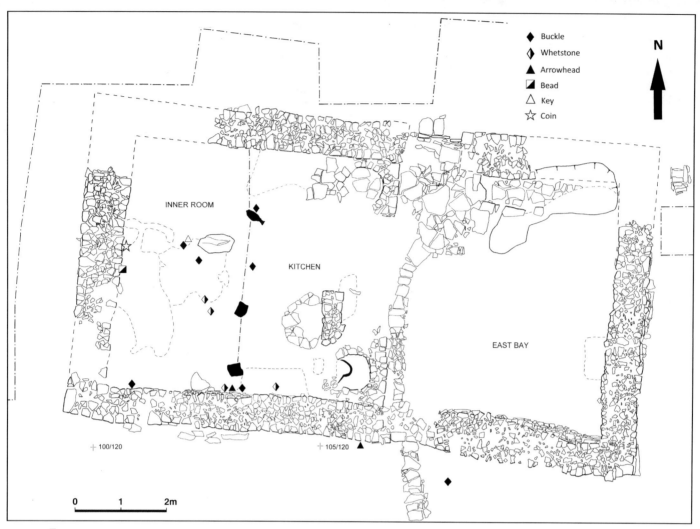

FIGURE 7.19

Period V Building 460 – distribution of personal items

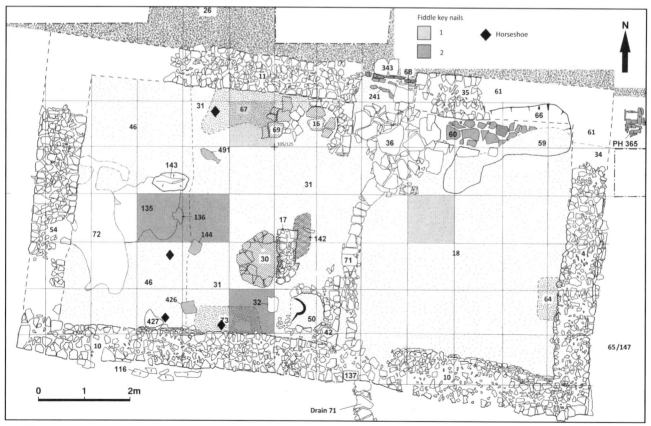

FIGURE 7.20

Period V Building 460 – distribution of equestrian objects including fiddle-key nails

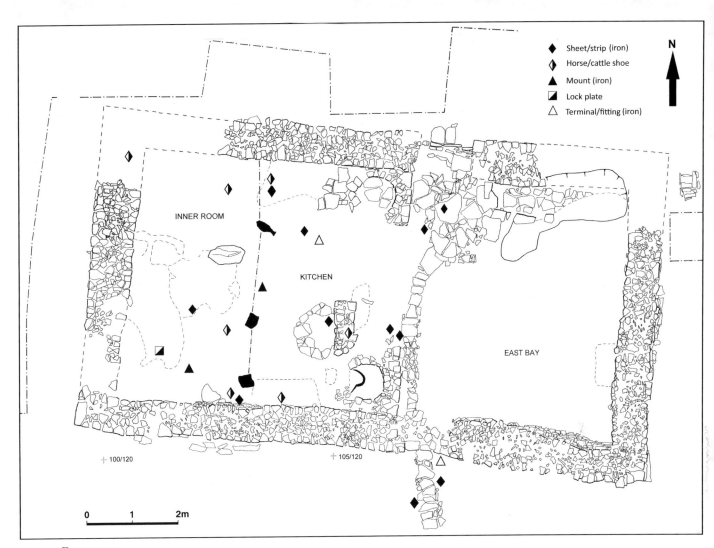

FIGURE 7.21

Period V Building 460 – distribution of miscellaneous objects

masonry was robbed out at this point and it remains unclear whether this apparent absence of finds indicates a particular activity or use, for example the position of a bed, that was distinct from the other parts of the bay.

The western bay represents the private 'inner chamber' of the house, where clothes and household valuables were evidently stored under lock and key and where presumably, at least some of the occupants slept, perhaps in a small cubicle to the north of the boulder and perhaps also in a small raised room or *solar* directly above, accessed via a ladder. Nonetheless, it appears quite likely that even the small space at ground level, totalling little more than 11 square metres, was used for a variety of different purposes (Kowalski and Goldberg (eds) 2008, 24). It may, as a consequence, have been further subdivided at ground level into three smaller zones arranged north to south; the northernmost a cubicle for sleeping, the middle part incorporating a table and craft area along with storage area for valuables, the latter secured in a small locked wooden chest, and the southern side used for meat and tool storage and/or household butchery. The inventory of domestic and other artefacts recovered from the three internal bays of Building 460 is detailed in Figure 7.37 below.

Period V, Building 463 and Structure 466: Byre and Kiln – Area A

The distribution of non-structural objects associated with these buildings (Figures 7.22 and 7.23) provides no clear indication of any particular medieval activity, although a general concentration of tools and domestic objects just inside the south wall of the byre indicates that the rear wall of the building may have incorporated shelves or perhaps a bench for the storage of general agricultural and craft equipment.

Period V–VI, Building 461 – Area B

Compared to Building 460 in Area A, the numbers of domestic and personal objects recovered from this building was very limited, both in terms of their range and number (Figure 7.29).

The assemblage is restricted to just two coins (Section 5.4), two iron keys, a scabbard chape and a boot plate, whilst tools are restricted to a single iron punch. Agricultural equipment is represented by two cattleshoes, whilst some small-scale metalworking may be indicated by a lump of waste galena and a simple lead disc. As with the structural objects from this area, the majority of the items were recovered from secondary contexts, either

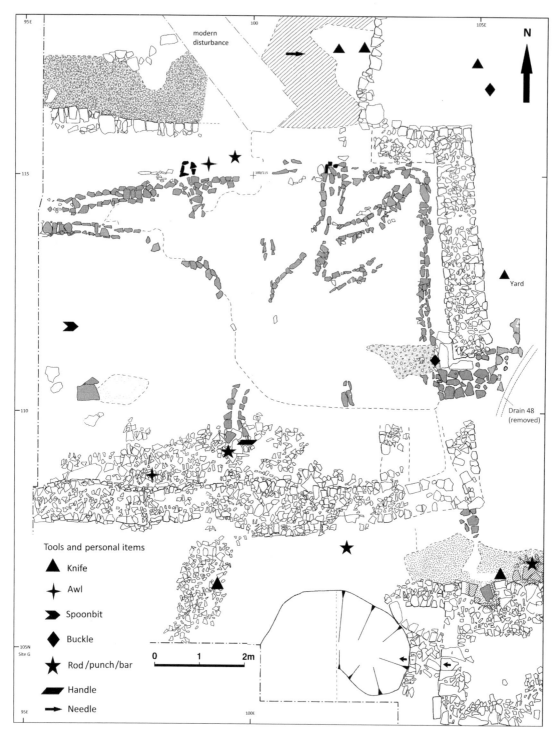

FIGURE 7.22

Period V Building 463 – distribution of tools and personal objects

reflecting casual loss on the adjacent trackway or post-depositional action as opposed to original location.

Period IV, Building 462 and Structure 465: Farmhouse and Byre – Area A

Just a handful of domestic artefacts could be securely associated with the occupation and use of Building 462 (Figure 7.10). As a group they suggest that the building was used for habitation, as similar types of domestic and craft activities are represented to those in the subsequent Period V building (Figure 7.37). However, unlike that later building, there are simply too few to provide any meaningful insight into precisely how the building was organised and used.

In the absence of any substantial floor deposits still fewer objects can be associated directly with Building 465 and its suggested use as an agricultural building of some kind is based largely upon the fact that it was subsequently replaced by Building 463 in Period V, a building whose function is more certain.

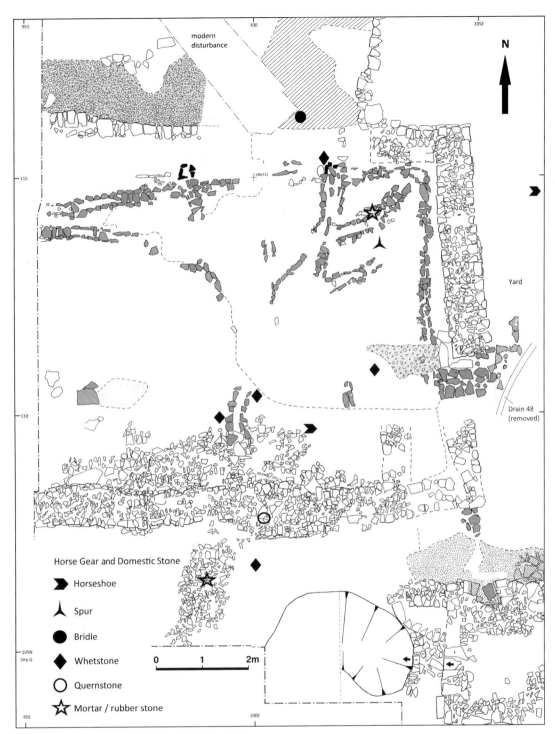

FIGURE 7.23
Period V Building 463 – distribution of horse gear and worked stone

Period III, Building 467 and Structure 468 – Area A

The information provided by the distribution of domestic and personal objects associated with these buildings (Figure 7.31) is relatively limited, foremost because of their generally secondary or tertiary contexts. The handful of stratified artefacts associated with Structure 468, a hammerstone and a fragment of quern, suggest some domestic and craft activity, but do little to clarify whether the structure was one of habitation or not. Artefacts associated with the occupation and use of Building 467 are more varied and numerous (Figure 7.31) and include a fairly standard range of domestic and personal objects; the former including several stone loom weights and bone pin beaters and the latter including two spur fragments and a pendant bell. There is some slight variation in the distribution of objects found inside the building and it is possible to distinguish a slightly greater number and range of objects in the west half, which could possibly reflect the location of a kitchen bay or an inner room. If this interpretation is correct it is of interest, as it mirrors the organisation of the later Period V

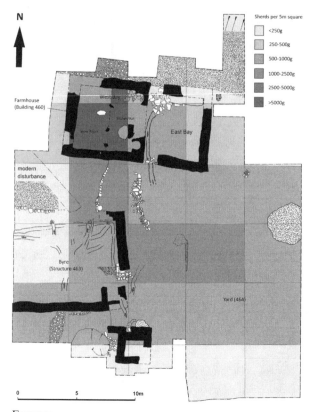

FIGURE 7.24

Area A Period V – distribution of ceramic ware 14 during CP5–6

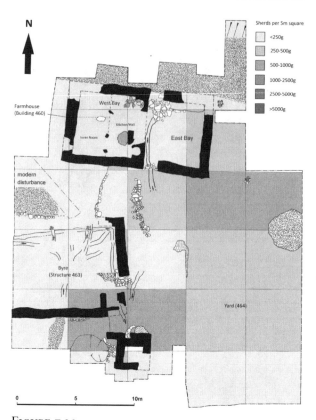

FIGURE 7.25

Area A Period V – distribution of ceramic ware 15 during CP5

building, Building 460, which incorporated this arrangement of internal rooms.

Period III, Building 477 and Structure 479 – Area H

The distribution of non-structural objects associated with these buildings (Figures 7.35 and 7.36) is once again limited by their secondary context and provides no clear-cut distinction in terms of the specific types of medieval activity undertaken in any particular part of the buildings. The range of objects is somewhat restricted, but includes a standard suite of domestic items including quernstones and knives as well as craft items, notably pin beaters used in weaving, a stitching hook, spindle whorls and possible loom weights. Other tools are confined to whetstones along with a small number of personal items including a key, an arrowhead, buckles and an earring, along with examples of horse gear. A single object of decorative metalwork and an iron terminal do no more than hint at the presence of internal furnishings.

Combined with the restricted range of pottery of CP2 and CP3 recovered from the structural features in Area H, the modest assemblage of non-structural finds, unlike the substantial nature of Building 477 itself, could indicate that the inhabitants were of fairly modest material wealth and standard of living. Set against this, the very presence of the small number of weapons and horse gear along with the earring and pendant is entirely consistent with the type and low numbers of artefacts recovered from late Saxon sites of documented higher status, for example those excavated at Flixborough, Humberside (Loveluck, 2007), Bishopstone, East Sussex (Thomas, 2010), Goltho, Lincolnshire (Beresford 1975) and West Cotton, Northamptonshire (Chapman, 2010), and indeed even at Yeavering (Hope-Taylor 1977).

Period V–VI, Building 461 – Area B

This building was, with the exception of the front (east) wall and flight of entrance steps, relatively poorly preserved and neither fully exposed or excavated. Nonetheless, the range of non-structural finds recovered from stratified deposits (Figure 7.29) indicates essentially domestic habitation and included an iron key (SF614), parts of an iron barrel padlock (SF57), an iron punch (SF615) and a scabbard chape (SF620). Structural ironwork was restricted to a handful of iron nails and a single hinge pivot. The floor deposits of the building also produced a silver penny of Edward I (SF 938, context 98) minted in AD 1300–1302 and a French silver *denier tournois* dated to the period AD 1205–1285. These latter indicate that the building was occupied around the same time as Building 460 in Area A, although evidence from reconstructed pottery sherds from inside Building 460 (Figure 7.28) suggests it may have remained in use after Building 460 had been abandoned.

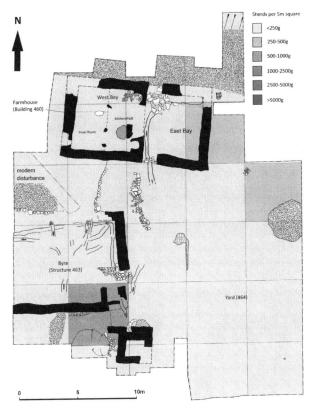

FIGURE 7.26

Area A Period V – distribution of ceramic ware 16 during CP5

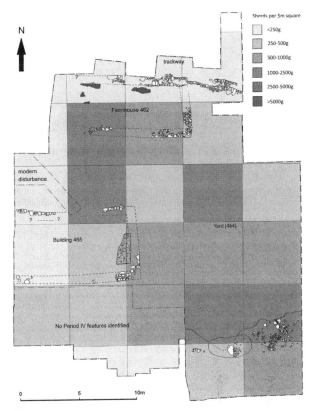

FIGURE 7.27

Area A Period IV – distribution of ceramic ware 4 during CP4–5

Other Evidence from Artefact Distributions

The Period V Farmstead in Area A

In addition to the distribution of structural, domestic and personal objects discussed for Buildings 460 and 463 above, a 5m square distribution plot of ceramic ware 14 pottery by weight (Figure 7.24; ceramic phases 5/6) shows a concentration within the western end of Farmhouse 460 and a fairly even spread within the yard [Structure 464] and extending into the eastern end of the byre [Structure 463]. In the final phase of medieval occupation (Phase V.2) domestic rubbish appears to have been disposed of at random across the yard. Metal, and possibly worked stone objects, were regarded as worth recycling and their lower numbers in the yard suggest many were selected for such. The only other discernible difference between the yard and the farmhouse assemblages is that cloth-related artefacts, including a spindlewhorl, a pin beater, a needle, shears and a stitching hook, are present in small numbers in the yard but entirely absent from the farmhouse. As it is unlikely that spinning and weaving would have been habitually undertaken in the open air, it is at least possible that these activities were no longer as important during the final phase of occupation.

The Period IV Farmstead in Area A

In addition to the structural and non-structural objects associated with Building 462, a 5m square distribution plot of ceramic wares 15 and 16 dated to ceramic phase 5 (Figures 7.25 and 7.26) shows two concentrations of Period IV activity; one in the northeast quarter of the yard [464] and a second to the southeast of Building 465. These concentrations stand out from the general background distribution of ware 4 pottery of ceramic phases 4–5 (Figure 7.27), which is present across much of the yard in low to moderate concentrations and in the area between Buildings 462 and 465, but seemingly not inside the latter. The concentration in the south side of the yard could perhaps reflect the location of rubbish or manure heaps.

The Period III Farmstead in Area A

The 5m square distribution plots for pottery of ceramic ware 4 (Figure 7.27; CP4–5) and ceramic ware 1 (Figure 7.32; CP2–4) indicate change across these periods. Ware 4 shows a fairly even spread across the yard and in the fill of the various pits and cut features forming Building 467. There is a slight reduction in pottery density in the area subsequently occupied by Building 465 in Period IV. In contrast, the distribution of ware 1 (Figure 7.32) shows a concentration of material in and over Pit Group 469, a more general spread across the yard [464] and a markedly reduced density in the area later occupied by Buildings 463 and 465.

Pit Group 469 [Features 319, 327, 346 and 357] produced relatively unabraded pottery totalling around

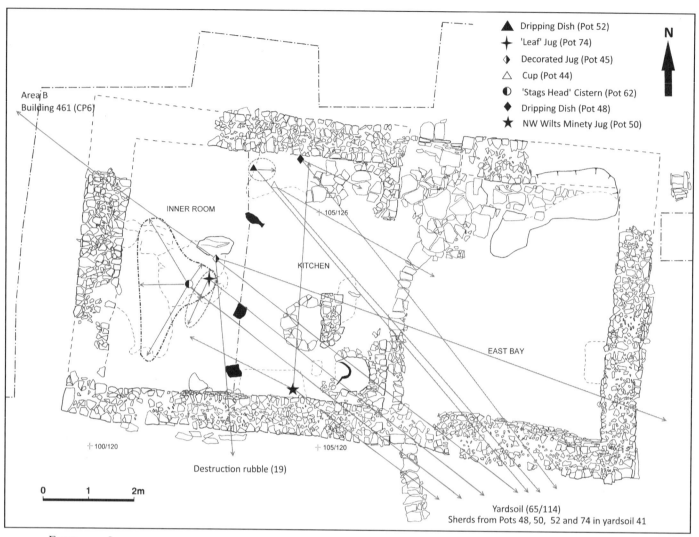

FIGURE 7.28

Area A Building 460 Period V.3 – breakage and movement of domestic pottery after abandonment

1kg with a mean sherd weight of less than 10g, which appears to reflect secondary refuse deposited during ceramic phases 3 and 4. Two of these features, Pits 319 and 357, also produced substantial deposits of charred grain probably reflecting domestic waste. The distribution also indicates that the area later occupied by Buildings 463 and 465 was not used to dump refuse at this time as earlier (CP1–2) pottery was common here. In view of this, it is possible that this area was already distinct and separate from the main part of the yard at this time, despite the fact that no structural evidence of any such division was evident.

The pits, postholes and trackway gullies, as well as features in the yard and the principal elements of Building 467, mostly produced abraded pottery with a mean sherd weight of less than 10g. This suggests that the majority of material derives from reworked secondary deposits and that its inclusion is incidental to the process of filling. Possible exceptions are Gullies 284 and 387 in Building 467 and the rectangular pit-structure, Structure 471 (Figure 4.2). The former produced relatively unabraded pottery sherds that could reflect primary domestic refuse, whilst the latter contained a large complete and inverted cooking pot (Figure 4.23) filled with stones, the reason for which was unclear but possibly not practical. These observations are relevant to the function of Structure 471 and the sunken-floor pits [Features 179, 221, 234 and 385] inside Building 467, as they indicate that they were not dug for rubbish disposal but intended for use as open cut features that were only later filled with soils derived from reworked secondary deposits.

The distribution of non-ceramic artefacts for this period (Figures 7.30 and 7.31) in the yard area shows a sparse scatter with no discernible spatial pattern. This albeit limited information indicates that domestic artefacts are slightly more common than other types and shows a slight concentration of quern fragments associated with Building 467. Craft tools, cloth-related artefacts and personal items are all very rare, whilst structural objects are restricted to a handful of iron nails and staples.

The Period III.1 occupation in Area A

The 5m square distribution plot of later 10th-century pottery (Figure 7.33; Fabric Types 13, 50,

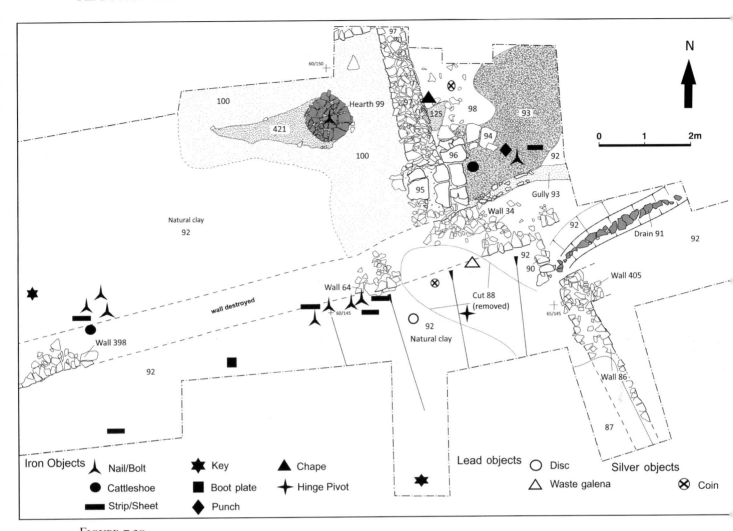

FIGURE 7.29
Area B Period V Building 461 – distribution of iron and lead objects

59 and 67) shows a restricted distribution that is most concentrated around the southern end of Structure 468. Most of this pottery is residual in later contexts and few other artefacts can be attributed to the period. The distribution alone is however of interest, both for its restricted extent and for its concentration inside the footprint of the suggested earliest Period III building.

The Period III Occupation in Area H

Pits 3017, 3019, 3029, 3049 and 3137, and Posthole 3088 (Figure 4.3) all produced over 1kg of relatively unabraded pottery with a mean sherd weight >10g, which appears likely to reflect artefacts in secondary contexts. The absence of any associated floor or occupation layers does not allow any more meaningful examination of the distribution of pottery sherds.

The small assemblages of non-ceramic objects, including personal items, horse gear, domestic objects and cloth-related items, plus a small number of structural nails and staples, were also recovered from secondary contexts and their significance has been discussed above, although it is worth noting that, unlike the Period III farmstead in Area A, craft tools for woodworking, leatherworking and iron-working are noticeably fewer or absent altogether.

Stage 3 – Abandonment and Site Formation Processes

The excavated assemblage is a modified version of the final occupation assemblage. The nature of the modification may be related to four processes that are firstly outlined and then discussed below in respect of Period V Building 460:

1 Natural decay processes
   Consideration of medieval documentary inventories suggests that decay will invariably have removed wooden furniture, vessels and tools as well as leather vessels, clothing and blankets etc.

2 Physical collapse
   Collapse is significant not only for physical damage but also for its levelling effect as items originally attached to walls or the roof structure will be recovered at ground level. Artefacts clustered along wall or partition lines may once have been placed on shelves or hung from pegs.

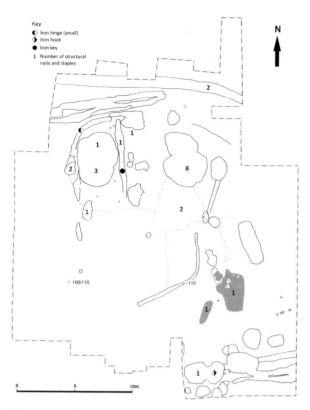

FIGURE 7.30

Area A Period III – distribution of structural metalwork

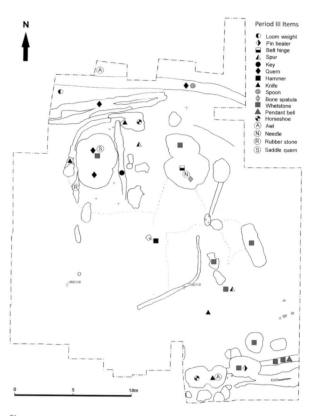

FIGURE 7.31

Area A Period III – distribution of domestic and other objects

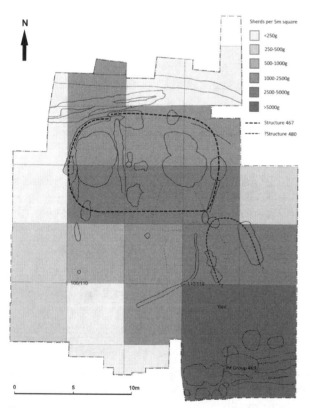

FIGURE 7.32

Area A Period III – distribution of ceramic ware 1 pottery sherds (CP2–4)

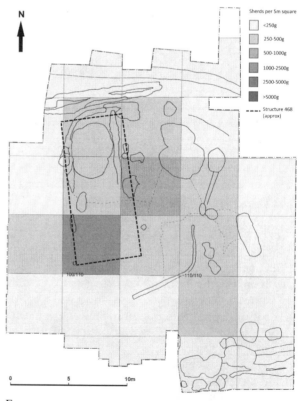

FIGURE 7.33

Area A Period III.1 – distribution of later 10th-century pottery sherds (CP1)

3 Post-abandonment scavenging
It is likely and usual that people will remove valuable items left abandoned if they can find them. More random disturbance may be expected from children and vandals.

4 The circumstances of abandonment
The process of site abandonment may be regarded as due to two processes; 'normal' where inhabitants leave in anticipated and usually favourable circumstances and 'catastrophic', as a result of sudden and unanticipated external forces such as war, fire, plague, eviction or some other natural disaster. Where abandonment is 'normal', we might expect to find only a few low value, old, broken or bulky items left behind and an assemblage that overall is little different from other excavated rubbish assemblages. Conversely, where abandonment is catastrophic, few if any items may be removed and the consequent difference from a 'normal' finds assemblage should be evident.

The application of these principles to the assemblage recovered from Period V Farmhouse 460 in Area A indicates the following:

Natural Decay

Clearly an important process but difficult to characterise directly. The presence of buckles suggests the former presence of clothing, whilst decorative mounts, terminals, small hinges and a lock plate are likely to be from wooden boxes or small storage chests. Sheet metal objects could reflect bindings from a variety of household objects. In each case these objects were surprisingly not removed but left in-situ.

Physical Collapse

The distribution of buckles, knives, whetstones, horseshoes and craft tools shows a concentration of find spots either side of the partition that separated the west and middle bays, probably as a result of these items being stored on shelves or hung on pegs or hooks. This is also possible for some of the ceramic vessels found adjacent to the partition line and alongside the north and south walls. However, the 'Stag's Head' cistern was found in-situ and upright on the floor, and it seems likely that other reconstructed jugs (Vessels 45 and 72) and at least two copper alloy vessels also formed part of a group of tableware that remained in-situ after abandonment.

Scavenging

The evidence indicates a phase of post-abandonment activity that appears to pre-date the large scale collapse of the building, but post-dates its final occupation. This is evident from the reconstructed pottery vessels found inside the building, of which a very small number of sherds were located outside the building and elsewhere on the site (Figure 7.28). This distribution, alongside other artefactual and environmental evidence, supports the suggestion that the house was probably open and unoccupied for a period prior to the onset of substantial collapse, a period that provided opportunities to remove a handful of (presumably interesting) sherds of pottery out of the building (and in one instance as far as Building 461 in Area B), but not it would seem for the wholesale clearance of recyclable items or objects with potential value from inside the farmhouse.

Sherds from Featured Pots 50 and 74 and from Dripping Dishes 48 and 52 were recovered from context 41, a soil deposit in the adjacent yard (Figure 7.28), along with a whittle tang knife, a horseshoe, an iron buckle, a ferrule and nails. Also nearby, albeit from the topsoil, was a silver penny dated 1278–1307. These seem likely to reflect artefacts removed from the western and central bays after the pots were broken, and therefore after occupation had ceased. Also at this time the Stag's Head cistern (Pot 62) was broken, the base of the vessel remaining upright and in-situ whilst the majority of the body sherds were spread westwards inside the western bay with just a couple of sherds moved into the eastern bay.

Jugs 45 and 50 and Bowl 73 (the latter not shown on Figure 7.28) could only be partially reconstructed and seem to have been more widely scattered, particularly in the case of Jug 45, a single sherd of which somehow reached excavation Area B [57]. This also indicates that the building in Area B probably remained open after the abandonment of Building 460. Disturbance is also indicated by the breakage and removal of the copper alloy cooking vessels, which are represented by five vessel feet and some repair sheets. A rotary quern also seems to have been broken and removed bar two pieces. The absence of strap hinges, hinge pivots or nails in the area of the north doorway indicates that it may well have been removed intact with fittings prior to major collapse.

The absence of virtually any artefacts from the eastern bay might be thought to indicate more systematic removal or scavenging from this part of the house. However, the plots for iron nails, pottery sherds and bone (Figures 7.6, 7.11 and 7.12) also show very low concentrations in this bay and it seems inconceivable that either the final occupants or subsequent scavengers would have entirely removed all classes of object from one bay whilst leaving rich deposits virtually untouched in the other two.

This suggested process of abandonment is further supported by the environmental evidence, which identified a group of unburnt hedgehog bones in the fill of Oven 42 and an owl pellet assemblage from the interior drain [71].

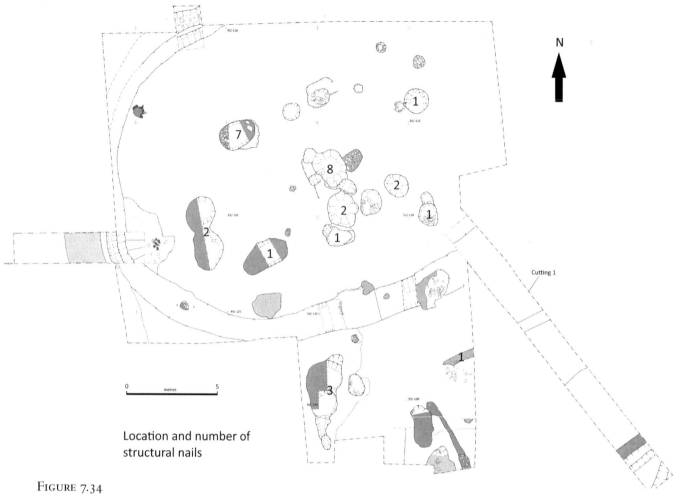

FIGURE 7.34
Area H Period III – distribution of structural nails

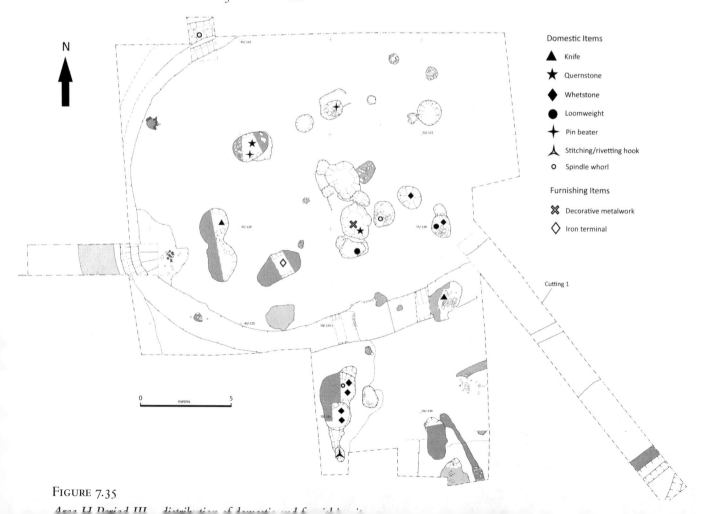

FIGURE 7.35
Area H Period III – distribution of domestic and furnishing items

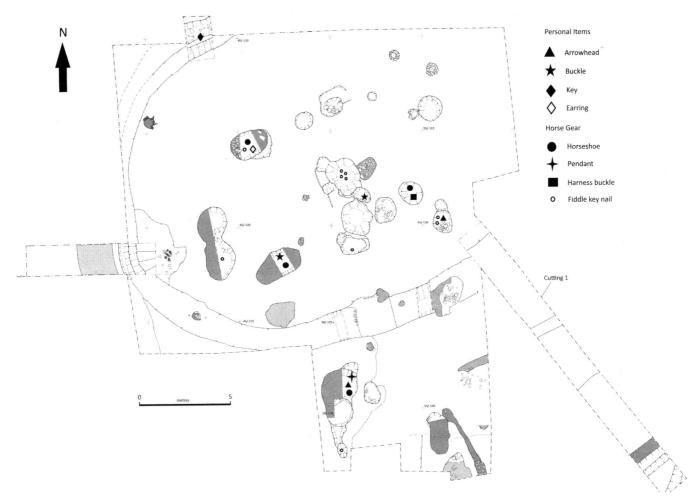

FIGURE 7.36
Area H Period III – distribution of horse gear and personal items

Circumstances of Abandonment

A coin recovered from floor layer 72 provides a stratified *terminus post quem* of AD 1351–1352 for the abandonment of Building 460. In addition, a comparison of the artefact assemblages recovered from the farmhouse [460] and its yard [464] shows that artefacts made from recyclable materials are proportionally far less common than pottery sherds in the yard but far more common inside the building (Figure 7.38).

When these artefact types are examined the variation in worked stone objects can be largely explained by structural stonework. With metal objects, however, a major factor is the size of the object: metal vessel parts and sickles are absent from the yard area whilst strap hinges, hinge pivots, craft tools, fittings and knives are rare. Particularly valuable items such as coins and beads are also absent, whilst small personal items such as buckles, keys, arrowheads and tweezers show less (but still some) sign of recycling, presumably a reflection of the fact that such small items are easier lost.

It is clearly not possible to distinguish with any certainty between the final actions of the departing inhabitants and the activities of later scavengers, although there is one identifiable action which does not fit the behaviour of the latter, namely the placing of a complete iron sickle (Figure 5.46, 68) inside one of the ovens [42]. The idea that this was an attempt to hide a valuable tool before leaving the house does not fit well with either of the suggested abandonment scenarios and its deliberate placement inside the oven could be an indication of rural folk-ritual as an act of termination, akin to similar votive deposits discussed by Hamerow in Anglo-Saxon contexts (Mark Gardiner pers comm).

According to the principles outlined above and the evidence from the site, it is therefore likely that this final episode of abandonment of Building 460 falls within the 'catastrophic' category. In contrast, the artefact patterns for the abandonment of the buildings recorded in excavation Areas B and H do not seem to reflect such a signature and as a result seem to belong to a 'normal' category of abandonment.

Artefact	Bay West (Chamber) Complete	Frag.	Total	Middle (Kitchen/Hall) Complete	Frag.	Total	East Complete	Frag.	Total
Jug	1	1	2	0	1	1	0	0	0
Cistern	1	0	1	0	0	0	0	0	0
Dripping dish	0	0	0	1	1	2	0	0	0
Bowl	0	0	0	1	1	2	0	0	0
Metal vessel	0	1 or 2[1]	1 or 2[1]	0	?1[1]	?1[1]	0	0	0
Knife	1	2	3[2]	4	1	5	0	0	0
Whetstone	1	2	3	1	1	2	0	0	0
Quern	0	0	0	0	1[3]	1	0	0	0
Rubber stone	0	0	0	1	0	1	0	0	0
?Food trough	0	0	0	0	1	1	0	0	0
Pot lid	0	1	1	0	0	0	1	0	1[4]
Awl	0	1	1	4	0	4	0	0	0
Punch	2	0	2	1	0	1	1	0	1
Spoon bit	1	0	1	0	0	0	0	0	0
Buckle	6	0	6	0	0	0	0	0	0
Bead	1	0	1	0	0	0	0	0	0
Door key	1	0	1	0	0	0	0	0	0
Coin	1	0	1	0	0	0	0	0	0
Arrowhead	1	0	1	0	0	0	0	0	0
Box/chest	0	?1[5]	?1	0	?1[6]	?1	0	0	0
Horseshoe	1	1	2	1	1	2	0	0	0
Fiddle key nail	4	0	4	3	0	3	1	0	1
Sickle	0	0	0	0	0	1	0	0	0

1 Five copper alloy feet – 2 vessels
2 Plus a bone knife guard
3 Two fragments probably from the same quern stone
4 Possibly reused building stone
5 Lock-plate and two mounts
6 Box hinge

FIGURE 7.37

Inventory of domestic objects from Period V Building 460

	Building 460 (%)	Yard 464 (%)
Iron objects	15.45	1.36
Copper alloy	1.31	0.23
Worked stone	3.13	0.33

FIGURE 7.38

Frequency of Area A Period V artefacts expressed as a percentage of the total number of pottery sherds

7.3 ARTEFACTUAL EVIDENCE FOR SETTLEMENT DEVELOPMENT – CONTINUITY AND CHANGE

In a bid to shed light on the signatures and processes of change during the life of the medieval settlement the following data were plotted in graph or table form:

– *Figure 7.39* – numbers of artefacts by material type from contexts in each ceramic phase, subdivided by excavation area and expressed in a bar graph. The graph emphasises that pottery sherds were by far the most common artefact type in all phases. Objects of stone, iron and, from CP5, copper alloy and lead, are the only other types of significance. A handful of bone (artefacts) were also recovered, but too few to register.

– *Figures 7.40 to 7.44* – these plots of total finds by area, type and ceramic phase illustrate clearly the steady rise in the material wealth and associated activity in Area A throughout the life of the settlement, along with the clearly defined and short-lived episode of settlement activity in Area H during the 11th century and the foundation and development of activity in Area B during ceramic phases 5 and 6.

– *Figures 7.45 to 7.47* – the frequency of iron, copper alloy and stone objects expressed as a percentage of the number of pottery sherds in each ceramic phase, subdivided by excavation area.

The graphs indicate that there is significant variation in the proportions of different materials through time. In ceramic phases 1 and 2 iron objects occur consistently at 4–5% of the pottery count in both areas A and H. In ceramic phase 3 there is a slight drop in Area H prior to the abandonment of that site, whilst in Area A the decline is dramatic, to less than 1%. There follows a slow increase in Area A

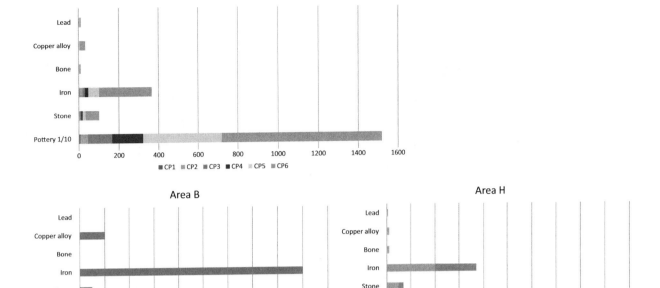

FIGURE 7.39

Total quantities of finds by excavation area and category

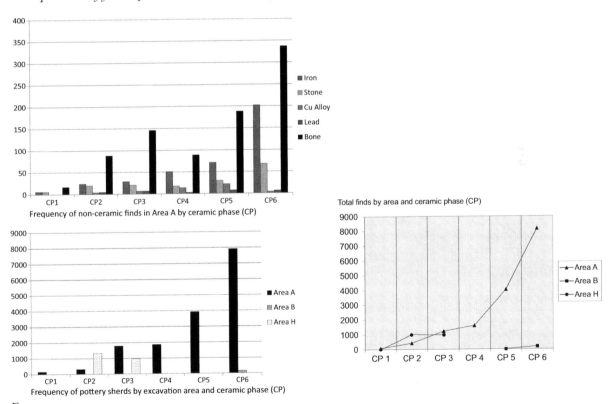

FIGURE 7.40

Total numbers of finds by excavation area, ceramic phase and material type

to 1.4% by ceramic phase 5 followed by a dramatic increase to 3.4% in ceramic phase 6. The plot for worked stone shows a broadly similar pattern of an early decline in ceramic phase 3 followed by levelling off and recovery only in ceramic phase 6. Copper alloy objects are too rare before ceramic phase 5 for any pattern to emerge, but thereafter show a substantial increase in frequency.

Discussion

The interpretation of these datasets is problematic since they record only the changing proportions of fragmentary residues. In order to reflect meaningful social conditions and change, the variations in the recorded material culture must correlate with variations in the availability of materials and objects to the inhabitants.

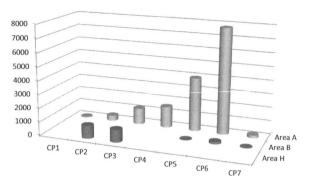

FIGURE 7.41

Total numbers of pottery sherds by excavation area and ceramic phase

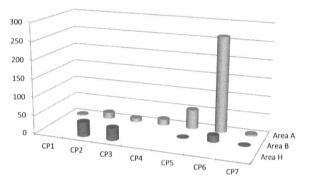

FIGURE 7.42

Total numbers of iron objects by excavation area and ceramic phase

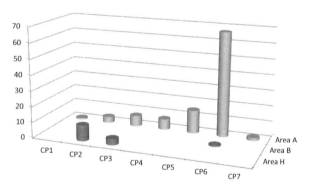

FIGURE 7.43

Total numbers of stone objects by excavation area and ceramic phase

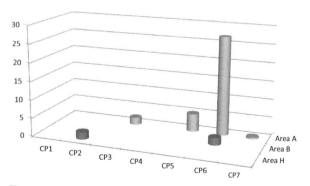

FIGURE 7.44

Total numbers of copper alloy objects by excavation area and ceramic phase

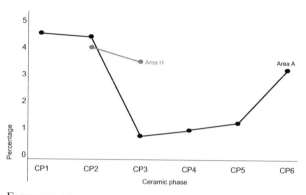

FIGURE 7.45

Comparative ratios of iron objects to pottery sherds in Areas A and H by ceramic phase

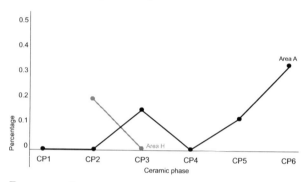

FIGURE 7.46

Comparative ratios of copper alloy objects to pottery sherds in Areas A and H by ceramic phase

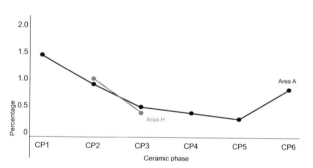

FIGURE 7.47

Comparative ratios of stone objects to pottery sherds in Areas A and H by ceramic phase

Pottery, the most common artefact type, was relatively cheap and used for domestic and agricultural purposes in all periods of settlement represented. Its frequency was therefore less subject to economic pressures than for example metalwork. A plot showing the quantities of pottery and waste animal bone by ceramic phase (project archive) and excavation area shows an approximately linear relationship between the two groups, indicating that there were no dramatic fluctuations in their relative proportions throughout the site's occupation. Metal objects would have been more expensive and valuable and have high potential for recycling; attributes that mitigate against their deposition in periods of social or economic pressure, when acquisition

Category	Object	CP1	CP2	CP3	CP4	CP5	CP6	CP7	U/S	Total
Domestic	Vessel (foot)	-	-	-	-	-	5	-	-	5
	Vessel (sheet)	-	-	-	-	-	2	1	1	4
	Knife	1	1	-	3	-	14	2	6	27
	Quern (rotary)	-	1	2	1	-	7	1	2	14
	Quern (saddle)	-	-	-	1	-	-	-	-	1
	Rubber stone	-	1	-	-	-	1	1	-	3
	?Food mould	-	-	-	-	-	1	-	-	1
	Mortar	-	-	-	-	-	1	-	-	1
	Pot lid	-	-	-	-	-	3	-	-	3
	Spatula	-	-	-	-	1	-	-	-	1
	Spoon	-	1	-	-	-	-	-	1	2
	Cookpot (type I)	★p	★c	★c	★c	★c	-	-	-	-
	Cookpot (type II)	★c	★c	★c	★c	★c	★c	-	-	-
	Cookpot (type III)	-	-	-	-	★p	★c	★c	-	-
	Jug/pitcher	-	?	★p	★p	★p	★c	-	-	-
	Westcountry dish	-	★p	★c	★c	★c	★p	-	-	-
	Cistern	-	-	-	-	-	★p	-	-	-
	Costrel	-	-	-	-	-	★p	-	-	-
	Dripping dish	-	-	-	-	-	★p	-	-	-
	Pancheon	-	?	?	★p	★p	-	-	-	-
	Bowl/cup	-	-	-	-	-	★p	-	-	-
Tools	Awl	-	-	-	2	1	7	-	4	14
	Punch	-	-	-	-	-	6	1	2	9
	Spoon bit	-	-	-	-	-	1	-	1	2
	Stone ?hammer	1	-	-	-	-	-	-	1	2
	Whetstone (type I)	-	-	-	1	-	3	-	2	6
	Whetstone (type II)	-	-	-	-	2	8	-	5	15
	Whetstone (type III)	-	1	1	3	3	12	-	7	27
	Whetstone (type IV)	-	-	3	1	5	3	-	7	19
Personal	Terminal	-	-	-	-	-	2	-	1	3
	Buckle	-	-	-	-	1	14	-	4	19
	Mount	-	-	-	-	-	4	-	1	5
	Strap/lace end	-	-	-	-	-	1	-	1	2
	Key	-	-	-	1	-	2	-	2	5
	Bead	-	-	-	-	-	1	-	-	1
	Coin	-	-	-	-	-	1	-	1	2
	Ring	-	-	-	-	-	1	-	-	1
	Brooch	-	-	-	-	-	-	-	1	1
	Tweezers	-	-	-	-	1	-	-	-	1
	Arrowhead	-	-	-	-	1	1	-	-	2
	Belt hinge	-	-	-	-	1	-	-	-	1
Cloth	Spindlewhorl	-	-	-	-	1	2	-	2	5
	Pin beater	-	-	-	1	-	1	-	-	2
	Needle	-	-	-	-	2	3	-	2	7
	Shears	-	-	-	-	-	1	-	2	3
	Heckle	-	-	-	-	2	2	-	12	16
	Stitching hook	-	-	-	-	-	1	-	-	1
	?Loom weight	-	1	-	-	3	15	2	3	24
Horse gear	Horseshoe	-	1	1	-	4	6	-	11	23
	Spur (fragment)	-	-	1	1	-	1	-	1	4
	Fiddle key nail	-	4	-	3	8	28	3	19	65
	Harness (misc.)	-	-	1	2	-	-	-	-	3
Agricultural	Cattleshoe	-	-	-	-	-	-	1	1	2
	Ox goad	-	-	-	-	1	1	-	-	2
	Sickle	-	-	-	-	-	1	-	-	1
	Ferrule	-	-	-	-	-	1	-	1	2
Structural	Strap hinge	-	-	-	-	-	9	1	2	12
	Hinge pivot	-	-	-	-	-	6	1	2	9
	Hinge	-	1	-	-	-	2	-	-	3
	Latch lifter	-	-	-	-	-	-	-	1	1
	?Hook	-	-	-	1	2	3	-	6	12
	Fitting	-	-	-	-	-	-	-	2	2
	Nail	1	4	4	5	18	116	24	98	270
	Bolt	-	-	-	-	-	2	-	1	3
	Staple	-	1	-	-	3	4	1	3	12
	Padstone	-	-	-	-	-	3	1	-	4
	Slate	-	-	-	-	-	4	-	-	4
	Pivot stone	-	-	-	-	-	1	-	-	1
	Handle (bowl)	-	-	-	1	-	-	-	1	2
	Barrel padlock	-	-	-	-	-	1	-	-	1
	Lock plate	-	-	-	-	-	1	-	-	1
	Sheet	-	1	1	-	5	20	5	18	50

★c=common ★p=present ?=possible

FIGURE 7.48

Inventory of finds recovered from late Saxon and medieval contexts in Area A by category and ceramic phase

Category	Object	CP1	CP2	CP3	CP4	CP5	CP6	U/S	Total
Domestic	Vessel (foot)	-	-	-	-	-	-	-	0
	Vessel (sheet)	-	-	-	-	-	-	-	0
	Knife	-	2	-	-	-	-	-	2
	Quern (rotary)	-	2	-	-	-	-	1	3
	Quern (saddle)	-	-	-	-	-	-	-	0
	Rubber Stone	-	-	-	-	-	-	-	0
	?Food Mould	-	-	-	-	-	-	-	0
	Mortar	-	-	-	-	-	-	-	0
	Pot Lid	-	-	-	-	-	-	-	0
	Cookpot (type I)	-	★c	★c	-	-	-	-	-
	Cookpot (type II)	-	★c	★c	-	-	-	-	-
	Jug/Pitcher	-	★p	★p	-	-	-	-	-
	Westcountry Dish	-	★p	★p	-	-	-	-	-
Tools	Awl	-	-	-	-	-	-	-	0
	Punch	-	-	-	-	-	-	-	0
	Spoon Bit	-	-	-	-	-	-	-	0
	Stone ?Hammer	-	-	-	-	-	-	-	0
	Whetstone (type I)	-	-	1	-	-	-	-	1
	Whetstone (type II)	-	3	-	-	-	-	-	3
	Whetstone (type III)	-	-	-	-	-	-	-	0
	Whetstone (type IV)	-	1	1	-	-	-	-	2
Personal	Terminal	-	2	-	-	-	-	-	2
	Buckle	-	1	2	-	-	-	-	3
	Mount	-	1	-	-	-	-	-	1
	Strap/Lace End	-	-	-	-	-	-	-	0
	Key	-	-	-	-	-	-	-	0
	Bead	-	-	-	-	-	-	-	0
	Coin	-	-	-	-	-	-	-	0
	Ring	-	-	-	-	-	-	-	0
	Brooch	-	-	-	-	-	-	-	0
	Tweezers	-	-	-	-	-	-	-	0
	Earring	-	1	-	-	-	-	-	1
	Arrowhead	-	2	-	-	-	-	-	2
	Chape	-	-	-	-	-	-	-	0
Cloth	Spindlewhorl	-	1	2	-	-	-	1	4
	Pin Beater	-	2	-	-	-	-	-	2
	Needle	-	-	-	-	-	-	-	0
	Shears	-	-	-	-	-	-	-	0
	Heckle	-	-	-	-	-	-	-	0
	Stitching Hook	-	1	-	-	-	-	-	1
	?Loom Weight	-	1	-	-	-	-	-	1
Horse gear	Horseshoe	-	4	-	-	-	-	1	5
	Spur (fragment)	-	-	-	-	-	-	-	0
	Fiddle Key Nail	-	5	5	-	-	-	-	10
	Harness (miscellaneous)	-	1	-	-	-	-	-	1
Agricultural	Cattleshoe	-	-	-	-	-	-	-	0
	Ox Goad	-	-	-	-	-	-	-	0
	Sickle	-	-	-	-	-	-	-	0
Structural	Strap Hinge	-	-	-	-	-	-	-	0
	Hinge Pivot	-	-	-	-	-	-	-	0
	Hinge	-	-	-	-	-	-	-	0
	Latch Lifter	-	-	-	-	-	-	-	0
	?Hook	-	-	-	-	-	-	-	0
	Fitting	-	-	-	-	-	-	-	0
	Nail	-	10	12	-	-	-	1	23
	Bolt	-	-	-	-	-	-	-	0
	Staple	-	5	2	-	-	-	-	7
	Pad Stone	-	-	-	-	-	-	-	0
	Slate	-	-	-	-	-	-	-	0
	Pivot Stone	-	-	-	-	-	-	-	0
	Barrel Padlock	-	-	1	-	-	-	-	1
	Sheet	-	3	5	-	-	-	3	11

★c=common ★p=present

FIGURE 7.49

Inventory of finds recovered from late Saxon and medieval contexts in Area H by category and ceramic phase

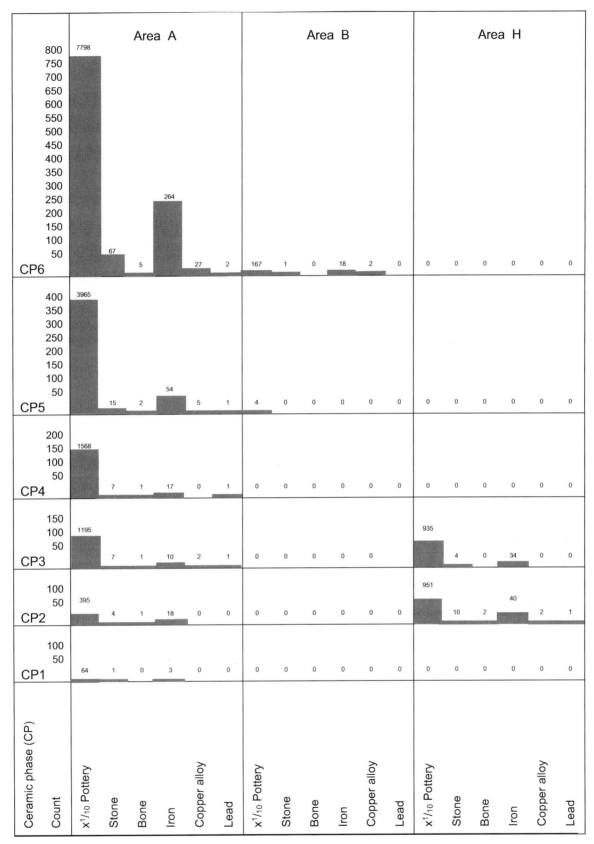

FIGURE 7.50

Total numbers of finds by count, area, category and ceramic phase.

would decrease but the intensity of recycling would likely increase. The fact that the incidence of stone objects appears to support this pattern indicates that the relationship may indeed reflect changing social conditions as opposed to a statistical anomaly.

There is no obvious or significant change in the types of archaeological contexts recorded during ceramic phases 1 to 4, which are predominantly negative cut features, pits, postholes, gullies and ditches, which produced primary and secondary domestic refuse. In ceramic phase 5, these types of negative cut feature are accompanied by layers of 'yardsoil' also containing domestic refuse. Ceramic phase 6 artefacts were mainly recovered from the yard and within the associated buildings, Farmhouse 460 and Byre 463. The former has been shown to contain a much higher proportion of metal and stone artefacts relative to pottery sherds, which is an indicator of the circumstances of its abandonment. This has skewed the relative figures for CP6 as contexts of this date in the yard [464] alone provide a percentage for ironwork of 1.36%, about the same as the figure for CP5. For copper alloy objects the CP6 figure is 0.23%, a slight increase from CP5.

If the case for these graphs measuring 'stress' on the settlement's economy is accepted, then they indicate an initial period of prosperity, during the late 10th and 11th centuries, which ends by the late 11th century, possibly soon after Conquest, with the abandonment of the settlement in Area H and dramatically increased economic pressure on the farmstead in Area A. Thereafter there seems to have been a gradual improvement in conditions with, possibly, a more dramatic resurgence beginning during the late 13th century which accelerates in the subsequent century. This indicated improvement in conditions appears consistent with the structural record, where the first stone buildings in Area A are constructed around the mid 13th century with subsequent wholesale rebuilding and expansion into Area B in the 14th century.

7.4 ARTEFACTS AND ECOFACTS – GENERAL CONCLUSIONS

Late Saxon *c*AD 950–1100 (Ceramic Phases 1–3)

Very few artefacts were recovered from the CP1 postholes and gullies recorded in Area A (Figure 7.48), so little can be deduced except that the range of pottery represented appears restricted. Cooking pots were small and usually heated indirectly (Type II cooking pots) whilst jugs and Westcountry dishes are not present. The presence of a knife indicates domestic activity.

In ceramic phases 2–3 the range of artefacts from Area A (Figure 7.48) increased and included a few domestic items (knife, spoon, whetstones and querns), some horse gear (horseshoes, a spur fragment, a pendant bell and fiddle-key nails) plus a few structural nails and a staple and some metal sheet fragments. Personal items and craft tools were absent, as were cloth-related objects except for a single possible loom weight. However, two pin beaters recovered from later contexts appear to be of 10th- to 11th-century type. The pottery assemblage is once again fairly restricted and dominated by cooking pots (Types I and II) but with very rare Westcountry dishes and jugs represented.

The 11th-century (CP2–3) farmstead in Area H produced a similar range of domestic artefacts (Figure 7.49) including knives, whetstones and quern stones as well as a range of horse gear (horseshoes, a pendant and fiddle-key nails) and structural ironwork (nails, staples and fragments of metal sheet). In contrast to Area A, however, a range of personal items (a buckle, earring and arrowheads), fittings (barrel padlock, terminal and a mount) and cloth-related objects (spindle whorls, pin beaters and a stitching hook) are all represented, but no other craft tools are present. The pottery is similar to the assemblage recovered in Area A, although items of tableware, jugs and lugged pitchers, the latter not represented in Area A, are represented in slightly greater numbers.

As a whole, the Area H assemblage is more varied and of perhaps slightly higher quality than that recovered from Area A. This difference may not be due to distortion of preservation caused by the abandonment of the site, as the majority of the Area H objects were recovered from ceramic phase 2 (i.e. pre-abandonment) deposits whilst none of the CP3 contexts produced finds indicative of an abandonment assemblage.

Medieval *c*AD 1100–1250 (Ceramic Phases 4–5)

Domestic occupation continued in Area A, as indicated by a similar range of artefacts to those of the previous century (Figure 7.48). These included knives, a bowl handle, whetstones and querns. The range and character of the pottery assemblage also changed little from the 11th century whilst associated activity is indicated by horse gear (a spur fragment and fiddle-key nails) along with a restricted range of structural ironwork, predominantly nails and fittings, including a wall hook, plus a key for a barrel padlock. Evidence of some development in the range of household activities is indicated by the presence of a few leatherworking tools (awls), whilst cloth production is represented by a bone pin beater.

This slight increase in the range of objects represented and the evidence for new craft production, ie leatherworking, is set against a possible background of economic stress, as outlined above, and could reflect evidence of a domestic response to such.

Medieval *c*AD 1250–1300 (Ceramic Phase 5)

Evidence for domestic activity is restricted to pottery, whetstones, a bone tool – possibly a spatula – and pottery (Figure 7.48). Glazed jugs, which previously had been exceedingly rare, become rather more common. The absence of other domestic artefacts may be due to chance, as no other artefact groups show a similar decline. Horse gear (horseshoes, a bridle piece, a pendant and fiddle-key nails) are well represented as are structural items and fittings (nails, staples, wall hooks and metal sheet). Leatherworking continues to be represented by a single awl as are cloth-related artefacts (spindle whorls, needles, heckles and possible loom weights). A general improvement in material wealth is indicated by the presence of a few personal items including a buckle, a belt hinge, tweezers and an arrowhead.

The assemblage indicates that craft production continued into the late 13th century with perhaps an increasing emphasis on wool and cloth. The presence of a few 'luxury' items could indicate some modest increase in disposable wealth.

Late Medieval cAD 1300–1375/1400 (Ceramic Phases 5–6)

The abandonment of the farmstead in Area A towards the end of the 14th century produces a very much larger and more complete artefact assemblage for this period (Figure 7.48) compared with those that preceded it. In contrast, the range of domestic artefacts is far greater and indicates changes, for example in domestic culinary practices. Metal cooking vessels appear to replace Type I cooking pots, whilst the introduction of dripping dishes and a stone mortar may indicate the increased importance of meat in the daily diet. Glazed jugs were common items of tableware and used alongside ceramic bowls and cisterns, the former possibly replacing wooden and leather receptacles. The numbers of Westcountry dishes decline to the extent that they may have no longer been used by the time the farmstead was abandoned.

Structural items of metal and stone (discussed above) are more varied and occur in greater numbers than recorded previously, and include nails, staples, strap hinges, a latch lifter, bolts, padstones and pivot stones. The numbers present, irrespective of what special circumstances led to abandonment, suggest that structural ironwork had become an increasingly significant part of building construction by this time. These are accompanied by iron items including hinges, a lock plate, mounts and terminals, indicating the presence of at least one wooden chest.

Horse gear continues to be represented by horseshoes, a spur fragment and fiddle-key nails. Tools of various kinds were also common: awls and a spoonbit indicate continued leatherworking and carpentry and are complimented by punches for ironworking and ox-goads, a sickle and ferrules pertaining to daily agricultural work. Cloth-related work is indicated by the presence of spindle whorls, pin beaters (although some may be residual), needles, shears, heckles and a stitching hook, although these latter types of craft tool, unlike the former, were noticeably absent from the interior of Farmhouse 460, possibly indicating that cloth-related work was not undertaken, in the house at least, during the final phase of occupation (Period V.2).

A range of personal items, including buckles, a lace-end, keys, a jet bead, coins, a ring and an arrowhead, are far more common than in earlier periods with a particular concentration (Figure 7.19) recovered from the western bay of the farmhouse.

An objective assessment of this period compared to the earlier periods is complicated by the abandonment assemblage preserved inside Farmhouse 460, which is much richer in metal and stone artefacts than the reworked and secondary refuse deposits of this phase of occupation, or indeed of those that preceded it. This may over-emphasise the extent of development from CP5 to CP6. Nonetheless, there is still evidence for an increase in material wealth in this period as measured by the ratio of metalwork and pottery (Figure 7.45). In addition, the variety of artefacts increases in all categories at a time when the farmhouse in Area A undergoes wholesale rebuilding and a new dwelling is built in Area B. Judging by the numbers of leatherworking and ironworking tools, it seems likely that craft production may have played a role in increasing prosperity although, conversely, cloth-related crafts may have actually declined by the time of abandonment.

The artefact data for Period V in Area A highlights a significant paradox: that the farmstead was abandoned rapidly, perhaps overnight, at a time when its material prosperity appears to have been at it greatest for some 300 years.

7.5 THE AGRICULTURAL AND DOMESTIC ECONOMY

Agriculture

The late Saxon and medieval animal bone finds (Section 5.13), combined with the environmental evidence (Section 5.14), indicate that the economic base of the settlement was that of 'producer' as opposed to 'consumer' throughout the period of late Saxon and medieval occupation, with livestock dominated by the rearing and use of cattle and sheep and cultivated crops overwhelmingly represented by bread-type wheat. In this respect at least the foundations of the agricultural economy at Eckweek appear little different from the great majority of late Saxon and medieval rural settlements excavated in southern England in the past thirty years or so.

Livestock

Simon Davis' bone report notes that there is little significant change, either in the variety of species represented, or in their proportions or patterns of slaughter, from the later 10th to the 14th century, with the majority of large mammals represented, comprising in excess of 80% of the total assemblage, derived from locally killed beef and mutton. Pig meat was also fairly consistently and uniformly represented throughout the late Saxon and medieval phases, the numbers indicating that they amounted to around 10% of the livestock, the majority of which were slaughtered for meat as young animals, before two years of age. This seemingly stable system of livestock management and use, albeit one that may have incorporated some slight change of emphasis by the later medieval period, indicates a regime of animal husbandry whose foundation of three principal livestock taxa was already essentially in place at Eckweek by the later 10th century, a system for which there is increasing evidence elsewhere in England from the mid-Saxon period onwards (Hamerow 2012, 155–156).

A large proportion, perhaps the majority, of the sheep and cattle represented in the assemblage appear to have survived to maturity, although a significant number of sheep were slaughtered for meat, most likely for domestic consumption, before two years of age. Nonetheless, the substantial numbers of mature sheep present, the overall proportion of which appears to increase slightly with time, suggest they were routinely retained on the hoof for the production of milk and by the 12th century increasingly for the fleece, the latter a widespread phenomenon linked with the growth nationally of the wool industry. By the mid 14th century Eckweek lay in a zone that produced wool of high quality, whose best value (between £6 and £7 per sack) was only exceeded by that produced in Herefordshire and the Forest of Dean (Walton 1991, fig. 163).

The age range for the slaughter of cattle appears more variable, possibly a reflection in part of the need to retain a mainstay of mature and experienced plough oxen, whilst slaughtering other animals as and when required for prime beef, ideally when around three years old. Further uncertainty concerning the precise husbandry of cattle is introduced by the undoubted importance of dairy produce; milk and its by-products – curds and whey, butter, cheese and buttermilk. Even so, this picture is still probably overly simplistic as beef 'on the hoof' stock kept for fattening and sale at market rather than home consumption, may also have formed at least part of the regime of livestock management, particularly in the later medieval period as part of a fully monetised market economy (O'Connor 2013). Nonetheless, whilst present in significantly fewer numbers overall compared to those of sheep, beef is likely to have represented a more important meat source than mutton throughout the period of late Saxon and medieval settlement (Davis this report).

Throughout the extended period of medieval settlement, the day-to-day diet of the population, one based upon bread and cereal-based food, was supplemented by a range of other animals, most notably chicken (and/or pheasant), goose and rabbit along with smaller numbers of mallard, partridge, woodcock and rook, the latter eaten in the English countryside into the 20th century. This range of protein appears to have been further supplemented on occasion by market-bought marine fish, including herring and eel recovered from Period III contexts in Area A. Remains of herring and freshwater eel are commonly recovered on both rural and urban medieval sites (Aston 1988) the former traded, most likely cured, inland from coastal or larger urban markets, for example Bristol. Both were common in Anglo-Scandinavian York by the late Saxon period (O'Connor 2013) and in Somerset at nearby Shapwick (Gerrard with Aston 2007, fig. 22.26) where herring were one of the commonest fish types represented with bones recovered from deposits dating from the 11th to the 17th centuries. Eels, overwhelmingly freshwater varieties, but also including a few marine Conger, were also represented at the Shapwick sites from the late Saxon period onwards (Davis this report). Wild game is essentially absent throughout the period of settlement, a feature that appears common for rural medieval settlements of all but the highest status (Davis this report), although its complete absence is perhaps surprising, especially for the earlier, pre-Conquest, phases (CPs 2–3) of medieval settlement where the structures, at least Building 477 in Area H, are suggested likely to reflect rather more important, possibly thegnly, occupants. This possibility is to some extent supported by the low numbers of horse bones, in particular the assemblage from Area H, the relative proportions of which are consistent with assemblages recovered by excavation at documented higher status sites such as Bishopstone (Thomas 2010) and Goltho (Beresford 1975; 1987).

Cultivated Crops

The report by Wendy Carruthers on the charred plant remains (Section 5.14) highlights a very uniform and consistent sequence of cultivated and natural plant remains, the character and range of the cultivars having seemingly already been established by the early 11th century and which remained essentially unchanged thereafter until the final phase of 14th-century activity recorded in Area A.

The plants identified indicate that the main crops being grown throughout the period consisted overwhelmingly of cereal grains of rivet wheat and bread wheat type free-threshing wheats. Barley and possibly oats were minor crops throughout, whilst rye was scarce and probably only growing as a weed. The total quantities of charred cereals recovered from samples peak significantly in the late 11th century (CP3; Carruthers this report), although this could at least in part reflect the availability of suitable depositional environments, namely pits, ditches and other similar cut soil features. Significant amounts of other cultivated food crops were also grown alongside cereals, including field beans, cabbages, peas and possibly carrots, although leguminous crops as a whole appear to have been much less common in the later medieval period – Period V and later.

The main depositional pathway for the preservation of charred material was in pits (21 of the 24 richest samples) and, to a lesser extent, in other similar negative soil features. The richest samples from the period of medieval settlement as a whole are associated with activity during Period III (CPs 2–3), the 11th century, both in Area A and Area H. The best samples were recovered from a group of pits (Group 469) located at the southern end of the yard in Area A and from postholes representing principal earthfast foundations for timber Building 477. In the later ceramic phases (CPs 4–5) in Area A, the few rich samples recovered came from a more diverse range of features including pits, a spread and a gully associated with a stone farmhouse, Building 460. Whilst present in all medieval phases, the periods that produced substantially greater volumes of charred cereals deriving primarily from domestic activities (notably mostly free of processing chaff) were also of Period III (cAD 1000–1100), in particular ceramic phase 3. Samples from Period V features (cAD 1275–1325), specifically ceramic phase 5, were also rich, although the total volumes of cereals present were significantly lower than those from Period III features. No rich samples were dated to either CP1 or CP6, the former in large part a consequence of the small number of features identified, although the absence of any rich material from the nine late medieval samples taken from CP6 features is less easy to explain.

Alongside the apparent peak in cereal grains, almost all of the vetch-rich (*Vicia sativa*) samples were also recovered from Period III (CPs 3 and 4) features, particularly samples containing seeds large enough to have been cultivated vetch, often called common or spring vetch (*Vicia sativa* subspecies *sativa*), which was grown as an important fodder and/or green manure crop in the Middle Ages. It is worth noting that horses thrive on common vetch, even better than on clover and rye grass; the same applies to fattening cattle, which feed faster on vetch than on most grasses or other edible plants. A common if rather restricted range of medieval garden vegetables is also represented in the assemblage, including cabbages, beans, peas and possibly carrots.

In concluding, Wendy Carruthers notes the similarities of the crops grown at Eckweek with other excavated medieval sites in Somerset and further afield, and the general absence of luxury foods. In this respect the assemblage is consistent with the crops and foodstuffs that would have been available to a middle ranking peasant household with 17 acres of well-drained land whose calcareous soils were ideal for the growing of wheat.

The charred plant data highlights two particular aspects of arable and horticultural cultivation during the period of medieval settlement at Eckweek. Firstly, the general uniformity of the varieties of cereals and plants represented, in combination with the overwhelming predominance of wheat (Carruthers this report Figure 5.82) in all the late Saxon and medieval phases, indicates that a regime of agriculture incorporating intensive cereal cultivation, and thereby, by inference an associated common-field system, was already established at Eckweek well before the Conquest and probably by the later 10th century. If so, this supports the hypothesis of Michael Costen, who suggests that common-field agriculture was already the established norm in Somerset (at least that part east of the Rivers Parret and Tone) by 1066. Moreover, Michael Costen sees the gradual adoption of the common-field in Somerset during the 10th century as integrally linked with the growth of a larger aristocratic elite, the reform of the monastic houses, most notably Glastonbury Abbey, and, critically, the introduction of the heavy plough; a combination of social and technological developments that led to a more intensive agriculture and greater agricultural surplus overall (Costen 2011). Secondly, and perhaps as a natural consequence of the changes noted above, is the suggestion that there is a substantial increase in the production of bread wheat and indeed cereals generally by CP3 at Eckweek, the later 11th century (see the various summary lists by Carruthers). This apparent peak is combined with the greatest incidence of cultivated vetch, as noted above an important fodder crop and green manure, along with unspecified vetch, pulses and peas (Carruthers this report). At face value this peak in the quantity and range of cultivated crops may well indicate an equivalent peak in the prosperity of the settlement during the second half of the 11th century that was followed by a subsequent decline. Factors associated with the suitability of depositional environments during Period III noted above may have led to preferential preservation of charred remains, although, if not, a similar pattern of economic growth peaking in the late 11th century and some subsequent reversal may also be evident from the analysis of associated artefact numbers.

Finally, differences identified in the types and proportions of weed seeds present alongside the charred cereals in Period III deposits (Carruthers this report) may indicate that the contemporary farmsteads identified in Areas A and H, although seemingly operating alongside one another, were being run as essentially separate concerns; either where the crops were derived from separate lands that had different weeds, or, where they were processed differently or with greater/lesser intensity after harvest. This apparently minor difference in the charred plant remains may nonetheless be of some relevance in terms of the ownership of the two Period III farmsteads (Section 5.14).

Exchange, Trade and Market Connections

The 10th century appears to have marked a general expansion and intensification of trade and economic activity in Somerset (Costen 2011, chapter 8). It was an expansion founded upon agricultural surpluses and driven by the need to satisfy the increasing demands of royal taxation and also in part by the growth of a middle-ranking and aristocratic warrior elite and their increasing demand for weapons and luxuries (Costen 2011, 75–76), the *Geld*. This shift was accompanied, not surprisingly, by an increasingly monetised day-to-day economy that facilitated an increasingly varied trade in both labour and agricultural products, the latter most importantly represented by cash crops of wool and grain.

The 10th century also saw the emergence of a native pottery industry in Somerset (McCarthy and Brooks 1988, 191–197), an area that, excluding small numbers of imported continental and Mediterranean wares brought into high status establishments, most notably at the reoccupied hillfort at Cadbury-Congresbury which produced sherds of fine tableware and amphora of the late 5th and 6th centuries from the eastern Mediterranean and Carthage areas (Fowler *et al* 1970), had been essentially pottery-free for some 400 years. Its appearance by the middle of the century in recognisable fabrics and forms at regional centres such as Cheddar (Rahtz 1979), Ilchester (Pearson T 1982), Bristol (Ponsford 1974) and Taunton (Pearson T 1984), indicates a number (probably many) of separate small-scale, but nonetheless systematic production centres, the precise location of which remain unknown. The appearance of this industry also defines (and indeed dates) the earliest phase (CP1) of medieval settlement in Area A at Eckweek, where its very presence confirms that the use of domestic pottery, and the trade that brought it, had already reached the lower ranks of rural society by the mid 10th century. The small number of fabrics and the restricted range of forms represented at Eckweek in the CP1 assemblage suggest pottery vessels with rustic characteristics broadly similar to vessels available elsewhere in Somerset were used in relatively low numbers until the turn of the millennium, after which (ceramic phase 2) both numbers and range expanded significantly. In addition, the presence of just two sherds of glazed Stamford ware, albeit both residual from later contexts, raises the possibility that the rudimentary range of domestic pottery available to the occupants during the later 10th century, which it is reasonable to assume was being produced inside the emerging county and most likely within the normal day-to-day range of the settlement, may have been complimented by at least one fine glazed piece of tableware traded from the kilns operating in distant Lincolnshire (Kilmurry 1980). The quantity and (still restricted) range of pottery present in 11th-century contexts (CPs 2 and 3) indicate substantially increased availability and probably also affordability, although the absence of any exotic traded vessels (apart perhaps from the several lugged pitchers from Area H) overwhelmingly suggests both intra-county production and trade. It is not until the middle of the succeeding 12th century (CP4 at Eckweek) that small numbers of exotic glazed and decorated tablewares from Bristol Ham Green (ware 17 at Eckweek), the Bath area (represented by a range of new and distinctive Westcountry dishes (FT75 etc.), Wiltshire (Naish Hill and Minety type wares, Eckweek wares 15, 16 and 7) and possibly South Somerset Donyatt (Eckweek ware 14) begin to appear more frequently. This gradual expansion in the variety and availability of traded ceramics continues at increased pace in the succeeding century and culminates in the 14th century with the great variety of fine and decorated domestic pottery and tableware represented in the CP5–6 abandonment assemblage that was preserved inside Farmhouse 460 in Area A. The assemblage demonstrates how completely the trade in and use of pottery had pervaded rural society by that date.

Objects of metal, in particular iron, appear to follow a similar trajectory to that of the pottery, with relatively small but slowly increasing numbers of objects (Figure 7.39) present in features and deposits of pre-Conquest date (CPs1–3). The majority of the objects, for example the structural nails and horseshoes, are likely to have been produced by a smithy located in the vicinity of (and perhaps within) the settlement, although no evidence of significant ironworking was identified by excavation in any period on the site.

The iron objects recovered from CP1–3 contexts in Areas A and H (Figures 7.48 and 7.49) confirm that nails and staples were being used in small numbers in the 11th-century timber buildings, along with a few domestic fittings, miscellaneous iron sheet and horseshoes. Again, all these objects were probably produced by a smithy located in or close to the settlement. Objects of greater technical quality, in particular knives, arrowheads, buckles and personal items, the barrel padlock and key, the awl, the spur and the earring, reflect items that are likely to have originated further afield and been traded into the settlement. Whilst this latter group certainly represents a restricted range of objects compared to those recovered from later medieval phases on the site, many of the items are either personal objects, weaponry or horse gear, all of which may have a particular bearing on the social status of the inhabitants of both of the Period III farmsteads. The metalwork assemblage from the subsequent (CP4) farmstead in Area A is, if anything, less extensive and varied than that of the Period III farms and it is not until ceramic phase 5, the later 13th century, that the number and variety of objects expands significantly, an increase that, like the pottery, culminates in the variety of domestic, personal and agricultural objects included in the abandonment assemblage (Figures 7.37, 7.48, 7.49 and 7.50) of Building 460. This trend is also expressed in the numbers and variety of copper alloy objects (Section 5.6), the majority of which were probably produced outside the boundary of the modern county and brought in by trade (Costen 2011). Evidence for more distant, trans-continental trade is restricted to the four honestones of Norwegian ragstone recovered from 14th-century contexts in Area A that originate from the area of Telemark in southern Norway (Moore 1983; Section 5.8 this report).

8
SYNTHESIS

8.1 PREHISTORIC ACTIVITY

In view of the substantial range of prehistoric, Romano-British and Anglo-Saxon archaeology recorded by Bill Wedlake at nearby Camerton (Wedlake 1958) between the 1930s and the 1950s, the discovery of significant late prehistoric settlement related activity in Area H at Eckweek (Section 4.3), just over 2km distant, should not have been a surprise.

Wedlake's excavation work at Camerton was located adjacent to two very substantial Bronze Age barrow monuments (Wedlake 1958, Barrows 1 and 2) on a site where he identified artefacts, features and structures reflecting activity from the Neolithic to Anglo-Saxon periods. The principal evidence recorded included a sequence of early Iron Age activity that incorporated a series of large enclosure or defence ditches (Phase 3) and a later roundhouse (Phase 4). These were followed by features and deposits indicating an extended period of Romano-British activity that included the construction of the *Fosse Way*, possibly along with an associated military station (Wedlake 1958, plate III), and the subsequent development of a substantial Roman roadside settlement whose occupation continued into the 4th century. The sequence of activity culminated in the formation of an Anglo-Saxon cemetery at Camerton Tyning, just to the north of the later Roman roadside settlement.

The remains of the early Iron Age ditches and the roundhouse were located in the extreme eastern part (Seven Acre Field) of the Camerton site, where they were cut by features associated with the *Fosse Way*, now the modern A367. The Phase 3 ditches were of a V-shaped profile and varied between 3m and 5m in width. On the basis of their morphology, Wedlake concluded that they were likely to have served a defensive function and goes on to acknowledge that the extent of the Iron Age activity was likely to have been far greater than that which he recorded. In particular, he notes the presence of the hillfort just to the east of Camerton at nearby Braysdown and the discovery of a human burial and a bronze-working crucible during construction work close to the Red Post Inn at Peasedown St John.

Excavations undertaken by Cotswold Archaeology in 2004–2005 less than 500m to the south of the Eckweek site, in advance of the construction of the Wellow Lane Business Park revealed a deep ditch of middle to late Iron Age date that was suggested to reflect part of a field system located in the vicinity of a contemporary settlement. The ditch, Ditch C (Rowe and Alexander 2011, fig. C), was discontinuous and approximately 5m wide and 1.8m deep, quite similar to the form of Ditch 3161 recorded in Area H at Eckweek (Figure 4.6).

The features recorded by excavation in Areas H and I at Eckweek, combined with the evidence from the geophysical survey (Figure 4.1), indicates one and possibly two extensive and discontinuous Iron Age boundary ditches (geophysical features M5, M6, M8, M13 and M14), which appear to define the northwestern corner of a large enclosure that extended beyond the survey area to the south and east. The part of the ditch recorded in Cuttings 1 and 2 in Area H, where the presence of a terminal indicates the position of an entrance or gateway, was accompanied by an earthfast timber palisade or stock-control fence that was located on the north side of the ditch. The preservation of the postholes suggests that a bank which accompanied the ditch was located on the south side, although no direct evidence is provided by the sequence of ditch fills to support this hypothesis. Evidence for associated settlement activity is restricted to the assemblage of early-middle Iron Age pottery, which includes sherds of traded Droitwich salt container (Section 5.1), part of a bronze-working crucible and a fragment of bronze wire, possibly a personal item. The recovery of this significant assemblage from just two small archaeological cuttings indicates a relative abundance of artefacts in this area and, despite the absence of any significant numbers of animal bone, suggests a focus of contemporary settlement, yet to be identified archaeologically, was located nearby.

In combination, the evidence from the sites at Camerton, Eckweek and the Wellow Business Park indicate an extended period of intensive later prehistoric agricultural and settlement-related activity across large parts of the Camerton and Peasedown St John plateau, where the evidence for extensive linear earthworks is consistent with an increasingly centralised and coercive social hierarchy and dominant pastoral economy in the region proposed by Cunliffe (1991, 385). That said, the evidence to date for the Iron Age period on the Camerton plateau, whilst significant, is clearly very far from complete and further detailed study to define and properly characterise late prehistoric settlement of the area is to be welcomed and will undoubtedly yield important new evidence.

8.2 LATE SAXON AND MEDIEVAL SETTLEMENT

Period III – the pre-Conquest and early post-Conquest settlement

Activity in Area A attributed to CP1 indicates that this particular farmstead and at least some of its principal features, including the remains of at least one timber building, the boundaries of the farmstead plot and the route of the adjacent trackway, were already established by the mid 10th century, or soon after, on a site that had not been occupied previously. The possibility that there was some unspecified activity in the study areas prior to the 10th century cannot be ruled out completely, as settlement sites in Somerset as a whole prior to the mid 10th century appear to have been entirely aceramic for over 300 years (Costen 2011). That said, the total absence of any structural features, deposits or stylistically earlier artefacts from the site indicates that the farmstead in Area A and the slightly later farmstead in Area H were both established at locations that had not been occupied before.

Nonetheless, the likelihood that these farmsteads probably emerged from an earlier local pattern of dispersed settlement is indicated by evidence from nearby Wellow Lane, where the excavations by Cotswold Archaeology (Figure 1.4) in 2004–2005 (Rowe and Alexander 2011, fig. 5) in advance of development identified a D-shaped enclosure (Period 5, Enclosure D) that contained at least two contemporary timber structures (Structures A and B). The activity was not dated by artefacts, although a pair of AMS radiocarbon determinations (Wk-18623 and Wk-18624) taken from material filling the enclosure ditch produced closely comparable middle Saxon (*c*AD 650–850) dates. If the activity recorded at Wellow Lane does indeed reflect the foundation of post-Roman settlement in the locale of Eckweek, it would add support to the model that envisages the emergence of a new chapter of rural settlement in the region in the period between the 6th and 8th centuries (Turner and Wilson-North 2012).

The remains of the earliest building identified by excavation in Area A, Structure 468, indicate that whilst it was a fairly insubstantial structure overall, it is nonetheless quite likely to reflect a dwelling, one whose size of approximately 10m long and 5m to 6m wide conforms to a simple two-square module, where the areas to either side of the central doorway consist of two approximately equally sized quadrangles. Certainly the small principal earthfast foundations that were preserved are broadly consistent with a widespread mid to late Anglo-Saxon building tradition, the remains of which have been recorded on many sites in southern and eastern England (Hamerow 2012). The few artefacts associated with the structure provide little by way of detail concerning the day-to-day activities of its occupants, although the environmental evidence indicates that the character and range of cultivated crops, and by inference a formalised manorial landscape and an associated regime of convertible husbandry (Christie and Stamper 2012) based upon large communal open fields in which they were grown, had already been established by the end of the 10th century. If so, this would be consistent with evidence from elsewhere in the region, most notably Shapwick, where there appears to have been an extensive reorganisation of the agricultural landscape and a restructured and intensified pattern of settlement during the 10th and 11th centuries, albeit at Shapwick leading to the emergence of a fully nucleated village (Gerrard with Aston 2007, 974–981).

The agricultural base of the settlement appears to have intensified during the first half of the 11th century as it underwent a period of dynamic and rapid change. This is signified in Area A by the abandonment of Building 468 and the construction of a larger and very much more substantial dwelling, Building 467, which was laid out on a new alignment alongside the trackway and inside a farmstead plot and yard defined by successive ditches. The dwelling incorporated some of the elements of earlier timber structures of the late 1st millennium AD recorded elsewhere in England, including opposing entrances in the side walls and at least two interior bays, one larger and one smaller, separated by a partition wall that had a lockable door. In addition, it was founded upon a small number of larger principal posts and rafters, a general structural development that seems to emerge gradually and to culminate in the 11th and 12th centuries (Gardiner 2014, fig. 1). That said, the plan form of Building 467, reconstructed from the excavated evidence in Figure 8.1, in particular the deeply hipped or rounded gable ends, has no *exact* parallel in the archaeological record of the region, although the 11th-century earthfast building recorded at Brent Knoll (D Young 2009), along with a number of other later medieval stone buildings excavated on Dartmoor, for example Barn 2 and Barn 3 at Houndtor (Beresford 1979) and the longhouse at

SYNTHESIS

Hutholes, Widcombe (Gent 2007 and Christie and Stamper 2012, fig. 9.3), display a broadly similar overall plan-form. That the building at Eckweek incorporated two sets of large sunken-floor features is undoubted, although whether these were covered with a floor of wooden planks, considered most likely by the writer, remains unproven; the reconstruction by Jennie Anderson, shown in Figure 8.1, assumes this was the case. It is of interest that the origins of the medieval term '*Bordar*' is suggested to stem from the continental Latin *borda*, a 'plank' or 'planked hut' (Thorn Section 2.3 this report). It can be said that the sunken features represent diagnostic elements of a type of 11th-century building that appears to date to be unique in the South West region and a building type whose defining characteristics seem to reflect an amalgamation of late Saxon principal post construction and the earlier Saxon *grubenhauser* tradition. In conjunction with the associated assemblages of domestic and personal artefacts and environmental evidence, this episode of settlement expansion and reconstruction appears to represent strong physical evidence for the '*intensification and quickening of activity at all levels of society in late Anglo-Saxon Somerset*' suggested by Michael Costen (2011).

Both these principal 11th-century buildings recorded at Eckweek are larger in terms of overall footprint than the majority of timber 'hall' buildings so far identified at higher status settlement sites elsewhere in England, for example the range of earthfast buildings identified at Bishopstone, the Period 5 Hall at Goltho or other 11th- to 12th-century structures considered by Gardiner (2014, fig. 1). Moreover, one can speculate that the large size and seemingly special-purpose design of Building 477, a reconstruction of which is shown in Figure 8.3, which could have incorporated some sort of partial upper storey and/or an integrated turriform structure (Structure 476), all set inside an oval or D-shaped enclosure defined by a shallow ditch and external bank (gestures that could never have provided a real defence) with a diameter of roughly 30m, combine to seemingly satisfy the key requirements of the *Promotion Law*, foremost of these being a defendable or fortified manor house (the Anglo-Saxon 'burgh gate') along with a tower or bell-house – the emblems of position that signified the thegnly class (Reynolds 1999, 123-135). Mark Gardiner suggests that the presence of a defined enclosure ditch around a late Saxon building, indicated in Area H at Eckweek by both the geophysical survey (Figure 8.2) and excavated evidence, is a strong indicator of enhanced status and a feature consistent with documentary references in the Law of Ine of Wessex, which specify fines for breaking into the defended (enclosed) premises of a nobleman, an ealdorman or King's *thegn*. The Saxo-Norman manorial complex at Trowbridge, Wilts (Graham and Davies 1993) was set in a similar if slightly larger sub-round enclosure (Enclosure 2, which measured approximately 50m in diameter), as was the Period 5 manorial hall at Goltho, also dated to the 11th century, although the latter was defined by a ditch and bank that was large enough to have been truly defendable. Figure 8.3 provides an artistic reconstruction of how the buildings and the enclosure recorded in Area H may have been designed to display such thegnly status just prior to the Conquest.

In his recent review of the archaeology of Somerset (2011) Michael Costen raised the possibility that the farmstead recorded in Area A at Eckweek (the only excavated farmstead that Dr Costen was aware of at the time of writing) may have belonged to the important Anglo-Saxon thegn, Alstan of Boscombe, who is recorded as the owner of one of two tiny 'manors' at Eckweek before 1066. If so, it may well have been his single unnamed villain or *Bordar* tenant (along with a single slave) who actually lived in Building 467 and farmed the virgate of land attached to it in 1066. Dr Costen goes on to note that the second of the two Domesday manors at Eckweek, whilst only slightly larger, was held entirely in demesne, that is to say it represented the home farm of the estate and land that was administered by the lord for his profit rather than let to tenants (Dyer 2002, 137). If correct, the tenurial arrangement of the two separate Period III farmsteads prior to 1066 might explain the apparent differences in the status of their principal buildings, one possibly the holding of a relatively low ranking and unfree tenant farmer and the other administered by the lord, possibly the Saxon thegn, Alwaker, the second of the two principal landowners recorded in Domesday at Eckweek prior to 1066 (Thorn Section 2.3 this report), with a single resident *Bordar*. This is indicated by the structures themselves, the range of artefacts each area produced, in particular, the slightly greater number of items of horse gear, weapons and personal items of increased luxury recovered from Area H and the similarly slightly greater number of craft and domestic objects recovered from Area A. It is further suggested by the environmental evidence, which indicates that each may have farmed land of differing quality and/or processed crops in slightly different ways. Despite these apparent differences, the excavated evidence indicates that each farmstead was in its own way prospering in an organised and productive agricultural landscape, a reconstruction of which is shown in Figure 8.4. In addition, it is to be noted that these possible slight differences in the character of the two Period III assemblages need not necessarily represent different social status, as a number of late Saxon high status sites, for example Yeavering (Hope-Taylor 1977) and Springfield Lyons (Tyler and Major 2005), all produced very low numbers of artefacts generally.

Reynolds has suggested that, at least in respect of settlement forms, '*the use of 1066 as a defining horizon is not particularly helpful*' (Reynolds 2003, 100). At Eckweek, this appears only partially true as the excavated evidence indicates an episode of dramatic change during the later 11th century (CP3), which appears broadly to coincide with the period of Conquest. The changes, whatever their precise nature, led to a contraction of the settlement as a whole and, most significantly, included the complete and total abandonment of the suggested demesne farmstead and thegnly residence located in Area H. The extent of abandonment across the settlement appears, however, to have been selective, as the farmstead in Area A undoubtedly continued to be occupied into the 12th century much as before and possibly included at least one episode of major repair or reconstruction of Building 467.

The precise sequence of events that led to this dramatic reversal in the fortunes of the settlement remain unknown although, like the majority of former Anglo-Saxon lands in England, Domesday records the transfer of ownership of both Eckweek manors after 1066 from the Saxon thegns, Alstan of Boscombe and Alwaker, to new Norman lords, the Count of Mortain and Walter of Douai respectively. Nonetheless, the abandonment (or indeed outright destruction) of a potentially valuable asset, namely the substantial building and associated structures and facilities in Area H, makes no obvious sense in terms of either tenure or economy and some other explanation could be plausible. The Domesday entry confirms that the larger of the two estates continued to operate at a similar value after 1066 (although presumably now centred at a different location) under the new lordship of Walter of Douai – one can speculate that perhaps the Saxon lord, the important thegn Alwaker, had been particularly troublesome during the period of Conquest, and as a result brought down a punishment that led to the removal of all trace of his former centre of administration and status, his thegnly hall. This soap-opera storyline is no more than that and is not directly supported by either the documentary or excavated evidence: a rather more prosaic explanation is that the thegnly building, of overambitious design that required large-scale structural support just to keep it from falling down, was simply an anachronism after the Conquest, one that became increasingly difficult to maintain and, in the end, was abandoned and left to collapse, never to be rebuilt.

Period IV – Transition During the Later 12th and 13th Centuries

The Period III farmstead buildings in Area A were entirely rebuilt in stone around AD 1200 (CP4) after the pits and sunken floor features of the Period III timber building had been fairly rapidly filled, possibly deliberately in preparation. Period IV also marks a general cessation of ditch and pit digging throughout the farmstead, as the boundaries of the plot formerly defined by ditches and pit groups are demarcated by new stone revetments and earth-retaining walls.

This change of building tradition marks a major period of transition in the built environment at Eckweek and a watershed that has been identified nationwide in the period between *c*AD 1150 and 1250, one where earthfast timber construction is replaced by the adoption of stone sill or sleeper walls (Gardiner 2014). This building innovation appears to have coincided with the increasing use of cruck-paired and end-cruck roof structures, something that Christopher Dyer (1994, 133–167) considers to be more than coincidence, and one that marks a move away from the use of principal post rafters. A similar shift in rural building tradition, involving the increasing use of a range of specialist craftsmen, is recognised across large parts of the country (Dyer 2002, 160–178) and appears, at least in part, to be driven by the adoption of new techniques of precise woodworking and construction methods generally (Gardiner 2014). The date at which stone was adopted as the principal method to build entire walls or support timber superstructures varies across the country, although the late 12th- to early 13th-century date for Period IV at Eckweek is consistent with similar rural buildings in stone recorded elsewhere in the region, for example Buildings 4016/R and 4016/Y at Shapwick (Gerard with Aston 2007, 405–417) and at nearby Barrow Mead just 8km to the northeast of Eckweek, where the Period III stone buildings were dated by the excavator to the 13th century (Woodhouse 1976). A further complex of manorial buildings that included two separate stone dovecotes, was recorded at Harry Stoke near Bristol (Young 1995).

Building 462 represents the farmstead dwelling that replaced Building 467 in Period IV, which was laid out directly alongside the existing trackway, its north wall built directly over the filled Period III trackside ditch. However, the plan of the building is incomplete and the structural features and associated deposits that were preserved along with it are limited. In addition, unlike subsequent Period V Building 460, the numbers and range of stratified artefacts that can be directly associated with the use of the building were relatively few. This, combined with the fact that the adjacent and contemporary building, Building 465, whilst also only partially excavated, appears to have been the larger of the two, with a minimum interior floor area of approximately 50 square metres, makes assigning a likely use problematic. As a result, it is certainly possible that it and not Building 462 was the main farmstead dwelling. If Building 462 was indeed used as the main dwelling it appears to have had a significantly smaller internal floor area, at approximately 30 square metres, than the timber building that preceded it. In addition, the absence of any significant amounts of associated demolition rubble could reflect the use of low sleeper walls used to

SYNTHESIS

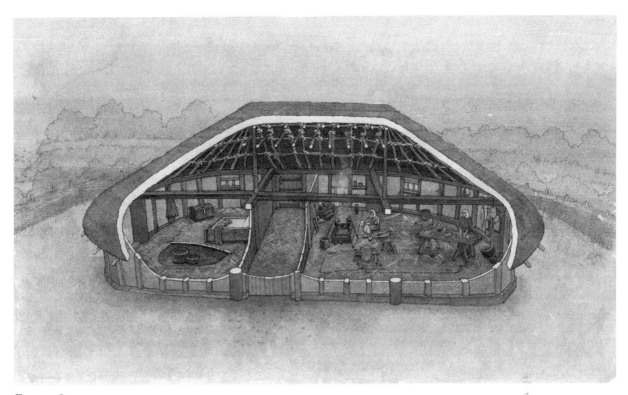

FIGURE 8.1

Reconstruction drawing showing the interior of Period III Building 467 in Area A. Looking north

support a timber superstructure founded upon pairs of raised crucks. The absence of significant amounts of residual Period IV wall masonry alone does not represent firm evidence that sleeper walls were used in the building, as the stone may simply have been removed or reused when the building was demolished and replaced in Period V. Nonetheless, the move from a ground-fast to a ground-set timber superstructure is widely acknowledged to coincide with the emergence of masonry foundation walls and new construction techniques, changes that were as much concerned with extending the life of a building as with the increased scarcity of timber and the availability of suitable local stone, the latter certainly available locally at Eckweek.

The agricultural economy associated with the occupation of stone Buildings 462 and 465 during the period, broadly between *c*AD 1200 and 1275, appears little different from that which preceded it, either in terms of animal husbandry or the types of crops that were being cultivated, although it seems likely that the increased variety of domesticated animals represented in the later medieval assemblage as a whole (Figure 5.72) probably begins to expand in Period IV. The range of domestic objects is dominated by pottery (Figures 7.39 and 7.41), which includes the same rather restricted range of cooking and storage pots, although the numbers of vessel in wares 1 and 2 appear in decline (Figure 5.34) whilst the incidence of vessels in ware 4, in particular Westcountry dishes that were perforated in the side or base with either two or four holes, increases markedly. The reason for this increase is not clear, although the use of these particular (and often very fragile) vessels is often associated with draining liquid as part of dairy processing or, perhaps less obviously, as bee-skeps for the production of honey (McCarthy and Brooks 1988, 110).

Finds other than of pottery recovered from stratified Period IV (CP4) contexts are fairly limited, but include a small collection of standard domestic, personal and agricultural objects including knives, an awl, a spur, miscellaneous fragments of iron sheet, and an ox-goad (Figure 7.48); these representing little more in either number or range than that recovered from the preceding Period III buildings. This apparent absence of any significant numbers of associated artefacts may reflect nothing more than differential preservation alone, or, alternatively, could conceivably indicate a period of reduced economic growth in the settlement. However, if it were the latter, it would be contrary to the widely accepted period of population growth and agricultural and economic expansion that is documented nationally during the late 12th and 13th centuries (Dyer 2002, 155–186) and contradict the extensive and costly reconstruction of the farmstead buildings in Area A.

Unlike the subsequent Period V farmhouse, the artefacts associated with the Period IV farmstead (Figure 7.48) provide little direct evidence to elucidate how the buildings were organised or used. Nonetheless, the remains of the buildings alone seem to reflect a household whose fortunes were broadly on-the-up, quite possibly the households headed by Baldwin de Ekewike or his contemporary, Henry de Hekewike, who are both documented landowners at Eckweek between AD 1200 and 1243 (Figure 2.4).

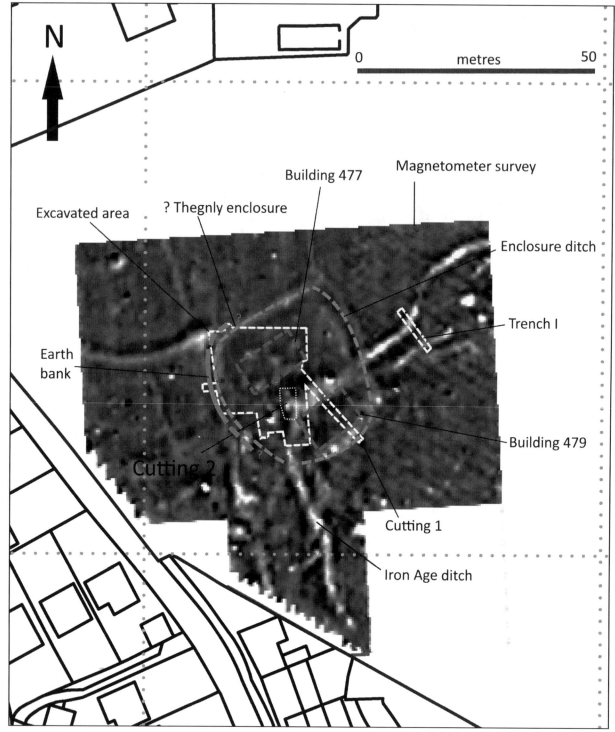

FIGURE 8.2

Detail of the magnetometer greyscale data from Area H with principal 11th-century Period III features superimposed

Period V – Prosperity and Expansion in the Late 13th and Early 14th Centuries

The Period IV farmstead buildings in Area A, the dwelling and byre, were demolished and entirely rebuilt in stone [Buildings 460 and 463] towards the end of the 13th century (CP5). A further stone structure, an oven or corn-dryer [Structure 466], was also constructed in Area A towards the south side of the yard along with a simple stone base for a corn or fodder stack [473]. At the same time an entirely new stone dwelling, Building 461, was built a short distance to the northeast in Area B (Figure 1.7), on a prepared and level platform formed alongside the trackway. These events, combined with evidence from the geophysical survey, which indicates a series of further similar stone buildings in the area of Trenches J and K, points to a period of redevelopment and expansion of the settlement generally during the latter part of the 13th and early 14th centuries, growth that is also reflected in the material wealth of the occupants and the fabric and form

SYNTHESIS

FIGURE 8.3

Reconstruction drawing showing the 11th-century Period III 'thegnly hall' and its compound in Area H. Looking north east

of the structures themselves, whose construction is likely to have required substantial outlay of capital for materials and the employment of specialist craftsmen, for example stonelayers, carpenters and thatchers (Blair and Ramsay 1991; Dyer 2002).

Buildings 460 and 463 and Structures 466 and 473 represent the final phase of occupation and activity in Area A – it is these structures and associated deposits that were most completely preserved and that defined the majority of the earthworks visible on the site in the modern era. The boundaries of the farmstead plot appear to have remained essentially unchanged generally and continued to be defined by revetted earth banks, although it is perhaps surprising that neither of the new buildings directly reused the footings of the Period IV buildings, the footprint of the enlarged farmhouse [Building 460] being entirely offset from that of Building 462 and set back from the trackway (Figure 4.2). The largely undisturbed preservation of the Period V structures provides a large body of information with which to reconstruct both the form and arrangement of the buildings and how the space inside each was organised and used (Figures 4.5 and 7.5). The latter is greatly informed by the range and distribution of artefacts located inside the main dwelling, Building 460 (Section 7.2). The height of the farmhouse [460] wall foundations, combined with the quantity of rubble [Layers 3 and 12 etc] that was preserved over and around them (Figure 4.62A), provides some indication as to the original height of its walls and, thereby, clues concerning the nature of the building's superstructure. The in-situ remains of the walls indicate an original height of no less than 500mm. The presence of the extensive rubble deposits confirms that they were originally higher, although how much so remains speculation since the volumes of rubble that were excavated were not measured and the amounts that had been removed by stone robbing (evident from Robber Pits 37 and 45) is unknown – nonetheless, the amount of rubble present indicates that the walls were originally significantly higher and (in the opinion of the writer), as an absolute minimum half as great again, at least 750mm and quite possibly 1m in height. Even so this inferred maximum still indicates that the walls did not rise to eaves height but provided support for a timber sill and frame founded on a raised cruck blade superstructure (for examples see Alcock and Miles 2013, 55–78), the interstices of which would have been most likely infilled with wood-wattle, clay or cob. An artistic reconstruction of the building as it may have appeared around AD 1350, showing its internal organisation, is shown in Figure 8.5.

The plan of each of the 14th-century buildings was, despite later episodes of stone robbing, essentially complete and the quantity and variety of associated artefacts, especially those from the farmhouse [460], provide a detailed insight into the organisation and use of internal space (see Section 7.1 above for a detailed discussion). The footprint of the farmhouse, which totalled approximately 74 square metres externally with an internal floor area

FIGURE 8.4

Reconstruction drawing showing the 11th-century Period III settlement at Eckweek. Looking north

of some 53 square metres, was significantly larger than Building 462 and broadly equivalent to that of the Period III farmhouse, Building 467.

The evidence for the agricultural economy associated with the occupation of the Period V farmstead during the period cAD 1275 to cAD 1400 appears broadly unchanged from that of Period IV, both in terms of the range of animal husbandry and the types of crops that were being cultivated and processed. The evidence does seems to reflect a peak in terms of the range of animals (Section 5.13) and cultivated crops (Section 5.14) represented, although there is some evidence that the overall level of agricultural production may have been diminishing by Structural Phase V.2 (CP6), broadly the mid 14th century, when the overall quantity of residual cereals present appears to fall significantly compared to earlier periods and, within that smaller assemblage, the relative proportion of wheat falls whilst there is an equivalent small rise in the amount of oats and, to a lesser extent, barley. This subtle change may simply be a consequence of preservation although, if so, this would be surprising given that the preservation of the associated material culture peaks in CP6 (Structural Phase V.2–3).

The range and numbers of structural, domestic, agricultural and personal objects recovered from Period V contexts increase substantially compared to earlier periods (Figures 7.39, 7.48 and 7.50). However, as before, the finds assemblage is dominated by pottery, which now incorporates a new and varied array of cooking and storage vessels (Figure 5.34) that includes both utilitarian and fine tableware vessels produced at new regional centres, for example vessels from South Somerset, NW Wiltshire (including Minety-type wares) and the area of Lacock in Wiltshire. Whilst the source of very many of the ceramic fabrics identified on the site remains unknown, there does appear to be a relative predominance of fabrics from recognised kilns to the south and east of the site, a feature that could reflect the predominant manufacturing centres that were trading wares into rural Somerset during the 14th century. If so, this suggests that products from the Bristol area, in particular the wide range of utilitarian and tableware vessels produced at the Bristol Redcliffe kilns, were being traded into the area only in relatively lower numbers at the time.

Non-ceramic finds were also represented in large numbers (and, moreover, either in, or very close to their original position) which allow a detailed insight into the organisation and use of space inside both the farmhouse and the adjacent byre building, one that is rarely observed in an archaeological context – as a result we can be confident that the distributions and the conclusions that are drawn from them (Section 7.2) are well-founded. In combination, the detailed evidence provided by the Period V farmhouse itself, combined with its associated distribution of artefacts, illuminates a peasant house whose internal arrangement, despite its cramped size, incorporated elements of a domestic culture that

FIGURE 8.5
Reconstruction drawing showing the interior of 14th-century Period V Farmhouse 460 in Area A. Looking north

was common to both peasant and lord alike and one that suggests the life of the relatively lowly medieval family of the 14th century was lived in a surprising degree of comfort and even, as David Clark (2013) suggests, some modest elegance. Clark goes on to suggest that a visitor entering the house would easily recognise the signs of common and private spaces and the hierarchy of activity within them, whatever the relative social status of the household was. As such, the principal subdivisions of the house, consisting of entrance cross-passage, a combined hall/kitchen, inner room and store or workshop, have been interpreted previously to reflect a scaled-down version of the high status hall, where the central hall-hearth represented an area of public character and a defining characteristic that in turn led to a private room, variously termed parlour, chamber or *celer*, which often had a simple floored room above, the *solar*, reached by a stair or ladder. Although this slimmed-down and rationalised interpretation remains a hypothesis, each of the building elements are either represented or possible in Building 460, although whether their greatly reduced scale managed to convey the same message seems hard to believe, to the writer at least. According to contemporary inventories, the hall was used for sitting and eating, cooking and serving, and usually contained a trestle table, a bench and a chair (Dyer 1994). A similar range of activities appear to have been undertaken in the hall/kitchen bay, although there is no direct evidence for what, if any, furniture the tiny room contained. However, since a bench and table would have represented the focus of the peasant hall (as it was in the lord's hall) where the sitting place or bench at the 'high end' of the hall (the part closest to the inner room or chamber) expressed the patriarchal status of the owner, it seems reasonable to assume that there was one. On that basis, the position of the hearth, which was slightly offset to the south side of the room, may reflect the need for some small open space against the partition wall to accommodate a table and bench. The presence of the two small ovens or boiling kilns clearly demonstrates that in this peasant house the room merged the roles of both kitchen and hall, an interpretation underlined by the range of domestic and cooking vessels that were preserved as dense concentrations of sherds in the areas directly in front of both ovens. This concentrated and varied use of the kitchen-hall space is consistent with both contemporary illustrations and modern reconstructions of medieval food preparation (for example see Michaelmore and Moorhouse 1987), where not only foodstuffs, for example flitches of bacon, but the gamut of domestic objects, tools, agricultural implements, horse-gear and weapons were kept alongside one another, either hanging from walls or stored on shelves. The distribution of artefacts found inside the central room (Figures 7.6 to 7.8 and 7.11 to 7.21) certainly appears to support this picture of a space that was pretty much jam-packed at the best of times, one that the reconstruction shown on Figure 8.5 illustrates well.

The inner room or chamber (Figure 4.5) appears to have been equally as crowded as the hall-kitchen, with domestic, personal and other equipment (Figures 7.6 to 7.8 and 7.11 to 7.21), the range and quality of which indicates that they reflect the household's most valuable possessions, including a lockable wooden chest and the best ceramic and metal tableware. The fine tableware including the Stag's Head cistern and glazed jugs was found in a close group in association with the feet and remnant sheeting from at least one and probably two bronze bowls. This close arrangement could indicate that they were all set on a small table, although the very limited space available makes this unlikely. The chest, seemingly set directly alongside against the gable wall, also appears to have held a range of personal objects including a coin, a rosary (bead) and possibly several buckles. It may also have held several tools including a spindle whorl, several knives (at least one of which had a proper metal guard) and punch, although it is possible that at least some of these may have been stored on shelves attached to the wall over the chest. The chamber is generally regarded to have incorporated the main sleeping area of the house, although there is no direct evidence for the location of a bed or similar, other than the absence of finds generally in the northern third of the room. This, combined with the suggestion of some further separation of this part of the bay, as indicated by the extent of a soil layer [72] and the boulder [143], could certainly reflect the space for a bed or a simple mattress (or just a large bundle of straw) although, as has already been noted, the absence of finds could simply be due to disturbance by later stone robbing [Pit 45]. The possibility that the chamber bay was storeyed with a further room above, a feature termed the *solar* that appears to have been increasingly common in later medieval peasant houses (Dyer 1994, 149–154), remains a possibility, although direct evidence for such, other than the enigmatic boulder, was lacking.

The inventory of artefacts (Figures 7.37 and 7.48) recovered from the interior of the Period V farmhouse appears broadly consistent with a number of similar documented late medieval household inventories for middling and better-off peasant households working up to a yardland (approximately 24 acres), for example those cited by R. K. Field in Worcestershire (Field 1965, 105–145 and in particular tables I–III), which make for useful comparison. On the basis of the documentary sources for the settlement (Section 2), the excavated inventory, which unlike those cited by Field (1965) excludes all perishables of wood, cloth or similar, includes most of the principal household items and belongings of a fairly well-to-do tenant peasant farmer, one defined by Christopher Dyer (2002) as a '*small scale landowner mainly engaged in agricultural production from a yardland or less*' – possibly the goods of the household headed by either Thomas Ekewyke or John Toukere of Ekewyke, both of which are referred to as landowners in contemporary documents between 1349 and 1362 (Figure 2.4). Objects commonly listed in contemporary medieval inventories and represented in the archaeological assemblage recovered from the building include wooden chests, often valued between 2 and 3 shillings each, brass (copper alloy) pans and cauldrons, these some of the most valuable domestic items, iron sickles and agricultural tools, pottery basins and ewers, horse gear and, on rare occasions, domestic ovens or kilns. Contemporary inventories also list items that are clearly missing from the excavated assemblage, but which we can expect to have been present – these include trestle tables, benches, stools and a wide range of other wooden objects, mattresses, bedding and clothes. Estimating the total value for these household goods is problematic, although Christopher Dyer (Dyer 2013, 19–27) cites a series of Yorkshire inventories where their value on death ranges between £6 and £20. He goes on to note that judging from the inventories, the majority of peasant households owned little in the way of luxury goods and that their most prized possession was often a cart with iron tyres, or a prized ox, either or both of which could have been kept at Eckweek in the adjacent byre building [463].

The excavated remains of the Period V farmhouse provide a rare and detailed insight into what was probably a pretty typical 14th-century tenant peasant household. This insight is a consequence of special preservation, as opposed to an unusual status of the occupants, and illuminates the principal setting for a typical and probably unremarkable family life in a home that was central to the work of the holding, housing and feeding the family and labour force; a place where, in spite of the limited space that was available, the mode of living and notions of orderliness and separation (Kowaleski and Goldberg 2008, 29) were important – a multi-functional home certainly, but also one whose evident organisation supports the model of '*interior spaces ... imbued with social meaning*' (Clark 2013).

Period V, Phase V.3 – Decline and Abandonment in the Later 14th Century

Sometime soon after AD 1352, a date provided by a 4d groat of Edward III recovered from the latest floor layer in the inner room, the prosperous farmstead in Area A, shown reconstructed at its height in Figure 8.6, was abandoned. It was never reoccupied, although the adjacent property in Area B, Building 461, appears to have continued in use for some time afterwards, probably into the 15th century. The documentary sources for the settlement (Figure 2.4) include a reference of AD 1440 to '*a toft, formerly a messuage*' that may denote the abandoned (and by implication largely demolished) farmstead in Area A. The reason for the abandonment of the farmhouse is not attested by the archaeology or the documentary sources, although the excavated assemblage indicates that many, if not all, of the fittings and furnishings of the house were left in-situ. As has already been discussed, this in itself suggests some unforeseen and possibly catastrophic circumstance, a strong contender for which is (of

SYNTHESIS

FIGURE 8.6

Reconstruction drawing showing the 14th-century Period V farmstead in Area A. Looking north

course) any of the four episodes of epidemic that ravaged the country between AD 1348 and *c*1373 (Horrox 1994). The archaeology does not allow the date of abandonment to be more closely defined, although it is interesting to note that the final documentary reference to Eckweek landowner Thomas Ekewyke (Figure 2.4) is dated in the same year the coin was minted, around two years after the end of the so-called 'first pestilence', whilst that of a second landowner, one John Toukere (the Tucker) of Ekewyke, is named in a later document of 1362.

Appointing an episode of plague or a similar unforeseen epidemic as the reason for abandonment of a settlement is today deeply unfashionable and there are indeed other reasons that could explain why so many household objects were not removed from the farmhouse in Area A. One is the possibility that the majority of the household items found in the building represented 'Principalia'; household goods claimed by the landlord as seigneurial property after a tenant left the property. If so, it is still difficult to understand why the lord did not then collect these goods if no new tenant was available or, alternatively, why they were not over time thoroughly scavenged. An alternative explanation for the abandonment could concern the secondary consequence of the epidemics, equally elusive archaeologically, which led to a period of increased social and economic pressure that is documented throughout rural England after 1348 (Dyer 2000; Fryde 1996, 8–29). These pressures were in part due to a scarcity of agricultural workers and a consequent if gradual rise in the wages that they could demand, an imbalance that increased the numbers of freelance and itinerant workers in the countryside and led to further abandonment of tenant farmsteads and rural settlements already reduced by epidemic. These changing circumstances led to the 'Statute of Labourers' being issued in 1351 by Edward III, an Act designed to restrict wages to pre-1348 levels. Further reorganisation of the rural landscape after 1348 also involved the amalgamation of earlier land holdings and this too might explain why the farmstead was not subsequently reoccupied when the documentary references examined by Nick Corcos (Figure 2.4) continue to show a close interest in the holdings of agricultural land at Eckweek well into the 15th century.

Whether the inhabitants of the 14th-century farmhouse in Area A did indeed succumb to epidemic, their home and goods left very much intact and to be avoided by survivors elsewhere in the settlement, or survived, only to up-sticks at short notice and perhaps move on to a new place with better prospects, we will never know for sure. What we can be sure of is that the farmstead in Area A, which had been occupied continuously for almost 500 years, remained abandoned and largely untouched for the following five hundred.

BIBLIOGRAPHY

Abrams, L, 1996 *Anglo-Saxon Glastonbury: Church and Endowment*, Woodbridge

Albarella, U, (in press) *Central England: A Review of Animal Remains from Saxon, Medieval and Post-medieval Archaeological Sites*. English Heritage, Research Report Series

Albarella, U and Davis, S J M, 1994 *The Saxon and Medieval Animal bones Excavated 1985–1989 from West Cotton, Northamptonshire*, HBMC AM Laboratory report 17/94, London

Albarella, U and Davis, S J M, 1996 'Mammals and birds from Launceston Castle, Cornwall: decline in status and the rise of agriculture', *Circaea* 12, 1–156

Alcock, L, 1980 'The Cadbury Castle sequence in the first millennium BC', *Bulletin of the Board of Celtic Studies* 28, 656–718

Alcock, N and Miles, D, 2013 *The Medieval Peasant House in Midland England*, Oxbow Books, Oxford

Alcock, N, Barley, M, Dixon, P and Meeson, R, 2014 *Recording Timber-Framed Buildings: An Illustrated Glossary*, Council for British Archaeology Practical Handbook in Archaeology 5

Allen, C A, Firman, R J, Knight, D and Williams, D F, 1994 'Fabrics' in D Knight, 'Excavations of an Iron Age Settlement at Gamston, Nottinghamshire', *Transactions of the Thoroton Society* 96, 17–90 (40–3)

Anderson, R, 2008 *Annotated List of the Non-marine Mollusca of Britain and Ireland*, Conchological Society of Great Britain and Ireland, London

ApSimon, A, 1959 'Iron Age pottery', in P A Rahtz and J C Brown, 1959 'Blaise Castle Hill, Bristol 1957', *Proceedings of the University of Bristol Spelaeological Society* 8, 147–171

ApSimon, A, Rahtz, P A and Harris, L G, 1957–1958 'The Iron Age A ditch and pottery at Pagans' Hill, Chew Stoke', *Proceedings of the University of Bristol Spelaeological Society* 8, 97–105

Archibald, M M, 1987 'Medieval coins' in G Beresford, *Goltho: The Development of an Early Medieval Manor c850–1150*, English Heritage Archaeological Report 4, 1158

Archibald, M M, 2010 'Coins' in A Chapman, *West Cotton, Raunds: A Study of Medieval Settlement Dynamics AD450–1450*, Oxford, 394–395

Armitage, P L, 1983 'The early history of English longwool sheep', *The Ark* 10, 90–97

Armstrong, P, 1977 'Excavations in Sewer Lane Hull 1974', *East Archaeologist* 3, Hull Old Town Report Series 1

Armstrong, P, Tomlinson, D and Evans, D H, 1991 *Excavations at Lurk Lane Beverley, 1979–82*, Sheffield Excavation Reports 1, J R Collis, Sheffield

Arnold, D E, 1985 *Ceramic Theory and Cultural Process*, Cambridge University Press, Cambridge

Ashby, S, 1999 *Bone and Antler Combs*, The Finds Research Group AD700–1700 Datasheet No.40

Aston, M A, 1983 'Deserted farmsteads on Exmoor and the lay subsidy of 1327 in west Somerset', *Proceedings of the Somerset Archaeological and Natural History Society* 127, 71–104

Aston, M A, 1986 'Post-Roman central places in Somerset', in E. Grant (ed), *Central Places, Archaeology and History*, 49–77, University of Sheffield

Aston, M A, 1988 'Land Use and Field Systems', in M A Aston (ed), *Aspects of the Medieval Landscape of Somerset*, 82–97, Somerset County Council

Aston, M A (ed), 1988 *Medieval Fish, Fisheries and Fishponds in England*, British Archaeological Reports 182

Aston, M A, Costen, M D, Hall, T and Ecclestone, M, 2007 'The later Medieval furlongs of Shapwick: attempts at mapping the 1515 survey, in C Gerrard with M A Aston (eds) 2007, 74–101

Aston, M and Lewis, C (eds), 1994 *The Medieval Landscape of Wessex*, Oxbow Monograph 46, Oxford

Aston, M A, 1994 'Medieval settlement studies in Somerset', in M Aston and C Lewis (eds), 219–238

Atkinson, D R, 1965 'Clay tobacco pipes and pipemakers of Marlborough', *Wiltshire Archaeological and Natural History Magazine* 60, 85–95

Ballard, A, 1906 *The Domesday Inquest*, London

Barker, P A, 1964 'Excavation of the moated site at Shifnal, Shropshire, 1962', *Transactions of the Shropshire Archaeological Society* 57, part 3, 194–205

Barrett, J C, 1980 'The prehistoric pottery', in R Price and L Watts 'Rescue excavations at Combe Hay, Somerset', *Proceedings of the Somerset Archaeological and Natural History Society* 124, 25–27

Barton, K J, 1963 'The medieval pottery kiln at Ham Green Bristol', *Transactions of the Bristol and Gloucestershire Archaeological Society* 82, 95–126

Bates, D, 1986 *A Bibliography of Domesday Book*, Royal Historical Society, London

Bates, D, 1998 *Regesta Regum Anglo-Normannorum: the Acta of William I (1066–1087)*, Oxford

Bates Harbin, S W, 1936 'Somerset enrolled deeds', *Somerset Record Society* 51

Bayliss, A, Freeman, P and Woodward, A, 2000 'The radiocarbon dates', in J C Barrett, P W M Freeman and A Woodward *Cadbury Castle Somerset; the Later Prehistoric and Early Historic Archaeology*, English Heritage Archaeological Report 20, 370–372

Bennett, J, 1985 *Sea Mills, The Roman Town of Abonae*, City of Bristol Museum and Art Gallery Monograph 3

Beresford, G, 1975 *The Medieval Clay Land Village: Excavations at Goltho and Barton Blount*, The Society for Medieval Archaeology Monograph Series 6

Beresford, G, 1977 'Excavation of a moated house at Wintringham, Huntingdonshire', *Archaeological Journal* 134, 257–276

Beresford, G, 1979 'Three deserted settlements on Dartmoor: A report on the late E Marie Minter's Excavations' *Medieval Archaeology*, 23

BIBLIOGRAPHY

Beresford, G, 1987 *Goltho: The Development of an Early Medieval Manor c850–1150*, English Heritage Archaeological Report 4

Beresford, M W, 1954 *The Lost Villages of England*, Lutterworth

Berkeley, Fitzhardinge, F W, Baron of, and Jeayes, I H, 1892 *Descriptive Catalogue of the Charters and Muniments in the Possession of the Right Honourable Lord Fitzhardinge*, Bristol

Bigelow, M M, 1879 *Placita Anglo-Normannica: Law Cases from William I to Richard Preserved in Historical Records*, London (reprinted New York, 1970)

Bintley, M D J and Shapland, M G (eds), 2013 *Trees and Timber in the Anglo-Saxon World*, Medieval History and Archaeology, Oxford University Press, Oxford

Bird, S, 1987 'Roman Avon', in M A Aston and R Iles (eds), *The Archaeology of Avon*, 52–71 Avon County Council

Blair, C, Blair, W J and Brownsword, R, 1985 'An Oxford brasiers' dispute of the 1390s', *Antiquaries Journal* 66 (1), 83–90

Blair, J, 2005 *The Church in Anglo-Saxon Society*, Oxford

Blair, J and Ramsay, N (eds), 1991 *English Medieval Industries*, The Hambledon Press, London

Boardman, S and Jones, G, 1990 'Experiments on the effects of charring cereal plant components', *Journal of Archaeological Sciences* 17, 1–11

Brenchley, W E, and Warrington, K, 1993 'The weed seed population of arable soil II. The influence of crop, soil and methods of cultivation upon the relative abundance of viable seeds', *Journal of Ecology* 21, 103–127

Brett, C J, 2007 'The manors of Norton St Philip and Hinton Charterhouse, 1535–1691', *Somerset Record Society* 93

BGS, 2000 British Geological Survey 2000 Frome. England & Wales Sheet 281 Solid and Drift Geology. 1:50,000, Keyworth, Nottingham: BGS

Bronk Ramsey, C, 1995 'Radiocarbon calibration and analysis of stratigraphy: the OxCal program', *Radiocarbon* 37, 425–430

Bronk Ramsey, C, 1998 'Probability and dating', *Radiocarbon* 40, 461–474

Bronk Ramsey, C, 2001 'Development of the radiocarbon calibration program OxCal', *Radiocarbon* 43, 355–363

Bronk Ramsey, C, 2009 'Bayesian analysis of radiocarbon dates', *Radiocarbon* 51, 337–360

Brown, L, 2012 'The pottery', in R Thomas, J Oswin and L Brown, 'A late Bronze Age/earliest Iron Age settlement on Bathampton Down, Bath', *Proceedings of the Somerset Archaeological and Natural History Society* 155, 204–207 (206–207)

Brownsword, R, Pitt, E and Symons, D, 1983–1984 'The analysis of some metal objects from Weoley Castle', *Transactions of the Birmingham and Warwickshire Archaeological Society*, 93, 33–39

Brunskill, R W, 1994 *Timber Building in Britain*, Gollancz, 40–49

Brunskill, R W, 2000 *Vernacular Architecture – An Illustrated handbook*, Faber & Faber

Brunskill, R W, 2007 *Traditional Farm Buildings and Their Conservation*, Yale University Press

Bulleid, A and Gray, H St G, 1911 *The Glastonbury Lake Village*, 1, Glastonbury

Bulleid, A and Gray, H St G, 1953 *The Meare Lake Village*, Taunton

Burke, J F, 1834 *British Husbandry; Exhibiting the Farming Practice in Various Parts of the United Kingdom*, 2 vols, Baldwin and Cradock, London

Campbell, G, 1994 'The preliminary archaeobotanical results from Anglo-Saxon West Cotton and Raunds', in J Rackham (ed) *Environment and Economy in Anglo-Saxon England*, Council for British Archaeology Research Report 89, 65–82

Carruthers, W J, 1995 *Charred Plant Remains from Eckweek, Peasedown St John*, unpublished archive report BATRM 1997.1

Carruthers, W J, 1997a 'Plant remains', in A G Vince, S J Lobb, J C Richards and Lorraine Mepham, *Excavations in Newbury, Berkshire 1979–90* Wessex Archaeological Report 13, 141–145

Carruthers, W J, 1997b 'Plant remains', in J W Hawkes and P J Fasham, *Excavations on Reading Waterfront Sites, 1979–1988*, Wessex Archaeological Report 5, 78–94

Carruthers, W (unpublished) 'The carbonised and waterlogged plant remains', in S Ford, *Charnham Lane, Hungerford*

Chadwick Healy, C E H, 1897 'Somerset pleas; rolls of the itinerant justices', *Somerset Record Society* 11

Chaplais, P, 1986 'William of St Calais and the Domesday Survey' in J C Holt (ed) *Domesday Studies: Papers Read at the Novocentenary Conference of the Royal Historical Society and the Institute of British Geographers*, Woodbridge, Winchester, 65–77

Chapman, A, 2010 *West Cotton, Raunds: A Study of Medieval Settlement Dynamics AD450–1450*, Northamptonshire

Christie, N and Stamper, P (eds), 2012 *Medieval Rural Settlement – Britain and Ireland AD800–1600*, Oxbow Books, Oxford

Clark, D, 2013 'The medieval peasant house – towards a new paradigm?' *Vernacular Architecture Group* 44, 1–5

Clarke, H, 1984 *The Archaeology of Medieval England*, British Museum, London

Clarke, H B, 1985 'The Domesday satellites', in P H Sawyer (ed) *Domesday Book: A Reassessment*, London, 50–70

Clay, P, 1981 'The small finds – non-structural', in J E Mellor and T Pearce, *The Austin Friars, Leicester*, Council for British Archaeology Research Report 35, 46–52

Clayton, T, 2015 *Coins of England and Great Britain*, www.coins-of-the-uk.co.uk, site accessed March 2015

Cleal, R M J, 1995 'Pottery fabrics in Wessex in the fourth to second millennia BC', in I Kinnes and G Varndell (eds), *Unbaked Urns of Rudely Shape*, Oxbow Monograph 55, 185–194, Oxbow Books, Oxford

Coates, R, 1999 'New light from old wicks: the progeny of Latin vicus', *Nomina* 22, 75–116

Coleman-Smith, R and Pearson, T, 1970 *Excavations at Donyatt and Nether Stowey, Somerset*, Donyatt Research Group, Southampton

Coleman-Smith, R and Pearson, T, 1988 *Excavations in the Donyatt Potteries*, Phillimore, Chichester

Collingwood, R G, 1930 *The Archaeology of Roman Britain*, Methuen, London

Collinson, J, 1791 *The History and Antiquities of the County of Somerset*, R Cruttwell, Bath

Corcos, N J, 2002a *The Affinities and Antecedents of Medieval Settlement: Topographical Perspectives from Three of the Somerset Hundreds*, British Archaeological Reports British Series 337, Archaeopress

Corcos, N J, 2002b 'Bourne and Burrington: a Burnantūn estate?', *Proceedings of the Somerset Archaeological and Natural History Society* 144, 117–138

Corcos, N J, 2007 'Enclosure at Shapwick: a brief history 1515–1839', in C Gerrard and M Aston 2007, 101–107

Corcos, N J, 2011 'Chew and Chewton: a pre-Conquest river estate north of Mendip', in J Lewis (ed), *The Archaeology of Mendip*, 275–297, Heritage Press

Corcos, N J, n.d. 'Fieldnames and Archaeology', on Wikiarc, moderated archaeology resource website; http://www.wikiarc.org/fieldnames

Cosh, S R and Neal, D S, 2005 *Roman Mosaics of Britain, Vol. 2: South-West Britain*, Illuminata for the Society of Antiquaries of London

Costen, M D, 1979 'Place-name evidence in South Avon', *Avon Past* 1, 13–17

Costen, M D, 1983 'Stantonbury and district in the tenth century', *Bristol and Avon Archaeology* 2, 25–34

Costen, M D, 1988 'The late Saxon landscape: the evidence from charters and placenames', in M A Aston (ed) *Aspects of the Medieval Landscape of Somerset*, 32–47, Somerset County Council

Costen, M D, 1992 *The Origins of Somerset*, Manchester University Press, Manchester

Costen, M D, 2011 *Anglo-Saxon Somerset*, Oxbow Books, Oxford

Courtney, P, 2004 'The small finds' in K Rodwell and R Bell, *Acton Court – The Evolution of an Early Tudor Courtier's House*, English Heritage, 365–396

Cowgill, J, de Neergaard, M and Griffiths, N, 1987 *Knives and Scabbards, Medieval Finds from Excavations in London*, HMSO

Cra'ster, M D, 1966 'Waterbech Abbey', *Proceedings of the Cambridge Antiquarian Society* 59, 75–94

Crummy, N, 1988 *The Post Roman Small Finds from Excavations in Colchester 1971–1985*, Colchester Archaeological Report 5, Colchester Archaeological Trust Ltd

Cunliffe, B, 1976 *Excavations at Portchester Castle (Volume II: Saxon)*, The Society of Antiquaries of London

Cunliffe, B, 1977 *Excavations at Portchester Castle (Volume III: Medieval)*, The Society of Antiquaries of London

Cunliffe, B, (ed), 1979 *Excavations in Bath 1950–1975*, Committee for Rescue Archaeology in Avon, Gloucestershire and Somerset, Excavation report 1, 4–71, Bristol

Cunliffe, B, 1991 *Iron Age Communities in Britain* 3rd edition, Routledge, London

Currie C R J, 1988 'Early vetches in Medieval England: a note', *Economic History Revue* 2nd Series, 41, 114–116

Darby, H C, 1977 *Domesday England*, Cambridge University Press, Cambridge

Davies, P, 2008 *Snails: Archaeology and Landscape Change*, Oxbow, Oxford

Davies, P, 2010 'Land and freshwater molluscs' in T O'Connor and N Sykes (eds) *Extinctions and Invasions: A Social History of the British Fauna*, 175–180, Windgather Press, Oxford

Davis, S J M, 1988 *Animal Bones from Dodder Hill, a Roman Fort Near Droitwich (Hereford and Worcester), Excavated in 1977*, Ancient Monuments Laboratory report 140/88, HBMC, London

Davis, S J M, (unpublished 1991) *Faunal Remains from the Late Saxon-Medieval Farmstead at Eckweek in Avon, 1988–1989 Excavations*, Ancient Monuments Laboratory Report 35/91, HBMC, London

Davis, S J M, 1992a *A Rapid Method for Recording Information about Mammal Bones from Archaeological Sites*, Ancient Monuments Laboratory report 19/92, HBMC, London

Davis, S J M, 1992b *Saxon and Medieval Animal Bones from Burystead and Langham Road, Northants; 1984–1987 Excavations*, Ancient Monuments Laboratory Report 71/92, HBMC, London

Davis, S J M, 2000 'The effect of castration and age on the development of the Shetland sheep skeleton and a metric comparison between bones of males, females and castrates', *Journal of Archaeological Science* 27, 373–390

Davis, S J M and Beckett, J, 1999 'Animal husbandry and agricultural improvement: the archaeological evidence from animal bones and teeth', *Rural History* 10, 1–17

Deniz, E and Payne, S, 1982 'Eruption and wear in the mandibular dentition as a guide to ageing Turkish Angora goats,' in B Wilson, C Grigson and S Payne (eds), *Ageing and Sexing Animal Bones from Archaeological Sites*, 155–205, British Archaeological Reports British Series 109, Oxford

Dickinson, F, 1889 'Kirby's quest for Somerset', *Somerset Record Society* 3

DoE, 1990 Planning Policy Guidance Note 16 (PPG 16), Archaeology and Planning, Department of the Environment, London

Domesday Book (Alecto). This edition of Domesday Book consists of (1) facsimiles of Great Domesday Book (R W H. Erskine (ed), Great Domesday, a Facsimile Text, London, 1986) and Little Domesday Book (G Martin and A Williams (eds), Little Domesday, A Facsimile Text, London, 2000); (2) a general volume (Williams and Erskine (eds), Domesday Book Studies, London, 1987); (3) a Library edition, 6 volumes (London, 1986–1992); (4) a 'county' edition (30 volumes, London 1986–1992) consisting of a series of boxed county volumes with an introduction, article on the administrative topography of the county ('Hundreds and Wapentakes'), a facsimile, translation, bibliography and map, together with the Domesday Book Studies as a common separate volume. The translation (poorly reformatted by electronic means and without marginalia) is available in a single volume: A Williams and G H Martin (eds) *Domesday Book: a Complete Translation*, Penguin Books, London 1992

Domesday Book (Phillimore), J Morris (ed), *Domesday Book: History from the Sources*, 38 vols (Chichester, 1975–1992). This edition contains all the Domesday counties plus the Boldon Book (vol 35), and Indices of places, persons and subjects (vols 36–38). This edition of Great Domesday and Little Domesday, with the exception of Yorkshire, (vols 1–29; 31–34) is now available in electronic form and is being thoroughly revised; the latest state is available both from the Arts and Humanities Data Service at Essex University as study number 5694 (http://www.data-archive.ac.uk/findingdata/snDescription.asp?sn=5694) and from the Hull University website (http://edocs.hull.ac.uk) or from the Domesday Explorer website (http://www.domesdaybook.net/). Domesday Somerset awaits revision

Domesday Book (Record Commission). *Domesday Book*, 4 vols, Record Commission (London, 1783–1816)

Vol 1 contains Great Domesday

Vol 2 contains Little Domesday (a bulkier 'survey' of the East Anglian counties)

Vol 3 is entitled Libri Censualis Vocati Domesday Book, Additamenta ex Codic. Antiquiss. and comprises the Liber Exoniensis, the Inquisitio Eliensis (the 'Ely Enquiry'), the Liber Wintoniensis (the 'Winton' or 'Winchester' Domesday) and the Boldon Book. (This is vol. 4 in some bindings.)

Vol 4 contains the General Introduction and Indices; it was also published separately as H Ellis, General Introduction to Domesday Book, 2 vols (London, 1833; reprinted 1971).

Vols 1–2 were transcribed by Abraham Farley and his work is referred to as 'Farley'.

Vol 3 was edited by H Ellis and the transcription of the Liber Exoniensis was carried out by Ralph Barnes, chapter clerk of Exeter Cathedral.

(DB = Thorn, C and Thorn, F, (eds), 1980 *Domesday Book, 8, Somerset*, Phillimore)

(DB Exon, 1783 *Libri Censualis Vocati Domesday-Book. Additamenta ex Codic. Antiquiss*, Record Commission, London)

Douglas, D C and Greenaway, G W, 1981 *English Historical Documents, ii. 1049–1189*, 2nd edition, London

Dowden, W A, 1962 'Little Solsbury Hill Camp; report on the excavations of 1958', *Proceedings of the University of Bristol Spelaeological Society* 9 (3), 177–182

Draper, S, 2002 'Old English wic and walh; Britons and Saxons in Post-Roman Wiltshire', *Landscape History* 22, 39–43

Draper, S, 2009 'Burh place-names in Anglo-Saxon England', *Journal of the English Place-Name Society* 41, 103–118

Draper, S, 2011 'Language and Anglo-Saxon landscape: towards an archaeological interpretation of place-names in Wiltshire', in N J Higham and M J Ryan (eds), *Place-Names, Language and the Anglo-Saxon Landscape*, 85–104, Boydell

Driesch, A von den, 1976 'A guide to the measurement of animal bones from archaeological sites', *Peabody Museum Bulletin* 1, Harvard University, Cambridge Massachusetts

Dunning, G C, 1962 'The bronze skillet from Stanford in the Vale, Berkshire', *Berkshire Archaeological Journal* 60, 98–100

Dyer, C, 1989 *Standards of Living in the Later Middle Ages*, Cambridge University Press, Cambridge

Dyer, C, 1994 *Everday Life in Medieval England*. Hambledon Press

BIBLIOGRAPHY

Dyer, C, 2000 *Everyday Life in Medieval England*. Hambledon Press, London

Dyer, C, 2002 *Making a Living in the Middle Ages*, Yale University Press

Dyer, C, 2010 'Villages in crisis: social dislocation and desertion, 1370–1520', in C Dyer and R Jones (eds), 28–45

Dyer, C, 2013 'Living in peasant houses in late Medieval England', *Vernacular Architecture Group*, 44, 19–27

Dyer, C and Jones, R, (eds), 2010 *Deserted Villages Revisited*, University of Hertfordshire Press

Ekwall, E, 1936 *Studies on English Place-names*, Wahlström and Widstrand, Stockholm

Ekwall, E, 1960 *The Concise Oxford Dictionary of English Place-names*, 4th edition, Oxford University Press, Oxford

Ellis, S E and Moore, D T, 1990 'XIII stone objects: petrology and provenance, 2. The hones', in M Biddle (ed) *Winchester Studies 7(i) Artefacts from Medieval Winchester – Object and Economy in Medieval Winchester*, 279–287 Clarendon Press, Oxford

Ellison, A, 1982 'Prehistoric pottery', in P J Leach *Ilchester I*, 124–126, Committee for Rescue Archaeology in Avon, Gloucestershire and Somerset, Bristol

English Heritage, 1991 *Management of Archaeological Projects (2)*, English Heritage

Evans, J G, 1972 *Land Snails in Archaeology*, Seminar Press, London

Evans, J G, 1991 'The land and freshwater Mollusca', in S P Needham, *Excavation and Salvage at Runnymede Bridge 1978*, 263–274, British Museum Press, London

Evison, V I, Dunning, G C, Hodges, H W M and Hurst, J G, 1974 *Medieval Pottery from Excavations: Studies Presented to Gerald Clough Dunning*, Baker, London

Eyton, R W, 1880 *Notes on Domesday*, T Kerslake and Co, Bristol

Faith, R, 1994 'Tidenham, Gloucestershire, and the history of the English manor', *Landscape History* 16, 39–51

Faith, R, 1997 *The English Peasantry and the Growth of Lordship*, Leicester University Press

Feet of Fines *Somerset Record Society* 6, 12, 17 and 22

Feudal Aids, *Inquisitions and Assessments Relating to Feudal Aids with Other Analogous Documents Preserved in the Public Records Office AD1284–1431*, 6 volumes, State Papers (London, 1899–1920)

Field, R K, 1965 'Worcestershire peasant buildings, household goods and farming equipment in the later Middle Ages', *Medieval Archaeology* 9, 105–145

Finberg, H P R, 1964a *The Early Charters of Wessex*, Leicester University Press

Finberg, H P R, 1964b 'Charltons and Carltons', in H P R Finberg, *Lucerna: Studies of Some Problems in the Early History of England*, 144–160, Macmillan, London

Finn, R, Welldon, 1963 *An Introduction to Domesday Book*, Longmans, London

Fowler, P, Gardiner, K and Rahtz, P, 1970 *Cadbury Congresbury, Somerset, 1968*, Bristol, The University Press

Fryde, E B, 1996 *Peasants and Landlords in Later Medieval England*, Alan Sutton Publishing

Galbraith, V H, 1961 *The Making of Domesday Book*, Oxford University Press, Oxford

Galbraith, V H, 1974 *Domesday Book: Its Place in Administrative History*, Oxford University Press, Oxford

Gardiner, M, 2000 'Vernacular buildings and the development of the later Medieval domestic plan in England', *Medieval Archaeology* 44, 159–179

Gardiner, M, 2011 'Stacks, barns and granaries in early and high Medieval England: crop storage and its implications', *Arqueologia Medieval* 5, 23–38

Gardiner, M, 2013 'The sophistication of late Anglo-Saxon timber buildings' in D Bintley and M Shapland (eds), *Trees and Timber in the Anglo-Saxon World*, 45–78, Oxford University Press, Oxford

Gardiner, M, 2014 'An archaeological approach to the development of the late medieval peasant house', *Vernacular Architecture Group* 45, 16–28

Gelling, M, 1967 'English place-names derived from the compound wicham', *Medieval Archaeology* 11, 87–104

Gelling, M, 1977 'Latin loan-words in Old English place-names', *Anglo-Saxon England* 6, 1–13

Gelling, M and Cole, A, 2000 *The Landscape of Place-names*, Shaun Tyas

Gent, T, 2007 'The re-excavation of a deserted medieval longhouse at Hutholes, Widecombe in the Moor, Dartmoor', *Devon Archaeological Proceedings* 65, 47–82

Geological Survey of Great Britain 1965 Frome, England and Wales Sheet 281, Solid and Drift edition. One inch geology map, Ordnance Survey, Chessington, Surrey

Gerrard, C J and Aston, M, 2007 *The Shapwick Project Somerset: A Rural Landscape Explored*, Society for Medieval Archaeology Monograph 25

Gerrard, C M, 1987 *The Bristol Type Series and Local Fabrics*, unpublished typescript report for Bristol City Museum and Art Gallery

Gerrard, C M, 1988 *A View from the Balk. Some Aspects of Recent Research into Mmedieval Ceramics in Somerset and Avon*, unpublished typescript report for Bristol City Museum and Art Gallery

Giovas, C M, 2009 'The shell game: analytic problems in archaeological mollusc quantification', *Journal of Archaeological Science* 39, 1557–1564

Good, G L and Russett, V E J, 1987 'Common types of Earthenware in the Bristol region', *Bristol and Avon Archaeology* 6, 35–43

Goodall, A R, 1980 'Copper Alloy and Lead Objects' in N Palmer 'A beaker burial and Medieval tenements in The Hamel, Oxford', *Oxoniensia* 45, Fiche 2B13

Goodall, A R, 1984 'Non-ferrous metal objects' in A Rogerson and C Dallas *Excavations in Thetford 1948–59 and 1973–80*, East Anglian Archaeological Report 22

Goodall, A R, forthcoming in *The Archaeology of York*

Goodall, I H, 1975 'Iron objects' in G Beresford, 79–91, 96–98

Goodall, I H, 1976 'Iron objects' in T G Hassall, 298–303

Goodall, I H, 1977 'Iron and lead objects' in G Beresford, 257–276

Goodall, I H, 1977 Iron and lead objects in P Armstrong, 63–68

Goodall, I H, 1987 'Iron objects' in G Beresford, 177–187

Goodall, I H, 1991 'Iron objects' in P Armstrong *et al*, 137–147

Graham, A and Davies, S, 1993 *Excavations in Trowbridge, Wiltshire, 1977 and 1986–8*, Wessex Archaeology Report 2

Grant, A, 1982 'The use of tooth wear as a guide to the age of domestic ungulates', in B Wilson, C Grigson and S Payne (eds), 'Ageing and sexing animal bones from archaeological sites', 91–108, *British Archaeological Reports* British series 109, Oxford

Green, F, 1979 'Phosphate mineralisation of seeds from archaeological sites', *Journal of Archaeological Science* 6, 279–284

Green, F, 1980 *Grain Deposits from the 12th Century Granary at Lydford, Devon*, Ancient Monuments Laboratory Report 3108 (old series), English Heritage, London

Green, F J, 1984 'The archaeological and documentary evidence for plants from the medieval period in England' in W van Zeist and W A Casparie (eds) *Plants and Ancient Man: Studies in Palaeoethnobotany, Proceedings of the 6th Symposium of the IWGP*, A A Balkema, Rotterdam, 99–144

Green, H S, 1984 'Flint arrowheads: typology and interpretation', *Lithics* 5, 19–39

Greene, E, 1892 'Pedes Finum, or Feet of Fines', *Somerset Record Society* 6

Greig, J R A, 1991 'The British Isles', in W van Zeist, K Wasylikowa and K-E Behre (eds) *Progress in Old World Palaeoethnobotany*, A A Balkema, Rotterdam, 299–334

Grenville, J, 1997 *Medieval Housing*, Leicester University Press

Grenville, J, 2008 'Urban and rural houses in the late Middle Ages', in M Kowaleski and P Goldberg (eds)

Griffiths, N, 2014 *Horse Harness Pendants*, Finds Research Group 700–1700, Datasheet 5

Griffiths, R, 1979, 'Excavation of a Medieval house at Whaddon, Buckinghamshire', *Records of Buckinghamshire* 21, 46–53

Grundy, G B, 1935 *The Saxon Charters and Field Names of Somerset*, Somerset Archaeological and Natural History Society

Gutierrez, A, 2007 'Bone, ivory and antler objects' in C J Gerrard and M Aston, *The Shapwick Project, Somerset, A Rural Landscape Explored,* The Society for Medieval Archaeology Monograph 25, 790–796

Hall, L J, 1983 *The Rural Houses of North Avon and South Gloucestershire 1400–1720*, City of Bristol Museum & Art Gallery Monograph No 6

Hallam, E and Bates, D (eds), 2001 *Domesday Book*, Stroud

Hallimond, A F, 1939 'On the relation of chamosite and daphnite to the chlorite group', *Mineralogical Magazine* 25, 441–465

Hamerow, H, 2002 *Early Medieval Settlements – the Archaeology of rural Communities in Northwest Europe 400–900*, Oxford University Press, Oxford

Hamerow, H, 2006 '"Special deposits" in Anglo-Saxon settlements', *Medieval Archaeology* 50, 1–30

Hamerow, H, 2012 *Rural Settlements and Society in Anglo-Saxon England*. Oxford University Press, Oxford

Hamilton, N E S A, 1876 *Inquisitio Comitatus Cantabrigiensis nunc Primum e Manuscripto Unico in Bibliotheca Cottoniana Asservato Typis Mandata; Subjicitur Inquisitio Eliensis*, London

Harvey, S P J, 1986 'Taxation and the ploughland' in P Sawyer (ed) *Domesday Book; A Reassessment*, 86–103, Edward Arnold, London

Hassall, T G, 1976 'Excavations at Oxford Castle 1965–1973', *Oxoniensa* 41, 298–303

Hayfield, C and Greig, J, 1988 'Excavation and salvage work on a moated site at Cowick, South Humberside, 1976', *Yorkshire Archaeological Journal* 61, 41–70

Hearne, T, 1723 *Hemingi Chartularium Ecclesiae Wigorniensis*, 2 volumes, Oxford

Hewett, C A, 1982 *Church Carpentry*, Phillimore & Co. Ltd

Higham, N J, 1990 'Settlement, land use and Domesday ploughlands', *Landscape History* 12, 33–44

Hillman, G C, 1981 'Reconstructing crop husbandry practices from charred remains of crops', in R Mercer (ed) *Farming Practice in British Prehistory*, 123–162, Edinburgh University Press

Hillman, G C, 1982 'Crop husbandry at the Medieval farmstead, Cefn Graenog', in R S Kelly, 'The excavation of a Medieval farmstead at Cefn Graenog Clynnog, Gywnedd', *Bulletin of the Board of Celtic Studies* pt.4, 29, 901–906

Hobhouse, E, 1887 'Calendar of the register of John de Drockensford, Bishop of Bath and Wells 1309–1329', *Somerset Record Society* 1

Holmes, M, (in press) *Southern England: A Review of Animal Remains from Saxon, Medieval and Post Medieval Archaeological Sites*, English Heritage, Research Report Series

Holmes, T S, 1896/7 'The Register of Ralph of Shrewsbury, Bishop of Bath and Wells 1329–1363', *Somerset Record Society* 9 and 10

Hooke, D, 1998 *The Landscape of Anglo-Saxon England*, Leicester University Press

Hooke, D, 2011 'The woodland landscape of early Medieval England', in N J Higham and M J Ryan (eds), *Place-names, Language and the Anglo-Saxon Landscape*, 143–174

Hope-Taylor, B, (ed), 1977 *Yeavering: An Anglo-British Centre of Early Northumbria*, Department of the Environment Archaeological Report 7, HMSO, London

Horrox, R, 1994 *The Black Death*, Manchester University Press

Hunt, W, 1893 'Two Chartularies of the priory of St Peter at Bath', *Somerset Record Society* 7

Hylton, T, 2010 'Other finds' in A Chapman, 335–424

Illingworth, W and Caley, J, 1812, 1818 *Rotuli Hundredorum*, Record Commission, 2 volumes, London

Jacomet, S (and collaborators), 2006 *Identification of Cereal Remains from Archaeological Sites*, 2nd edition, Archaeobotany Laboratory IPAS, Basel University. English Translation by James Greig

Jarrett, C, 2013 'Clay tobacco pipes' in V Ridgeway and M Watts, *Friars, Quakers, Industry and Urbanisation, The Archaeology of the Broadmead Expansion Project, Cabot Circus, Bristol, 2005–2008*, Cotswold Archaeology Monograph 8, 215–237

Jeayes, I H, 1892 *Descriptive Catalogue of the Charters and Muniments in the Possession of the Rt Hon Lord Fitzhardinge at Berkeley Castle*, C T Jefferies and Sons Ltd, Bristol

Jones, J, 2009 'Plant macrofossil remains', in S Rippon *Landscape, Community and Colonisation: The North Somerset Levels During the 1st to 2nd Millennia AD*, Council for British Archaeology Research Report 152, 230–236, York

Jones, R, 2010 'Contrasting patterns of village and hamlet desertion in England', in C Dyer and R Jones (eds), 2010, 8–27

Jones, R and Page, M, 2006 *Medieval Villages in an English Landscape: Beginnings and Ends*, Windgather Press, Oxford

Keats-Rohan, K S B, 1999 *Domesday People, a Prosopography of Persons Occurring in English Documents 1066–1166: I Domesday Book*, Woodbridge

Kellaway, G A, and Welch, F B A, 1948 *Bristol and Gloucester District, British Regional Geology*, HMSO, London

Kelly, S E, 2007 'Charters of Bath and Wells', *Anglo-Saxon Charters 13*, Oxford University Press for the British Academy

Kemp, B R and Shorrocks, D M M (eds), 1974 'Medieval Deeds of Bath and District, *Somerset Record Society* 73

Kempe, D and Harvey, A (eds), 1983 *The Petrology of Archaeological Artefacts*, Oxford

Kerney, M P, and Cameron, R A D, 1979 *A Field Guide to the Land Snails of Britain and Ireland*, Collins, London

Keynes, S and Lapidge, M (eds and trans), 1983 *Alfred the Great: Asser's Life of King Alfred and Other Contemporary Sources*, Penguin

Kilmurry, K, 1980 *The Pottery Industry of Stamford, Lincolnshire, AD850–1250*, British Archaeological Reports 84

Knight, D, Marsden, P and Carney, J, 2003 'Local or non-local? Prehistoric granodiorite-tempered pottery in the East Midlands', in A Gibson (ed) *Prehistoric Pottery: People, Pattern and Purpose,* British Archaeological Reports International Series 1156, 111–125, Archaeopress, Oxford

Kowaleski, M and Goldberg, P (eds), 2008 *Medieval Domesticity – Home, Housing and Household in Medieval England*, Cambridge University Press

Lane, T and Morris, E L, 2001 *A Millennium of Saltmaking: Prehistoric and Roman Salt Production and Distribution in the Fenland*, Lincolnshire Archaeology and Heritage Reports Series 4, Heritage Trust for Lincolnshire, Heckington, Sleaford

Leach, P J, 1982 *Ilchester Vol I: Excavations 1974–5*. Western Archaeological Trust Monograph 3, Bristol

Leach, P J, and Aston, M (eds), 1984 *The Archaeology of Taunton – Excavation and Fieldwork to 1980*, Western Archaeological Trust Monograph 8

Lefebvre des Noettes, R J E C, 1931 *L'Attelage. Le cheval de selle à travers les âges Contribution à l'histoire de l'esclavage*, Picard, Paris

Lewis, C P, 2011 'The invention of the manor in England', *Anglo-Norman Studies* 34, 123–150

Liebermann, F, 1903 Die *Gesetze der Angelsachsen* i, Halle

Loveluck, C P (ed), 2007, *Rural Settlement, Lifestyles and Social Change in the Late First Millennium AD: Anglo-Saxon Flixborough in its Wider Context. Excavations at Flixborough 4*, Oxbow Books, Oxford

Loyn, H R, 1962 *Anglo-Saxon England and the Norman Conquest*, Longman, London

BIBLIOGRAPHY

Mabey, R, 1972 *Food for Free*, Collins, London

McCarthy, M R, 1974 'The medieval kilns on Nash Hill, Lacock, Wiltshire', *Wiltshire Archaeology and Natural History Magazine* 69, 97–145

McCarthy, M R and Brooks, C M, 1988 *Medieval Pottery in Britain, AD900–1600*, Leicester University Press

MacGregor, A, 1987 'Objects of bone and antler' in G Beresford, 188–193

McKinley, R, 1990 *A History of British Surnames*, Longman, London

McSloy, E R, 2013 'Metal and other small finds' in V Ridgeway and M Watts, *Friars, Quakers, Industry and Urbanisation: The Archaeology of the Broadmead Expansion Project, Cabot Circus, Bristol, 2005–2008*, Cotswold Archaeology Monograph No 5

Mahany, C, Burchard, A and Simpson, G, 1982 *Excavations at Stamford, Lincolnshire 1963–69*, Society for Medieval Archaeology Monograph 9, London

Maitland, F W, 1897 *Domesday Book and Beyond*, Cambridge University Press, Cambridge

Margary, I, 1973 *Roman Roads in Britain*, 3rd edition, John Baker Ltd, London

Mears, R and Hillman, G, 2007 *Wild Food*, Hodder and Stoughton

Melville, R V and Freshney, E C, 1982 *The Hampshire Basin and Adjoining Areas, British Regional Geology*, HMSO, London

Mepham, L, 2000 'Prehistoric pottery', in V Birbeck 'Excavations on Iron Age and Romano-British settlements at Cannards Grave, Shepton Mallet', *Proceedings of the Somerset Archaeological and Natural History Society* 143, 41–116 (72–79)

Metcalf, D M, 1960 'The currency of "Deniers Tournois" in Frankish Greece', *The Annual of the British School at Athens* 55, 38–59

Michaelmore, D and Moorhouse, S, 1987 *The Medieval Kitchen and its Equipment*, a synopsis of papers presented to a joint meeting of the Finds Research Group and the Medieval Pottery Research Group

Miles, A E W and Grigson, C, 1990 *Colyer's Variations and Diseases of the Teeth of Animals*, Cambridge University Press

Miller, G S, 1912 *Catalogue of the Mammals of Western Europe (Europe exclusive of Russia) in the Collections of the British Museum*, British Museum (Natural History) Department of Zoology, London

Mills, A D, 2011, *A Dictionary of British Place-names*, 2nd edition, Oxford University Press, Oxford

Minitt, S, 2007 'Coins recovered from fieldwork by the Shapwick Project, Appendix 8', in C Gerrard and M Aston, 1158–1160

Moffett, L, 1991 'The archaeobotanical evidence for free-threshing tetraploid wheat in Britain', in I E Hajnalov (ed), 'Paleoethnobotany and archaeology: IWGP 8th Symposium Nitra-Nov Vozokany 1989', *Acta Interdisciplinaria Archaeologica* VII, 233–243

Moffett, L, 2007 'Crop economy and other plant remains', in A Hardy, B M Charles and R J Williams, *Death and Taxes: the Archaeology of a Middle Saxon Estate Centre at Higham Ferrers, Northamptonshire*, Oxford Archaeology Monograph 4, 158–178

Moffett, L C, unpublished 1987 *Cultivated Plants and Domestic Activities: The Evidence from the Charred Plant Remains from Dean Court Farm, Oxon*, Ancient Monuments Laboratory Report 202/87

Moffett, L C, unpublished 1991 *Plant Economy at Burton Dassett, a Deserted Medieval Village in South Warwickshire*, Ancient Monuments Laboratory Report 111/91

Mook, W G, 1986 'Business meeting: recommendations/resolutions adopted by the 12th International Radiocarbon Conference' *Radiocarbon* 28, 799

Mook, W G and Waterbolk, H T, 1985 'Radiocarbon dating', *Handbook for Archaeologists* 3, Strasbourg (European Science Foundation)

Moore, D T, 1978 'The petrography and archaeology of English honestones', *Journal of Archaeological Science* 5, 61–73

Moore, D T, 1983 'The petrological aspects of some sharpening stones, touchstones and milling stones' in D R C Kempe and A P Harvey (eds) *The Petrology of Archaeological Artefacts*, Oxford University Press, Oxford

Moore, J, 1986 'Post-mortem of an invasion' in *National Domesday Committee, Domesday: 900 Years of England's Norman Heritage*, London, 67–82

Morris, E L, 1982 'Iron Age pottery from Western Britain: another petrological study', in I Freestone, C Johns and T Potter (eds) *Current Research in Ceramics: Thin-section Studies*, British Museum Occasional Paper 32, 15–27 British Museum, London

Morris, E L, 1983a *Salt and Ceramic Exchange in Western Britain during the First Millennium BC*, doctoral dissertation, University of Southampton

Morris, E L, 1983b, 'Petrological report, Droitwich briquetage containers and Seriation analysis by fabric type of the Iron Age pottery' in A Saville and A Ellison 'Excavations at Uley Bury Hillfort, Gloucestershire 1976', in A Saville *Uley Bury and Norbury Hillforts*, Western Archaeological Trust Excavation Monograph 5, 14–19, Western Archaeological Trust, Bristol

Morris, E L, 1985 'Prehistoric salt distributions: two case studies from Western Britain', *Bulletin of the Board of Celtic Studies* 32, 336–379

Morris, E L, 1987 'Later prehistoric pottery from Ham Hill', *Proceedings of the Somerset Archaeological and Natural History Society* 131, 27–47

Morris, E L, 1988 'The Iron Age occupation at Dibble's Farm, Christon', *Proceedings of the Somerset Archaeological and Natural History Society* 132, 23–81

Morris, E L, 1994 'Production and distribution of pottery and salt in Iron Age Britain: a review', *Proceedings of the Prehistoric Society* 60, 371–93

Morris, E L, 1998 'Prehistoric pottery', in J I McKinley 'Excavations at Ham Hill, Montacute, Somerset 1994 and 1998', *Proceedings of the Somerset Archaeological and Natural History Society* 142, 77–137 (91–107)

Morris, E L, 2007 *Iron Age Pottery (45–53 West St, Bedminster, Bristol; BSMR 22276)*, client report submitted to Avon Archaeological Unit Ltd, Kingswood, Bristol

Morris, E L, 2009 'Prehistoric pottery and briquetage', in P Leach 'Prehistoric ritual landscapes and other remains at Field Farm, Shepton Mallet', *Proceedings of the Somerset Archaeological and Natural History Society* 152, 11–68 (34–46)

Morris, E L, 2012 'Iron Age ceramics: pottery and briquetage', in J Proctor, 'The needles eye enclosure, Berwick-upon-Tweed', *Archaeologia Aeliana* 41 (fifth series), 19–122 (52–78)

Morris, E L, and Woodward, A, 2003 'Ceramic petrology and prehistoric pottery in the UK', *Proceedings of the Prehistoric Society* 69, 279–303

Morris, J, 1980 *Domesday Book 8; Somerset*, Phillimore, Chichester

Morris, R, 1989 *Churches in the Landscape*, Dent, London

MPRG 2001, *Minimum Standards for the Processing, Recording, Analysis and Publication of Post-Roman Ceramics*, Medieval Pottery Research Group. Occasional Paper 2

Murphy, P and Locker, A, unpublished 1988 *Barton Bendish, Norfolk: Plant and Animal Macrofossils from a Rural Medieval Site*, Ancient Monuments Laboratory Report 199/88

Murphy, P, 2004 'Charred plant remains from Late Bronze Age/Early Iron Age and Middle Iron Age contexts' in R Havis and H Brooks 'Excavations at Stansted Airport, 1986–91. Vol 1', *East Anglian Archaeology* 107, 65–78 Volume II; 327–339, 350–459

Musty J W G, 1973 'A preliminary account of a medieval pottery industry at Minety, North Wiltshire', *Wiltshire Archaeology and Natural History Magazine* 68, 79–88

Musty, J W G, Algar, D J and Ewence, P F, 1969 'The medieval pottery kilns at Laverstock, Salisbury', *Wiltshire Archaelolgia* 102, 83–150

NE 2009, *Agricultural Land Classification: Protecting the Best and most Versatile Agricultural Land*, Natural England, Technical Information Note TIN049

Neal, D S, Wardle, A and Hunn, J, 1990 *Excavation of the Iron Age, Roman and Medieval Settlement at Gorhambury, St Albans*, English Heritage Archaeological Report 14

Noakes, J E, Kim, S M and Stipp, J J, 1965 'Chemical and counting advances in liquid scintillation age dating', in E A Olsson and R M Chatters (eds) *Proceedings of the Sixth International Conference on Radiocarbon and Tritium Dating*, 68–92, Washington DC

O'Connor, T, 1982 *Animal Bones from Flaxengate, Lincoln c870–1500*. The Archaeology of Lincoln 18 (I). London, Council for British Archaeology

O'Connor, T, 2013 *Livestock and Animal Husbandry in Early Medieval England*. Quaternary International

O'Donovan, M A, 1988 *Charters of Sherborne*, (Anglo-Saxon Charters 3), London

Orme, B J, Coles, J M, Caseldine, A E and Bailey, G N, 1981 'Meare Village West 1979', in J M Coles (ed), *Somerset Levels Papers* 7, 12–69, Somerset Levels Project

Payne, S, 1969 'A metrical distinction between sheep and goat metacarpals', in P J Ucko and G W Dimbleby (eds) *The Domestication and Exploitation of Plants and Animals*, 295–305, Duckworth, London

Payne, S, 1987 'Reference codes for wear states in the mandibular cheek teeth of sheep and goats', *Journal of Archaeological Science* 14, 609–614

Payne, S and Bull, G, 1989 'Components of variation in measurements of pig bones and teeth, and the use of measurements to distinguish wild from domestic pig remains', *Archaeozoologia* 2, 27–65

Payne, S and Munson, P J, 1985 'Ruby and how many squirrels? The destruction of bones by dogs', in N R J Fieller, D D Gilbertson and N G A Ralph (eds) *Palaeobiological Investigations; Research Design, Methods and Data Analysis*, 31–39, British Archaeological Reports International Series 266

Peacey, A, 1979 *Clay Tobacco Pipes in Gloucestershire*, Committee for Rescue Archaeology in Avon, Gloucestershire and Somerset Occasional Paper 4

Peacock, D P S, 1968 'A petrological study of certain Iron Age pottery from western England', *Proceedings of the Prehistoric Society* 34, 414–427

Peacock, D P S, 1969 'A contribution to the study of Glastonbury ware from southwestern Britain', *Antiquaries Journal* 49, 41–61

Peacock, D P S, 1977 'Ceramics in Roman and medieval archaeology' in D P S Peacock (ed) *Pottery in Early Commerce*, Academic Press, London

Peacock, D P S, 1979 'Petrology of Fabrics A-H', in P A Rahtz 1979

Pearson, G W, 1979 'Precise ^{14}C measurement by liquid scintillation counting', *Radiocarbon* 21, 1–21

Pearson, G W, 1984 *The Development of High-precision ^{14}C Measurement and its Application to Archaeological Time-scale Problems*, unpublished PhD thesis, Queens University Belfast

Pearson, T, 1982 'The post-Roman pottery', in P Leach, *Ilchester Vol 1: Excavations 1974–5*, 169–217

Pearson, T, 1984 'Medieval and post medieval ceramics', in P Leach and M Aston (eds), 142–144

Pelling, R, 2009 'Charred and waterlogged plant remains', in K Powell 'Excavation of a medieval site at West Wick, Weston-Super-Mare, Somerset', *Proceedings of the Somerset Archaeological and Natural History Society* 152, 179–182

Percival, J, 1948 *Wheat in Great Britain*, Duckworth & Co. Ltd, London

Phythian Adams, C V, 1996 *Land of the Cumbrians: A Study in British Provincial Origins, AD400–1120*, Scolar Press, Aldershot

Platt, C and Coleman-Smith, R, 1975 *Excavations in Medieval Southampton 1953–1969*, 2, Leicester University Press

Ponsford, M W, 1974 'Late Saxon pottery from Bristol' in V I Evison *et al*, 120–122

Ponsford, M W, 2001 'Excavations at a Saxo-Norman Settlement, Bickley, Cleeve, 1982–89', *Proceedings of the Somerset Archaeological and Natural History* 146 (2002) 47–112

Price, R, 2014 *Bristol Pipemakers and their Families, of the 16th to 20th Centuries*, unpublished research material on CD

Rahtz, P A, 1979 *The Saxon and Medieval Palaces at Cheddar*, British Archaeological Reports 65

Rahtz, P and Hirst, S, 1974 *Beckery Chapel, Glastonbury: Excavations 1967–8*, Glastonbury Antiquarian Society, Bristol

Reimer, P J, Bard, E, Bayliss, A, Beck, J W, Blackwell, P, Bronk Ramsey, C, Buck, C E, Cheng, H, Edwards, R L, Friedrich, M, Grootes, P M, Guilderson, T P, Haflidason, H, Hajdas, I, Hatté, C, Heaton, T J, Hoffmann, D L, Hogg, A G, Hughen, K A, Kaiser, K F, Kromer, B, Manning, S W, Niu, M, Reimer, R W, Richards, D A, Scott, E M, Southon, J R, Staff, R A, Turney, C S M, and van der Plicht, J, 2013 'IntCal13 and Marine13 radiocarbon age calibration curves 0–50,000 years cal BP', *Radiocarbon* 55, 1869–1887

Reynolds, A, 1999 *Later Anglo-Saxon England – Life and Landscape*, Tempus Publishing Inc

Reynolds, A, 2003 'Boundaries and settlements in later sixth to eleventh-century England', in D Griffiths, A Reynolds and S Semple (eds) *Boundaries in early medieval Britain*, ASSAH 12, 98–139

Robertson, A J, 1956 *Anglo-Saxon Charters*, 2nd edition, Cambridge University Press

Roffe, D, 2000 *Domesday: The Inquest and the Book*, Oxford University Press

Roffe, D, 2007 *Decoding Domesday*, Woodbridge

Round, J H, 1895 *Feudal England*, London

Rowe, M and Alexander, M, 2011 'Multi-period archaeology at Wellow Lane, Peasedown St John: excavations 2004–5', *Proceedings of the Somerset Archaeological and Natural History Society* 154, 53–70

Russett, V J R, 1985 *Marshfield: An Archaeological Survey of a Southern Cotswold Parish*, Avon County Planning Department, Bristol

Ryan, M J, 2011 'That "Dreary old question": the hide in early Anglo-Saxon England', in N J Higham and M J Ryan (eds), *Place-Names, Language and the Anglo-Saxon Landscape*, 207–223, Boydell

Saville, A and Ellison, A, 1983 'Excavations at Uley Bury Hillfort, Gloucestershire 1976', in A Saville (ed), *Uley Bury and Norbury Hillforts*, Western Archaeological Trust Excavation Monograph 5, i-iv and 1–24, Western Archaeological Trust, Bristol

Sawyer, P H, 1968 *Anglo-Saxon Charters: An Annotated List and Bibliography*, Royal Historical Society Guides and Handbooks, 8, London

Scollar, I, Tabbagh, A, Hesse, A and Herzog, I 1990 *Archaeological Prospecting and Remote Sensing*, Cambridge University Press

Scott, E M, Aitchison, T C, Harkness, D D, Cook, G T and Baxter, M S, 1990 'An overview of all three stages of the international radiocarbon intercomparison', *Radiocarbon* 32, 309–319

Shorrocks, D M M (ed), 1974 'Medieval deeds from the Walker-Heneage Manuscripts', in 'Medieval Deeds of Bath and District', *Somerset Record Society* 73

Smith, A H, 1970 *English Place-name Elements, Parts I and II*. Cambridge University Press

Smith, G H, 1979 'The excavation of the hospital of St Mary of Ospringe, commonly called Maison Dieu', *Archaeologia Cantiana* XCV, 81–184

BIBLIOGRAPHY

Smith, S V, 2010 'Houses and communities: archaeological evidence for variation in medieval peasant experience', in C Dyer and R Jones (eds), 64–84

Smith, W, 2007 'Medieval charred plant remains', in D E Y Young 'Iron Age, medieval and recent activity at Whitegate Farm, Bleadon, North Somerset', *Proceedings of the Somerset Archaeological and Natural History Society* 151, 65–73

Smith, W and Campbell, G, 2007 'Medieval plant macrofossils and waterlogged wood', in C Gerrard and M Aston, *The Shapwick Project, Somerset. A Rural Landscape Explored*, Society for Medieval Archaeology Monograph 25, 857–864

Soil Survey of England and Wales, 1983 *Soils of England and Wales: Sheet 5 – South West England, 1:250,000 Soil Map*, Lawes Agricultural Trust, Harpenden

Spencer, E, 1925 'Occurrences of spherulitic siderite and other carbonates in sediments', *Quarterly Journal of the Geological Society London* 81, 667–705

Spink, 2000. *Standard Catalogue of British Coins: Coins of England and the United Kingdom*, London

Spufford, P, 1963 'Continental coins in late Medieval England', *British Numismatic Journal* 32, 127–139

Stace, C, 2010 *New Flora of the British Isles*, 3rd edition, Cambridge University Press

Steane, J M and Bryant, G F, 1975 *Excavations at the Deserted Medieval Settlement at Lyveden: Fourth Report*, Northampton Museum and Art Gallery 12

Stephenson, C, 1947 'Notes on the composition and interpretation of Domesday Book', *Speculum* 22, 1–15

Stevenson, W H, 1907 'A contemporary description of the Domesday survey', *English Historical Review* 22, 72–84

Straker, V, Campbell, G and Smith, W, 2007 'The charred plant macrofossils', in C Gerrard and M Aston 2007

Stuiver, M and Kra, R S (eds), 1986 'Calibration issue, proceedings of the 12th International ^{14}C conference', *Radiocarbon* 28 (2B), 805–1030

Stuiver, M and Polach, H A, 1977 'Reporting ^{14}C data' *Radiocarbon* 19 (3), 355–363

Stuiver, M and Reimer, P J, 1986 'A computer program for radiocarbon age calculation', *Radiocarbon* 28 (2B), 1022–1030

Stuiver, M and Reimer, P J, 1993 'Extended ^{14}C data base and revised CALIB 3.0 ^{14}C Age calibration program', *Radiocarbon* 35 (1), 215–230

Tate, W E, 1948 *Somerset Enclosure Acts and Awards*, Somerset Archaeological and Natural History Society, Frome

Taxatio, 1802 *Taxatio Ecclesiastica Angliae et Walliae Auctoritate Papae Nicholai*, T Astle, S Ayscough and J Caley (eds), Record Commission IV, London

Thomas, G, 2008 'The symbolic lives of late Anglo-Saxon settlements: a cellared structure and iron hoard from Bishopstone, East Sussex', *Archaeological Journal* 165, 334–398

Thomas, G, 2010 *The Later Anglo-Saxon Settlement at Bishopstone: A Downland Manor in the Making*. Council for British Archaeology Research Report 163

Thomas, R, 2005 'Zooarchaeology, improvement and the British agricultural revolution', *International Journal of Historical Archaeology* 9 (2), 71–88

Thompson, N P, 1970 'A medieval pit at Great Somerford', *Wiltshire Archaeology and Natural History Magazine* 65, 167–171

Thorn, C and Thorn, F, 1980 *Domesday Book: Somerset*, Chichester (Volume 8 of the Phillimore edition)

Thorn, C and Thorn, F, 1985 *Domesday Book: Devon*, Chichester (Volume 9 of the Phillimore edition)

Thorn, F, 2014 'The ancient territories of Frome and Bruton, Somerset', *Proceedings of the Somerset Archaeological and Natural History Society* 157, 1–51

Thorn, F and Thorn, C, 1982 *Domesday Book: Worcestershire*, Chichester (Volume 16 of the Phillimore edition)

Thorn, F and Thorn, C, 2001 'The writing of Great Domesday Book', in E Hallam and D Bates (eds), 37–72, 200–203

Timby, J, 2003 'Pottery', in C Bateman, D Enright and N Oakey 'Prehistoric and Anglo-Saxon settlements to the rear of Sherborne House, Lechlade: excavations in 1997', *Transactions of the Bristol and Gloucestershire Archaeological Society* 121, 23–96 (47–63)

Timby, J, 2013 'Later prehistoric and Roman pottery', in D Stansbie, R Brown, T Allen and A Hardy, 'The excavation of Iron Age ditches and a Medieval farmstead at Allcourt, Little London, Lechlade, 1999', *Transactions of the Bristol and Gloucestershire Archaeological Society* 131, 25–91 (46–49)

Tomber, R and Dore, J, 1998 *The National Roman Fabric Reference Collection: A Handbook*, Museum of London/English Heritage/British Museum

Turner, G, 1951 *Place-names of North Somerset*, unpublished Cambridge D. Litt. thesis

Turner, S and Wilson-North, R, 2012 'South-west England: rural settlements in the Middle Ages', in N Christie and P Stamper (eds), 135–150

Tusser, T, 1580 *Five Hundred Points of Good Husbandry* 1984 reprint, Oxford University Press

Tweddle, D, 1986 *Finds from Parliament Street and Other Sites in the City Centre, The Archaeology of York, Volume 17, The Small Finds, Fascicule 4*, Council for British Archaeology and York Archaeological Trust

Tyler, S and Major, H, 2005 *The Early Anglo-Saxon Cemetery and Later Saxon Settlement at Springfield Lyons, Essex*, East Anglian Archaeology III

Van Caenegem, R C, 1990–1991 *English Lawsuits from William I to Richard I*, 2 vols, Selden Society, London

VCH Somerset, *Victoria History of the County of Somerset*, various dates and volumes. Institute of Historical Research

Vince, A G, 1979 'The Medieval pottery: fabric types', in B Cunliffe (ed), 27–31

Wade, K, 1980 'A settlement site at Bonhunt Farm, Wicken Bonhunt, Essex', in D G Buckley (ed), *Archaeology in Essex to AD1500*, Council for British Archaeology Research Report 34, 96–103

Wainwright, G J, 1972 *Durrington Walls: Excavations 1966–68*, Society of Antiquaries of London

Walton, P, 1991 'Textiles', in J Blair and N Ramsay (eds), 319–54

Ward, G K and Wilson, S R, 1978 'Procedures for comparing and combining radiocarbon age determinations: a critique', *Archaeometry* 20, 19–31

Ward-Perkins, J B, 1940 *London Museum Medieval Catalogue 1940*, British Museum, London

Waterman, D M, 1959 'Late Saxon, Viking and early medieval finds from York', *Archaeologia* 97, 59–105

Watts, L and Rahtz, P, 1985 *Mary-le-Port Bristol Excavations 1962–1963*, City of Bristol Museum and Art Gallery Monograph 7, Bristol

Weaver, F W, 1889 *Somerset Incumbents*, Weaver, Bath

Wedlake, W J, 1958 *Excavations at Camerton, Somerset*, Camerton Excavation Club, Bath

Welldon Finn, R, 1973 *Domesday Book: A Guide*, London and Chichester

Whitehead, R, 1996 *Buckles 1250–1800*, Greenlight Publishing, Chelmsford

Whitelock, D, Douglas, D C and Tucker S I (eds), 1965 *The Anglo-Saxon Chronicle, a Revised Translation*, London

Whitfeld, M, 1981 'The Medieval fields of South-East Somerset', *Proceedings of the Somerset Archaeological and Natural History Society* 125, 17–29

Williams, A and Erskine, R W H, 1987 *Domesday Book Studies*, London; republished as Erskine and Williams, *The Story of Domesday Book*, Chichester 2003

Williams, D, 1990 'A note on the petrology of two Beaker sherds', in M Bell *Brean Down Excavations 1983–1987*, English Heritage Archaeological Report 18, 120, English Heritage

Williams, D and Woodward, A, 1990 'Fabrics', in M Bell *Brean Down Excavations 1983–1987*, English Heritage Archaeological Report 15, 121–123, English Heritage

Williams, D and Woodward, A, 2000 'The ceramic fabric series', in J C Barrett, P W Freeman and A Woodward *Cadbury Castle Somerset; The Later Prehistoric and Early Historic Archaeology*, English Heritage Archaeological Report 20, 325–326, English Heritage

Williams, E, 1990 'Curing chambers and domestic corn-drying kilns in SW England', *Proceedings of the Somerset Archaeological and Natural History Society* 134, 233–242

Williams, G, reference number LEIC-892AF6, Portable Antiquities Scheme Database, site accessed March 2015

Williams, J H, 1979 *St Peter's Street Northampton, Excavations 1973–1976*, Archaeological Monograph 2, Northampton Development Corporation

Wilson, D M and Hurst, D G, 1965 'Medieval Britain in 1964', *Medieval Archaeology* 9, 170-220

Witts, P, 2000 'Mosaics and room function: the evidence from some fourth-century Romano-British villas', *Britannia* 31, 291–324

Woodhouse, J, 1976 *Barrow Mead, Bath 1964. Excavation of a Medieval Peasant House*, British Archaeological Reports 28

Woodward, A, 1990 'The Bronze Age pottery', in M Bell *Brean Down Excavations 1983–1987*, English Heritage Archaeological Report 15, 121–145, English Heritage

Woodward, A, 2007 'Prehistoric pottery', in D Young, 31–81 (43–47)

Woodward, A and Bevan, L, 2000 'A quantitative analysis of pottery from Sites D, K, and N', in J C Barrett, P W M Freeman and A Woodward *Cadbury Castle Somerset; The Later Prehistoric and Early Historic Archaeology*, English Heritage Archaeological Report 20, 25–41, English Heritage

Woodward, J and Luff, P, 1983 *The Field Guide: A Farmland Companion*, Blandford Press, Poole, Dorset

Wrathmell, S (ed), 2012 Wharram – *A Study of Settlement on the Yorkshire Wolds, XIII: A History of Wharram Percy and its Neighbours*. York University Archaeological Publications 15, English Heritage

Young, A, 1813 *General View of the Agriculture of Oxfordshire* (reprint of 1969) David & Charles

Young, A C, 1995 'Excavations at Harry Stoke, Stoke Gifford, Northavon', *Bristol and Avon Archaeology* 12, 24–55

Young, D, 2007 'Iron Age, Medieval and recent activity at Whitegate Farm, Bleadon, North Somerset', *Proceedings of Somerset Archaeological and Natural History Society* 151, 31–81

Young, D, 2009 'Excavation of an early Medieval site at Brent Knoll, Somerset', *Proceedings of the Somerset Archaeological and Natural History Society* 152, 105–137

Youngs, F A, 1979 *Guide to the Local Administrative Units of England, I: Southern England*, Royal Historical Society Guides and Handbooks, 10, London

Zadora-Rio, E, 2003 'The making of churchyards and parish territories in the early medieval landscapes of France and England in the 7th-12th centuries: a reconsideration' *Medieval Archaeology* 47

Zohary, D and Hopf, M, 2000 *Domestication of Plants in the Old World*, 3rd edition, Oxford University Press, Oxford

Online sources consulted:

www.finds.org.uk. Portable Antiquities Scheme database: CUPL-5DB651; SOM-4BCE71; CORN-B2B042; CORN-E75F85; CORN-0C2D27.

www.finds.org.uk/database, site accessed March 2015.

www.finds.org.uk Portable Antiquities Scheme database: CUPL-5DB651; SOM-4BCE71; CORN-B2B042; CORN-E75F85; CORN-0C2D27.

www.fitzmuseum.cam.ac.uk, site accessed March 2015.

folk.uio.no/ohammer/past/. Past, free software for scientific data analysis, with functions for data manipulation, plotting, univariate and multivariate statistics, ecological analysis, time series and spatial analysis, morphometrics and stratigraphy.

INDEX

A367 (road) 8, 289
abandonment 75, 80, 270, 273, 275, 277 *see also* demolition; stone robbing
   11th century 55, 64, 82, 239, 250, 284, 290, 292
   14th century 58, 28, 93, 101, 106, 167, 255, 285, 298–299
   prehistoric 10
Acton Court 184–185, 187, 190, 213–214
agricultural buildings
   see also mills; farmhouses; farmsteads; yards
   byres 93, 105, 251, 254–255, 258, 267–268, 271, 284, 294, 296
   grain store 80
agricultural tools 177, 202, 254, 267, 293, 296–298 *see also* ironwork
agriculture 8–10, 17, 23, 28–29, 42, 182, 226–228, 285–288, 290–291, 293, 296 *see also* crop processing; crop rotation; manuring
Aldgyth 31–32
Alfred the Great 17, 38
Allcourt 117
Almodis 37
Alstan of Boscombe 291–292
Alwaker 36–38, 291–292
Ancient Monuments Laboratory 10, 167–168, 182, 221–222
Angevin dynasty 165
Anglo-Danish kings 42 *see also* Danelaw
Anglo-Saxon Chronicle 30, 248
Anglo-Saxon period 9–11, 13–16, 23–24, 27, 53–55, 61, 239
animal husbandry 168, 171, 182, 215, 218–221, 226–227, 230, 253–254, 260, 286–287, 290, 293, 296 *see also* livestock
Archaeological Resources Centre 220
arrowheads 177, 182, 191–192, 261, 270, 277, 284–285, 288
artefacts *see* bone objects; copper alloy objects; flint objects; ironwork; pottery; stone objects
   recording system 255
Ashgrove 10
Aston, Mick 1, 44
Æthelred 38
Austin Friars, Leicester 183
Avon (river) 8, 39, 231
Avon Archaeological Unit Limited 5
Avon County Community Environment Scheme 3
Avon County Council 1, 3, 5

Baggeridge 16, 23, 26–27
baking *see* breadmaking
Bampton 37
Banworth 39
barns *see* agricultural buildings
Barrack House 29
Barrow Mead 120, 134, 137, 142, 144, 151, 199, 204, 243, 292
basketry 182
Bath 1, 5, 8, 11, 16, 39, 115, 117, 151, 156–157, 163, 210, 243
   Citizen House 120, 144, 163
   church of 38
   Hospital of St John the Baptist 229
   Business Park 10
Bathampton Down 115
Bath and North East Somerset Historic Environment Record 9
Batheaston 29
Bathford 29
Bathwick 29
Bayeux, Bishop of 31
beads 102, 196–197, 199, 208, 214, 277–278 *see also* jet beads
Beazer Homes Limited 3

Beckery Chapel 120, 127, 134, 142, 144, 163
Bede 42
Bedminster 115
beds 231, 267, 298
Bellême, Mabel of 37
Bendish, Barton 232
Bengeworth 31
Berkeley Castle 17
Bickley 243
Bishopstone 249, 270, 286, 291
Black Death 28, 167, 299 *see also* epidemics
Blackdown Hills 199
Blaise Castle Hill 115
Bleadon 116, 232
Bolbec, Hugh of 34
bone objects 102, 167, 212–214, 278–279
   combs 212, 214
   needles 212
   pin beaters 212–213, 269
   rings 214
   spatula 284
   tools 212
   whistles 212–213
bones *see* faunal remains
Bonhunt Farm 248
Boscombe, Alstan of 36–38
boundaries *see also* enclosures 54–55, 58, 62, 64–65, 72–73, 80–85, 87–90, 101, 105–106, 109, 111, 250–251, 289, 292, 295
Box 27
brass 168
Braysdown 289
breadmaking 222, 228, 261, 286
Brean Down 115
Brendon Hills 38
Brent Knoll 290
Bridewell Lane 232
Bristol 36, 107, 114–115, 144, 153–155, 157, 167, 196, 199, 208–210, 214, 286, 288, 292, 296
   Castle 121, 127, 144, 153
   Museum 11, 120
   University of 120
Brittany, Count Alan of 34
Bronze Age 9, 53, 113, 191, 289
bronze-working 118, 289
Bruton 38–39
building materials 292, 295 *see also* structures; timber buildings
   bricks 49, 111
   ceramic 106, 118–119, 152
   cob 241
   daub 74, 78, 83
   plaster 75
   temper 230
   timber components 292–293
   wattle 67, 83–84, 238, 241, 252, 295
   worked stone 196
building traditions 250, 292
Burchill, Rod 130–131, 144, 153, 155
burials 11, 13, 109 *see also* cemeteries
Burton Dassett 229
Burystead 218
butchery 261, 267, 285–286 *see also* meat
butter 199, 286 *see also* dairying
byres *see* agricultural buildings

Cadbury Castle 114–115, 117
Cadbury-Congresbury 288
Calne 248
Cam Brook 5, 8, 16, 23
Camerton 8–9, 11, 13–15, 18–19, 39–40, 118, 289–290
Camerton Tyning 289
Cannards Grave 115
Canterbury 31, 167

Carlingcott 37, 40
carpentry 251, 258, 261, 285 *see also* woodworking
carts 254–255, 258 298
Castle Cary 37
Castle Neroche 120
cattle 220, 285–287 *see also* faunal remains; livestock
Cefn Graeanog 232
cemeteries 11, 13, 24, 106, 109, 289
Central Excavation Unit 167
Centre for Archaeology, Portsmouth 214
ceramics *see* building materials; pottery; tobacco pipes
cesspits 74, 224, 231–232, 244, 250 *see also* latrines
charcoal 72–73, 76, 78, 82–84, 90, 100–102, 107, 112, 243, 253–254
Chaselton hillfort 117
Cheddar Palace 9, 62, 120, 124, 134, 137, 142, 144, 163, 199, 208, 248, 288
cheese 286 *see also* dairying
Chepstow 153
chests 169, 173, 177, 187, 212, 214, 254, 261, 267, 275, 285, 297–298 *see also* security
Chew Stoke 117
Chippenham 120
Christianity 13
   material culture 102, 199, 214, 261, 298
Christon 115, 118
churches 13–16, 25–26, 32, 38–39
Church Field 232
Clarendon Palace 120
clay 65, 78, 83–84, 87, 91, 94, 97, 102, 104–105, 295
   extraction 87
   sources 114, 117, 147, 157, 159
Cleeve 243
climate 235–236 *see also* environment
clothing 183, 185, 267, 275, 298
Cnut of Denmark 31
coal-mining 1
cobbles 72–73, 78, 83–85, 92, 97, 100, 104, 107, 109–110
coins 11, 13, 52, 58, 165–167, 261, 267, 275, 277, 285, 298
   chronology 167
   denier tournois 165–167, 270
   Edward I 105, 166–167, 270
   Edward III 58, 102, 166–167, 298
   recording system 52
   Roman 53, 165–166
Colchester 169, 177
Combe Hay 16, 29, 40, 114
construction techniques *see* cruck construction; drystone masonry; structures; timber buildings
Conteville, family 37
cooking 182, 184, 187, 249, 285 *see also* pottery, cooking vessels
copper alloy objects 182–190, 278–280, 284, 288
   book clasps 184–185, 187
   bracelets 118
   buckles 183–185, 187, 190
   chapes 183–185
   chronology 187
   composition 187, 210–211
   decorative strips 185
   earrings 270, 288
   fittings 183, 187
   horse equipment 183, 190
   ingots 187, 210–211
   Iron Age 182
   jewellery 183, 185, 187, 190
   keys 184, 187, 190
   miscellaneous fragments 187
   modern 185, 187
   mounts 183–185, 187, 190

palstaves 11
pendant bells 183, 185, 187, 269, 284
production 184, 211
strap ends 183
tweezers 183, 185, 187, 190, 277, 285
vessels 184–185, 190, 211, 275, 298
wire 61, 182, 184–185, 187
corn drying 57, 105, 255, 258, 294
Cornwall 37
Corston 39–40
Cotswold Archaeology 289–290
Cotswold Hills 5, 196
Courseulles, Roger of 37
Coutances, Bishop of 31–32
Coventry Polytechnic 211
Cowick 233
craft production 93, 168, 182, 260–261, 267–269, 272, 284–285, 291
Crickley hillfort 117
crop processing 230–233, 250, 287, 291, 296
crop rotation 227–228, 231, 290
cruck construction 241, 243, 250–252, 257–258
curing 261 *see also* storage
Curry Rivel 38
cutler's marks 168–169, 177
Cynewulf 38, 40

dairying 29, 160, 199, 286, 293
Danegeld 42
Danelaw 145
Dartmoor 254, 290
Dassett, Burton 229, 232
Dawson, David 165
Dean Court Farm 229, 232
DELILAH 167
demolition 10, 49, 52, 84, 88, 99, 103–105, 107–108, 251, 292–294 *see also* abandonment; stone robbing
Denham, Varian 119
deserted medieval villages 24
destruction 104
Devizes 120, 209
Devizes Museum 120
Dibbles Farm 115, 118
diet 215, 219–222, 226, 228–230, 232–233, 285–286
ditches 49, 53–55, 59–62, 64–65, 72–73, 76–77, 80–87, 109–110, 250, 289–292
dogs 215, 218
Domesday survey 14, 17, 24–27, 29–31, 33–39, 42, 227, 291–292
  see also Exon Domesday; Great Domesday Book; Little Domesday Book
domestic objects 165, 196, 261, 264, 267–269, 273–274, 284, 291, 293, 296–297
Donyatt 124–125, 127, 131, 147, 154–155, 288
Douai, Walter of 36–37, 292
dovecotes 292
drainage 86, 90, 93, 95, 97, 99–101, 104–105, 112, 240, 253–254, 260
dress accessories 171, 182–183, 187, 190, 202
Droitwich 117
drying 244, 261 *see also* corn drying
drystone masonry 89, 91–95, 97, 99–100, 105, 107–109, 251, 258
Dunkerton 5, 8–9, 15–16, 40
Dunkerton Hill 11, 13
Durham 29
  Bishop of 29, 35
dwellings 28, 58, 64, 230, 240, 244, 250–251, 268, 290, 292, 294
dyeing 229

Eadgyth 37
earth resistance surveys 46–48
earthworks 5, 44–45, 49, 51, 58, 80, 85, 99, 106, 111, 290
East Wellow, Hampshire 17
Eckwick *see also* abandonment; Anglo-Saxon period; Bronze Age; environment; Iron Age; Romano-British period; structures; timber structures; Wellow
  documentary evidence 9, 14–29, 36–37, 39
  Domesday entry 36–37, 39
  excavation areas 51–52
  field names 22–23, 29, 228
  landscape 9, 14, 23–24, 41
  medieval period 9–11, 53–58, 61–106, 284–285, 292–299
  period I 53, 58–61, 289–290
  period II 53
  period III 53–55, 61–89, 290–292
  period IV 55–57, 89–93, 292–293
  period V 57–58, 93–106, 295–299
  period VI 58
  phasing 52–53
  post-medieval occupation 58, 196
  prehistoric occupation 9, 53, 58, 118, 191, 289
  recording methods 52
  site survey 44–45
Eckwick burial ground 11
Eckwick Farm 9–13, 28
Eckwick House 9, 11, 13, 23, 45–46, 48
Eckwick House Farm 1–5, 8, 44, 51, 58, 108–109
economy 284–288, 293–294, 296
Edgar 166
Edith of Wessex 32
Edward I 167
Edward III 218, 299 *see also* coins, Edward III
Edward the Confessor 32, 34, 36–38, 42
eels 244, 286
Ekewike, Baldwin de 293
Ekewyke, Thomas 18, 298–299
Ely Abbey 31, 34
Emma, wife of Walter of Douai 37
enclosures 8, 11, 55, 58, 62, 64, 73, 80–82, 87–88, 250, 289, 291 *see also* boundaries
English Heritage 1, 3, 119, 133, 167
English Heritage Ancient Monuments Laboratory 45
Englishcombe 39–40
environment 220, 227, 235–236
environmental samples 59 *see also* plant remains
epidemics 275, 299 *see also* Black Death
estates 14–16, 24, 32–33, 39–43, 291–292
Ethelred 42
Eu, William of 37–38
Evershed, Richard 120
Exon Domesday 30, 33–35, 37, 39

famines 228
Farleigh Hungerford 40
farmhouses 54, 57, 93, 105–106, 251, 284–285, 287–288, 293, 295–296, 298
farmsteads 89, 101, 109, 229, 231, 271, 287, 290–291, 293, 295, 298
Farnham 145
faunal remains 97, 214–221, 228, 280
  amphibians 220
  birds 215–218, 220
  cats 215–217
  cattle 215–217, 219–221
  deer 215
  dogs 215–217
  eels 286
  fish 220, 286
  goats 215–217, 220
  hedgehogs 215–217, 275
  horses 215–216, 218
  measurements 218
  mice 214, 218, 220, 222
  pathology 220–221
  pigs 215–217, 219–220
  preservation 215, 218
  rabbits 215–217
  sheep 215–217, 219–221
Field Farm 114–115
field systems 17, 24, 287, 290
fieldnames, post-Conquest 24
Fitzwilliam Museum 166
Flanders 37
  Count of 31
flax 179, 182, 231–232, 244, 253 *see also* textile production
flint objects 53, 190–195
  arrowheads 53
  raw materials 191
  recording system 52
Flixborough 270
flooring 75, 90–91, 240, 243, 245, 251–254
food production 261, 286 *see also* agriculture; crop processing; dairying
foodstuffs 120, 168, 199, 287, 297 *see also* butter; cheese; eels; game; meat
foraging 229, 232–233
fords 16, 27
Fosse Way 1, 8, 10–11, 15–16, 19, 289
fossils 158–159, 199, 208
foundations 63, 67, 72–73, 76, 86–88, 93, 97, 109, 240–241, 247, 250–251, 254, 258, 293
Foxcote 14, 25–26, 31–32, 40
Freshford 29

Frome 14–15, 38–41
fulling 244, 253 *see also* wool production
furniture 97, 169, 173, 253, 261, 263, 267, 270, 273, 275–276, 297–298 *see also* beds; chests

game 286 *see also* hunting; meat
Gardiner, Mark 5, 243
geld *see* taxation
Geoffrey, son of Walter of Douai 37
geology 5, 8, 46, 113–114, 120, 144, 156–159, 191, 196–197, 208
geophysical surveys 3, 5, 7, 10, 45–46, 51, 53, 58–59, 61, 73, 81, 88, 108, 289, 291, 294 *see also* earth resistance surveys; magnetometer surveys
Giffard, Walter 34
glass 111, 182 *see also* windows
Glastonbury 118, 134, 144, 163
Glastonbury Abbey 287
Gloucester 30, 33, 35, 211
  Earl of 17, 39
Godwinson, Harold 32
Goltho 167–169, 183–185, 187, 190, 210, 213–214, 244, 270, 286, 291
Great Domesday Book 29–30, 35–38, 42
Great Somerford 144
Greenland, Richard 209–210
Grubenhauser 243, 249

Ham Green 83, 153, 157, 165
Ham Hill 113, 115, 117
Hampton 31
Hanham 196, 208
Harcombe 191
Hassage 16, 26–27, 39
hay 226–227, 229–231
haystacks 93, 101, 104, 255, 294
hearths 87, 95, 100–102, 230–231, 243, 249, 253–255, 258, 260, 297
Hekewike, Henry de 293
Heming 33
Hemming 37
Henry II 165
Henry III 167
Hereford, Bishop of 33
Herlève 37
Higham Ferrers 229
hillforts 13, 117, 289
Hinton Charterhouse 14, 39–40
Historic England 5, 45, 237
hollow-ways 62, 85, 109 *see also* trackway
Holme Farm, Wellow 10
honey 160, 199, 287
horse gear 266, 269–270, 273, 277, 284–285, 288, 291, 297–298 *see also* ironwork
horses 28, 182, 215, 218, 227, 286–287
Houndtor 290
household objects 102, 169, 171, 182–183, 187, 190, 204, 275, 299
Huddox Hill 22
Hull 167, 211
Hungerford 232
Hunt, Jeffrey 209
Hunt, Thomas 209
Hunterwick 29
hunting 182, 215, 221 *see also* game; meat
Hunts, Thomas 209
Hutholes 291

Ilchester 113, 120, 137, 140, 144, 288
Iles, Rob 1
imports 145, 165, 187, 199, 202, 208, 229–230, 233, 288 *see also* trade
Ine of Wessex 291
inheritance 29, 32, 34, 38
Inquisitio Comitatus Cantabrigiensis 34
Inquisitio Eliensis 43
Iron Age 9–11, 13, 51–53, 59–61, 78, 113, 115, 182, 187, 224, 236, 289–290
ironwork 167, 182, 273, 278–280, 284–285, 288
  agricultural tools 177, 267, 293
  arrowheads 177, 182
  buckles 171, 182, 261, 275, 285, 298
  cattleshoes 171, 173, 182, 267
  chapes 177, 182, 270, 267–270
  door furniture 173, 252–253, 255, 257–258, 261, 275, 285
  ferrule 169, 275, 285
  fittings 102, 169, 171, 173, 182, 284, 288
  hinges 169, 171, 173, 175, 252, 255, 257–258, 261, 270, 285
  hooks 173, 175

INDEX

horse equipment 171, 173, 182
horseshoes 261, 275, 288
household objects 169, 171
ironworking tools 179, 261, 267
jewellery 169, 171
keys 177, 241–242, 252, 258, 261, 267, 270, 285, 288
knives 102, 167–169, 182, 261, 284, 288, 293, 298
leatherworking tools 179, 261, 288
locks 102, 177, 241, 252, 270, 288
miscellaneous objects 179, 182, 260, 270
nails 52, 171, 173, 175, 255–260, 270, 272–273, 275–276
needles 179
ox goads 177, 179, 182, 285, 293
punches 179, 261, 270
recording system 52
shears 167–169, 182, 271, 285
sickles 95, 177, 179, 182, 261, 277, 285, 298
spurs 171, 173, 182, 269, 288
staples 173, 175, 255–256, 258, 272–273, 285, 288
structural 173, 256, 258, 260, 270, 274, 276, 284–285
textile-working tools 179
utensils 169, 182
vessels 261, 265
weaponry 177, 182
weights 169
wood-working tools 179
ironworking 179, 182, 261, 273, 285, 288 *see also* metalworking

jet beads 214, 261, 285
Jones, Andrew 220
Juncus grass 254

Keele University 196
Keynsham 2, 39
Kidd, Alexander 3, 5, 109, 119–120
Kilmersdon 39, 41
kilns 57, 93, 100, 105, 120, 145, 151–152, 157, 165, 229–230, 253, 255, 288, 296–298
Kingston-upon-Thames 145
kitchens 253–254, 261, 269
Kitson, Peter 15
Knoll, Brent 243
Knoll Hill 22

land administration 41–43 *see also* estates
landholding 14, 16, 29–34, 36–38, 41–42, 89, 291–292, 298–299
landscape 8
Langham Road 218
Langley Burrell 120, 145
language 36
latrines 80, 244, 250 *see also* cesspits
Launceston Castle 218, 221
Laverstock 120, 145
Lawn Farm 244
lead objects 52, 112, 167, 182, 267, 273, 278–279
leather 168–169, 173, 183, 285
leather-working 179, 182, 260–261, 270, 273, 284–285
Lechlade 117
Leicester 183
Leigh-upon-Mendip 35, 209
Les Échelles, Hardwin of 34
Liber Eliensis 34, 41
Lichfield, Bishop of 39
lighting 199, 208, 253 *see also* windows
Limésy, Ralph of 37
Lincombe 29
lipid analysis 120, 160
Little Domesday Book 29
Little Solsbury 117
Liverpool, University of 120, 160
livestock 28, 30, 34, 182, 218, 226–227, 230, 285–286, 293, 296 *see also* animal husbandry
London 36, 145, 167–168, 177, 182, 211
loom weights 196, 199, 269–270, 284 *see also* spindle whorls; weaving
lords 33–34, 248, 250, 286–287, 297 *see also* thegns
Lovel, Ralph 37
Lozinga, Robert of 33
Ludgershall Castle 214
luxury goods 285, 287–288, 298 *see also* valuables; wealth
Lydeard St Lawrence 35
Lydford 232

Lyveden 183, 190

magnetometer surveys 45–49, 53, 58, 294
Maiden Castle 11
Malmesbury Abbey 37
malting 255, 258 *see also* corn drying
Maltwood Fund 3, 9
Malvern Hills 117
manors 14, 32, 37–38, 42, 248 291 *see also* estates
Manpower Services Commission 3
manuring 228, 230–231, 271, 287
markets 204, 220, 229, 286–287 *see also* trade
Marlborough 107, 209–210
Marshfield 191
Mary Le Port 144
May Hill 117
Meare 113, 118
measurements 41, 257
meat 215, 220–221, 261, 267, 285–286 *see also* butchery
Mendip 107
metal vessels 261
metalworking 93, 97, 118, 261, 267 *see also* bronze-working; ironworking
methodology 5
milling 204
mills 25–26, 31–32, 34, 38
mining 211
molluscs 233–236
monastic houses 287
Monceaux, William of 31
Montgomery, family 37
Morris, Elaine 131
mortar 106

National Heritage List 25, 27
Natural History Museum 196
Neolithic 191
Nether Stowey 120, 147
Newbury 229, 232
Newton St Loe 39–40
Nomina Villarum 39
Noon, Stephen 45
Norman Conquest 14, 23, 29, 37, 53, 183, 287, 291–292 *see also* Anglo-Saxon period
Normandy 31, 35
Norman period 30, 173, 239, 292
Northumberland 29
Norton St Philip 16, 26–27, 40–41, 209
nucleation 290

occupations 36 *see also* workers
Odo, Bishop of Bayeux 31, 35, 37
Old Sarum 35, 120
Old Wick, Weston 29
Ordnance Survey 28, 44
ovens 93, 95, 97, 100–102, 196, 230–231, 253–255, 260–261, 277, 294, 297–298
owls 220, 224, 275
oxen 227, 286, 298
Oxenham 227
Oxford 183–185
Castle 177

padstones 73, 84, 196–197, 252, 254–255, 257–258, 285
Pagans Hill 117
Paglinch 39
parishes 13–15
pasture 1, 8, 11–12, 28, 31–32, 34, 38, 41, 44, 227–228, 231, 287, 290 *see also* animal husbandry; hay; livestock
Paulton 114
Paxton 232
Payne, Andrew 1, 45
Peasedown St John 1, 8–10, 13, 15, 22–23, 39, 289–290
Braysdown road 11
cemetery 13–14
chapelry 15
Peglynch 25–26
personal care 168, 183, 187, 190, 212
pivot stones 196, 255
pits 72–78, 82–90, 92–94, 100–101, 223, 226, 233, 241
intercutting 77–78, 87
containing vessels 87
placenames 13–14, 16, 24–29, 35
plant remains *see* hay
beans 223–224, 229, 232–233, 286–287
black bindweed 61, 224

carbonised material 67
cereal grains 59, 61, 73, 78, 87, 100, 222, 224–233, 250, 286–287, 296
chaff 222, 226–227, 230–233, 250, 287
clover-type 61, 224
distribution 224, 226
fat hen 61, 224
grasses 225–227, 230–232
herbs and spices 229–230, 232–233
peas 224, 229, 232–233, 286–287
radiocarbon dates 237–238
sampling strategy 222
vegetables 227, 229, 286–287
ponds 44, 244
Portable Antiquities Database 166
Portsmouth 214
postholes 62–65, 67, 72–78, 80–81, 83–89, 99, 101, 240–241, 244–247, 249–250, 289
pottery 113–165 *see also* building materials, ceramic; tobacco pipes
Anglo-Saxon 119, 144, 160, 163, 272, 274
Bath 134, 137, 140
Bristol Ham Green wares 83, 120, 288
Bronze Age 53, 113, 115–117
Cheddar 62, 142, 144, 156, 158–159, 163
chronology 53, 58, 116, 119–120, 160, 238
cisterns 97, 102, 105, 147, 153, 165, 257, 261, 275, 285, 298
classification 133
cooking vessels 72, 133, 137, 140, 142, 144–145, 151–152, 157, 159–160, 163–165, 272, 284, 293, 296–297
crucibles 118
dripping dishes 102, 261, 275, 285
Droitwich salt containers 59, 117–118, 289
glazed 109, 133, 137, 140, 144–145, 147, 151–152, 154–155, 160, 164–165
Great Somerford wares 163
handmade 137, 140, 142, 164
imported 119, 145, 165
Iron Age 53, 58–59, 113–118, 289
jugs 97, 102, 109, 261, 275, 285
leaf decorated jugs 154, 257
lipid analysis 120, 160
Minety-type wares 144, 165, 288, 296
North West Wiltshire wares 120, 144, 296
petrological analysis 114, 120, 133, 155–156, 158–159
post-medieval 58, 107, 109, 111, 155
prehistoric 113
production 113–114, 118, 120, 157, 159–160, 164, 288
quantification 116, 280
recording system 52
Redcliffe wares 154–155, 165, 296
Romano-British 53, 118–119, 145
Saxo-Norman 119, 164
South-East Wiltshire wares 147, 160, 164
South Somerset wares 109, 120, 147, 155, 165, 296
Southwestern Glastonbury wares 114, 116
Stamford wares 145, 160, 164, 288
Surrey white wares 145
tablewares 109, 145, 296, 298
ware 1 133–134
ware 2 137, 293
ware 3 140
ware 4 140, 142, 271, 293
ware 5 142
ware 6 142–143
ware 7 144, 288
ware 8 145
ware 9 145
ware 10 145
ware 11 145
ware 12 145
ware 13 147
ware 14 147, 270–271, 288
ware 15 151
ware 16 151–152, 271, 288
ware 17 153–154
ware 18 154
ware 19 154–155
ware 52 155
prehistory *see* Bronze Age; Eckweek; Iron Age
Preston, Cirencester 144
project archive 5, 52, 109, 120, 132–133, 222, 224, 280
Promotion Law 250, 291 *see also* thegns
Puxton 232

Quantocks 38
quarries 36, 196
Queen's University Belfast 5, 237
querns 196–197, 199, 204, 261, 269–270, 272, 275, 278, 284 *see also* crop processing; breadmaking; milling

radiocarbon dates 52–53, 73, 83–84, 120, 237–238, 242, 290
Radstock 1–2, 8, 16, 41, 196, 208
Raunds 167, 187, 190, 210, 213–215
Reading Abbey 229, 233
rebuilding 54, 57, 86, 224, 240, 244, 248, 284–285, 291–292
recycling 271, 277, 280, 283
Redcliffe Hill 154
Red Post Inn 289
refuse 84, 97, 224, 230–231, 271–272, 284
Reinbald, priest of Frome 38
ridge and furrow 61
ring 285
ritual deposits 244, 277
Robert, son of Walter of Douai 37
Roberts, Jan 3, 52
Robert the Frisian 31
Rode 209
Roman Baths Museum 5, 120
Romano-British period 11, 13, 28–29, 53, 118–119, 131, 166, 179, 289
Roman road 10 *see also* Fosse Way
rosary beads 102, 199, 214, 261, 298
Rotuli Hundredorum 39
Rusham 22

Saint-Calais, William of 35
Salisbury, Museum 120
salt 117–118
    see also pottery
    Droitwich salt containers
Sandwich 187
scavenging 275
security 187, 241, 249, 252, 257–258, 261, 267, 290, 297
settlement patterns 23–27, 290
Shapwick 17, 167, 190, 212, 214, 232, 244, 286, 290, 292
sheep 218, 220–221, 227, 285–286 *see also* wool production
shells 59, 233–236 *see also* molluscs
Shenberrow Camp 117
Shepton Mallet 114–115
Sherborne 14–15
Sherborne House 117
Shifnal 183, 190
Shockerwick 29
Shoscombe 15, 22, 25–26, 39
Shrewsbury, Earl of 37
sieving 52, 214, 220, 231–232
site formation processes 273, 275
Skinner, John 13
Skuse, William 28
Slack, Colin 182
slag 61
slaves 24–25, 31–34, 36, 41, 43, 291
snails *see* molluscs
soakaways *see* drainage
social hierarchy 30, 32–33, 41, 43
social status 24, 55, 182, 215, 221, 229, 232–233, 239, 248, 250, 285–288, 291–293, 297–298
soils 8, 46, 77–78, 85, 93, 99, 101, 104, 107, 223–228, 231–233, 255, 272 *see also* yardsoils
soil samples 222
Somerset 9
    Record Office 27
    Vernacular Architecture Group 26
Southampton 213, 230
    University of 133
South Cadbury 214
South Petherton 38
South Stoke 23
spindle whorls 196, 199, 204, 208, 213, 270–271, 284–285, 298 *see also* loom weights
spinning 179, 271
Springfield Lyons 248–249, 291
Stanford-in-the-Vale 187, 190
Stansted 229, 232
Stantonbury 16
Statute of Labourers 299
stone objects 196–208, 265, 269, 277–280, 283–284 *see also* loom weights; querns

chronology 204
domestic 196–197, 199
petrological analysis 196, 208
recording system 52
sources 196, 199, 204, 208
tiles 243
whetstones 196–197, 199, 202, 204, 208, 261, 270, 278, 284, 288
stone robbing 93–95, 103–106, 108, 253, 267, 295, 298 *see also* abandonment; demolition
Stoney Littleton 16, 22, 24–25, 39–40
storage 54, 87, 182, 230, 249–250, 255, 260, 267, 293, 296
strike-a-lights 191–194
structures *see also* timber structures
    alignment 64, 239, 290
    Anglo-Saxon 240–243, 290–291
    entrances 240, 242, 246, 250, 252–254, 258, 260, 275, 289
    internal arrangements 65, 67, 74, 83, 86, 93, 101–102, 104, 240–242, 253–255, 257–258, 260–261, 295–298
    lifecycle 239
    roofing 74, 86–87, 95, 97, 152, 196, 228, 239, 241, 243, 246, 250, 252, 257 *see also* thatch
    solars 97, 248, 267, 297–298
    stone 55–57, 89, 93, 105, 109, 224, 250–251, 254–255, 290, 292–295
    structure 460 93, 101, 103, 251–252, 255–258, 260–267, 270–272, 275, 277, 294–295, 297
    structure 461 93, 105–106, 109, 167, 258, 267, 270, 273, 275, 294
    structure 462 84, 89–90, 92, 95, 250–251, 258, 260, 268, 271, 292, 295–296
    structure 463 93, 97–100, 104, 254–255, 258–259, 267–269, 294–295
    structure 464 90, 258
    structure 465 89, 91, 97–98, 250–251, 268, 271–272, 292
    structure 466 93, 98–100, 255, 294–295
    structure 467 64, 67, 72, 82–87, 89, 94, 239–240, 242–246, 258–260, 269, 271–272, 292–293
    structure 468 62–64, 239–240, 269, 273
    structure 469 250
    structure 471 244, 272
    structure 472 106
    structure 473 255, 295
    structure 474 85
    structure 475 73, 78–80, 82, 87, 245, 250
    structure 476 73, 78–79, 245, 248–249, 260, 292
    structure 477 248–250, 286–287
    structure 479 73, 77, 88, 270
    structure 480 244
    sunken floored 54, 65, 68, 83–84, 87, 107–108, 241–243, 249, 251, 258, 272, 291–292
    turriform 87, 239, 248–250, 260, 291
    upper storeys 248–249, 267
surnames 24, 26–28
Swaffham 34

Tadwick 29
Taunton 2, 199, 210, 288
    Castle 128, 134
    Museum 11, 120, 165
taxation 31–34, 36, 38–39, 41–43, 287–288
Tellisford 40
textile production 179, 182, 199, 212–213, 229, 244, 253, 271–273, 284–285 *see also* fulling; spinning; weaving; wool production
thatch 199, 228, 231, 243, 295
thegns 250, 286, 291–292, 295 *see also* lords
timber structures 52–55, 58, 61–65, 73–77, 80–81, 84–89, 109, 224, 226, 239–251, 258–260, 288, 290–292
    associated ironwork 173
    buttresses 76
    defences 289
    roofing 252
tinder 230
tithe maps 16–17, 22, 24, 26–28, 44, 196
tobacco pipes 5, 58, 107, 155, 187, 208–210
Toukere, John 28, 298–299
Tours 165
trackway *see also* hollow-ways 64–65, 72, 84–86, 96, 101, 104–105, 109–110, 290, 292, 294–295
trade 117–118, 145, 165, 196, 199, 202, 204, 286–289, 296 *see also* imports; markets
transport 104, 182, 298 *see also* carts

troughs 94–95, 199, 253, 260–261
Trowbridge 291
Tunley 13
towers 87, 239, 248–250, 260, 291
Twerton 39–40
Twinhoe 16, 27, 39

Uffculme 37
Uley Bury 116–117
Underhill, Edward 209–210
Upper Twinhoe 23, 27

Vair, Aubrey of 34
valuables 261, 267, 275, 280
Victoria County History 14
Vikings 42, 167–168, 173
Vince, Alan 142, 147
votive deposits 244, 277

wages 299
Ware, Davina 182
Waterbech Abbey 183, 190
watercress 244
waterlogging 86, 232
Wealden formations 158
wealth 285, 287
weaponry 270, 287–288, 291, 297
weaving 196, 212–213, 270–271 *see also* loom weights; textile production
Week Farm, Combe Hay 29
Wellow 5, 9, 13–17, 22–25, 39–40
    churches 13, 15
    Domesday entry 38–39
    estate 15, 17, 27, 40
    fields 17, 22–24
    Holme Farm 10
    parish 9, 14, 16, 27
    placenames 14–16, 22, 24
    post-Conquest 17
    pre-Conquest 23
    river 5, 8, 14, 16, 26, 40
    Roman Villa 11, 13–14, 119
    tithe map 23
    woodland 23
Wellow Lane 10, 290
Wellow Lane Business Park 289
Wells 14, 38, 40–41
Wessex Downs 191
Westbury Homes Limited 3
West Cotton 167, 270
Weston 29
Weston-super-Mare 115–116, 232
West Stow 243
West Wellow, Hampshire 17
Wharram Percy 253, 257
Whitegate Farm 116, 232
White Ox Mead 8, 10–11, 17, 19, 22–26, 39–40, 44
Whittokesmede, John 27
Whittoksmede 25
Wicken Bonhunt 248
Widcombe 291
William I 30–35, 37, 42
William II 33, 35
Wiltshire Downs 199
Winchester 36, 196, 199
    Bishop of 35
windows 252–253, 258, 260
Woodborough 25–26, 39–40
wooden objects 285
Woodix 29
woodland 8, 23, 27, 40–42
woodworking 179, 182, 251, 273, 292, 295
wool production 5, 179, 182, 204, 215, 227, 244, 253, 260, 285–286, 288 *see also* fulling; sheep
Worcester 211
Worcester F 33–34
workers 299 *see also* occupations
Wrangway 147

yards 46, 54, 62, 64, 70, 87, 92, 99–102, 105, 244, 251–254, 290
yardsoils 84–85, 89, 92, 94, 99–102, 104, 284
Yeavering 270, 291
Yeo (river) 39
Yeovil 39
York 167–168, 177, 183, 185, 220